BUILDING THE NEW EUROPE
Volume 1: The Single Market and Monetary Unification

CENTRAL ISSUES IN CONTEMPORARY ECONOMIC THEORY AND POLICY

General Editor: **Mario Baldassarri**, *Professor of Economics, University of Rome 'La Sapienza', Italy*

This new series is a joint initiative between Macmillan, St. Martin's Press and SIPI, the publishing company of Confindustria (the Confederation of Italian Industry), based on the book collection MONOGRAFIE RPE published by SIPI and originated from the new editorial programme of one of the oldest Italian journals of economics, the *Rivista di Politica Economica*, founded in 1911. This series is intended to become an arena in which the most topical economic problems are freely debated and confronted with different scientific orientations and/or political theories.

The 1990s clearly represent a transition period in which the world economy will establish new international relationships and in this context, new challenges and new risks will have to be faced within each economic system. Fundamental issues on which economic theory and policy have long based their reasoning over the last two or three decades have to be critically reviewed in order to pursue new frontiers for theoretical development and economic policy implementation. In this sense, this new series aims at being a "place of debate" between professional economists, an updated learning tool for students and a specific reference for a wider readership aiming at understanding economic theory and policy evolution even from a non-specialist point of view.

Published

Mario Baldassarri (*editor*)
KEYNES AND THE ECONOMIC POLICIES OF THE 1980s

Mario Baldassarri (*editor*)
INDUSTRIAL POLICY IN ITALY, 1945–90

Mario Baldassarri (*editor*)
OLIGOPOLY AND DYNAMIC COMPETITION

Mario Baldassarri, John McCallum and Robert Mundell (*editors*)
DEBT, DEFICIT AND ECONOMIC PERFORMANCE

Mario Baldassarri, John McCallum and Robert Mundell (*editors*)
GLOBAL DISEQUILIBRIUM IN THE WORLD ECONOMY

Mario Baldassarri and Robert Mundell (*editors*)
BUILDING THE NEW EUROPE
VOLUME 1: THE SINGLE MARKET AND MONETARY UNIFICATION
VOLUME 2: EASTERN EUROPE'S TRANSITION TO A MARKET ECONOMY

Mario Baldassarri, Luigi Paganetto and Edmund S. Phelps (*editors*)
INTERNATIONAL ECONOMIC INTERDEPENDENCE,
PATTERNS OF TRADE BALANCES AND ECONOMIC POLICY
COORDINATION

Mario Baldassarri, Luigi Paganetto and Edmund S. Phelps (*editors*)
WORLD SAVING, PROSPERITY AND GROWTH

Building the New Europe

Volume 1: The Single Market and Monetary Unification

Edited by

Mario Baldassarri
Professor of Economics
University of Rome 'La Sapienza'

and

Robert Mundell
Professor of Economics
Columbia University, New York

St. Martin's Press

in association with
Rivista di Politica Economica,
SIPI, Rome

First published in Great Britain 1993 by
THE MACMILLAN PRESS LTD
Houndmills, Basingstoke, Hampshire RG21 2XS
and London
Companies and representatives
throughout the world

A catalogue record for this book is available
from the British Library.

ISBN 0–333–58702–2

Printed in Great Britain by
Antony Rowe Ltd
Chippenham, Wiltshire

First published in the United States of America 1993 by
Scholarly and Reference Division,
ST. MARTIN'S PRESS, INC.,
175 Fifth Avenue,
New York, N.Y. 10010

ISBN 0–312–08977–5

Library of Congress Cataloging-in-Publication Data
The Single market and monetary unification / edited by Mario Baldassarri and Robert Mundell.
p. cm. — (Building the new Europe; v. 1)
Published in association with *Rivista di Politica Economica*.
Includes index.
ISBN 0–312–08977–5
1. Monetary policy—European Economic Community countries.
2. Monetary unions—European Economic Community countries.
3. European Monetary System (Organization)   4. Europe 1992.
I. Baldassarri, Mario, 1946– .   II. Mundell, Robert A.
III. Series.
HC240.B84   1993 vol. 1
[HG930.5]
338.94 s—dc20
[332.4'566'094]   92–189371
                                                          CIP

Contents

Preface

The single market and the monetary integration of European Economic Community countries, the reunification of Germany, and the Central and East European move towards the marketplace: these are the events and processes that will redesign the European political and economic spheres, creating great opportunities and fresh challenges for Europe and for the rest of the world. Europe in the nineties will take a new international policy direction, which may serve to strengthen supranationalism. The Community as a whole must ensure that these new steps make it possible to reconcile the economic interests of countries on the Continent and in the rest of the world.

The challenge is none the less fascinating to those in this 'profession', namely the economists who are called on to participate in the planning and the building of 'the new Europe'.

This is why we felt it would be stimulating and worthwhile to collect the analyses, ideas, observations, provocations and recommendations of economists from over 15 different European and non-European countries, and from 34 different universities. The diversity of backgrounds, cultures, and theoretical and practical experiences, it is hoped, will lead to the creation of a framework which, though less than homogeneous, forms an interconnected whole, a solid base which may provide some insight into future developments in the nineties.

The sheer number and length of the essays, analyses and provocative conclusions made it necessary to publish the collection in two separate volumes.

This first collection deals with the problems caused by the single market and by the monetary unification of EEC member states.

The second volume examines the problems of East European countries.

This book is divided into four sections. The first deals with *Basic Issues for Building the New Europe*. The second section, *Towards the Single Market: Problems and Perspectives*, comprises five essays on the themes that are fundamental to the single-market process, written by

Silvio Borner, University of Basel; Martino Lo Cascio, Università Tor Vergata, Rome; Richard Eckaus, Massachusetts Institute of Technology; Giovanni Caravale, Università 'La Sapienza', Rome; and Jurgen Kroger, EEC Commission, Brussels.

The third section is devoted to monetary unification and includes essays by Robert Triffin, University of Leuven; Michele Fratianni and Jurgen von Hagen, Indiana University; A. J. Hughes Hallet and David Vines, Daniel Gros, CEPS, Brussels; Wilhelm Kohler; Daniel Cohen, CEPREMAP, Paris; Andrew Tyrie, Nuffield College, Oxford; Francesco Farina, Università de Siena; Lucio Valerio Spagnolo, Università di Salerno; Peter Bofinger, Deutsche Bundesbank; John Williamson, Nuffield College, Oxford; Massimo Tivegna, Università Tor Vergata, Rome; Emil Maria Claassen, Université Dauphine, Paris; Norbert Walter, Deutsche Bank, Frankfurt; Miranda Xafa, IMF and Princeton University.

The fourth and final section studies the relationships between the 'new' Europe and the rest of the world, in essays by Charles P. Kindleberger of the Massachusetts Institute of Technology, Ippei Yamazawa of Hitotsubashi University and Gianni Fodella, Università de Milano.

Before beginning a detailed examination of the specific themes, the volume opens with two essays, the first by James Meade and the second by Robert Mundell, which provide an overall framework in which to fit this volume and the next, and make it possible to identify unifying elements within 'the new Europe'.

The first essay, written by James Meade of the University of Cambridge and Nobel laureate in economics, is titled, *The Building of the New Europe: National Diversity Versus Continental Uniformity*.

Socialism is dead, long live capitalism... but does capitalism really exist? This is the provocative premise of Meade, who seems to ask: 'How much socialism has seeped into capitalist systems, especially in western Europe? And when this happens, which parts are nurtured, and which parts are discarded?' It would seem that Meade hopes to create a summary of the best-case scenarios guiding economies towards the capitalism of the year 2000.

Various factors make it necessary to maintain national diversity within Europe. If this is true, then what should be the common thread uniting countries on the Continent? What should be left to the member states themselves, and what should fall under EC jurisdiction? Meade foresees the re-emergence of Europe-wide government and a new role for Europe in international relations. During this century, major conflicts within Europe led to the polarization of the world into two 'non-European' powers. The unification process 'recentres' the Continent, and, according to Meade, it is a challenge that is worth accepting even at considerable economic cost. Viewed from this angle, the Single Market is without a doubt an important step, but it is not sufficient on its own. 'We must go further' is the recommendation of one of the great European fathers of modern economics. Meade goes on to provide concrete analyses of the various issues related to the Single Market and monetary union, sparking debate with the parable of the ambidextrous economist and offering, with his usual acumen, opinions and suggestions of his own.

The second introductory essay, by Robert Mundell of Columbia University, deals with the theme of Monetary Policies for the new Europe.

The first section provides an in-depth analysis of the monetary policy alternatives of East European countries during their transition to market economies. Mundell proposes five basic options, evaluates the benefits, risks, and costs associated with them, and examines possible combinations to lower the costs and increase the benefits. He concludes by matching five instruments to five objectives: the instruments include the sale of public-sector assets, stabilization of exchange rates, restoring convertibility of currencies into gold, tightening of monetary policy and balancing of government budgets; the objectives are to avoid the vicious circle affecting economics, finance and budget, to control inflation, to step up currency reserves, to use monetary policy as a tool to hold inflation in check, to make the tightening of monetary policy a possible and practicable alternative and to aim at tying their currencies to the deutsche mark or to the ECU.

The second section evaluates the monetary policy options open to EC governments, in a brief overview of the 'revolutions' in favour of increased integration, beginning with the European Coal and Steel Community agreement in the fifties. Mundell asks how large the new Europe should be, what requirements East European countries will have to fulfill in order to be considered credible partners, and whether a single new currency or a system of '$n + 1$' currencies is the optimal solution. As for West European countries, the following options are examined: currencies linked to the dollar or the creation of a European dollar; the creation of an autonomous currency linked to a European currency, namely the deutsche mark: the creation of a basket of currencies; a return to the gold standard.

The main risk, Mundell concludes, is that Germany may be reluctant to accept a leadership role in the new Europe, since this unification process may provide fewer advantages to Germany than to other governments. It would therefore be advisable for the other countries to convince Germany, perhaps by conceding in other areas, to guide Europe into the future. Since Mundell is convinced that the sooner this happens the better, he suggests using the Bundesbank as the agent of the European Central Bank during the transition phase, and the deutsche mark as the basis for the new single currency. This strategy, which would place Germany at the helm of the unification process, would offer 'the best chance that the final destination will actually be reached'.

In the first section, *Towards the Single Market: Problems and Perspectives*, four essays cover issues of a general nature. Silvio Borner, in *Institutional and Constitutional preconditions for Growth Effects Resulting from European Integration*, explores the institutional and constitutional preconditions necessary in order to produce the potential growth effects of the integration process. In the early eighties, the Cecchini Report attempted to quantify the 'costs of non-Europe'. However, this attempt was little more than a static analysis. According to Borner, the dynamism of the future will give rise to more far-reaching consequences. The globalization of economic issues will bring about a globalization of government. It will be in the interest of some nations to take 'hard-binding' measures, so that their countries will somehow begin to adhere to European rules of behaviour, and share in the benefits of increased resources. Borner departs from this premise to make some interesting recommendations.

Trends in the growth of real saving in Western Europe are analyzed in a stimulating essay by Martino Lo Cascio, *Real Saving Growth in Western Europe: Exploring Future Patterns*, which asks 'who controls what?' in the new equilibria of aggregate demand and aggregate supply, and what connections link public debt, current-account expenditure and saving formation.

Much can be garnered from the vast store of theory concerning development economics. This is especially true as regards the countries of the Mediterranean and Eastern Europe. Richard S. Eckaus', *Some Lessons from Development Economics for Southern and Eastern Europe*, points out that due attention must be paid to the processes of human capital formation and to the speed of the integration process. Enthusiasm may push the imagination beyond the limits of what is actually feasible. The resultant failures may in turn cause dangerous temptations to arise.

The employment prospects in store for the Single Market are analyzed by Giovanni Caravale, in *Perspectives for Employment in Europe after 1992*. Will the invisible hand be sufficient to reallocate production processes and the 'labour factor' to maximize the benefits and the levels of employment? This question has no easy answer in economic theory; using the words of Joan Robinson, Caravale concludes: `we are [then] left in the uncomfortable position of having to think for ourselves'.

Integration between East and West Germany has sometimes been used as an example to be generalized within the European integration processes. Jurgen Kroger, in *Integration Problems of the East and West German Economy*, claims strong peculiarities of the German case, well distinguished with respect to the other Eastern European economies. Direct support granted by West Germany to the ex-DDR is like a Marshall Plan which cannot be generalized to other experiences. Indeed, East Germany may be in a position like West Berlin in the past. The crucial point in the German case still remains the wide productivity differentials between the two parts and the risk for the eastern Länder is to become some kind of Mezzogiorno. What pros? What cons?

The second section deals specifically with the process of Monetary Union. It opens with an insightful, provocative essay whose very title reveals the need to get to the bottom of the issue, the creation of a true International Monetary System. Its author, Robert Triffin, asks whether the letters IMS stand for International Monetary System, or, in the light of past experiences, 'International Monetary Scandal'.

The power of the United States and the dollar during the cold war years provide the basis for Triffin's powerful analysis of the most recent 'twenty years of confusion', during which the world's richest country was financed by the rest of the world. Triffin sees Europe-wide monetary unification not as 'the next best thing', but, rather, as the first step towards 'enlarging the system' to include the United States and rebuilding a true International Monetary System. Two conclusions are drawn concerning the specific process of European monetary unification. Firstly, as regards whether to maintain national currencies within a fixed exchange-rate regime or to create a single currency, Triffin is decidedly in favour of the latter option. Secondly, Triffin enthusiastically supports the notion that monetary union implies political union.

It is certainly not easy to summarize in this brief introduction the analyses, ideas and observations contained in the essays which make up the main body of this section on monetary unification. I will therefore highlight the salient points in the passages which follow.

Fratianni and Von Hagen, in *On the Road to EMU*, begin with a careful study of four 'alternative strategies', which are evaluated according to three phases of implementation. Which of these strategies is the right one? Their criteria include three main characteristics: credibility, flexibility during execution, and minimization of the costs of transition. In conclusion, the authors propose an interpretation of the Delors Plan according to the theory of public-sector decision-making.

Can a European monetary union be carried out without costs? This is the central issue of A.J. Hughes Hallet and David Vines, in *Adjustment Difficulties within a European Monetary Union: Can They Be Reduced?*

Loss of sovereignty and the need for a greater flexibility in fiscal policy must necessarily be considered. But in any case costs cannot be reduced to zero. Hence the problem of how to distribute them will have to be faced.

The use of the exchange rate as an adjustment instrument is often associated with a 'beggar thy neighbour' policy. On the other hand a fixed exchange rate can be a deterrent to prevent wage and price struggle and to control inflation. Wilhelm Kohler, in *Currency Unifica-*

tion and Real Exchange Rates, analyzes these issues with respect to national and regional problems leading to the need for interregional transfers within a currency union process.

Towards a Common Monetary Policy in the Transition: the Role of the ECU and Required Reserves is the title of the essay by Daniel Gros which describes how the debate is currently being speeded up as a consequence of European monetary union, and reveals the lack of emphasis on the problems of the transition, or actually achieving the goal. A common monetary policy is necessary 'during' phase two; in this sense, it is hardly difficult to imagine the decisive role of the system of required reserves, with the ECU as the final currency objective.

In *Monetary Union and its Implications for Fiscal Policy*, Daniel Cohen asks whether European monetary unification does not by its very nature reveal the need for a European Fiscal Union (EFU). This study centres on cooperative and non-cooperative games theory.

Andrew Tyrie, in *A Political Economy of Economic and Monetary Union*, focuses on four major points: the debate about EMU is primarily about politics and not economics; secondly, fears of irrecoverable loss of sovereignty are often exaggerated; thirdly, the Commission and some other analysts largely overweigh the economic benefits of further monetary integration; finally, the Delors Plan may have alternative routes to greater integration, its main objective is indeed a high degree of surrender of control over one's own monetary affairs, not simply the economic benefits of integration.

In *From the EMS to the EMU: the Role of Policy Coordination*, Francesco Farina identifies the principal characteristics of a regime of 'fixed but adjustable exchange rates'. He opposed the hypothesis of a symmetrical Europeam Monetary System and 'monetary discipline', and goes on to assert that controls on capital movements and interest rate differentials in relation to Germany have worked together as the complementary instruments of an anti-inflationary monetary policy aimed at causing a convergence of the German economy and those of other countries. This paper concludes with a detailed analysis of the problems posed by the transition.

The Role of the European System of Central Banks in the European Integration Process, the essay written by Lucio Valerio Spagnolo, seeks to support the idea of a unified Europe in which individual member countries do not simply delegate internal problems to the supra-national institutions; rather, they accept the fact that these institutions must create a common policy. This study, which centres on the unique role of the European central banks in the integration process, examines the varying situations that currently exist, and concludes that Europe no longer has 'time to decide that convergence. Tomorrow's historians, telling today's history, when asking themselves why Europe waited such a long time to become a united Europe, could find a number of reasons but not a satisfactory justification'.

Peter Bofinger's, *The Political Economy of the Hard-ECU Proposal* juxtaposes the hard-ECU proposal with the Delors Plan, and points out that the first recommendation 'lets the market decide' while the Delors Plan is criticized because it is linked to the decision-making of bureaucrats in Brussels. But if the hard ECU became reality, wonders Bofinger, then which market would decide? Who would participate in that market, and in what roles?

In conclusion, Bofinger asserts that the hard ECU is judged positively only by Great Britain and that in any case the hard ECU can only be the deutsche mark.

In *Aspects of the British Debate on EMU*, John Williamson presents a summary of a recent report, edited by him for England's Liberal Democratic Party, and deals with two specific problems that are particularly worrisome to those who believe that even today, a flexible exchange-rate regime is a useful economic policy instrument. As regards the hard ECU, he agrees with Peter Bofinger about the need to identify subsidy sources. As opposed to Daniel Cohen's thesis, Williamson stresses the need for coordinated, centralized fiscal policy. In sum, Williamson is in favour of a single currency, but only once all of the conditions have been identified.

The central theme of *The Fluctuations of the Mark/Dollar Exchange Rate and their Impact on European Rates: The Case of the Lira and the French Franc*, by Massimo Tivegna, is whether or not the dollar still plays a central role. The answer to this question seems to be a negative one. Tivegna asserts that it is the dollar that has been 'circling' the perfectly sound EMS, rising and falling erratically, as noted in a famous paper by Giavazzi and Giovannini. A comprehensive empirical study identifies 17 different stages and points out that a stable European area has already been created.

Emil-Maria Claassen turns again to the case of German monetary union in an attempt to examine the sequencing and timing of stabilization policies to be followed by other national experiences.

The concrete experiences of German monetary unification are widely presented by Norbert Walter, whose assessment of the speed of unification is decidely positive, since in his opinion there were no practicable alternatives. To be sure, grave problems have arisen and must be solved, but, according to Walter, from 1992 onwards even the Länder of the former German Democratic Republic will see the beginnings of an economic recovery. Given Germany's economic policy mix, composed of an 'expansive' budget policy and a `restrictive' monetary policy, one may be tempted to make comparisons with Reaganomics. However, Walter points out that major differences exist. One such difference, in fact, is that the balance-of-payments surplus will decline, but will remain a surplus; another is that inflation, despite some signs of an increase, will remain low. In conclusion, German monetary union will speed up the process of European monetary unification.

In the end, another national experience is proposed by Miranda Xafa, *EMU and Greece: Issues and Prospects for Membership*. Some estimates and figures are proposed to evaluate the feasibility and desirability for Greece of joining the EMU or to estimate EEC regional and social funds compensations required to make up for the forgone inflation revenues.

The fourth and final section analyzes the relationships between the new Europe and the rest of the world economy, namely the United States and Japan.

Europe in the World Economy is the essay written by Charles P. Kindleberger. As always, a fascinating historical, political and economic overview is given.

The dual process of EEC unification and integration with Eastern Europe generates an enormous need for capital within Europe. This will stem the capital flow of the past few years towards the United States, thereby jeopardizing monetary and exchange-rate stability worldwide. The inevitable migration flows from East to West could also, during the initial stages, slow down development in both East and West. Therefore, according to Kindleberger, the possibility of postponing the 1992 deadline cannot yet be ruled out.

Kindleberger departs from this premise to pose key questions regarding the world economic outlook and the role of the new Europe, and asks who can and should be the producers of 'public goods'. On the international scene, who will be responsible for guaranteeing the openness of markets to international trade, the stability of exchange rates, the coordination of macroeconomic policy, and the steady flow of capital? Who will be the 'lender of last resort?' Several possible answers exist: international agencies, the regionalization of issues, trilateralism or a group of five, seven, eight or ten. But that is not enough, says Kindleberger. New leadership is what is lacking. Reference is made to the crash of 1929, which according to Kindleberger was due to the loss of leadership in the United Kingdom.

In his view, Europe is overly intent on solving problems which, though important, are minor in the light of the above explanation. Europe should aim at becoming the needed world leader capable of becoming the supplier of primary 'public goods'. Hence Kindleberger's conclusion, that we are going through a transitional phase that can only lead to much-needed 'world government'.

Japanese perspectives, attitudes and strategy concerning the new Europe are put forward in the essay by Ippei Yamazawa. The author asserts that, notwithstanding the dangers of a fortress Europe `withdrawn into itself', Japanese investment on the Continent is not expected to slacken as firms 'nationalize' their European counterparts to gain a foothold 'in the new Europe'. That may create problems for Pacific Rim economies. But its 'global' strategy means that Japan's economy is already well placed to deal with either an open Europe, or a closed one.

There can be no question but that Japan has been carefully monitoring European developments, and has its own doubts and reservations. Nonetheless, even today Japan seems well equipped and ready to take on any turn of events.

Let us now examine the other side of the coin: can thenew Europe compete with Japan and the United States? This is the subject faced by Gianni Fodella who concludes: 'data and projections seem to indicate that the new Europe will be able to successfully compete with the United States, but will not match the competing power of Japan'. The perspectives of 'the producers'seem to prevail in Japan, the perspectives of consumers seem paramount in the United States. Europe is probably in between.

This concludes the brief and by no means exhaustive look at the essays of this collection, an attempt to identify the nexus underlying the studies and positions presented here.

One last duty remains: to express thanks in an informal way to the many colleagues and friends who agreed to contribute, with appreciable scientific involvement, to this 'experiment' in analysis and observation, and who also made it possible to publish insightful information on the process of building the 'New Europe'.

Mario Baldassarri

I - BASIC ISSUES FOR BUILDING THE NEW EUROPE

The Building of the New Europe: National Diversity Versus Continental Uniformity

James E. Meade
Cambridge University

1. - Introduction

This paper is concerned solely with certain internal economic aspects of the relations between the member countries which may come together to build a new European Community.

It does not deal with any of the political problems involved nor with any of the political or economic aspects of the relationship between the new Europe and the rest of the world. Within these limitations it is argued that there is a potential clash of far-reaching importance between two distinct major objectives. On the one hand, it is maintained that there are at present exceptionally strong reasons for preserving a large measure of freedom for the various countries of Europe to experiment in different diverse forms of liberal economic policies and institutions. On the other hand, it is maintained that there are powerful arguments in favour of building a strong centralised union structure to control, and unify certain economic policies and institutions in order to attain certain clear communal objectives. Some clash between these two principles is inevitable. But must one of these principles be for practical purposes abandoned in favour of the other or is some set of workable arrangements possible which will achieve the main advantages of both principles?

2. - The Demise of Communism

In this paper it is simply assumed that the new Europe should be built so as to be capable of incorporating the ex-communist countries of Eastern Europe, including perhaps ultimately Russia itself. The incorporation of such countries would, it is generally agreed, be dependent upon their having successfully switched from basic dependence upon a command-economy structure to basic dependence upon a structure of competitive free-enterprise market arrangements.

In discussing the economic implications of this requirement that members of the new Europe should promote competitive free-enterprise market structures, it is useful to distinguish between the advantages of free enterprise and the advantages of competition. Free enterprise implies that there are certain risk-bearing entrepreneurs who are free to take decisions to maximise the profit which they can obtain from the enterprise which they direct. One way of increasing profit is to reduce the cost of producing whatever is being produced. Free enterprise may thus be welcomed as offering high incentives to produce efficiently in the sense of getting as large an output of products as possibile from any given input of factor resources.

Competition strengthens this incentive to produce efficiently since otherwise the profit of the enterprise may be threatened by the lower cost and selling price of competitors' products. In addition a competitive search for profit brings it a quite different social advantage in so far as it attracts resources into the production of foods for which consumers express the highest values by offering the highest prices and into methods of production which employ the plentiful and thus the cheaper rather than the scarce and therefore more expensive factors of production.

Such are the economic advantages of a free-entreprise competitive market structure. But in certain situations serious monopolistic conditions are inevitable. In the case of a free-enterprise monopoly, such as a privatised national railway network, profit may be increased, not only by using a given amount of resources as efficiently as possible but also restricting the input of resources and the output of products in order to enjoy an excess profit by raising the selling prices of the products and squeezing the prices paid for the factor inputs. In this case the social advantage of using inputs efficiently may be more than offset by the social disadvantages of restricting the input and outputs of the monopolised concern. If the business had been nationalised and run by official managers under instruction to produce as much as possible subject to being able to sell the product at a price which covered the market cost of the factor inputs, outputs of products and inputs of factors might be increased more nearly to the socially optimal levels; but the profit incentive to maximise output per unit of input would be weakened. In such a case is a privatised free-enterprise market or a nationalised socialist market structure to be preferred?

Subject to some basic questions of this kind one may in general greatly welcome the extension throughout Europe of competitive free-enterprise market structures wherever they are possibile. From this it is very often implicitly if not explicitly inferred that a restriction of membership of the new Europe to countries which effectively promote competitive free enterprise market conditions removes any need for diversity in the national economic policies and institutions in the new Europe. Capitalism, it is contended, has knocked socialism out. All members of the new Europe will have familiar capitalist market economies. We can, therefore, concentrate attention on building a centralised union structure which helps these more or less uniform national capitalist structures to work harmoniously and efficiently together.

I believe this conclusion to be totally false. It is clear that, even in the absence of the problems raised by integrating the ex-communist countries into a new Europe there is need for much experimentation in developing liberal capitalist economies. Neither the extreme Thatcherism of the United Kingdom nor even the successful social market of Germany can be regarded as the end of the road in a search for the best form of liberal economy. It would be a grave obstacle to progress if changes in these structures could be tried out only on a uniform basis in every European country simultaneously.

But the transition of the ex-communist economies of Eastern Europe from a "Socialist" to a "Capitalist" way of life does raise these issues in a very clear way. When "Capitalism" versus "Socialism" is the subject of political discussion in the countries of Westrern Europe

"Socialism" is normally held to exhibit one or more of the three following features: 1) the State ownership and planned management of the land and capital resources of the community together with extensive State regulation of, and intervention in, many activities which remain in private hands; 2) a great emphasis upon State measures to ensure a more equal distribution of income and standards of living, and 3) social security, including the certainty of earning a living in conditions of full employment.

3. - The Ownership, Management and Regulation of the Country's Capital Wealth

There is in fact almost an infinity of various diverse ways in which the production of goods and services may be organised, planned and managed. I will mention only six typical varieties.

Variety one may be called *Command Socialism*, where there is a central economic plan instructing production units what to produce and what resources to use for their production and how to allocate their output to consumers. It is not competitive; it does not rely on free enterprise; and it makes no use of a market.

Variety two may be called *Marked Socialism*. With this system there is no competitive free enterprise, since all productive enterprises are State owned and established or disestablished by the central authority, the State owning all the capital invested in the various firms. But the managers of the firms are instructed to produce as much as they can, subject to covering their costs at current market prices of their imports and outputs, prices being adjusted so as to clear all markets.

The remaining four varieties of productive structure could meet the full requirements of a competitive free-entreprise market structure.

Variety three may be called the *Capitalist Company Structure* and is the familiar textbook pattern for the discussion of capitalism. There is private ownership of capital resources wiuth freedom to establish a new firm. In the firms the owners of the capital resources appoint the management. Labour is hired by the capitalist company at an agreed fixed rate of pay and the employer-owners of capital bear the risk receiving what income is left over from the market sale of the output of the firm after the payment of labour and other hired factors of production.

Variety four is the *Profit-Sharing Capitalist Company* in which the text-book capitalist company is modified by granting to workers in addition to any element of fixed wage a share in the residual profits of the firm, but with the owners of the capital still engaging the workers and making the main decisions about the working of the firm.

Variety five may be called the *Labour Cooperative* in which capital and labour reverse their roles. The workers hire the capital resources used in the firm; they manage the firm and take all decisions about its policy; and they bear the risks accepting as their pay what income is left over from the sales revenue of the firm after paying the agreed sums for the hire of capital, land, and other productive resources.

Variety six may be called the *Labour-Capital Partnership.* The firm is run by partners some of whom contribute work to the firm and some risk-bearing capital. The partners share in the management and risk-bearing of the firm and they divide the residual profit of the concern between them in predetermined shares according to the amount of work and/or risk-bearing capital which they put into the firm. In this structure neither capital hires labour nor labour hires capital, but worker and capital partners together decide on the management of the firm including decisions about the terms on which new worker or capital partners should be engaged by the firm.

There can, of course, be many mixtures of these various forms of competitive free-enterprise market structures. In any one economy there may be some capitalist companies, some profit-sharing capitalist companies, some labour-managed cooperatives, and some labour-capital partnerships. Moreover a single firm may be constructed on a mixture of forms. For example in a labour-capital partnership some workers may be hired by the partners at a fixed wage and some capital funds may be lent at fixed interest to the partnership by outsiders who are not partners.

The existence of certain socialist elements in the production processes adopted by the members of a new Europe cannot be ruled out of court. Thus a nationalised railway network could be operated on full market socialist principles, selling its products and buying its inputs in an uncontrolled free market. Even elements of command socialism will inevitably exist in socialised activities producing such public goods as defence and law and order and may well by choice be adopted in other activities such as those of a national educational system or a national health service in which the outputs are not subject to market sales but are produced and allocated according to a central plan, but in which various degrees of market socialism or indeed of full competitive free-entreprise may be adopted for the supply of various ingredients into these services.

Moreover, so-called socialist intervention in the management of a country's economic resources can include not only those cases in which the resources are owned and/or operated directly can include not only those cases in which the resources are owned and/or operated directly by some State organisation. It covers also many forms and instances of State intervention by means of regulation and control of private concerns operating otherwise in a free market. Town and country planning, the control of monopolistic mergers between private companies, the setting of maximum prices, and the quantitative restriction of the output of pollutants are examples of such interventions.

Clearly not all elements of State ownership, management, fiscal interventions and direct regulation of industrial and similar activities can be ruled out in the economies of new Europe. Thee are many possibilities for legitimate diversity and experimentation in mixtures of different forms of structure within an economy which is generally based upon the principles of competitive free-enterprise markets.

4. - The Distribution of Income and Wealth, Social Security and Full Employment

The other main features with which the ideology of the old socialist countries of Eastern Europe may be associated are the distribution of income and wealth, social security and full employment. These ideas are so closely interconnected that it is convenient to discuss them together.

All European governments take some measures to relieve the poverty of those citizens who are destitute and indeed to effect some measure of general redistribution of income and wealth. But there are a number of questions to be asked. First, there is the question of degree. At what point, if any, do egalitarian measures become such a soaking of the enterprising rich and subsidisation of the idle poor as to prohibit membership of a community built on the principle of free enterprise? Second, can the measures normally employed in the present capitalist countries be usefully supplemented by measures of a more socialist type? Third, how far can any diversification of national experiments in redistributive and other social policies be accommodated in a new European Economic Community?

The varieties and the implications of different redistributive and other social measures are so numerous that it is impossible to present a *catalogue raisonnée* of all possible experiments. I intend, therefore, to describe one country's particular experiment in combining a reliance on competitive free enterprise markets with a somewhat socialist apparatus for a more egalitarian distribution of income and wealth and for greater social security and fuller employment. I raise the question whether it would, in principle, be possibile for this particular country, without any basic reformulation of these social policies, to join an economic community composed of the existing Western European countries. One can in this way well illustrate all the main problems of integrating different social objectives and experiments into a single economic community based on competitive free-enterprise markets.

The country which I have in mind is the island of Agathotopia which I visited in 1988 and whose attempt to combine a reliance on competitive free-enterprise markets with a radical emphasis on these social objectives I greatly admired (1).

_____

(1) A more detailed accountt of my visit to Agathotopia may be found in MEADE J.E.: «Agathotopia: The Economics of Partnership», Edinburg, Aberdeen University Press for The David Hume Institute, *Hune Paper*, no. 16, 1989; an Italian edition, *Agathotopia L'Economia della Partnership*, Milano, Feltrinelli, 1989. For the purpose of the present paper it is not necessary to enquire into the details of the island's existence and other institutions nor to ask whether any European country would in fact ever be likely to act quite like the Agathotopians. The only relevance for the present paper is to provide a list of many measures any one or combination of which a European country might wish to adopt.

The Agathotopians accept the fact that they cannot rely on competitive free-enterprise markets working efficiently unless they allow the markets to determine the price of the factors of production, that is to say, of capital, of land of different qualities in different regions, and of labour of various skills and training. It is only if the producers of goods and services can compete for the hire or purchase of the various factors of production that free markets will have the effect of attracting the factors of production into the industries and the methods of production that will produce the greatest amount of what the competing purchasers of the final products most desire to consume. The result will determine the incomes of the various owners of different resources of land and capital and of the various workers of different skills, training and localities. In particular the distribution of the revenue from the sales of manufactures products between return on capital and income of labour will depend upon the relative scarcity of labour and of capital resources, the degree to which consumers want goods and services which are capital-intensive or labour-intensive in their production, and the extent to which new technologies are relatively labour-saving or capital-saving. In their own economy the Agathotopians recognise the fact that these conditions are such that for the general range of industrial workers, apart from those with special skills or abilities, full employment depends upon the acceptance of a relatively low income from work. The demand for a higher rate of pay would involve a restriction of the demand for the labour, leaving some unfortunate workers in unemployment.

They have reacted to this situation in two ways.

First, they have taken a number of far-reaching measures to ensure that rates of pay are very responsive to labour market conditions and are very flexible in particular in a downward direction if that proves to be necessary to preserve full employment.

Second, they realise that it would have been impossible to move seriously in the direction of such flexibility in rates of pay if they had not taken equally far-reaching steps in providing for every citizen a basic income in addition to his or her income from work or from the ownership of wealth. Such a basic income constitutes a major instrument in the redistribution of income as well as being an essential element in mitigating the otherwise universal insistence on receiving a rate of pay sufficiently high to provide a given real standard of living.

To deal with the first of these two sets of problems the Agathotopians have a very extensive set of rules and institutions to promote competition through the outlawing of every kind of combination between individual productive units for the purpose of dividing the market, of maintaining prices or of preventing the entry of new competitors. Where any marked monopolistic power is unavoidable as in the case of many public utilities they set maximum levels for selling prices and other charges. They apply these same principles relentlessly to the labour market making it in effect very difficult for combinations of workers to take industrial action in order to prevent the management from employing additional workers at lower rates of pay.

In addition they have instituted a system of compulsory arbitration to settle any dispute about rates of pay in any sizeable productive unit, the arbitrators being required to set the wage at a level which will promote employment. This is designed not merely as an additional safeguard against pressures by inside employed workers for the raising of rates of pay above the level necessary to attract outsiders to the concern, but also to prevent employers with monopsonistic powers from keeping rates of pay below the level necessary to attract new labour to the concern.

The Agathotopians realise that none of these wage-fixing institutions can prevent capitalist and workers in any successful business from getting together to share an increase in their prosperity by raising simultaneously the wage rates and the dividends received by the firm's insiders rather than by reducing prices, selling a greater output and employing more workers to the advantage of deprived outsiders. They have tackled this problem in two ways.

First, to put some curb on such inflationary agreements among insiders they have introduced a scheme, covering all sizeable firms, under which any rise in the average rate of pay in excess of a given moderate norm is subject to an inflation tax.

Second, they have promoted a widespread structure of what they call *discriminatory labour-capital partnerships*. The Agathotopians have a great preference for the partnership form of structure in which the worker's reward takes the form not of a contractual rate of wage but of a share in the concern's profit or rather in the net value added by the concern. They encourage it by means of extending certain tax privileges to such forms of industrial organisation. But the danger is that any such partnership which is especially successful and whose members are for that reason receiving returns on their partnership shares which exceed the market rates of return which are being earned elsewhere in the economy will have no incentive to expand their successful enterprise. To expand indefinitely by offering to additional partners the same share of profit which the existing partners are themselves enjoying would lead to a reduction of the incomes of all partners down towards the outside competitive levels.

The Agathotopians have met this problem by insisting that a labour-capital partnership should receive favourable tax treatment only if it were ready to adopt what they call the principle of discrimination in their plans for expansion. In the case of a successful discriminating labour-capital partnership, this requires the partnership to offer to new partners whatever terms of membership are needed to attract them without any obligation to offer them terms which are as high as those already enjoyed in the existing exceptionally successful partnership. By this means a successful partnership, which ought in the public interest to expand, can attract new partners without any reduction of the incomes enjoyed by the existing partners. However, this principe. of discrimination between the terms of engagement for existing and for new additional partners implies the abandonment of the principle of equal pay for equal work.

The Agathotopians have managed to operate a rasonably success-ful full employment policy by accompanying the measures for the downward flexibility of money wage payments so long as any substan-tial number of workers were unemployed with a combination of monetary and fiscal policies designed to maintain a steady 5% per annum rate of growth of their money GDP, i.e. of the total of money expenditures on their domestic products.

They recognised that it was impossible to put into effect the general measures just discussed unless pay was supplemented by another source of income to offset the prospect of possible low and risky rate of pay. This purpose was in part achieved by the familiar means of State provision on an equal basis to all citizens of educational and health services. But in addition to this they rely on two less familiar arrangements.

First, they devised their structure of taxation in such a way as to encourage a more equal distribution of ownership of private wealth and so of the receipt of investment income. For this purpose they exempted all net savings from their income tax base by the simple process of adding to the tax base all sales of capital assets and exempting from the tax base all purchases of capital assets. But they combined this with a moderate annual wealth tax on all holding of capital assets above a given level together with heavy taxation on transfers of wealth by gift *inter vivos* or by bequest on death. The result was that citizens with little wealth could accumulate savings up to a given level free of tax, while further accumulations by savings or by transfers of wealth from other citizens were penalised.

Second, there are no personal or other tax-free allowances under their income tax (other than the exemption of tax on net savings). But in place of such personal allowances the State pays free of tax to every citizen a basic income which depends solely upon the age of the citizen, a distinction being drawn between the payment to a child or to an adult of working age or to a pensioner.

This basic income is paid at a generous rate to every citizen, rich or poor, and it thereby imposes an extremely heavy burden on the Agathotopian government's budget. They have been prepared to accept the need for a relatively high and progressive schedule of tax for their savings exempt income tax and for their duties on transfers of wealth *inter vivos* and at death. But such sources of revenue could not be sufficient to finance the hideous expense of paying a substantial tax-free benefit to every citizen, rich or poor. They have supplemented their tax revenue by three exceptional measures.

First, the Agathotopians are very green and have taken far-reaching steps to curtail every form of pollution. They have refrained in every case from doing this simply by issuing restrictions on the amount of any polluting element which any producer or other economic agent is permitted to emit. Still less are they willing to use the method of subsidising non-polluting competitors of any polluting activity. They have in every case acted by imposing a tax or other charge on polluting activities at a rate sufficient to achieve the desired reduction of that activity. In those cases where more direct quantitative regulation of a pollutant seems necessary they have acted by auctioning to the highest bidders the quota rights to produce the pollutant. They have in addition imposed an important tax on advertisement of different kinds on the grounds that the extensive promotion of unnecessary consumerism is a form of social pollutant. They have raised a very substantial revenue by these taxes and charges which are not merely revenue-raisers but whose indirect effects are wholly desirable.

Second, they have imposed a surcharge on the first slice of each citizen's taxable income. The reason is as follows. Much the cheapest way of guaranteeing a minimum income to every citizen is to pay a conditional basic income to every citizen but to withdraw the payment pound for every pound of other income received by the citizen. In this case no one receives any payment above whatever is needed to supplement his or her other income up to the basic minimum. The revenue needed for guaranteeing a basic income is minimised, but all incentive to earn additional income at the bottom of the scale is removed since such income is docked pound for pound as it is earned. An unconditional basic income with no surchange, on the other hand, does not penalise earnings at the lower level, but it is intolerably expensive if it is paid at an adequate rate to every citizen, rich or poor. A surcharge on the first slice of other income is a compromise. The need for other revenue is reduced at the cost of a partial, but only partial, extra disincentive against earning income at the bottom of the income scale.

Third, in marked contrast with the representative capitalist economies of Western Europe the Agathotopians have no State national debt. On the contrary they have a State national asset. Over the past years by heavy taxation of a form which is paid out of private savings or private holdings of wealth they have managed to pay off any original national debt and in addition to accumulate for the State a national asset. The surplus capital funds thus accumulated are invested by the State through investment trusts and similar private financial institutions indirectly in private competitive free enterprises. The State does not manage these enterprises. It, like many a private rentier, merely enjoys the beneficial ownership of the profit made by private enterprise of one kind or another. The net result is that the State instead of having to raise tax rates to pay interest on a national debt receives indirectly a substantial proportion of the yield on privately managed capital assets without having to raise tax rates for that purpose.

To reach this position the government in any capitalist country with an existing national debt would have to go through a process of what may be called Topsy Turvy Nationalisation. If a private company is nationalised with an issue of national debt to raise the funds to compensate the previous private owners, the State over the management of the concern but does not benefit financially from the ownership in so far as the interest payable on the national debt is raised *pari passu* with the profits earned by the nationalised enterprise. But if on the contrary the capital funds are raised by an annual levy on private wealth and are then used to redeem the national debt or are invested by the State on the stock exchange indirectly in part ownership of a range of businesses which remain in private management, the State does not nationalise the management of any private enterprise but does acquire a partial beneficial ownership in a range of otherwise private concerns. It is to be noted that this process of topsy turvy nationalisation would present a formidable fiscal problem for the capitalist countries of Western Europe starting off with a large national debt, whereas in the case of a socialist country of Eastern Europe the result might well be achieved merely by refraining from selling the whole of the beneficial ownership of all the State-owned assets to the private sector.

There could clearly be a very great variety of experiments in this catalogue of institutions and policies for the promotion of flexibility of prices and rates of pay, for the maintenance of full employment, and for the redistribution of income and wealth in a competitive free-enterprise market framework, which I have illustrated from the Agathotopian experiment. The question arises whether diversification in this sort of experimentation would be compatible with the requirements of an effective economic union of the countries concerned. It is to the requirements of such a union and to the question of the degree to which such requirements would preclude national experimentation that I will now turn.

5. - The Role of Politics and of External Relations

This paper is confined to a discussion of the distribution of the distribution of economic functions inside a European Community between the national governments and the central Community authorities. It purports therefore to exclude all considerations of political matters and of relations of the Community and its members with other parts of the world. These distinctions between the political and the economic and between the internal and the external problems of the new Europe are inevitably artificial. In fact in the final choice of designs for a new European Community both political and external aspects must play a very significant role.

No doubt it will and should be a requirement of the new Europe that the governments of the member countries, as well as the governmental authorities of the community itself, should be based on the political principles of liberal democracy. The design of such liberal democratic structures presents great problems and is of the utmost importance. But for the purpose of this paper in discussing the distribution of internal economic functions the national governments and the central Community authorities we may simply assume that appropriate efficient governmental institutions exist at both the national and the central level to carry out the relevant internal economic functions.

But there are other important objectives of the political arrangements in a new Europe. The political structure may well be designed so as to produce what may be called internal cohesion between the member nations and external influence *vis-à-vis* the nations of the outside world. In the present century two world wars have arisen as a result of the nations of Europe fighting each other, the cohesion that a political union might create can thus be very highly valued even if it carries with it little or no economic advantages—indeed even if it carried with it only economic disadvantages. Moreover political union can enhance the influence and power which the constituent members can exert in world affairs; and for this purpose it may be argued that it is not politically sufficient simply to promote a single market within Europe, but that political arrangements should be such as to enable Europe to exert a powerful unified influence over would political and economic institutions and policies.

These aspects of a new European political structure, namely their effects on internal cohesion and external influence, inevitably have effects upon internal economic developments which in turn have implications for the distribution of economic functions between the national governments and the central authorities with in a new European Community. Defence arrangements provide an outstanding example. Suppose that defence became a direct function of the new European Community. This 1) would promote internal cohesion by giving the various member nations a function which they had to perform jointly together; 2) would increase their power and influence vis-a-vis the rest of the world; and 3) by necessitating a large increase in the central authority's budget would greatly affect the internal distribution of economic functions between the national governments and the central Community authority.

There are many other political and external institutional arrange-ments which have internal economic implications of this kind. The following are three examples: 1) the choice of a customs union rather than a free trade area basis of a European single market; 2) the common agricultural policy of the European Community, and 3) the proposals for a single currency in a European monetary union. All three of these institutions have two very important features.

First, they give the central political authority a task for the member countries to decide and administer jointly: a single set of imports levies in the case of the European economic customs union; a single set of support prices and subsidies in the case of the common agricultural policy; and a single structure of money rates of interest in the case of the European monetary union. Second, all of them draw a sharp distinction between the inside members and the outside foreigners, the insiders sheltering behind the common tariff against foreigners' products, or enjoying the agriculture subsidies which are not available to foreign farmers, or dealing in a single money which is distinct from the foreigner's money.

These features in all three cases promote the internal cohesion of the Community and increase its bargaining power and other forms of external influence *vis-à-vis* rest of the world. But they also have important implications for the distribution of economic functions within the Community: the customs union determines a single set of uniform harmonised import duties and shifts revenue from the national budgets to the central budget; the common agricultural policy implies, like defence, a heavy centralised fiscal burden; and a common currency shifts the determination of monetary policies, such as the setting of rates of interest, from national central banks to a central monetary authority.

Thus in fact a complete disregard of political and external considerations is not really possible in considering the distribution of economic functions between national and central authorities within the new Europe. However, having looked this problem squarely in the face, we will pass on to consider that distribution with the minimum possible reference to the implications of political and external factors.

6. - The Principle of Subsidiarity and the Parable of the Ambidextrous Economist

In the current discussion of economic decisions about European union much reliance is often put on the principle of subsidiarity, namely the principle that, in the ascending hierarchy of authorities from paterfamilias to neighbourhood council to regional council to national government to European Community, anything which can be done well at a lower level should be left to that level and only those things which cannot be done well at the lower level should be assigned to decision and administration by a higher level of authority. This sensible federalist doctrine can no doubt in many cases be of great help. I take environmental control as an example. Certain forms of pollution — or more generally of what economists would call external diseconomies — may be very local in their incidence, such as the noise emitted by various local activities. Other forms of pollution may be very widespread in their effects, such as the chemical pollution of the atmosphere or of sources of water, in which case a polluting activity in one locality may have its effect over a wide territory of a continent or even of the whole world. The principle of subsidiarity can then clearly point to the assignment of the control of the former type of pollution to a local or national authority and of the latter type to a European or world authority.

Much lip service is paid to this doctrine of subsidiarity. But it is in fact in direct opposition to the idea described in the previous section that the internal cohesion of a new Europe can be strengthened by finding positive tasks for the central Community authorities to perform. On occasion one feels that the principle has for this reason been reversed and that the assignment of a given function to a Community authority is recommended provided that it can be efficiently performed at the centre and regardless of the question whether it could be equally well or even better performed at the national level.

But even in the absence of any anti-subsidiarity tendency of this kind, the application of this comforting principle of subsidiarity does not present a simple solution to the great majority of problems of clashes between the relative advantages of national diversification and continental unification. It will be my purpose in what follows to point out that time and time again there are certain clear advantages in leaving a matter to the unfettered choice of a national government and at the same time there are certain quite different but equally clear advantages in devising a uniform continental solution for the problem. In such cases the pros and cons of the various possible solutions must be weighed up against each other in making the final choice, the principle of subsidiarity playing the very minor role of suggesting that if the other pros and cons seem to be evenly balanced the chairman's casting vote, as it were, should go in favour of the national authority.

At this point I introduce the parable of the ambidextrous economist. President Truman, we are told, instituted a search for a one-armed economist so that when he sought advice on an economic decision he would not be told that on the one hand there was a case for, but on the other hand a case against, a particular decision. I believe that president Truman was at fault in this desire. Indeed, that very great President himself had, I believe, on his desk a placard which read «The Buck Stops Here». There is almost always a case for and a case against an economic decision; in such cases it is the duty of

an economic adviser to explain the economic technicalities of the case
for and of the case against; it is the duty of the President to decide
between the two. In a number of instances where the case for or the
case against a particular proposal seems to me to be overwhelming I
will play the role of the President and decide what should be done. But
I shall frequently play the role of the ambidextrous economist and will
describe a number of cases where there is a much more evenly
balanced clash between the case for national diversification and the
case for continental uniformity, It is for the reader then to play the
political role of the President and make the final choice between
alternative solutions. One must not fall into the vulgar error of
believing than an economic adviser is useless because he or she
confines his or her advice to a statement of the economic case on the
one hand for, and on the other hand against, a particular policy.

On this principle I shall proceed to discuss such possible clashes
under two main headings which cover, I think, the two basic sets of
problems which are the subject matter of current debate about
European economic and monetary union, namely the formation of a
single economic market and of a single monetary unit.

7. - The General Nature and Economic Objectives
   of a Single European Market

The general purpose is to remove all direct and indirect obstacles
to the free movement of goods, services, capital and labour between
the separate competitive free-enterprise market economies of the
European countries so as to transform the whole into one uniform
competitive free-entreprise market. The economic advantages expected from such a transformation are those so well expounded long
ago by Adam Smith and Ricardo.

First, free trade in products between countries with different
factor endowments will enable each constituent country to concentrate on the goods and services in the production of which it has a
comparative adavantage with the result of an increase in the total
output of goods and services.

Second, free trade will extend the size of the total market for goods and services and thus enable a greater advantage to be taken of the reduced costs of production which may result from Adam Smith's division of labour in a large scale of production. In some cases a market of an extent no less than that offered by the whole European continent may be required to enable any one European producer to take full advantage of the economies of large-scale production. In other cases each separate European national market might be of sufficient extent to enable one or at the most a very limited number of national producers to take full advantages of the economies of scale. In such a case the organisation of a single market covering the whole European continent could ensure that there was much more effective competition in what would otherwise be a structure of national enterprises, each able to exploit monopoly powers in its own protected national market.

Finally, the freedom of movement of labour or capital from the localities in which it is relatively plentiful and cheap to the localities in which it is relatively scarce and expensive will supplement the cost-reducing effects of free trade in increasing the output of the products of labour and capital.

The action needed to construct such a single market would seem to be obvious, easy and straightforward. Remove all national or continental governmental obstacles to freedom of movement of goods, service, capital, and labour and the problem is solved. There is much truth in this simple prescription; but, alas, for reasons to which I have already alluded in earlier sections of this paper, the answer is a good deal more complicated than that. There are at least three groups of basic reasons why simple laissez-faire is not enough.

The first general set of complicating factors can be grouped under the heading of those resulting from monopolistic conditions. Where economies of scale are so large relatively to the market that there is room for only one or two productive units to service the given market, free competition cannot be relied upon to produce the optimum output of the product. Producers will have some incentive to restrict output and to raise prices above cost because there is no room in the market for new competitors producing on a scale which would make their entry profitable. This phenomenon can take many forms ranging from that of a single railway network covering the whole geographical area to that of a small local producer protected by heavy cost of transport of products into his area from outside sources or protected by the attraction of a special brand name of the product.

A second general set of complicating factors can be grouped under the heading of external economies or diseconomies. By the term external diseconomies economists describe situations in which a private producer or consumer imposes a social cost on society for which he or she makes no payment, the most obvious cases being those in which the activity causes some form of pollution the social cost of which does not enter into the market cost of the good as it is produced or consumed. By external economies the economist describes a situation in which some economic activity produces a social good for which the private producer or consumer obtains no market benefit, an example being the invention of some new unpatented product or method of production of which competitors can take advantage without making any market payment to help to meet the cost of the initial research involved in perfecting the invention. A single market will be working efficiently only if some means can be found of bringing these external social costs or benefits into account in determining what are the real benefits to society of producing one product instead of another or of using one method of production rather than another. But this involves some form of state intervention to tax or otherwise restrict activities with high external diseconomies and to subsidise or otherwise promote those activities with high external economies.

The third general set of complicating factors can be grouped under the heading of distributional effects. As has already been argued at length in section 4 of this paper an economy which is based on competitive free-enterprise market arrangements will lead automatically to a given distribution of income and wealth among the citizens of the community which may not be considered acceptable.

In all of these three cases of monopolistic conditions, of environmental pollution and of the distribution of income and wealth State intervention in the market may be needed. In all three cases the questions arise: How unacceptable must the adverse effects become for positive intervention in the market to be legitimate? What forms should such interventions take? And should any such interventions be operated on diverse national principles or by a continental authority on a uniform basis?

In the next section I will try to illustrate the possible answers to these questions by applying them, very superficially I fear, to a select number of issues which are currently debated in connection with the building of a new Europe. In examining these specific questions I shall, on the principle of subsidiarity, assume that the starting point is that the continental authority should do nothing; it should rely upon laissez-faire to construct an effective single market. Starting from this basis I shall then ask whether in any particular instance there is an economic case for active intervention at the continental level, bearing in mind that such active continental intervention may tale a positive or negative form. By negative continental intervention I mean that the continental, authority merely prohibits the national use of certain policies or institutions e.g. it prohibits a national government from discriminating in favour of its own nationals in making contracts for governmental purchases of goods and services. In the case of such negative continental interventions the central authority must, of course, have powers and procedures for ensuring that these prohibitions are respected by the national authorities. By positive continental intervention I mean the design by the central authority of a policy or institution which requires the relevant positive action to be taken by the continental authority itself, as in the case of a common tariff of import duties or a common set of subsidies in the case of agriculture. It is not easy to draw a sharp distinction between negative and positive interventions by the continental authority; but the distinction is, I think, sufficiently sharp to be a useful one.

The basic objective of a single market is, as has already been discussed, to promote competition through freedom of movement of goods, capital and labour. In the case of positive interventions in the single market which are left to the decision of the national authorities, I shall draw a distinction between what may be called uncompensated and compensated freedom of movement. The idea behind this distinction can be made clear by a simple example. There is a tax of 10% in country A on a particular product. In country B there is no tax. Uncompensated freedom of movement of the good from B to A would mean the absence of any tax on the import of good by A from B, and this would five the producers of *B* a 10% "unnatural" tax advantage over the producers of the good in *A*. A 10% duty on the import of the good from *B* would represent what I would call compensated free entry for the good into *A*. This has real meaning because a 20% duty which would give *A*'s producers a 10% advantage over *B*'s producers would in my terminology mean that there was not freedom of movement of the good, even though there might be no quantitative quota restriction on the amount of the good that was permitted to move from *B* to *A*. The application of the idea of compensated freedom of movement is not at all easy, as I hope to show; but as a means of clarifying some of the basic underlying issues in the discussion of the treatment of clashers between national diversity and continental uniformity it can, I believe, be useful.

8. - Some Specific Single Market Issues

8.1 *Agriculture*

Many relevant issues are raised by the Common Agricultural Policy (CAP); but I shall not discuss them in this paper. My official reason for not doing so is that it is impossible to consider the CAP without discussing the commercial relations of the members of the European Community with outside non-member countries; and I am strictly excluding relations with outside countries from the scope of this paper. An additional personal reason for excluding the CAP from this paper is to avoid the apoplectic fit which I might suffer if I started to do so. I can claim to be one of the founding fathers of the GATT; I have always worked for movements towards freedom of trade on a world-wide basis and have abhorred the construction of tight regional discriminatory protective devices. That the governments of the EC members should have risked endangering the whole future of the GATT for the sake of the political votes of a group of uneconomic farmers seems to me to be an unspeakable outrage. At this point I break my promise not to discuss the external relations of the European Community by asking the question whether the so-called capitalist countries could not be enlightened enough to apply to their mutual trade the principles of competitive free-enterprise markets, the application of which they are welcoming so heartily for the ex-communist countries.

8.2 *The Social Charter and the Redistribution of Income and Wealth*

On the principle of subsidiarity, as already explained, I start the examination of this wide range of labour market and other social interventions in the market on the assumption that such interventions should be left to the national governments and that the function of the European Community in these matters is to ensure the free competitive movement of goods and of factors of production between the member countries. On examination there is much to be said for continuing to rely in the main on this principle in the case of these social measures.

The are great differences in the standards of living in the various member countries. Any attempt to lay down a meaningful minimum wage for all workers in the Community as an equalising device at the lower end of the income scale would have disastrous effects. If such a regulation were strictly confined to the wage for labour it would be extremely unfair to a country which adopted the Agathotopian policy of tackling unemployment by combining a low wage with a high basic income from other sources or which adopted the profit-sharing principle of combining a low fixed rate of wage with a high share of profit for the workers. If an attempt were made to set a meaningful minimum, it would at least be necessary to include receipts from a basic income, from a share of profits or from other similar sources in the definition of the "wage". This together with other problems such as the treatment of part-time work through the decision whether it was the hourly rate of pay or weekly earnings to which the minimum referred would raise great administrative problems, the regulation and policing of which would require a considerable central bureaucratic staff.

But the basic argument against such central intervention does not depend upon these administrative problems. A minimum rate of pay which had any meaning for the member countries with existing high standards would be a device which protected them from being undercut by the products of member countries whose uncontrolled rates of pay would be below the minimum. As far as real differences in the productivity of labour in different European countries are concerned, it is freedom of movement of goods, of capital, of enterprise, and of workers between the countries which could provide a really effective equalising factor. The concentration of production on labour-intensive products in those countries where labour is plentiful and on capital-intensive products in those countries in which capital equipment is plentiful, together with free exchange of the products between the two types of country, would promote total production as well as helping to equalise earnings. And a similar tendency would result from the free flow of capital from economies in which it was plentiful into economies in which it was scarce and form the free migration of workers from economies in which labour is cheap to economies in which it is expensive.

There is a similar strong argument for leaving questions affecting the choice of institutions and other arrangements for wage-fixing and of the structure of competitive production units to the decision of the national governments rather than to attempt to devise central regulations covering the participation of workers in the management of such units. Different countries may produce different mixes of what I have called «market socialism», «capitalist companies», «profit-sharing companies», «labour managed cooperatives» and «labour-capital partnerships» with different arrangements about wage-fixing and about labour participation in the management of the concerns. By ensuring free competition between them the central European authority can make its best contribution to the choice of the most appropriate structures.

There remains, however, one very important set of problems in this field with which the simple attribution to the national governments of these social policies does not cope satisfactorily. Where differences in standards of living are due to differences in real underlying economic conditions, the proposed laissez-faire attitude of the central authority is likely to be the appropriate answer. But such differences may themselves well be the result of differences in national regulations, institutions, and policies rather than of differences in the underlying supply, demand, and productivity of the available economic resources. Suppose that countries A and B are very similar in their real underlying economic resources; that A has adopted a wide range of institutions and policies to redistribute income and wealth in an egalitarian direction; but that B has interfered very little with the distribution of income and wealth which results from the free play of the competitive markets. Low-paid unskilled workers might migrate from B to A to enjoy the favourable tax, social security, basic income advantages in A, while highly-skilled high-paid worekers and successful entrepreneurs might migrate from A to B, carrying their capital funds with them, to enjoy the relatively favourable tax treatment which they would receive in B. At the extreme such a situation could lead to a most inefficient and undesirable concentration of all the poor low-productive factors in one country with all the rich high-productive factors in the other.

One result might be that country A would decide to abandon or to modify its egalitarian interventions. Free competition between A and B in the Community market would have induced a convergence in national policies, in this case probably in the direction of scrapping egalitarian experiments.

A second possibility is that the central Community authorities should introduce regulations for the harmonisation of the relevant national institutions and policies. This would imply that some egalitarian intervention should take place but on the same scale and by the same means in all the national economies. This solution raises the great problems of deciding what the uniform scale and methods should be and implies the building of an effective central bureaucratic apparatus to administer and enforce the harmonised procedures. It also has the disadvantage of eliminating the possibility of diverse experimentation in the different national arrangements.

A third possibility is that the central Community authority should allow free national experimentation in these policies but should itself introduce and administer a positive form of egalitarian intervention of its own. For example it might itself raise a general community levy or tax of some form and use the proceeds to pay a modest Basic Income to all the citizens of the member countries. The national governments could be left to top this up with their different national schemes. Movements of people and capital would as before put a brake on the most extreme egalitarian experiments; but the existence of the modest Community scheme would mean that the outcome of the competition between the national experiments would be less markedly in-egalitarian than would otherwise have been the case. This solution would permit more national experimentation and would involve a less complicated central bureaucratic apparatus than the solution through centrally administered full national harmonisation.

A fourth possibility is to allow complete national freedom of experimentation in this field but to attempt to offset the effects of competition between the different national schemes by modifying the forces of competition through the introduction of what I have called compensated freedom of movement of goods, capital, and workers. Workers would be free to migrate from country B to country A, but they would not enjoy the extra egalitarian benefits which were offered in A over and above those that were offered in B. Capital could flow from A to B but would remain subject to any extra egalitarian tax or other treatment to which it was subject in A. I will return later to the question to what extent such compensated freedom is a practical possibility.

Meanwhile I claim the privilege of the ambidextrous economist and leave the choice between these solutions of the problem to the reader's Presidential decision.

8.3 *Norms and Standards for Health, Safety and Similar Reasons*

The formation of a single market for the European Community clearly requires the removal of national regulations of particular activities which are designed simply to protect national producers, or traders, against the competition of the producers and traders of other members of the community. But often the problem is not as simple as that. Thus imports of goods may be controlled on the grounds that the foreign goods may carry with them a threat to the health or safety of the consumers. Regulations excluding foreign banks or other financial institutions from providing their services in the domestic market may be imposed in order to protect local standards of operation for the financial security of the creditors of the institutions. Medical, legal, or other practitioners may be required for similar reasons to have aquired recognised national qualifications, often obtainable only by lengthy and costly training.

Some national procedures may be protective of national producers without any other important justification, such as regulations which require governmental procurement to give preference to national supplies. But many regulations, while they have an important, perhaps a predominant, protective effect, may also have a legitimate and important purpose in the protection of the consumer. This is a field in which there is a clear need for Community action to ensure that necessary regulations exist to protect the health, safety and security of consumers of goods and services without imposing unnecessary protection to local suppliers. In fact a great deal of tedious and detailed work has been done and is in the process of being done to apply this principle to a large number of particular activities.

I shall not attempt to discuss these individual cases in this paper because this is a field in which, if one assumes that all are agreed on the basic principle of a single market, there is no basic inevitable clash between national and community interests. The only problem is to search for a method which prevents the use of such regulations for national protective purposes with the minimum of detailed community regulation. Wherever possible, the best method for this purpose is the rule that member countries should recognise the national norms and standards of each other. Country *A* should allow free import of goods and professional services and personnel from country *B*, provided these goods and services satisfy the norms and standards which country *B* lays down for the consumption of country *B*'s products in country *B*. This rule would have to be accompanied by some basic Community minimum requirements which each country's national norms and standards would have to satisfy. But subject to that provision, the method allows the maximum possible national diversity of norms and standards with the minimum amount of central bureaucratic administration.

8.4 *Control of Monopolies*

Another closely related but more difficult set of problems arises in
cases in which important monopolistic structures are inevitable. In
fact we live in a world of imperfect competition in which monopolistic
elements are to be found in most, if not all, markets. Everyone is
familiar with the danger that a monopolist may restrict output in
order to raise the price of the product and to make an undue profit at
the expense of the consumer. The basic weapon against such monopolistic action lies in a competitive economy in which there is freedom
for new suppliers to enter the monopolist's market to take advantage
of the monopolistic profits with the result of increasing supplies and
bringing the price of the product down.

Why then does freedom of competition not suffice to remove all
monopolistic activities? The answer lies in the phenomenon of "increasing returns to scale"; in order to produce a good or service at a
low cost one must have a sufficiently large market to be able to
produce on an economically large scale. This principle applies over
the whole range of activities from the village shop to the gigantic
industrial combine. The village shop operates in a market which
enjoys a modest protection due to cost of transport and of customer
movements. The villager finds it cheaper to walk round to the village
shop to buy a loaf of bread rather than to take the train or bus to the
nearest large shopping centre. The village shop is thus able to charge a
somewhat higher price than the neighbouring large shopping centre.
No competing village shop enters a small village market because there
is not room for two to be able to conduct the business on a scale
which is sufficient to reduce the costs to a tolerable level. The same set
of considerations on a very different scale will explain why there is
room for only one or two producers of, say, cars, each able to
preserve some degree of monopolistic profits. Low costs of production
may require an assembly line which will handle a very large output;
and the demand for cars may be such that there is room for only one
or two assembly lines producing on an economic scale.

So long as the separate nations of Europe could take steps to
protect their industrias from competing imports, a good might well be
produced separately in each country on a scale which was not

sufficient to enjoy all the available cost-reducing advantages of a large-scale production. The removal of national trading obstacles by the formation of the single market would then enable one country's productive unit to undercut and expand at the cost of another country's productive unit or to merge voluntarily with another country's productive unit and to concentrate the two national productions onto one production unit. In other words it might well result in the concentration of the national units into one or two much larger units. The result could be a real saving in cost for the Community as a whole combined with a concentration of activity and profit in one central locality at the cost of the other nations whose production units had been absorbed into the concentrated central unit. Here is the possibility of a very real clash of interest between the production of the good at the lowest possible cost for the Community as a whole and the desire of a nation to avoid the danger of becoming a deindustrialised depressed region and to maintain some diversity in its industrial structure. In view of these considerations what shoul be the policies of the member nations and of the community?

A merger will have two effects. On the one hand, it will increase the monopolistic powers of the merged concerns; on the other hand, the merger by increasing the scale of operations of the single concern may well reduce the costs of production of the combined output. Whether or not the merger should be permitted must depend upon whether or not it is judged that in the particular case the disadvantage of increased monopolistic power is or is not outweighed by the opportunities for real cost reductions. But should the judgement and control be a function of the national authorities or of a central Community authority?

In so far as the proposed merger is confined to two or more concerns operating in, and providing services for, a particular country it would seem clear that on the principle of subsidiarity the decisions should remain with the national authorities. It is arguable that even in the case of a proposed merger between concerns operating in a number of national markets — and it should be remembered that many large concerns are in any case multinationals operating in many national markets — each nation should have the power of preveting a merger of a concern located in its territory, even when the merger concerns business located in other territories. Such a power may be needed to preserve its industrial base and the diversity of its enterprise. But on the other hand it would appear that in such cases there should be a central Community authority to judge whether the whole balance between increased monopoly power and reduced costs weas such a to make the merger desirable for the Community as a whole. But in this case the questions remain how far and by what means should the Community authority take into account national interests in the diversity of their productive activities. The present ambidextrous economist does not know the answers and once more leaves the Presidential decisions to the reader.

Where a large-scale productive structure is needed in order tto attain low and economic costs of production, a limitation of the misuse of the inevitable monopoliostic power may be attempted through the control of the monopolist's selling price. A similar result may be achieved even more directly by the nationalisation of the enterprises concerned (as, for example, in the case of a country's generation and distribution of electricity), the managers of the nationalised concern being instructed to produce on as large a scale as is compatible with setting prices at a sufficiently high level to cover costs plus a moderate rate of profit. In such cases there is a wide range of systems for price-fixing which may be available. Where increasing returns to scale are still operating the average cost of producing a unit of the product will be higher than the marginal cost, that is to say, than extra cost incurred by adding some additional units to the total output The average cost will be lowered because the additional units of output add less to the total cost than the existing average cost. In such cases there is a strong case for charging prices on a discriminatory basis which allows some or all units of production to be sold at the low marginal cost while the average cost is covered by charging additional sums on some other basis.

Two examples may be given. The electricity supplied by a nationalised concern may be sold at a low marginal cost when it is exported to consumers in other countries where it can compete with and undercut the local producers and at a higher price to the domestic consumers. Alternatively the electricity may be sold to all consumers at the low marginal cost while a fixed standing charge based on some criterion other than the amount of electricity consumed is added to the electricity bill of each domestic consumer. The foreign importing country may be charging a single average cost price for all its output. It may, therefore, argue that discriminatory prices of the kind outlined in these two examples represent a case of dumping in which the exported electricity is sold at a lower price than that charged in one form or another to the domestic consumer. The question therefore arises whether there should be Community regulation over such national pricing systems even though they are designed to increase the sales and so to reduce the costs of the monopolistic producers. If so, should some Community action take the form of prescribing such pricing systems or of allowing the importing countries of such products to impose a compensating import duty equal to the excess of the export's average cost of production over the price charged for the export? The latter solution would allow a diversity of national experimentation in that a system of charging low marginal-cost prices to the units sold to its own domestic consumers could be applied in the exporting country while tax-inclusive average prices were charged in the importing country.

Finally, one may note that the monopolistic powers of some producers are positively maintained and reinforced officially by patent laws. Such arrangements are justified by the fact that the great costs of research and development of new products and of new methods of production would not be undertaken if the results could immediately be used by all competing producers without making any contribution to the cost of producing the invention. Patent rights give the inventer a monopoly of the use of the invention for a given period of years. The longer the period during which the monopoly profit from the protected use of the invention can be enjoyed, the greater the incentive to produce such inventions but the longer the period during can be enjoyed, the greater the incentive to produce such inventions but the longer the period during which other producers and consumer cannot maket use of the knowledge. The question arises whether there should be any special Community regulations to prevent the misuse of the patent system by one member country at the expense of others through granting strict patent rights for excessive periods to its national inventors of what may be very simple innovations. It is questionable whether the situation needs any special Community regulation over and above the existing general international arrangements in this field.

8.5 *Externalities and Environmental Problems*

Interventions of one kind or another in the working of competitive free-enterprise markets are needed in those cases in which there are social costs or benefits involved in the activity which are not charged or paid in the workings of the private price mechanism. The cost of pollution of the air or the sea or river water by the discharge of deleterious gases or chemicals of one kind or another is a most important example which is of great topical interest.

Where it is possible without too much difficulty there is great merit in controlling such pollution by a system of taxes or other charges or levies on the amount of pollution which each individual polluter is causing. If the polluter is taxed at so much per unit of the socially harmful gas or chemical which his or her activity causes it is equivalent to a simple supplement of the private production costs — of capital, raw materials, and labour — which the activity entails. Such a form of intervention has all the merits of competitive free-enterprise market arrangements. It leaves private producers and consumers in competition with each other to choose what they will produce and consume, including in the costs and prices in the market the social as well as the private costs of production. The social costs are charged on those who are doing the social damage and this gives them an incentive to change their methods of production which matches the social need for them to do so. But at the same time it allows for the fact that some polluters will be able to change their methods of production more easily and with less loss of output than others. To avoid the tax those who can change easily will change more than those who can change only at great private cost; and it is economically sound that, if the discharge of a harmful element is to be reduced to a given tolerabe level, the reduction of the discharge should be undertaken by those who can most easily do so.

Finally this method of control of pollution has an outstanding advantage over other methods of direct regulation; it raises tax revenue for the government in question. All governments need tax revenue. Most forms of taxation carry with them some undesirable disincentive effects such as the possible effects of a progressive income tax on the incentives and opportunities of entrepreneurs to expand their businesses. But levies on pollution constitute a method of tax which not only raises revenue but does so in a way which improves economic incentives in competitive free-enterprise market conditions.

Unfortunately, however, the application of the method of taxing the polluter can present grave administrative costs and technical difficulties. It requires some physical and administrative means for measuring the amount of pollution caused by each polluter. Such measurement may be technically difficult or even impossible. In such cases it may be possible to restrict the amount of pollution by more crude means. For example, it might be laid down that one particular polluting method of production should in all cases be prohibited. Such a regulation might reduce the polluting element to an unnecessarily low level and would make no distinction between those who could reduce pollution at little cost and those who could do so only at great cost. Direct and crude regulation of this kind should be employed only where the administrative and other costs of charging pollution taxes are too high.

So much for the methods of environmental control. One must also draw a distinction between the cases in which a private polluting activity affects only the social costs in a local region of one country and those cases in which the polluting activity affects social costs over a wide area which includes many countries. We may start with a sharp distinction between an activity which affects only one member country of the European Community and an activity whose social costs affect all the countries of the Community.

The principle of subsidiarity suggests that in the case of a purely local environmental social cost (as in the case of town and country planning of the use of land resources or of noise abatement in a given locality) the responsibility of control should lie with the national government, which would be free to use whatever method of control it chose to use. In the case of an activity which pollutes on a European continental scale the argument for using a Community pollution tax is very strong in all cases in which such taxation is a practical possibility. For the reasons already given it would represent the appropriate method for supplementing a European continental structure of competitive free-enterprise market arrangements. It would also have the great advantage of providing the central Community with a tax revenue. But where a continental pollution could not be controlled by a continental pollution could not be controlled by a continental pollution tax, the function of the central Community authority could be reduced to a determination of the quantitative extent to which each member should reduce its emission of the pollutants, leaving it to each national government to determine the means by which its quantitative target should be attained.

But the scope of polluting activities is not confined to those which affect one member country alone and those which affect all the European member countries. Some polluting activities (e.g. the discharge of chemicals into a river) may affect some but not all of the member countries of the Community, or may affect a group composed of one or more members countries together with one or more non-member countries (e.g. the discharge of chemicals into a river flowing through a number of different countries). This suggests that schemes of pollution control may be best devised between groupings of countries which may differ in their composition and which may or may not contain countries which are, as well as countries which are not, members of the European Community.

This subject of environmental control is, as everyone now knows very well, of the greatest importance; but it is at a very early stage of discussion and application. I myself feel unable to say more than that those forms of environmental pollution which affect all or a majority of the European countries raise problems of the kind which I have described and which certainly call for appropriate treatment by a central Community authority.

8.6 *Harmonisation of Taxes and Subsidies*

It is in the setting of taxes and subsidies that the most difficult and important clashes between national and continental interests can occur. The general problem is clear. If one decides to build a perfect single market in which no governmental interventions have any effect in distorting the relative adavantages of producing or consuming one nation's products rather than another's or of working or of holding capital or of living in one national area rather than another, there must be complete harmonisation of all taxes or subsidies throughout the area of the single market. Otherwise there will inevitably be some distortion of choice. On the other hand such complete and perfect tax harmonisation would remove all possibility of effective diversity in the national designs of economic institutions and policies.

The problem of finding an appropriate balance between legitimate and illegitimate diversity of national fiscal arrangements raises an extremely wide range of very complicated issues. It is possible in this paper only to scratch the surface of the problem by giving a few simple examples of the sort of issues involved.

Taxes which are laid simply on a nation's import or a nation's export of a particular good or service should clearly be ruled out be a general Community regulation against such national protective devices. But indirect taxes oin the whole national consumption or on the whole national production of a commodity are not in the same way obviously protective.

An indirect tax which is levied on all domestic production of a product with exported production paying no tax but all imports being subject to the tax, is clearly a tax on domestic consumption regardless of the source of the taxed good. Similarly an indirect tax which is levied on all production whether it is consumed domestically or is exported but without levying any tax on imports of the products is clearly a tax on domestic production of the taxed good regardless of its destination. In order to prevent the most obvious protective uses of indirect taxation it is clear that a national indirect tax should be either a tax on the national consumption whatever the source of the good or a tax on the national production whatever the destination of the product.

But such a simple rule would not suffice to rule out the design of structures of indirect taxes which in fact had a very marked protective effect. For example, in the case of VAT which is a tax on national consumption, harmonisation would mean that the tax must be im-.

posed on all items of consumption at the same uniform rate of tax. But in the interests of diversification it can be argued that the different nations should be permitted to differentiate between their scales of VAT and of other indirect taxes as between one class of goods and another. The legitimate grounds for such differentiation might be: 1) on distribution grounds (i.e. to tax expenditure on luxuries more heavily than expenditures on necessities) or 2) on environmental grounds (i.e. on the grounds that the consumption of the good caused an environmental evil.). However if complete freedom of choice of tax scales were permitted, there would be nothing to prevent all goods which were imported in large quantities by the natin being taxed at exceptionally high rates which would give an incentive to the home consumers to shift their purchases away from foreign on to domestic products. For example, in the UK a heavy consumption tax on wine and a low tax on beer could encourage the British habit of swilling home-brewed beer instead of sipping French wines.

A similar problem arises with the indirect taxation of production. If a nation levies particularly high rates of tax on products which it does not export and particularly low rates on products which it does export, it would in fact be paying the equivalent of a subsidy on its exports.

Considerations of this kind raise the question whether and, if so, how and to what extent the member nations should be required to consult with, and possibly to acquire the consent of, some Community authority with regard to the structures of their indirect taxes. One conceivable procedure would be: 1) to allow freedom to the constituent member countries to impose their own rates of indirect taxes; 2) to require them in any case to define and treat each such tax as either a tax on consumption regardless of origin of the good or as a tax on production regardless of destination of the production; 3) to allow other member countries to appeal to some Community body on the grounds that a member's structure of indirect taxes was in fact having an undue discriminatory effect on the offending member's imports or exports; 4) to require the accused member to justify its structure on certain clearly defined grounds such as a desirable redistribution of income or the protection of the environment; 5) to produce an award by the Community body as to the degree of unjustifiable tax or subsidy there was was on the complaining members' imports or exports of particular types of goods; and 6) to allow the injured members on the basis of «compensated freedom of movement of goods» to offset the effect of the unjustifiable tax or subsidy by an offsetting subsidy or tax on their own imports from or exports to the offending country. But the question remains whether or not any procedure of this kind could possibly be made workable.

I turn now from indirect to direct taxes and subsidies. In this category one may include taxes on income, on wealth, and on capital transfers and subsidies to income such as the payment of social benefits of one kind or another. In so far as these taxes or subsidies are levied on, or paid to, residents of a given nation and in so far as persons never change their residence, there are no insuperable problems involved in failing to harmonise the structure or rates of the various national regimes. There would need to be an agreed Community system of double tax relief which ensured that it was the tax regime of the country in which the taxpayer was resident which was operative in the case of any transaction. Thus if a taxpayer resident in country A received income in respect of work done or capital invested in couny B, the income would be subject to A's income tax and would not be charged under B's income tax regime. Similarly wealth held in B by a resident of A would be subject to A's wealth tax and would not be charged under B's wealth tax; and country A's social benefits would be paid to residents of A and B's to residents of B. However in the case of a capital transfer tax there could be a problem. Suppose some capital were transferred from a resident of A to a resident of B. If the capital transfer tax of A was payable by the benefactor and that of B was payable by the beneficiary, there would be a case of double taxation. Whereas if the capital transfer tax was payable by the beneficiary in A and by the benefactor in B both parties would be exempt from tax.

In this last case there would need to be some Community agreement about the way in which this kind of situation should be treated; and there could be other cases for which special rules would have to be agreed, for example for the treatment of the income of a discretionary trust some of the potential beneficiaries of which might be residents of A and others residents of B. But in general the principle of applying the tax regime of the country of residence of the person liable to pay the tax would be clear in its application. The problem would be simply that of avoiding evasion. For this purpose Community procedures for co-operative action between the various national revenue collecting authorities could be most helpful. In the extreme, if there was a single Community revenue collecting administration applying the various national regimes on behalf of the various national governments, the opportunities for tax evasion would be greatly reduced.

So far so good. But as has been already shown in the discussion of social problems, differences in fiscal arrangements for the redistribution of income and wealth may give rise to very serious problems in a Community in which there is free movement of persons between the various member countries. Egalitarian country *A* with a high basic income might attract all the poor, inefficient, or idle citizens while incentive-minded country *B* attracted all the rich, efficient and active members of society together with their capital resources.

Movement from one place of residence to another is, of course, not costless particularly in a continent in which languages differ from country to country. Some degree of diversity in tax regimes would be possible without leading to great movements of taxpayers. But if fully free uncompensated changes in rsidnce were allowed, this would set a very effective limit to the degree of diversity in national tax regimes which were practicable. Those who adovcated egalitarian measures on a large scale would have to persuade all — or at least the most important — nations of the Community to make more or less simultaneously the same sort of tax changes, the extreme version of which would imply complete tax harmonisation and the complete disappearance of experimental national diversity.

But may there not be some form of compensated freedom of movement of persons which would increase the feasibility of national diversity in tax regimes? Theoretically there is one simple rule which would solve the whole problem, namely a rule that while persons were free to change their actual residences they could not change their legal residence for purposes of direct-tax regimes. Thus a national of *A* who had migrated to *B* would still be taxed under *A*'s tax regime. If such a rule were possible, the problem would disappear.

Citizens would still have an economic incentive to move from A to B if and only if their pre-tax incomes were greater in B than in A. The taxes they would pay would depend upon A's tax schedule, but presumably the actual revenue would accrue to B's government, since the persons concerned would now for all intents and purposes be citizens of B enjoying the advantages and responsibilities of that country. It is perhaps not inconceivable that in the end, particularly if there were a single Community administration for the collection of the member countries' direct taxes, a solution somewhat on these lines might be possible. But it does not sound like a political possibility at the moment. I must leave it to the reader to consider whether there are more feasible methods of introducing some rough compensatory measures which would offset in part or whole some of the undesirable effects of diverse direct-tax regimes. Or would the existence of large diversities in national fiscal policies for redistribution of income and wealth necessitate the continuation of direct controls over migration between the member nations?

Such undesirable tax effects are to be expected not only as a result of the differences in the redistributive effects of taxation which I have just discussed. If country A exempts all net savings from its income tax and thereby turns it into a tax on consumption expenditures, while country B operates a straightforward income tax, there will be an incentive for citizens to be residents of A while they are saving for the future and their expenditure is low and to become residents of B when they are living on their past savings and their expenditures are greater than their income. Does this mean that A and B must jointly decide to operate either an income tax or an expenditure tax? Or could the citizens be treated as not having changed their legal residence for tax purposes when they move for A to B? Or could some rougher form of tax compensation be devised so that they pay some penalty on what they have saved tax free in A, when they move to B?

There are other forms of tax which I have not discussed and which raise similar problems. For example, a corporation tax is a tax on profits, i.e. on a form of income, which is payable not by a person but by a corporation. Differences in rates and structures of such a tax may thus affect incentives to expand production in one plant in A

rather than in another plant in B and in the case of a multinational company operating both plants it will give rise to incentives to keep the companies' accounts in such a way as to concentrate the profit return in the lower-taxed plant, for example, by selling intermediate products at an exceptionally high price when they move from the low-taxed to the high-taxed plant. Once again the question arises whether tax harmonisation is on balance desirable in order to remove these unwanted incentives.

This discussion of tax harmonisation has been very superficial, but it is hoped that it has served to show how basically important the question is in the search for a balance between the requirements of national diversity and continental uniformity.

9. - European Monetary Union

A very special case of possible conclitct between the merits of diversity and uniformity arises in the monetary field in choosing between a single European currency and a European set of national currencies with variations in the rates of exchange between them.

There are certain clear advantages in having a single European currency. The most obvious and familiar of these is the saving of the cost and inconvenience involved in having to change a domestic currency into a foreign currency for purposes of foreign trade, tourism, capital investment and other forms of transaction with foreigners, together with the ease of making comparisons between domestic and foreign prices and costs. Closely allied to this is another advantage, namely the removal of the uncertainty as to what the future rates of exchange will be between a domestic currency and various other currencies. The exporter of goods from A to B who contracts to produce them at a given price in B's currency will bear no exchange rate risk if B's currency is the same A's, but will bear a serious risk if B's currency may depreciate in terms of A's currency over the period of the contract; and in the absence of offsetting measures foreign exchange rates are notoriously volatile in their fluctuations.

For some countries membership of a Community with a single

currency — or with monetary arrangements like the ERM which greatly restrict exchange rate variations — may enable the country to resist inflationary pressures. For example suppose that a country is threatened with a high rate of inflation because of upward thrusts of money wage costs due to its wage-setting institutions. It may find it politically easier to take the necessary restrictive monetary and fiscal measures to fight such inflation if these measures are essential to maintain a given agreed exchange rate for its currency in terms of its competitor's currencies than if the restrictive measures are taken merely to avoid the rate of national inflation from rising above some nationally determined target level. There may be little or no real economic difference between the two methods. A given degree of restriction of money expenditures with the same consequential degree of recession and unemployment may be needed in both cases to break the wage cost-push inflation. The difference is basically a political one. The preservation of an internationally agreed exchange rate mechanism may be a more persuasive and credible argument than the prevention of a national index of inflation from rising above a target level and may thus have a greater effect in inducing wage bargainers to set less inflationary wage rates.

But probably the strongest argument in favour of a single European currency has little or no economic content but is straightforwardly political. A single currency gives the Community authorities a very important positive function to perform jointly — namely, the issue and administration of a single non-inflationary currency — in a way which distinguishes the countries concerned sharply from the outside world. Thus, like a flag it presents to the world a great symbol of unity. Such considerations may well be by far the nost important ones in the case of a European monetary union with a single currency, but they are not basically economic.

But a structure of separate national currencies with the possibility of variations in the rates of exchange between them also has certain clear advantages. The first of these is the much greater case of making any necessary adjustments between the general level of money prices and costs in one country and in another. Such situations may arise in a number of ways. Suppose that countries A and B concentrate on two different types of tradeable products, A concentrating on the manufacture of consumer goods and *B* on machinery and similar capital equipment. Suppose that the world demand for *A*'s product falls and for *B*'s products rise. Equilibrium in the world markets will require a general fall in the price of *A*'s products relatively to *B*'s products. Or suppose that *A* and *B* are producing very similar manufactured goods in competition with each other, but that *A*'s money wage costs have risen more rapidly than *B*'s. Such a development might occur through a higher rate of increase of output per head in *B* than in *A* or from a difference in institutions and customary procedures for the fixing of money wage rates, leading to a higher rate of increase of money earnings per head in *A* than in *B*. In either case a reduction of the general level of money prices and costs in *A* relatively to those in *B* is needed to restore *A*'s competitive position.

If *A* and *B* share the same currency, the process of readjustment requires an absolute reduction in *A*'s and/or an absolute rise in *B*'s money prices and costs. Such adjustments will be brought about in the markets by a slow and piecemeal procedure with the fall in the demand for *A*'s products causing reduced output and unemployment separately plant by plant in a whole range of industrial plants and companies. This process must continue on a scale sufficient to lead gradually to the necessary reduction in the general level of money prices and costs, while the rise in the demand for *B*'s products gradually causes a plant-by-plant rise in *B*'s money wages and policies. If, however, *A* and *B* have different currencies, the whole adjustment can be achieved without a prolonged period of plant-by-plant adjustment and without unemployed resources in *A* by means of a single once-for-all depreciation of *A*'s currency in terms of *B*'s.

In deciding whether *A* and *B* should share a single currency or should retain separate national currencies the merits of exchange-rate variations as an instrument of adjustment between the two countries must be set against the merits of a single currency in reducing costs and uncertainties in transactions between the two countries. There are at least four important factors to be considered in assessing the relative merits of the two exchange-rate mechanisms.

First, the greater is the size of any natioal or regional economy, the greater is likely to be the value of its internal transactions relative to the value of its transactions with the outside world. For this reason the relatively small economy will suffer relatively bigger transactions costs from having a separate currency of its own, monetary transactions with outsiders being large relatively to monetary transactions with insiders. A separate currency is more appropriate, the larger is the volume of internal transactions relative to external transactions.

Second, in deciding whether to join a monetary union sharing a single currency with other countries, a country should take into account the structures of its own economy and of the economies of the other members of the monetary union. The smaller the probability of a need for the real terms of trade between its products and the products of the rest of the union to be adjusted from time to time (i.e. for the price of its products to vary relatively to the price of the products of the rest of the union), the smaller would be the relative merits of retaining its own separate national currency.

Third, the greater the flexibility of its own money costs and prices in response to changes in demand and supply, the smaller would be the advantages of retaining its national currency. A particular and important example of this is the ease with which its wage-fixing institutions and procedures allow money-wage costs to rise and fall in its various industries and occupations as a result of an increase or decrease in the demand for labour at each point in the economy. The greater the flexibility, the less the need for exchange-rate variations as a means of adjustment of a general disequilibrium.

Fourth, the greater the ease of movement of labour and capital from regions in which there is an inadequate demand for their services to regions in which they are scarce and fully employed, the less need will there be for a reduction in the prices of the factors of production in the former regions relatively to their prices in the latter regions and the less, therefore, the need for a depreciation of the former currency in terms of the latter.

There is one other important merit in having a set of different national currencies. A currency must be managed by the relevant monetary authority with some set of financial objectives in view. One such objective — and it is often considered to be the only objective — will be the prevention of inflation or at least the prevention of the rate of inflation from rising above a moderate target level. But there are many ways of measuring the degree of inflation. The commonest measure is the rate of increase of a price level. But there are many different price levels. To take the ordinary cost of living index has grave dangers. For example, suppose there to be a sharp rise in the price of imported oil which enters into the cost of production of the economy's consumer goods and services. In order to prevent an inflation of the cost of living wage costs will have to be reduced absolutely by an amount necessary to offset the rise in the cost of the oil inputs. It would be difficult enough to resist an absolute rise in wage rates to offset the rise in the cost of living due to the increased cost of imported oil. But to obtain an absolute reduction in money wage rates sufficient to offset the rise in the price of oil might well need a restrictive financial policy on a scale which would cause a very large recession and growth in unemployment in order to cut wage rates sufficiently. Exactly the same problem would arise if it was decided to raise the rate of VAT or of other indirect taxes as a means of raising revenue. To offset the resulting rise in the cost of living would require an absolute reduction of money wage rates.

A more appropriate price index might be an index of the costs of production of the economy's output of goods and services exclusive of costs of imported raw materials and of indirect taxes (i.e. a GDP deflator). Such an index would not require an absolute reduction of wage costs to offset any rise in the price of imports or in indirect taxes. But it might still be liable to lead to serious recessions and unemployment. Suppose there were a rise in the price of imported oil which was allowed to lead to a rise in the cost of living rather than needing to be offset by an absolute reduction in wage rates. It would still be necessary to prevent the rise in the cost of living from leading to the absolute increase in wage rates which might be demanded in order to offset the rise in the cost of living. To prevent such increases in money wage costs there might have to be a serious recession and cutback in the demand for lavour. To obtain an immediate reversal of a 1% rise in wage demands might involve an immediate cutback of, for example, 5% in the demand for labour.

There is another measure of wage inflation which would call for a much less drastic cutback in the demand for labour in such conditions. This alternative would be to control the rate of rise in the total value of home production of goods and service exclusive of imported materials and of indirect taxes instead of controlling the rate of rise in the price per unit of such output (i.e. to substitute the total money GDP for the GDP deflator). Any undesired increase in money wage rates by raising the money price of output would, of course, raise the total money value of the output by a corresponding amount. But to obtain an immediate reduction of 1% in the value of total output could not at the worst lead to more than a 1% reduction in the demand for labour. A 1% reduction in the value of total output would be brought about by a 1% reduction in the level of output and employment event if there were no response at all in reducing the money wage rate and the money cost-price of output. For this reason taking the money GDP stead of a price level would be liable to cause much less sudden and sharp variations in the levels of output and employment. It would thus reduce the risks involved in joining a full monetary union with a single currency for a country whose institutions and procedures led to rather rigid wage-rate settlements.

There are thus many possible measures of inflation. A set of different national currencies would thus make room for a greater diversity of national experiments in the control of inflation, not only by allowing for different levels for any given inflation target but also by the choice of different methods of measuring inflation. In particular it would not rule out an experiment with an index of money GDP instead of a money price index as setting the inflation target. But it different countries were maintaining different inflation targets, there would have to be a possibility for at least moderate adjustments in their exchange rates.

There is one other important set of financial considerations which have important implications for the choice between a single uniform European currency and a set of independent national currencies. It should be the objective of the financial authorities not only to keep the economy on a given inflation target (whether this be a price target or a money GDP target), but also to keep the economy on what may be called a wealth target. This latter target might take the form simply of maintaining a certain budget balange between the government's tax revenue and its current expenditures on goods and services, in order to avoid the possibility of the government simply eating up the country's wealth by borrowing all private savings to finance a govern-

mental excess of current spending. Alternatively, the wealth target
might aim at keeping the level of public plus private savings at a given
target level. Whatever precise indicator is chosen for the wealth target
— and there is every reason to regard diversity of natinal experiment
in this sphere being in itself a desirable feature — there will then be
two policy instruments (namely, monetary policy controlling the rate
of interest and fiscal policy controlling the rate of tax) available to aim
at the two financial targets, (namely the inflation target and the
wealth target whatever precise form these may take).

It is often taken for granted that the obvious course is to assign
the use of the monetary weapon solely to the control of the monetary
target (e.g. to raise or lover the rate of interest as it is desired to lower
or to raise the rate of price inflation) and the use of the fiscal weapon
solely to the control of the wealth target (e.g. to raise or lower the rate
of tax as it is desired to raise or lower the budget balance). But this is a
mistaken idea. Monetary restriction will reduce the amount of
expenditures on goods and services. This reduction in demand will
help to reduce prices, but it will also reduce the incomes of these
producing the goods so that not only the revenue from indirect taxes
will fall as the result of lower sales but the revenue from direct taxes
will also fall as a result of lower expendable money incomes. Thus
monetary restriction will lower the inflation index and wil also lower
the tax revenue and thus the budget balance indicator. Fiscal restriction in the form of a rise in the rate of tax will raise the budget balance
but it will also lead to a fall in the demand for goods and services and
thus to some fall in the rate of price inflation. Thus both financial
weapons will affect both financial targets. The way to use them
efficiently so that both targets are maintained simultaneously is to use
them jointly and simultaneously to produce the jointly desired effect
on both targets. To use them with separate assignments, setting
monetary policy to control price inflation without any consideration of
its effect on the budget balance and setting fiscal policy to control the
budget balance withouth any consideration of its effect on price
inflation is at its best a very clumsy and inefficient procedure which
will enable the two targets to be reached only after a prolonged
process of adjustment and readjustment. At the worst if fiscal policy is
relatively more effective as a controller of price inflation and monetary

policy relatively more effective as a controller of the budget balance, the independent operation of monetary policy to control price inflation and of fiscal policy to control the budget balance will lead to a disastrous instability of the system (2).

The first solution would be to settle for a system of independent national currencies so that each national authority could control both its monetary and fiscal policies for the joint control of its own inflation and wealth targets. This would necessitate come degree of flexibility between the nations exchange rates, though it would be perfectly possible and desirable to devise a set of European rules and institutions for the conduct of foreign exchange policies which prevented unnecessary volatility in exchange rates but allowed for those moderate exchange rate variations which will be needed to harmonise the diverse national financial targets.

The second solution would be to institute a single European currency to be shared by all the member countries with a single European central bank to administer its issue, but at the same time to centralise a sufficient part of the fiscal operations of the European Community in a centralised Community budget in order to enable Community monetary and fiscal authorities jointly to design a joint monetary-fiscal policy for the control of inflation, while paying proper

---

(2) The dangers and disadvantages of assigning monetary policy exclusively to the control of inflation and fiscal policy exclusively to the control of budget balances are increased by the formation of a monetary union with a single currency. The formation of the union will cause much of the foreign trade of each constituent member nation to be transformed into the domestic trade of the union so that the ratio of foreign to domestic trade is much reduced. This has a double effect: 1) the fall in leakages of expenditures on imported goods causes the multiplier to be higher in the union. This means that both monetary policy and fiscal policy are more effective in controlling domestic expenditures and so in controlling both inflation and the tax base. But fiscal policy unlike monetary policy becomes less effective in controlling the budget balance. With a higher multiplier a given rise in the rate of tax will have a larger effect in decreasing consumption expenditures and thus in restricting the tax base; and this will reduce the tax yield from any given rise in tax rate. 2) when interest rates are raised to fight inflation, any consequential appreciation of the rate of exchange will have a smaller effect in reducing the cost of living in the union in which the price of imports is a smaller component of cost by living price index. This factor will reduce the effect of monetary policy on inflation. For these reasons the relative effects of monetary policy on inflation and of fiscal policy of budget balances will both be reduced by the formation of the union, so that the case for the esclusive assignment of monetary policy to the control of inflation and of fiscal policy to the control of budget-balance is doubly weakened.

James E. Meade

regard to the need not to upset national fiscal plans for the maintenance of their wealth targets. Such a situation might automatically result if for other purposes the European Community needed to develop its own considerable budget and tax revenue, as for example would be the case if joint expenditure on a single defence force became part of the Community's function. But in the absence of such a development one would need to endow the Community with a Community rate of tax (such as a Community VAT) which it could vary in order to help to regulate the total of money expenditures in the Community, but the revenue from which would be assigned to the various countries in which the revenue was raised. What needs to be avoided is a European central bank issuing a single European currency with the sole object of maintaining an inflation target in terms of that currency but without regard to any fiscal effects, the independent national budgets being subject to a scattered set of independent fiscal authorities acting without any regard to the inflationary or deflationary effects of their decisions.

I will cease the ambidextrous waving of my two arms and reveal my Presidential decision which is to advocate something on the times of the British proposal for the issue of an additional European currency which, following their notation, I will call a hard ECU. It seems to me to be a good way of reconciling as well as one can the conflicts which I have mentioned between the merits of a single European currency and of a set of independent national currencies.

Let me quickly state the main features of the proposals as I would like them to be made (3). Let there be a European Bank with the responsibility of issuing a new currency, the hard ECU. Its would be to control the issue so as to stabilise in terms of the hard ECU an index of the rate of price inflation or alternatively, as I would prefer, an index of the rate of price inflation or alternatively, as I would prefer, an index of the rate opf growth of the Community's total money GDP. Any member country or group of member countries could adopt the hard ECU as their national currencies thus forming a full monetary union with the European central bank as their single operative central

---

(3) The basic features of these proposals are described in the Appendix to this paper.

bank. Any other member country would be free to link its currency to the hard ECU in a way designed to rule out unnecessary fluctuations in the hard ECU value of its national currency but to permit such exchange rate variations as were planned to maintain equilibrium between its own plans for inflation control in terms of its own currency and the European central bank plans for its inflation control in terms of the hard ECU. Such planned variations would need to have the agreement of the European central bank authorities. Personally I think that they might often take the form of a planned crawling peg between the national currency and the hard ECU, changes in the rate of crawl being agreed from time to time with the European central bank.

Such a system would allow for the early formation of a full monetary union by those countries which were ready and desired immediately to do so, for a period of adjustment for those who wished to do so but were not ready to do so, and for a continued use of a suitably controlled but variable linkage with the hard ECU for those countries who wished to maintain indefinitely the experiment of having one currency for domestic purposes and another currency for foreign transactions for one reason or other, such as a choice of different forms of inflation or wealth target or a continuing divergence in wage and price setting mechanisms. The whole system would be a remarkable example of a new monetary experiment without, one would hope, nations which opted for one form of use of the hard ECU being regarded as superior or inferior to those who opted for another.

The Basic Features of an Independent Hard ECU

The following are 12 basic features of the hard ECU arrangements described in the last two paragraphs of the main text.

1) Every currency system requires a legal tender by means of which obligations expressed in terms of the currency must in the last resort be met. The legal tender consists of hard ECU bank notes.

2) These bank notes are issued by a European central bank (ECB) with a strong independent Governor and Board of directors.

3) The initial assets and liabilities of the ECB are constituted in the following way. The national central banks (NCBs) pay into the ECB an incorporation of their holdings of gold and foreign exchange in return for hard ECU deposit liabilitites of the ECB. The assets of the ECB are further augmented by the payment into the ECB of bonds or bills denominated in hard ECUs and issued by the national governments and/or the NCBs of the constituent member countries in return for holdings of ECB hard ECU deposit liabilities. The constituent governments guarantee the solvency of the ECB.

4) All accounts, transactions, assets and liabilities of the European Community and of all its institutions and organisation are denominated in hard ECUs. All tax payments or other payments by the national governments to the Community's budget are this payable in hard ECUs.

5) At the outset the existing ERM obligastions of the national Governments are continued with the exception that the existing exchange-rate grid is abolished and is replaced by an obligation to peg each national currency to the hard ECU with the existing permitted margins of fluctuation. The grid which sets a separate linkage between each pair of national currencies is a clumsy method of controlling exchange rates. It was preferred to a direct linkage of each national currency with the existing soft ECU because the grid required no currency to depreciate unduly in terms of any other currency (includ-

ing the hardest currency in the group), whereas a linkage with the soft ECU required only a performance no worse than the average of the currencies in the group. The existence of a hard ECU makes the grid system unnecessary.

6) The ECB sets an interest rate structure at which it will negotiate to borrow or lend hard ECUs in transactions with the NCBs, the national governments, the Community organisations and a wide range of other financial institutions both inside and outside the Community.

7) The obligation of the ECB is to raise or lower its interest rate structure in terms of the hard ECU so as to stabilise an inflation index measured in terms of hard ECU prices. This index could be a price index covering the total output of goods and services of all the member countries, or, preferably, an index of the money value in terms of hard ECUs of that total output of goods and services. For the construction of such indices national values would be converted into hard ECU values at the current market rates of exchange.

8) The obligations of the NCBs would be to preserve their ERM pegs on the hard ECU by appropriatre adjustments in their interest rate structures in terms of their own national currencies.

9) The Governor and Board of directors of the ECB would not include the Governors of the NCBs. There would thus be no grey area of mixed responsibilities. The ECB would be responsible for setting hard ECU interest rates to control inflation in terms of the hard ECU. The NCBs would be responsible for setting national currency interest rates to maintain their pegs on the hard ECU.

10) It is essential that the ECB should be aware of the inflationary or deflationary effects of current fiscal policies and that fiscal authorities should be aware of the inflationary or deflationary effects of current monetary policies on their tax bases and so on their budgetary revenues. For this purpose there would be a process of continuous consultation between the monetary and fiscal authorities of the Community in order to coordinate monetary and fiscal policies so as to devise a joint strategy in control of inflation and of budget balances.

11) The setting up of this ECB structure could be regarded as stage two of the *Delors Report*. The member countries which were

ready and wished to do so could fix their pegs on the hard ECU rigidly and irrevocably and could then adopt the hard ECU in place of their national currencies. The NCBs of such countries would then become the local offices of the ECB. The system would be so flexible that not all member countries need adopt this full EMU solution at the same moment. Indeed a single country could at any time elect in agreement with the ECB to adopt the hard ECU as its national currency.

12) Any member country which wished to do so could continue indefinitely to link its currency with the hard ECU without ruling out any possible future changes in the exchange rate between its national currency and the hard ECU. For example, it could simply maintain its existing ERM obligations under which any change in its peg would have to be agreed with the ECB. New forms of linkage with the hard ECU could be devised to replace the ERM type of linkage. For example, a crawling-peg type of adjustment might be appropriate in certain circumstances. But the overriding rule would be that membership of the ECB group would be conditional upon the member country maintaining a linkage of its currency with the hard ECU on terms which were accepted as suitable by the ECB.

Monetary Policies
for the New Europe

Robert Mundell
Columbia University, New York

Introduction

Only a few years ago Europe looked very different. The cold war was still hot, East Europe was captive, the Germanies were divided and the Soviet Union was an evil empire. Today, freedom has been reborn in Eastern Europe and democracy has spread like wildfire. The end of the cold war signals the beginning of an as yet undefined New Era.

In Eastern Europe, the dismantling of socialism has proved to be easier than reconstructing capitalism; initial euphoria has already been dulled by the fact of harsh economic reality. The design for the new post-socialist societies is still unclear and so is the optimum path of the transition. Whatever the new system, however, stable monetary arrangements are necessary. In this introduction, I will start with a consideration of the main alternatives for monetary stabilization in Eastern Europe.

In Western Europe, on schedule in plans for completion of the common market by 1993, center stage is being occupied by plans for monetary union. There are not many alternatives that satisfy the conditions of both political and economic feasibility. The second part of the paper relates to the costs and benefits of the economic options and political alternatives.

1. - Monetary Options for Eastern Europe

Europe has become again a geographical expression, not a continent divided by an iron curtain. In the new Europe, what is going to be the relationship between the Eastern European countries and the Economic Community? Once the transition phase to democratic capitalism is accomplished, the answer is surely that they should have the right to become members of the Community. To speed the process, it would be helpful if they could do so in stages. The first stage is for the potential partners of the EC to put their economic affairs in order.

Except for debt forgiveness, which is partly a global obligation, responsibility for reform rests with the governments. Fundamental transformations are needed: privatization, open markets, entre-preneurial education, fiscal reform and monetary stabilization. The main difficulty to be overcome is the inertia of the bureaucracies that stand to lose by the dismantling of socialism. Without enlisting their cooperation or otherwise compensating them (as Reuven Brenner emphasizes) they have the power to block the transition.

Entrepreneurial capitalism involves the allocation of resources guided by profit incentives. The profit-motive cannot be mobilized without a stable currency. The inconvertibility of most East European currencies stems from the overhang of excess money supplies. The focus of monetary reform must therefore be to eliminate the currency overhang, in many countries a substantial fraction of the money supply. It is necessary to bridge the gap between supply and demand either by reeducing the supply or reducing the demand. Five possibili-ties are relevant:

1.1 *Inflation and Devaluation*

This approach, which was implemented in Poland (1) in 1990, has the defect of setting in motion a wage-price spiral that makes it

---

(1) JEFFREY SACHS and the International Monetary Fund played a prominent role in establishing the plan for the Polish reform.

difficult to sustain monetary and fiscal discipline, leading, ultimately, to further devaluation.

1.2 *Currency Confiscation*

This is the solution (2) that was adopted by West Germany and Japan, under the auspices of occupation authorities, in 1948. One defect is that it, like the inflation option, arbitrarily penalizes those who have held savings in the form of cash; another defect is that it breeds expectations that it might be repeated; and a third is that it conflicts with inter-generation equity in treating equivalently people of different age groups. It is a policy that could be accomplished only under an authoritarian (or, as in the 1948 cases of Germany and Japan, an occupation) government.

1.3 *Gold Standard*

This proposal (3) urged for the Soviet Union because of its gold production and reserves, avoids the defects of inflation or confiscation, and, if feasible, would have a salutary effect on expectations. There are, however, four objections to it: *a)* it is doubtful that the Soviet Union has sufficient gold reserves to mop up the overhang (4) and establish credibility; *b)* commitment of its gold reserves to internal monetary circulation is not necessarily the best use of the Soviet

---

(2) Under the euphemism of currency reform, this approach has been recently proposed for the East European countries by Rudiger Dornbusch.

(3) The gold currency plan has been proposed for the Soviet Union by Jude Wanniski of Polyconomics, and Governor Wayne Angell of the Federal Reserve System.

(4) Soviet gold reserves are a state secret so it is not possible to make a precise analysis. It seems unlikely, however, that Soviet reserves are higher than, say, 70 million ounces, and are probably substantially lower. At $400 an ounce, reserves would be valued at $28 billion. Assume the overhang is 30% of total deposits, or 150 billion rubles, out of a total money supply of 500 billion rubles. Without devaluation — rejected by Wanniski and Angell — there would be a vast gap between the level of gold reserves and the size of the overhang. A successful convertibility plan would, of course, increase the demand for money, reducing the overhang; and conversions of rubles into gold (assuming they are sterilized) would reduce internal liquidity. Even taking into account these possibilities, the Soviet gold stock may not be adequate.

Union's gold reserves and *c)* the ruble exchange rate would fluctuate with the vicissitudes of the gold market, arbitrarily destabilizing the domestic economy; none of the other countries, with much stronger economies and larger gold reserves has risked convertibility into gold.

1.4 *Foreign Exchange Standard*

A variant of the gold standard solution free of one of its defects involves stabilizing the ruble exchange rate against dollars or marks, using gold reserves as collateral for the acquisition of foreign exchange reserves to establish partial external convertibility. A monetary freeze — which assumes a balanced budget — combined with economic growth would eventually eliminate the overhang and allow a gradual movement to full convertibility. A disadvantage of this approach is that it is slow and risks losing the momentum of a transition process that demands faster results (although the program could be accelerated with stabilization loans).

1.5 *Sales of State Assets*

Instead of using gold sales to mop up the liquidity, as in paragraph 1.3, an alternative is to sell non-gold assets owned by the state: land, houses, apartments and factories, followed by sterilization of the proceeds. For a state (the Soviet Union) that owns 95% of all property, a reduction in state ownership of only 5% would suffice to mop up the excess liquidity (5).

A combination of option in paragraph 1.5 and 1.4 represents the best chance for monetary stability. By using property sales to eliminate the overhang, the defect of option in paragraph 1.4 its slowness eliminated. By utilizing gold for collateral to acquire foreign exchange, and exploiting the possibility of stabilization loans from the

---

(5) To illustrate with a rough calculation, on the basis of figures supplied by the Gosbank, suppose Soviet GNP is 1 trillion rubles; state-owned assets are 3 trillion rubles; and the money supply is 500 billion rubles. Various calculations suggest that the overhang is of the order of 150 billion rubles so that sales of only 5% of state-owned assets would suffice to absorb it.

West (6) the ground work for a convertible ruble can be built. In the instrument-target approach to economic policy, we have fine instruments and five targets: Asset sales — to mop up the overhang; exchange rate stabilization — to establish price stability; collateralizing gold — to acquire a foreign exchange reserve; monetary freeze — to restore confidence; budget balance — to make possible the monetary freeze.

Monetary stability is a *sine qua non* for a successful market economy. But monetary stability is impossible without fiscal balance. Fiscal problems may be exacerbated if the loss of revenue from state-owned assets that become privatized is greater than the expenditure savings from the subsidization of loss-making state enterprises; value-added taxes in the European style would be the best foundation for the fiscal systems of countries seeking entry to the Community.

Once the fiscal reforms necessary for achieving budget balance are established, convertibility has a chance to succeed. It is not sufficient to "peg" exchange rates, buying and selling foreign currencies. A commitment to convertibility will be credible only if it involves the mechanism for adjusting the balance of payments. Money supplies must be allowed to rise or fall according to whether there is a surplus in the balance of payments. An automatic system is more likely to be credible than a discretionary system. At the beginning, to establish credibility, central banks should operate like currency boards, backing marginal changes in the quantity of money with additional foreign exchange reserves.

Into what asset or currency should East European currencies on the road to stabilization be made convertible? Under the gold, silver or bimetallic standards, countries had the easy option of stabilizing the price of a precious metal. Under the Bretton Woods system a country could have selected the dollar which had limited (7) convertibility into gold. Since 1971 none of these options have been available. The feasible candidates for Eastern Europe are now the dollar and the

---

(6) And the International Monetary Fund, which the Soviet Union is expected to join in the near future.

(7) The dollar was *de jure* convertible into gold for "monetary purposes" for foreign central banks at the official price, but US citizens were not allowed to hold gold; gold became inconvertible *de facto* in the 1960s.

DM. The dollar is still the most important currency area, but the DM area, when it is transformed into a genuine ECU area, will have important geographical advantages for East European countries. Despite the extra global advantages of the dollar area, there would be significant advantages, for those countries expecting to become candidates for membership in the Community, to adopting from the start the DM. The decision for any particular country, however, will depend on the alternatives opened up by monetary changes in the rest of the world.

The revolution in Eastern Europe creates a new situation. The profound change in relations between the Soviet Union and Eastern Europe will mean a shift from bilateralism to multilateralism, involving substantial future gains. However, the elimination of the subsized price of Soviet oil to East European customers, combined with the collapse of the Soviet capacity to import will cause great adjustment stress in Eastern Europe, forcing a redirection of trade. Eastern Europe should now be speedily integrated into the world economy. But will this integration would be helped or impeded by joining the Economic Community?

It would certainly benefit most of the East European countries if they could join quickly the Economic Community. The European Community is fluid enough to accept applicants from Central and Eastern Europe. A major obstacle in the transition process for Eastern Europe in the absence of a capitalist institutional framework, and infrastructure. Just as West Germany was able to provide for East Germany ready-made legal, social, political and economic institutions, so the Economic Community could provide, at a less intimate level of integration, the institutional infrastructure for those East European countries that wanted it.

2. - Monetary Options for Western Europe

Europe has been integrated in the past, but always by coercion. The present happy experiment seeks to unite Europe by consent. Initial motives were Franco-German enmity, fear of invasion by the Soviet Union and emulation of the United States. All of these motives have, if not disappeared, become much less important. There remains nevertheless the problem of curbing any future tendency of a united Germany to dominate.

2.1. *The Western European Revolution*

Economic events provided the entry points for integration from diverse beginnings. These included the European Coal and Steel Community in the early 1950s, the focus on coordinated decision-making in what was then the OEEC, and the *Treaty of Rome*, which itself followed on the heels of the failure, in 1954, of the European Defense Community. In the 1950s, political union was only a far-fetched goal as the final centerpiece of a pan-Europa dream. But the spectacular success of the EEC since its inception in 1956, in "victory" over EFTA, and new outside stimulus accelerated thinking on the monetary and political dimension.

The weakness of the dollar has always provided grist for the mill of European monetary integration. The crisis of the international monetary system in the late 1960s had led to a discussion of the European-currency project even before the Bretton Woods system collapsed in August 1971. Europe was caught unprepared to engineer a joint float at that time, of even in the spring of 1973 when the Smithsonian system was breaking down. The crisis accelerated the preparatory work for the actual organization of the EMS when the dollar again weakened in the late 1970s (8).

The events planned for the beginning of 1993 are in practice irreversible. The twelve members of the Economic Community have thrown in the towel on the economic nationalism manifested in tariffs and exchange barriers in commodity and financial markets. This makes for a grand economic and financial space of 3000 million people with a gross Community product matching that of the United States itself. This immense protected market gives Europeans full

---

(8) Other outside factors were 1) the growth of Japan as a major competitor for Europe in world markets; 2) the common dilemma posed by the oil crises of the 1970s; and 3) the need for common action on questions of the environment and resource depletion.

opportunity to exploit the economies of scale once available only to the United States, giving rise to competition, new techniques of production, greater efficiency, and recovery of start-up fixed costs over much longer production runs. Nations are no longer the dominant economic planning space for the members of the European Community.

Europeans will be, as they are to a certain extent already, free to locate capital, businesses and persons across national boundaries, leading to increased economic homogeneity. The huge labor market will confirm the natural migration from low-wage to high-wage countries, reinforcing the effect of intra-Community free trade in equalizing wage rates. The opening of the Community to new members from low-wage countries in Southern Europe will reinforce the flow of unskilled labor to high-wage Northern Europe. International differences in economic ability and education will continue to exist even with wage-rate equalization due to differences in education, abilities and skills. Other barriers to migration based on culture, religion and language will remain long after legal barriers have fully disappeared.

Capital movements will be relentless once financial barriers have been fully lifted. Capital will continue to move from high-wage to the low-wage countries, reinforcing migration effects in equalizing factor prices. Other things equal, each capitalist tries to match his capital with the cheapest labor in the common market, maximizing returns. The capital movements also proceed in search of land values, from areas where land is expensive to areas where land is cheap; rents are thus equalized by the international exchange of ownership titles. These capital movements automatically produce current account surpluses in the capital-exporting countries and deficits in the capital-importing countries. In the long run they also store up potential future problems of international capital indebtedness.

The equalization of equivalent-factor prices enhances efficiency and Community-wide productivity. The greater the initial differences in factor prices, the greater the inefficiencies to be corrected — by a combination of free trade and factor movements — and the greater the gains from integration. Per capita incomes will continue to differ because of unequal distributions of both human and physical capital.

Despite factor-price equalization, countries with high proportions of skilled labor, productive land and net international creditor positions will naturally have higher per capita incomes. Free trade does not eliminate poverty.

2.2 *One Currency or* n + 1?

The cutting edge of the European policy curve is monetary integration, embodied in debate on the creation of a European currency and a European Central Bank. There are two main tracks. One creates a currency that would replace other currencies; the other creates a currency additional to the others. The former implies an irrevocably-unified monetary policy and thus a big jump in the direction of political integration. The other makes out of the basket ECU an additional currency, printed and used as reserves or adopted as its own currency by any willing nation; the ECU approach is in turn sub-divided into the "hard" and "not-so-hard" ECUs, with momentum ont he side of the latter. The choice between the one-currency plan and the $(n + 1)$ currencies plan will determine the pace of European monetary union, but not necessarily its final resting place.

It is important not to exaggerate the differences between a system of national currencies with fixed exchange rates and a unified currency system (9). It is true that a common currency implies a centralized monetary policy, in essence control over the money supply vested in the hands of a single central bank, whereas a fixed exchange rate system allows some degree of decentralization of monetary policy. The difference, however, is not as great as it first appears. A

---

(9) Among monetary options, Milton Friedman ranks a fixed exchange rate system below either a flexible rate system or a monetary union. I do not agree with this ranking. First of all, either a monetary union or a fixed rate system would be inferior to a flexible rate system if the rest of the world were unstable; and superior to it if the world were stable. Credible fixed exchange rate systems existed under the gold standard, bi-metallism and even the Bretton Woods systems; and fixed rate systems thrived in most imperial dependencies before 1914. I think the source of the basic difference between us is that I conceive of a fixed exchange rate system as implying an automatic or semi-automatic monetary policy that sustains equilibrium in the balance of payments; whereas Friedman thinks of a fixed exchange rate peg combined with an independent (Friedman-type) monetary policy with sterilized central bank intervention that destroys the adjustment mechanism.

truly fixed exchange rate system even with separate national currencies leaves little scope for independent national monetary policies.
Confidence in the exchange rate parity requires affirmation of a
commitment to a mechanism for adjusting the balance of payments.
Countries must allow their money supplies to increase or decrease
according to whether they have a surplus or deficit in the balance of
payments. Under a system in which both spot and forward exchange
rates are fixed indefinitely, there is little difference, except transac-
tional convenience, between a fixed exchange rate system and a
monetary union. Other examples close to the monetary union side of
the spectrum include a currency board system, by which a country
maintains full backing for domestic currency in the form of international reserves.

The major difference between the case of fixed exchange rates
and the hard-ECU plan lies in the retention by the member states of
the "right" to devalue (or revalue). This right reserves for the national
State an important element of "monetary sovereignty". The main
advantage of this right is a country's ability to protect itself against
any inflationary of deflationary policies in the currency area as a
whole. It would be important, however, only if an individual country
thought the monetary policy of the unin were going to be more
unstable than its own.

Preservation of the right to devalue or revalue also has costs.
Expectations of devaluation will mean speculation against a country's
currency. A discount will appear in the forward exchange market
pushing up domestic interest rates above the interest rates prevailing
in currencies that are expected to remain stable or appreciate. If the
devaluation does not take place, a capital-importing country will have
been saddled with a much higher cost of capital than would otherwise
be necessary.

Devaluation, however, has considerable costs akin to a mind of
moral hazard. Once a government shows its willingness to meet
problems of, say, excessive wage expansion by devaluation, it sets in
motion a train of events that make it necessary to repeat the operation. A high "propensity to devalue" in a country means both higher
nominal interest rates and a faster rate of increase of wage demands;
it provokes a race between the devaluing monetary authorities and the

wage-setting labor-management negotiators; when devaluations are fully expected they no longer work. The countries that have gone the route of inflation and depreciation in the 1970s and early 1980s — Italy, Britain and Canada are prominent examples — still experience the after-effects in the form of high interest rates, forward market discounts and higher than normal unemployment.

Against powerful arguments against devaluation, it remains an important, not to say vital, weapon in the policy arsenal of a sovereign power, a last recourse of governments with budget deficits they cannot otherwise finance. Because of the critical political implications, debate on the subject has become polarized. There is no possibility of compromise between the two positions; the alternatives, not complements. But it is unlikely that the debate will be settled on economic grounds alone.

An important issue is the sentimental, patriotic attachment to national currencies; a country's money is its patrimony, that goes to the heart of the social contract. Although the sentiment is universal, countries will nevertheless be affected differently. Size plays a role. The small countries have less to lose since their currencies are not used much internationally. Of the four major countries in Western Europe, Britain has the oldest currency with an unbroken record of continuity going back almost a millennium, the oldest existing currency in the world; the pound, however, has been tarnished by inflationary monetary policies after World War II. Germany, experiencing two shattering currency conversions in the twentieth century, has fewer grounds for sentimental attachment to its currency; on the other hand, Germany certainly can take pride in its monetary stability since the currency reform of 1948, a record rivalled only by three other countries (Switzerland, Holland and Japan). By creating a more balanced country, the unification of Germany will make Germany even more viable and stable as an independent currency area. For very different reasons, therefore, Britain and Germany will feel that they have the most to lose from scrapping the national currency (10).

---

(10) France has special responsibilities in the CFA franc area and, perhaps for this reason, has followed a monetary policy which, over the past three decades, has kept the franc close to the dollar.' It could be argued that France and Italy stand to lose most from the failure of monetary union and would thus have adequate compensation for the replacement of their own currencies for a European currency.

2.3 *The Options*

The options for EMU include the following: 1) using a currency outside the monetary union; 2) using a currency inside the monetary union; 3) creating a synthetic currency; and 4) using a commodity currency like gold (11). It cannot be emphasized too strongly that unbacked currencies have little chance of surviving in the absence of a strong central government.

2.3.1 Using the Dollar

Given a history of money replete with currency failures, it is safer to rely on an existing currency or asset than to construct something entirely new. Among currencies outside the Community area, the natural choice is the dollar. It is the most liquid (12) currency in the world and, over the last century, has been the most stable. In the Bretton Woods era, it was the only currency convertible into gold. Even since the breakdown of the Bretton Woods system, the dollar has held its value as good as or better than all except five currencies (13). Long-term interest rates have been among the lowest in the world and at the long end of the maturity spectrum — that bell-weather of confidence — US govenment bonds have the longest maturity — thirty years — of any in existence.

Politics aside, the dollar could be a prime candidate for a European currency itself or the backing for one. Set up a European Central Bank (ECB) with a Board of Governors composed of national central bank governors with weighted votes. The EC members could exchange their gold and dollar reserves for Europas issued by the ECB and the national governments could then assign monetary policy to

---

(11) I leave outside of consideration here the possibilities of a tabular standard (which amounts to indexing money) and a commodity reserve standard.

(12) The liquidity of a currency is a function of its ability to withstand shocks, which depends on the rate of decline in its marginal utility as additional quantitative of currency are increased. Because this is a direct function of the amount outstanding, the marketability or liquidity of a currency is an increasing function of the size of a currency's transactions domain.

(13) The yen, the Swiss franc, the mark, the guilder and the shilling.

ensure convertibility of national currencies into Europas. Over a transition period, national currencies could be gradually exchanged for Europas until all national legal tender notes were replaced. Europas could be kept convertible at a fixed rate into dollars by the ECB during the transition period. Eventually, as Europas acquired confidence as an independent currency, they could be weaned from the dollar, establishing independent monetary properties. An international exchange rate system could then be devised coordinating the Europa with the dollar and the yen.

The case against the dollar, however, is formidable: *a)* the United States would continue to gain seigniorage from the use of its currency as reserves; *b)* the dollar has undergone periods of weakness and strength that fluctuate with the business cycle and US economic policy and this instability would be transmitted to Europe; *c)* the European currency movement has been inspired by the desire to get out from under the thumb of American monetary policy; the anti-American wing of the European integration movement would reject the possibility out of hand; *d)* by fixing rates to the dollar, Europe commits itself to a monetary rule without a reciprocal commitment (e.g. Bretton Woods type convertibility) from the United States, putting itself in a satellite position; and *e)* the United States has not heeded the advice of Europeans over almost four decades to correct its balance of payments or budget deficits. Based on the seigniorage argument alone, the optimum rate of inflation is higher for a reserve currency country than any other (14). These disadvantages probably make the dollar a non-starter.

2.3.2 Using a European Currency

A second alternative is to use one of the existing European currencies. The mark would be the natural choice. Germany is the largest economy in Europe and the third largest in the world. The mark has been the second strongest major currency over the past four

---

(14) See my paper «The Optimum Balance-of-Payments Deficits» in SALIN P.-CLAAS-SEN E. (eds.): *Stabilization Policies in Interdependent Economies*, Amsterdam, North Holland Press, 1972.

decades and its consistently anti-inflationist posture has earned the Bundesbank respect and credibility. Europeanization of the mark would be the most straightforward choice for a European currency.

A multiple of the mark could be designated as the European unit of account. Suppose 1 Europa = DM 10. The transition process could be managed as follows. Set up a European Central Bank with a Board of Governors composed of national central bank governors with weighted votes. The ECB authorizes the Bundesbank, designated as agent for the ECB, to accept European currencies in exchange for Europa currency notes (or deposits denominated in Europas), converted at the market exchange rate equivalents of 10-DM notes.

After *E*-day, production of national currencies would cease. National currency notes would then be exchanged for Europa notes at the ECB (or the Bundesbank, in its capacity as agent). Responsibility for union monetary expansion after E-day would then devolve upon the ECB. Europa expansion would arise through the purchase of foreign assets (dollars and other foreign exchange) and domestic assets of the member countries (government bonds or other eligible paper).

2.3.3 Creating a Basket Currency

Because of political objections to the adoption of the dollar or the mark, basket currencies have been at the heart of most reform plans. The idea of using a combination of two assets as money goes back to the electrum of the Lydians of the ancient world, and received the influential support of no less an authority than Alfred Marshall (15). Baskets of paper currencies are a more recent phenomenon. The existing ECU, deposits issued by the European Monetary Cooperation Fund (EMCF) against the gold and dollar deposits made by the

---

(15) Marshall called his plan calling for a mixture of a fixed weight of gold and silver as the unit for money "symmetallism"; he later dropped the idea as unworkable. In 1970 (before the breakdown of the Bretton Woods system), I developed a currency plan for the European Commission in which the unit of account would be a fraction of one ounce of three precious metals — platinum, gold and silver — in a proportion than would be subject to periodic review.

monetary authorities of the member states, is defined as a basket of currencies composed of specific amounts of the currencies of the members; each currency share is weighted more or less in line with GNP and foreign trade. Use of the currently existing basket ECU would establish a rate of inflation equal to the average of the EMS members.

The "hard ECU" plan achieved some distinction and notoriety when it was advanced two years ago with the support of the Thatcher government to keep Britain in the forefront of the debate over monetary union. The hard ECU involves national currency weights fixed in nominal terms, so that a country's weight in the ECU would be eroded by inflation and depreciation. Because the hard ECU would never depreciate against any currency, it would automatically be the strongest currency with lower interest rates on assets denominated in it than any other currency.

If the standard ECU plan errs on the side of inflation, the hard ECU plan errs on the side of deflation insofar as any one large member could throw the currency area into deflation (16); it is also likely that the country proposing it (Britain) would be the last country to adopt it as an alternative to its own currency.

Use of an ECU basket avoids the invidious jealousies associated with choice of the dollar or the mark or another living currency. There are some arguments against it: 1) like the SDR, it is not independent, being first evaluated against the US dollar before being translated into other currencies; 2) there are so many options with respect to weights, and method by which it is introduced that it will be difficult to negotiate a plan that will be a satisfactory alternative to the national currencies; 3) it will be difficult for the public to understand a currency that is defined as a basket of national currencies that no longer exist; 4) because of policy uncertainty about changes in the composition or future of the basket, it would remain an uncertain asset in which to denominate long-term contracts. It would be extremely difficult, if not impossible, to create sufficient confidence in an unbacked European basket currency without the support of a central fiscal authority.

---

(16) In the current state of inflation in all countries including Germany, this might turn out to be an advantage rather than a defect.

2.3.4 Using Gold

Europe, counting Switzerland, possesses three fifths of the world's monetary gold reserves. The EC countries alone hold 375 million ounces, or 464 million, counting the gold reserves of the EMCF (in exchange for which the EMCF issued ECUs to the member countries), compared to 262 million ounces for the United States. There will be gold in the monetary future of Europe.

Gold could be used to give confidence to a European currency. At $350 an ounce the EC country's gold is worth over $161 billion. Foreign exchange reserves amount to close to about $290 billion. A gold Europa coin (or rather some multiple of it) could be a useful symbol of a European monetary unity. But what would be the relation between gold and currencies? A gold-convertible paper Europa would create a European currency that would fluctuate relative to the US dollar with the price of gold. At the same time such a monetization of gold would itself have a feedback effect on the value of gold.

A more interesting proposal would be to create a basket currency composed not only of the national currencies, as the ECU is, but also of gold. A gold component in the basket would lend to its long-run stability. The assets of the ECB could include gold, dollars and national currencies, and the ECU or Europa could, in principle, be convertible into the basket of assets the ECB holds. The inclusion of gold in the basket would partly compensate for the absence of an all-Europe government backing the currency.

Gold also represents one opening through which the Soviet Union could re-enter the international monetary system. Gold could be used for inter-bloc settlements. The possibility of an international gold reserve currency — perhaps in connection with the SDR — might become an inviting option in the future.

Concluding Remarks

Theory deals in abstractions, but economic policy must cope with the real world. Economics is itself an abstraction, but policy must consider political variables. On economic grounds alone, the best chance for creating a successful European currency would be to adopt an existing currency, the dollar or the mark. On economic grounds, but rejecting the dollar, the Europa would be the ghost of the mark.

On political grounds, however, two factors work in opposing directions. The populations of other countries in the Community — other things equal — might object to the use of a Europa that was, even only initially, a thinly disguised 10-DM note (or some other multiple). Against this, however, it could be said that other things are not equal, that Germany has the largest economy, and that German management of its currency, through alternating political parties, has been exemplary. It might also be noted that the plan to use the DM merely travels to the same destination by a different route.

The other political factor concerns the costs and benefits of the monetary union from the standpoint of the different countries. Just as large countries tend to gain less than small countries from free trade, so large countries gain less than small countries from monetary integration. To some extent, therefore, Germany gains less than the other countries in the Economic Community and this may be a factor making Germany ultimately reluctant to take the final step of scrapping the most successful currency in Europe for a pig-in-a-poke. German rejection of the ECU would derail monetary union just at a time when its momentum, in Europe as a whole, is reaching a peak. It is worth making concessions to Germany (although no German has suggested this solution) just to make sure that Germany gets aboard the monetary European train. The alternatives are much worse.

Is time on the side of or against European monetary and political union? The new European momentum that was stimulated by the weak dollar is upstaged by the outbreak of peace and freedom in Eastern Europe. The end of the cold war allows nationalism (and racial and religious bigotry) to come once more to the forefront. Unless the European movement is pampered, the power configuration of the Europe of the middle 1990s might regress to that of the nations before 1914. In a world of independent nationalities the power of big nations is magnified. After Germany has fully digested its Eastern part, anti-integration, nationalistic forces could be aroused. In this scenario procrastination reduces the chances for completion of monetary union.

The fast track provides the surest approach to monetary union. This involves using the Bundesbank as agent for the European Central Bank for the transition period and the DM as the initial backing for the new currency. The end goals is the same but the Bundesbank route, committing Germany, would offer the best chance that the final destination will actually be reached.

II - TOWARDS THE SINGLE MARKET:
PROBLEMS AND PERSPECTIVES

Institutional and Constitutional Preconditions for Growth Effects Resulting from European Integration

Silvio Borner
University of Basel

1. - The Importance of Institutions to Economic Growth

The question of the connection between growth and institutions is not new. Adam Smith dealt with the necessity of a legal system which guaranteed property rights. The so-called «old institutionalists» remained rooted, however, in a highly descriptive representation of institutions. The renaissance of «institutionalism» can, on the one hand, be explained by the political upheavals (1); on the other hand, there are certainly internal economic reasons: various theoretical trends which have, during the past 30 years, dealt with the influence of different institutional regulations, have attained a degree of formality which has brought them recognition in the mainstream.

Before we analyze the importance of institutions to growth, we would like to deal with the definition of institutions. We follow North ([13], p. 6) who defines institutions as «rules, enforcement characteristics of rules, and norms of behaviour that structure repeated human interaction. Hence, they limit and define the choice set of neo-classical theory».

---

(1) For example, the upheavals in Eastern Europe show clearly the need for institutional reforms when there is a change from a planned to a market economy.

Advise: the numbers in square brackets refer to the Bibliography in appendix.

North does not intend to explain institutions per se but only to examine their consequences on the usual (neoclassical) choice or decision behavior of the actors. In other words, the traditional theory shows how decisions can be optimized under given restrictions (choice set). The institutional view simply goes one step, but a decisive one, further: in its normative version it tries to optimize the choice set, i.e. to minimize the transaction costs of the economic subjects by establishing rules of law and enforcing them through the state (2).

The unhappy experience with governments in most countries in most phases of history primarily has to do with the "rulers'" exercise or preservation of power. First of all, inefficient rules make it easier for a ruling elite to extort excessive taxes or rents or even brides from the population and secondly, more efficient rules would threaten important interest groups who protect and support the elites. In most political systems, therefore, the choice of norms and rules is anything but optimal. The same is true *a fortiori* for their enforcement. This second difficulty, which is very closely linked to the first, lies in the necessity for a «third party», for a State which lays down the property rights, and makes available the law. In other words, the whole State legal system represents a central prerequisite for the development of a differentiated, complex, long-term-oriented and thus, in the long run, growth-oriented economy. Besides all the risks of an economic or technical nature, the enforcement risks of this third party are often overwhelming.

One cannot combine a highly differentiated economy and modern technology with political anarchy and legal despotism (3). But with the State a new problem appears. The State institutions become a breeding ground for rent seekers of all colours. Whoever has control over the laying down and enforcement of rules can use this position of power to line up advantages for themselves (subsidies for producers, protectionism against foreign competition, appearance of bureaucracies, etc.). And all this again raises the transaction costs of the private

---

(2) See BORNER-BRUNETTI-WEDER [6].

(3) We have examined elsewhere in more detail the delicate question as to how far direct democracy, by inconsistent distribution struggles and rent-seeking cartels, shakes the foundations of the legal prerequisites for an innovation-driven market economy (See BORNER *et* AL., [5] and [6].

actors. This is the fundamental dilemma: «If uou want to realize the potential of modern technology, you cannot do with the State, but you cannot do without it either» (4). Unfortunately, this deterioration of institutions is also clearly visible in modern democracies (5).

And so we come to the question of the determinants of political systems. What are the optimum institutions for the development of objectives, laying down of norms and enforcement of rules? Unfortunately, it is impossible to answer these questions, even on a purely logical basis; for, unlike the Walras market system without institutions, there is no analogous model of reference for politics or the state (Arrow paradox). In the long run, this is ture for politico-economic systems of the public choice theory type. If one endogenizes the factor «politics» one can no longer use the non-political Walras equilibrium as a model of reference for welfare and, for example, define all rent-seeking costs (including pure redistribution) as losses of prosperity. The crucial question then shifts to another level: which institutional foundations — in the market as well as in politics — promise most politico-economic efficiency? (6). Theory as well as history can demonstrate which institutional patterns represent decisive obstacles to growth; for example, badly defined property rights, arbitrary applications by a corrupt judiciary or discretionary scope of the executive. Yet even if one knew which institutional prerequisites were necessary and sufficient for growth, one would still not know how to put them into practice, particularly when powerful interests are in conflict with more efficient institutions. Analogous to the way in which the market functions, one must start from the assumption that the introduction or improvement of competitive elements is, in fact, «always a good thing». In our opinion, this institutional view of competition (in contrast to the instrumental view of traditional industrial organisation theory) is also applicable to politics: it is, in fact, «always better» to make political structures contestable.

The position which has been put forward here does not amount to a demand for minimum state influence, but rather for a contestability of the State by the greatest possible competition inside it and

---

(4) See NORTH [14], p. 425.
(5) See OLSON e.g. [15].
(6) See also BAGHWATI [4].

outside of it, in order to limit its discretionary power — and hence the institutional uncertainty this induces (7).

2. - From the Nation-State to EC '92

The benefit from having a State as a third party to contracts greatly enhances the range and scope of contracting possibilities and therefore increases gains from trade and specialization. The primary function of the State is thus to be an impartial third party to contracts, which secures the enforcement of agreed terms (8). We have already mentioned that there is another side to this coin: the problem of committing the State to exercise its duty and nothing else! This situation has been labeled a «principal-agent» (9) relationship. The principal being the people, who delegate the task of enforcing contracts to the agent, the State. The problem arises from the dilemma, that in order to exercise its function as third party to contracts, the State has to be equipped with powerful enforcement and control mechanisms, such as a police force or an army. But this monopoly of power can also be abused. The problem of an optimal social contract thus becomes one of binding the State to use its monopoly in the exercise of power in the interest of its constituencies.

So this marks a critical trade-off. On the one hand a society has a need for a powerful State in order to be able to contract efficiently and realize the gains from trade. The society will therefore be willing to give some power to this third party in exchange for the enforcement of contracts: this is what we call the social contract. On the other hand the emergence of this powerful third party poses the problem of controlling and/or limiting its range.

It is my central hypothesis that the EC '92 project will only produce additional and permanent growth effects if it is based on the

---

(7) See BORNER *et* AL., [5] and [6].

(8) Of course the State provides a number of other public goods, but in the approach we take here these are disregarded. Our focus is primarily on the legal and political institutions of a State that exercises its most «primitive» functiono.

(9) A basic reference for the notion of «Principal-Agent» is JENSEN-MECKLING [11].

contestability of national institutions within a federal union with maximum economic and political sovereignty of European citizens.

The effects of an enlargement of markets on welfare and growth is one of the cornerstones of economic research in Europe. The reason for this is the new dynamism of the European Community which plans to build a common market under the heading EC '92. in short, European markets will become much larger because twelve formerly relatively separated countries will form one unified market by 1992. Of course, many barriers to free movement of goods, services, capital and people have been brought down before. But common rules for European competition will make a quantitative and qualitative difference.

EC '92 is based theoretically on a broad research program under the heading *The Costs of Non-Europe, Cecchini Report* (10). This study attempted to work out the basic effects of increased market size and to quantify the possible gains. In the next paragraph we will briefly describe these effects in three categories. But the *Cecchini Report* calculated only the so called static, or once-and-for-all effects of market enlargement. New developments in neo-classical growth theory argue that such static analysis seriously underestimates the potential welfare gains. The newest publications show that the increased market size will also affect the growth rate through positive externalities.

3. - Static Welfare and Dynamic Growth Effects of Market Size

Static welfare gains can be subdivided into three broad effects: better allocation, economies of scale and increased competition.

1. - *Allocation:* a larger economy leads to more specialization and to more efficient production. The larger the number of transaction partners, the more the individual can specialize in its comparative advantage. In a completely specialized economy everybody can do the

---

(10) See the summary in COMMISSION OF THE EUROPEAN COMMUNITIES [10].

thing he does best and obtain all other activities and goods on impersonal markets.

2. - *Economies of Scale:* a second source of higher welfare are economies of large numbers, if fixed outlays lead to sinking average costs for bigger production lots. Such scale economies can arise in many activities, especially production, research, marketing, management or financing. This effect can be very important for many smaller nations, if fixed initial investment outlays suddenly break even in bigger markets.

3. - *Competition:* a third advantage of larger markets stems from increased competition if monopolistic inefficiencies are challenged by new competitors. More competition leads to two favourable developments. First, and for our purpose potentially very important: the new challengers work towards the elimination of monopolistic rents and establish the law of one price throughout the whole market. Secondly, the former monopolists lose their safe haven of high rents and have to eliminate internal inefficiencies.

Potentially more important than the static welfare effects of market size are dynamic growth effects. The difference in the expressions — in the first case welfare in the second growth — is intentional. Static gains theoretically change only the level of GDP (11). Even if these once-and-for-all welfare effects may be large, they can be dwarfed by potential dynamic growth effects.

The key notion to understanding these growth effects in «positive externalities» (12). Such externalities are created if new knowledge arises because of technological progress. If a firm improves a production process by research and development or simply by means of learning by doing, it cannot completely prevent other firms from imitating, or using for free, at least parts of the new knowledge. But for the imitating firm, this new knowledge is an externality because it did not have to sacrifice resources for its development. New growth theory builds neo-classical models around this general idea and

---

(11) See for example Lucas [12], p. 12.
(12) For a detailed discussion of this motion and its crucial effects on growth see Romer [17].

generates the basic result that the external effects of knowledge are fundamental for understanding growth. That such effects may be very important follows from the general nature of the good «knowledge». To create the first item of say a new design for a product is very costly but all further uses of this design generate practically no additional costs. In other words: «knowledge goods» can be accumulated on a per capita basis literally ad infinitum.

The better the transaction system (the lower the transaction costs) the more positive externalities can be expected from a given «unit of investment of innovation». This could be the most important effect of a larger European market. And this importance is even reinforced by the positive effects of competition on the incentives to innovate. Dynamic gains arise from the fact that the harsher competition in a larger market forces the firms to innovate intensively if they want to stay in the market. We again observe a double positive effect: first, the rate of innovation is enlarged and second, the larger market enhances the diffusion process of the positive externalities generated by these very innovations. A decrease in institutional uncertainty entrails a speeding up of such social learning.

4. - EC '92: Institutional Stimulus for Growth

Institutional reforms which encourage competition in the markets, as well as between state regulation systems, should act as a stimulus to growth. It is these expansions of markets on the one hand and supranational competition between state systems of regulation on the other which should have an effect on the European single market when it exists. The catchword «Eurosclerosis» which, particularly at the beginning of the '80s, dominated politico-economic discussion, has today disappeared to a large extent. The highly developed countries of Western Europe were primarily sclerotic because rent-seeking processes had led to ever more industrial cartels which were protected from competition. According to Olson [15], this is a logical result of long political stability. Interest groups had plenty of time to get themselves organized and influence the political process to their own advantage. There many domestic-oriented industries which were only able to avoid necessary structural changes because of protectionist measures. This process of increasing rent-seeking activities leads inevitably to the systematic erosion of institutions encouraging competition. All this is to change now: with a large, open domestic market, economic and political competition should be helped to a definite breakthrough. The static gains of which there are estimates for this EC single market in the *Cecchini Report*, will lead to improvement of levels but not to permanent changes in growth rates. Past thinking has been that profits were to be expected in particular from the regeneration of the institution «competition» in the European domestic market. Baldwin [1] has created a dynamic system of growth, accounting for the EC '92 project along these lines, which has attracted a great deal of attention.

Baldwin, who refers explicitly to Romer [16], stays close to the existing model style of the *Cecchini Report* and attempts to supplement the static efficiency gains with medium-term of permanent dynamic growth effects. In this he bases his ideas on the one hand on Cobb-Douglas production functions, with economy-wide scale returns, and on the other hand on increased innovations as a result of the growing market, to which Romer himself had already drawn attention. Baldwin's empirical calibrations of these dynamic effects, in part, show dramatic rises in prosperity profits due to European integration (13). The big response to these mathematical exercises puzzles the institutionally-oriented economist. It was clear, in any case, that the object of the single market was not those few little one-time growth percentages in national income. Either the European market is a genuine liberalization cure — and then it really is only a question of the dynamic growth effect resulting from the institutional intensification of competition — or the common market is a purely political production of potential bureaucracies with the aim of central conformity.

In the latter case there is every possibility that the common market would not even generate static one-time rises in the gross

---

(13) All this reminds me of the time when I was a student in the fifties, when a visiting Soviet growth theoretician filled the black-board with production functions and predicted that the Soviet Union would overtake all Western countries in GNP/per capita by 1990.

national product: in particular if it represents externally a purely defensive answer to the worldwide formation of blocks and internally a conspiracy against competition by the leading industrial and social (or socialist) interests. In other words, in the long term, whether or not the common market raises the growth rate will be primarily decided by the legal and political environment, the new market structures and, not least, the corporate strategies of the eurocompanies.

An analysis of growth effects *à la* constitutional economics or in a public choice framework would, in our opinion, give better-quality predictions. The domestic market will result in growth effects if — and only if — the EC succeeds in realizing the following preconditions:

1) realization of a simple, transparent and liberal constitution in politics and the economy which effectively limits the influence of the State and allows the greatest possible scope for private initiative;

2) if competitive federalism within the EC leads to competition between the former national rules and regulations and helps the most efficient of them to assert itself;

3) if an egalitarian social order for the whole EC is dispensed with, so that the various regions enter into a more intensive exchange on the basis of their differences, i.e. if the adjustment of productivities and incomes is the final consequence of the domestic market and is not decreed to be the prime prerequisite;

4) if power building by monopolies and cartels, including European trade union cartels, on the goods as well as the factors, markets can be prevented by an institutional competition policy, i.e. if the contestability on all European markets increases significantly;

5) and finally, if the institutional foundations of macroeconomic policy, particularly monetary and fiscal policies, are also so laid down that they remain, as far as possible, shielded from national and/or sectoral interests.

Unfortunately, there is no room for such considerations either within the framework of a static efficiency analysis in the style of the *Cecchini Report*, or in mathematical exercises *à la* Baldwin. «In applied work it is essential that the model employed gives an intuitively acceptable description of the economy as we observe it. The model described in this paper (Baldwin, S.B.) may be an elegant way of building a growth model based on R&D, but it is not rich enough to capture the policy change which it is trying to study (EC domestic market) (14).

5. - Principles for Institutional Reform in Europe

The Homeric account of Ulysses and the sirens has a lot of explanatory power for what follows in this paragraph. According to the saga, Ulysses correctly anticipated that he would not, any more than any other man, be able to resist the tempting songs of the sirens. He was, nevertheless, able to «subvert certain inclinations of his future self» (15) by binding his hands to the mast of his ship. It may be that this Homeric account is the basis for the notion of «hand binding». The idea is to precommit oneself credibly to a certain future choice. The problem of credibility is obviously only solved if the alternative option is no longer present at the relevant moment — wehn temptation comes.

We may be stretching the metaphor a little too far but the central idea of institutional reform is, in our view, to design institutions that accomplish this «hand-binding».

We economists like to give advice. This is not only a source of our income but it also makes us feel important. On the surface it is rather easy — if done in the traditional way which Coase aptly labelled «blackboard economics». One draws with chalk or (even better) formulates in mathematical terms a model of an ideal economic system and then, comparing it with what we observe (or claim to observe) we prescribe what is necessary to achieve the ideal state. «The analysis is done with great ingenuity but it floats in the air» ([9], p. 28). In the language of the Ulysses tale, blackboard economics would entail showing why it is bad to follow the temptation of the sirens and the conclusion would be that the temptation should be

---

(14) See VENABLES [19], p. 275.
(15) See BRENNAN-KLIEMT [8], p. 125. We were inspired with this symbolism by the Logo of the journal *Constitutional Political Economy*; a representation of Ulysses bound to the mast of his ship.

resisted. It would not mention the rule that enables the tempted to resist temptation. In point of fact, economic policy involves a choice among alternative institutional arrangements. Economic policy that really matters is a change in the rules of the game.

If the problem of private contracting could be solved by introducing a third party, why should there not be a similar solution to the problem of the social contract? But, shouldn't there be a fourth party to constrain the third party? And a fifth party to restrain the fourth? This route obviously doesn't take us far because we enter into an infinite regress and the problem of who is to control the controllers and how is not solved.

In the example of Ulysses, the limitation was introduced in the form of self constraint. Such self-constraints are quite familiar in everyday life. We leave the car at home to avoid drunken driving after a party. Self-constraints between two contracting parties are more complex because this requires more sophisticated enforcement mechanisms (16). Unfortunately the scope of such mutually binding contracts is limited (and therefore restricts the number of potential transaction partners) and leads to the necessity of having a third party as an enforcer and often also as a producer of rules — and with this we fall back into the trap of infinite regress. There is no ideal way to solve this basic paradox of democratic rule.

We therefore have to look for alternative mechanisms that introduce the necessary constraints. We call our conceptual framework covering all these constraints «political contestability». Contestability means that there is a set of institutions which ensure competition within the State and competition from outside the State.

Perhaps contestability is best described in the domain of the market (17). A contestable market is one where access or entry is possible and the result is that the actions of the firms in the market are

---

(16) With regard to Swiss labour-management relations, such a self-binding contract has been in effect for more than 50 years. The secret of this success story is that the contract does not specify what the parties have to agree on but rather how they are to proceed in the case of disagreement. Specifically the mutual pledge is to stick to peaceful procedures and therefore not to use either strikes or lockouts. This kind of contract has a stabilizing mechanism similar to the ones which can stabilize a repeated prisoner's dilemma on the efficient equilibrium.

(17) The term Contestable Market was introduced by BAUMOL *et* AL. [2].

constrained by the potential entry of new firms. As soon as the «insiders» try to reap too large a (monopoly or oligopoly) rent, the entry of new competitors erodes their discretionary power. In the political process the mechanism of contestability ensures that the potential rents from the discretionary power of the executive are competed away in a similar manner.

Basically there are two main avenues to minimize the risks of growing government intervention.

(i) Internal Constraints. These include all rules breaking up power within the country by either giving more power to the individual, i.e. enlarging the domain of individual (property) rights, or by dividing power within the different government agencies, e.g. by decentralization and federalism. «True federalism is competitive with regard to public goods just as an open market is for private goods. Each governmental unit is required to measure its competition and to implement strategies that lead to survival and, it is hoped, to establishing a cushion for future growth». (Swartz-Peck [18], p. 41).

(ii) External Constraints. These are based on the principle of «hand-binding» by giving away some national sovereignty. The fact that power on certain issues is delegated to supranational bodies creates the necessary credibility that the power is not going to be abused. The common feature of external constraints is that they limit in some form or other the domain of national sovereignty. At first sight, a loss of national sovereignty may seem totally inacceptable. As we have explained, a national State-apparatus is necessary to guarantee the «rules of the game». But national sovereignty can be vertically divided in a federal system and thereby introduce institutionalized political competition within the State. This is the main reason why a true «Federal European Union» with a European Parliament and a European Court is called for: everything stopping short of such a true Federal Union will not institutionally guarantee the four freedoms, which are at the core of the single market. Without central enforcement of the basic rights and rules, competition in the Federal Union will be neither efficient nor fair.

Nationalism is bad enough in football stadiums but it is definitively worse in the arena of economic policies creating trade wars or comfortable niches for protected suppliers. Just as in the 19th century modern nation states evolved in order to make the industrial revolution really happen, the next century will see a rise of supranationality. Too many global problems defy national treatment and too many interdependencies render national rules ineffective (global warming, the ozone layer, worldwide migration, etc.).

Why do countries voluntarily join GATT? In every country there are vested interests that lose on free trade agreements. These pressure groups will therefore try to influence the political process in order to conserve their rents. To join GATT means to commit oneself to free trade. The individual government can no longer be held responsible for unpopular measures against structurally weak sectors of the economy, the blame lies with the supranational body. Thus supranationality may serve as a welcome constraint that provides a credible precommitment to a certain policy direction. Joining international institutions and accepting their rules in the abstract and beforehand is a very good way to self-binding. This is the true secret of the European integration success story if it really does come about.

Both the unchecked growth of government as well as the march of the interest groups through the institutions take place within the confines of the nation-state. National interests of all shades are mustered to legitimize inefficient interventions. This is true especially for all kinds of protectionism, for import substitution and for national security reasons.

«Openness» of the economy has thus been a very important brake on interventionism, rent-seeking and other procedures leading to high institutional uncertainty and transaction costs. Once goods and services and factors of production are mobile, we enter a new type of international competition: the competition of different national regulatory systems for mobile factors of production or for location of footloose economic activities. A big hope for EC '92 growth effects is connected to this new aspect of relative attractiveness of «rules» or institutions: we expect that good rules will drive out bad ones and stable rules drive out unstable ones. Integration in Europe will therefore be growth-producing not only because of further economies of scale or reductions in tariffs but also because of increased competition between national enabling conditions.

Of course, higher degrees of economic openness or integration mean a loss of increasing parts of national sovereignty. But in a relatively peaceful area such as Europe, this is nothing to be regretted on *a priori* grounds. National sovereignty is not really a final goal such as individual freedom or, in our view, competition. Few principles have been misused and abused as often as national sovereignty. Oversized national armies, unnecessary national airlines, harmful national protection, wasteful national infrastructures are all examples of the same type of misuse of national sovereignty.

6. - The Bernholz Plan: How to Limit the Growth of a Federal European Government and to Contain the Influence of Specific Interests

We have seen that there is a need for a State to secure contracting efficiencies, but there is also a tendency for discretionarity. Building a European constitution means to optimize between the «good» constructing efficiencies and the «bad» discretionarity. Additionally, it is also well-known that democratic systems with market economies show, if unchecked, a strong tendency towards increasing state activity (Olson [15], Weede 1986, Bernholz [3]). As a consequence, the motivation of individuals to work efficiently, to engage in risky productive activity and to innovate, is weakened, whereas the removal of intra-European barriers to the movement of people, goods and services tends to weaken and perhaps even to reverse the growth of government in member States. A growth at the federal European level has to be expected, as soon as Europe-wide interest groups and parties have been fully established. A European constitution has thus to contain provisions to check such tendencies.

My colleague from the University of Basel, Peter Bernholz [3] has had the courage to come up with specific proposals. Let me conclude with his most important points:

1) the *Declaration on Human Rights of the Council of Europe*, should be part of the constitution;

2) member States have the right to secede from the union. Provinces and localities (bordering another member State) the right to

secede from nation States. Regions with ten million inhabitants or more can by majority vote of the population declare themselves to be independent member States of the Union;

3) other European States have the right to join the Union, if they fulfill the following conditions: *a)* they have a constitution, organization and legal system guaranteeing the rule of law and democracy; *b)* they have market economies with dominating private property; *c)* they accept the constitution and the laws of the European Community;

4) the jurisdiction of the EC is limited to foreign policy, foreign trade policy, defence, the enforcement of free intra-community movement of people, goods, services and capital, anti-cartel and anti-monopoly policy constitution and to market-consistent measures concerning community-wide pollution. Market-consistent measures include preferably strong property rights concerning non-pollution and a corresponding tort law as well as pollution taxes and fees in preference to regulations, whenever feasible;

5) the activities of the Community are financed by a single tax, namely a proportional income tax. Increases of the tax rate are subject to unanimous consent of the European Council and to a popular *referendum* if at least half a million citizens ask for it with their signatures (the advantages of a single tax in limiting government activity are discussed in Brennan and Buchanan [7]);

6) subsidies and transfers of the federal government to firms, scientific, cultural and sports organizations, to communities, provinces and member States are forbidden, as are obligatory transfers among member States. Voluntary transfers by member States to each other are only allowed if they do not conflict with the goals of the Community. Present transfers and subsidies of the European Community are frozen for two years and then gradually phased out over eight years;

7) a centralized harmonization of national tax and social security system, of tax rates and of national regulation is forbidden;

8) the Community supports a free trade policy and the principle of free capital movements. This requirement may be waived for a limited period only with the purpose to motivate other nations to advance free trade in goods and services and free capital movements.

Both the European Parliament and the Council of the Union can each veto such measures;

9) each citizen has the right to conclude with his partners contracts, to incur debts or to give credit in any unit of account they select. Payments can be made in any currency or commodity they prefer. Taxes can be paid in any convertible currency at the exchange rate of the day;

10) banks are allowed to issue claims, credits and money in any unit of account they select. The proprietors or shareholders of banks issuing currency are subject to unlimited liability;

11) each individual, firm, community, province, member State and the federal government has the right to sue at the European Court any violation of the European constitution and of European laws to which he is or they are subject. All regulations and restrictions hindering the free movement of people, goods, services and capital in the community are illegal.

7. - Summary and Conclusions

1 - Institutions are the decisive growth factor. With the collapse of socialism (both as an ideology and as an experiment) history has not come to an end but rather entered a new phase — the phase of functional competition between nations (or single markets) with different variations of capitalist rules.

2 - Good rules for guaranteeing free and efficient private contracting are not easily found, but much more difficult to implement and maintain. All types of common-good ideologies, rent-seeking interest groups and even plain majority voting in democracy can and usually will lead to a deterioriation of a liberal economic/political order (in those few times and places where it ever got a foothold in the first place).

3 - The constitution is the set of mega-rules: on the one hand it lays down the procedure on how rules are changed and on the other hand the basic human rights of the individual. Whenever talking about political union in Europe, we should be talking about a «European Constitution».

4 - The cornerstones of a liberal Constitution are inalienable rights of the individual, both as a sovereign economic agent as well as a sovereign citizen. But in order to make full use of his rights, the individual needs a third party, a strong but limited State.

5 - Competition is a creative process not only in the economic but also in the political sphere. Economic contestability of any kind of market power is therefore always a good thing. But contestability of State authority is equally always as good.

6 - Political competition in this sense can be promoted in two different ways: one is by what I call internal constraints, that is, by constitutional safeguards limiting the State (for instance by federalism, qualified majorities in case of rule changes, etc.). The second is external pressure, that is, competition between different sets of national rules for the so-called relative attractiveness.

7 - The EC offers a historically unique chance for fundamental economic and political reform (as was the modern nation-state in the last century).

8 - The EC constitution should aim at a federal union. A new super-nation-state would just replicate the shortcomings of the old nation state, whereas a purely economic union could not prevent the individual nation from inventing new forms of protection.

9 - The European constitution should, therefore, establish a strong supranational European government, but strictly limit its competence.

10 - The nations within this federal union would lose parts of their sovereignty but would not cease to exist as «States» with rule-making power according to the subsidiarity of federalism.

11 - national competition for relative attractiveness would eliminate bad regulations and innovate good ones. In order to institutionalize this type of competition between regulatory systems within the European federation harmonization must stick to the very few essential property rights.

12 - The European federation should not become a closed club but remain open to all those nations accepting the basic rules of the game. Maybe the Community should not even protect the old nation states from splitting and/or allowing new federal members to be formed by regions of different nations.

BIBLIOGRAPHY

[1] BALDWIN R.: «The Growth Effects of 1992», *Economic Policy*, no. 9, 1989, pp. 247-81.

[2] BAUMOL W.J. - PANZAR J.C. - WILLIG R.D.: *Contestable Markets and the Theory of Industry Structure*, New York, Warcourt Brace Jovanovich, 1982.

[3] BERNHOLZ P: «Democracy, Competition and Subsidiarity: Essential Foundations of European Political Union», Frankfurter Institut, *Discussion on European Economic Policy*, no. 3, 1990.

[4] BHAGWATI J: «Is Free Trade Passé after All?», *Weltwirtscahftliches Archiv*, no. 125, 1989, pp. 17-44.

[5] BORNER S. - BRUNETTI A. - STRAUBHAAR TH.: *Schweiz AG - Vom Sonderfall zum Sanierungsfall?* Zürich, Verlag Neue Zürcher Zeitung, 1990.

[6] BORNER S. - BRUNETTI A. - WEDER B.: «Institutional Obstacles to Latin American Growth and Proposals for Reform», *WWZ-Studie*, no. 26, 1990.

[7] BRENNAN C. - BUCHANAN J.: «The Reasons of Rules», *Constitutional Political Economics*, Cambridge, Cambridge University Press, 1985.

[8] BRENNAN G. - KLIEMT H.: *Logo Logic, Constitutional Political Economy*, vol. 1, no. 1, 1990, pp. 125-7.

[9] COASE R.H.: *The Firm, the Market and the Law*, Chicago, 1988.

[10] COMMISSION OF THE EUROPEAN COMMUNITIES: «The Economics of 1992», *European Economy*, no. 35, March 1988.

[11] JENSEN M. - MECKLING W.: «Theory of the Firm: Managerial Behavior, Agency Costs and Ownership Structure», *Journal of Financial Economics*, October 1976, pp. 306-60.

[12] LUCAS R.: «On the Mechanics of Economic Development», *Journal of Monetary Economics*, no. 22, 1988, pp. 3-42.

[13] NORTH D.: «Institutions and Economic Growth: An Historical Introduction», Cornell University Conference on: *The Role of Institutions in Economic Development*, New York, Ithaca, 1986.

[14] — —: «Institutions, Transaction Costs and Economic Growth», *Economic Inquiry*, Vol. XXV, 1987, pp. 419-27.

[15] OLSON MANCUR: *The Rise and Decline of Nations*, New Haven, Yale University Press, 1982.

[16] ROMMER P.: «Increasing Returns and Long-Run Growth», *Journal of Political Economy*, no. 94, 1986, pp. 1002-37.

[17] — —: «Endogenous Technological Change», *Journal of Political Economy*, forthcoming, 1990.

[18] SWARTZ TH. - PECK J.: «The Changing Face of Fiscal Federalism», *Challenge*, December 1990, pp. 41-6.

[19] VENABLES A.: *Comments to Baldwin: The Growth Effects 1992*, 1989, pp. 273-5.

Real Saving Growth
in Western Europe:
Exploring Future Patterns

Martino Lo Cascio
Università «Tor Vergata», Roma

Foreword (*)

The increasing integration of Western Europe economies due to and coupled with institutional factors, such as the new rules for capital, labour and services free movements across state boundaries, and the perspective of a European currency, is bound to introduce substantial shifts in the past trends of main macroeconomic aggregates.

If one were to single out the indicator that best characterizes the major problem of West European economies in the last decade, the choice would fall on the unemployment rate, which was in the 1980s twice as high as in the 1970s. Also, the width of the subsequent gap between "potential" and "actual" output growth has been viewed as one of the leading causes of current unbalances within the OECD area. The issue today is whether and how policy should be used to lead the economy towards the potential output, reducing some of the record unemployment.

There are three major interpretations of Europe's low growth and high unemployment. The first claims that unemployment depends on

---

(*) Simulation results have been carried out by a research group on International Econometric Modeling directed by Martino Lo Cascio, II Università di Roma Tor Vergata. The other members of the group were Margherita Carlucci, Nino Cingolani, Stefano Di Palma, Giorgio Garau, Tiziana Todini.

Advise: the numbers in square brackets refer to the Bibliography in appendix.

excessively high real wages, coupled with a slowdown in productivity growth. The second interpretation refers to rigidities and non-wage labour costs, including «tenure arrangements, severance pay and regulation of hours, all of which work to impair a firm's flexibility in the optimal use of labour, thus raising the effective labour cost» (Dornbush [2]).

These two separate sources of unemployment may interact with effect of an increasing weight of the services sector in the structure of final demand. During the 1950s and 1960s, qualitative as well as quantitative developments in final demand were primarily directed towards manufactured products; this had a positive effect on the economic system as the manufactured products multiplier is higher than the one for agriculture or services. This was associated to a change in relative prices: decreasing real prices of manufactured products, particularly of durable goods, encouraged new consumers' spending patterns.

During the 1990s a new trend, started in the previous decade, reached growing incidence: the saturation of marked growth capabilities for some manufactured goods, the increasing demand for both public and private services (i.e. changes in consumer attitudes and in political environment), together with the slowdown in international trade growth (the most sensitive to relative prices among the components of final demand) induced a higher real wage growth with respect to productivity increase (Lo Cascio [9]).

The third explanation of unemployment in Western Europe points at the lack of demand, which calls for new Keynesian policies (Dornbush [2]). None of the above explanations is supported by unambiguous empirical evidence, since the three phenomena interact and, to my knowledge, no comprehensive model incorporates them.

Then, going back to policies, an eclectic approach is needed. This should take into account that:

— many variables normally treated as exogenous must be properly considered as endogenous, according to a Fischer-type analysis (Fischer [4]);

— conventional wisdom, both on theoretical and political grounds, defines constraints for policies aimed at the control of: *(i)* the inflation rate; *(ii)* the magnitude of public debt; *(iii)* the size of current account imbalances; so that many potential degrees of freedom for policy variables fade away.

We need first of all to consider the effect of shifting the above constraints from individual countries to the entire EEC area, in order to properly evaluate Western countries' future growth patterns in the perspective of: *a)* a new round of trade liberalization that includes services (whose impact has been measured in the *Cecchini Report*); *b)* free movement of labour and financial assets; *c)* a common currency for the twelve EEC countries.

In fact, at the end of this institutional process, there will be:

1) a "fine-tuning" problem for aggregate supply and demand (i.e. inflation) of the entire EEC area: that means bringing about a convergence of actual trends in prices and productivities among countries;

2) a problem of EEC public debt instead of single European countries' public debt;

3) a problem of EEC current account balance and reciprocal capital account positions, no longer between individual countries but between the whole area and the rest of the world, as a counterpart of the diversion of real saving flows within the area and between the area and the rest of the world.

In linking these perspectives with the above mentioned need for policies, it is also necessary to consider that the new prospects for the European Community actually induce a change in the rules of the game for both public and private agents operating in each country.

A healthy debate has developed over the progress of the EEC integration and particularly the creation of the EMU. As an extreme simplification, the underlying question concerns the loss of a degree of freedom in the adjustment of the economy real magnitudes in connection with a non-fixed exchange rate system (allowing the re-alignment on the part of individual EEC countries).

Whether policies aimed at guiding exchange rates may favour a real adjustment of a country's economy or may actually delay it is a matter of argument. Likewise the debate is open with respect to the most appropriate policies in the transitional stage and the benefits or losses to individual countries. The purpose of this research is not to take in these controversial issues, but rather to explore the long-run perspectives for the European economy, with particular attention to the mechanism of growth financing in the hypothesis of an actual EMU implementation, and to compare those perspectives with the ones envisionable should the integration process come to a halt.

As statistical information on impulse-reaction process following institutional changes is still unavailable, exploration of long run conditions in a radically different institutional framework is only feasible provided that one can work with few structural relationships. The outline of this paper is the following. In the first paragraph the rationale and essential structure of the econometric estimates and solutions developed are briefly described. The model firstly concerns the relationships that define long-run demand-supply equilibrium for individual EEC countries. Domestic and external relative prices are considered, which allows to include in the analysis both competitiveness and terms of trade distributional effects that, in turn, affect propensity to save. In order to simulate the shares of output, saving and investment within the EEC area in the new institutional framework, another model is developed. Its purpose is to capture the performance of particular sub-areas when convergence hypotheses on policies and structural conditions are introduced. These models must be properly viewed in a scenario framework rather than as a forecasting exercise.

In the second paragraph the main results, both in their quantitative aspects and qualitative implications, are discussed. To better appreciate the differential effects produced by the new institutional rules with respect to the existing ones, two sets of figures are presented for long-term rates of growth, savings formation, investment requirements and financing needs, external positions and a few other indicators. The two sets of results are obtained from two alternative sets of hypotheses: *(i)* continuity of policies (monetary, fiscal, current account balance control, etc.) at the individual country level; *(ii)* adoption of global policies for the entire EEC area.

In the third paragraph some conclusions are drawn regarding the impact of the new EEC institutional rules on the reduction of the existing gap between potential and actual output and employment levels. Induced effects on the world economy are also examined.

1. - The Analytical Framework

The economic literature provides several alternative approaches to deal with long-term demand and supply equilibrium paths. Conventional methods, at least in the empirical literature, entail ecletic approaches in which traditional demand-oriented models take into account the supply side by centering the core of feed-back loops for the supply side on accounting identities, price and import-export behavioral relationships. Relevant for supply-side analyses, in the solution, are the adjustment procedures by rescaling policy variables (i.e. quantity of money, Government demand, exchange rate in order to take into-account the constraints on the country's external position or debt size).

Up to now these models provide the most exhaustive explorations of future trends for a number of countries. In spite of their formal complexity the results must be viewed as detailed and consistent databases for scenario simulations rather than proper forecasts. Furthermore, as Gilli [5] has shown, their solutions are based on a sub-block of few truly interdependent relationships upon which the rest of the system equations has a weak influence, representing, in fact, a block triangular subsystem.

In the last decade a number of different approaches have been developed, whose philosophy is focused on: *(i)* use of modern time series analysis; *(ii)* macroeconomic relationships having sound microfoundations. The resulting models assume an optimizing behavior on the part of the various agents and include expectations (for all, see Nickell and Hendry [12]). With few but very important exceptions, these models concern problems related to particular markets and, by their very design, do not address all the questions at issue.

Furthermore, cointegration based models and VAR techiniques have been used to test and estimate interdependent and dynamic models without defining *a priori* which variables are exogenous, and for the purpose of catching the causal relationships only in terms of temporal sequences between shocks affecting the trend of few aggregate macroeconomic and policy variables (Fischer [4]). The main result of this approach, in my view, lies in the finding that most policy variables have a predominant endogenous nature. On the other hand, these conclusions (see also Pagano [13]) are of limited value as for their implications to the questions at issue.

The approach followed in these models' specification and estimation does not specifically belong to any of the above mentioned modeling philosophies, although it aims to capture their essential findings in order to address the questions we are concerned with.

1.1 *Investment-Saving Functions*

When working in a comprehensive empirically-oriented framework, a crucial role in the specification and estimation of an econometric model is played by the national accounting identities. The most important among them is the following relationship:

$$(1) \qquad\qquad M - E = I - S$$

where M and E represent the import and, respectively, the export of goods, while S and I denote domestic saving and, respectively, investment including those of the public sector.

Equation *(1)* can be viewed as an *ex post* accounting constraint or, more properly, as an *ex ante* equilibrium constraint. Both interpretations involve many theoretical questions, and empirical assumptions mainly related to the lack of correspondence between the definition of the economic variables concerned and what the data actually used in the analysis represent. The latter, by their very construction, implicitly incorporate their own specific theoretical background (consider, for instance, index-number based figures for real aggregates or deflators). Consider equation *(1)* as the *ex ante* steady-growth equilibrium condition: the current account $E - M$ and the $S - I$ may be considered as functions of a number of variables, including *GDP* or final domestic demand, world demand, the exchange rate and the interest rate, via domestic and international prices. The country or area demand/supply or external balance equilibrium is determined by the intersection of the $E - M$ and $S - I$ functions. Thus, for instance, the external balance reflects changes in import-export behavior as well as changes in domestic saving and investment behavior.

Suppose we have some estimates of long-term import and export growth rates satisfying the additional constraint $M - E = 0$; the related import-export equilibrium prices are the result both of the international economic environment and of policy variables satisfying the above mentioned constraints. In this case the long-term steady growth paths for output and other macroeconomic variables are defined by $S = I$ functions. One fact that must be taken into account and that is not often considered in explicit form, is that the domestic-to-external prices ratio may alternatively represent: *(i)* competitiveness and *(ii)* terms of trade. An increase in competitiveness — defined by policy variables according to the structural conditions prevailing in a given economy — weill positively affect output provided that the long-term Marshall-Lerner conditions are satisfied. At the same time, the corresponding decrease in terms of trade will negatively affect the share of real savings made available to internal investment. In this context, the characteristics and the rationale behind the model defined in the following pages should be self-evident. First, since the propensity to save *(PMS)* equals $1 - PMC$ (where *PMC* is the propensity to consume), we can start from a consumption function of the following type:

(2) $$C_t = \mu_0 + \alpha_1 C_{t-1} + \beta_0 Y_t + \beta_1 Y_{t-1} + \varepsilon_t$$

where C_t and Y_t represent consumption and income at constant prices. This formulation is consistent with Modigliani's *life-cycle* hypothesis, provided that the estimation is subject to the appropriate restriction. Equation *(2)*, on the other hand, can be viewed as the estimable specification of the relationship:

$$C_t^* = \mu_0 + \beta Y_t^* + \varepsilon_t$$

where C_t^* and Y_t^* are non-observable variables representing expected consumption and income levels, or of:

$$C_t = \mu_0 + (B(L)/A(L)) Y_t$$

where $A(L) = 1 - \alpha_1 L$ and $B(L) = \beta_0 + \beta_1 L$ are two polynomials of the first order representing the relationship between C_t^* and the series

C_t and between Y_t^* and the series of Y_t according to a distributed lag scheme.

Equation *(2)*, thus, represents a dynamic specification of the relationship between consumption and income that, given the number of available sample points, seems judicious from the point of view of time-series statistical estimation. If the variables appearing in equation *(2)* are expressed in logarithmic form, in the steady-growth situation characterizing most traditional development models one can expect $\beta = B(L)/A(L) = 1$ i.e. that the income elasticity of consumption in the long run be equal to 1 or, in other words, that long-term average and marginal propensity to consume be constant and take the same value. This implies the restriction:

(3) $$\alpha_1 + \beta_0 + \beta_1 = 1$$

If we set $\gamma = 1 - \alpha_1$ equation *(2)* can be written as:

(4) $$lnC_t = \mu_0 + (1 - \gamma)\, lnC_{t-1} + \beta_0 lnY_t + \beta_1 lnY_{t-1} + \varepsilon_t$$

or else:

(5) $$lnC_t - lnC_{t-1} = \mu_0 + \beta_0\,(lnY_t - lnY_{t-1}) + \gamma\,(lnY_{t-1} - lnC_{t-1}) + \varepsilon_t$$

Equation *(5)* represents the well known ECM version of the consumption function proposed by Hendry et Al. [7].

Using yearly data and series having about 20 observations it is difficult to verify the restrictions due to the need to keep the distributed lags within a first order scheme. It is possible, however, to test both the significance of the relationship *(2)* and the godness of fit of the more restrictive specification *(5)* (i.e.: of restrictions *(3)*) to the data.

If these restrictions are accepted: β_0 represents the short-run elasticity of consumption with respect to income; γ gives the elasticity speed of adjustment to actual income with respect to expected income and $\gamma\,(lnY_{t-1}/lnC_{t-1})$ is the correction factor that keeps the growth path of short-run consumption along its equilibrium trajectory.

Analogously, in the steady-growth case we would have:

$$ln(C_t / C_{t-1}) = dC/C = dY/Y$$

This way we would be able to define the entire set of parameters:

$$PMC = exp\left\{\left[\mu_0 - (1 - \beta_0)\frac{dY}{Y}\right]/\gamma\right\}$$

that represent the constant equal average and marginal propensity to save for a given income growth rate, and which take upon different values as the long-run steady growth of income varies. So, the values *PMS* = 1 − *PMC* represent the corresponding values for the average and marginal propensity to save which are constant for a given steady growth rate but change as a function of varying long-run output growth trends.

So far, we haven't considered in the model the income distribution effects on propensity to save due to domestic-to-external relative prices, i.e. due to changes in terms of trade. In the long run horizon the assumption of no influence of domestic to external relative prices on the propensity to consume or to save could be appropriate. In a steady-state situation these relative prices can be viewed as a random variable adding up to the residual term ε, defining a random walk of consumption around μ_0.

Even in a long run equilibrium situation, however, Scandizzo [15] has argued and demonstrated, for a given country, the theoretical consistency of prolonged *deficit/surplus* in current accounts and corresponding *surplus/deficit* in capital or financial assets' accounts. If the model is extended to include another residual area (or the other relevant countries), it follows that steady growth paths for more interdependent areas are consistent with different constant growth rates of their respective prices.

Furthermore, as required on statistical grounds, when dealing with a more comprehensive model thats must include short-term behavior as well as *ex ante* demand-supply disequilibrium, it is necessary:

a) to introduce — even ignoring the proportions and extensions of Scandizzo's analysis — relative prices in the specification of the consumption (saving) function. This function must of course lead to well-behaved estimates when the model collapses to the steady-state situation;

  b) to take into account the existence of a systematic gap between the economic variables involved and the data currently utilized. In particular, since it is difficult to understand what the real meaning of constant prices income figures is (other than its purchasing power), in estimating equation *(5)* I introduced the *GDP* time series as a proxy for income. The differences between the two aggregates ultimately depend on domestic to external relative prices (shifts over time in prices, interest and change rates will in turn affect factors' income inflows, outflows and balance).

  These considerations explain why in specifying equation *(5)* I introduced the variable $\Delta lnPREL$, representative of the rate of change of the ratio between export and import prices in US dollars. Thus, the consumption function becomes:

(5bis)
$$C_t = C_{t-1}\, exp\, \{\mu_0\, \Delta\, lnPREL + \\ + \beta_0\, (lnY_t - lnY_{t-1}) + \gamma\, (lnY_{t-1} + lnC_{t-1})\} + e_t$$

  If, in the steady-state equilibrium case, $\Delta\, lnPREL = 0$, the long-run average and marginal propensity to consume *PMC* is equal to one (zero income growth rates), then, according to economic theory the difference between the long-run average and marginal propensity to save *PMS* equals zero.

  The model to estimate the long-run accumulation rate is based on a simple approach along the lines of development economics traditional theory. Investment is viewed as an accumulation process towards the desired level of the capital/output ratio. Therefore, the current share It/Yt of investment over the GDP is a function of the current output growth rate dY/Y.

  Conditions set by economic policy or by social rigidities, may constrain the speed at which current propensity to invest adjusts to the desired level. For these reasons the model can be specified, by introducing the term I_{t-1}/Y_{t-1}, along the lines of a partial adjustment process. The estimated specification is thus of the form:

(6)
$$\frac{I_t}{Y_t} = a_0 + a_1 \frac{dY_t}{Y_{t-1}} + a_2 \frac{I_{t-1}}{Y_{t-1}} + \varepsilon_t$$

where we can expect $0 < a_2 < 1$, and $k = 1 - a_2$ represents the speed of adjustment of the actual propensity to the desired capital/output ratio. In the steady-growth situation, we have:

$$\frac{I}{Y} = \frac{a_0}{1 - a_2} + \frac{a_1}{(1 - a_2)} \frac{dY_t}{Y}$$

The higher k is, the lower is the growth of investment requirements per unit of output as income growth rate rises. In a fully developed economy, a higher relative weight of depreciation in gross investment and lower reduction in the marginal efficiency of capital strenghtens the role of biased technical progress relative to the scale economies available with a higher degree of accumulation.

1.2. *The GDP Share Equations for EEC Countries*

Consider the total supply provided by an individual area that must meet total demand of an integrated area including the above mentioned countries. Furthermore, assume for each country a system of production functions in an aggregate variable q_j representing the availability of primary factors (the suffix indicating country j).

A generic production function for the EEC area may thus be written as:

(7) $a = a(q_1, \ldots, q_n)$ (n = number of countries in the area).

Denoting with p_j ($j = 1, \ldots, n$) a primary inputs' aggregate price vector, let us consider the optimization problem:

(8) $Max\ a = a(q_1, \ldots, q_n)$

(9) sub to $\Sigma_j p_j q_j = Y$

where: Y stands for current income = net output value of the whole area.

Constraint *(9)* ensures that the sum of individual countries' supplies equals the area's total demand (both supply and demand must be at constant prices). Then, solving the optimization problem *(8)* and *(9)* the supply functions may be written as:

(10) $q_j = q_j(p_1, \ldots, p_n; Y)$

Now, we need to specify either the production functions' *(7)* or, in alternative, the supply function *(10)* analytical form. A particularly simple choice for the area production function is the following:

(11) $a = \Pi_j(q_j - c_j)^{\beta_j}$

where c_j and β_j are unknown parameters, with $\Sigma_j \beta_j = 1$, which leads, through the maximization problem *(8)* and *(9)* to the country supply function:

(12) $q_j = c_j + \dfrac{\beta_j}{p_j}(Y - \Sigma_j p_j c_j) \qquad j = 1, \ldots, n$

The economic interpretation of the unknown parameters c_j and β_j is self-evident. At a first glance, c_j could represent the total output share due to a given country's specialization within the EEC area, showing zero elasticity to relative price changes. On the other hand, β_j could be interpreted as the elasticity of total area supply (net of c_j share) to each country's primary inputs, or as each country's marginal share of the EEC market.

In econometric estimation it is necessary to allow for shifts over time in c_j specification, as non-price competitiveness of each country's supply changes over time. Furthermore, data set inherent biases must be considered, namely those concerning value added at constant prices (used as a proxy for total primary factors input) and deflators standardized with exchange rates indexes (a proxy for relative prices by countries).

Internal technical progress (factor augmenting scale) may bias the quantity of inputs required in each period, as well as their quality (with a mechanism somewhat similar to increasing returns to scale). Thus, systematic biases may be assumed in quantities and prices trajectories, as resulting from the data, and in the corresponding variables as defined by economic theory.

In this context, equation *(12)* must be considered as a relationship between latent q_j^* and p_j^* variables, so that the set of equations:

$$(12bis) \qquad q_j^* = c_j^* + \frac{\beta_j}{p_j^*}(Y - \Sigma_j p_j^* c_j^*) \qquad j = 1, \ldots n$$

must be extended to include the following

$$(13) \qquad q_j = \Psi_j(q_j^*) \qquad \text{and} \qquad p_j = \phi(p_j^*)$$

(see Trivellato [16] for a general discussion on model estimation under systematic measurement errors in the data set).

It has been shown (Fontela-Lo Cascio (1)) that a sound specification of equation *(12bis)* couples with *(13)* results in the following reduced form:

$$(14) \qquad q_j^t = c_j^* \left(\frac{q_j^{t-1}}{q_j^{0-1}}\right)^{b_j} + \frac{\beta_j}{p_j}\left[Y - \sum_j p_j c_j^* \left(\frac{q_j^{t-1}}{q_j^{0-1}}\right)^{b_j}\right]$$

$$j = 1, \ldots n$$

where q_j^0 stands for the constant-price GDP of the base year. The equations *(14)* can be econometrically estimated under the assumptions of a static specification of the error terms and a dynamic specification of the economic behavioral relationships (see in a similar context Rossier [14]).

---

(1) See FONTELA E. - LO CASCIO M.: «Quality Indices in the National Accounts Framework», *Economic Systems Research*, forthcoming, 1991.

2. - Thinking about the Future of EEC
in the New Institutional Framework

In summarizing the reasons behind European unemployment (and the gap between actual and potential ouptput), Dornbusch [2] utilizes the Mundell (2) diagram. This shows along the *MM* line the locus of real wages and aggregate demand combinations where the level of output supplied by profit-maximizing, competitive firms equals the level of real spending.

«To meet a higher level of demand given capital, material price and technology, a lower product wage is required so as to stimulate employment and output. The vertical schedule denotes the full employment level of output». (Dornbusch [2]).

GRAPH 1

REAL WAGES, AGGREGATE DEMAND

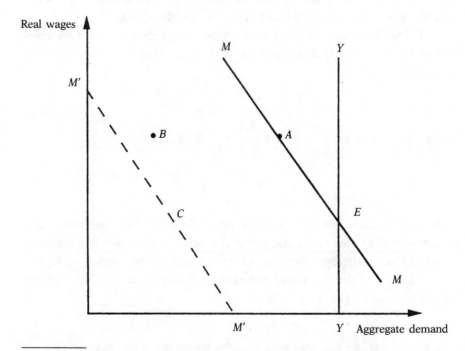

(2) See MUNDELL R.: *International Economics*, New, York, MacMillan 1968.

In the equilibrium point E, the classical model full employment is reached through flexible wage rate schedule. Point A defines the gap between potential and actual level of output due to excessively high real wages, other rigidities or non-wage labour costs. Point C reproduces situations of insufficient demand, while point B stands for both lack of demand and too high real wages.

Introducing dynamic and expectations, we may interpret Graph 1, without loss of generality, by redefining the variables on the axes as expected long term growth rates. Thus, YY represents the full employment rate of growth and MM the combinations of rates of real wages and real aggregate demand. Rethinking the present European situation in terms of Graph 1 is a very difficult task, since we cannot really distinguish between the three cases A, B and C, nor we can claim that all real situations are taken into account.

Suppose that Graph 1 refers to a single country or area that takes prices (including interest rates) as exogeneously given, since they are fixed in a world context. Moving along the MM curve from A to E implies also a loss of purchasing power due to a deterioration of ferms of trade, that can shift downwards the MM curve to the $M'M'$ one. So, if the slope of MM does not change, reaching full employment income becomes impossible as a higher wage flexibility does not guarantee that a reduction of demand due to the loss of purchasing power be offset by foreign demand. Furthermore, even in this stylized context, we need to introduce external demand and supply as a function of competitiveness and policy constraints (such as the current account balance) in order to take into account substitution of foreign demand for domestic demand.

It could be useful to refer to Graph 2, which reproduces the reasoning of the above described econometric methodology. In it, PMS and PMI denote long-term propensities to save and, respectively, to invest, while the shifts in PMS due to $\Delta lnPrel$ are denoted by dashed lines and the bold line represents all solutions for which the output rate satisfies demand/supply constraints.

In the second section of Graph 2 the corresponding solution points consistent with the $M - E = 0$ constraint are represented. As can be seen, there is an inconsistency between the two policies aimed to achieve symultaneously internal demand-supply balance (control of

GRAPH 2

EXCHANGE RATES, COMPETITIVENESS
AND GROWTH RATE IN THE LONG RUN

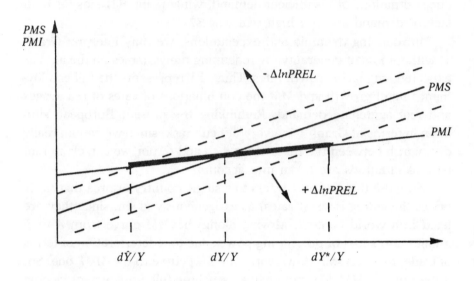

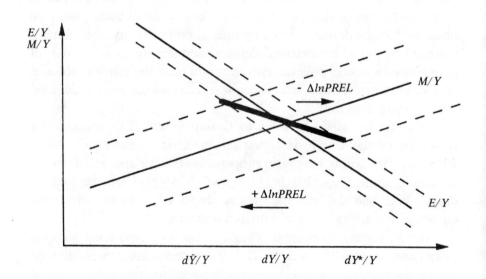

inflation) and trade balance, when the actual rate is "forced" to move towards the potential rate. Degrees of freedom for economic policy measures, other than those directed to change structural relationships, do not abound: among them a significant role is played by measures, such as a change in the institutional framework, that modify the rules of the game for economic agents.

Point *A* now describes the feasible rate of growth *dy/y* satisfying both demand-supply (inflation) and external balance constraints, provided that real interests prevailing at world level are consistent with the feasible rate of internal growth (Graph 3). A more accommodating monetary policy, an increase in government spending, a downwards shift of the exchange rate should improve *dy/y*, to the right of *A*, provided the *PMS* shifts downwards or doesn't move. But all three policy measures entail, everything staying the same in the international context, a fall in the country/area prices relative to international prices. For a third of the above policies this is obvious; also a drop in real exchange rate or, more generally, in export prices relative to world prices, must be foreseen (both on behavioral and current accounts balance grounds) in the first two cases as well.

GRAPH 3

UNDEREMPLOYMENT GROWTH RATE

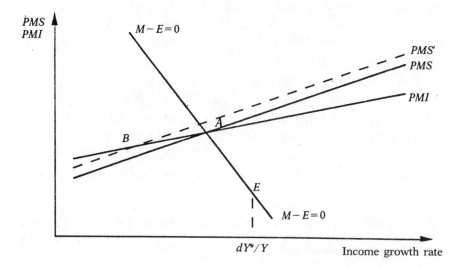

Theoretical statements established in paragraph 1 suggest that if relative prices decrease the *PMS* curve shifts upwards (see Graph 3). Point *B* shows the first round consequences of the above-mentioned policies: the corresponding rate of growth is lower than the "feasible" one and implies a deficit in current accounts.

A more restrictive monetary policy, such as a reduction in government expenditure or at least a re-evaluation, can improve economic conditions of the country/area. The constraints' consistency of these policies strongly depend on cross point slopes of the *PMS* and *PMI* curves (3) and on the shifts induced in *PMS* by equilibrium $\Delta lnPREL$, whose values on turn depend on point elasticities of imports to output and to relative prices. Historical patterns of policy variables, different by country and, for some country, even over time, suggest a fine-tuning, beyond which still remain the long-term structural conditions and economic agents' behaviour coupled with institutional framework. In the last decades, few occurrences had changed the previous long-term trends: *a)* demographic and political environment; *b)* technology trajectories; *c)* Bretton Woods agreements; *d)* EEC institution; *e)* non-convertibility of dollar followed by increase in oil prices.

Will the new Europe change the previous trends? The response to this question could come from the following econometric estimates.

Tables 1 and 2 report the main statistical results for demand-supply models referred to Germany and the whole EEC area (estimates for single EEC countries are available, even if unpublished). The sample period is 1960-1988 and the data set has been derived from OECD and Eurostat time series.

Solutions for these models have been obtained introducing Δln-*PREL* historical trends to represent the effects of fine tuning economic policies that satisfy both internal and external constraints. This in turn implies positive rates in German export prices, negative rates for the rest of Europe. Thus, I obtained the following figures for Germany's *PMS* and *PMI* which, with further calculations, lead to the corres-

---

(3) Restrictive policies may even have counter-intuitive effects with respect to trade balance if the slope of *PMI* is always higher than that of *PMS*. This is the case of some developing countries (BAGELLA M. - LO CASCIO M. [10]).

TABLE 1

CONSUMPTION FUNCTIONS

$$C_t = C_{t-1} * EXP(\mu_0 * \Delta LPREL + \beta_0 (lnY_t - lnY_{t-1}) + \gamma (lnY_{t-1} - lnC_{t-1})) + e_t$$

| | Parameter μ_0 | | Parameter β_0 | | Parameter γ | | Statistics | |
	Value	T	Value	T	Value	T	R^2	DW
Germany	0,078	1,92 (0,066) (*)	0,597	5,92 (0,00) (*)	0,042	3,69 (0,001) (*)	0,998	1,48
EEC	0,112	3,88 (0,001) (*)	0,84	10,21 (0,000) (*)	0,024	2,28 (0,031) (*)	0,999	1,66

(*) Two tail test.

TABLE 2

INVESTMENT FUNCTIONS

$$\frac{I_t}{Y_t} = a_0 + a_1 \frac{\Delta Y_t}{Y_{t-1}} + a_2 \frac{\Delta I_{t-1}}{Y_{t-1}} + \varepsilon_t$$

| | Parameter a_0 | | Parameter a_1 | | Parameter a_2 | | Statistics | |
	Value	T	Value	T	Value	T	R^2	DW
Germany	0,028	2,69 (0,012) (*)	0,262	4,60 (0,000) (*)	0,839	18,62 (0,000) (*)	0,937	1,43
EEC	0,038	4,78 (0,000) (*)	0,401	7,34 (0,000) (*)	0,769	19,62 (0,000) (*)	0,965	2,13

(*) Two tail test.

ponding figures for the rest of Europe (*RES*). This procedure is outlined in Table 3.

TABLE 3

SOLUTION PROCEDURE FOR THE CASE
WITH CURRENT ECONOMIC POLICIES

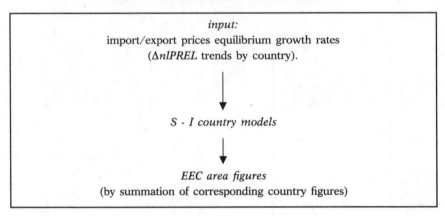

These results are presented in Tables 4 and 5 and also in Graphs 4 and 5, while Graphs 6 and 7 refer to the whole EEC area, obtained summing up Germany's and *RES'* results.

TABLE 4

LONG-TERM *PMS* AND *PMI* AS FUNCTION OF GROWTH RATE
GERMANY

Growth rates	PMS	PMI
1.0	0.081	0.190
1.5	0.124	0.198
2.0	0.164	0.206
2.5	0.203	0.214
3.0	0.240	0.223
3.4	0.275	0.231
4.0	0.308	0.239
4.5	0.340	0.247
5.0	0.371	0.255
5.5	0.400	0.264
6.0	0.427	0.272

TABLE 5

LONG-TERM *PMS* AND *PMI* AS FUNCTION OF GROWTH RATE
EEC AREA

Growth rates	PMS	PMI
1.0	0.090	0.190
1.5	0.132	0.198
2.0	0.172	0.206
2.5	0.210	0.214
3.0	0.247	0.223
3.5	0.282	0.231
4.0	0.315	0.239
4.5	0.346	0.247
5.0	0.377	0.255
5.5	0.405	0.264
6.0	0.433	0.272

GRAPH 4

LONG-TERM PROPENSITY TO SAVE (*PMS*)
AND TO INVEST (*PMI*)
CURRENT POLICIES CASE
GERMANY

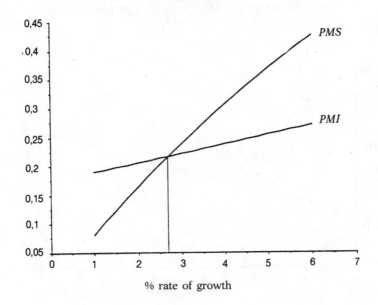

% rate of growth

GRAPH 5

LONG-TERM PROPENSITY TO SAVE (*PMS*)
AND TO INVEST (*PMI*) CURRENT POLICIES CASE
REST OF EEC

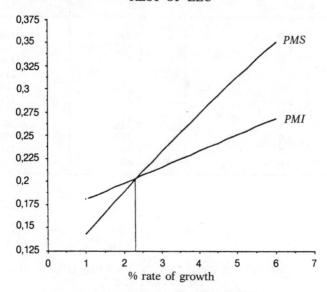

GRAPH 6

LONG-TERM PROPENSITY TO SAVE (*PMS*)
AND TO INVEST (*PMI*) CURRENT POLICIES CASE
EEC AREA

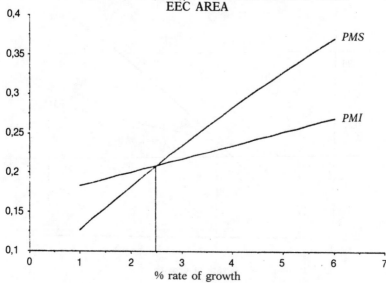

GRAPH 7

LONG-TERM PROPENSITY TO SAVE (*PMS*)
AND TO INVEST (*PMI*) CURRENT POLICIES CASE (*)
EEC AREA

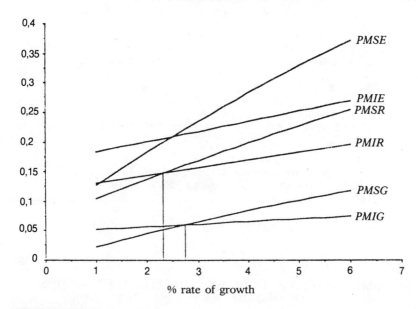

% rate of growth

(*) *PMSR* = *PMS* (rest of EEC)   *YR/YE*
    PMIR = *PMI* (rest of EEC)   *YR/YE*
    PMSG = *PMS* (Germany)   *YG/YE*
    PMIG = *PMI* (Germany)   *YG/YE*

The equilibrium growth rates for Germany (2,8%), *RES* (2,3%) and the whole EEC (2,5%) are consistent with those projected in baseline scenarios by the main international forecasters (for instance, *DRI* gives the same values for the next 5 years, which become 0,3-0,5% higher around the year 2010).

To simulate the new institutional framework for EEC countries, I used the solution of the model for the whole EEC area as starting values. Therefore, I introduced a very rough hypothesis of equalization of prices' growth rates by country. Eventually, to take into account the shift from single countries' to the whole area's public budget and current accounts constraints, I put $\Delta \ln PREL = 0$. This procedure is outlined in Table 6. Resulting values for *PMS* and *PMI* are showed in Table 7 and Graph 8.

Table 6

SOLUTION PROCEDURE
FOR THE NEW INSTITUTIONAL FRAMEWORK CASE

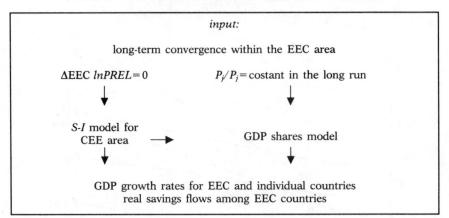

Table 7

SIMULATED LONG-TERM *PMS* AND *PMI* AS A FUNCTION
OF GROWTH RATE, EEC AREA

Growth rates	PMS	PMI
1.0	0.064	0.183
1.5	0.094	0.192
2.0	0.124	0.201
2.5	0.152	0.209
3.0	0.180	0.218
3.5	0.206	0.227
4.0	0.232	0.235
4.5	0.257	0.244
5.0	0.281	0.253
5.5	0.304	0.261
6.0	0.327	0.270

In the new context all European countries will compete in the
same market, their firms facing the same total EEC demand, similar
prices and increasing convergence in technical progress and productivity.

GRAPH 8

LONG-TERM PROPENSITY TO SAVE (*PMS*)
AND TO INVEST (*PMI*)
NEW INSTITUTIONAL FRAMEWORK CASE
EEC AREA

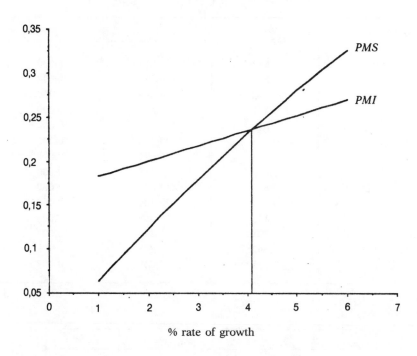

% rate of growth

To measure long-term trajectories for single countries or subareas I applied the GDP share model described in paragraph 1. Its coefficients and statistics are presented below (Table 8).

The estimates reported below have been obtained assuming a 4% growth rate for the whole area and an equal GDP price index by country (see Tables 9 to 11 and Graphs 9, 10).

Even in the hypothesis of a constant rate of growth for European GDP, constant output growth for each country could be expected only in a very long time horizon. In this regard, a crucial role is played by actual differences in specialization, productivity, internal factor technical progress, output quality.

TABLE 8

FUNCTIONS OF GDP SHARES

$$q_j^t = c_j^* \left(\frac{q_j^{t-1}}{q_j^0-1}\right)^{b_j} + \frac{b_j}{p_j}\left[Y - \sum_j p_j c_j^* \left(\frac{q_j^{t-1}}{q_j^0}\right)^{b_j}\right]$$

Parameters	Value	T	Two tail test
c_1^*	682	241,012	0.000
c_2^*	554	126,175	0.004
c_3^*	842	154,899	0.000
c_4^*	471	181,834	0.000
c_5^*	671	429,815	0.000
b_1	0.853	25,715	0.000
b_2	0.743	6,095	0.004
b_3	0.823	11,418	0.000
b_4	0.858	14,192	0.000
b_5	0,810	20,380	0.000
b_1	0.137	4,854	0.008
b_2	0.221	6,294	0.003
b_3	0.342	14,845	0.000
b_4	0.145	6,445	0.003

	R^2	DW
$j=1$ FRA	0.997	1,713
$j=2$ UK.....................	0.964	1,427
$j=3$ FRG	0.997	2,005
$j=4$ ITA.....................	0.994	1,515
$j=5$ RES	0.999	2,057

However, a synthetic view of saving flows within the EEC countries could be obtained applying the demand-supply models by country. The results are shown in the last three graphs (11-13).

TABLE 9

EEC COUNTRIES GROSS DOMESTIC PRODUCT
NEW INSTITUTIONAL FRAMEWORK CASE
(billion ECU at constant 1988 prices)

Year	Fra	UK	FRG	Ita	Res	EEC
1990	857	749	1,123	770	862	4,361
1995	1,011	899	1,424	965	1,007	5,306
2000	1,200	1,084	1,785	1,201	1,186	6,455
2005	1,432	1,311	2,220	1,485	1,406	7,853
2010	1,714	1,591	2,746	1,827	1,676	9,553
2015	2,057	1,933	3,385	2,240	2,005	11,620
2020	2,474	2,352	4,162	2,741	2,405	14,134
2025	2,978	2,865	5,109	3,348	2,892	17,194
2030	3,589	3,492	6,264	4,086	3,483	20,915

TABLE 10

EEC COUNTRIES OUTPUT GROWTH RATES
NEW INSTITUTIONAL FRAMEWORK

Year	Fra	UK	FRG	Ita	Res
1990-1995	3.34	3.71	4.89	4.64	3.14
1995-2000	3.47	3.80	4.64	4.48	3.30
2000-2005	3.58	3.88	4.47	4.35	3.45
2005-2010	3.66	3.93	4.35	4.24	3.56
2010-2015	3.71	3.97	4.28	4.17	3.64
2015-2020	3.75	4.00	4.22	4.12	3.70
2020-2025	3.78	4.02	4.18	4.08	3.75
2025-2030	3.80	4.04	4.15	4.06	3.78

TABLE 11

EEC COUNTRIES OUTPUT SHARES
NEW INSTITUTIONAL FRAMEWORK CASE

Year	Fra	UK	FRG	Ita	Res
1990-1995	0.19	0.17	0.26	0.18	0.19
1995-2000	0.19	0.17	0.27	0.18	0.19
2000-2005	0.18	0.17	0.28	0.19	0.18
2005-2010	0.18	0.17	0.29	0.19	0.18
2010-2015	0.18	0.17	0.29	0.19	0.17
2015-2020	0.18	0.17	0.29	0.19	0.17
2020-2025	0.17	0.17	0.30	0.19	0.17
2025-2030	0.17	0.17	0.30	0.20	0.17

GRAPH 9

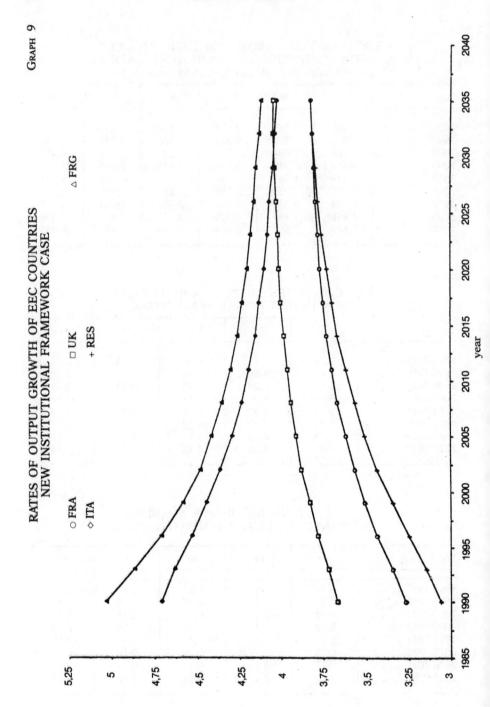

RATES OF OUTPUT GROWTH OF EEC COUNTRIES
NEW INSTITUTIONAL FRAMEWORK CASE

○ FRA   □ UK   △ FRG
◇ ITA   + RES

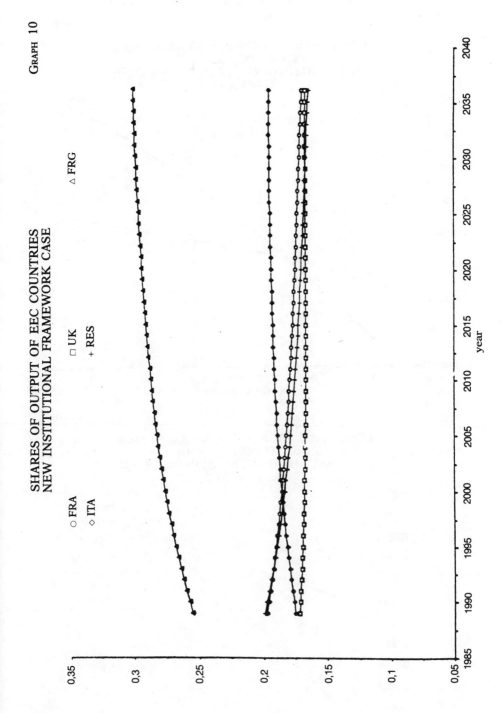

GRAPH 10

SHARES OF OUTPUT OF EEC COUNTRIES
NEW INSTITUTIONAL FRAMEWORK CASE

○ FRA   □ UK   △ FRG
◇ ITA   + RES

year

GRAPH 11

LONG-TERM PROPENSITY TO SAVE (*PMS*)
AND TO INVEST (*PMI*)
NEW INSTITUTIONAL FRAMEWORK CASE
GERMANY

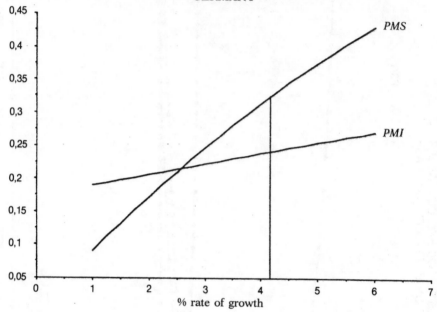

GRAPH 12

LONG-TERM PROPENSITY TO SAVE (*PMS*)
AND TO INVEST (*PMI*)
NEW INSTITUTIONAL FRAMEWORK CASE
REST OF EEC

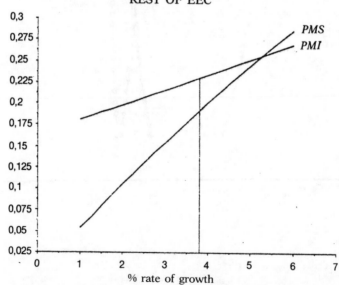

GRAPH 13

LONG-TERM PROPENSITY TO SAVE (*PMS*)
AND TO INVEST (*PMI*)
NEW INSTITUTIONAL FRAMEWORK CASE (*)

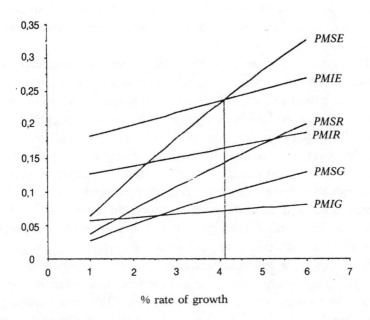

% rate of growth

(*) *PMSR = PMS* (rest of EEC)   *YR/YE*
    PMIR = PMI (rest of EEC)   *YR/YE*
    PMSG = PMS (Germany)   *YG/YE*
    PMIG = PMI (Germany)   *YG/YE*

The additional real saving flows within EEC area could be expected to equal a share between the 3% and the 5% of the area's GDP (between 9% and 15% in the case of Germany).

Time profiles show for Germany a dramatic increase in output growth rates in the next ten years (2% above last decade trends), as a counterpart of net saving outflows directed to the other partners. To some extent, a major impact in the next decade could be expected also for Italy, while for other EEC countries output growth rates will reach Germany's (and Italy's) levels only after the year 2000.

3. - Concluding Remarks

It is intuitively obvious that EEC future rate of growth cannot be determined without taking into account current conditions and likely evolution in the other developed countries, the raw materials producer countries, the newly industrialized countries, the developing nations, and vice versa.

The number of factors that can affect a long-term global economic scenario or projection, and their degree of uncertainty, due to political reasons (East European institutional revolutions and Gulf crisis are today examples, but many others could occur), result in manifold alternative paths for the future of EEC countries. Particularly the German unification requires in-depth analysis of many difficult factors, even though it is likely that convergence policies in EEC area will be improved rather than discouraged as a result. So, the fiugures presented in paragraph 2 represent only suggested magnitudes for the purpose of an introductory discussion of the issues and of the need for attitude changes in each country.

It is important to evaluate these magnitudes from two perspectives. The first perspective is connected to the particular type of analysis developed, aimed at indicating the EEC countries' approximate growth and the savings flow required for its financing in the hypothesis of continued integration and of creation of the EMU vis-à-vis the correspondent trends that can be envisioned in the absence of substantial institutional innovations. The analysis, therefore, does not cover the conditions through which the EMU becomes possible, nor the costs and benefits realized in the transitional stage: it only provides, instead, two reference frameworks for two extreme cases. The limitations in this approach are obvious. However it has some merits that deserve to be mentioned. In the debate concerning the "transitional stage" and the feasibility conditions, the background picture is that of the current trends. But this introduces some distortions concerning the hypotheses to adopt and the assessment of the advantages/disavantages of various economic and monetary integration policies among countries. In particular, a fact not accounted for in the solution to the n-players game, is that cooperative solutions are more likely to occur as output levels and financial resource availability increase, like in the case shown by the EMU implementation scenario.

The characteristics of the financing of structural convergence processes, the relaxation of some constraints within each country (though partly offset by those imposed by EEC policies) will not, in the transitional case, be those of an area strongly integrated in both monetary and economic terms. However, ignoring them in the evaluation of the EMU operational conditions and of its policy implementation stages would be a mistake. Approaching the potential attainable growth path, defeating the low resource employment level (a key issue in the last 15 years for EEC countries) are results capable to modify the existing mechanisms that presently allow a reconciliation of diverging interests among EEC countries. The above consideration introduces the second perspective for the analysis of the experiences developed.

In case of a strengthening of EEC integration and of EMU implementation, it appears clear that all EEC countries and/or subareas will know a new long-term wave, calling for an unprecedented effort directed to manage: (*i*) the convergence of taxation levels and structures coupled with transfer systems for public services financing; (*ii*) the new financial market, highly affected by the new institutional framework. Furthermore an 1,5% increase in EEC GDP will increment the area demand, on the international market, of about 1,5-2,5% approximately.

Due to the high level of interdependence reached by the world economy, the current and capital account imbalances are also expected to lessen. The current tendency of short-term financial flows to amplify both real economy growth differences and divergences in national cycle profiles will be discouraged while the ability of international capital market flows to meet long-term productive investment will be improved. The magnitude of the diversion in real saving flows trend by countries and areas considered in the present analysis is consistent with the highest values projected by international institutions in their long-term forecasts and scenarios.

BIBLIOGRAPHY

[1] CARLUCCI M.: «Il prodotto lordo potenziale: aspetti definitori e misure», in ISCONA, *Proceedings of Conference on: La contabilità nazionale per gli anni '90*, Roma November 22 1990.

[2] DORNBUSCH R.: *Dollars, Debts and Deficits*, Massachusetts, London, MIT Press, 1986.

[3] EEC: *Research on "Cost of Non-Europe"*, Bruxelles, EEC 1988.

[4] FISCHER S.: «Relative Price Variability and Inflation in the United States and Germany», *European Economic Review*, no. 1-2, 1982.

[5] GILLI M.: «Causor, a Program for Analysis of Recursive and Interdependent Causal Structure», *Cahier du Departement d'Econometrie*, no. 3, 1984.

[6] HENDRY D.F.: «Econometric Modeling: the Consumption Function in Retrospect», *Scottish Journal of Political Economy*, no. 30, 1983.

[7] HENDRY D.F. - WALLIS K.F. (eds.): *Econometric and Quantitative Economics*, Oxford, Blackwell, 1984.

[8] LEFF N.H. - SATO K.: «The Prospects for Higher Domestic Savings Rates in Latin America», *Journal of Policy Modeling*, no. 4, 1987.

[9] LO CASCIO M.: «Technology and Terms of Trade», in HIERONYMI O.: *Technology and International Economy*, London, Macmillan Press, 1987.

[10] LO CASCIO M. - BAGELLA M.: «Debt and External Savings in Latin American Countries», *Rivista di Politica Economica*, October, 1990.

[11] LO CASCIO M. - CARLUCCI M. - CINGOLANI N.: «Divergent Sectorial Path in Productivity and Long-Term Inflation», *Economic Systems Research*, no. 2, 1990.

[12] NICKELL S.: «The Modelling of Wages and Employment» in HENDRY D.F. - WALLIS K.F. (eds.): *Econometric and Quantitative Economics*, Oxford, Blackwell, 1984.

[13] PAGANO M.: «Relative Price Variability and Inflation: the Italian Evidence» *European Economic Review*, no. 2, 1985.

[14] ROSSIER E.: *Contribution Aux Explications Dynamiques de la Consommation Semi-Agregée*, Berne, Lang, 1974.

[15] SCANDIZZO L.: «The Effects of Capital Flows on National Saving», *Rivista di Politica Economica*, October 1990.

[16] TRIVELLATO U.: «Modelli di comportamento e problemi di misura nelle scienze sociali: alcune riflessioni», *Proceedings of the XXXV Scientific Meeting of the Società Italiana di Statistica*, Padova, 1990.

Some Lessons from Development Economics for Southern and Eastern Europe

Richard S. Eckaus
Massachusetts Institute of Technology, Cambridge, (Mass.)

Major economic policies are now, often, perhaps even most often, based on analogy. This is partly because economic theory provides relatively little guidance for the major structural transformations being considered or underway and time and data are lacking to do careful studies. Thus, what seems to have worked or not worked in one country and time is used to justify trying or not trying the policy again in another place and time. This application of analogies is unavoidable, but it is also dangerous, if the analogies are not applicable.

Analogies are being applied intensively to the economies of Southern and Eastern Europe, including the Soviet Union, as these countries change their economic compass headings. The analogies have, for the most part, been drawn mainly, if not exclusively, from the experiences of the advanced industrialized countries. Yet the countries of Southern and Eastern Europe do not fit into that category. These countries, for the most part, fall into the «upper middle-income» class of *developing* countries, according to the World Bank rankings, with the exception of Spain and Ireland, and, of course, treating Italy as a Northern European country. Spain and Ireland are at the bottom of the World Bank category of «industrial market economies», with Ireland's per capita income less than two thirds that of Italy, the next highest country in the ranking (1).

It seems more reasonable, therefore, to look for suggestions and guidance for Southern and Eastern Europe in the experiences of developing countries, searching for examples of successful policies and warnings of what to avoid. This is a first and incomplete attempt.

The implication that there are clear "lessons" to be learned from development economics might appear suspect, in view of the contentious quality of much of the discussion in this field. Yet there is no less contention about policy of the advanced industrial countries, though, perhaps, it is more polite. Moreover, I believe that, in fact, there are some generalizations that can be made that would command wide support among development economists.

This survey will concentrate on microeconomic issues. A great deal has been learned about the pathologies of macroeconomics in recent years from the various debt and stabilization crises around the world. Again, the analogies may not be exact, but they are fruitful. By contrast, the microeconomic transformations contemplated present relatively new problems, while microeconomic theory has remained focused on the examination of existing market structures, rather than the creation of new institutions and structures. One can, therefore, make the case that analogies are a more important guide to microeconomic policies, because microeconomic theory is less useful in providing recommendations for structural change.

It will be useful to distinguish between two types of issues and the lessons that are relevant to them. There are the grand, strategic issues of economic structure: of centralized vs. decentralized decision-making, of openness or autarky, of enforcing competition or allowing monopolies, and so on. Then there are tactical issues, related to implementation.

---

(1) Actually the per capita incomes of five small or island «upper middle income», developing countries are higher than those of Spain and Ireland. There are, of course, important differences among the Southern and Eastern European countries. Spain and Ireland, although distinctly below the rest of the EEC countries in per capita income and other measures of development are substantially above Greece in these measures, which is, in turn, substantially above Portugal. It is not possible, now, to rank the countries of Eastern Europe and the Soviet Union.

Advise: the numbers in square brackets refer to the Bibliography.

Many of the lessons I propose will have a somewhat different relevance for Southern as compared to Eastern European countries and the Soviet Union, because they have different problems, structures and resources. There will be some common elements, however. There is no doubt that my "lessons" will be controversial. That is partly because the literature is a large one, and I cannot claim to fully command it. It is also because there is still a lack of consensus and new insights are constantly becoming appearing that warrant revisions.

Like a good general, the start will be made with strategy before proceeding to tactics.

1. - Strategic Lessons

1.1 *Individual Economic Incentives Are Powerful Instruments*

The record is clear that, where there is a choice between individual and social actions, with similar objectives, individual economic incentives are, by far, the most reliable means of sustaining the required efforts and achieving the goals. The most successful economic records have been built by these incentives. The evidence is so overwhelming that it is really not necessary to cite the obvious examples.

It is important to heed the qualification of «similar objectives», for economic theory tells us that, even in a perfectly competitive world, there would be many and important circumstances in which individual actions are systematically inconsistent with overall economic welfare. Distributional objectives, natural monopolies, public goods and certain types of externalities provide the obvious examples. Thus, some caution is required in applying this lesson (2).

Reliance on individual incentives for effective action is clearly a necessary condition rather than a sufficient one for economic develop-

---

(2) See Lewis W. Arthur [11].

ment. Individual economic incentives have not, in themselves, been sufficient for success in many countries, including the Southern European countries, with their long history of underdevelopment, now, fortunately, mainly past.

It is really the negative evidence, that is critical. The history of the centrally planned economies, as is now becoming more and more clear, must lead to the conclusion that their command systems did not lead to sustained economic development. They did achieve impressive economic transformations in some cases, though at enormously high cost in human and economic terms. The explanations for this history are still not entirely clear and what we have are mainly caricatures and slogans. How much of the failure was due to the extremist quality of the centralization? How much is inherent in any bureaucratic system of control? We really do not know the answers to these questions (3).

Patriotism and social commitment have, no doubt, been responsible for the mobilization of extraordinary individual and social effort in times of war and revolution. No doubt it has sustained great struggles. There are many examples. Yet, when the outside threat weakens, so has the patriotic commitment. So it is also with revolutionary fervor. When the revolution grows old and requires the participation of persons without revolutionary fervor, individual economic incentives again come to be important.

There have been periods during revolutions when it was thought to be possible to create a «new kind of economic man», who would respond only to social, not individual, incentives. Perhaps the appeals to these incentives were not implemented effectively; perhaps they could be effective in some other kind of setting. The lesson is, nonetheless, that it must, at the least, be extremely difficult to count on such appeals as a way of implementing policy.

Yet it would be dangerous to deny that there is an important economic role for social motivations, as distinct from individual economic incentives. There is a necessary social cohesion that must provides the climate within which individual economic incentives can flourish and lead to desirable outcomes. This social cohesion affects

---

(3) For insightful discussion, however, see KORNAI J., [9].

confidence that agreements will be honored, laws obeyed and that the political environment will permit the realization of economic gains.

It might appear that the lesson of the importance of individual economic incentives has been learned so well that there is no reason to emphasize it. Yet, even in the fully industrialized countries, there is continued recourse by political leaders to appeals to social motivations to achieve overall economic goals. And, more importantly, there is continued reliance on regulatory procedures and tax policies that are not fully consistent with individual economic incentives and are difficult to enforce. Observance of government regulations and taxes depends on the intensity of social cohesion, but it is also plausible that some care must be taken in placing too heavy a burden of compliance on volunteerism. One precept from development experience is that there are great differences among countries in the ability of their governments to rely on individual compliance with regulations and taxes. There are, for example, not many countries that can use effectively a personal income tax system that requires a relatively high degree of voluntary individual compliance.

While the strength of individual incentives is an important lesson, it is also important to learn its limits. There are many voices that appear to argue that the creation of opportunities for individual economic incentives will, by itself, insure the transformation of the formerly centrally planned countries to efficient and growing economies. The record of development shows that is not likely.

1.2 Markets Matter!

This lesson is about the existence, the structure and the importance of markets. First, with respect to existence, it is clear that, outside of the centrally planned economies, one of the primary processes of development has been the creation of markets to mediate an ever-widening set of transactions. At the family level, in the course of development home production moves into the commercial arena and markets emerge to mediate new kinds of transactions, e.g., for prepared foods, for medical care, for life and casualty insurance, for the financing of education. At the commercial and production levels, market also emerge, e.g. for resource inputs, for office services, for business insurance, for design and repair services, for subcontracting and, very importantly, for finance. These markets help make specialization possible with resulting increases in personal skills and, in some cases, advantages in larger scale production.

With respect to market structure, the good news is that development experience confirms economic theory that market structure matters, in the sense that the economic efficiency of price and output decisions made by firms is affected by the structure of the markets in which they operate. The bad news is that the experience does not provide an unequivocal guide with respect to the kind of market structures that are most effective, except, perhaps, that the internal markets need not follow the theoretical guidelines for competition. In such diverse countries as Japan, Korea, Brazil and Mexico, there are high degrees of concentration in important sectors that have also been quite successful. Some of these sectors had to, or elected to, compete in international markets.

The combination of good news and bad news makes the lesson rather equivocal. Is there a kind of market structure that is just right? It is easier to say that there is a kind of market structure that is almost always, but not quite always, just wrong. That is unregulated monopoly. It may not be primarily because of the static inefficiency that is associated with monopoly, although there is room for debate as to whether the deadweight losses are really as small as claimed. What is more obvious from the experience of both developing *and* developed countries is that monopolists become lazy, resistant to or unaware of technological changes and unresponsive to new market opportunities.

An important subtext of this lesson is that it would be incorrect to argue that the lessons of experience demonstrate that countries in the course of development need as complete a set of markets as exist in already industrialized countries in order to be successful. This needs to be stressed because there are evangelists for markets in the industrialized countries who will claim that a full complement is necessary for development. Stock and bond markets with substantial volumes of activity are, in particular, relatively rare in successful developing countries and even in the industrialized countries. It should not be expected that such markets are necessary prerequisites to progress in Southern and Eastern Europe.

There is a special aspect of this lesson related to macroeconomic policy, which has its basis in the structure of financial markets and institutions. It is that in order to manage monetary policy central banks do not need to have all the tools of the US Federal Reserve Board of Governors. The central banks in most of the countries of Latin America functioned reasonably well for many years in managing their countries' money and credit by use of quantitative controls, including direct controls on credit. The same was true, until recently, of the Banco de Portugal, which is now shifting to open market operations.

There are advantages in being able to use open market operations. However, those require markets that, in turn, require a degree of sophistication of financial markets that is not always present in developing countries and cannot be expected in Eastern Europe.

It is of more than passing interest that small scale personal banking and personal credit facilities have proved relatively easy to establish in Latin America. The *financieras* of several countries, that specialize in consumer deposits and lending serve useful functions. These are worth considering in both Southern and Eastern Europe. In other forms they are present in the already industrialized countries, providing services to markets that the conventional commercial banks were slow to recognize, perhaps another example of the unresponsiveness of a monopolized sector, in this case, the commercial banks.

1.3 *Government Intervention*
Is Often Necessary to Make Market
Systems Work Both Efficiently and Humanely

This may appear to be the opposite of the prior lesson, but it is, rather, a complementary lesson. It is in at least partial contrast to the argument, often made with vehemence, for liberalization in its broader classical meaning. That means elimination of all kinds of government "interventions" in domestic markets as well as in international markets. It would, justifiably, do away with interest rate ceilings and wage rate floors, subsidies and price controls oin consumer or producer goods, as well as licensing of investment and other direct allocation rules, such as those for imported goods. But it would also abolish or constrain other inteventions such as urban zoning, professional licensing, pure food and drug laws, public disclosure requirements in financing, and so on. A frequently cited caricature of the broad scope sometimes given to liberalization policies is that the only policy that government should follow to achieve efficient use of resources and effective development is to remove any interferences that would prevent, «getting the prices right», and should then step back and allow the economic to operate. It is not popular to be "interventionist" in the present world climate, yet the limitations of liberal policies need to be understood. Although this is certainly not the place for a complete review, a short reprise may be helpful. First, it should be remembered that the politics of the replacement of neoclassical liberalism was, basically, popular dissatisfaction with some of the ways in which markets had worked: monopoly pricing of goods and services, monopsony power in factor, especially labor, markets, sale of adulterated and deceptive products. It is no more likely that capitalist mentality has been transformed in the past hundred years or so than it is likely that a new kind of worker motivation has evolved. Secondly, it is well recognized that there are all kinds of reasons why markets will not work perfectly.

While the criticisms of imperfect markets have been used to justify policies of government intervention, that is, strictly speaking, not a necessary deduction. Improvement in the quality of the markets is another alternative that should be pursued, but may not always be practicable. There are no completely general solution. One can bring from developing countries all sorts of examples in which government interventionism has been constructive, as well as examples in which it has been obstructive to economic efficiency and growth.

1.4 *An Open, Outward Oriented Economy*
Will Develop Faster

This lesson is carved in stone as one of the axioms of the EEC, at least with respect to inter-EEC trade. So it may appear that the only point in introducing the maxim here is to praise it. Since, however, the meaning of the lesson has often been misinterpreted and that meaning may still be important for policies of the Eastern European countries and the Soviet, it is worth examining again.

There are books upon books upon articles that claim to demonstrate the lesson and this is not the place to undertake a full fledged review of the literature. It is useful to recall what it does not say. First, with respect to the source of the lesson, there are, of course, the Ricardian and Hecksher-Ohlin theories of international trade argue that, in good markets, there are potential gains from international specialization. The reminder is worthwhile that these theories say little about the distribution of the gains from trade. Moreover, the conventional trade theory does not argue that, «the more trade the better». The optimal shares will certainly vary from country to country depending on natural endowments, relative factor availabilities and all the other factor mentioned in international trade textbooks.

There are more recent theories which argue that, if a country has some degree of monopoly or monopsony power, there may be gains from exercising that power rather than acting as a price taker. There are even more recent theories that argue that economies of scale and some non-competitive trade practices may also generate benefits if firms do not behave strictly competitively.

The empirical evidence on the relations between openness and economic growth, with one important recent exception, consists mainly of country studies with a modest amount of analytic comparison. For developing countries there are the well known and striking cases of the newly industrializing countries that have grown quite rapidly in large part from the even more rapid expansion of their export sectors. This is among the most frequently cited evidence for the benefits of openness (4).

One problem with interpreting the openness success stories is that, in some cases, at least, the export push has been associated with vigorous protection of the domestic market. This makes the point that there can be a difference between «openness» and export promotion.

---

(4) The literature is quite large. For summaries of country studies see BHAGWATI J. [1] and KRUGER A. [10].

In some cases, the successes of openness are really successes of export promotion (5).

Another difficulty is that it is not easy to know whether the experiences are representative examples or quite special cases. For example, a target of 30% of GNP generated by export demand implies quite a different degree of penetration of world markets in the case of a small country or island economy than for a large country. It is also questionable as to whether this type of performance, which was achieved in some cases in the 1970s and 1980s, is still feasible in the increasingly protectionist atmosphere of the 1990s.

It is clear simply from looking at the raw statistics that a relatively large share of exports in total value added, and, therefore, a relatively large share of imports in final demand, are not, in themselves, guarantees of economic growth. Ireland and Portugal are examples of this point. Much better than casual examination of the data is the recent paper by Quah and Rauch which investigates the relationship between openness and economic growth with sophisticated econometric techniques (6). The hypothesis of the paper is that, if there is such a relation, it should be evident not only in the most dramatic cases, but at all degrees of openness. Their result, which is striking because, it differs from the lesson conventionally told for developing countries, is that they do not find such a relation. Yet, on reflection, that conclusion is quite consistent with what our economic theory would lead us to expect.

Import substitution has acquired such a bad name in much of the development literature that it needs to be reaffirmed that some growth of import substituting industries in developing countries and Southern Europe and Eastern Europe should be expected and is desirable. The logic is strainghtforward: development implies industrialization; pursuit of comparative advantage will, in general, imply that some of that industrialization should be in esports and some should be in import substituting goods. The infant industry argument for protection is also alive and well and being put into practice in

---

(5) Park Yung-Chul [15].
(6) See Quah Danny - Rauch James E.: *Openness and the Rate of Economic Growth*, unpublished, Dec. 13, 1990.

much of the developing world as well as in advanced countries, where it is still being used to justify closing of domestic markets. The history of Japanese development provides some excellent examples (7). It would, therefore, be mistaken to make a fetish of opposition to import substitution.

1.5 *Microeconomic Balance Among Industries* *Is Less Important than Overall Macroeconomic Balance with the Exception of Domestic Provision of Nontraded Goods and Services, Especially Those of Infrastructure*

At an early stage of systematic thinking on development problems, there was an intense debate over the advantages and disadvantages of «balanced growth». The idea has been revived in recent years in theoretical contributions to the "new growth" (8). A precise definition of "balance" was not provided by either side in the first debate and has still not been provided in the second round (9). Presumably, however, the idea is that there is some particular sectoral composition of output that would lead to a higher rate of growth than otherwise.

Both the early and the more recent emphasis on "balance" in economic growth arose mainly from considerations on the demand side, it is claimed that, in order for new investments to successfully market their products, incomes must grow rapidly enough to absorb the output of the new undertakings. That, in turn, requires investments in other undertakings, whose output could also be absorbed by the general rise in incomes.

The original opposition to the prescription for balanced growth was a supply side argument: that price "balance, still undefined, was not possible and, anyway, «imbalance» would create the price incent-

---

(7) For a definitive survey of protectionist arguments, see BHAGWATI J. [2].

(8) See ROSENSTEIN-ODAN P.N. [16] and MURPHY R. - SHLEIFER A. - VISHNY R. [14].

(9) The definition of «balanced growth» used in dynamic economic theory, that, «the mutual, proportions in which commodities are produced remain... constant», (SOLOW R.S. - SAMUELSON P.A. [17], p. 412) is certainly not the definition desired by development economists.

ives necessary to stimulate investment (10). As a theory of investment, it claimed, therefore, that «ordinary profits» would not be enough to induce investment in developing countries. The profits had to be extraordinary, as a result of supply bottlenecks. In retrospect, at least, it seems to be an implausible argument.

There are several, even more damaging criticisms of both the original and more recent balanced growth theories. The first is their reliance on the assumption of a closed economy. The output of new investments is virtually always small, relative to the size of the world market so the output of new undertakings can find an export market if their quality and price are competitive. If they are not, they should not be undertaken. A second criticism is that new investments seldom produce new products, but compete for markets with existing products. Again, if the quality and price of the output of the new undertaking are competitive, they can find a market.

The idea that a particular oputput composition will generate a higher growth rate than other compositions is found in other places in economic theory and the debate over development. It was part of the von Neumann «turnpike» theorem that there was a particular combination of outputs that would move the economy along more rapidly than any other combination (11).

It was a much less abstract, Stalinist economic doctrine that investment in heavy industry was the key element in rapid industrialization. There is a theoretical analysis that would provide some justification for such a policy under special conditions. In a closed economy, the higher the rate of investment, the larger the proportion there must be of investment in the capital forming sectors (12). However, economies need not be closed and capital goods can be imported. For large countries, however, the amount of capital goods imports required in a development program would, in turn, be relatively large as would be the corresponding exports to pay for such imports. Moreover, given the scale of the requirements, it would be possible for large countries to achieve, in domestic production, the economies of scale that exist in such industries. For large countries,

---

(10) Alfred Hirschman was the major expositor. See HIRSCHMAN A. [8].

(11) See VON NEUMANN J. [18].

(12) See DOMAR E. [5].

therefore, it might be expected that a capital goods industry would be a rational development. Even in a closed economy, as the composition of output shifted toward consumer goods the composition of investment would also have to change away from heavy goods industries.

The last point is especially relevant to the Eastern European countries and the Soviet Union now. As their economies shift toward production of consumer goods, they will find excess capacity in the capital goods industries. Unless they can "dump" the output of those industries abroad, it will be necessary to close down some of the enterprises. Even "dumping" requires that the quality be suitable for export, which may be more achievable for unfinshed than finished products (13).

The qualification in the lesson was with respect to production of nontraded, especially infrastructural goods and services. That deserves a lesson of its own.

1.6 *Inadequacies and Inefficiencies in Infrastructure Burden the Entire System of Production and Consumption*

It is the nature of infrastructure, in fact it is almost the definition, that these goods and services are inputs to nearly every producing sector as well as to investment and final consumption. That means that supply bottlenecks in the infrastructure sectors will constrain the entire economy. There is much evidence in developing countries of this happening. One of the most recent large scale examples is provided by the constraints on recent development in India as a result of inadequate capacity in power and railroads (14).

There are important differences in the dependence of the various sectors on the particular infrastructure sectors. Agriculture, for example, makes relatively few demands for electric power and communications. Financial services do not require much electricity, though it must be reliable, but do need efficient communications. The point is that planning infrastructure investments by projecting past

---

(13) Not only must physical capacity in many "heavy" industries be closed down, but the state ministries that found their justification in continued expansion of those industries must be dealt with. That may be the hardest part.

(14) See, for example, DHAR P.N. [4].

demand growth will lead to mistakes, if the sectoral composition of output is changing.

There is a growing tendency in developing countries to transfer inefficient infrastructural enterprises from the public to the private sector, as a means of transforming them into more effective suppliers. The environment and incentives for private enterprise in the infrastructural area are of a different kind than in other sectors. In order to make wise investment decisions, enterprises are required to project the patterns of growth in the economy as a whole, or at least certain geographic areas. That is more difficult than projecting the market for a particular product that will substitute for other products in domestic and foreign markets.

Regulation of private firms in infrastructure sectors is necessary, because they are, characteristically, natural monopolies. One of the lessons of developing countries, and advanced economies, as well, is that such regulation can impose great inefficiencies (15). Infrastructure firms have been used to subsidize the entire economy and/or particular sectors or groups of consumers, by fixing their prices below costs. They have been forced to use particular technologies or had the scale of their plants restricted below minimum efficient size. Because of their position in the structure of production, the resulting inefficiencies impose burdens on the entire economy.

Another lesson from history is that, without regulation infrastructural firms will behave just as monopolies are expected to behave. The slide into monopolistic practices is the most natural model of behavior for them. Privatization, itself, will not resolve the difficulties of efficient infrastructure supply.

2. - Tactical Lessons

The distinction between strategy and tactics is not always a clear one, particularly at the level at which I will discuss tactics, which is not in terms of administration. So it may be that these tactical lessons will appear to some to be strategic.

---

(15) See MacAvoy P. [12].

2.1 *Avoid Big Mistakes*

One could add, «of course, and avoid small mistakes as well». However, only someone with great hubris would think that all mistakes can be avoided. The long form of this lesson is, «since mistakes are inevitable, avoid commitments, or prepare insurance, that will prevent mistakes from becoming disasters». As a hypothesis that has not been tested, I would propose that, characteristically, more damage is done to development prospects from the consequences of major mistakes than from the slow grind of inefficiency. Perhaps that view is affected by the international debt crisis, which is, almost certainly, the single most widespread and largest blunder in developing countries of the post-World War II period (16).

One reason for undiversified government policies may be that it is more difficult for political leaders to sell «mixed» strategies to the public than to sell «pure» strategies. The resort to war may provide an extreme example. It might be expected, solely from the desirability to maintain a diversified policy, that whenever war is waged, that conditions for settlement would be offered simultaneously. Yet sending mixed messages may make it impossible to carry out the war policy effectively. Yet it is also conceivable that the specialist advisers to policymakers are also victims of fads and infatuations with particular policies, that they, no more than the common man, like to live with uncertainty and persuade themselves of their precision.

There may be a professional tendency among economists to think that all economic decisions and changes that occur are small ones. These assumptions about market adjustments make it possible to use the differential calculus, to which we are all addicted. The assumption is naturally carried over to a view of the world. Yet developing economies often face events that cannot be perfectly foreseen and that are, for them, "big", e.g. crop faillures, large interest changes, debt crises, large new entrants into markets, changes in foreign macro-economic conditions that have a major impact on export markets, technological changes, political realignments and upheavals and so on.

---

(16) As an analitical treatment of the debt crisis, see FAINI R. - DE MELO JAIME [7].

In addition, in contradiction to the conventional «rational expectations» assumption, not only are the consequences of policy not foreseen with certainty, there are many opportunities for miscalculations that have nothing to do with stochastic processes. Some of the miscalculations arise from the fact that information is not available, or potential users do not know where to find it or how to evaluate it, even when it exists. Moreover, the phenomenon of economic decisions being made on political grounds — and the turning out badly — is well known.

The process of making large commitments certainly often looks like rational decisionmaking. What appears to be a good idea emerges, for example: the land in a large region seems ideal for growing ground nuts. So why not do it on a large scale and get large benefits? There seems to be enough water for a very large, rather than small, irrigation project. Why not use all of it? It is possible to borrow at a nominal rate that is close to or even less than the inflation rate, so why not do it on a large scale and reap large benefits from the low positive or negative real rate of interest?

The risks involved are either quite unrecognized or set aside as of no consequence. It is easier to think that tomorrow will be like today than to work out the possible changes that might occur and assign probabilities. Assignment of probabilities is, of course, no classroom exercise. Nature will not have provided us with the exact frequency distribution of possible outcomes, so the probabilities will have to be subjective, and, therefore, liable to controversy.

Of course, if all goes well, large commitments will appear very farsighted. If the commitment was only partial, there will be recriminations that there was not a larger stake. When things go badly, on the other band, there is a tendency to think that the whole idea may have been wrong, when, in fact, the dice simply fell the wrong way on this particular occasion while, on another occasion, they might fall differently. If the initial stake was relatively small, so will be the losses and the idea might be tried again.

The combination of the uncertainty and the relatively large scale of important influences on growth requires a different attitude toward decisions than is customary in policymaking. One of the lessons of economic theory, which is a lesson about economic management, is that in the face of the risky ventures, diversification of portfolios of undertakings is an optimal policy.

In contrast, the history of economic decisions in industrialized, as well as developing countries, is replete with examples of undivided commitment to particular policies and projects that involve a high proportion of available resources, as if there were no risk at all. These include very large investment projects, often undertaken by government enterprise or by public authorities. There are any number of examples: ground nuts in Ghana, the Sines project in Portugal, the aluminum and fertilizer plants in Aswan, Egypt, and so on.

There are, however, examples of private firms similarly making commitments that involve a large proportion of their assets to a single project or type of undertaking. The observe of the excessive borrowing by developing countries was the excessive lending by the large international banks. That was preceded or followed by the large, and apparently unwise, commitments by banks to energy projects and, finally, to real estate development. This series of mistakes has been responsible for large loan losses and deterioration of the capital conditions of banks from Japan to Europe.

Complementary to the mistake by banks in lending very large amounts to developing countries was the mistake of such countries in borrowing those amounts. That provides another, obvious example of an undiversified policy decision. When their own and world economic conditions changed so that it was impossible for the borrowing countries to maintain their debt service, the international financial system was managed by the banks and governments of the countries of the lending banks so that all the costs of adjustment were placed on the borrowing countries. The outcome has been disastrous for most of the borrowing countries. The decade of the 1980s lost much of the gains of the 1970s.

A less obvious but extremely important example of an undiversified portfolio is the commitment by governments to an exclusive sectoral allocation or macroeconomic policy. An example of this is the across-the-board adoption of import substitution policies in many developing countries. Interestingly, Korea, a country whose export promotion is touted as an example of "openness", may be thought of as having, by its protection of its domestic market, followed a diversified policy.

The broadening of the EEC common market arrangements and the formation of a EEC monetary union and central bank may provide another example of an undiversified policy. While politicians may assert that they are sure that all countries will benefit from all the proposed policies, we know that economic analysts are still at an early stage of trying to understand how these policies will, in fact, work. On the other hand, it can be argued that this is a case in which the risks to the most vulnerable members of the Community are recognized and steps are being taken, represented by large flows of «adjustment finance» to reduce that vulnerability.

The current argument that the conversion of the centrally planned economies to market systems must be done in one great sweep another undiversified policy program. It is justified with metaphors about not being able to cross a great chasm in two jumps. The reasoning behind it remains obscure; certainly economic theory has nothiong to say about it. Perhaps it rests on social psychology, but economists have no special claim to expertise in this area.

In contrast, we know that the industrialized economies are blends of private markets and government regulation and enterprise. These blends function reasonably well. This is another analogy that is not exact, but at least it is not a metaphor.

2.2 *Microeconomic Mistakes Will Contaminate Macroeconomic Policy and Vice Versa*

The separation of responsibility and authority in government institutions and the expertise among economists leads naturally to a disassociation of macroeconomic and microeconomic decision making. Macroeconomic policy decisions often overlook, or make unrealistic assumptions about microeconomic policy and behavior and similar mistakes are made in microeconomic policy formation. Yet one of the lessons of development is that effective economic policy, especially when major reforms are being considered, requires coordination of both types of decisions.

There are many examples of microeconomic or macroeconomic

programs that have been unsuccessful because they did not take into account their consequences in the other arena. The most dramatic cases that spring first to mind are the comprehensive stabilization programs designed to reduce hyperinflation in some Latin American countries.

These were notable for a number of reasons, including their attempt to integrate microeconomic and macroeconomic policies. They were often undone, however, by inconsistent microeconomic decisions: government wage adjustments or government budgeting of particular projects or programs in excess of targets (17).

The scope available to Southern European countries to exercise independent macroeconomic policies will become more limited to the degree that monetary and Central bank policies are coordinated. That is likely to create a temptation to increase the dependence on micro-economic policies, for which there may be a greater latitude, to achieve macro goals.

In another area, the advice on macroeconomic policies to the countries of Eastern Europe is likely to be cleares and more effective than the microeconomic reform proposals. As argued above, the requirements for macroeconomic viability and the means for achieving it are more obvious than are the requirements and means of microeconomic reform and efficiency. And, in fact, microeconomic theory has almost nothing positive to say about economic reform, except to "somehow" create good markets. By comparison there is relatively clear guidance from macroeconomic theory about what will and will not work well. The lesson is that while macroeconomic stability is essential, it will not be achieved without an effective micro economy. That is more difficult to create because it requires many institutions at the local level.

2.3 *The Time Horizon for Creation of New Popular Economic Institutions is a Long One*

The word "popular" is used in the present context as meaning, «of the people», to make the contrast with new administrative institu-

(17) See BRUNO M. - DITELLA G. - DORNBUSCH R. - FISCHER S. [3].

tions as, for example, a central bank. As a lesson of history, this is familiar. The slow change of institutions is a staple of historians. Almost nothing in the past seems to have happened rapidly. Historians will explain that even the major realignments of borders and governments after wars and revolutions have had their roots in the previous temporally slow evolutions of populations and institutions. Even the remarkable events of the last two years in Eastern Europe may, in retrospect, be seen, with some merit, as the most recent stage in a process with earlier manifestations in the abortive Hungarian uprising in 1956 and the «Prague Spring».

The lesson has significance because institutional changes are being urged on the countries of both Southern and Eastern Europe by international advisers and international organizations. In some cases they are designed to perform new functions; in other cases they are intended to replace existing institutions. One of the prime examples of the former are the proposals to create or expand stock and bond markets in both Southern and Eastern European countries. Hardly had the Soviet Union and the countries of Eastern Europe declared their intention to adopt market reforms than some enthusiasts proposed the creation of stock markets in these countries.

Without denigrating at all the role of stock markets in the US economy, it is important to appreciate how long it took for them to become respectable and useful in their present roles and how many other changes were necessary for these things to occur. The New York stock market was a large and active market, with a limited degree of participation outside of New York, itself, even in the 1920s. It took the reforms of the 1920s to make it fully respectable. And all this happened after many years of evolution of the market system in the US (18).

An example of the importance of the historical evolution of conditions for a new stock markets, that may be persuasive because it is more contemporary, can be found in Latin America in the 1970s and 1980s. In the early 1970s the Organization of American States began a project to propose and assist financial reforms in Latin America. One of the projects that emerged was the creation of stock

---

(18) See MICHIC R.C. [13].

markets in a number of the countries of Latin America. Considerable effort was put into the design of these markets. Perhaps there was some long lasting effect of all the effort, but it was modest at best. The stocks markets were alien institutions that had no clear and important role in the economies.

One way of making a big mistake is to build a major program on a market institution that is not viable in the particular environment. This should be kept in mind in considering proposals for mutual funds that would hold shares in privatized government enterprises. Mutual funds have achieved great success in the US and a few other countries in a relatively short period of time, but in all cases the success was built on well established preconditions.

Even more "ordinary" markets require some time, as well as effort, to develop. The conditions of contemporary labor and real estate markets in developed countries reflect the evolution of several hundred years, an evolution that was stopped, at a relatively early stage, in the Soviet Union and much of Eastern Europe. Product markets may be simpler, but it is striking that developing countries do not have the proliferation of consumer protection authorities of the industrialized countries, or, if they do exist, such authorities function, as a whole, much less well.

There is an obverse side to this argument: the destruction of a non-market institution may also be a big mistake because of the difficulty of creating an effective replacement. Government fixed price food shops, for example, are more than simple goods distribution systems. They are primary, if somewhat inefficient, instruments of a welfare society. Replacing these fixed price food shops by private markets may well improve the efficiency of food distribution, but it will not carry out the other functions of the fixed price stores.

2.4 *The Time Requirements for the Implementation of New Capacity is Also Long*

It is a conventional assumption of economists that investment in one year yields productive capacity in the succeeding year. It is an obvious lesson of development, as well as of careful observation of developed countries, that the assumption is incorrect. It takes time to put up new productive capacity. While there have been few studies of this gestation period, either in developed or developing countries, the condition is well known.

Productive capacity is a «sandwich» composed of different elements: buildings, building facilities; machines; power supplies, transporation ports, and so on. Each one of these may have a somewhat different construction time that depends, in part, on how intense the effort is. Moreover, the order in which the construction takes place is usually, if not fully determined by technology, variable only within modest limits.

The «gestation periods» for different types of capacity will vary between one and 8 years, or even longer. In the US two and a half to three years or four years are required to build most types of new manufacturing facilities. Five to seven years are required for new thermal power plants. And all of this presumes that the design and the blueprints are available. If new designs are required, that can add a year or even more.

The shorter periods are associated with small additions to capacity, perhaps just buying a new machine. The longer periods are necessary to build entire new plants. If a plant is being changed from one use to another, it will generally be the case that only the building shell itself and some of its facilities will be convertible. Even in this case, however, the generation time may be shortened considerably, since building construction is often the slowest part of the process.

For developing countries, there are few, if any, systematic studies of gestation periods. Casual empiricism suggests that construction times in developing countries are a quarter to one half longer than in industrialized countries.

In addition to a gestation process, there is also often a «maturation» process involved in the creation of new capacity. It takes time for a work force to learn how to use the facility, to work out the inevitable "bugs" and develop effective schedules (19).

The longest periods required for creation of new capacities are necessary for, «human capital», i.e. educated people: fifteen years for

---

(19) For a comparison of gestation periods in centrally planned and market economies see ELLMAN M [6].

a college educated person and two to four years more for a professional school education. Necessary work experience extends the training time. If training managers takes five to seven years or more of experience, in addition to an undergraduate college education and a business school degree, it is one of the protracted investment processes.

Fortunately there is some substitutability among types of education and some substitutability between experience and education. Often the substitution is only one way. Engineers can become managers and with experience and modest training may become good managers. Managers cannot become engineeers without going to engineering school.

All of this means that quick transformations of productive capacity and creation of new efficient capacity are quite unlikely and promises based on such new capacity are bound to be unfulfilled. It means in Southern Europe that, if there is large scale new investment in manufacturing facilities, those will only begin to pay off in regular employment and income after three or four years. It also means that it may be necessary to staff the facilities with foreign experts until enough local technical staff are trained.

The implications for Eastern Europe aree similar, but, perahps, even more profound. Much new investment will be required as the composition of output changes toward consumer goods and in order to produce at world quality standards. New worker and technical skills may be necessary and, certainly, new managerial skills. While some conversions of plant and equipment are possible, those are likely to be modest. Thus, no quick transformations and overall improvements in standards of living will occur.

Conclusions

These are only some of the possible lessons from development that are relevant for Southern and Eastern Europe. There are more lessons, but my time and space are exhausted.

There are many more ways of making mistakes than of getting the development process working smoothly. There are some general lessons but no detailed blueprints that can be copied from one country to another. To summarize, one might say, «There is no magic», or as one colleague put it, «there is no fairy dust that will transform economies and societies». It is a difficult, often painful and usuallly long process. It would be misleading and, perhaps, even dangerous to suggest otherwise.

BIBLIOGRAPHY

[1] BHAGWATI J.: *Anatomy and Consequences of Exchange Control Regimes*, Cambridge (Mass.), Ballinger Publishing Co., 1978.

[2] — —.: *Protectionism*, Cambridge, MIT Press, 1988.

[3] BRUNO M. - DITELLA G. - DORNBUSCH R. - FISCHER S.: *Inflation Stabilization: The experience of Israel, Argentina, Brazil, Bolivia, and Mexico*, Cambridge, MIT Press, 1988.

[4] DHAR P.N.: «The Indian Economy: Past Performance and Current Issues», in LUCAS R.E.B. - PAPANEK G.F.: *The Indian Economy: Recent Development and Future Prospects*, Boulder, Westview Press, 1988, pp. 3-23.

[5] DOMAR E.: «A Soviet Model of Growth», *Essays in The Theory of Economic Growth*, New York, Oxford University Press, 1957.

[6] ELLMAN M.: *Socialist Planning*, Cambridge, Cambridge University Press, 1987.

[7] FAINI R. - DE MEO J.: «Adjustment, Investment and the Real Exchange Rate in Development Countries», *Economic Policy*, n. 11, October 1990, pp. 491-502.

[8] HIRSCHMAN ALFRED: *The Strategy of Economic Development*, London, Yale University Press, 1958.

[9] KORNAI J.: *Overcentralization in Economic Administration*, London, Oxford University Press, 1959.

[10] KRUEGER ANNE O.: *Liberalization Attempts and Consequences*, Cambridge (Mass.), Ballinger Publishing Co., 1978.

[11] LEWIS W. ARTHUR: «Development and Distribution», *Employment, Income, Distribution and Develoment Strategy, Problems of Developing Countries: Essays in Honor of H.W. Singer*, New York Holmes & Meier, 1976, pp. 15-47.

[12] MACAVOY P.W.: *The Economic Effects of Regulation*, Cambridge, MIT Press, 1965.

[13] MICHIC R.C.: *The London and New York Stock Exchanges, 1850-1914*, London, Allen & Unwin, 1987.

[14] MURPHY K.M. - SHLEIFER A. - VISHNY R.: *Industrialization and the Big Push*, mimeo, 1988.

[15] PARK YUNG-CHUL: «Korea», in DORNBUSCH R. - HELMERS F.L.C.H. (eds.): *The Open Economy: Tools for Policymakers in Developing Countries*, Oxford, Oxford University Press, 1988, pp. 336-47.

[16] ROSENSTEIN-RODAN - PAUL N.: «Problems of Industrialization of Eastern and Southeastern Europe», *Economic Journal*, n. 53, June-September 1943, pp. 202-11.

[17] SOLOW R. - SAMUELSON P.A.: «Balanced Growth Under Constant Returns to Scale»; *Econometrica*, vol. XXI, n. 3, July 1953, pp. 412-24.

[18] VON NEUMANN J.: «A Model of General Economics Equilibrium», *Review of Economic Studies*, vol. 13, n. 1, 1945-1946, pp. 1-9.

Perspectives for Employment in Europe After 1992

Giovanni Caravale
Università «La Sapienza», Roma

1. - Introduction

The purpose of my paper is to offer some reflections on the prospects of employment policy in Europe after 1992. This I shall try to do — however briefly — in the light of two quite different groups of elements: *(i)* on the one hand the abundant work carried out both under the auspices of official European institutions and elsewhere — in some way to envisage what will happen after the 300 measures embodied in the 1985 European Commission *White Paper* will have been enacted by the end of 1992; *(ii)* on the other hand the picture that emerges at present in the field of macroeconomic theory — the theory, I wish to stress, that should constitute the logical basis for the definition of the lines of economic policy, with special reference to the problem of employment.

The conclusion — a provisional one, of course — towards which my reflections seem to point is that while unemployment will continue to be, in 1992 and after, a major problem for European economies (or for *the* European economy), the help governments and institutions will be able to draw from macroeconomic theory is unfortunately going to be very limited, in consequence of what has been recently termed the «collapse of theoretical consensus» (Milgate [12], p. 65) (*). The upshot of the argument is the emphasis on the responsibility

---

(*) *Advise:* the numbers in square brackets refer to the Bibliography in the appendix.

which lies upon the shoulders of each one of us in the profession to overcome the *impasse* in which economists risk appearing like blacksmiths at the end of the era of horse transport; a state of affairs which is strikingly similar to that described by John Maynard Keynes in December 1935, in his «Preface» to the *General Theory*: «the deep divergences of opinion between fellow economists — he wrote — have for the time being almost destroyed the practical influence of economic theory, and will, until they are resolved, continue to do so» (Keynes [9], p. 146).

2. - Employment after 1992 - The «Cecchini Report» and the «Bakhoven Report»

2.1 Let me come to the first point, the prospects for employment after 1992.

The standard reference work for the analysis concerning Europe after 1992 is what is commonly called the *Cecchini Report* (Cecchini [6]). Technically speaking, this, as we all know, is not a forecast of what will happen in 1992 with the elimination of non-tariff barriers, but rather an attempt to set out what is the cost of technical, fiscal and physical barriers now in existence (border controls, restrictions on public procurement, differences in the conditions at which financial services are available, lack of standardization, heterogeneous fiscal treatment, etc.).

The logic of the *Cecchini Report* is equally well known. The evaluation of the benefits of a single European market is made indirectly, through the observation of the discrepancy of prices now existing in the Community: the idea behind this is that in a single market the differences will be eliminated, and the system will spontaneously tend towards the lowest price in the range.

According to the *Report* the removal of non-tariff barriers will bring about a cost reduction which on the whole will produce higher price-over-cost margins, and lower prices. The decrease in prices will stimulate demand and therefore lead to an increase in the production of goods and services, which in turn will allow exploitation of comparative advantages and economies of scale.

The removal of barriers on the other hand will favour new entries in the market and increase the level of competitive pressure thus stimulating a restructuring of industries through innovations and technical progress. The benefits will not be limited to the micro-economic level, that is to the companies and consumers «who buy and sell [in the market]»; they «will [instead] ripple out into the economy at large. Public deficits will be eased, under the dual impact of open public procurement and the economy's regeneration. Inflation ...will be cooled down by the drop in prices provoked by open markets...» (Cecchini [6], p. XIX).

The fully optimistic evaluation, however, gives way to a slightly more prudent attitude when it comes to the prospect for employment. The *Report* recognizes for instance that: «...medium-term policies for sustainable economic growth are [in the present situation]... inhibited by fears of their short-term impact on jobs, despite the stronger employment outlook they herald in the longer run» (Cecchini [6], p. 92); but hastens to add that EC market integration will loosen (among others) also this particular constraint on growth, «even if the gains [in terms of employment] will come in the medium term», (Cecchini [6] *ibidem*).

More specifically: «...in the short term productivity gains [arising from economic integration] might mean a degree of job loss, but this dip in employment will be progressively filled and then spectacularly built on... The short-term difficulties are inseparable from the longer run benefits. To be eaten the cake has got to baked» (Cecchini [6], p. 97).

As a whole, the favourable medium-term effect on employment-according to the *Report* — would be to reduce the jobless rate by around 1.5 percentage points (Cecchini [6], p. 97).

Official optimism is enhanced by the prospects of the monetary unification. The following are significant examples from the recent study of the European Community (Commission of the European Communities, Directorate-General for Economic and Financial Affairs [8]): «...The addition of a single currency to the single market more than doubles the number of businessmen who would expect a very positive impact on the European business climate» (p. 9);

«...Simulations presented in this study suggest that [if a fully

credible European monetary union is realized] the economy would
not only be more efficient and less inflationary, but also subject to less
variability of prices and output levels» (p. 10);

«...Model simulations suggest that with the European monetary
union — as compared to other regimes — the Community would have
been able to absorb the major economic shocks of the last two decades
with less disturbance in terms of the rate of inflation and, to some
extent also, of the level of real activity. This is of renewed relevance,
given that the Gulf crisis of summer 1990 once again subject the
Community to a potentially damaging economic shock» (p. 11).

2.2 A wholly different evaluation is, on the other hand, offered
by the *Bakhoven Report* (Bakhoven [1]). This *Report* has been
published in March 1989 by the Netherlands Central Planning Bureau
as an attempt to update, specify and correct the results of the
Cecchini Report. Its critical attitude is made evident from the outset:
«First, the CPB is interested in the *expected* consequences of the
White Paper measures while the EC study intended to quantify the
potential effects. [Second], the CPB has different views about some of
the assumptions underlying the EC study. Finally, the CPB has at its
disposal a world model (CPB-WM) with which all the macroeconomic
calculations could be made, while the EC had to rely on ...different
models, partly incomplete (Hermes) and partly obsolete (Compact)»
(Bakhoven [1], p. 2).

In the *Bakhoven Report* the prudent evaluation of the *Cecchini
Report* turns into open pessimism as far as the problem of employment is concerned. With the estimated increase in labour productivity
the prospect, according to the *Bakhoven Report*, is in fact that of *a
reduction of employment by 1.2% after six years*, which may mean
something like 1.5 million more unemployed.

2.3 The point is important and it is therefore legitimate to raise
the question of the degree of realism of these conflicting evaluations.
It is certainly difficult to answer, but two types of observations may be
offered for a critical reflection on the conclusions reached by the
Cecchini Report.

On the one hand I wish to emphasize the fact that the essentially
static nature of the analysis carried out by the *Cecchini Report* may

produce a certain under-estimation of the favourable long-term dynamic effects of the creation of a single market in 1992. Reference, from this point of view, to Pasinetti's distinction between the *phase of trade* and the *phase of industry* (Pasinetti [13]) may be in order.

On the other hand we have however a whole series of aspects, which represent serious limitations of the analysis carried out by the *Cecchini Report*, suggesting that the estimates are over-optimistic. Let me list the main ones, in a very sketchy manner:

a) the approximate nature of the estimates, many of which are based on surveys of business opinions;

b) the almost complete absence of considerations relating to the nature of the markets, in many of which oligopoly is the rule and segmentation is therefore not likely to disappear after 1992 (1). In fact, as Matutes recently emphasized (Matutes [10], p. 10), «in tight oligopolistic markets, with few national producers and strong economies of scale ...entry of new firms is not likely to occur [and] it is not clear ...[why there should be] much hope for stronger competition after 1992». Although the prospects are better for the sectors where there are no natural barriers to entry and where small and medium enterprises are the norm, it seems difficult to anticipate on balance a favourable effect of greater competition on prices;

c) the unrealistic assumptions underlying the *Report* for what concerns the degree of flexibility of the European economy, from the viewpoint of prices, technical requirements, tax systems etc. The goal of complete equality — which has not been reached in other federal countries like the United States or Canada — is likely to prove even more difficult to achieve in the European market, characterized, as this is, by profound differences in current behaviour, legislation, tastes, culture and language;

d) the omission of any consideration whatsoever of possible strains of adjustments and imbalances in the regional effects of the European integration. This aspect appears particularly important in

---

(1) «The reaction of companies has already been shown to be complex as they can invest, acquire, set up joint ventures and *use all sources of moves to try to perpetuate competitive advantage,* leading to "imperfect" outcomes far from a single market. In public procurement, a further source of substantial gain, whatever the legislation, the scope for continuing preferences and inefficiencies by public purchasers is considerable» (MAYES [11], p. 1209, italics added).

the light of the experience of the unification of Italy in the 19th century with its effects, which we still feel, on the underdeveloped South;

e) finally, the absence of any analysis of the likelihood of agreement or disagreement between the member states on the political plane — an element which is going to play a crucial role in the difficult process of integration after 1992.

2.4 In the light of all this it seems possible to conclude that it is highly likely that unemployment will continue to be a major problem for the European economy after 1992: in the medium term its absolute size will not be favourably affected by the integration process, and is likely to show a substantial increase.

In 1988 unemployment in the EC countries was about 14.6 million units, representing a rate well above 10% of the total labour force. Now, if the *Bakhoven Report* hits the mark, the integration process will not improve this picture and is likely on the contrary to make it even worse bringing the total amount of unemployment close to the dramatic figure of 16 million units after six years (more or less the amount of unemployment in the US during the great depression).

2.5 Further strains on the labour market in Europe are very likely to derive from three sets of distinct circumstances (the extreme brevity with which I shall mention them here should by no means be taken to mirror the degree of historical and economic importance I attach to them):

a) the process of German unification which, at least in the short and medium term, will have to face the employment consequences of the necessary attempt to harmonize the efficiency of the productive apparatus of the former Democratic Republic with that of the Federal Republic;

b) the radical process of change which has taken, and is still taking place, in the countries of what was formerly called the Communist Bloc. One of the probable consequences of this process is a significant phenomenon of emigration. Although likely to concern primarily North American countries, this will presumably refer to Europe as well, in a measure which it is now impossible to ascertain. Some commentators have mentioned the figure of 3 million people. Many of these would be in search of a stable employment — and it is unlikely that EEC countries will take a prejudicially negative attitude towards their requests to settle down in Europe;

c) the limitations that — in the event of a European Monetary Union — the existence of a single currency will imply for the economic policy of each member country. Although the loss of the exchange rate variation as a policy tool is not viewed as a serious one by the recent *EEC Report* ([8], p. 11), the question is by no means simple since this loss may end up by rendering more difficult the defence of employment in situations of economic strain (2).

We may perhaps be allowed to conclude that the perspective for employment in the New Europe seem to leave very little room for the optimistic, even triumphant, attitude of the *Cecchini Report.*

3. - Macroeconomic Theory Today

In this context, what is the help that we can expect governments and institutions to be able to draw from macroeconomic theory? After all this is what economics — or to use the old, and more appropriate term «Political Economy», should be there for: interpreting the world and indicating ways to solve the economic problems of the time.

The answer to this question must however be very cautious. The present situation of macroeconomic theory is deeply unsatisfactory both when it comes to the question of adequately explaining unemployment, this outstanding feature of our present experience, and in suggesting workable remedies for the problem.

Not only do we have a great number of competing theories, but even the framework within which these are developed and the criteria by which they are compared and criticized are not agreed upon.

The «collapse of theoretical consensus» has an inevitable counterpart in the arena of policy debate: «Alternative theories of the desirable role of Government policy abound, and *laissez-faire* is back on the agenda, to a degree inconceivable even fifteen years ago» (Milgate [12], p. 65).

---

(2) The complexity of the matter is emphasized in CIOCCA P. [7].

Now, I do not know if there has ever been anything like an age of theoretical consensus; what is certain is that our days are those of paralyzing disagreement among theorists.

This is certainly not the occasion for attempting an accurate survey of competing macroeconomic theories. It may be useful, however, to recall a basic distinction between two groups of macroeconomic theories from the viewpoint of policy implications.

There is, first, a group of analyses whose main policy implication is the denial of any scope for an active and systematic State intervention: either *laissez-faire*, or predefined "automatic" rules of behaviour for certain crucial variables. I have in mind especially the theoretical stand that goes under the name of «New Classical Macroeconomics», which embodies the resurgence of the ancient myth of the invisible hand. The assumptions on which NCM is based — especially for what concerns the level and use of the relevant information on the part of economic agents — have no counterpart in the world in which we actually live and seem instead to have something to do with what could be termed (borrowing from psychiatry) a kind of *delirium omniscientiae* (3).

On the other hand a second group of interpretations of the functioning of contemporary economic systems imply the necessity of a continuous and flexible management of economic policy on the part of public authorities.

Within this latter wide range of theories it seems important to emphasize in particular the difference between what may be called *the imperfectionist approach* to macroeconomics and the *unemployment equilibrium interpretations* of the economic system.

According to the *imperfectionist approach* the task of economic theory is the analysis of frictions and rigidities (imperfections) which interfere with the *normal* operation of the economic machine, which by itself would be capable of bringing about an *optimal* situation for the system (full employment, efficient allocation of existing resources, etc.). The task of economic policy is accordingly that of re-establishing the conditions for the *normal* operation of the economy. This type of vision represented orthodoxy *before* Keynes's *General Theory*, char-

---

(3) On this point see also CAFFÈ [2], p. 28.

acterized important lines of interpretations of this work, and is still at the heart of contemporary developments in the theory of employment — for example the economic theory of labour contracts.

On the other hand adherents to what I have called the *unemployment equilibrium interpretations* believe that there is no inherent tendency to self-adjustment, to full employment in particular; that on the contrary modern economic systems tend towards a position of less than full employment, and that this position is not to be considered as a transient *dis-equilibrium* due to imperfections of some sort — a position from which the system will spontaneously tend to move away — but rather as a full position of equilibrium; that is as a centre of gravity for the economy (Caravale [3], [4], [5]). In this perspective the task of economic policy is obviously far more important and demanding.

The debate between adherents to these two different approaches is complex and subtle. I shall limit myself to saying that, in my view, the present situation and the perspectives for employment in Europe after 1992 — on which I had to say a few words above — seem to represent a confirmation of the validity of the latter *vision* of the functioning of the economic system.

4. - Conclusion

The presence of imbalances and disharmonies — of which the employment problem is but one example — turns the idea of a smooth, perfectly functioning market mechanism into a remote and foggy picture — and fully justifies, in my view, a "return" to the spirit of Keynes's legacy. Far from being obsolete and old-fashioned — as the adage "there are no Keynesians under the age of forty" meant to imply some ten years ago in the US — this vision grasps the fundamental characteristics of the world in which we live and shows its great ethical and economic significance.

The "moderately conservative implications" of the *General Theory* could then represent the point of reference for the definition of the framework of a renewed, *rational*, and active economic policy; an economic policy inspired in particular by Keynes's own prescription according to which "certain central controls [should be established] in matters which are now left in the main to individual initiative" (Keynes [9] p. 377-8).

In this perspective, both at the national and at the Community level, demand management (implying the systematic presence of the State in the economy) still appears indispensable. This management should rigorously avoid the defense of *parasitic* positions in the system — something which has unfortunately, and very heavily, characterized the Italian experience. At the same time it should be realized through a set of measures tending to reach two objectives: *(i)* the defence of full employment — in the very apt expression of Federico Caffé, «an objective upon which depends the very notion of civilized society» (Caffé [2], p. 30); and *(ii)* the establishment of the degree of social consensus necessary to the enforcement of an effective incomes policy for price stability and growth.

Demand management should be accompanied by more specific, or structural interventions. For instance: *a)* a system of unemployment allowances connected with measures tending to re-qualify the unemployed with a view to faciliting their re-absorption in sectors where there is more demand for labour. The correction of the present imbalances — shortage of highly qualified, and excess of less qualified workers — has in addition a particularly important role to play in the longer run since the competitive performance of the European Community appears to depend largely on this factor; *b)* appropriate anti-trust legislation aiming at an acceptable compromise between the economic efficiency of firms and the defence of a "pluralistic" society based on the distinction of roles and functions of the various agents (private and public); *c)* an environment policy capable of reconciling the development of productive forces with the defence of acceptable and enjoyable conditions of life.

Although the advantages and the disadvantages of Europe's economic and monetary integration are difficult to evaluate on a purely analytical basis (4), the project is certainly fascinating from the political viewpoint, and in all probability positive from the economic viewpoint (especially in the longer run).

---

(4) This point is emphasized in Ciocca P. [7].

The process of integration, complex and costly as it certainly is, cannot however be left entirely to the «invisible hand», or to the «magic of the market». It must be guided by a set of rational measures in the fields I have endeavoured to indicate above.

Unfortunately, the practical content of all these measures cannot be defined in advance, once and for all, on the basis of Keynes's message, or anyone else's message.

To use Joan Robinson's words «we are [thus] left in the uncomfortable position of having to think for ourselves» (Robinson [14] p. 98).

BIBLIOGRAPHY

[1] BAKHOVEN A.F.: *The Completion of the Common Market in 1922: Macroeconomic Consequences for the European Community*, The Hague (Holland), Central Planning Bureau, March 1989.

[2] CAFFÈ F.: *La solitudine del riformista*, Turin, Bollati Boringhieri, 1990.

[3] CARAVALE G.: «The Neo-Keynesian School: Some Internal Controversies», *Atlantic Economic Journal*, December 1987.

[4] — —.: «Keynes and the Concept of Equilibrium» in SEBASTIANI I.M.: *The Notion of Equilibrium in the Keynesian Theory*, forthcoming, London, Macmillan, 1991.

[5] — —.: «The Notion of Equilibrium in Economic Theorizing», Presidential Address, *International Atlantic Economic Conference*, mimeo, Rome, 1991, to published in *Atlantic Economic Journal*, Sept. 1991.

[6] CECCHINI P.: *The European Challenge, 1992 — The Benefits of a Single Market* Wildwood House Ltd, 1988.

[7] CIOCCA P.: «L'unione monetaria d'Europa fra politica ed economia», *L'Impresa banca*, no. 3, September 1990.

[8] COMMISSION OF THE EUROPEAN COMMUNITIES: *One Market, One Money - An Evaluation of the Potential Benefits and Costs of Forming an Economic and Monetary Union*, Brussels, October 1990.

[9] KEYNES J.M.: *The General Theory, of Employment Interest and Money*, The Collected writings of J.M. Keynes, Vol. VII, London, Macmillan, 1973.

[10] MATUTES C.: *Some Considerations About 1992*, address presented at the "Atlantic Economic Society" International Conference, Barcellona, 1989 (mineo).

[11] MAYES D.G.: «Review of M. Emerson et Al., "The Economics of 1992"», *The Economic Journal*, December 1989, pp. 1208-10.

[12] MILGATE M.: «Controversies in the Theory of Employment», *Contributions to Political Economy*, vol. 7, 1988, pp. 65-82.

[13] PASINETTI L.L.: *Structural Change and Economic Growth - A Theoretical, Essay on the Dynamics of the Wealth of Nations*, Cambridge, Cambridge University Press, 1981.

[14] ROBINSON J.: *Economic Philosophy*, Chicago, Adline Publ. co., 1962.

Integration Problems of the East and West German Economy

Jürgen Kröger (*)
Commission of the European Communities, Brussels

1. - Analogies for Economic Catching-up Process

In the past, various models have been devised for the transformation of a capitalist economy into a centrally planned economy, but no such models exist for the reverse process. Consequently, economic theory and the political process are having difficulty in keeping up with the rapid development towards a market economy in Eastern Europe. Internal German development is playing a special role here. A monetary union has been concluded with the former GDR, on condition that the framework is created for a market-orientated economy. The fundamental political aim was that the promotion of economic prosperity in East Germany rather than administrative measures taken by the Federal Republic of Germany should put an end to the tide of migrants which followed the opening of the internal German frontier. The German economic, monetary and social union was seen as a signal and a promise that the difference in living standards would be reduced in the foreseeable future and encouraged positive expectations regarding economic prospects.

(*) In spite of numerous discussions with and comments from colleagues coming from his daily work in the Commission services, the views can only be attributed to the author.

1.1 *The "Economic Miracle" Model*
of the Federal Republic of Germany

At first glance, it seems as though the development of the East
German economy could follow a course similar to that taken by the
Federal Republic of Germany at the end of the war. Here too a currency reform marked the transition from a planned economy to a fully
market-orientated system. As a result of war production, the capital
stock was misallocated and in part destroyed. The economic starting
conditions prevailing at that time are comparable to the present situation in East Germany, where the capital stock is largely out of date
and therefore economically obsolete. The present capital stock position
in East Germany may be much more serious, it is true. However, the
financial backing from the Federal Republic of Germany greatly out-
strips the financial support to West Germany's post-war economy provided by the *Marshall Plan*, which is generally seen as having applied
the initial spark to West Germany's economic miracle.

The positive dynamic of the West German economic miracle has
basically been due to the following factors. The inflow of workers
from the previously German areas in the East combined with a high
performance potential created a fertile environment for investment.
What is more, the Federal economy had the benefit of strongly
expanding demand, due not least to an undervalued currency at that
time. Important domestic sectors were protected from the competition of the world market, largely because of the relatively modest
integration of the commodity, and more especially the financial
markets. In the course of the fifties and early sixties the efficiency of
the German economy was also favoured by a relatively modern capital
stock compared to that of other countries.

Although a similar scenario would be desirable for the East
German economy, the differences between the starting conditions for
the present-day East Germany and post-war West Germany are
obvious. Essentially there are three basic considerations arguing
against a repetition of the economic miracle. In the first place, the
monetary union means that the East German economy is immediately
exposed to world competition. Because of greater market integration
and an overvalued — measured in terms of East German productivity

— currency, the effects will be far more serious. Secondly, important preconditions for a high yield on capital do not exist: on the one hand, the wage-level measured against labour productivity seems too high, and on the other, there are considerable industrial-location problems due to the inadequate infrastructure. Thirdly, and perhaps the most crucial difference, the economic actors (entrepreneurs, employees and consumers) in East Germany are able to choose between an economically developed area — the Federal Republic of Germany — and an area faced with a protracted catching-up process. In the fifties and sixties, such a choice did not exist in the Federal Republic of Germany. All in all, it must be assumed, therefore, that an independent economic catiching-up process will not occur within the area of East Germany.

1.2 *Mezzogiorno*

The absence of investment in East Germany carries with it the danger that the area could become an economically backward region inside Germany like the Mezzogiorno has been in Italy. The East German market could be supplied by producers from the Federal Republic of Germany of other European countries without any need to set up major production units in East Germany. Highly trained and adaptable workers would migrate to the economically prosperous area. Less adaptable workers and the older population would stay at home. The region would become heavily dependent on government transfers, withouf itself being able to make any substantial contribution to prosperity.

Against this, there are weighty considerations which argue against the East German area falling into a permanent underdevelopment. Firstly, the East German territory was an important German and European hub of industry before the war. Just as the other East European countries are improving their economic development, so the former GDR area will probably be able to pick up the threads of this tradition. Secondly, the opening-up of Eastern Europe is likely to eliminate quickly the regionally-peripheral status which the East German area has occupied hitherto. Indeed, it could work itself into a central position on the European stage. Thirdly, it may also be assumed that centres like Berlin or others in the south of the former GDR will be able to develop their own economic pull.

The general economic trend towards the service sector may be of distinct benefit here. A more than proportional share taken by the East German economy in service and leisure activities falls into line with the future structural requirements of German economic development viewed as a whole. Nevertheless, it has to be recognised that any important service sector needs an industrial basis. Lastly, East Germany has a reservoir of relatively well-trained labour. If the performance of this labour potential can be mobilized, there is no real reason to assume that in the final analysis it cannot be as economically successful as the labour force of the Federal Republic of Germany.

In summary, it is fair to say that, while the danger of East Germany becoming a "Mezzogiorno" in the long run cannot be entirely dismissed, this phenomenon can be avoided by suitable policy measures (see below).

The crucial question is whether an East German Mezzogiorno can be avoided until the rest of Eastern Europe is recovering.

1.3 *West Berlin*

In a way, the present state of East Germany is comparable with West Berlin in the fifties. Because of its marginal position, West Berlin had no attraction for manufactures. The market could be supplied from West Germany, and the labour force was increasingly migrating to the economically flourishing area. Long-term and extensive financial aids were needed to halt and reverse this trend.

It follows from this that East Germany needs a massive regional development programme offering a wide range of short-term attractions, and especially investment incentives and wage subsidization, to persuade people to stay home. The incentive scheme for zonal border areas provides a further example for a programme of this kind to be eventually transposed to East Germany.

The difference from West Berlin lies in the fact that in the medium term East Germany can overcome its peripheral status, both in regional terms and with regard to the technical and organizational facets of economic life. To the extent that the disadvantages as a place of production can be eliminated over time, the East German territory can develop its own potential for economic prosperity. Therefore, public assistance should be provided on a massive scale in the short term but can be degressive in character right from the start.

2. - Adjustment Problems in the East German Economy

2.1 *Recent Developments*

Although the present economic situation remains uncertain in many respects, the first months of unity have unveiled the large adjustment needs which face the former GDR. So far, the implications for the real economy have been much more important than the monetary consequences.

Political discussions primarily centre on the question of the implied costs of unification.

Recent developments confirm that German monetary union has to be assessed primarily as a shock to the real economy. Industrial production fell substantially (by more than one third from 12 months earlier). In particular, consumer goods industries (food processing, textiles, light industry) experienced a huge drop in production. Since then, other indicators have confirmed a significant reduction in the demand for goods produced in East Germany. In the investment goods sectors, the drop in production may be lagged, as current production largely depends upon prior domestic and foreign orders and export subsidies.

The fall in production has led to a rapid increase in unemployment and part-time employment (nearly 3 million people are underemployed). The measures introduced in order to cushions the social effects of unemployment suggest that part-time employees should largely be considered as unemployed. Short-term prospects are very gloomy. In addition to a further rise in unemployment in the industrial sector, severe employment risks exist particularly in agriculture and also in the public sector, which is heavily over-staffed.

So far, the introduction of the DM has had no important implications for inflation. Monetary union has increased the purchasing power of East German residents. Moreover, a very substantial part of East German internal demand has shifted towards imported products. However, the somewhat higher inflation rate recorded in West Germany during the recent months is primarily due to the oil price hike rather than to supply bottlenecks. Moreover, the monetary aggregates have not exceeded the target growth rate of 4-6% in 1990. The additional demand effect to West German products has obviously been cushioned by a higher production exceeding normal capacity utilization in some sectors, reduction in stocks, and higher imports. Nevertheless, during the first months of 1991, monetary growth has accelerated.

Important problems have arisen in the financial situation of both the enterprise sector and the public sector in East Germany. Enterprises still rely on credit lines with the Treuhandanstalt (1). Liquidity credits were granted until 31 May 1991, although on a more selective basis. These funds have mainly been used to cover the operating costs of production rather than to finance new investment. Therefore, a reduction of the production costs of these enterprises through increased efficiency, in preparation for competition has not yet been achieved. Recourse to normal bank credits without risk coverage by the Treuhandanstalt is rare, although this would contribute to achieving a more effective allocation of production factors, as well as facilitating a more appropriate assessment of the viability of individual enterprises by private banks.

2.2 *Public Finances*

Major uncertainties relate to prospects for the public finances. As political unification now makes it impossible to look at both public deficits independently, the correct approach is to look at the all-German consolidated budget for general government. Low tax revenues and immediate expenditure commitments have led to a substantial disequilibrium in the East German public sector, which, however, is

---

(1) The Treuhandanstalt is a quasi-public body which owns the whole of the formerly state-owned property of the GDR. It aims at the restructuring and privatization of this property. For the time being, it is also granting credit to enterprises in order to help them cope with short-term liquidity problems.

largely balanced by transfers from West Germany. As an order of magnitude, the direct and indirect budgetary impacts will amount to about 100 bn DM in 1990 and at least 150 bn DM in 1991.

Given the high degree of uncertainty, these figures have to be interpreted with care, particularly as major risks exist in the following fields: *a)* the level of unemployment may be very high in the short term; *b)* the liquidity needs of the enterprise sector may become very large, exceeding the credit limits of the Treuhandanstalt; i.e. reconstructing the enterprise sector may burden the public sector more than expected; *c)* subsidies to stabilize basic living conditions, e.g. in housing and energy prices, may become unavoidable for social reasons; *d)* wages may increase to higher than expected levels; *e)* the newly-created local authorities will also need substantial liquid resources in order to fulfill their obligations and to begin infrastructural improvements in East Germany.

In addition to budgetary flows, further risks relate to the need to take over debt and to consolidate the all-German public sector. In this respect, the former debt of the GDR state insurance and health scheme are important. The debt of the Treuhandanstalt together with equalization claims arising from the asymmetric rate of conversion for debts and assets has reached significant levels too. Enterprise debts will probably be largely transformed into public debt also, if privatization of enterprises is successfully achieved. Debt service requirements will therefore grow significantly and will reduce the room for manoeuvre of German fiscal policy for the foreseeable future, certainly if no revenue enhancing measues are taken.

2.3 *The Productivity-Wage Dilemma*

The future development of the East German economy will crucially depend upon expectations about returns on new investment. In addition, the survival of existing enterprises will also depend upon the relation between production costs and sales prices. However, economic unification limits the instruments available to East German enterprises to achieve high profits. Firstly, sales prices have equalized for tradeable goods and services and secondly, monetary union implies the same capital costs throughout the union. Therefore, the only important market instrument to counter the current lower level of productivity in East Germany would be a favourable wage differential.

Although the requirement of moderate wage formation in East Germany is generally correctly acknowledged, it is highly doubtful whether wages can be maintained at a level consistent with the prevailing productivity levels. The forecast speed of alignment between East and West German wage will have a critical impact on the adaptation process of the East German economy. Therefore, it deserves closer consideration.

Various mechanisms supporting a rapid alignment of wages are identifiable: the price reform which has not yet been completed together with the introduction of a system of taking consumption, is leading to a rise in the price level, a rise which may provoke an exaggerated subjective response. In turn, this is already giving rise to wage claims which are in fact incompatible with the productivity level. An aggravating factor is that sales prices for East German products will probably have to be substantially lowered if they are to be sold at all. The periods for which the new wage agreements are to extent are extremely short, and wage rises have mainly been agreed in terms of lump sum increases. However, further adaptation of the wages structure will be necessary to improve motivation and hence the performance of labour. This will probably lead to a further rise in the average wage level.

To the extent that employees in areas close to the border can also find a job in the Federal Republic, this spill-over will have repercussions in East Germany. The Berlin labour market will probably be very seriously affected. In the civil service, large pay differences cannot really be accounted for by differences in productivity. New investments in East Germany will create high-productivity jobs and demand well-trained labour. It is likely that the wage level for such jobs will approximate to that in the Federal Republic. Furthermore, it is probable that in many areas the middle management will come from the Federal Republic. If the salaries of corresponding East German employees remain well below the level of their West German counterparts, this could lead to an unacceptable degree of distortion in the pay pyramid. In other words, the model of a "colonization" of

East Germany is hardly plausible. It must be assumed that the trade unions in both economic areas, though inspired by different motives, well press for rapid wage alignment.

As a result, the cost alignment of the most important factors of production (i.e. capital and labour, with the exception of the special case of land), would mean alignment of the market capital/labour ratio throughout the currency area. Essentially, this could take place in two different ways: either by the increased offer of labour by East German workers in the area of the Federal Republic or by investments in East Germany.

If movements of labour generated no social costs, it would be a matter of indifference which of the two adaptive strategies was adopted. In practice, however, things are liable to be different. Any massive East-West migration would encounter active resistance in the Federal Republic as it would aggravate the housing problem, jeopardize entrenched positions on the labour market and impose an additional burden on the social fabric. In East Germany, a large-scale emigration of labour would aggravate the regional problem. The least mobile and efficient workers and the older population would stay at home. Again, social tensions could not be ruled out here — though the reasons would be different. It follows from this that the public interest will be best served if capital flows are directed towards East Germany in order that the risk may be reduced.

In the short term, a difficulty arises from the fact that movements of labour can take place more quickly than the transfer of physical capital. Consequently, the alignment of wages between the two regions as the result of private decisions, i.e., searching for a job in the territory of the Federal Republic, could happen more rapidly than is in the public interest. However, there is one important factor reducing labour mobility: housing, which at the same time is a source of social tension.

2.4 Risks and Opportunities
of Introducing a Convertible Currency

The introduction of the DM to the East German region simultaneously presents opportunities and risks. On the one hand, it enables a catching up without a balance-of-payments constraint, it provides direct and almost unlimited access to world financial markets, it reduces the exchange-rate risk of investing in East Germany and it provides modern Western technology at relatively low prices. These are very favourable conditions for a rapid reconstruction of the East German economy. In these respects, catching up might prove easier than in other centrally-planned economies moving towards market-based economic structures.

On the other hand, the East German economy is immediately confronted with competition on the world market. The immediate and full convertibility of the Ostmark has revealed the inappropriate products structure and inefficient production methods which exist in East Germany. Given the rigidities in the labour market and the upward pressure on wages, a fixed exchange rate at the West German productivity level denies existing East German enterprises the possibility of compensating for their inappropriate product mix by lowering prices on the world market. In this respect, other Eastern countries have the opportunity to adjust to world market conditions more gradually by reducing real wages through devaluation, thus protecting the "competitiveness" of existing production.

In these circumstances, the preference must be to inject high levels of investment in new activities in East Germany rather than to keep alive existing uncompetitive enterprises. Emphasis should be placed on fostering new investment which will have a high level of productivity. The immediate adjustment pressures require that only production units with long-term survival prospects should be maintained. Otherwise, financial resources needed for new productive investment will be wanted. Moreover, large and ultimately unjustified subsidies provided to existing enterprises will impede new investment by protecting these enterprises from competition.

All in all, the introduction of the DM in the East German economy has limited the choice between a gradual and a much more rapid adjustment process. Encouraging new investment with a high marginal rate of return and scrapping old structures is the only way to survive the pressures of world competition. Appropriate incentives provided for private investment (see below) together with a large infrastructural programme can help to provide the favourable investment climate which is necessary to attract private capital. In the medium term, a high rate of return will only be achieved by a modern capital stock with a high level of total factor productivity operating in an integrated world economy.

2.5 *The Transition to a Market Economy*

The introduction of the DM to the East German territory is the foundation on which market behaviour can be established; nevertheless, this is not guaranteed. The legal framework of the social market economy now applies to the East German territory but there are obvious obstacles to the implementation of efficient interrelations between economic agents. Firstly, market economic behaviour has to be learned by economic agents; secondly, an effective competition policy has to be established; thirdly, the framework of economic regulations must not be simply copied from the FRG, without assessing the economic consequences for the territory of East Germany.

Past experience of extremely regulated structures has prevented economic agents in the former GDR from behaving rationally in a market sense. For the consumer, the intertemporal choice between consumption and saving was largely unattractive. Consumption was determined by supply and a distorted price system rather than demand. The introduction of the DM has immediately eliminated supply shortages without, however, changing consumer behaviour. The drastic demand shift from products produced in East Germany to imported goods even for basic consumption items such as food, the failure to gather information on quality and prices by buying in the FRG, and the relatively low importance of the standard determinants of consumption, i.e. income expectations and interest rates, are evidence of continuing irrational economic behaviour i.e. rent-seeking behaviour still dominates.

Establishing economic rationality is even more important in the case of producers. Production in the past has not been orientated towards demand — because of supply shortages — and profitability aspects have not been important. This has led to very inflexible production processes and poor quality products. Not surprisingly, only minor attempts were made to defend markets after the introduction of the DM in order to regain markets, it is necessary to improve the marketing of local products, to estabilish an efficient distribution system and to use the price instrument more flexibly.

After more than 40 years of a centrally planned economy, an effective framework for competition has now to be established. A rapid privatization and dismantling of existing monopolies is a necessary condition for competition. In the short term, stronger competition is needed in the retail sector; this will not be easily achieved, as the retail sector is highly concentrated. Thus, the consumer does not have choice and existing shops are behaving as mini-monopolies. In addition, co-operation between Western enterprises and East German shops might lead to a blas towards Western products as East German suppliers are hindered by an inefficient distribution system.

2.6 *Achieving Economic Prosperity in East Germany*

The necessary catching-up process has to be supported by economic policies mainly to compensate for transitional disadvantages of East Germany as a place of production. Thus, it will be of crucial importance to improve the conditions for investment in East Germany relative to West Germany. Otherwise, East Germany may remain an economically underdeveloped area with structural disadvantages possibly aggravated by emigration of skilled workers. Investment in the GDR should be encouraged with a view to the competitive advantages of the East German territory and structural difficulties which currently exist in the German or even European economy.

Special support should be given to sectors in which prospects are favourable. Nevertheless, in order to compensate for the overall disadvantages facing East Germany as a place of production, a general review of regional policies is required. Investment incentives which favour the territory of West Germany should be abolished and special transitory incentives could be introduced for investment in East Germany. Measures might be taken as soon as possible to reduce uncertainties which are already leading to the postponement of decisions at the private level. Special investment subsidies could be large at the outset but should be gradually phased out. Direct investment subsidies might be preferable to lowe taxation. Lower taxes only favour enterprises which are already making profits, while many existing East German enterprises will record losses for quite a time. Moreover, the liquidity effect of direct investment aid is very important for East German enterprises as they are heavily liquidity constrained. Finally, with a general tax cut for East Germany, West German enterprises could be favoured disproportionately as they would be able to transfer profits to East Germany through intra-company operations.

A regional development plan for East Germany might comprise the following elements:

— improving infrastructure, if necessary by shifting public projects to the territory of East Germany in order to reduce the obvious absorption problems in East and West Germany. Within the unified Germany, the marginal rate of social return of infrastructural and environmental investment is much higher in East Germany than elsewhere;

— abolition of investment incentives and production subsidies in the West German economy;

— direct investment aid rather than higher depreciation allowances or lower taxes in order to begin rebuilding the capital stock in East Germany;

— fostering the creation of new enterprises by giving income support during the starting phase, by providing a guarantee on risk capital and by lowering capital costs. Establishing small- and medium-sized enterprises is the clue for an efficient market economy and the precondition for a high degree of competition.

3. - The Performance of the Unified German Economy

The rapid integration of the East German economy into the unified Germany makes it increasingly inappropriate to consider both economies separately. The currently favourable developments in West Germany largely reflect short-term adjustment problems in East Germany. For example, the shift of internal East German consumption towards imports after the introduction of the DM has boosted demand in West Germany. The relatively healthy condition of the

West German budget balance might lead to an incorrect assessment if the financial imbalances in East Germany are not considered. Finally, the still widening trade surplus in West Germany.

In a unified German context, the short-term macroeconomic implications can be seen in: *a)* a substantial gap between aggregate supply and demand in the union; *b)* large asymmetries in the German labour market; *c)* a significant relaxation of fiscal policy.

3.1 *The Supply Gap*

Recent figures confirm that unification has rendered a significant part of the East German capital stock economically obsolete; thus potential output of the region has been severely reduced. Meanwhile, the conversion of the Ostmark into DM has increased the purchasing power of East German residents as for the time being the price index has decreased. Clearly, higher wage settlements since then have added further to purchasing power and demand.

In the short term, the gap between aggregate demand and supply in the German economy has been largely filled by higher production (production probably exceeding normal capacity utilization) by running down stocks of final goods and by higher imports. However, some markets e.g. for used cars, have experienced significant price increases. For the period ahead, the gap between demand and supply may become even larger for two reasons. Firstly, wages and thus consumption demand in East Germany may continue to increase ahead of productive capacity. Secondly, higher investment in East Germany will initially have considerable demand effects while supply will increase only after some time.

Appendix 1 attempts to illustrate the large adjustment needs. The significant fall of aggregate supply relative to demand because of the economic obsolescence of large parts of the East German capital shock, together with growing demand supported by an expansionary fiscal policy, creates the need for a considerable reduction of the current account balance. By 1991 the current account surplus might have to disappear completely in order to close the gap betweem supply and demand in Germany.

A substantial catching up in East Germany per capita income to about 75% of the West German level by the end of the decade, would imply that the supply gap would initially become even larger, suggesting an all-German current account deficit in order to balance domestic savings and investment. Later, when supply is responding, the gap will be closed. Nevertheless, the need for large transfer of resources to reconstruct East Germany is clearly apparent.

Any sustained gap between demand and supply requires an adjustment of the real exchange rate, which can be achieved either via a nominal exchange rate adjustment or via higher inflation and a corresponding real appreciation. In this respect, the recent appreciation of the DM against the dollar fits the picture. Moreover, the demand-supply gap can also be addressed by a policy designed to encourage imports. To the extent that the East German demand profile is now similar to that of other industrialized countries, the import share may adjust to similar levels without any exchange rate adjustment. In addition, demand for imports should be supported by reducing trade barriers which still exist in many sectors. Early adoption of Community internal market proposals by the German authorities is therefore advisable. Finally, trade relations with Eastern European countries should be intensified. Higher exports from these countries would reduce the demand-supply gap in Germany while helping to mitigate the external constraint facing these countries.

3.2 *Labour Market Asymmetries*

The second very important effect of German unification concerns the labour market. The shift in demand has improved employment prospects in the West German economy. However, this shift has considerably worsened employment prospects in the East German economy. Low demand for labour together with the need for structural changes and higher labour efficiency makes very high unemployment unavoidable in the East German economy, at least during the transition period.

An important asymmetry in the labour markets of East and West Germany concerns the wage level. The average wage level in the East is at present around 50% of the West German level. This figure is, however, misleading as the wage gap is much lower for unskilled workers, particularly if one considers wages net of rent. As wages in East Germany are not differentiated according to economic efficiency, wage differentials are very much wider for skilled workers. A ratio of 1:3 or greater may exist in specific professions.

A further asymmetry relates to skills. In ideologically influenced jobs, e.g. economists and administrators, skills in East Germany are probably inappropriate to a market-based economy. As regards workers, modern production techniques must be learned. For the time being, regional and professional flexibility seems to be at a low level in East Germany.

It is unlikely that these asymmetries will persist in the long term, but integration of both labour markets may imply social costs of adjustment, e.g. through large-scale migration. Therefore, although German economic policy has traditionally not played an active role in the labour market, a review of this stance may prove necessary.

3.3 Relaxation of Fiscal Policy

The third important macroeconomic implication of German unification is a significant relaxation of fiscal policy. This relaxation is largely the counterpart of transfers to prevent a fall in the purchasing power of the East German population. The swing in the fiscal policy stance might be as large as 5% of GDP between 1989 and 1991. Given the deterioration in the financial balances of other sectors, particularly the enterprise sector, the disappearance of the overall German current account surplus is therefore consistent with the saving-investment equilibrium.

As a safeguard against the inflationary impact of such a change in the policy mix, fiscal policy should aim to limit the expansionary effect of the transfers to East Germany. First of all, subsidies which favour investment in regions and sectors in the West German economy should be cut. Secondly, infrastructural and environmental investment expenditures should be shifted to East Germany where the marginal rate of return is higher. Thirdly, if tax increases become unavoidable, direct tax measures should be considered as well as indirect tax measures so as to contribute to a more balanced development of after-tax wages and incomes in both areas.

In the medium term, a catching up in the East German economy will certainly contribute to economic growth in the unified German economy. Nevertheless, it has to be accepted that the benefits of higher economic growth will need to be channeled towards an improvement in the economic conditions in East Germany i.e. an increase in real income towards the level of West Germany, an improvement in the quality of the housing stock, infrastructure and the environment, a reduction in the large fiscal deficits and servicing of the higher debt level. To the extent that new private investment in East Germany represents a shift from the West rather than a genuine addition to total investment, the growth in the potential output of West Germany may even be temporarily reduced somewhat.

The fundamental change in the public finance situation is illustrated in Appendix 2. Assuming a continuation of the formerly very healthy trend, together with moderate economic growth, the public debt level would have been on a declining trend in the medium term. In the new situation in which the initial public debt level is larger because of debt takeover, public deficits will probably be rather persistent and higher interest rates are probably unavoidable. The public finance situation will probably not become unsustainable, but the long-term level of the debt will be significantly larger than it would have been in the non-unified Germany. Moreover, a significantly larger recorded public sector deficit does not necessarily imply a larger primary deficit which seem, however, necessary to accompany the East German catching-up process. Thefore, the need to consolidate public finance in Germany will become a heavy burden.

4. - Repercussions on the European Economy

4.1 *Demand Effects Versus Tighter Monetary Conditions*

The gap between aggregate supply and demand in Germany will certainly boost imports in the short term. The import leakage in the re-oriented consumer demand in the new five Länder will be large so that European partner countries will benefit from the demand pull. The change in the overall trade pattern of the former GDR suggests that all Community countries will establish similar trade links as those already existing with other industrialized countries; in the short term, exports to the former GDR will accelerate while the flow of imports from the former GDR will be determined by the rate of reconstruction in its capital stock. Therefore, it can be expected that all Community countries will run a current account surplus with the former GDR.

Exports to Germany might grow further as capacity shortages become greater in West Germany; production bottlenecks are already emerging in some sectors. On the world market, Germany might lose market shares because priority might be given to provide resources for reconstructing East Germany.

Empirical evidence of bilateral export behaviour already suggests a significant increase in exports to Germany (see Appendix 3). In particular Denmark, the Benelux countries and France seem to be benefiting from the demand pull effects in Germany. These effects may become stronger to the extent that the need for imports is still veiled by a run-down in stocks of final goods in Germany, the prevailing high level of production cannot be sustained and demand may accelerate further ahead of growth in potential output.

However, the net growth effect will also depend upon the tighter monetary conditions prevailing in the EMS after German unification. Despite the fact that interest rates have been increasing significantly more in Germany than in other Community countries, all EMS partner countries have experienced a real appreciation of their currencies in particular against the dollar. It is doubtful as to whether European central banks would have accomodated the significant fall in the dollar without the anticipated stimulating effect of German unification.

4.2 EMU - Related Issues

4.2.1 Exchange Rate Dynamics

To a certain extent, Germany can be compared to a country in which a significant part of the economy has to catch up by improving or replacing the prevailing capital stock. In the long run, there is the prospect of building up a modern economy by implementing advanced technologies in the private sector, to establish industries which coincide with future needs and to bring the infrastructure to an advanced level. Then, East Germany might exhibit similar features as West Germany in the 1950s and early 1960s when the capital stock embodied greater technical progress relative to that of other countries.

Nevertheless a dilemma might develop in the EMS Community to the extent that tighter monetary conditions might become necessary in Germany in order to accompany the structural adjustment and catching-up process in East Germany without inflationary pressurres. It has to be recognised that any sustained gap between demand and supply requires an adjustment of the real exchange rate which can be achieved via a nominal exchange rate adjustment or via higher inflation. Clearly higher inflation is not the preferred option for the Bundesbank.

If tighter monetary conditions will became necessary in Germany in order to avoid overheating in the German economy, tensions in the EMS might the develop as monetary tightening could be inconsistent with the domestic needs of the other countries. Therefore an exchange-rate adjustment could become an option, if the Bundesbank is using monetary policy as a short-term stabilizing instrument.

The dilemma for the other countries is aggravated by negative credibility implication of a realignment. These may be somewhat reduced if the DM appreciates *vis-à-vis* all other EMS countries. Financial markets would then consider the realignment being triggered by inner-German developments. Moreover, a DM appreciation against all other EMS countries would be less detrimental for the convergence process in the EMS.

It has been argued that over time a real depreciation of the DM is required if higher investment is adding to overall supply. This adjustment will probably be much more easily achieved by lower inflation in Germany compared to other countries. Therefore, in the medium term and given an initial real appreciation of the DM nominal exchange-rate stability would become consistent with some disconvergence in inflation rates in the EMS i.e. a positive inflation differential in favour of Germany.

4.2.2 The Anchor Problem

German unification may alter the anchor role of the DM in the EMS in three respects: firstly, it has made more difficult the definition of the appropriate domestic stance of monetary policy; secondly, the appropriate domestic stance may contradict the requirements of partner countries and thirdly, monetary variables have become less reliable indicators of monetary policy.

The appropriate stance of monetary policy will depend upon the size of the supply gap and the implied inflationary threat. Uncertainties exist as to the size of the fiscal expansion i.e. to what extent can expenditure increases be compensated by higher revenues or expenditure cuts in other areas, the size and time profile of private and public investment in East Germany, the part of the capital stock to be scrapped in East Germany, and the contribution of other countries' resources i.e. what is the speed and profile of the reduction of the current account surplus. Moreover, the integration of the East and West German labour markets could have a favourable supply-side effect too, if wage pressure is reduced by high unemployment in the medium term.

Therefore, defining the appropriate stance of monetary policy has become much more difficult and a pre-emptive tightening would involve speculative elements. Nevertheless, if and when recorded inflation has already increased the adjustment costs of subsequently reducing inflation could be large.

As regards the functioning of the EMS, it has always been argued that domestic demand shocks should not be remedied by monetary means. Therefore, when the need for an exchange-rate adjustment has arisen, non-monetary policies have also been adjusted. The particular case relating to German unification is that a significant domestic shock occuring in the anchor country.

On the more technical level, interpretation of money indicators may become more difficult at least during the period of transition. Firstly, monetary aggregates may become more volatile if the velocity of money changes, in particular in East Germany. As initially all financial assets were part of M3 and an adjustment towards non-monetary financial assets can be expected (in West Germany the relation between M3 and non-monetary assets is roughly 1:1), M3 should fall in East Germany until the portfolio adjustment is completed. Moreover, as the banking system is fairly underdeveloped in East Germany, velocity could grow even faster suggesting that monetary expansion should be lower than otherwise.

Uncertainties exist also as to the interpretation of interest rates. An increase in long-term interest rates could be either due to an increase in inflation expectations and an expected future tightening of monetary policy or to an increase in the expected real rate of return. In order to discriminate between these factors, the development of the real exchange rate will have to become a more important, market based indicator for monetary policy.

To the extent that intermediate monetary indicators in other countries would remain relatively more reliable, the anchor role of the EMS system is at least partly transfering to those countries. Due to its relative size, this transfer of role applies primarily to France. This, however, means that the degree of freedom given by the decreasing differential of interest rates with Germany should not be used at the expense of price stability. All in all, the question of the optimality of asymmetry which has so far characterized the working of the ERM should be reconsidered in present circumstances.

4.2.3 The Optimal Currency Area

The opening up of the inner-German border and the movement in other Eastern countries towards market economic structures will add a new dimension to the economic integration process in Europe. Trade with Eastern countries will accelerate considerably. Firstly, during the catching-up process, investment goods will have to be imported by those countries and secondly, if industry has become competitive on the world market the Eastern countries will participate in the international division of labour. To the extent that East Germany can become the bridgehead in this process, Germany will probably be more significantly affected than Community partner countries. The question arises as to whether, in the longer term, the EMS area would then be a less optimal model of monetary coordination.

On the micro-level, it should not be expected that German industry will favour Eastern markets more than traditional Western markets. Due to the likely undervaluation of the Eastern currencies, exports to these countries will probably not consist of highly advanced technology (in contrast, East Germany because of the overvaluation of the DM relative to productivity will probably demand highly advanced technology). Therefore, if exports to traditional markets were to continue, Germany through accelerating imports could even become more integrated.

On the macro-level, in accounting terms, the counterpart of the German current account surplus has been a deficit in some partner countries. The German current account suruplus will significantly decline and possibly find its counterpart also in an easing of Eastern countries' deficits. Therefore catching-up might become more difficult in particular as higher interest rates increase the disciplinary effects on the public sector and some investment might be crowded out or in other words an overvaluation of the currency might become less easily sustainable if autonomous capital inflows dry up. Therefore, catching-up countries may have to postpone their economic development towards the average EMS level if German unification would significantly increase capital shortages on the world financial market.

All in all, it should be clear that, as long as the main principles of macroeconomic and microeconomic behaviour are largely coherent with respect to, for example, the level of savings, profits and wages, and stability-oriented policies, neither German unification nor developments in Eastern Europe should alter the long-run prospects of achieving stronger monetary integration in Europe.

1. - The Supply-Demand Gap in the Unified Germany

German unification has led to a substantial gap between supply and demand. A significant part of the East German production capacity has become obsolete in economic terms while demand is being stabilised by supporting disposable income; this has not been done by a redistribution from West to East but by public borrowing, leading to a large public sector deficit. The quantitative magnitude of this gap will have a decisive influence on economic policy recommendations as it will determine the medium-term inflationary threat. In order to illustrate the significance of the problems, two scenarios have been defined.

The first scenario assumes no catching up in East Germany. However, potential output in West Germany is likely to accelerate more than without unification. Potential output is assumed to accelerate by about half a percentage point. The drop in East German supply has been set at 30% in 1990 and a further 20% in 1991, the latter mainly because of an overhang effect. The initial size of the East German economy has been assumed to be 12% of the West German economy. Assuming that potential output of West Germany has been 100 in 1989, the overal supply of Germany is 112 in 1989. As the curent account surplus has been around 5% of GDP in 1989, total domestic demand has been 107 in 1989. The following table summarises the assumptions.

The second scenario assumes a significant catching-up process over the next 10 years in East Germany. It is assumed that per capita income (supply) reaches 75% of the West German supply level by 1999. As such a catching-up will require very large investment in East Germany, some replacement of investment can be expected and growth of production capacity would be somewhat lower (25% per year) in West Germany. The increase of East German potential will have to be as large as 16% per year in order to achieve the assumed

TABLE 1

ASSUMPTIONS UNDERLYING SCENARIO I - NO CATCHING UP
(West German GDP of 1989 equals 100)

Supply feature	1989	1990 (%)	1991 (%)	1992-1999 (%) for year
Former FRG	100	+ 3	+ 3	+3
West Germany	100	+ 3	+ 3.5	+3.5
East Germany	12	− 30	− 20	+3.5
Demand				
Total domestic demand	107	+ 4	+ 3.5	+3

catching-up. The demand effect of additional investment is large at the beginning (capital output ratio = 3.5) expaining the larger increase of demand in the first years of the catching-up process. The scenario neglects multiplier effects which would strengthen demand growth even further. Because of the shift in demand to East Germany, demand growth is assumed to be somewhat lower than in Scenario I.

The following three graphs illustrate the implied supply-demand dynamics, admittedly in a stylized way. In the scenario where East

TABLE 2

SCENARIO II - CATCHING-UP

Supply	1989	1990	1991 (%)	1992 (%)	1993 (%)	1994-1999 (%)
West Germany	100	103	+ 3	+ 2.75	2.75	2.75
East Germany	12	− 30%	− 20	+16	+16	+16
Demand						
Total domestic demand without demand effect of additional investment in East Germany	107	+ 4%	+ 3.5	+ 3	+ 3	+ 3
Additional demand effect of East German growth in potential				+ 3.1	+ 0.4	+ 0.5

Germany is not catching up but West Germany is growing more rapidly, the change in the supply-demand relationship is significant. The current account deficit will have to disappear in the short run in order to close the gap of demand and supply. In the years 1991-1994 even a small current account deficit is required to provide the necessary resources. One might argue that Graph 1 overemphasizes the adjustment needed in the short run given that Germany is still running a current account suruplus. However, one should not forget that German monetary union was implemented in the middle of 1990 and, at present, German production is above normal capacity utilization rate — a situation which cannot be sustained. Moreover, the problem might also be veiled by running down stocks and by increasing order shocks. Actually, very recent figures confirm a large drop in the current account surplus.

Scenario II suggests that a current account deficit can hardly be avoided in a positive scenario of rapid catching up in East Germany. The order of magnitude of the deficit may be significant; indeed, according to the assumption made in this scenario, it may reach 4% of GDP.

GRAPH 1

DEMAND: SCENARIO I AND SCENARIO II

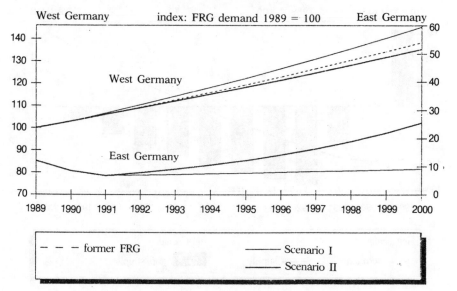

GRAPH 2

SCENARIO I

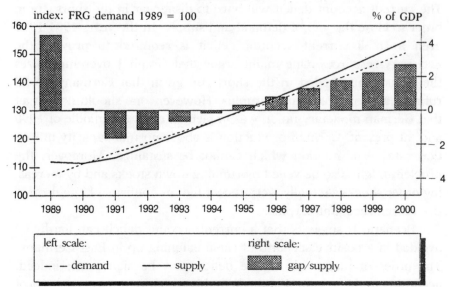

GRAPH 3

SCENARIO II

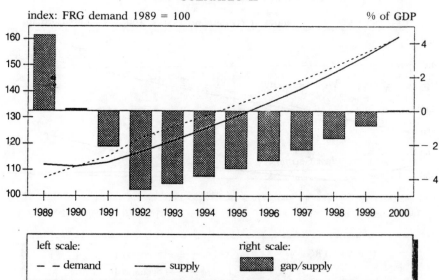

2. - Public Finance Dynamics After German Unification: an Empirical Illustration

This appendix illustrates the development of the German debt level which may materialize because of the budgetary implications of unification. However, the underlying assumptions are very uncertain and the static elements of the method used are obvious. The following two tables summarise the assumptions underlying the two scenarios.

TABLE 3

SCENARIO I
PUBLIC DEBT DYNAMICS (WEST GERMANY)
WITHOUT UNIFICATION (*)

	1990	1991	1992	1993-1999
Assumptions				
Real growth (% ch.)	3.5	3.0	2.75	2.75
Budget deficit (% of GDP)....	0.5	1.0	1.0	1.75
Inflation rate (%)............	2.7	2.5	2.5	2.5
Nominal interest rate (%)	7.0	7.0	7.5	7.5

(*) For 1990 and 1991 the figures correspond to the Commission forecast of Autumn 1989, 1992-1999 own assumptions.
The initial public debt level was 43.6% of GDP in 1989.

TABLE 4

SCENARIO II
PUBLIC DEBT DYNAMICS (GERMANY)
WITH UNIFICATION

	1990	1991	1992	1993-1999
Assumptions				
Real growth (% ch.)	1.0	0.5	2.5	3.0
Budget deficit (in % of GDP)	3.4	5.0	5.0	4.0
Inflation rate (%)............	2.8	3.9	3.5	3.0
Nominal interest rate (%)	9.0	9.7	10.0	9.25
Real growth West Germany (% ch).....................	4.3	3.1	2.0	

The debt level has been increased by 5% of GDP in both 1990 and 1991 because of the necessity to take over debt, stemming from various sources in the former GDR.

The differences in the two scenarios are significant. Without unification and a continued sound budgetary position, the debt level would have maintained its downward trend (Graph 4). Unification may significantly alter this feature. The initial debt take-over, the high public sector deficit (incl. treuhandsantalt) and higher interest rates will involve an additional burden for fiscal policy. Given the assumptions underlying the scenario, public debt will rise to a level which is almost twice as large as in the first scenario. By the end of the decade the public debt level may reach 58% of GDP as compared to 37% of GDP in the first scenario.

In the unification scenario, the debt servicing requirement (interest payments) accelerates quite rapidly even in the short term because of the takeover of debt and the higher level of interest rates. All in all, interest payments may increase by more than 2% of GDP, reducing the room for manoeuvre for fiscal policy.

GRAPH 4

GERMAN UNIFICATION: PUBLIC DEBT DYNAMICS

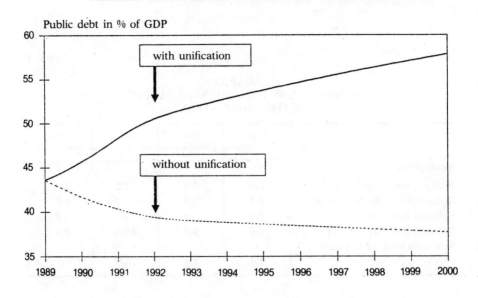

GRAPH 5

GERMAN UNIFICATION: PUBLIC SECTOR INTEREST PAYMENTS

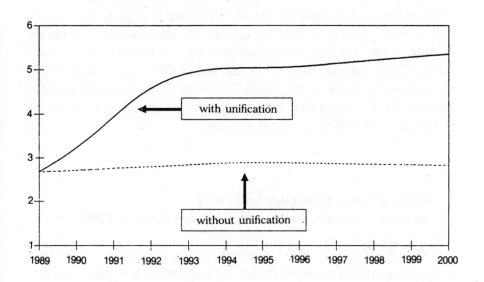

GRAPH 6

GERMAN UNIFICATION: PRIMARY BALANCE

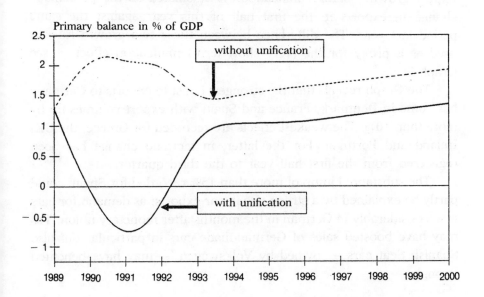

Although, in the short term, the primary balance shows a deficit as compared to the large surplus which would have materialised without unification, the differences are much smaller in the medium term. Although it is assumed that the total deficit only declines to 4% of GDP in the medium term, the primary surplus will have to show a similarly large surplus compared with the scenario without unification. This suggests that reducing the public sector deficit will probably prove to be very difficult. Given the huge financial needs in East Germany, a significant reduction of the primary surplus from the prevailing level will be required anyway.

3. - Early Effects of German Unification on Other Community Countries, Third Quarter 1990

The Bundesbank trade statistics reveal a strong turnaround in import growth (12 month rate) between June and July, coinciding with the implementation of the monetary union. For each member country we calculate the percentage change in exports to Germany in the third quarter against the same quarter last year. Export growth "before unification" is calculated as the percentage change in exports in the first half of this year against the same period last year. The difference between these two growth rates is used as a proxy for the (very short term) unification effect — see Graph 7.

The Graph reveals that the strongest boost to exports to Germany has come in Denmark, France and Spain with export volumes up by more than 10%. The weakest effects are recorded for Greece, the UK, Ireland and Portugal. For the latter, in fact, no change has been registered from the first half year to the third quarter.

The substantial jump of more than 15% recorded for Spain, could partly be explained by a strong rise in car exports; as demand for cars rose considerably in German in the months after monetary union. Ths may have boosted sales of German-made cars in particular but also Spanish Seat cars — owned by Volkswagen — may have benefited strongly.

GRAPH 7

GROWTH OF EXPORT TO GERMANY
BEFORE AND AFTER UNIFICATION (*)

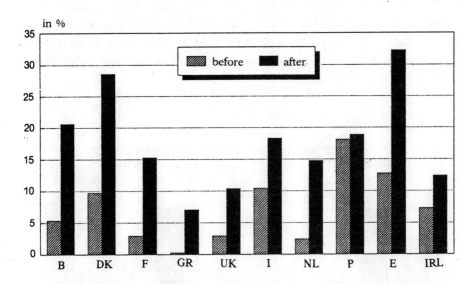

(*) Before: (1. Halfyear '90 / 1. Halfyear '89): change in %.
   After: (Jul-Nov '90 / Jul-Nov '89): change in %.

Germany as an export market differs in importance for the various member contries. Whereas more than 25% of all Greek and Dutch exports go to Germany less than 15% of total British, Spanish and Irish exports are directed towards Germany (see Table 5). Therefore, a given change in exports to Germany will have different effects on the overall export performance in particular countries.

TABLE 5

EXPORTS TO GERMANY IN PERCENT OF TOTAL EXPORTS, 1989

B	DK	F	GR	UK	I	NL	P	ES	IR
19.8	18.2	18.7	25.1	12.7	17.4	28.1	15.8	11.1	12.2

212 *Jürgen Kröger*

Thus, even though the recorded rise in exports from the UK and Ireland is almost of the same magnitude as that recorded for the Netherlands, the effect on the overall exports is much stronger for the Netherlands (see Graph 8). For Spain, Germany is a relatively less important export market. Hence, although Spanish exports to Germany have increased by more than that of any other Community country, the impact on total Spanish exports has been no higher than for France and Denmark.

GRAPH 8

ADDITIONAL EXPORTS TO GERMANY
AFTER UNIFICATION AS % OF TOTAL EXPORTS (*)

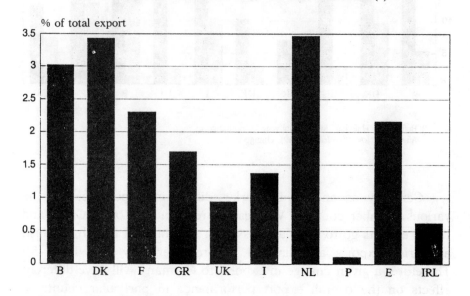

(*) Calculated on a full-year basis.

The next step is to take into account the degree of openness of the various Community countries i.e. the share of exports in GDP.

The higher this share, the higher will be the effect on production of a given increase in exports. Of all Community countries, Belgium and Netherlands have the highest share of exports in GDP (see Table 6); Spain, France and Italy having the lowest. When translated into a

TABLE 6

TOTAL EXPORTS OF GOODS IN PERCENT OF GDP, 1989

B	DK	F	GR	UK	I	NL	P	ES	IR
60.5	27.3	18.7	14.5	18.3	16.4	48.3	28.5	12.32	59.9

direct full-year impact on GDP, therefore, Belgium and Netherlands appear to be the two most affected countries, with Denmark and France slightly below. Production and thus employment in Greece, the UK and Portugal, on the other hand, are barely affected.

GRAPH 9

ADDITIONAL EXPORTS TO GERMANY
AFTER UNIFICATION AS % OF GDP (*)

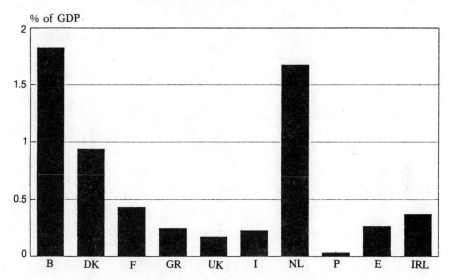

(*) Only direct impact, calculated on a full-year basis (no multiplier effect).

The results shown should be modified by taking into account the multiplier effects and import leakages. This would presumably alter the "ranking" of countries according to how much they are affected.

Thus, due to less import content in Danish and notably French production, the dynamic (multiplier) effects of German unification in these countries would be samewhat higher than in the very open small economies of e.g. Belgium and Holland. A more precise answer requires econometric simulations.

III - EUROPEAN MONETARY UNION

IMS: The International Monetary System or... Scandal?

Robert Triffin
University of Leuven

«Vingt fois sur le métier remettez votre ouvrage.
Polissez-le sans cesse et le repolissez». Boileau

Introduction

The IMS acronym can only be interpreted today as meaning «The International Monetary Scandal» rather than the «International Monetary System».

This paper aims at making understandable, even to the — much sought-after — man in the street, the root causes of a few of the major policies and institutional arrangements underlying the actual disaster and gloomy future prospects confronting his daily life: awesome rates of unemployment reminiscent of the 1930's, unprecedented world inflation, wasteful and suicidal armament expenditures in even the poorest countries of the world, etc., etc.

The first section offers an economic explanation that highlights a major blindness of virtually all analysts, responsible for the calamitous distortion of their policy advice.

The second — and probably most important — one spells out the political imperatives that dominate inevitably economic policy, and may hopefully reverse tomorrow the cold war policies of yesteryears?

The third and fourth revert, in this light, to the recent developments and future perspectives of the worldwide and regional components of the international monetary system.

1. - Economic Analysis

I hope that the reader will appreciate the brevity of Table 1: it is not easy to summarize on a single page both the mechanism and the results of the functioning of our international monetary system — or scandal? — over the last four decades: from the end of 1949 to the end of 1989.

Its significance as to the sources of reserve assets is brought out even more briefly in Table 2.

1.1 *The Mechanism*

The mechanism (Table 1) analyzes the creation of gross reserve assets, measured in US dollars, into three components: 1) the traditional «gold standard», *i.e.* the volume of gold reserves at $35 per ounce; 2) the fold or paper «exchange standard», under which I group with "foreign exchange assets" the so-called bookkeeping profits

TABLE 1

SOURCES OF WORLD MONETARY RESERVES
(1949-1989)

	in billions of dollars				in % of total			
	1949	1969	1979	1989	1949	1969	1979	1989
I. *Gold standard*	33	39	36	36	73	49	4	3
II. *Foreign exchange standard*..........	11	34	777	1,052	23	43	92	92
a) Gold appreciation	—	—	496	380	−1	—	59	33
b) Foreign exchange reserves	11	34	281	672	—	—	33	58
III. *International Monetary Fund*........	2	7	32	60	4	8	4	5
a) SDR holdings ..	x	x	16	27	x	x	2	2
b) Reserve positions	2	7	15	33	4	8	2	3
Total	45	79	845	1,149	100	100	100	100
20 years % increase....	+75		+13,529					
	1949-1969		1969-1989					

TABLE 2a

CREDIT RESERVES
(in billions of dollars)

Year end	1949	1959	1969	1979	1986	1987	1988	1989
Assets	12,6	19,5	40,2	313,2	475,7	672,5	687,6	732,4
Industrial countries	6,5	12,5	26,7	156	271,1	413,8	433,9	461,9
USA	1,5	2,0	5,1	7,8	37,5	34,7	36,7	63,6
Other	5,1	10,5	21,6	148,2	233,6	379	397,1	398,3
Third world	6	6,9	13,5	157,2	204,7	258,7	253,7	270,5
OPEC	0,5	1,6	2,8	72,3	61,6	67,6	55,8	56,3
Other	5,5	5,3	10,7	84,8	143,1	191,1	198	214,2
Liabilities	−11,1	−17,1	−38,6	−309,3	−475,7	−671,1	−685,7	−731,5
Industrial countries	−11	−16,8	−37,3	−296,5	−426,3	−619,7	−641,9	−691,2
USA	−3,2	−10,6	−17	−221,5	−295,7	−427,2	−434,9	−482,6
Other	−7,8	−6,2	−20,3	−75	−130,6	−192,6	−206,9	−208,6
Third world	−0,1	−0,3	−1,3	−12,9	−49,4	−51,4	−43,8	−40,3
OPEC	—	—	−0,1	−1	−1,9	−2,8	−2,6	−4,2
Other	−0,1	−0,3	−1,1	−11,9	−47,5	−48,6	−41,2	−36,1
Net assets	+1,5	+2,3	+1,7	+3,8	—	+1,4	+2,9	+0,9
Industrial countries	−4,5	−4,3	−10,6	−140,5	−155,3	−205,8	−208,1	−229,3
USA	−1,7	−8,6	−11,9	−213,7	−258,3	−392,4	−398,2	−419,1
Other	−2,8	+4,3	+1,3	+73,2	+103,3	+186,6	+190,1	+189,7
Third world	+6	+6,6	+12,3	+144,3	+155,3	+207,3	+210,1	+230,2
OPEC	+0,5	+1,6	+2,7	+71,4	+59,7	+64,7	+53,2	+52,1
Other	+5,5	+5	+9,6	+73	+95,5	+142,5	+156,9	+178,1
Dollars for SDR	1,00	1,00	1,00	1,3173	1,2232	1,419	1,345	1,31416

TABLE 2b

FOREIGN EXCHANGE

Year end	1949	1959	1969	1979	1986	1987	1988	1989
Assets	10.9	16.2	33.5	281.2	408.7	599.2	622.4	672.0
Industrial world	*4.9*	*9.4*	*20.8*	*133.5*	*223.1*	*361.4*	*283.9*	*413.0*
United States........	—	—	2.8	3.8	17.3	13.1	17.4	44.6
Other	4.9	9.4	18.0	129.7	205.8	348.4	366.5	368.4
Third world	*6.0*	*6.8*	*12.7*	*147.8*	*185.6*	*237.8*	*138.5*	*259.0*
OPEC	0.5	1.6	2.7	67.0	46.3	51.3	44.5	48.9
Other	5.5	5.2	10.1	80.7	139.3	186.4	194.0	210.2
Liabilities ($-$)	10.9	16.2	33.5	281.2	408.7	599.2	622.4	672.0
Industrial world	*10.9*	*16.2*	*33.5*	*281.2*	*408.7*	*599.2*	*622.4*	*672.0*
United States........	3.2	10.1	18.0	217.3	289.7	420.2	428.3	476.2
Other	7.7	6.1	15.5	63.9	118.9	179.0	194.1	195.9
Third world					Assumed insignificant			
OPEC								

Net assets	×	×	×	×	×	×	×	×
Industrial world	-6.0	-6.8	-13.4	-147.8	-185.6	-237.8	-238.5	-259.0
United States........	-3.2	-10.1	-15.2	-213.5	-272.4	-407.1	-411.0	-431.6
Other	-2.8	$+3.4$	-1.8	$+65.7$	$+86.8$	$+169.3$	-172.4	$+172.7$
Third world	$+6.0$	$+6.8$	$+12.7$	$+147.8$	$+185.6$	$+237.8$	$+238.5$	$+259.0$
OPEC	$+0.5$	$+1.6$	$+2.7$	$+67.0$	$+46.3$	$+51.3$	$+44.5$	$+48.9$
Other	$+5.5$	$+5.2$	$+10.1$	$+80.7$	$+139.3$	$+186.4$	$+194.0$	$+210.2$

resulting from the unavoidable appreciation of gold market prices in terms of the "reserve currencies" when their indebtedness feeds an excessive growth of foreign exchange reserves; 3) the creation of truly «international» fiduciary reserves, *i.e.* the «SDR holdings» and «reserve positions» of countries in the IMF.

Last, but not least, line II shows the growing role of the exchange standard in the mechanism of reserve creation: from 23% of gross reserves as of the end of 1949 to 92% today. Its pace of increase declined sharply from the 1970's ($745 billion) to the 1980's ($276 billion), but only because the enormous gold price increase of the 1980's ($494 billion) was followed by a decrease ($-$ $5 115 billion) in the 1980's. The other, and causal, component, *i.e.* the amount of foreign exchange reserves, increased on the contrary at a faster pace, from $248 billion in the 1970's to $390 billion in the 1980's.

Parts II and III of the table show the consequences of this mechanism upon the regional constellation of reserve claims and debts.

1.2 *The Results*

1) As far as fiduciary claims (part II) are concerned, the recorded results are at the opposite pole from common sense and from the goals often reiterated in pious resolutions of the Assembly of the United Nations: *a)* the Third World finances the industrial countries, at a level reaching $145 billion at the end of the 1970's and rising to $236 billion at the end of last year (see lines II); *b)* the poorest countries, *i.e.* the non-oil-exporting countries of the third world are by far the major creditors; *c)* the basic source of this insane lending pattern is the role of foreign exchange reserves, the other, but insignificant, SDR and IMF credit claims conforming, on the contrary, to the common sense prescription of the United Nations requiring the richest countries to lend to the poorer (see lines II B and II C); *d)* this pattern of net foreign exchange resefves is, of course, to be expected under the «exchange standard»: so-called "reserve currency countries" — especially the United States — have no need to accumulate reserves as long as they can settle their deficits with their own IOU's;

and the other countries have plenty of reasons to accumulate a large portion of their global reserves in interest-earning foreign exchange on them rather than in sterile — even costly — gold hoards. It is also, however, nonviable in the long run, not only because the growing indebtedness of reserve-center countries is bound, at some point, to instill bearish expectations about their currency and deter further purchases, but also because the "beneficiairy" (?) countries cannot stand forever the handicap of an increasing uncompetitiveness of their overvalued currency in world trade.

2) As far as gold holdings are concerned, the richer countries of the industrial world were, of course, the main reapers of the bookkeeping profits resulting from the huge increase of market gold prices and peaking at $496 billion at the end of the 1970s, but dropping to $380 billion at the end of the 1980s.

The share of the United States in these profits was far smaller than that of the other industrial countries whose gold holdings are now 2.5 times those of the United States, having more than quadrupled in volume from 1949 ($5.4 billion) to 1989 ($22.3 billion), while those of the United States dropped from $24.6 billion to $9.2 billion.

1.3 *The Link Between the Mechanism and the Results*

These observations bring us back to the core of the problem: the logical absurdity and disastrous results of the use of a new national currencies as the major, or sole, instrument of international monetary reserves.

1) The first shortcoming of this system is the basic asymmetry it creates in the settlement of balance-of-payments disequilibria. These normally redistribute unchanged international reserves between surplus and deficit countries, gradually imposing readjustment policies upon the latter as their reserves decline to unacceptably low levels. Contrariwise, the deficits of a reserve-center country may be financed mostly — or even overfinanced — by an increase of world foreign exchange reserves, with little or no decline of gross reserves for that reserve-center country and, therefore, no imperative pressure for the readjustment of inflationary policies.

2) The second shortcoming is that this process may easily degenerate into a self-feeding spiral of inflationary reserve increases, since these are themselves reinvested in the reserve centers and increase the ability of their leaders — official and private — to pursue inflationary policies for any purposes they may wish, even if often totally repulsive to the ultimate, unwitting, lenders.

The incomprehensible lack of awareness of this defect by virtually all economic analysts distorts calamitously their policy advice.

3) The third shortcoming is the stimulation of lending by poorer and less adequately capitalized countries to richer countries, far less dependent on foreign capital for their economic developent.

1.4 *The "Exchange Standard" Historical Debate*

The major political significance of the «gold exchange standard» of former times as well as of the «paper exchange standard» of today was clearly perceived nearly 200 years ago by Immanuel Kant in the fourth article of his *Perpetual Peace: A Philosophical Essay* (1795): no national debts shall be raised by a state to finance its foreign affairs: «No objection can be taken to seeking assistance, either within or without the State, on behalf of the economic administration of the country; such as, for the improvement of highways or in support of new colonies or in the establishment of resources against dearth and famine. A loan, whether raised externally or internally, as a source of aid in such cases, in above suspicion. But a credit system, when used by the powers as a hostile, antagonistic instrument against each other and when the debts under it go on increasing indefinitely and yet are always liquid for the present (because all the creditors are not expected to cash their claims at once), is a dangerous money power. This arrangement — the ingenious invention of a commercial people in this century [England] constitutes, in fact, a treasure for the carrying on of war; it may exceed the treasures of all the other States taken together, and it can only be exhausted by the forthcoming deficit of the exchequer — which, however, may be long delayed by the animation of the national commerce and its expansionist impact upon production and profits. The facility given by this system for engaging in war, combined with the inclination of rulers toward it (an inclination which seems to be implanted in human nature), is therefore a great obstacle in the way of a perpetual peace. The prohibition of it must be laid down as a preliminary article in the conditions of such a peace, even more strongly on the further ground that the national bankruptcy, which it inevitably brings at last, would necessarily involve in the disaster many other States without any fault of their own; and this would damage unjustly these other States. Consequently, the other States are justified in alying themselves against such a State and its pretensions».

The «Sterling exchange standard» continued to grow nevertheless in the 19th century with the expansion of the British empire, throughout which the national currencies of dominions and colonies were uniformly backed by — and issued against — equivalent claims on the Bank of England.

The extension of this practice to independant foreign countries was cleverly argued by UK participants at the international monetary conferences called in Brussels, Geneva, etc. to tackle the shortage of gold — at its former prices in national currencies — as legal reserve requirement for national money supplies vastly increased by wartime inflation and postwar reconstruction. It was never legally agreed at these conferences, whose concluding remarks had to record the dire warnings issued by various delegates, particularly by the Belgian Prime Minister and Minister of Finance, Léon Delacroix, who argued forcefully for an alternative solution, more necessary today than ever, to end the scandalous abuses of any unbridled «exchange standard»: the creation of an «international institute of issue and control» which "would operate, in the first place, as a vast clearing-house of exchange. It would make all possible use of compensation and would superintend the settlement of all transactions... In so far as compensation would be impossible and especially for the purpose of settling temporary differences... the Institute will permit the liquidation of transactions by the issue of «gold bond» (anticipating by more than a quarter of the century Keynes' proposed "bancors").

In the failure of agreement on Delacroix's proposals as well as the British and any other ones, the «gold-exchange standard» grew considerably throughout the 1920's. The Gold Commission of the League of Nations was still debating its defects and vulnerability when events confirmed the fears of the critics. The gold-convertibility of the pound Sterling had to be suspended on September 21, 1931, its foreign indebtedness having grown far beyond its dwindling gold reserves. The huge exchange losses encurred as a result by various foreign central banks exceeded, of course, the interest-earnings that had led them to accumulate Sterling assets as reserves, and they all returned for a while to a strict «gold bullion standard» obviously too deflationary to be tenable in the long run, and replaced in fact, following the second world war, by a «dollar standard» whose functioning and results have been analyzed above (paragraph 1.1 and 1.2).

Jacques Rueff, Fritz Machlup and myself were the most profligate critics of the system, fundamentally in agreement about its defects, but with basic differences of emphasis and in proposals for reform.

Rueff and I were primarily concerned with the disastrous shortcomings of the huge foreign exchange component of international monetary reserves, while Machlup earmarked most of his sarcasm for the logical absurdity of its gold component.

Rueff, however, argued for a pure «gold standard» from which all fiduciary reseves would be eliminated and replaced, to avoid an unbearable, deflationary reserve shortage, by a once-and-for-all increase in the price of gold. I vainly tried to convince him that this solution was a will-o'-the wisp, since you could not erase from the memory of our policy-makers the knowledge that they could impose on the public the absorption of enormous amounts of paper money, far beyond what they would have dreamed possible in the days of the gold standard. Even if a particular government might be willing to give up such a convenient policy tool, none could commit its successors to renounce it for ever.

Machlup and I were in complete agreement about the ideal system: 1) the adoption of a single reserve instrument, in the form of truly international reserve deposits with the International Monetary Fund; 2) the adjustment of reserve creation to the requirements of optimal, feasible growth rate, .*i.e.* in a presumed range of 3% to 5%, through a similar rate of growth of the IMS net loans and investments' portfolio; 3) the earmarking of these loans and investments for agreed high priority objectives, among which the financing of development in the less capitalized countries, but also others, such as the fight against pollution, contagious diseases, etc. (Such objectives should be contrasted with those that have predominated the "exchange standard": the financing of the Vietnam war and of the explosion of military expenditures).

1.5 *The Richest Country of the World Becomes its Major Borrower*

Most of this analysis and of these conclusions are identical to those on which an intellectual — if not political — consensus was reached in June 1974 by Jeremy Morse's Committee of Twenty, after ten years of continuous debates and negotiation between Finance Ministers, Governors of central banks and their experts.

About sixteen years went by, however, without any agreement on a reform deemed as urgent as essential for the restoration of an orderly monetary system. Why?

One of the main obstacles was obviously the reluctance of short-sighted US politicians to abandon the "extravagant privilege" denounced by Président de Gaulle: the possibility of financing most of the US deficits through the acceptance of the national US currency as an international settlements medium by foreign central banks, commercial banks and other large international investors. This, however, was to be expected: it reduced the US need for unpopular tax increases or reductions of expenditures, even if contrary to the longer-run national interest.

I would put the major blame, therefore, on the other countries for being willing to extend persistently such financing to the US, in increasingly huge amounts, at the cost of a world inflation without precedent in man's history. But how can this be explained?

First of all, by bureaucratic routine, the negotiating difficulties of agreeing on an alternative world currency to be created *ex nihilo*, and the reluctance of foreign firms in competition with US firms at home or abroad to abandon the advantage derived by them from the resulting overvaluation of the dollar.

Secondly because the disadvantages of such financing are confined primarily to a few countries with huge surpluses, primarily Japan and Germany.

The June 1990 OECD Economic Outlook estimates show that as much as 80% of the reported $763 million US deficits of the last six years (1984-1989) were financed by these two countries: $394 billion (52%) by Japan and $5 212 billion (28%) by Germany. Other countries, except the so-called NIC's (newly industrialized Asian countries), were in deficit, or had only moderate surpluses. They felt no strong interest in abandoning their overcompetitiveness vis-à-vis the United States.

Table III totalizes the OECD space estimates for these six years and reorganizes them in a manner designed to highlight the share of major country groups and of each industrial country in total and net world surpluses and deficits. The concentration on a few countries only is striking, Japan, the Asian NICs and Germany accounting for 82% of the surpluses and the United States alone for 61% of the deficits.

I have ventured, however, to eliminate in my Table the $360 billion statistical discrepancy of reported estimates by deducting from the US deficits the amounts mentioned in the explanatory note of page 38 as due to a reporting convention used only by the United States and which will be corrected in future publications.

With this correction, deficits are shown only for the countries of the Third World (− $217 billion) and appropriately equated to the surpluses (+ $217 billion) of the industrial world, and the US deficits drastically reduced from $763 billion to $403 billion, still nearly double, however, those of the 160 countries of the Third World taken together!

Last, but far from least, the acquiescence of central banks and other official institutions to such enormous and persistent financing of US external deficits is the political counterpart of their countries' dependence on the US nuclear umbrella as a crucial contribution to their own defense against Soviet aggression or blackmail. US defense expenditure averaged 6.25% of GNP over the last six years (1984-1989) as against little more than 3% in Germany and 1% in Japan. These two countries recognized that this was the main explanation both of their enormous balance-of-payments surpluses ($606

TABLE 3

WORLD NETWORK OF CURPENT ACCOUNT SURPLUSES AND DEFICITS = NET CAPITAL EXPORTS OR IMPORTS: 1984-1989

Surplus = net capital exports

	$ billions	% of world
I. Industrial world	886	100
a. Outside Europe	517	58
Japan	394	44
Major Asian NICS	123	14
b. USSR and Eastern Countries	75	8
c. Western Europe	294	33
1) European Communities	256	29
Germany	212	24
Netherlands	30	3
Belgium and Luxembourg	14	2
2) Switzerland	38	4
II. Third world	—	—
III. World	886	100

Deficit = net capital imports | **Region's net**

	Deficit $ billions	Deficit % of world	Region's net $ billions	Region's net % of world
I. Industrial world	− 669	76	+ 217	+ 24
a. Outside Europe	− 512	58	+ 5	+ 1
United States	− 403	45		
Australia	− 51	7		
Canada	− 39	4		
New Zewland	− 9	1		
b. Europe	− 157	18	+ 212	+ 24
1) European Communities	− 126	14	+ 130	+ 15
United Kingdom	− 60	7		
Italy	− 23	3		
Denmark	− 15	2		
Greece	− 12	1		
France	− 10	1		
Spain	− 6	1		
Ireland	− 1	—		
Portugal	—	—		
2) Other countries	− 31	3	+ 82(*)	+ 9
Finland	− 11	1		
Sweden	− 10	1		
Norway	− 6	1		
Turkey	− 2	1		
Austria	− 1	—		
Iceland	− 1	—		
II. Third world	− 217	24	− 217	+ 24
OPEC	− 49	6		
Other	− 168	19		
Asia	− 86	10		
Latin America	− 51	6		
Africa	− 31	3		
III. World	− 885	100	×	100

(*) including USSR and Eastern Countries.

Source: Oᴇᴄᴅ: *Economic Outlook*, no. 47, June. 1990, Tables 84 on p. 172-73, on p. 164 and R20 on p. 213.

billion) and of the similarly enormous deficits of the United States ($763 billion) (1). They accepted therefore the US argument that they should invest most of their surpluses in such a way as to finance the disproportionate contribution of the US to the world defense expenditures jointly regarded by all of them as essential to face the threat of USSR aggression or blackmail.

They hardly could, however, convince their parliaments and public opinion to increase domestic taxation — or reduce expenditures — in order to subsidize the enormous budgetary deficits of the richest country in the world. It was much easier, politically, to ask their central banks to absorb the dollar overflows in the private market, and to encourage thereby their commercial banks and other large investors to invest also in the United States. This would preserve, or even increase, the exchange rate overvaluation of the dollar and its undercompetitiveness vis-à-vis foreign contries' exporters and importers in would markets.

This is undoubtedly the main explanation of foreing acceptance of huge and persistent accumulation of paper dollar claims, as long as the US favored such discrimination against itself in world markets, including the US domestic market itself, in order to prevent a fall of the dollar exchange rates. At some point, however, US trade lobbies would rebel against this unfair handicap and force the Administration to readjust downward the overvalued dollar rates. This could always be achieved easily by official declarations "talking down" the dollar supplemented if necessary by official market sales of paper dollars whose issue could be increased at will by the US authorities.

This explains the fantastic fluctuations of US exchange rates, totally unrelated — or even opposite — to the evolution of the balance of payments on current account. Its rate vis-à-vis the main rival currency, the deutshe mark, thus moved from 2.82 marks per dollar in March 1973 to 1.71 in Juanuary 1980, 3.47 in February 1985, and record lows of less than 1.50 at the end of 1990.

---

(1) The difference between these recorded surplus and deficit estimates being explained by other countries' surpluses, but mostly by unexplained "errors" and omissions. (Table 3).

2. - Political Imperatives

The enormity of world military expenditures, guesstimated today at about $1,000 per year — of which more than $300 billion for the United States alone — is undoubtedly the major source of the inprecedented economic, financial and monetary disequilibria confronting us all today in our daily life. They reflect, of course, all too understandable and legitimate concerns for national security, highlighted in the old slogan: «*si vis pacem, para bellum*» (2).

This slogan may have had some validity in former days, when the economic and human costs of military aggression might be deemed outweighed by the conjectured benefits of territorial conquest and occupation. It has, however, become merely absurd since any conceivable benefits of this sort must now be measured against the risks of nuclear escalation and mutual assured destruction, baptized "MAD" by its proponents themselves.

Yet, until very recently, the mass media, financed by the "military-industrial complexes" denounced by President Eisenhower in his farewell address as a major threat to democracy, continue to divide the world simplistically into two opposite camps: the peace-mongering nations — their own, of course, and their allies — and the warmongering ones: imperial America for the USSR and, for the United States, the "evil empire" of Soviet Russia and its subjugated nations.

Public opinion was led thereby to accept an over-rearmament race under which the United States sought its security, and that of its allies, thorugh the military superiority of NATO over the *Warsaw Pact*, and the USSR sought its own security, and that of its allies, through the military superiority of the *Warsaw Pact* over NATO. Needless to say, they could not both succeed simultaneously, and the race went on uselessly therefore with two consequences: 1) worldwide inflation, since military expenditures increase spendable incomes without any parallel increase of available goods and services on which they can be spent, nor of the real wealth from which taxes can be

---

(2) «If you wish peace, prepare for war!».

levied; 2) the growing threat of "preventive" aggression by the power deeming itself in danger of losing the race, or of miscalculation by either superpower of the other's intentions, such as — reportedly — the radar misreading of a flight of birds, etc. This diminished, rather than strengthened, the security of both and their allies.

As for the — approximately 180 — countries other than the two superpowers, most of them were resigned to seek their national security in military alliances subordinating their pretended national sovereignty to the hegemony of either of the two superpowers, and accepting in all but in name the status of "satellites", or "protectorates" complying more or less supinely with the policies of their protector. Worst of all, they could not but be aware that the "nuclear umbrella" protecting them was far more likely to remain unused, or to be used only over their territory rather than over the territory of their protectors, in view of the understandable reluctance of these to accept the risk of mutual destruction of their own military bases and population centers.

In the meantime, the "cold" war of the superpowers continued to entail a multiplicity of "hot" foreign an civil wars for the satellite countries of the Third World, with millions of military casualties and death from starvation.

Who could doubt the longing of statesmen and of public opinion for switching from this suicidal and inflationary over-rearmament race to a mutual reduction of overbloated defense expenditures, enabling a joint pursuit of optimal rates of real rather than nominal GNP gowth, and of leisure time compatible with decent living standards? (3). Yet this commonly shared goal would remain inaccessible through mere negotiations as long as each persisted on negotiating only from strength, as adamantly advised by the "hawks", in the United States as well as in the USSR.

It is of course true that it takes two to preserve peace, but only one to impose war on both. The old observation of Clemenceau is still

---

(3) Reducing thereby unemployment rates for the richer countries, and enabling the poorer ones to approximate living standards obviously unattainable for the world as a whole if the former continue to devote productivity increases to material consumption, such as two, or more cars per household, etc.

valid: war is too serious an affair to be left to the generals, and disarmament negotiations are bound to fail — as they have indeed for nearly 60 years, since the 1929 Aristide Briand initiative in the League of Nations — as long as politicians feel bound to leave them in the hands of their military establishment experts. The switch from a costly and dangerous over-rearmament race to a mutual race toward disarmament could be initiated unilaterally, without any danger whatsoever, by either of the two superpowers if their statesmen and public opinion recognized at long last that the time-worm slogan of «*si vis pacem, para bellum!*» should be replaced today by President Rooveselt's slogan: «the only thing to fear is fear itself!». Since each of the protagonists was suddiciently armed atomically to destroy several scores of times every citizen of the opponent country, it could safely afford to reduce its overflowing arsenal by a few percents, or much more, and hope that his protagonist would follow suit.

The opponents of such a disarmament race, in the United States as well as the Soviet Union, long continued nevertheless to argue that this was a Utopian and dangerous dream because the other country could not be trusted to give up its over-rearmament policies; and their military allies, in NATO as well as in the Warsaw Pact, remained equally anxious to preserve the nuclear umbrella of their "protector".

Having visited together more than 90 countries, my wife and I have discovered a universal truth that should obviously be — but rarely is — incorporated in all textbooks about international politics: in every country, public opinion and mass media are persuaded that the danger of war comes from some other country, but never from their own. This obviously, cannot be true.

The truth is that there exists in every country two types of minds: *a)* those who feel insecure, and seek their security in making sure that they are stronger than their feared opponent or opponents. But this inevitably means that the latter will feel insecure, and leads therefore to a dangerous re-armament race, or even to pre-emptive aggression; *b)* those who understand that their own security can best be guaranteed by the security of their conceivable opponents.

Drastic cuts in military expenditures should, at long last, prove feasible in the disarmament negotiations between the two superpowers. These, however, are likely to tarry, or even fail, if they are left in the hands of military negotiators (4). The switch from an inflationary and lethal over-rearmament race to a mutual race toward disarmament should be initiated, even umilaterally at the start, by either of the major protagonists without endangering in any way its own security. An MIT (Massachusetts Institute of Technology) committee report to President Reagan concluded in June 1987, that «the superpowers could achieve their goal of deterring attacks with drastically fewer nuclear arms. . . since a limited attack on the United States, involving only one percent of the Soviet strategic nuclear arsenal, could set off a collapse of the US economy that would last decades . . . The Soviet Union is even more vulnerable» (5).

This would mean that either of them could slash its present nuclear arsenal even by as much as 99% — let us say 50 to 90% — and hope that the other would follow suit.

2.1 *A Pax Russo-Americana?*

The Gorbachev Revolution should, at long last, usher in a new era of peace and cooperation, eliminating hundreds of billions of dollars per year of military waste, and permitting both: 1) the reduction of global expenditures to a non-inflationary level; and 2) an enormous increase in the financing of productive investments, particularly for the less capitalized countries of the Third World.

The implications of this revolution for international monetary reform were spelled out as constructively as concretely in the unprecedented and revolutionary statement of the delegate from the USSR Institute of World Economics, Dr. D.V. Smyslov, at the Round Table East-West Conference on *The Future of the Global Economic and Monetary System*, held at Szirak (Hungary) on August 28-29, 1988 (6).

In brief, Dr. Smyslov's paper repudiated the former USSR call for a return to gold, and asserted that the policy of the new administra-

---

(4) As convincingly argued by Alva Myrdal in numerous publications.

(5) See the summary provided on June 22, 1987 by our best, truly global newspaper: *The International Herald Tribune.*

(6) Edited by M. Szabó-Pelsöczi, with Foreword by Robert Triffin, Institute for World Economics of the Hungarian Academy of Sciences, Budapest, 1990.

tion was to seek full participation in worldwide monetary, financial and economic groupings and institutions, such as the International Monetary Fund, the World Bank, GATT, etc. This, however, should entail the fundamental reforms long advocated by Triffin for the international monetary system, particularly the replacement of the dollar by a truly international monetary unit.

Moreover, Russia was also ready to use the ECU as an alternative to the SDR, especially if the United States' opposition continued to delay the worldwide reforms deemed necessary by most other countries, and particularly by the European Community.

These proposals have been encapsulated since in President Gorbachev's call for a common «European house», encompassing the United States as a stabilizing element (7), and expanding the European Community, as foreseen by President de Gaulle, from the Atlantic to the Urals.

President Delors has suggested instead the name of «European village» for the forthcoming association of a «USSR House» and a «European Community house» that would obviously include the former statellites of the defunct *Warsaw Pact* (8).

3. - The Internationalization of the Exchange Standard

I have indefatigably and endlessly reiterated for more than thirty years the obvious rudiments of a rational world monetary system, substantially endorsed in the swan song of Jeremy Morse's Committee of Twenty, after ten years of debates and negotiations between Ministers of Finance, Governors of Central Banks and their economic advisers (9).

International monetary reserves should be held exclusively — except possibly for modest and strictly limited amounts of working

---

(7) Assuaging, e.g., European fears of the predominant might of the newly reunified Germany.

(8) See the Statement on the broad lines of Commission Policy of President Delors to the European Parliament at Strasbourg on 17 and 18 January 1989, p. 18.

(9) See IMF: *International Monetary Reform. Documents of the Committee of Twenty*, 1974.

funds — in the form of International Reserve Deposits (IRD for short) with the IMF rather than in gold, national reserve currencies, Special Drawing Rights and Reserve Positions with the Fund, as is the case today.

IRD transfers would therefore become also the only way for Central Banks to settle overall balance-of-payments surpluses or deficits on current and capital accounts; and the IMF would become a clearing house, through which bilateral surpluses and deficits could cancel each other, leaving only a much smaller multilateral net surplus or deficit to be financed through a gain or loss of IRD reserves.

Clearing houses were, of course, the ancestors from which Central Banks developed gradually and naturally in the nineteenth century. Could one expect, therefore, a similar evolution of the IMF from a world clearing house into a world Central Bank?

Yes, as far as credits are concerned, including the famous "lending of last resort" which is one of the main functions of Central Banks. The universal acceptance of IRDs would enable the IMF to extend unlimited credits to its members. I have suggested that it would be necessary, therefore, to reassure prospective surplus (creditor) countries against inflationary IMF policies by inserting in its statutes a presumptive limitation to a growth rate of, let us say, 3% to 5% yearly the Fund's ability to increase world reserves through the expansion of its loans and investments portfolio.

Overenthusiastic followers, however, as well as dire critics of what they regarded as my naïve Utopianism misinterpreted this proposed clearing house as a World Central Bank. I had to disabuse them repeatedly in this respect by pointing out that I regarded it as wildly premature to imagine that it could play on a world scale the third and essential function of a full-fledged Central Bank, *i.e.* to create a world currency, or even to guarantee the enduring stability of exchange rates between the national currencies of all member countries (10).

---

(10) See, for instance, my answer to Senator Paul H. Douglas, Chairman of the Joint Economic Committee, in *Gold and the Dollar Crisis*, first edition, Yale University Press, May 1960, and my article «A Tardy Autopsy of the Keynes Plan for an International Clearing Union: its Merits and Drawbacks» in ALAIN BARRÈRE (ed.): *Keynesian Economic Policies*, Macmillan, 1990.

The 3% to 5% presumption mentioned above should normally prevent the wild inflationary and deflationary disorders typical of — and flowing from — the old gold exchange as well as the present paper exchange standard. It could, however, be set aside by special majority vote under exceptional circumstances such as, for instance, the two explosions of oil prices in 1973 and 1979.

The worldwide monetary reforms just outlined would serve the national long-term interests of the United States as well as of the rest the world, but are adamantly resisted: *a)* by powerful politicians benefiting from the "extravagant privilege" denounced by President de Gaulle and enabling them to elude unpopular tax increases or reductions of expenditures and *b)* by private interest groups profiting from the hegemony of the dollar in the investment of foreign exchange reserves and other working funds.

The resumption of the aborted negotiations concerning the fundamental international monetary reforms deemed essential and urgent by the Committee of Twenty, sixteen years ago, continues to be repeatedly shelved by the "summit meetings" of the major financial powers. Attention is centered instead on the discussion of exchange rates, the United States expecting other countries to defend the rate of the dollar whenever it wishes to prevent its depreciation, but without forgoing the possibility to "talk" or force it down whenever it deems it preferable in order to reduce its foreign deficits and fight otherwise insuperable protectionist lobbying pressures by firms and trade unions threatened by bankruptcy and unemployment (11).

Other countries should obviously do whatever they can to stimulate and facilitate the participation of the United States in the restoration of a worldwide monetary order by using — as suggested by an old American slogan — both "the carrot and the stick": *a)* the "carrot" by couching their own reforms and policies in a manner susceptible of contributing to the solution of the US dollar problem as well as to minimize, as far as possible, their present overdependence

---

(11) See, for instance, a March 24, 1987 speech of H. Robert Heller, Governor of the Federal Reserve Board, pointing out that: «entire industries have disappeared in the United States during the period of the dollar rise, while new ones were created in the countries whose currency depreciated». The rise of the previously non-existent Japanese car industry is a case in point.

on the vagaries of the dollar; *b)* the "stick" by denying the US the "extravagant privilege" of financing the perpetuation of US policies prejudicial to all concerned.

The countries of the European Community are best able to take the leadership in such regional aggrements, as outlined in section IV below.

4. - Regional Monetary Cooperation

4.1 *Its Usefulness as a Complement to Worldwide Cooperation*

Regional monetary cooperation should not be viewed simply as a temporary second-best to worldwide cooperation, pending full US participation in the latter. It should also permanently supplement worldwide cooperation by exploiting as fully as possible other opportunities for fuller mutual cooperation and commitments negotiable only among closely interdependent countries, united by common traditions or forced by history to accept the hegemony of a powerful neighbor.

The present oligocentric world political, military, economic, financial and monetary system is obviously far from ideal in this respect. It should be reformed, but will never disappear entirely. In the monetary field as in others, all powers should not be concentrated at the top, but distributed between the center and various groups and subgroups as they are indeed, even in relatively homogeneous countries, between provinces, cantons, shires, departments, municipalities, etc.

As for the IMF, it should reserve its limited time and competence to deal with problems insoluble at a lower level, leaving it for instance to the EMF to deal with payments problems between France and Germany, to the CMEA to deal with those between Hungary and Rumania, and to other similar continental, and particularly sub-continental groups in Asia, Africa, and the Pacific, to deal with those among their members.

Such a decentralization of the defunct Bretton Woods system would help rally to it both many disaffected countries of the Third World and non-member countries of the Communist World.

4.2 *The European Community*

4.2.1 The First Twenty Yars (1958-1978):
Paralysis of the European Drive

Paradoxically, the first twenty years of the European Community were marked by an enormous regression of European monetary cooperation. The United Kingdom argued that the very success of the European payments union should spell its termination in favor of a worldwide restoration of convertibility, based as before primarily on the pound and the dollar as the main intruments of international settlements and reserve accumulation, and eliminating therefore the EPU unit-of-account as a rival of Sterling.

The EPU was replaced by the EMA (European Monetary Agreement) under which most clearing transactions were returned to the private market, and credit provisions no longer included partial automatic financing of *intra*-European balance-of-payments deficits by the countries in surplus. Offical cooperation centered mostly on international consultation and cooperation of central banks through the International Monetary Fund, the Group of Ten and the BIS (Bank for International Settlements) and mutual swap agreements with the Federal Reserve System (12).

A momentous new step toward European monetary union was expected from the first Summit Meeting of Heads of State or Government at The Hague in December 1969. Jean Monnet, the Father of Europe, had convinced Willy Brandt to call such a meeting to create a European Reserve Fund, with which Central Banks would be required to hold an agreed portion of their international monetary reserves: 20% initially, rising gradualy to 100% at the final stage of full monetary union (13).

---

(12) See the admirable booklet of ABRAHAMS J.P. - LEMINEUR-TOUWSEND C. on *The European Monetary Choices, 1950-1980*, reproducing their April 1981 article in the «Cahiers de la Faculté des Sciences Economiques et Sociales de Namur».

(13) I helped Jean Monnet prepare for Chancelor Brandt the necessary documentation, which neither the Bundesbank nor the Ministry of Finance was willing to provide him. See my «Note sur ma Collaboration avec Jean Monnet» in *Temoignages à la Mémoire de Jean Monnet*, Fondation Jean Monnet pour l'Europe, 9 novembre 1989, pp. 529-34, particularly p. 532.

This simple, concrete and immediately practical proposal was, unfortunately "kicked upstairs" into a more ambitious proposal for full "monetary union" subject, however, to preliminary, transitory provisions extending over ten years, and spelled out in the 1970 Werner plan: the gradual elimination of exchange margins and *de facto* stabilization of exchange rates.

Ten, and even twenty years have elapsed without full implementation of these provisions.

4.2.2 The Resumption of European Negotiations: Copenhagen 1978

The resumption of the drive toward European monetary unity can be dated from the 1978 IMF meeting at Copenhagen. It should be credited primarily to three statesmen and their experts: Roy Jenkins (assisted by Michael Emerson) from the European Community, Helmut Schmidt (and Horst Schulmann) from Germany and Valéry Giscard d'Estaing (and Bernard Clappier) from France (14). Their intellectual agreement led with amazing rapidity to the adoption of the European Monetary System in March 1979.

4.2.3 The European Monetary System: 1979-1990

The EMS has two basic objectives: 1) as long as different national rates of inflation cannot be (?) evened, to stabilize *Real* exchange rates of currencies through appropriate realignments of their nominal rates; 2) to reduce as sharply as possible national rates of inflation, thus making it possible to preserve also the stability of nominal rates.

---

(14) The former Chairman of the IMF, Jean-Paul Schweitzer, should also be mentioned for his courageous denunciation at the Annual Meeting of 1970 of the inflationary excesses of paper dollar accumulation by central banks, his daring assertion of «the need for the United States to settle its balance of payments with primary reserve assets... [and] to make a contribution toward a general realignment of currencies,... suggesting [in effect] that the dollar be devalued». This speech was widely applauded by the audience, but prompted his dismissal by President Richard M. Nixon, as well as his two successive secretaries of the Treasury, John B. Connally and George P. Shultz, on the expiration of Mr. Schweitzer's second term in 1973.

A first indication of its performance was the fact that realignments between the participating currencies could be agreed promptly within brief week-end meeting and have become much sparser in number and importance.

For the seven major fully participating countries that form the core of the system, the average pace of inflation — measured by cost-of-living indices — were large and very disparate in the first four years (March 1979 - March 1983), but were slashed down in the last seven years (March 1983 - March 1990) to a range of from about one fifth for the Netherlands to less than one third for Italy. Consequently, the realignment of nominal exchange rates vis-à-vis the ECU dropped also to a yearly average of from plus 1.19% for Germany and the Netherland's to minus 1.12% for Italy, compared to from plus 3.34% for Germany to minus 4.30% for Italy (Table 4).

This progress toward price and exchange rate stability contrasts sharply with the smaller progress of the United Kingdom and the United States in this respect, but especially with the switch from appreciation to depreciation for the exchange rate of the pound sterling and particularly the dollar.

It is unanimously agreed today that the EMS has succeeded, far beyond the hopes of even its most fervent advocates, to perform the essential function of any exchange-rate system, i.e. to stabilize real exchange rates within the European Community at competitive levels consonant with desirable capital movements from its more developed to its less develped participating countries.

This should assuage the initial fears which prompted the national central banks of most of the Community countries — particularly the German Bundesbank — to oppose faster progress toward European monetary union because this might force the surplus countries to extend inflationary financing to partner countries unable to avoid excessive or persistent balance-of-payments deficits.

These fears have proved totally unfounded, enabling me to spare the reader a description of the complicated provisions of EMS for mutual financing designed to avoid, minimize or postpone exchange-rate realignments. "Medium-term financial assistance" and "short-term monetary support" were never used at all. Only "very short-term monetary support" was resorted to occasionally, for relatively insig-

TABLE 4

PROGRESS TOWARD EUROPEAN MONETARY UNITY: 1979-1990
(% changes)

Country	Realignment of nominal exchange rates				Cost of living increases			
	Total		Yearly Average		Total		Yearly Average	
	1979-1983	1983-1990	1979-1983	1983-1990	1979-1983	1983-1990	1979-1983	1983-1990
Germany	+ 13.34	+ 8.32	+ 3.34	+ 1.19	21.94	11.19	5.49	1.60
Netherlands	+ 9.01	+ 8.30	+ 2.25	+ 1.19	23.79	8.03	5.95	1.15
Belgium	− 11.06	+ 4.85	− 2.77	+ 0.69	34.48	22.30	8.62	3.19
Luxembourg	− 11.06	+ 4.85	− 2.77	+ 0.69	36.49	18.37	9.12	2.62
Denmark	− 11.91	+ 3.05	− 2.98	+ 0.44	47.86	33.71	11.97	4.82
France............	− 14.64	+ 0.01	− 3.66	—	57.42	30.08	14.36	4.30
Italy.............	− 17.21	− 7.84	− 4.30	− 1.12	90.55	59.01	22.64	8.43
Ireland	− 7.59	− 6.45	− 1.90	− 0.92	84.39	146.00	21.10	20.86
Greece	− 21.96	− 60.33	− 5.49	− 8.62	126.20	195.19	31.55	27.88
Portugal					115.23	154.46	28.81	22.07
Spain					69.96	62.95	17.49	8.99
United Kingdom					49.92	41.98	12.48	6.14
United States......					37.19	29.16	9.30	4.17
Switzerland					37.87	43.26	9.47	6.18
Japan					18.27	10.13	4.57	0.65

nificant amounts — totalling rarely more than 2 billion ECUs — and promptly repaid each time.

This is due, however, to the fact that countries resorted relatively little to the treaty provisions for compulsory financing of so-called "marginal" interventions whenever their exchange-rates reached 2.25% above or below their agreed bilateral central rate vis-à-vis any other member currency, except the Italian lira whose margin was provisionally enlarged to 6%, and the pound sterling which entered the system only in November 1990.

Most interventions were "intra-marginal" and financed, as previously, in dollars, rather than in ECUs or member currencies.

4.3 *Future Perspectives*

The repeatedly reaffirmed objective of full economic and monetary union is inseparable of course from political union, and raises therefore crucially difficult problems of implementation, geographic scope, and relationships with other parts of the world.

4.3.1 Cooperation in the Solution of the International Dollar Crisis

What is most certain in this regard is that it should and would eliminate the hegemony of the US paper dollar in future European settlements and reserve accumulation, which should take place instead in ECUs or IRSs.

This would aggravate enormously the international crisis of the dollar if the Community did not insert its own policies and institutional development within the world framework, as stressed in the preceding section of this paper. The fulfillment of its economic and monetary union should therefore be seen as a way to cooperate far more effectively than would be possible otherwise to solve the dollar problem.

It would, first of all, enable the monetary authorities of a United Europe to sterilize in the forms of "consols" the vast overhang of short-term dollar indebtedness inherited from former US balance-of-payments deficits and threatening at any time a collapse of the dollar on the world exchange markets. Such "consols" could recover the prestigious attraction which they held in the nineteenth century, if the US agreed to convert into ECUs or into the creditor's currency, the deposits and securities now denominated in paper dollars and held more and more reluctantly. Such "consols", escaping exchange risk, would be a most appropriate form of investment for the European Federal Reserve Banks, for commercial banks and for other firms and individuals, and require lower interest rates than present dollar obligations.

Secondly, the European monetary authorities should admit that the United States cannot possibly eliminate overnight its huge internal (budgetary) and external deficits. They should therefore, agree to accumulate themselves some further amount of US consols over the next two or three years, and encourage other official institutions (including the IMF), firms and individuals to do the same as long as the US authorities commit themselves to implement jointly agreed programs in this respect.

4.3.2 The Three Stages of the *Delors Plan*

As far as the European Community is concerned, three stages are envisaged in the *Delors Plan*, approved by the European Council meeting in Dublin on June 25 and 26, 1990.

Its first phase should center on a greater convergence of the economic and monetary policies of member countries and a much more rigorous coordination of their decision-making authorities. Notable in this respect is the appointment in August 1990 by the Committee of Governors of Central Banks of six top-level experts to form the core of the research department of the forthcoming European Central Bank.

The second — least clearly delineated — stage should center on the parachievement of such a European Central Bank, on a federal model inspired by German as well as American experience, and promoting the use of the ECU: *a)* as a "parallel currency" substitute for the dollar in international settlements; and *b)* as an alternative for present national currencies in domestic transactions.

Numerous policy statements of government leaders — such as Mrs Thatcher, at one extreme and Chancelor Kohl, at the other — have made it clear that a core of countries are determined to proceed fairly rapidly in this direction, leaving the door open for other countries, particularly the United Kingdom, to join them later, but refusing to accept any veto from them.

The unification of Germany is accelerating this progress, now seen as indispensable to build a European Germany rather than a German Europe.

Two intergovernmental conferences have been convened: *a)* to discuss the Treaty amendments necessary for the completion of economic and monetary union and to be ratified by national Parliaments before the end of 1992; and *b)* to start work on the development of the Community into political union.

4.3.3 An Irrevocable Stabilization of Exchange Rates or a Single European Currency?

Sceptics and opponents never tire to repeat the obvious, i.e. the difficulties — or even impossibility? — to surmount a major obstacle: the unwillingness of national political and financial leaders to accept the mergers of sovereignties enrailed in the harmonization of budgetary and monetary policies indispensable to the irrevocable stabilization of exchange rates.

Fifteen exchange-rate realignments have indeed been deemed necessary, over the twelve years of functioning of the EMS (March 1979-March 1991) to restore sufficient equilibrium in their balances of payments to avoid: *a)* excessive or persistent financing of the countries in deficit by the countries in surplus; *b)* and, as a result, an averaging of inflation rates unacceptable to the latter.

Germany refuses, understandably and rightly, to run the risk of becoming the "milk cow" *(vache à lait)* of inflationary Community partners! It recognizes that the EMS, as it now operates, has succeeded beyond the highest hopes of its advocates, and contrary to the dire predictions of its initial opponents — such as the Bundesbank — to achieve the most essential role of any exchange-rate system, i.e. to stabilize real exchange rates between participating currencies, in contrast to the huge and erratic fluctuations of other currencies, particularly the dollar, vis-à-vis the ECU. The opponents of ECU, on the other hand, use this very success as an argument to be satisfied with the present system and to give up the ambition of stabilizing nominal exchange rates.

Yet, the stabilization of nominal exchange rates appears far more possible today than would have been imagined at the inception of the EMS.

The size and disparity of the realignments vis-à-vis the ECU deemed necessary over twelve years of existence of the EMS ranged in the first four years (March 1979-March 1983) from about plus 13% for Germany and 9% for the Netherlands to minus 11% for Belgium and Luxembourg, 12% for Denmark, 15% for France and 17% for Italy, but in the following seven years (March 1983-March 1990) only plus 8% for both Germany and the Netherlands 5% for Belgium and Luxembourg, 3% for Denmark and 0.01% for France to minus 6% for Ireland and 8% for Italy (15).

The countries most determinated to progress toward European unity thus accept today as realistic the stabilization of exchange rates entailed in monetary union.

Most people, however, still regard such stabilization as fully equivalent to the merger of national currencies into a single currency. In reality, the advantages of a merger would be enormous: *a)* obviously, by eliminating the billions of national currency units unnecessarily wasted today in settling daily transactions among residents of different participating countries (16); *b)* but also making it possible to elicit from the general publc stabilizing capital movements from the countries in surplus to the countries in deficit. The opposite is most often the case today, because mere proclamations of intention by central banks and government officials fail to convince the public that exchange-rate fluctuations are no longer possible, or even probable.

---

(15) See Table 4, p. 4.

(16) Last estimated at between 13 to 19 billion ECUs, i.e. about 0.5% of GDP per year for the Community as a whole, and up to 1% for smaller member States. Even more significant is the estimate that the decrease of exchange risks would stimulate a reduction of 0.5% in the rate of return demanded by market investors and lead thereby to real output gains accumulating over time to 5% of the Community's GDP.

The replacement of national currencies by the ECU would be much more difficult to reverse and should incite capital movements to respond primarily, or even exclusively, to interest-rate differentials. Central banks could be relied upon to push official rates in the desired direction if market forces alone did not do so sufficiently; c) last, but not least, the promoters of European political union would obviously regard a single currency as a vital symbol of such a union.

The actual pace of progress toward European monetary and political integration, as well as its punctual successes and failures, will be determined primarily in the future as they have in the past, by the ability of France and Germany to lead the process through bilateral policy cooperation and institutional agreements which other Community countries are invited to join at their own pace, but with no veto from any of them, even Britain.

A first momentous step in this direction was taken in 1963 by a Franco-German treaty between President de Gaulle and Chancellor Adenauer. A second was the signing, in 1988, of two additional protocols creating a Defense and Security Council and an Economic and Financial Council.

Continuous progress has emerged since then from the bimestrial meetings between the President of France and the Chancellor of Germany, and is now expected to accelerate as a result of the reunification of Germany in October 1990. Everybody agrees that a European Germany is now the only possible alternative to a German Europe, and that full economic and monetary union should be achieved before January 1, 1993.

APPENDIX

Comparison with IFS Estimates

My table differs considerably from the estimates of international reserves of International Financial Statistics.

1. - The major difference, of course, is that the IFS table does not include any estimates of "reserve liabilities" and "net reserves". I calculate the latter in the same way of the Survey of Current Business of the Commerce Department calculates the "net investment" position of the United States, *i.e.* by deducting from "US assets abroad foreign" (and international) assets in the United States (17).

2. - My reserve assets estimates also differ substantially from those published in IFS:

2.1 Gross reserves, with gold holdings measured at market prices and at 35 SDRs per ounce, are identical to the "all countries total reserves" recorded on lines 010 of the two penultimate paragraphs of IFS table (such as on pages 70 and 71 of the the 1989 Yearbook), converted from SDRs into dollars. Their breakdown between gold holdings and total reserves minus gold (labelled "fiduciary reserves" in my table) differs substantially (by more than $3.5 billion, for instance, at $35 per ounce, and than $40.2 billion at market price, at the end of 1989) for the following reason. The IFS bizarrely includes under "foreign exchange, in millions of SDRs" the gold holdings held by European Community countries as swap deposits with the BIS (Bank for International Settlements) and with the EMCF (European Fund for

---

(17) My table's estimates of net US reserves differ, however, from those of the Survey for a variety of reasons, such as:

a) the calculation of gold asset at market prices, rather than at the irrelevant official parity at which the dollar is no longer convertible into gold;

b) the inclusion of "statistical discrepancies" — formarly labelled "errors and omissions" — as unrecorded liabilities as was done until 1900, and since May 1986 in several Federal Reserve Bulletin articles;

c) the inclusion in the foreign official liabilities of my table of those held by foreign central banks indirectly through foreign branches of US banks, and recorded in the Survey as liabilities to private banks abroad.

Economic Cooperation, better known as Fecom, or Fonds Européen de Coopération Monétaire), valued at contractual prices close to market prices, and whose legal ownership and attendant exchange risks are totally retained by each country separately.

The global value of these gold holdings, measured in SDRs, is recorded in the bottom paragraphs of the IFS gold tables (on pages 66 and 67, for instance, of the 1989 Yearbook), but their regional breakdown is included only at SDR $35 per ounce — and not at market price — in the IFS "Total Reserves" tables.

My table calculates their value: 1) at $35 per ounce, by deducting from these IFS "Total Reserves" tables my estimates of "Total Reserves minus Gold", corrected as indicated above, *i.e.* excluding gold swaps with the FECOM and the BIS; 2) at market price, by multiplying these $35 per onuce estimates by the ratio between the IFS global estimates of gold at market price and at $35 per ounce.

2.2 The IFS tables use different — and therefore non-additive — units of measurement: the SDR for fiduciary assets, ounces for gold assets, and either $35 per ounce of gold or the gold market price for the gold component of total reserves.

I use instead the US dollar as a uniform measurement unit: 1) in order to make possible the addition of regional estimates into world estimates; 2) because international settlement, reserve assets and reserve liabilities are still contracted mostly in dollars, the SDR unit of measurement being used only for Fund transactions which constitute an insignificant fraction only of global settlements and reserve accumulation. These dollar estimates can, of course, be converted easily into ECUs, deutsche marks, or any other currency deemed more appropriate today than the dollar for the analysis of monetary developments in different parts of the world for which the dollar valuation is becoming less significant than was the case in former years.

It should be noted that these obbious shortcomings of IFS and Survey of Current Business statistical estimates are unfortunately carried over in most other standard publications, such those of the OECD (Organization for Economic Cooperation and Development), and invalidate partly therefore the economic analysis of the books and articles based on them.

IMF ACCOUNTS

Year end	1949	1959	1969	1979	1986	1987	1988	1989
Assets	1.7	3.3	6.7	31.9	67.1	73.3	65.2	60.4
Industrial world	*1.6*	*3.1*	*5.9*	*22.5*	*47.1*	*12.2*	*43.8*	*48.9*
United States	1.8	2.0	2.3	4.0	20.1	21.6	19.4	19.0
Other	0.1	1.1	3.6	18.5	27.7	30.6	30.4	29.9
Third world	*0.1*	*0.2*	*0.8*	*9.4*	*19.3*	*21.1*	*15.4*	*11.5*
OPEC	—	—	0.2	5.3	15.3	16.2	11.3	7.4
Other	0.1	0.2	0.6	4.1	3.9	4.9	4.1	4.1
Liabilities (1)	− 0.2	− 0.9	− 5.1	− 28.1	− 67.1	− 71.9	− 63.2	− 66.0
Industrial world	*− 0.1*	*− 0.6*	*− 3.8*	*− 14.9*	*− 18.4*	*− 21.0*	*− 19.4*	*− 19.2*
United States	—	− 0.5(2)	− 1.0(2)	− 4.2	− 6.0	− 7.0	− 6.6	− 6.4
Other	− 0.1	− 0.1	− 2.8(3)	− 10.7	− 12.4	− 14.0	− 12.8	− 12.7
Third world	*− 0.1*	*− 0.3*	*− 1.3*	*− 13.2*	*− 48.9*	*− 50.8*	*− 43.8*	*− 46.9*
OPEC	—	—	− 0.1	− 1.0	− 1.9	− 2.8	− 2.6	− 4.2
Other	− 0.1	− 0.3	− 1.1	− 12.3	− 46.8	− 48.0	− 41.2	− 42.7
Net assets	+ 1.5	+ 2.3	+ 1.7	+ 3.8	—	+ 1.4	+ 2.0	+ 5.6
Industrial world	*+ 1.5*	*+ 2.5*	*+ 2.1*	*+ 7.7*	*+ 29.4*	*+ 31.2*	*+ 30.4*	*+ 29.7*
United States	+ 1.5	+ 1.5	+ 1.3	− 0.2	+ 14.1	+ 14.7	+ 12.8	+ 12.6
Other	—	+ 1.0	+ 0.8	+ 7.8	+ 15.3	+ 16.5	+ 17.6	+ 17.2
Third world	—	*− 0.1*	*− 0.4*	*− 3.8*	*− 29.4*	*− 29.6*	*− 28.6*	*− 35.4*
OPEC	—	—	+ 0.1	+ 4.3	+ 13.4	+ 13.4	+ 8.7	+ 3.2
Other	—	− 0.1	− 0.5	− 8.1	− 42.9	− 43.1	− 37.2	− 38.6

(1) Including contigent liabilities for SUR allocations.
(2) IMF gold deposits and investments $ 500 in 1959 and $ 1,019 in 1969.
(3) Of which $ 40 million IMF gold deposits and investments.

TABLE 5b

IMF CREDITS AND INVESTMENTS

Year end	1949	1959	1969	1979	1986	1987	1988	1989
Asset (reserve position)	1.7	3.3	6.7	15.5	43.2	44.6	38.0	33.5
Industrial world	*1.6*	*3.1*	*5.9*	*10.2*	*28.1*	*28.9*	*26.2*	*25.7*
United States	1.5	2.0	2.3	1.3	11.7	11.4	9.7	9.0
Other	0.1	1.1	3.6	8.9	16.4	17.5	16.5	16.6
Third world	*0.1*	*0.2*	*0.8*	*5.3*	*15.1*	*15.8*	*11.8*	*7.9*
OPEC	—	—	0.2	3.9	13.2	13.6	9.7	5.7
Other	0.1	0.2	0.6	1.4	1.9	2.2	2.0	2.1
Liabilities (+)	-0.2	-0.9	-5.1	-10.5	-40.9	-41.5	-34.4	-31.3
Industrial world	*-0.1*	*-0.6*	*-3.8*	*-2.2*	*-0.7*	*-0.5*	—	—
United States	—	-0.5	-1.0	—	—	—	—	—
Other	-0.1	-0.1	-2.8	-2.2	-0.7	-0.5	—	—
Third world	*-0.1*	*-0.3*	*-1.3*	*-8.3*	*-40.9*	*-41.5*	*-34.4*	*-31.3*
OPEC	—	—	-0.1	—	-0.1	-0.7	-0.6	-2.2
Other	-0.1	-0.3	-0.1	-9.3	-40.8	-40.8	-33.8	-29.1
Net assets	+1.5	+2.3	+1.7	+3.0	+2.4	+3.2	+3.7	+2.2
Industrial world	*+1.5*	*+2.5*	*+2.1*	*+7.6*	*+27.4*	*+28.4*	*+26.2*	*+25.7*
United States	+1.5	+1.5	+1.3	+1.3	+11.7	+11.4	+9.7	+9.0
Other	—	+1.0	+0.8	+6.3	+15.7	+17.0	+16.5	+16.6
Third world	—	*-0.1*	*-0.4*	*-2.6*	*-25.1*	*-25.2*	*-22.5*	*-23.5*
OPEC	—	—	+0.1	+3.9	+13.1	+12.9	+9.2	+3.5
Other	—	-0.1	-0.5	-6.5	-38.2	-38.1	-31.8	-27.0

TABLE 5*c*

SDR ACCOUNTS

Year end	1979	1986	1987	1988	1989
Assets (holdings)	+ 16,4	+ 23,8	+ 28,7	+ 27,1	+ 26,9
Industrial world	+ 12,3	+ 19,7	+ 23,3	+ 23,6	+ 23,2
United States	+ 2,7	+ 8,4	+ 10,3	+ 9,6	+ 10,0
Other	+ 9,6	+ 11,3	+ 13,0	+ 14,0	+ 13,3
Third world	+ 4,2	+ 4,2	+ 5,4	+ 3,5	+ 3,7
OPEC	+ 1,4	+ 2,1	+ 2,6	+ 1,4	+ 1,7
Other	+ 2,8	+ 2,0	+ 2,7	+ 2,1	+ 2,0
Contingent liabilities (−) (allocations)	− 17,6	− 26,2	− 30,4	− 28,8	− 28,2
Industrial world	− 12,6	− 17,7	− 20,5	− 19,4	− 19,0
United States	− 4,2	− 6,0	− 7,0	− 6,6	− 5,4
Other	− 8,4	− 11,7	− 13,5	− 12,8	− 12,5
Third world	− 5,0	− 8,6	− 9,9	− 9,4	− 9,2
OPEC	− 1,0	− 1,8	− 2,1	− 2,0	− 2,0
Other	− 4,5	− 6,7	− 7,8	− 7,4	− 7,2
Net assets	− 1,1	− 2,4	− 1,7	− 1,7	− 1,7
Industrial world	− 0,3	+ 2,0	+ 2,8	+ 4,2	+ 4,2
United States	− 1,4	+ 2,4	+ 3,3	+ 3,0	+ 3,5
Other	+ 1,1	− 0,4	− 0,5	+ 1,2	+ 1,7
Third world	− 0,8	− 4,4	− 4,5	− 5,9	− 5,5
OPEC	+ 0,4	+ 0,3	+ 0,5	− 0,6	− 0,3
Other	− 1,2	− 4,7	− 5,1	− 5,3	− 5,2

(1) Only in case of withdrawal or liquidation.

On the Road to EMU

Michele Fratianni - Jürgen von Hagen
Indiana University, Bloomington

Introduction

The European Community (EC) is preparing itself to embark on a highly ambitious project: monetary union. Since its foundation in 1958, the EC has spent much time, effort, and political capital trying to build a monetary union. In fact, the vision of a European monetary union is as old as the EC itself (1). But never did the chances for success look as good as today. There are several reasons for the renewed interest in monetary union: the general perception that the European Monetary System (EMS) has benefitted its participants through closer coordination of monetary policies (2); the progress with the single market program, the belief that the gains from economic integration will be even larger when combined with monetary union, and, not the least, the quest for greater political integration of the EC countries.

This paper deals with the transition to a European economic and monetary union (EMU). Taking the goal of EMU as given, we are interested in the strategic problems of transforming the current EC monetary arrangement into a monetary union. We center our discussion on the blueprint presented by the Committee for the Study of Economic and Monetary Union (*Delors Report* [3]), composed of central bank representatives. In this report, all EC central banks

---

(1) For a historical review, see VON HAGEN [17], FRATIANNI, VON HAGEN [7].

Advise: the numbers in square brackets refer to the Bibliography in the appendix.

(2) For an assessment of the EMS, see FRATIANNI - VON HAGEN [5], [6], [7], as well as VON HAGEN [17] for a discussion of the relevant literature.

acknowledged for the first time the common goal of creating a monetary union in Europe. The stature of the Committee members and the fact that their strategy was officially endorsed by the European Council at its 1989 Madrid Summit make the *Report* the inevitable standard against which one must measure alternative approaches to EMU.

We begin our paper (paragraph 1) by reviewing the *Report*. Its strategy for EMU rests on three fundamental concepts: the choice of the EMS as the basis to construct a monetary union (MU); "parallelism", the principle according to which economic union (EU) and MU must progress simultaneously; and the call for binding fiscal restraints. With regard to the latter, we will restrict our attention in this paper soley to the strategic aspects arising in the transition phase (3).

In paragraph 2, we compare the Delors strategy for EMU with alternative strategies, including the "hard ECU" proposal of HM Treasury [14]. The comparison helps to pinpoint some of its important characteristics. Parallelism creates a bias for centralized market intervention and regulation, and conserves capital market inefficiencies. In paragraph 3 we discuss the criteria guiding the choice between alternative strategies for EMU: credibility, flexibility, and the cost of transition. The Delors strategy seeks to enhance credibility by imposing the fixed exchange rate mechanism of the EMS on all EC countries during the transition phase. However, the additional constraint implied by the EMS lacks credibility itself, and does not address the sources of the credibility problem. If the process to EMU is based on democratic consensus instead of bureaucratic intervention or on cooperation of independent central banks, the apparent trade-off between credibility and flexibility in the transition vanishes. The capital market distortions implied by the Delors strategy make the transition process unnecessarily costly and raise the chances of a disruptive rather than smooth transition.

In paragraph 4 we develop a public-choice interpretation of the Delors strategy. Our view is that the proposal is a rational response of EC central bankers to the growing threat of fiscal dominance in a

---

(3) For a discussion of the role of fiscal policy in a monetary union see FRATIANNI - VON HAGEN [5], VON HAGEN - FRATIANNI [18], [19], [20], [21] (1990). VON HAGEN [16].

future economic and monetary union. Standard open-economy macroeconomics predict that national fiscal policies are ineffective within a highly integrated economic union and flexible exchange rates. Rational fiscal policymakers will try to centralize fiscal policy to regain leverage. Since most likely the EC is not politically mature for fiscal centralization, the next best alternative for the fiscal authorities is to gain control over the effective policy instrument, monetary policy. For this purpose, they will push for fixed exchange rates in the EU. We argue that the three fundamental featues of the Delors strategy — the EMS as a basis for EMU, parallelism and fiscal rules — represent the central bankers' reaction to the threat of being dominated by the fiscal authorities in this way. They serve to maintain policy authority at the national level for the foreseeable future and ensure that the European central bank be politically independent of Treasury ministries. The market inefficiencies on which the Delors strategy rests are the inevitable price to pay for achieving these political goals.

The concluding paragraph 5 takes up some of the issues in the current policy debate over the transition to EMU.

1. - The «Delors Report»: A Strategy for Monetary Union (4)

The *Delors Report* consists of three main parts, one dealing with economic union; another one dealing with the construction of EMU; and a third one dealing with fiscal policy in a monetary union. In this paragraph, we focus on three aspects of the *Report*: The principle of parallelism, the choice of the EMS as the basis for MU and the recommendation for binding fiscal restraints on national governments. Consider first some critical passages from the *Report*.

1.1 *Economic Union*

«The success of the internal market program hinges to a decisive extent on a much closer coordination of national economic policies...

---

(4) Much of the following discussion draws on FRATIANNI - VON HAGEN [6].

This implies that in essence a number of the steps towards economic and monetary union will already have to be taken in the course of establishing a single market in Europe» (par. 14).

«Economic and monetary union would represent the final result of the progressive economic integration in Europe» (par. 16).

1.2 *Monetary Union*

The *Report* defines monetary union as a «...currency area in which policies are managed jointly... The single most important condition for a monetary union would, however, be fulfilled only when the decisive step was taken to lock exchange rates irrevocably» (par. 22).

«The adoption of a *single currency*... might be seen... as a natural and desirable further development of the monetary union... The replacement of national currencies by a single currency should therefore take place as soon as possible after the loking of parities» (par. 23).

«A new monetary institution would be needed because a single monetary policy cannot result from independent decisions and actrions by different central banks... [This institution] should be organized in a federal form, in what might be called a *European System of Central Banks* (ESCB)... The System would be committed to the objective of price stability;... should be independent of instructions from national governments and Community authorities» (par. 32).

1.3 *Progress in Three Stages*

«*Stage one* represents the initiation of the process of creating an economic and monetary union. (par. 50) ...[it] would center on the completion of the internal market... would strengthen economic and fiscal policy coordination...» (par. 51).

«[It] would include all Community currencies in the EMS... [But] realignments of exchange rates would still be possible...» (par. 52).

«The *second stage* could begin only when the new treaty had come into force» (par. 55).

«...While the ultimate responsibility for monetary policy decisions would remain with national authorities,... a certain amount of exchange reserves would be pooled... [and] regulatory functions would be exercised by the ESCB in the monetary and banking field in order to achieve a minimum harmonization of provisions (such as reserve requirements or payment arrangements) necessary for the future conduct of a common monetary policy» (par. 57).

«The *final stage* would commence with the move to irrevocably locked exchange rates...» (par. 58) ...with the ESCB assuming all its responsibilities as foreseen in the treaty...» (par. 60).

«...The Council of Ministers... would have the authority... to impose constraints on national budgets... to make discretionary changes in Community resources... and to apply... structural policies...» (par. 59).

1.4 *Parallelism*

«Economic union and monetary union form two integral parts of a single whole and would therefore have to be implemented in parallel» (par. 21).

The principle of "parallelism" (par. 42) is an important axiom of the *Report*. Parallelism rests on the claim that monetary unification and economic integration cannot proceed fruitfully if they are pursued independently of each other. The reasoning behind "parallelism", however, remains vague. On the one hand, «achieving monetary union is only conceivable if a high degree of economic convergence is attained» (par. 21).

On the other hand, the *Report* fails to establish why reaching EU requires MU: «The creation of a single currency area would add to the potential benefits of an enlarged economic area because it would remove intra-Community exchange rate uncertainties and reduce transactions cost... At the same time, however, exchange rate adjustments would no longer be available as an instrument to correct economic imbalances within the Community...

The role of MU for EU is thus ambivalent; MU may add or subtract from the benefits due to EU. MU forces the EC to give up exchange rate flexibility which otherwise offers valuable degrees of freedom in the process of adjustment to an integrated market. Exchange rate flexibility allows changes in relative prices between countries without fluctuations in their output price levels. Relative price adjustments are necessary to absorb idiosyncratic supply and demand shocks rate flexibility is the more valuable, the more important are idiosyncratic shocks compared to common shocks (5). Idiosyncratic shocks result mainly from are independent changes in national economic policies, including legislation for regulating goods and financial markets and for income redistribution. It seems plausible to assume that the importance of idiosyncratic shocks will increase in the process of building an integrated European market, as different countries in the Community need to abolish different types of country-specific regulations and policy interventions. In contrast, the theory of fiscal federalism suggests that idiosyncratic shocks will loose importance once the single market has been established. Free mobility of goods and factors severely limits the scope and incentives for uncoordinated policy interventions. Exchange rate flexibility will thus be very valuable in the process of integration, but loose importance when EU has been achieved. This suggests that the optimal sequence is to first achieve EU and then add MU to it (6). The *Delors Report* disgregards the different roles of exchange rate fixity in the process to and in the established EU. Insisting on parallelism, instead, the *Report* proposes: «Community policies in the regional and structural field would be necessary in order to promote an optimum allocation of resources and to spread welfare gains throught the Community» (par. 29).

That is, if the additional constraint of imposing EMU in the transition period causes strains in the EC, market interventions at the Community level will be used to alleviate the tensions. In this way, relying on "parallelism" creates a predisposition for bureaucratic regulation, which contradicts the spirit of deregulation embedded in the *Europe 1992* program. Furthermore, the concept of parallelism suggests a requirement for fine-tuning the two processes to assure that monetary union does not trail behind or go ahead of economic integration. Again, such fine-tuning creates a predisposition for

---

(5) See VON HAGEN [17] and VON HAGEN - FRATIANNI [19] for a detailed discussion.
(6) See GOODHART [13] for a discussion.

centralized Community decisionmaking instead of relying on market forces to realize the single market.

A second implication of parallelism is that it enforces a gradual approach to the creation of MU. Given that economic integration is necessarily a gradual process involving changes in private sector behavior, parallelism deprives the Community of the alternative to establish MU in one step by a general monetary reform. As pointed out by Giovannini [11], one reason for adopting a gradual approach may have been that the Delors Committee realized the political dimension and difficulties of monetary unification and did not want to preempt what it considered important political decisions in the timing of the process. Thus, «The question of when these stages should be implemented is a matter for political decision of when these stages should be implemented is a matter for political decision» (par. 15).

«The conditions for moving from stage to stage cannot be defined precisely in advance; nor is it possible to foresee today when these conditions will be met. The setting of explicit deadlines is therefore not advisable» (par. 43).

A second justification for the gradual approach seems to be the belief that it reduces the cost of building new institutions. This is most clearly stated in the *Report* discussion of stage 2: «Stage two must be seen as a period of transition to the final stage and would thus primarily constitute a training process leading to collective decision-making, while the ultimate responsibility for policy decisions at this stage would remain with national authorities» (par. 55).

The Committee seems to have been convinced that the gradual process would give the new institutions time to learn the skills necessary for their functions.

2. - Alternative Strategies to Achieve EMU

The most fundamental choice in proposing a strategy for monetary union regards the timing of the events. Taking the goal of EMU as given, there are several ways to reach thisa end. For a better understanding of the dynamic processes involved, we compare several alternative strategies in Table 1. All scenarios share the same ultimate

TABLE 1

ALTERNATIVE PATHS TO EMU

| | EU | | MU | | | |
	goods & services	capital	EMS	ESCB	FR	Comment
	Y					integrated goods markets
A1	Y	Y				integrated goods and financial markets (Europe 1992)
A2	Y	Y		Y	Y	monetary reform for EMU
B1	Y	Y				Europe 1992
B2	Y	Y		Y		centralized policy coordination with flexible exchange rates
B3	Y	Y		Y	Y	EMU
C1	Y	Y				Europe 1992
C2	Y	Y			Y	decentralized but coordinated policies (e.g. gold standard)
C3	Y	Y		Y	Y	EMU
D1	Y		Y			*Delors* stage one
D2	Y		Y	Y		*Delors* stage two
D3	Y	Y		Y	Y	*Delosr* stage three = EMU

Legend:
EU   = economic union including financial intergration;
MU   = monetary unions;
EMS = enlarged European monetary system;
ESCB = central monetary authority;
FR   = irrevocably fixed exchange rates.

objective, EMU, and the same basis, full integration of the markets for goods and services. From this starting point, the completion of EU requires to eliminate all remaining constraints in the financial markets which currently hamper the free flow of capital within the EC. The steps leading to MU, in contrast, introduces new constraints on monetary policymaking until a unified monetary system is achieved. Thus, EU and MU are qualitively different. The purpose of the following discussion is to evaluate different ways of timing the elimination and addition of constraints on the road to EMU.

Scenarios *A*, *B* and *C* complete EU, first. At this stage, the EC would consist of fully integrated and widely deregulated financial and goods markets, the notion of «Europe 1992». National monetary policies remain autonomous and exchange rates flexible until EU is completed, allowing free adjustment of real exchange rates through nominal exchange rate changes. After this stage, the question is when to impose the new constraints leading to MU. Scenario A proposes to introduce MU in one act through a Community-wide monetary reform. This reform would simultaneously transfer all monetary policy authority to the newly created European central bank (ESCB) and abolish all nominal exchange rate variation among EC currencies. This "radical" option must be compared against a variety of alternatives which all achieve MU through a gradual process.

Scenario B and C take different routes after the establishment of EU. Step B2 adds an ESCB, which would coordinate the monetary policies of the members. At this point, the ESCB is an independent institution most likely comprised of representatives from all participating central banks. Its function would be to formulate consistent monetary policies for all members and to monitor their implementastion. Policy coordination would occur with flexible exchange rates, preserving the additional degrees of freedom to adjust to idiosyncratic shocks and to converge to a common monetary policy at individually optimal speeds. The fact that exchange rates are flexible does not imply that coordination is loose. It can consist of common policy rules, such as monetary targeting. Monetary policy would still be executed at the national level, leaving the national authorities with the freedom to choose their own operating regimes and instruments to implement the common strategy. However, the national authorities would be responsible to the ESCB for the successful implementation. Step B3 finally fixes all EC exchange rates, clearing the way for MU. At this point, the ESCB is transformed into an independent monetary authority for the EC with the power to formulate and enforce monetary policy in the Community as a whole.

In comparison, scenario C rests on a system of decentralized policy coordination with fixed exchange rates. At stage C2, all participants commit to truly fixed exchange rates, but they retain their individual monetary authorities. This is comparable to the gold standard, although no metallic or commodity money is necessary to implement this step. Stage C2 does, however, require a well-specified "anchor" for monetary policy in the EC determining the common inflation rate. Depending on the rules for intervention and steriliz-ation, this role could be assigned to a "dominant" member or to an outsider by targeting the common exchange rate with an outside currency (7). Policymaking is decentralized, but each monetary authority must assure the fixity of the exchange rate. Step C3 then adds the ESCB as the central policy authority, which assumes the full authority over EC monetary policy at this stage. Compared to scenario B, scenaio C has the advantage that decentralized coordi-nation is easier to implement and to monitor (8). On the other hand, C imposes a tight constraint on exchange rates and therefore gives up flexibility in the adjustment to idiosyncratic shocks at an earlier stage than B.

In the Delors scenario D, the road to monetary union starts from an enlarged EMS including all EC members in the exchange rate mechanism (ERM). The ERM requires only a small degree of policy coordination, because it explicitly permits discrete realignments of exchange rates and, hence, persisting differences in inflation rates among the member countries. The possibility of realignments, how-ever, exposes the ERM to the danger of speculative attacks. The more likely a realignment, the more certain becomes the profit from speculating against the central banks' ability or willingness to main-tain the parities. An increasing likelihood of a realignment therefore triggers speculative capital flows, which force central bank interven-tions and depletion of their reserves and precipitate the realignment. In view of this threat, the ERM needs capital and exchange controls to survive. Indeed, despite the common perception that capital and exchange controls are being fully dismantled in the EC, their reimposi-tion remains possible under current EC regulations, if short-run capital movements cause significant strain in foreign exchange markets and disturb the execution of monetary policy in a member country (Bofinger [2], p. 433; Key [15], p. 596). Therefore, D1 does

---

(7) According to a popular view, the Bundesbank plays such an anchor function in the EMS. Recent empirical evidence has not supported this view. See e.g. FRATIANNI - VON HAGEN [5]; VON HAGEN - FRATIANNI [19], [20], and VON HAGEN [17] for a review of this literature.

(8) See FRATIANNI - VON HAGEN [5] for a discussion of the monitoring problem in international coordination.

not complete EU. Instead, EU and MU are both reached only in the final stage of the Delors strategy. In this sense, making the EMS the basis of MU leads one to accept parallelism.

The ESCB is added to the EMS in stage two (*D2*), but its functions remain vague. The authority over monetary policymaking still rests with the national authorities at this stage. Some aspects of central banking may be transferred to the ESCB to give the new institution an opportunity to acquire the skills necessary in stage three. In this way, the Delors strategy provides for the coexistence of central and decentralized decision making, which is bound to create conflicts between the institutions. Since there are no rules nor institutions to resolve such conflict, there will be more room for discretionary political action in the conduct of monetary policy. The result is not only additional uncertainty about monetary policy, but a predisposition for decisionmaking processes and outcomes that reflect political opportunism rather than economic rationale. Such institutional conflict does not arise in the other scenarios because the Community authority replaces national monetary authorities rather than coexisting with them.

Finally, the transition from step *D2* to *D3* implies the simultaneous abolition of capital controls, the ending of the EMS, the imposition of irrevocable fixed exchange rates and the transfer of full monetary policy authority to the ESCB. Compared to the alternatives, the move to stage three requires both the elimination of the remaining constraints on capital and the addition of new constraints to reach MU. The final step of the Delors strategy is therefore less evolutionary that the alternatives and carries the danger of greater disruptions.

In November 1989, the British Treasury put forth an alternative strategy for EMU called *An Evolutionary Approach to EMU* (HM Treasury [14]). The Treasury's proposal is a variant of our scenario *B*. While it accepts the enlarged EMS as a starting point, it envisions a stage one which focuses on the completion of the economic union rather than a strengthening of the exchange rate mechanism in the EMS. Thus, stage one should include «the dismantling of longstanding barriers to the movement of people, goods and services... the strengthening of competition policy, the liberalization of capital movements, the strengthening of coordination of economic and monetary

policies, the inclusion of all currencies in the ERM on equal terms»
(par. 4).

In addition, restrictions barring the residents of one country from
using another country's currency should be removed to strengthen
currency substitution and competition. The proposal rests on the
belief that the completion of EU would create sufficient pressures on
national monetary policies to enforce the convergence of inflation
rates at a low level and eliminate exchange rate variability. In
particular, depreciating realignments would become politically and
economically unattractive because they undermine the credibility to a
price stability commitment. Furthermore, with increased currency
substitution more inflation-prone currencies would be driven out of
transactions, which would reduce the monetary authority's incentive
for inflation. The result would be an EU in which all participating
currencies would be used interchangeably and have «more or less
fixed exchange rates» (par. 23). That is, the evolutionary approach
does not lead to MU itself, but rather attempts to lay the "sound
foundations" on which MU could be build if the Community so
wishes.

Another strategic proposal has recently been advocated by
Giovannini [11]. Giovannini accepts the principles of parallelism and
building EMU on the EMS from the *Delors Report*. His strategy is
therefore a variant of scenario *D*. He adds four main elements to the
Delors strategy. First, realignments should no longer be permitted in
the EMS, so that exchange rates would already be irrevocably fixed in
stage one. Second, the participating governments would declare their
willingness to counteract turmoil in the foreign exchange and the
money markets due to speculative capital flows by speeding up the
final implementation of EMU. Third, Giovannini gives more content to
the functions of the ESCB during stages one and two. Specifically, the
ESCB would consist of an Exchange-Rage Stabilization Authority
(ERSA) concerned with maintaining intra-EMS parities, and a Board
of Central Bank Governors, whose role would be to propose monetary
policy strategies for the member countries and to watch over the
operations of ERSA and the consistency of the national policies. The
national authorities would still retain their domestic monetary policy
instruments. With that, just like the Delors strategy, the proposal lacks

a clear separation of responsibilities. There are no provisions regarding the sterilization of ERSA foreign exchange interventions, and the effective authority of the Board over ERSA remains unclear. The proposal therefore shares with the *Delors Report* the weakness of setting up an uncertain institutional environment. Finally, Giovannini proposes a currency reform at the beginning of stage three, which would fix all bilateral EMS exchange rates to unity. In this way, the EC could keep currencies with different denominations and yet maximize the transparency of its price system.

Long before the current proposals, the *All Saints' Day Manifesto* [1] rejected the idea of a sudden currency reform to reach EMU on the ground that it gave the people no choice on the matter. This political reservation is shared by the Treasury proposal which criticizes the *Delors Report's* penchant for bureaucratic and centralized solutions. The *Manifesto's* own proposal is again a variant of our scenario *B*. It proposed the introduction of inflation-proof money as an alternative to existing national monies. With a guarantee of a zero real rate of return, governments cannot penalize money holders and, therefore, cannot profit from generating unanticipated rates of inflation. With such a parallel currency, the *Manifesto* argued that the cost of adjusting to a common inflation rate would not be as high as if exchange rates were to be set rigidly at a given date. Such a proposal implies that the 12 national monetary authorities would follow money supply or quantity rules; that exchanges rates among national monies would be flexible; and that the conversion rate between the parallel national monies would be flexible; and that the conversion rate between the national currencies would be set by the authorities according to a crawling peg formula. Only when all national monies were replaced with the inflation-proof currency would the ESCB gain control of its supply.

3. - Choosing a Strategy for EMU

Reviewing the alternative proposals for EMU, three criteria seem to be most important in guiding the choice of a strategy: credibility, flexibility, and the prospective economic cost of transition. In this section, we discuss the individual criteria and apply them to the Delors strategy and its alternatives.

3.1 *Credibility*

Following game-theoretical literature, we call a commitment to a monetary policy goal or an institution announced at time *t credible*, if pursuing the goal or preserving the institution remains an optimal strategy of monetary policy when the monetary authority can revise its policy at a date later than *t*. Credibility requires that deviating from a prior announcement results in less desirable outcomes for the policy-maker. Breaking the commitment must either result in unfavorable economic outcomes or carry a sufficiently high cost to the policy-maker. The economic importance of credibility stems from the role of expectations in private sector behavior. Unless an announcement is credible, it will not change private sector expectations, and hence will not direct private sector behavior in the desired way. Pursuing the announced policy will then generally no longer be optimal itself, and the desired goal may not be achievable.

The main advantage of our scenario *A* is that it maximizes credibility of the commitment to the goal, EMU. By setting up the MU in one step, no doubt about the commitment to EMU is left. In contrast, all gradual strategies (*B*, *C* and *D* and their variants) suffer from the possibility that the private sector may not believe in the governments' commitment to EMU, because there is no clearly perceived penalty for abandoning this goal in the future. There is thus a danger in the gradual approach that the failure to convince the private sector becomes an obstacle in the realization of EMU.

The Delors proposal and the Giovannini proposal seek to overcome this credibility problem by sending strong signals to the markets about the firmness of the governments' commitment to EMU. The *Delors Report* calls for the full EMS membership of all EC countries and the formulation of convergent policies (par. 39). However, such formulations would remain mere declarations of intent and by themselves would not add credibility. Similarly, although leaving the EMS may be politically very unattractive and hence embed a penaltry, EMS membership adds little credibility as long as realignments are possible and give each member substantial room for independent policy. Giovannini's proposal recognizes this weakness of the *Report*. It attempts to strengthen credibility by abolishing realignments and adding the provision that the final monetary reform be precipitated in the case of exchange or money market turmoil. Abolishing realignments certainly would enhance the value of EMS membership as a signal of commitment, because it equates parity changes with the politically unattractive move out of the EMS. However, as Giovannini ([11], p. 9) puts it himself, «ostensibly fixed exchange rates have been changed before). As long as national interests are politically rated higher than the Community, the probability of realignments will always be nonzero in the EMS.

Giovannini's provision to speed up the final reform aims at shielding the fixed exchange rates against speculative attacks. It is based on the view that destabilizing speculation is the main threat the EMS faces in the transition phase. If the commitment to swift monetary reform in response to speculative capital flows was credible, it would lower expected speculative profits and thereby prevent speculation from destabilizing the system. Yet, this view escapes the more fundamental issue of what determines the expectations that drive speculative capital flows, i.e. what makes speculators believe that a parity change is approaching. In the absence of convincing empirical evidence that speculation is mainly driven by "animal instincts" or "sunspots", such expectations are likely to combine information about economic fundamentals with beliefs about the authorities' objectives (9). The likelihood of a realignment is the larger, the more severe are idiosyncratic shocks in the system and the more persistent are individual deviations from the common inflation

---

(9) Indeed, GIOVANNINI ([11], p. 5), contends that irrational speculation is empirically significant. He speaks of «speculative pressures that were not dictated by fundamentals (i.e., self-fulfilling speculation) "and" non-fundamental speculation "by which" speculators provoke exchange-rate turbulence for their own profit». Giovannini goes on in a rather bold methodological move citing the fact that «to-date, no, sensible model of the foreign exchange market based on fundamentals has been able to explain the extreme short-run volatily and unprecedented long-run swings of the dollar "as empirical evidence showing that" speculative activity in the foreign exchange markets is not tightly linked to the fundamentals»; inference based on ranking the axiom that researchers have the true model at hands higher than the hypothesis of fundamentals-driven speculation.

trend. Furthermore, it is the larger, the stronger the incentive for the national authorities to pursue domestic goals which are inconsistent with the fixed exchange rate. Fixed exchange rates are exposed tyo speculative attacks, if for one or both of these reasons speculators believe that the probability of a realignment is sufficiently large. But, in an environment of dominant idiosyncratic shocks and national interests, the concept of speeding up the final reform to monetary union is void and, hence, lacks credibility itself: the political feasibility of a swift reform presupposes consensus that fixed exchange rates are optimal (10).

A first conclusion emerging from credibility considerations is that fixing exchange rates during the transition phase to EMU does not, bu itself, enhance the credibility of the governments' commitment to the ultimate goal. On the contrary, imposing fixed exchange rates may damage the credibility of the goal of EMU if, at a later stage, the constraint is given up. To avoid such damages, the transition phase should be characterized by an institutional environment which itself is credible in the face of idiosyncratic shocks and dominant national interests, such as our scenario *B*.

At the heart of the credibility problem lies the governments' temptation to use monetary policy in the pursuit of domestic goals other than price stability. The second conclusion emerging from these considerations is, therefore, that in order to enhance the credibility of the commitment to EMU, this temptation must be removed. There are two fundamental ways to achieve this. One is to assure that national politicians can seek no political reward from breaking away from the path to EMU: The greatest credibility of the commitment to the goal would come from the democratic consensus that EMU is a desirable goal. If EMU is carried by a majority of the voters, politicians will seek no gain in deviating from the way to it. This seems to be behind the position of the British government and its rebuke of the bureaucratic approach favored by the Delors Commission. The alternative is to take the authority over monetary policy away from government politicians and place with independent, national central banks. As the example of

---

(10) GIOVANNINI ([11], p. 10), argues more optimistically that, if the alternative was to postpone the union and undo the EMS, political obstacles might be reduced.

Germany's Bundesbank demonstrates, independent central banks have no incentive to use monetary policy to pursue short-run oriented economic goals and will focus on the common target of price stability instead (11). This seems to be the fundamental view of the Bundesbank. Although setting up independent central banks first may seem like a step backwards from EMU, this would create the basis for placing the transition to EMU under the control of monetary authorities all credibly committed to price stability. This joint commitment and the independence from the political to price stability. This joint commitment and the independence from the political sector would provide the necessary credibility to the goal of EMU. Neither of these two solutions needs exchange rate fixity as a signal of commitment, which, ultimately, is an attempt only to cure symptoms instead of source of the credibility problem.

3.2 *Flexibility*

The *Delors Report*, Giovannini [11], and the British Treasury proposal all underline the uncertainty the EC faces in the transition phase. Greater financial integration necessarily causes changes in the empirical performance of money demand and financial sector institutions with the result that monetary control becomes more difficult. In addition, the possibility of severe economic shocks affecting the Community in the transition phase cannot be excluded and demands possibilities for adequate economic policy response. This would suggest that monetary policy retain flexibility during the transition. Retaining flexibility is, of course, the principle behind our scenario *B*. It should be noted, however, that introducing EMU at once in scenario *A* does not imply to give up flexibility of economic policies per se. EMU requires a different solution of the assignment problem, giving Community monetary policy the task of dealing with common shocks to all countries and fiscal policy the task to deal with idiosyncratic shocks. EMU does not mean that the EC has no instrument to tackle the latter. During a gradual transition phase, however, while

---

(11) For a discussion of central bank independence see NEUMANN (1991) and VON HAGEN - FRATIANNI [21].

the assignment problem has not been solved entirely, the flexibility of exchange rates adds valuable degree of freedom.

Giovannini [11] speaks of a trade-off between credibility and flexibility in the transition phase. As discussed above, his and the Delors proposal foresee to fix exchange rates as a signal of credible commitment to the goal of EMU. Our discussion above implies that such a trade-off exists only if the Community is not prepared to address the sources of the credibility problem and favors the exchange rate approach instead. The apparently unfavorable trade-off is easily resolved if the commitment to EMU is made credible by building its political base or by entrusting it to independent central banks.

3.3 *Cost of Transition*

A guiding principle in the *Delors Report* is the assumption that institutions need time for "learning by doing" in order to minimize the cost of potential errors of economic policy. This is a valid concern, as the new monetary environment in a EMU will be largely unknown. Yet, again, the question arises, is the transition based on an enlarged EMS the appropriate way to minimize the cost of transition?

The non-vanishing probability that countries in the EMS can resort to realignments as well as exchange and capital controls means that real interest rates under the Delors strategy will embed a compensation for this risk (12). This risk premium drives a wedge between relative marginal productivities of capital and relative real rates of return. Relying on the EMS, the Delors strategy thus creates an inefficiency which is resolved only in the final step and which does not arise in scenarios *A, B,* and *C.* This inefficiency raises the cost of transition relative to the alternative scenarios. The Delors strategy therefore embeds a tendency to move quickly to the final stage to avoid this additional cost. This discourages valuable learning by doing in the new environment, and adds unnecessary uncertainty to the process of building MU.

---

(12) GIOVANNINI [12] shows that eccessive *ex-post* real rates of return in Italy and the Netherland comparing to Germany in the late 1980s can be explained by the positive probability of a realignment perceived in the market.

The *Report* views the ESCB in stage two as a «training process leading to collective policymaking» (par. 55). Bofinger [2] correctly argues that such training is unlikely to be successful, because the ESCB will find it difficult to attract qualified people willing to invest in an institution of little importance and reputation. The German Council of Advisers to the Finance Ministry [4] warns that a weak institution like the ESCB of stage two would specialize in activities like coalition building, logrolling and infighting that would prevent the creation of a politically independent Community monetary authority. Thus, the learning phase of an ill-defined institution poses the risk of resulting in adverse performance of the ultimate ESCB.

4. - A Public Choice Interpretation of the Delors Proposal

We have pointed out that the Delors Committee's approach to MU has a number of strategic deficiencies. In light of these deficiencies, the question arises: what is the motivation underlying the Delors Committee's proposal. Public choice theory suggests that the central bankers on the Committee sought to pursue their own interests. To develop an interpretation of the *Report* consistent with that notion, we start by sketching how EU will change the environment for fiscal policymaking in the Community. Assume that the «Europe 1992» program is successful in the two important dimensions of goods market and financial integraition. Stronger goods market integration will increase intra-EC trade and raise the share of exports and imports in each country's GNP. Financial market integration, independent of the type of exchange rate regime, will increase the international substitutability of financial assets within the region, particularly at the shorter end of the markets. Thus, each economy in the region becomes more "open" and more closely integrated in the regional capital markets.

In the present context, the important implication of these two trends is that national fiscal policies are likely to lose much of their power to control national output and employment, even in the short run. The traditional literature on fiscal federalism argues that greater openness reduces the Keynesian spending multipliers, since a larger percentage of the induced demand spills over to the rest of the Community. Second, standard open-economy macroeconomics, typified in the Mundell-Fleming model, predicts that with rigid prices, flexible exchange rates and perfectly integrated capital markets, fiscal policy becomes ineffective in a small country. A domestic fiscal expansion momentarily raises the domestic eate of interest, which induces capital inflows and an appreciation of the domestic currency and results in a complete crowding out of net exports. In contrast, fiscal policy remains effective under fixed exchange rates, because its domestic interest rate effect forces the monetary authority to expand the money supply to offset the country is large enough to affect permanently domestic and world interest rates will the bond-financed increase in government spending succeed in raising domestic output under flexible rates (13).

Progress towards EU therefore implies a that the power of the national fiscal policy-makers in the EC vanishes. Public choice theory suggests that fiscal policy-makers will seek ways to restore their leverage. Given the completion of EU, there are two ways for them to do so. Coordination of fiscal policies among the EC members offers a way to overcome the relative size problem and to gain market power in international capital markets. While each individual country would seem relatively small, the combined size of their financial markets can be expected to be large enough for a coordinated fiscal expansion to raise world interest rates. Second, by fixing exchange rates among the community countries, fiscal policy-makers can exert power over the instrument that remains effective even with EU, namely monetary policy. The process of goods and financial market integration, thus, sets in motion two tendencies among finance ministries: a move towards coordination and a predisposition for fixed exchange rates. It is noteworthy in this respect that the legal power to choose exchange rate regimes generally rests with the finance ministries or the central governments, not the central banks.

To the EC central bankers these tendencies must appear as a serious threat to their own political power and independence. According to standard macroeconomic analysis, the imposition of truly fixed

---

(13) See, for example, FRENKEL - RAZIN [9].

exchange rates will degrade national monetary policy to a minor role
(14). Furthermore, fiscal policy coordination will reduce the relative
power monetary policy has compared to the fiscal authorities. Our
interpretation rests on the assumption that central bankers take these
developments of fiscal policy as given. In designing the future EC
monetary regime, they therefore have a strong incentive to select
strategies that diminish the perceived danger of fiscal dominance.

To interpret the strategy proposed in the *Delors Report* as a
rational response of EC central bankers to this threat requires to show
how the Delors strategy, if adopted, would reduce such a threat. We
focus on two elements. The first is the *Report's* insistence a building
MU gradually and on the foundations of the EMS. The critical
characteristic of the EMS here is that monetary policymaking remains
at the national level. Far from being a true fixed exchange rate
arrangement, the exchange rate mechanism explicitly allows for
realignments and therefore requires only a small degree of policy
coordination. The *Report* is very clear in this respect. During stage
one, it proposes to extend «the scope of central bank autonomy» (par.
52) — i.e., to strengthen the position of monetary policymakers
vis-à-vis their governments — and to include all Community currencies in the exchange rate mechanism. The main common policy
institution at this stage, the Committee of Central Bank Governors
would merely formulate and express opinions and write an annual
report (par. 52). Similarly, during stage two, the «ultimate responsibility for policy decisions would remain... with the national
authorities» (par. 55). The transfer of policy authority to the ESCB
would occur only in the final stage. In essence, the creation of the
ESCB within the existing EMS raises the probability that the national
monetary authorities see their interests represented in the ESCB and
at the same time lowers the probability of building a truly supranational and independent ESCB.

The small degree of coordination implied by the EMS need not

---

(14) We emphasize that our interpretation is built on the assumption that central
bankers predominantly reason along the lines of the Mundell-Fleming framework of
analysis. The fact that the latter represents the intellectual core of most empirical
models studying questions of national policy and international policy coordination gives
empirical concreteness to our assumption.

exclude, of course, that closer coordination may take place for a prolonged period of time, should this serve the interests of the central bankars. The recent experience since the 1987 realignment has made this quite clear. Such coordination, however, is less evidence of a "new EMS" (Giavazzi and Spaventa [10]) than of the simple fact that the adoption of similar policies may occur even without much formal coordination. We conclude that the Delors strategy, while suggesting that the way to MU is best achieved though a gradual strengthening of the EMS, serves to minimize the loss of policy authority for the central banks during this process.

The second critical element for the development of our interpretation concerns the call for binding fiscal rules in a MU. These rules are designed to guarantee independence to the ESCB in the final stage of MU through «exclusion of access to direct central bank credit and other forms of monetary financing» and to limit the scope of independence of national fiscal policy (par. 33). The former has an obvious justification in a monetary union committed to price stability (par. 32). But, as noted above, there is no evidence that quantitative limits on national budget deficits can assure fiscal discipline. Referring to the authority of regional and national policy-makers in macroeconomic management, the *Report* states: «...given their potential impact on the overall domestic and external situation of the Community and their implications for the conduct of a common monetary policy, such decisions would have to be placed within an agreed macroeconomic framework and be subject to binding procedures and rules» (par. 19).

To put it more plainly, the mere fact that fiscal policies interfere with monetary policymaking is sufficient to justify restrictions of the governments' scope for independent decision making. Obviously, the Delors Committee understands well the enhanced power of fiscal policy on aggregate demand when monetary policy is forced to hold exchange rates constant. The Delors Committee did not favor fiscal coordination per se uncoordinated fiscal policies, but rather takes as given the tendency for coordinated policies upon which it wants to place restraints to safeguard the leverage of monetary policy. Binding rules are called for to limit the discretionary actions of the fiscal authorities. As a result, the balance of decision making power in the future MU would shift towards central bankers.

Interpreting the *Delors Report* as a rational response of the EMS central-bankers to curb the threat of fiscal dominance, it is easy to make sense of the peculiarities of its strategy for MU. Its inefficiencies and biases are the price to be paid for maintaining monetary policymaking at the national level as long as possible. The end result is likely to be an ESCB consisting of a collection of national interests instead of a true Community institution standing above particular interests.

5. - Conclusions

As the Community prepares for the December 1990 intergovernmental monetary conference aimed at revising the *Rome Treaty*, a controversy has emerged concerning the speed of the transition. For example, Peter Norman in the *Financial Times*, «Confusion Reigns on the Road to EMU», 9-17-'90) states: «Mr Pöhl, influenced by Germany's difficult experience with monetary union, voices his concern about early institutional changes to Europe's monetary system in a speech in Munich [given at the Mont Pelerin Society General Meeting on the 3rd of September] before the Rome meeting. Spain put forward an alternative to Mr. Delors' fast track plan in Rome, that envisages moving to stage two at the beginning of 1994. Stage two would then last for an extended period of five or six years to enable EC economies to converge before EMU's third and final stage».

Andrew Fisher in the *Financial Times* of September 21, 1990 («Bundesbank Adds a Voice to Bonn's go Slow Chorus on EMU») report the conditions the Bundesbank considers «indispensable» for moving to stage three of the *Delors Report*: convergence of inflation rates, harmonization of central bank statutes, rules on budgetary discipline, and full implementation of EU. Given the strength of these conditions, one may conclude that the Bundesbank wants a lengthy transition.

This position conforms with the Bundesbank's historical antipathy against fixed exchange rate arrangements. Today, this antipathy can no longer take the form of total opposition to EMU, but emerges by raising objections to an early implementation. In particular, an exchange-rate union is not acceptable for the Bundesbank unless the economic preconditions have been met. The views of the Bundesbank do not differ fundamentally from those of the British government under Mrs. Thatcher, although Mrs. Thatcher even rejected the goal of MU.

The Bundesbank cannot, however, be equated with the German government. Her views on MU have not been shared by Chancellors Willy Brandt, Helmut Schmidt, and Helmut Kohl. The Chancellors have tended to look at the process of economic and monetary integration in Europe as part of a broader process whose ultimate objective is political unity. The experience of German monetary union is a vivid example of such a process. Assessing the implications of German monetary union for EMU Helmut Schmidt (*Die Zeit*, September 14, 1990) remarks: «...it became obvious that the [German] government was quite capable of brushing aside the concerns of the Bundesbank for higher political reasons —why not similarly in the case of the EMS».

Politically, Germany is more likely to side with France and Italy than with the Bundesbank on the issue of the speed of implementation of MU. Our prediction, indeed, is that the objections of the Bundesbank to the speed of transition will not be consequential in the decision-making process. Those member countries in favor of a speedy transition will point to the fact that German monetary union came in spite of the low degree of economic integration between the countries. Helmut Schmidt (*Die Zeit* September 7, 1990) puts it cogently: «[The Bundesbank's] central argument in obstructing or in any case in slowing down the process was and is that a full harmonization of all aspects of EC economic policies must be reached first, and then monetary policies could be brought under one hat, almost coronating the common market this way... the German "coronation theory" of the late 1980s is the manifestation of economic nationalism and bureaucratic turf-preservation of the Bundesbank».

Apart from the credibility considerations discussed above, the Chancellor-Franco-Italian alliance has two reasons to speed up the transition phase. The first can be found in the distribution of influence in the current EMS. Empirical analysis shows that France and Italy are underrepresented in the monetary policy-making process (15). By forming a common central bank, France and Italy would likely gain more influence and the power of the Bundesbank would be reduced. The second argument is predicated on the hypothesis that an early implementation of stage three would facilitate economic and eventually political integration. In particular, completing EMU can be viewed as a strategy to assure Germany's lasting integration into the West European community of nations and the Western Alliance.

With Britain's recent entry into the EMS, the options of building EMU on a foundation other than the EMS may be lost. The important question then is, is there a non-disruptive way to achieve MU starting from the current EMS? There are two feasible alternatives. The first is to move from the EMS directly to EMU, that is the path described by stages D1 and A2 of Table 1. Elsewhere (von Hagen and Fratianni [18]) we have argued that such a strategy would enhance monetary policy reputation and lock in the gains of inflation achieved so far in the EC. The other possibility is to soften the ERM but rely on a centralized institution like the ESCB for coordinating national monetary policies, that is the path described by D1, B2 and B3. In this scenario, national central banks should be freed from government influence and EU should be completed during steps D1 and B2. As we have already noted, the first pathwould maximize credibility, but the second one might have the advantage that it is easier to monitor and easier to implement. Both alternatives have the advantage over the Delors proposal of avoiding the unnecessary uncertainties and the lack of credibility resulting from the ambiguities of its stage two.

---

(15) See VON HAGEN - FRATIANNI [20].

BIBLIOGRAPHY

[1] ALL SAINTS' DAY MANIFESTO FOR EUROPEAN MONETARY UNION: *The Economist*, November 1975, reprinted in FRATIANNI MICHELE - THEO PEETERS (eds.): *One Money for Europe*, London, MacMillan, 1978.

[2] BOFINGER PETER: «Zum Bericht zur Wirtschafts-und Währungsunion in der Europäischen Gemeinschaft des Ausschusses zur Prüfung der Wirtschafts-und Währungsunion - Delors Bericht» *Kredit und Kapital* no. 22, 1989, pp. 429-47.

[3] COMMISSION OF THE EUROPEAN COMMUNITIES - COMMITTEE FOR THE STUDY OF ECONOMIC AND MONETARY UNION: «1. Report on Economic and Monetary Union in the European Community; 2. Collection of Papers Submitted to the Commitee for the Study of Economic and Monetary Union», *Delors Report* Luxembourg, Office for Official Publications of the European Communities, 1989.

[4] COUNCIL OF ECONOMIC ADVISORS TO THE GERMAN MINISTER OF ECONOMICS: *Europäische Währungsordnung*, Bonn, 1989.

[5] FRATIANNI MICHELE - VON HAGEN JÜRGEN: «The European Monetary System Ten Years After», in MELTZER H. ALLAN - PLOSSER CHARLES (eds.): *Carnegie-Rochester Conference Series on Public Policy*, vol. 32, 1990.

[6] — — - — —: «Public Choice Aspects of European Monetary Union», *Cato Journal*, forthcoming, 1990.

[7] — — - — —: *The European Monetary System and European Monetary Union*, Westview, forthcoming, 1991.

[8] FRENKEL JACOB - RAZIN ASSAF: «The Mundel-Fleming Model a Quarter Century Later: a Unified Exposition», *International Monetary Fund Staff Papers*, vol. 34, no. 4, 1987, pp. 567-620.

[9] GIAVAZZI FRANCESCO - SPAVENTA LUIGI: «The New EMS», in DE GRAUWE PAUL - PAPDEMOS LUCAS (eds.): *The European Monetary System in the 1990s*, forthcoming, 1990.

[10] GIOVANNINI ALBERTO: «The Transition to European Monetary Union», Princeton University, *Essays in International Finance*, no. 178, 1990.

[11] — —: «European Monetary Reform: Progress and Prospects, Columbia University, *Working Paper*, November 1990.

[12] GOODHART CHARLES: *The Delors Report: Was Lawson's Reaction Justifiable*, London School of Economics, typescript 1989.

[13] KEY SIDNEY J.: «A Financial Integration in the European Community», Washington, Board of Governors of the Federal Reserve System, International Finance, *Discussion Paper*, no. 349, 1989.

[14] H.M. TREASURY: *An Evolutionary Approach to Economic and Monetary Union*, Paper distributed prior to the meeting of ECOFIN, 13, 1989.

[15] VON HAGEN JÜRGEN: «A Note on the Empirical Effectiveness of Formal Fiscal Restraints», *Journal of Public Economics*, forthcoming, 1990.

[16] — —: «Monetary Policy Coordination in the EMS», in FRATIANNI MICHELE - SALVATORE DOMINIK (eds.): *Handbook of Monetary Policy*, Greenwood Press, forthcoming, 1991.

[17] VON AGEN JÜRGEN - FRATIANNI MICHELE: «Credibility and Asymmetries in the EMS», in ARGY VICTOR - DE GRAUWE PAUL (eds.): *Selecting and Exchange Rate Regime: The Challenge for the Smaller Industrial Countries*, Washington (DC), International Monetary Fund, 1990.

[18] —— · ——: «Policy Coordination in the EMS with Structural and Stochastic Asymmetries», Indiana University School of Business, *Working Paper*, 1990.

[19] —— · ——: «German Dominance in the EMS: Evidence from Interest Rates», *Journal of International Money and Finance*, 1990.

[20] —— · ——: «Monetary and Fiscal Policy in a European Monetary Union: some Public Choice Considerations», in WELFFENS PAUL J.J. (ed.): *The EMS: From German Dominance to European Monetary Union*, 1990.

Adjustment Difficulties Within a European Monetary Union: Can they be Reduced?

A.J. Hughes Hallet - David Vines (*)
University of Strathclyde and CEPR - University of Glasgow and CEPR

1. - Introduction

1.1 *Two Key Issues in the EMU Debate*

Economic and monetary Union (EMU) could bring many benefits. There will be undoubted efficiency gains, as transactions costs and exchange-rate uncertainty are eliminated. Monetary union might also provide an enduring basis for Central Bank independence and price stability. And the ECU as a single currency would, with its weight and quality, become a major international currency, which could bring benefits for the international monetary system. But we must realise that there may also be problems.

First, EMU implies a common monetary policy which in turn implies the loss of national sovereignty over monetary policy. This would not matter if all national economies faced the same shocks, had the same structure, and possessed policymakers with the same preferences. In that case all countries would desire to follow the same

(*) We are grateful to Myrvin Anthony for his help with calculations and Strathclyde University for financial support. In writing this paper we have benefited from discussions with Jacques Melitz, from comments by Karl-Otto Pöhl, Richard Portes and Alberto Giovannini, and from suggestions made at a seminar at the Australian National University in July. Ian McDonald made helpful comments on the wealth target issue discussed in section 3. We would also like to thank Warwick McKibbin for permission to use his algorithm DYNGAME in computing the adjustment scenarios described in section 4. None of these people should be held responsible for what follows.

monetary policy anyway. But, if there are differences in shocks, structure, or preferences, union will impose a constraint upon national monetary policy; and this constraint could reduce welfare.

Second, in the face of such a monetary constraint there may be implications for fiscal policy of two rather different kinds. First, union brings a danger of "excessive deficits": the risk that there would be pressures in favour of undue monetary accommodation, coming perhaps from Eurofed governors closest to countries with very big budget deficits and debt service burdens. Second, since monetary hands will be partly tied, fiscal policy may need to respond differently in the different countries to differences in shocks, structure and preferences: the monetary constraint of union may lead to the need for greater fiscal flexibility. The difficulty is that, unlike monetary policy, flexible fiscal changes are difficult to introduce.

These problems have been addressed in two recent papers, and we will build closely on these analyses.

Begg [1] examines both sets of issues. He presents a small, but very illuminating, theoretical model which he uses to study the dynamics of adjustment to shocks which differ across countries. In his model forward-looking wage setters, who partially understand the nature of the regime in which they find themselves, play a crucial role. Our model will be almost identical to that which Begg uses (1). Begg's analysis provides two valuable insights. First, joining a monetary union will change the speed of adjustment to shocks within the union, because one possible part of an adjustment process — namely exchange-rate changes — will be removed. Wage setters will perceive this and alter their behaviour, thus reinforcing the effect. Second, policymakers can use fiscal accommodation to alter the adjustment path, if it is felt to be of the wrong speed; and the anticipation of such policies by wage setters will have further implications for the underlying dynamics. In sum Begg's analysis provides an important springboard for our own.

Masson and Melitz [10] concern themselves only with the second, fiscal policy, issue. They use a real econometric model (the IMF's

---

(1) Interestingly we wrote down this model in an earlier paper (HUGHES HALLETT and VINES [8]) before seeing Begg's treatment.

Advise: the numbers in square brackets refer to the Bibliography in the appendix.

Multimod model) to study particular real world shocks. They conclude «Our simulations have illustrated cases in which there would be clear value to the retention of fiscal flexibility, because of different initial conditions (or asymmetric shocks) and different preferences» (p. 25). But these authors do not study quite the same sets of shocks as those which interest us, and they set up the policy problem in a different way from that considered by either Begg or us.

1.2 *Two Sets of Shocks*

Our model of the EMU — like that of both Begg and Masson and Melitz — contains two countries, "France and Germany". For simplicity the structures of these countries are assumed to be identical, and so are the underlying preferences of their governments. We thus concentrate on the problems caused by asymmetric shocks, i.e. shocks which impinge differently on France and Germany. We study adjustment in the face of two particularly important shocks of this kind. First we consider the effect of an inflation shock in Germany, but no such shock in France, the kind of outcome which might emerge from German reunification. Second we investigate the consequence of a transfer of demand from France to Germany, caused, say, because French consumers come to prefer German goods rather than their own.

2 - Adjustment Problems Within a Monetary Union

2.1 *Responses to shocks*

We now review briefly the economics of dealing with our two types of shocks within a monetary union.

2.1.1 Inflation Differences

Are national labour markets integrated enough — or likely to become so — for Europe to become an «optimal currency area» in the

Mundell [11] sense? This sense requires that potential labour mobility would be great enough within the union to rapidly remove unemployment in any of its regions. In the extreme, labour mobility would also eliminate the potential for autonomous cost-push wage pressure in a particular region. It would thus also eliminate any need for currency depreciation in order for the competitiveness of a region to be preserved; and at the same time it would render currency depreciation useless as a device for rectifying any such resulting losses of competitiveness.

European labour markets are clearly so segmented that this view cannot be appropriate. (Eichengrees [6] argues that that view is inappropriate in the US, and that Europe is more segmented than the US). Instead rapid adjustment within a union might still be possible for expectational reasons: the integrated monetary discipline which is known by wage setters to exist within a monetary union might of itself dampen any wage pressures in the member economies, and make the two separate labour markets behave more like one market.

Our empirical view is that adjustment problems can and will remain. One example is the difficulties which the United Kingdom now faces having joined the ERM of the EMS, given the UK's present inflation rate: it may need to cut its interest rates by more than seems appropriate for domestic anti-inflation reasons. Similarly Spain, Portugal and Italy would encounter difficulties in an immediate move to full monetary union; needing as they do for various reasons interest rates as high as those at present. EMU might even impose an unwanted constraint upon high interest rates in Germany itself, if, as seems possible, reunification in Germany leads to a large boom in Germany. Such a boom might lead German policymakers to want higher interest rates — to control inflation in Germany — than those wanted throughout the union to control inflation in the union as a whole.

The general nature of the problem is well known and is summarised by Masson and Melitz [10]: «As a rule, fixed exchange-rate regimes are successful in handling shocks hitting all of the members similarly, as they avoid opposing efforts to move the exchange rate. Asymmetric shocks, on the other hand, tend to require flexibility of . . . exchange rates».

2.1.2 Inter-Regional Wealth Transfers

It is sometimes claimed that «the balance-of-payments problem of an individual country will go away if the country joins a monetary union». Protagonists of this point of view suggest that, for example, the «Scottish balance of payments is not a problem». In a narrow sense this is true. But a monetary union, like that of Scotland with England, might transform the potential for balance-of-payments problems into a potential for decumulations of wealth on a regional basis. It might do this by impeding the adjustments of competitiveness necessary to remove continuing wealth transfers within the union through continuing current account deficits. Again Masson and Melitz [10] note that: «Social transfers to affected regions through national fiscal systems exist in many countries on a scale that far exceeds the current level of such transfers in the Community . . . In the absence of a major Community-wide mechanism of transfers a country hit by an adverse country-specific blow might be tempted to move out of a monetary union and devalue».

This discussion relates to the *Delors Report* where it is argued that adjustment in national fiscal policies might be necessary to prevent "involuntary" continuing transfers through current account imbalances, institutionalising a centre vs periphery differential. Our point will be to explore what these restrictions might be, and to display their costs (2).

2.2 *Alternative Exchange-Rate Regimes*

In the light of this discussion we ask which exchange-rate regimes might make life easier with respect to these two key problems of inflation differences between countries, and wealth transfers.

To do that we focus on three regimes:

a) a pure float. This is studied purely as a benchmark, and

---

(2) There has been much discussion about whether there should be «binding rules» for these fiscal adjustments, (see (DELORS [4])). In our view the «bindingness» of the fiscal rules is not the point, but the possible «costliness» of them, in the absence of large interregional transfers.

certainly not because we are in any sense advocating it as an alternative policy regime for Europe;

b) a hard monetary union. This involves a complete permanent locking of currencies (or a new currency - for our purposes the differences are immaterial);

c) we briefly touch on a regime of exchange-rate bands, much like the current ERM scheme, and consider the consequences of progressively tightening those bands.

We have examined both co-operative and non-co-operative versions of the each regime as a way of examining whether exchange rate fixing — here in the form of monetary union — can act as a surrogate for co-operation.

3. - The Formal Model

3.1 *Model Setup*

We use a multi-region adaption of the Taylor overlapping contract model of Taylor [12]. There are three regions: «Germany», «France» (which together make up «Europe»), and the «United States». In both France and Germany aggregate demand, the interest rate, and prices are all endogenous. The US, however, is «large» in relation to the European economies and so we treat US output, interest rates, and prices as exogenous.

The model is forward looking, in two ways. First, wage and price setters are forward-looking. However wage earners do not fully understand the systems's responses or the consequences of their actions. This can lead to unstable behaviour and, rather than the normal forward-looking jump to a stable solution, wage setting has to be tied down with a terminal condition and/or some backward looking effects. As in Begg's paper, that comes from sluggishness in the wage and price setting, to reflect the fact that wages cannot be immediately adjusted to their market clearing level following a shock. Inflation is perfectly anticipated in the real interest-rate calculations which affect aggregate demand decisions.

Second, exchange rates between Europe and the US are

determined according to uncovered interest parity, and exchange-rate developments are perfectly anticipated, apart from the effects of initial shocks. That implies that any movements in the French-German exchange rate are perfectly anticipated.

Consumption is not forward looking, for simplicity, as in Begg's paper. A forward-looking consumption function might lessen the need for active fiscal policy as consumers conduct inter-temporal consumption smoothing, (and hence prevent wealth decumulation), without any need for an explicit government policy in this area. There is wide disagreement in the theoretical literature on whether this would happen, and (like Begg) we simply assume that it does not for the reasons given in Blanchard [2]. A full model listing appears in an appendix to this paper.

3.2 *The Specification of Policy Targets and Policy Instruments*

3.2.1 Targets

We take inflation to be a paramount objective of policy and its control to be essential for any monetary union or other monetary system proposals. We still want to examine the extent which different monetary union schemes can crease price discipline, but a minimal or reduced cost to output growth. Hence output is a second target of policy.

Our third target will be a wealth target. Previuos work has sometimes taken the balance on the current account of the balance of payments as a third policy objective (e.g. Masson and Melitz [10]). But with monetary integration and capital mobility, the current account is becoming less and less important per se. We generalise from a current account measure — which relates only to the accumulation of foreign wealth — to the accumulation of wealth as a whole, through domestic investment as well as the current account. By adding together domestic investment and the current account surplus, one is, in effect, taking national savings as the third target. Even if the current account becomes unimportant in a monetary union, the impact of a region's/nation's aggregate wealth on that region's welfare and development is still very important (see again Scotland and England).

3.2.2 Instruments

The policy instruments are the nominal interest rate, r, and an index of fiscal stance, g. Use of the interest rate, as the monetary instrument rather than the money stock, corresponds to actual practice, and is not subject to the «indeterminacy of the price level» critique because here the interest rate is endogenous, and manipulates in precisely the way required to control the inflation rate (3). treating the interest rate as a policy instrument allows us to sidestep the issue of currency substitution which Begg analyses in detail: given the interest rate which results from policy decisions, currency substitution determines the way in which money holdings emerge as a consequence.

3.3 *Policy Design Framework*

Let unstarred variables denote German variables, and starred variables denote French ones.

3.3.1 Policy Targets

   (*i*)   Inflation: Δpc, Δpc^*
   (*ii*) output: y, y^*
   (*iii*) wealth: w, w^*

3.3.2 Policy Instruments

   (*i*) nominal interest rate: r, r^*
   (*ii*) index of fiscal stance: g, g^*

---

(3) It is also common in «closed-loop» models: see, e.g. Edison-Miller and Williamson [5].

For each of the regimes studied below, our approach will be to carry out inter-temporal optimisation over 60 periods (a «long run»), in order to determine the best outcome possible in response to shocks to the system; given any constraints which the regime imposes on the movements in fiscal and monetary policy instruments. Since we are only interested in the adjustment process in a monetary union, we take equilibrium values to define the target path for each variable: i.e. capacity output levels, with zero inflation, zero policy interventions and balance on current accounts and wealth. The welfare functions used in the optimisations then penalise squared deviations of each target and instrument from its target or baseline value in each period. For Germany that welfare function may be written as:

$$(1) \qquad U = \Sigma \left[\Delta pc^2 + \alpha y^2 + \beta w^2 + \gamma r^2 + \delta g^2 \right]$$

where: $\qquad \alpha = \delta = 1, \ \beta = 0.1 \ \gamma = 0.$

Deviations in inflation, output and government expenditure (from their pre-shock positions) are all taken to be equally costly, in the absence of any clear way to choose other weights. Deviations in interest rates are not penalised per se, and the penalty on wealth is set at one-tenth of the other penalties because wealth cumulates over time.

There is a similar function for France

$$(2) \qquad U^* = \Sigma \left[\Delta pc^{*2} + \alpha y^{*2} + \beta w^{*2} + \gamma r^{*2} + \delta g^{*2} \right]$$

where: $\qquad \alpha = \delta = 1, \ \beta = 0.1 \ \gamma = 0.$

preferences are therefore identical (both in aspirations and in relative priorities) between countries, and all regimes will be compared using the same welfare fuctions, evaluated, for simplicity, over the first five years only. But, as will become clear, the welfare functions actually used to compute optimal policies will, for certain regimes, necessarily differ from welfare function used to evaluate the outcomes. This complication should be borne in mind in what follows.

Welfare function outcomes for all regimes are brought together in a final table (Table 9).

As a benchmark for these comparisons, we take a free float exchange-rate regime. It is important to stress that floating is offered as a benchmark for comparisons and not necessarily as an alternative regime. Floating will certainly not be a candidate regime if the benefits from central bank independence and price stability, or from lower transactions costs and exchange-rate uncertainty, are judged to be the main advantages of monetary union. Nevertheless we still need a yardstick for calibrating any redistributional or adjustment difficulties implied by monetary union, in order to investigate whether those difficulties imply that a single currency will tend to unite or divide the European economies.

3.4 *Formal Specification of the Regimes*

3.4.1 The Pure Float Benchmark

In this regime policymakers in the two countries separately pursue their own objectives without any cooperation. Thus Germany uses r and g to maximise U in equation *(1)*; France uses r^* and g^* to maximise U^* in equation *(2)*.

3.4.2 Full Monetary Union: a Hard EMU

There are several ways in which a hard EMU could be defined. We will use one which perhaps comes closest to that described in the *Delors Report*: full integration of national monetary systems (and policy). The European currency unit (ECU) becomes a common currency and there can only be one monetary policy. The European Central Bank sets the short-term interest rate in ECUs.

This policy regime is compatible whith a number of different exchange-rate regimes for the EMU against the dollar. In this paper we assume that there is a free float of the EMU against the dollar exchange rate in the hard EMU regime.

In terms of our model, each country will target European inflation, output and wealth:

$$1/2 \, (pc_t - pc_t^* - 1 + pc_t^* - pc_{t-1}^*); \; y_t + y_t^*; \; \text{and} \; w_t + W_t^*$$

in addition its own inflation, output and wealth variables. In a cooperative framework, that comes down to optimising an equally weighted average of *(1)* and *(2)* using a single monetary policy, $r = r^*$, and cooperatively chosen fiscal expenditures, g and g^*, subject to indentical dollar exchange rates for the franc and mark (the single currency assumption).

3.4.3 Exchange-Rate Bands

Germany and France use r and g, and r^* and g^*, to maximise U and U^* respectively, but noncooperatively where an extra target of a_t^* $- a_t - p_t + p_t^*$ is added to both objective functions. That extra target represents the deviations of the nominal franc-mark exchange rate from its equilibrium (parity) value. The weight on those squared deviations my be raised to tighten the implied band.

4. - Simulation Results

In our detailed simulation analysis we have used the simulation model described in paragraph 3 to illustrate the adjustment strategies and outcomes to be expected under three different types of external shock or difficulty. The detailed outcomes are displayed in Table 1 to 10 in the Appendix. In those tables the figures denote deviations from pre-shock (equilibrium) values, in obvious units of measurement.

The first group of results (Tables 1 and 2) consider symmetric inflation shocks which are unanticipated by the policy makers and the private sector. These are presented as background to our analysis of asymmetric shocks.

The second group (Tables 3 and 4) consider unanticipated country specific (asymmetric) inflation shocks; and the third group

(Tables 5 and 6) consider a case of symmetrically offsetting current account shocks. Our symmetric inflation shocks are 10% to each country and indicate the sensitivity of each policy regime to a general supply-side disturbance, like the change in oil prices experienced in late 1990. The asymmetric inflation shocks are 20% to Germany and zero in France. These represent the financial consequences of a country-specific disturbance like German reunification. Finally matching current account shocks of + 5% in Germany and − 5% to France represent the kinds of changes to current accounts which led to pressure for a DM revaluation which was proposed but ruled out in late 1989.

4.1 Results: Symmetric Inflation Shocks

4.1.1 The Non-Cooperative Free-Float Benchmark (Table 1)

Symmetric 10% inflation shocks, under free-floating causes two types of policy response.

First, in order to control inflation, interest rates are increased in both real and nominal terms. That causes both the franc and the DM to appreciate against the dollar (but not against one another) in real terms, and for that reason both economies contract. Notice that the anti-inflation policy does not bring the price level back to its original path; although inflation itself is eliminated fairly rapidly, prices actually end up some 20 to 30% per cent higher by the end of the period. As a result, the nominal exchange rate will need to depreciate to maintain competitiveness; and, anticipating this, policymakers actually make that accommodation right from the start. But, with prices being sticky, the depreciations are needed throughout the adjustment process.

Second there is a fiscal contraction to control wealth losses. As a result of the real interest-rate increases and real appreciation just discussed, investment, the current account, and wealth all fall. This is counteracted by cuts in government spending, although wealth goes on falling cumulatively until year 3. The subsequent policy moves become more subtle. The real exchange-rate appreciation is reversed

TABLE 1

FREE FLOAT WITH SYMMETRIC (10%)
INFLATION SHOCKS

	Years	1	2	3	4	5
German economy						
Output	(%)	− 7.30	− 4.56	− 2.93	− 1.88	− 1.20
CPI inflation	(D)	9.82	4.11	2.71	1.76	1.14
Real money supply	(D)	− 10.21	− 6.28	− 3.97	− 2.51	− 1.58
Real exchange rate	(%)	− 2.54	− 0.69	0.09	0.45	0.57
Wealth	(%)	− 1.09	− 1.38	− 1.38	− 1.25	− 1.07
Nominal exchange rate	(%)	7.46	13.29	16.72	18.82	20.08
Real interest rate	(D)	1.85	0.78	0.36	0.12	0.00
G	(%)	− 0.74	− 0.85	− 0.73	− 0.60	− 0.48
Current account	(%)	0.07	0.20	0.22	0.21	0.18
Investment...........	(%)	− 1.15	− 0.49	− 0.22	− 0.08	− 0.00
French economy						
Output	(%)	− 7.30	− 4.56	− 2.93	− 1.88	− 1.20
CPI inflation	(D)	9.82	4.11	2.71	1.76	1.14
Real money supply	(D)	− 10.21	− 6.28	− 3.97	− 2.51	1.58
Real exchange rate	(%)	− 2.54	− 0.69	0.09	0.45	0.57
Wealth	(%)	− 1.09	− 1.38	− 1.38	− 1.25	− 1.07
Nominal exchange rate	(%)	7.46	13.29	16.72	18.82	20.08
Real interest rate	(D)	1.85	0.78	0.36	0.12	0.00
G	(%)	− 0.74	− 0.85	− 0.73	− 0.60	− 0.48
Current account	(%)	0.07	0.20	0.22	0.21	0.18
Investment...........	(%)	− 1.15	− 0.49	− 0.22	− 0.08	− 0.00

(%) is percent deviation from unchanged baseline;
(D) is change from unchanged baseline.

in order to reverse the recession and bring wealth back on track, while continued fiscal contraction prevents this from causing inflation.

Overall, the timing of these changes clearly shows policymakers putting a premium on solving their inflation problem first, and then recovering the wealth target later on. Indeed as so often in problems of this kind, the key lies in obtaining the right *sequence* of policy changes. Floating enables that issue to be addressed in a flexible way that monetary union would find more difficult. It is also important to remember that this is a noncooperative policy regime. There is no constraint which prevents European policymakers from trying to offload their inflation on each other by seeking to appreciate their exchange rates against each other in a «beggar thy neighbour» fashion (but see footnote (4)).

4.1.2 Hard EMU (Table 2)

In the hard EMU regime the balance of policy responses changes. The reasons for this are as follows.

First, there is less monetary contraction. This is because all policy decisions are taken cooperatively and there is a unified monetary policy. The monetary authorities of France and Germany no longer seek to appreciate their exchange rates against each other, and so the incentives for each of them to introduce a monetary contraction are now less. This is a classic result: the coordination in the union stops the members attempting the «beggar thy neighbour» interest-rate contractions which occurred under free floating, and obviates the need for defensive responses involving yet higher interest rates in a vain attempt to achieve some relative currency appreciation. That allows better outcomes for output together, with smaller wealth losses and smaller monetary contractions (4).

---

(4) One might have expected the cooperative case to show up as a definite welfare improvement in Table 9. Cooperation within the union stops members attempting «beggar the neighbour» policy contractions and prevents each country imposing unwanted spillover effects on its partner. Tha might allow better outcomes and/or smaller policy interventions as countries suffer fewer unfavourable spillovers and need less in the way of defensive policy responses. (COOPER [3], HUGHES HALLETT [9]).

This effect may be counteracted by the fact that our policy designs are restricted to being «time consistent», in which policymakers cannot merely rely on a reputation for promises of future disinflation to be believed. They can only implement policies which, predictably, they would not wish to renege on in the future. With reputation, governments may announce a tightening of monetary policy, now and in the future, and restrain inflation in part directly and in part through expectations. Without reputation, the expectational channel is blocked, so that policy is weakened and a more inflationary outcome will occur. Thus the absence of reputation leads to a weakening of policy impacts. This goes against the strengthening of policy effectiveness identified above, and may just serve to overturn the presumption that cooperation within the union would improve welfare.

It is not obvious why a monetary union would in itself improve the reputation of monetary policymakers compared with that under free floating. (Statements by the Governor of the Bundesbank at the time of writing indicate a concern to this effect). Therefore, in studying both monetary union (of both hard and soft varieties) and free floating, we restrict ourselves to time consistent policies which do not rely on any reputational effect.

TABLE 2

SYMMETRIC HARD EMU
WITH SYMMETRIC (10%) INFLATION SHOCKS (*)

Years		1	2	3	4	5
German economy						
Output	(%)	−4.25	−3.34	−2.63	−2.07	−1.63
CPI inflation	(D)	9.94	6.55	5.15	4.06	3.19
Real money supply	(D)	−7.60	−5.97	−4.71	−3.72	−2.93
Real exchange rate	(%)	−0.91	−0.74	−0.63	−0.52	−0.42
Wealth	(%)	−0.04	−0.08	−0.08	−0.08	−0.07
Nominal exchange rate	(%)	9.09	15.79	21.05	25.21	28.50
Real interest rate	(D)	0.16	0.11	0.11	0.10	0.08
G	(%)	−1.10	−0.87	−0.67	−0.52	−0.40
Current account	(%)	0.14	0.11	0.08	0.06	0.04
Investment	(%)	−0.10	−0.07	−0.07	−0.06	−0.05
French economy						
Output	(%)	−4.25	−3.35	−2.64	−2.08	−1.64
CPI inflation	(D)	9.94	6.55	5.15	4.06	3.19
Real money supply	(D)	−7.59	−5.97	−4.71	−3.72	−2.93
Real exchange rate	(%)	−0.91	−0.75	−0.63	−0.52	−0.42
Wealth	(%)	−0.04	−0.08	−0.08	−0.07	−0.6
Nominal exchange rate	(%)	9.09	15.79	21.05	25.21	28.50
Real interest rate	(D)	0.15	0.11	0.11	0.09	0.08
G	(%)	−1.10	−0.87	−0.66	−0.51	−0.40
Current account	(%)	0.14	0.10	0.07	0.05	0.04
Investment	(%)	−0.10	−0.07	−0.07	−0.06	−0.05

(*) (%) is percent deviation from unchanged baseline;
(D) is change from unchanged baseline.

However one shouldn't make too much of this point since one would still expect «beggar thy neighbour» monetary contractions by Europe as a whole against other countries (there is no cooperation outside Europe), and Table 9 shows that the credibility constraint discussed in footnote (4) reduces the scope for better coordination. In fact, the Europe-wide contractions never appear. Instead we get a shift in policy mix to fiscal contractions, and hence a depreciation of the EMU. As a result, inflation is disciplined more slowly and prices now end up higher by more up by about 30 to 35% overall. That means the degree of accommodation is actually larger than in Table 1; the ECU must depreciate by more against the dollar than did the nominal exchange rates of France and Germany in the free float case. But, by way of compensation, the extra depreciation implies that the policy-induced falls in output are smaller.

Second, stronger fiscal contractions are required to compensate for weaker monetary control and to assist in the disciplining of inflation. It is this change in policy mix (to larger fiscal interventions and less monetary contraction) which causes the EMU depreciation, and the worse inflation but better output results. Full monetary union therefore requires greater fiscal flexibility. At the same time there are no wealth transfers, current account imbalances or investment losses to speak of.

In sum the monetary union regime has both costs and benefits. The costs are slower disinflation and a requirement for greater fiscal flexibility. The benefits are smaller output losses and the smaller instrument required movements. One's view of the outcomes will therefore depend upon one's ranking of these costs and benefits.

4.2 Asymmetric Inflation Shocks

With asymmetric shocks, things start to look very different. Our shock is a (very large) 20% inflation shock in Germany alone, scaled so that the average shock in Europe is the same as in the symmetric case just considered. It is designed to display the possible policy responses to inflation which results from a boom in one country, rather than in Europe as a whole.

4.2.1 Free Float (Without Cooperation)

Under a non-cooperative floating regime (Table 3), «German reunification» delivers a substantial inflationary shock within the German economy, but very little of the losses are transferred to the French economy. There is a small inflationary spillover in the year after the shock, but that is squeezed out of the system by a small French monetary contraction in the same year and a substantial appreciation against the mark as a result of German policy. The result

TABLE 3

FREE FLOAT WITH ASYMMETRIC (20%, 0%)
INFLATION SHOCKS (*)

Years		1	2	3	4	5
German economy						
Output	(%)	− 14.23	− 9.03	− 5.88	− 3.83	− 2.49
CPI inflation	(D)	18.56	7.86	5.26	3.47	2.29
Real money supply	(D)	− 19.38	− 12.22	− 7.90	− 5.10	− 3.29
Real exchange rate	(%)	− 5.48	− 2.34	− 0.87	− 0.09	− 0.29
Wealth	(%)	− 2.07	− 2.64	− 2.67	− 2.43	− 2.09
Nominal exchange rate	(%)	14.52	24.84	31.21	35.25	37.80
Real interest rate	(D)	3.14	1.47	0.78	0.38	0.15
G	(%)	− 1.48	− 1.69	− 1.45	− 1.20	− 0.96
Current account	(%)	− 0.11	0.35	0.46	0.48	0.44
Investment	(%)	− 1.96	− 0.92	− 0.49	− 0.24	− 0.09
French economy						
Output	(%)	− 0.37	− 0.09	− 0.03	− 0.07	− 0.08
CPI inflation	(D)	1.09	0.36	0.16	0.05	0.00
Real money supply	(D)	− 1.04	− 0.34	− 0.04	− 0.09	0.13
Real exchange rate	(%)	0.40	0.95	1.04	0.98	0.85
Wealth	(%)	− 1.10	− 0.11	− 0.09	− 0.07	− 0.05
Nominal exchange rate	(%)	0.40	1.74	2.23	2.38	2.35
Real interest rate	(D)	1.55	0.09	− 0.06	− 0.13	− 0.15
G	(%)	0.01	− 0.01	− 0.01	− 0.01	− 0.00
Current account	(%)	0.24	0.05	− 0.02	− 0.06	− 0.07
Investment	(%)	− 0.35	− 0.06	0.04	0.08	0.09

(*) (%) is percent deviation from unchanged baseline;
(D) is change from unchanged baseline.

of these adjustments is therefore very little inflation or output or wealth loss in France. Prices rise by no more than 2% overall, and the output losses are negligible. Floating enables France to largely insulate her economy.

Germany, by contrast undertakes both monetary and fiscal contractions. The first 3 years sees large output losses (up to 14%) as the price for disciplining inflation. These problems are eventually removed but their initial impact is quite large and involves an initial loss of wealth, which only gradually begins to be corrected. As one might expect the policy responses, and the disturbances to output, the price level and wealth, are about twice what they were in Germany under the Europe-wide inflationary shock of Table 1. But adjustment is slightly faster because Germany is more open as an economy than Europe, and so imports disinflation faster with any given degree of currency appreciation.

Notice that, although inflation is brought under control in Germany, the price level in Germany actually ends up 42% higher. Floating exchange rates enable Germany on its own to accommodate German inflation by depreciating against the franc and dollar, just as in Table 1 they allowed Europe as a whole to accommodate European inflation.

There are thus two key features of these results, both of which are in a sense well known, but both of which are important for the comparison with monetary union. First floating isolates France from German disturbance. Second floating enables Germany to accommodate the entire inflation disturbance.

4.2.2 Hard EMU

Under the hard EMU regime (Table 4) the responses to our asymmetric inflation shock are savagely strong. Monetary conditions are tightened Europe-wide, and the speed of inflation discipline in Germany is greater than in the floating case discussed in Table 3. Essentially the inability of Germany to depreciate vis-à-vis France causes a loss in German competitiveness and a German slump output-price inflation (not shown here) is stopped dead in its tracks, with the result that the high nominal European interest rate causes a high real interest rate in Germany, and hence a second recessionary impulse in Germany. France gets a boom from its emergent trade surplus with Germany. That causes inflation on France, with the consequence that real interest rates in France are in fact low, giving a second boost to the French boom.

There is also a very large wealth transfer from Germany to France and elsewhere, associated with both German appreciation (which has caused a current account deficit) and the high real interest rate in Germany (which depresses investment). Fiscal policy is powerless to assist in correcting this. In fact fiscal expansion is required to partly

TABLE 4

SYMMETRIC HARD EMU
WITH ASYMMETRIC INFLATION SHOCKS (*)

	Years	1	2	3	4	5
German economy						
Output	(%)	− 20.05	− 8.84	− 3.55	− 1.63	− 1.07
CPI inflation	(D)	12.79	4.57	4.13	3.73	3.19
Real money supply	(D)	− 23.40	− 11.46	− 5.63	− 3.27	− 2.36
Real exchange rate	(%)	− 10.87	− 3.78	− 0.07	1.18	1.29
Wealth	(%)	− 8.24	− 11.38	− 11.09	− 9.48	− 7.69
Nominal exchange rate	(%)	9.13	15.81	21.06	25.22	28.50
Real interest rate	(D)	7.09	3.71	1.25	0.11	− 0.23
G	(%)	3.23	0.93	− 1.17	− 2.02	− 2.05
Current account	(%)	− 3.81	− 0.82	1.07	1.69	1.64
Investment	(%)	− 4.43	− 2.32	− 0.78	− 0.07	− 0.14
French economy						
Output	(%)	11.55	2.15	− 1.72	− 2.52	− 2.20
CPI inflation	(D)	7.09	8.53	6.18	4.38	3.20
Real money supply	(D)	8.19	− 0.49	− 3.80	− 4.17	− 3.50
Real exchange rate	(%)	9.13	2.33	− 1.18	− 2.22	− 2.14
Wealth	(%)	8.32	11.53	11.26	9.63	7.83
Nominal exchange rate	(%)	9.13	15.81	21.06	25.22	28.50
Real interest rate	(D)	− 6.75	− 3.48	− 1.03	0.08	0.39
G	(%)	− 5.43	− 2.67	0.16	1.00	1.25
Current account	(%)	4.10	1.03	− 0.91	− 1.58	− 1.56
Investment	(%)	4.22	2.18	0.64	− 0.05	− 0.24

(*) (%) is percent deviation from unchanged baseline;
  (D) is change from unchanged baseline.

correct the loss in otuput which the adjustment process brings about. (This result exactly mirrors Begg's argument discussed in the introduction). Moreover fiscal activity has to be higher in *both* countries to compensate for the restriction on relative monetary adjustments.

Two features of the inflation-control process in the monetary union are worth emphasizing.

First, more discipline is imposed on German prices in a monetary union. In the floating regime, we saw that, although German inflation was eventually removed, German price levels permanently diverged from those in France (which hardly moved). That divergence was accommodated by depreciating the mark against the franc. But, in the

monetary union case, no accommodating depreciations of the mark
are allowed: German and French price levels must rise by the same
amount as each other in the long run, and this fact severely curtails
the overall rise in German prices (to 36% instead of 42%) while French
prices rise 36% instead of 2%. Summarising «monetary union does not
allow relative accommodation of inflationary shocks».

Second, union spreads the accommodation to German inflationary pressure throughout Europe: it causes French prices to rise
(5). In fact, in our experiment, in response to the German inflation
shock, prices in both France and Germany go up by more than half of
what happens to German prices under a float and the European price
index rises by more than it does under the floating regime. For Europe
as a whole, the degree of accommodation is therefore higher (6) than
under floating. (Such accommodation is possible under monetary
union, because, although there is no mark-franc depreciation, both
currencies depreciate against the dollar by enough to accommodate
the Europe-wide rise in prices). We discuss the reason for this below.
The important point is that monetary union does not of itself (7)
eliminate accommodation. It merely spreads it, from the country in
which the inflation originates, to the whole of Europe. Thus: «monetary union does not *prevent* absolute accommodation of inflation
shocks, so that (relative) inflation discipline does not ensure (absolute)
price discipline».

These two points may be significant for a real-world Europe with
many countries, each of different sizes. Small and inflation-prone
countries may like monetary union because of the price level discipline which they can «buy» from larger better disciplined countries.
But they do this partly through exporting the accommodation of

---

(5) Obviously since German inflation begins above French inflation and never
drops below zero, and because in the end German and French prices must rise by the
same amount, there must be a period when French inflation goes above German
inflation. This happens from year 2 onwards.

(6) This is the same result as we observed when comparing Tables 1 and 2. The
point is that since Germany is half of Europe, a similar degree of accommodation would
see prices rise throughout Europe under monetary union case by half of the amount by
which they rose in Germany alone under floating.

(7) This is not to deny that joining a monetary union might change the preferences
of policymakers.

inflation to the whole of Europe. Lacking an overall nominal anchor, such a system may only work well if a large economy is prepared to act as disciplinarian. Yet larger non-inflation prone economies may not like to do this since it would compromise the absolute discipline which they might have achieved on their own. To some extent, they lose their grip on their own inflation.

In our own exercise, the «spreading» of accommodation throughout Europe under monetary union makes the outcomes for Europe as a whole appear better under monetary union than under floating (Table 9). This is because our performance measure penalizes extremes of any kind (8), and monetary union spreads the extreme German inflation to produce more moderate levels of inflation for all in Europe.

However monetary union has clearly made the distribution of benefits across countries much worse; the average outcomes in Table 9 are better than the national outcomes evaluating outcomes for Europe as a whole obscures adjustment difficulties at the national level, in particular those associated with the transfer of inflation and hence relative real exchange-rate movements, which lead to wealth transfers (which are partly offsetting and therefore ignored when considering Europe as a whole), and the very large output movements (which are again partly offsetting at the European level). That result explains why accommodation is actually greater, and absolute (but not relative) discipline weaker, than in the floating regime. Convexity of preferences means policy will try to avoid very large disturbances. Hence a policy which tries hard to remove the 20% inflation shock within Germany will try less hard (and more than proportionately so) when it comes to counteracting the lower Europe-wide inflationary pressures which result from the spreading action of monetary union. As a result it becomes desirable to reduce the degree of discipline somewhat. In other words a European Central Bank with the same degree of independence as the German Bundesbank is likely to try less hard to eliminate inflation than would an equally cautious Bundesbank.

---

(8) The loss function is quadratic.

4.3 *Offsetting Current Account Shocks*

The current account shocks consist of a diversion of demand from France to Germany equivalent to 5% of the GDP of each country. Without any policy response, such a shock would cause excess demand and inflation in Germany, and a continuing wealth transfer from France to Germany.

Tables 5 and 6 show what we might expect from such an intra-European shift in spending: outcomes considerably worse for each individual country than for Europe as a whole. Indeed, for the symmetrical regimes of free floating and hard EMU we would not expect any change in any European outcomes at all since without any policy response at all such an intra-European shock would leave all European aggregates unchanged.

4.3.1 Free Float (Without Cooperation: Table 5)

In a floating regime, exchange-rate movements can largely neutralise this shock. An appreciation of the DM could, in principle, correct the intra-European current account imbalances entirely, and thereby completely remove the excess demand in Germany and the corresponding output fall in France. That would also remove the wealth transfer between France and Germany. But such an exchange-rate movement would not be costless: it would cause price inflation in France and deflation in Germany. It is preferable, therefore, to leave some residual boom in Germany, together with some wealth movements associated with the real interest-rate changes necessary to shape the real exchange-rate adjustments over time.

Notice that the pattern of adjustment which emerges sees the level of prices drifting up in Germany, and down in France. Part of the adjustment process therefore sees upward price level accommodation in Germany to the demand shock there (and vice versa in France). Overall the disturbances to output and wealth are relatively small. And because the exchange rate bears the burden of adjustment the required policy responses — which are equal and opposite — are small also. In particular, little fiscal flexibility is needed.

TABLE 5

A FREE FLOAT WITH SUSTAINED OFFSETTING
(+5%, −5%) CA SHOCKS (*)

	Years	1	2	3	4	5
German economy						
Output	(%)	4.52	2.93	1.94	1.29	0.85
CPI inflation	(D)	−0.99	2.21	2.97	3.50	3.86
Real money supply	(D)	3.68	1.59	0.29	−0.58	−1.16
Real exchange rate	(%)	−2.30	−3.25	−3.79	−4.13	−4.34
Wealth	(%)	1.18	1.76	2.06	2.20	2.25
Nominal exchange rate	(%)	−2.30	−0.63	2.04	5.34	9.08
Real interest rate	(D)	−0.95	−0.53	−0.34	−0.21	−0.13
G	(%)	−0.05	0.15	0.18	0.18	0.16
Current account	(%)	0.58	0.24	0.09	0.01	−0.03
Investment............	(%)	0.60	0.33	0.21	0.13	0.08
French economy						
Output	(%)	−4.52	−2.93	−1.94	−1.29	−0.85
CPI inflation	(D)	0.99	−2.21	−2.97	−3.50	−3.86
Real money supply	(D)	−3.68	−1.59	−0.29	−0.58	1.16
Real exchange rate	(%)	−2.30	3.25	3.79	4.13	4.34
Wealth	(%)	−1.18	−1.76	−2.06	−2.20	−2.25
Nominal exchange rate	(%)	2.30	0.63	−2.04	−5.34	−9.08
Real interest rate	(D)	0.95	0.53	0.34	0.21	0.13
G	(%)	0.05	−0.15	−0.18	−0.18	−0.16
Current account	(%)	−0.58	−0.24	−0.09	−0.01	0.03
Investment............	(%)	−0.60	−0.33	−0.21	−0.13	−0.08

(*) (%) is percent deviation from unchanged baseline;
    (D) is change from unchanged baseline.

4.3.2 Hard EMU (Table 6)

This time there can be no relative exchange-rate movement — no exchange-rate «separation» occurs — and so there can be no long-term price-level accommodation either. Tying the monetary instruments together removes the policy flexibility just at the time when policymakers should do equal and opposite things in order to cope with the equal and opposite shocks in otherwise identical economies. That restriction, which effectively neutralises any monetary policy response altogether, would be very expensive in this sort of situation if

A.J. Hughes Hallett - David Vines

TABLE 6

SYMMETRIC HARD EMU
WITH PERMANENT CURRENT ACCOUNT SHOCKS (*)

	Years	1	2	3	4	5
German economy						
Output	(%)	1.57	0.96	0.58	0.38	0.28
CPI inflation	(D)	0.00	0.72	0.58	0.43	0.32
Real money supply	(D)	1.57	0.96	0.58	0.38	0.28
Real exchange rate	(%)	0.00	− 1.26	− 2.27	− 3.02	− 3.58
Wealth	(%)	5.11	9.23	12.48	15.04	17.09
Nominal exchange rate	(%)	0.00	0.00	0.00	− 0.00	− 0.00
Real interest rate	(D)	− 1.26	− 1.01	− 0.75	− 0.56	− 0.43
G	(%)	− 4.72	− 3.63	− 2.64	− 1.84	− 1.23
Current account	(%)	4.32	3.24	2.31	1.59	1.03
Investment............	(%)	0.79	0.63	0.47	0.35	0.27
French economy						
Output	(%)	− 1.57	− 0.96	− 0.58	− 0.38	− 0.28
CPI inflation	(D)	0.00	− 0.72	− 0.58	− 0.43	− 0.32
Real money supply	(D)	− 1.57	− 0.96	− 0.58	− 0.38	− 0.28
Real exchange rate	(%)	0.00	1.26	2.27	3.03	3.59
Wealth	(%)	− 5.11	− 9.24	− 12.48	− 15.04	− 17.09
Nominal exchange rate	(%)	0.00	0.00	0.00	− 0.00	− 0.00
Real interest rate	(D)	1.26	1.01	0.75	0.56	0.43
G	(%)	4.72	3.63	2.64	1.84	1.23
Current account	(%)	− 4.32	− 3.24	− 2.31	− 1.59	− 1.03
Investment............	(%)	− 0.79	− 0.63	− 0.47	− 0.35	− 0.27

(*) (%) is percent deviation from unchanged baseline;
(D) is change from unchanged baseline.

it were not possible to substitute a very active fiscal policy in compensation. Once again the fiscal flexibility is crucial to the monetary union idea, and the symmetry in Table 6 clearly shows that any attempt to impose a common fiscal policy within a union (for example by restricting national budget deficits) would have potentially disastrous consequences for output and inflation. As it is, the potential output and inflation losses are quite small since fiscal contraction in Germany immediately compensates for the expansion of demand coming from the positive shock to net exports. The cost of this is a continuing wealth transfer from France to Germany which is only gradually corrected as the adjustment process gets underway.

In the floating case, adjustment happened in the short term through exchange-rate separation — the DM appreciated immediately — and the process allowed price levels to drift apart over the longer term. Here adjustment requires a gradual rise in output prices in Germany (and fall in France) which only gradually changes the real exchange rate, but — subject to this change in relative prices — the price levels are locked together in the longer term. And it is possible that the real DM exchange rate will need to appreciate further in the longer term too correct the short- to medium-term wealth transfer from France to Germany. Hence, as we would expect this regime performs much worse for each of the countries than does the free-floating regime.

5. - On Price Anchors and Price Stability in a Monetary Union

The main difficulty with a monetary union based on fixing or stabilising exchange rates is that, while it can successfully eliminate inflation and inflation differentials, it does not stabilise prices as such. Tables 1 to 6 clearly show steadily rising price levels in response to exogenous shocks, even if inflation itself is removed. Monetary union is therefore, in seafaring terms, acting as a sheet anchor but not as a fixed (or absolute) anchor. This happens simply because there is still a rest of the world and Europe cannot isolate itself from that. The single currency can float up and down against non-European currencies just as much as any national currency would in a floating regime; and there is no reason therefore to expect that the European monetary authority would be any less accommodating in their monetary control of the EMU than the national monetary authorities would be, just because the European economy is larger than its component parts. This argument is of course quite different from that put forward in the official analysis where it is assumed that the EMU can *never* (be expected to) depreciate against any other currency (European Economy ([7], p. 315). Our conclusions are therefore quite different. So long as Europe remains an open trading economy with respect to the rest of the world, the possibility of an EMU depreciation to accommodate inflationary pressures exists and exchange-rate stability within the union does not guarantee price stability.

5.1 *The Price Effects*

What happens if we provide a fixed price anchor to ensure price stability? This could be done by pegging the ECU to the price of gold (say), or a specified basket of commodities, or by progressively hardening the ECU by preventing it being devalued against any other currency. Do the outcomes of a monetary union improve with this extra condition? That is easily examined by replacing Δpc and Δpc^* in *(1)* and *(2)* by pc and pc^* respectively. The results for output and prices under asymmetric (German) inflation shocks, being the case which throws the lack of a price anchor into high relief, are sketched in Graphs 1-4, together with the corresponding «sheet anchor» results already discussed from Tables 3 and 4. [Tables 7 and 8 contain the results for the remaining variables].

It is clear, from Graphs 1 and 2, that inserting a fixed price anchor does the trick; not only is inflation eliminated, but the price levels are stabilised too. Under floating we get the usual insulation of the French economy; prices peak at 2% higher than their original level in year 1, but then return to their baseline (barring slight oscillations) by year 3. (That contrasts with a permanent rise of 1.75% in the «sheet anchor» case). In Germany, however, price stability is also now restored by year 7; prices peak at the much lower level of 17% above base in year 1 and then fall back quickly, in contrast to a 42% rise by year 11 in the «sheet anchor» case. Once again if there are any oscillations, they are negligible.

Under a hard EMU regime we get the same stabilisation of price levels — a more rapid disciplinary of prices than under floating for Germany (at least in the early years), but with rather less success in stabilising prices than under floating in the case of France (as we might expect since insulation is no longer possible). Germany now sees prices peak at only 15% up on the baseline in year 1, and fall more slowly than under floating so that they both have prices 13% above base in year 2. From year 3 onwards the monetary union

Table 7

THE FLOATING REGIME
WITH A FIXED PRICE ANCHOR (*)

	Years	1	2	3	4	5
German economy						
Output	(%)	− 29.19	− 12.87	− 3.91	0.15	1.48
CPI inflation	(D)	17.29	− 4.37	− 4.97	− 3.81	− 2.38
Real money supply	(D)	− 29.98	− 11.98	− 2.66	1.23	2.24
Real exchange rate	(%)	− 10.36	− 2.71	1.43	3.17	3.54
Wealth	(%)	− 4.57	− 6.77	− 7.33	− 6.97	− 6.23
Nominal exchange rate	(%)	9.64	11.23	9.47	6.97	4.82
Real interest rate	(D)	7.64	4.15	1.74	0.36	− 0.27
G	(%)	− 2.72	− 1.25	− 0.76	− 0.68	− 0.72
Current account	(%)	0.20	0.63	0.87	.095	0.92
Investment...........	(%)	− 4.78	− 2.54	− 1.09	− 0.23	0.17
French economy						
Output	(%)	− 1.81	− 0.19	0.52	0.64	0.50
CPI inflation	(D)	2.03	− 0.48	− 0.70	− 0.54	− 0.30
Real money supply	(D)	− 2.72	− 0.41	0.62	0.84	0.71
Real exchange rate	(%)	0.66	1.91	2.45	2.48	2.25
Wealth	(%)	− 0.51	− 0.72	− 0.72	− 0.63	− 0.51
Nominal exchange rate	(%)	0.66	2.50	2.94	2.75	2.34
Real interest rate	(D)	1.25	0.53	0.03·	− 0.23	− 0.31
G	(%)	0.06	0.14	0.10	0.03	− 0.02
Current account	(%)	0.27	0.15	0.05	− 0.01	− 0.05
Investment...........	(%)	− 0.78	− 0.33	− 0.02	0.14	0.20

(*) (%) is percent deviation from unchanged baseline;
(D) is change from unchanged baseline.

solution shows a higher price level than the floating regime and final price stability is achieved more slowly. So while monetary union with a fixed price anchor exercises a sharper discipline against price inflation in the short term, it actually takes longer to return prices back to their original level than would floating with the same anchor. But either regime is preferable to monetary union without a price anchor (where prices permanently rise by 33%).

In France, the spreading effects of monetary union ensures price stability in weaker than under floating — but the degree of instability is a lot less than the «sheet anchor» results in Table 4. With a fixed price anchor, prices peak at 10.5% above the baseline in year 2 —

TABLE 8

THE HARD EMU REGIME
WITH A FIXED PRICE ANCHOR (*)

	Years	1	2	3	4	5
German economy						
Output	(%)	−28.56	−12.21	− 4.08	−0.65	0.62
CPI inflation	(D)	15.60	− 3.93	− 3.57	−2.74	−2.08
Real money supply	(D)	−28.84	−11.65	− 3.19	0.27	1.41
Real exchange rate	(%)	−11.45	− 3.65	0.36	1.74	1.94
Wealth	(%)	− 7.84	−10.70	−10.40	−8.96	−7.40
Nominal exchange rate	(%)	8.55	9.10	7.98	6.20	4.35
Real interest rate	(D)	7.80	4.01	1.38	0.20	−0.19
G	(%)	0.70	− 0.59	− 1.85	−2.12	−1.85
Current account	(%)	− 2.97	0.05	1.70	2.08	1.89
Investment...........	(%)	− 4.87	− 2.51	− 0.86	−0.12	0.12
French economy						
Output	(%)	4.98	− 1.75	− 2.95	−1.91	−0.63
CPI inflation	(D)	4.20	4.87	0.48	−1.71	−2.26
Real money supply	(D)	4.71	− 1.19	− 2.06	−0.99	0.16
Real exchange rate	(%)	8.55	0.91	− 2.18	−2.62	−2.11
Wealth	(%)	8.88	11.71	11.04	9.22	7.38
Nominal exchange rate	(%)	8.55	9.10	7.98	6.20	4.35
Real interest rate	(D)	− 7.64	− 3.09	− 0.43	0.51	0.61
G	(%)	− 7.64	− 2.82	0.51	1.90	2.14
Current account	(%)	4.11	0.45	− 1.52	−2.06	−1.92
Investment...........	(%)	4.77	1.93	0.27	−0.32	−0.38

(*) (%) is percent deviation from unchanged baseline;
    (D) is change from unchanged baseline.

compared with a peak of 2% under floating and 36% in a monetary
union without a price anchor. Moreover the price anchor returns
prices to their original level after 8 years or so under a monetary union
(compared to 5 years under a float, and never with a sheet anchor).

5.2 *The Output Losses*

The gains which a fixed price anchor brings in terms of greater
price stability (and lower inflation) have their costs in greater output
instability. For Germany, a fixed price anchor provides a considerably

GRAPH 1

PRICE LEVELS, GERMANY

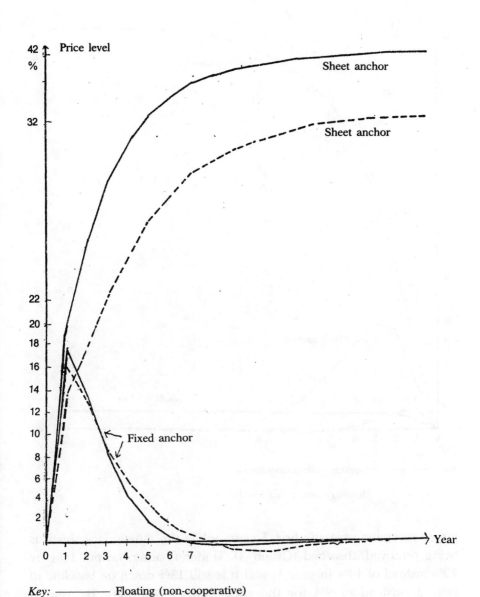

Key: —————— Floating (non-cooperative)

– – – – – Monetary union (hard EMU)

GRAPH 2

PRICES LEVELS, FRANCE

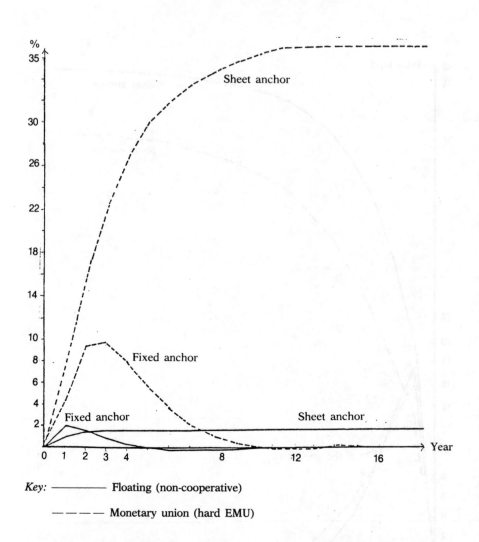

Key: ——————— Floating (non-cooperative)

— — — — Monetary union (hard EMU)

larger recession over the first 3 years while the inflationary shock is being removed/absorbed (Graph 3). Under floating, output falls by 29% instead of 14% in year 1, and it is still 13% down on baseline in year 2 (instead of 9% for the sheet anchor solution). By year 3 however the stronger discipline of a fixed anchor begins to pay

GRAPH 3

OUTPUT LOSSES, GERMANY

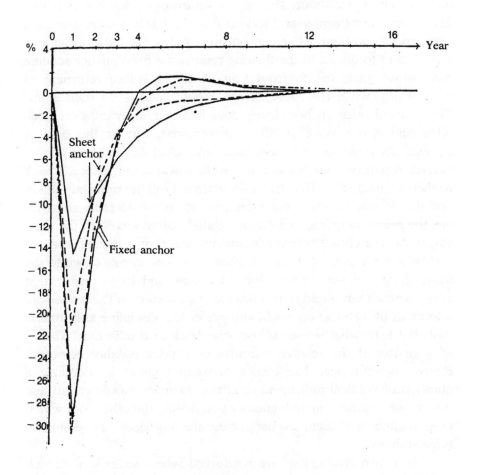

Key: ————— Floating (non-cooperative)

———— Monetary union (hard EMU)

dividends with output only 4% down (compared to 6% under the sheet anchor regime) and from years 4 to 10 output actually rises up to 2% above base before returning to its equilibrium level. The sheet anchor solution recovers its equilibrium level more slowly and without rising above it.

Monetary union produces the same pattern but in a more exaggerated form the peak losses are still 29% (in year 1) with a fixed anchor, but 20% without. The rate of return to equilibrium is a little faster thereafter (from year 2 to year 6 or 7). The losses are now 12% with, and 8% without, a fixed anchor in year 2; 4% in either scheme in year 3, and so on. As in the floating regime the fixed anchor scheme has output gains of 1% from years 5 to 11 before returning to equilibrium, while the sheet anchor scheme shows no such gains. Thus a fixed price anchor clearly does induce greater inflation discipline and hence price stability, as required, but at the cost of significantly larger output losses while that discipline is being administered. A part of those losses can then be made up as prices fall back to their original level. The effects show up in both the monetary union and the floating regimes, but monetary union considerably strengthens the price discipline, and the associated output losses, in the early stages. So the choice between monetary union or a floating regime, and between a fixed or a sheet anchor for prices, comes down to the same thing. Do you prefer sharp discipline and larger adjustment costs, with a more rapid return towards equilibrium in the immediate aftermath of a shock; or would you prefer less discipline and smaller costs but somewhat slower adjustments back to equilibrium? That is all a matter of the relative priorities over price stability vs output (employment) losses. The choice between regimes is therefore a question of political judgement, and not (as many would claim) one where one regime is unambiguously better than the other. But which even regime is chosen, exchange-rate stability does not guarantee price stability.

These two conclusions are reinforced when we look at French output behaviour with the extra discipline of a fixed price anchor (Graph 4). The floating regime shows the usual insulation property, (but the output losses (in year 1) are exaggerated by the extra disciplines of a fixed price anchor. Monetary union shows this effect much more clearly with large output gains (5% with a fixed anchor, but 9% without) while price discipline is being administered in the German half of the union, but significant output losses in years 2 or 3 to year 8 when Germany starts to recover and France needs to eliminate the transferred inflation. The induced cycle of adjustments,

GRAPH 4

OUTPUT LOSSES, FRANCE

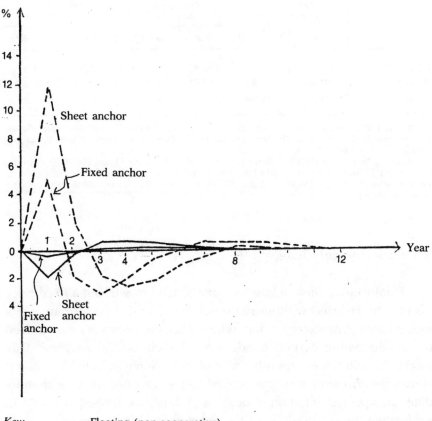

Key: ————————— Floating (non-cooperative)

— — — — Monetary union (hard EMU)

with peaks of + 5% to + 9% and troughs of − 3%, are much clearer than in the German case and show that this time monetary union slows up the adjustment back to equilibrium (as does the lack of a fixed price anchor). So the conclusions remain the same in the periphery countries: the choice between regimes is a matter of preferences over targets and time, and exchange-rate stability does not secure price stability.

TABLE 9

OBJECTIVE FUNCTION VALUES
FOR YEARS 1 TO 5 INCLUSIVE (*)

	Symmetric inflation shocks		Asymmetric inflation shocks		Asymmetric demand shocks	
	float	hard EMU	float	hard EMU	float	hard EMU
Germany ..	108.16	120.41	403.83	436.35	39.49	65.37
France	108.16	120.41	0.67	239.16	39.49	65.02
Europe	244.15	189.46	244.16	189.10	0.00	0.05

(*) All policies derived from noncooperative decision making and a standard quadratic loss function described in section 3. The European objective reflects the aggregate targets (and average inflation) as noted in section 3.

Cooperative policy making in a floating regime yields 108.88, 108.88 and 240.69 for Germany, France and Europe under symmetric inflation shocks. Under asymmetric inflation shocks the corresponding figures are 398.39, 1.72 and 240.29; and under the demand shocks they are 42.4, 42.41 and 0.

5.3 *Exchange-Rate Bands*

Finally could these adjustment costs, with or without a fixed price anchor, be reduced without too much loss in price performance in a looser form of monetary union, where exchange rates are constrained to remain within certain bands around their official parities? That might provide a less expensive way of disciplining inflation because it allows governments a strictly limited degree of freedom to accommodate unexpected inflation shocks, and hence a limited amount of exchange-rate «separation» in the short term. Many countries would probably regard this as a useful from of «insurance», allowing them to adjust exchange rates a bit when extreme circumstances and large output losses demand it. But it is an insurance policy which would not be invoked in the normal course of events of «average» sized shocks. A limited degree of flexibility would therefore allow them to maintain their preferences for price stability vs. output losses even when asymmetric shocks would otherwise call large short-term output adjustment.

We have examined this option by introducing an explicit exchange-rate target term into (1) and (2); the «sheet anchor» case. We could regard the floating regime with asymmetric inflation shocks (Table 3) as an ERM system with extremely wide exchange-rate bands (i.e. the exchange-rate target has zero weight, but the equilibrium exchange rate is the parity or target value). A number of realignments would be required since the implied Fr./DM band starts at ± 14% and widens to ± 36% (Table 10). Can we get more price discipline, without much extra output cost, by tightening the band to the typical ERM limits of ± 2.5% or ± 6%? We can model that by increasing the penalty given to deviations of the Fr.-DM exchange rate from its equilibrium level. Table 10 shows that when that penalty reaches 3 times that on inflation or output deviations a weak form of ERM (± 6% bands) will be operating from year 2. When that penalty ratio reaches 5, the stronger (± 2.5% bands) form will be operating by year 2. And even stronger penalties will progressively harden the scheme to something like the hard EMU. However even when the penalty ratio is 5 we fail to get quite as good outcomes as in the hard EMU scheme (Table 3) in the earlier years. Things follow the same pattern, but output losses and inflation are both slightly larger for Germany (and smaller for France) over years 1 to 3. By years 4 and 5 output and inflation looks better in both countries under the band regime. So exchange-rate bands do not impose such strong discipline, but they incur some extra costs in Germany, in the early stages of adjustment. But the disturbances induced imply less lasting damage (although these differences are quantitatively small). The spreading effect, in which victims as well as sinners must share the pains of adjustment as well as the benefits of discipline, are also weakened. These are the

TABLE 10

THE MARK-FRANC EXCHANGE RATE BANDS
IN % DEVIATIONS FROM PARITY

Penalty ratio	Years	1	2	3	4	5
0		± 14.5	23.4	29.2	33.0	35.6
1		± 18.2	9.9	4.3	1.5	0.3
3		± 15.0	6.0	1.8	0.3	0.1
5		± 13.9	2.4	0.3	0.1	0.1

advantages of the short-run exchange-rate separation made possible by retaining an insurance policy against asymmetric shocks.

However there are also costs. It is clear that, whatever band system, realignments are needed in year 1. No band system can cope with a shock that is the asymmetric in its impact, since the width in year 1 cannot be reduced below ± 14%. But the band can be tightened very fast thereafter, implying that exchange rates, prices, output etc. can be stabilised rapidly — and *more* rapidly than in the Hard monetary union scheme — *once* the insurance policy has been invoked. That is an advantage. However progressively tightening the band to get that result does incur greater output losses than wider bands with less stabilising power, and it does imply a very rapid redistribution of the original inflation shocks from Germany to France.

So while fairly tight exchange-rate bands will eliminate disturbances faster in the interests of greater stability, they very quickly redistribute the adjustment costs between participants (especially in terms of output and employment). Hence, while the insurance policy of limited short-run exchange-rate flexibility is very useful for getting a recovery underway, it does not allow us to dodge the price stability vs output costs which any monetary union scheme poses.

6. - Conclusions

Our conclusions may be stated as follows.

a) If all goes well, all regimes are much of a muchness. Symmetric shocks don't change that. But asymmetric shocks cause the relative merits of regimes to diverge. EMU schemes redistribute the costs of shocks, compared with floating which enables the costs of shocks to be largely localised where they occur. So if all countries share in the benefits of monetary union, they must also share in the costs of adjustment.

b) Without fiscal flexibility (or forward-looking wages) monetary union would perform much worse.

c) Monetary union allows no relative accommodation in the short run through exchange-rate separation. This imposes greater adjustment costs when dealing with relative shocks, although inflation is disciplined faster. Fiscal flexibility lowers the cost of this constraint and may be necessary to make these costs acceptable.

d) Monetary union does not prevent absolute accommodation to an inflationary shock: it may impose inflation in the «centre» countries. Thus, although individual prices may rise by less than in the absence of EMU, the spreading of inflation means more economies participate in the adjustment process and the European price index rise by as much as it does under a free float. Thus, viewed from within a purely European context, the strict *relative* price discipline will make monetary union look very attractive. But when Europe's performance is considered in relation to the rest of the world, the lack of *absolute* price discipline will make those benefits seem much less certain.

e) The choice between regimes is a judgement on the desirability of price stability over maintaining output or employment levels. But exchange-rate stability in a monetary union does not, in itself, ensure price stability.

f) Exchange-rate bands do not allow relative accommodation in the long run. But they do in the short run. This allows short-run shock absorption, which may be advantageous for reducing the costs of adjustment.

g) It is important to focus on welfare distribution within Europe. A hard EMU performs well for the European aggregate but badly for separate economies. Both hard and soft monetary union regimes have a greater effect on the distribution of performances than they do on average/aggregate performance. At the European level any regime may look good even under asymmetric shocks, but bad for individual countries. Therefore the real problem to be addressed involves obtaining a satisfactory distribution of costs and benefits, not one of ensuring better overall performance.

The model is in levels rather than logarithms, and is expressed in terms of deviations from a baseline trajectory. Unstarred variables are those for Germany; French variables have stars attached. All US variables are exogenous, and are therefore suppressed. (The US dollar exchange rate and the US current account deficit are obvious exceptions to this statement, but their levels are implicit from European variables). The mark and franc exchange rates are each expressed in terms of the dollar, rather than bilaterally.

The model is too complex to solve analytically, and we are forced into using numerical simulations. Parameters have been chosen so as to correspond in a stylized fashion with reality. We now list some key assumptions underlying the assumed parameter values.

(i) The Keynesian multiplier has a value of 2.0. (ii) The average and marginal propensity to import is 0.25 in both countries. This is on the low side for actual European countries, but here Germany should perhaps be thought of as including the low countries and France should be thought of as including Italy; this would make these numbers more appropriate. Initially trade is balanced between France and Germany, and between Europe and the US. (iii) 72% of French and German trade is trade between themselves. This means that the propensity of each to import from the other is 18%, and from the US 7%. (iv) Trade elasticities are of a standard size: the sum of the price elasticities of demand for exports and imports is 2.5. This means that a 1% depreciation of the mark, not matched by a change in the franc would, ceteribis paribus, improve the German current account balance by 2.5% of the initial level of exports (Or 0.625% of GDP). But of course, if the franc followed suit, the trade improvement would only be 28% (= 100% − 72%) of this.

The equations of the model are displayed in the following table. Equation (1) and (1.1) show the determination of aggregate demands. The real exchange-rate terms show the effects on the home country trade balance of home country and foreign country exchange rates.

The y^* term in equation *(1)* shows French demand for German exports, and vice versa in equation *(2)*. Equation *(2)* and *(2.1)* are the Phillips curves, which contain effects in both the level of and change in output. Equations *(3)* and *(3.1)* relate consumer prices to output prices and import prices (which are influenced by both exchange rates). Equations *(4)* and *(4.1)* show current account evolution and equations *(5)* and *(5.1)* show investment as depending on the real interest rate. Equations *(6)* and *(6.1)* show wealth evolution, which is the sum of domestic investment.

The Model

Equations

(1) $\quad y = 1.25a - 0.09a^* + 0.36y^* + 2.0inv + 2.0g$

(1.1) $\quad y^* = 1.25a^* - 0.09a + 0.36y + 2.0inv^* + 2.0g^*$

(2) $\quad p_{+1} = p + pc - pc_{+1} + 0.5y + 0.3\,(y - y_{+1})$

(2.1) $\quad p^*_{+1} = p^* + pc^* - pc^*_{+1} + 0.5y^* + 0.3\,(y^* - y^*_{+1})$

(3) $\quad pc = p + 0.25a - 0.18a^*$

(3.1) $\quad pc^* = p^* + 0.25a^* - 0.18a$

(4) $\quad ca = 0.625a - 0.45a^* - 0.25y + 0.18y^*$

(4.1) $\quad ca^* = 0.625a^* - 0.45a - 0.25y^* + 0.18y$

(5) $\quad inv = -\,0.625\,(r - p_{+1} + p)$

(5.1) $\quad inv^* = -\,0.625\,(r^* - p^*_{+1} + p^*)$

(6) $w = 1.05w_{+1} + ca + inv, \ w_0 = 0$

(6.1) $w^* = 1.05w^*_{+1} + ca^* + inv^*, \ w^*_0 = 0$

(7) $a_{+1} = a + (r - p_{+1} \, p)$

(7.1) $a^*_{+1} = a^* + (r^* - p^*_{+1} \, p^*)$

Variables

A star denotes a French variable; variables without stars are German variables. $A"_{+1}"$ subscript indicates a forward-looking variable.

Endogenous Variables   *Policy Instruments*

y : output g : government expenditure
p : output prices i : interest rate
pc : consumer prices
ca : current balance
inv : investment
w : wealth
a : real exchange rate in $ terms

and the current account surplus. In future work debt interest payments on net foreign debt will be included. Equation (7) and (7.1) show exchange-rate determination under perfect capital mobility under model-consistent expectations.

BIBLIOGRAPHY

[1] BEGG D.: *Alternative Exchange Rate Regimes*, Paper presented at a CEPR Meeting, Perugia, July, 1990.

[2] BLANCHARD O.J.C.: «Debt, Deficits and Finite Horizons», *Journal of Political Economy*, n. 93, 1985, pp. 223-47.

[3] COOPER R.N.: «Macroeconomic Policy Adjustment in Interdependent Economies», *Quarterly Journal of Economics*, n. 83, 1969, pp. 1-24.

[4] DELORS: *Report of Economic and Monetary Union in the European Community*, Brussels, Committee for the Study of Economic and Monetary Union, Commission of the European Communities, 1989.

[5] EDISON - H. WILLIAMSON J. - MILLER MARCUS: «On Evaluating and Extending the Target Zone Proposal», *Journal of Policy Modelling*, n. 9, 1987, pp. 199-224.

[6] EICHENGREEN B.: «Is Europe an Optimal Currency Area?», London, Centre for Economic Policy Research, *Discussion Paper*, n. 478, 1990.

[7] EUROPEAN ECONOMY: «One Market, One Money», Luxembourg, *EC Official Publications*, n. 44, October, 1990.

[8] HUGHES HALLETT A. - VINES D.: «Adjustment Difficulties Within a European Monetary Union: An Analysis and a Comparison with Alternative Regimes», paper presented to a CEPR Workshop, Perugia, 29 June-1 July, 1990.

[9] HUGHES HALLETT A.J.: «Anatomy and the Choice of Policy in Asymmetrically Dependent Economies», *Oxford Exonomic Papers*, n. 38, 1986, pp. 516-44.

[10] MASSON P. - MELITZ J.: «Fiscal Policy Interdependence in a European Monetary Union», London, Centre for Economic Policy Research, *Discussion Paper*, n. 414, 1990.

[11] MUNDELL R.A.: «A Theory of Optimum Currency Areas», *American Economic Review*, n. 51, 1961, pp. 657-65.

[12] TAYLOR J.: «Staggered Wage Setting in a Macro Model», *American Economic review Papers and Proceedings*, Vol. 69, n. 2, 1979, pp. 108-113.

[13] WILLIAMSON J. - MILLER M.: *Targets and Indicators: A Blueprint for the International Coordination of Economic Policy*, Washington, Institute for International Economics, 1987.

Currency Unification
and Real Exchange Rates

Wilhelm Kohler (*)
University of Innsbruck

1. - Introduction

In a well known passage, John Stuart Mill once wrote of different nations retaining separate currencies as being barbaric (1). It is by now more than twenty years ago (1969, The Hague) that the EC first decided to rid Europe of such "barbarism" by aiming for currency unification. Twenty years later, with the ongoing discussion of the specific Delors proposals, it might seem to many observers that currency unification for Europe has finally come to be "just around the corner". However, this discussion also reveals substantial differences between various officials and commentators as to how and when a European currency area might sensibly be achieved. More importantly, from a theoric point of view, the question can (and should) be raised if the sceptics should at all be accused of Millian "barbarism". As Frenkel has put it 15 years ago, the tardiness of the integration process might just as well reflect the "sound resistance of economic rationality to unsound political aspirations" (Frenkel [18], p. 217).

(*) I am grateful to Fritz Breuss, Jon-ren Chen, Karl Socher, and Theresia Theurl for discussions and comments on an earlier version of this paper.

(1) The exact quotation is: «So much of barbarism, however, still remains in the transactions of most civilised nations, that almost all independent countries choose to assert their nationality by having, to their own inconvenience and that of their neighbours, a peculiar currency of their own». The quote is from MUNDELL [45].

Advise: the numbers in square brackts refer to the Bibliography in the appendix.

The present paper is in the spirit of this question. The key issue addressed is whether or not variability of bilateral nominal exchange rates between the nations (or regions) of the prospective currency union (2) is of any importance for sufficient variability in real exchange rates, i.e., for real adjustment. Real exchange rates, like all other relative prices, will have to move in response to changes in the "real fundamentals" of the different economies (Dornbusch [14]), or else these economies will be threatened by unemployment. Thus, it would be wrong to conclude that a greater variability of real exchange rates as such implies greater misalignments.

In a Walrasian world where prices of all factors and goods are perfectly flexible, the above issue would never arise (3). But if, for some reason, economies are characterised by nominal price rigidities, nominal exchange-rate variability may act as a "surrogate price flexibility" in the process of real adjustment. In the event of currency unification, this kind of "surrogate price flexibility" is not completely removed because the union currency (or all union currencies) may still fluctuate (jointly) *vis-à-vis* third currencies, but it is restricted by the irrevocable fixity of bilateral exchange rates between the (former) union currencies (4). How strong a constraint this will be depends *a)* on the precise nature of the price rigidity, *b)* on the real (or sectoral) structure of the economies involved, *c)* on the type of real shocks (or, perhaps somewhat less dramatically, simply real changes) that have to be absorbed, one way or another, by the union countries, and *d)* on whether or not adjustment mechanisms other than exchange-rate changes are available.

---

(2) "Nation" and "region" are used as interchangeable terms in present paper.

(3) In such a Walrasian world, currency unification would, however, still not necessarily be optimal. It has sometimes been argued that an optimal tax system might imply different tax-rates for the inflation tax in different countries. If this is the case, differing currencies with flexible exchange rates are essential for devising optimum tax systems in different countries. See DORNBUSCH [12], GIAVAZZI [20], COHEN - WYPLOSZ [9], and CANZONERI - ROGERS [7], for recent elaborated arguments of this kind with respect to the EC. An earlier presentation of the argument can be found in LAIDLER [38]. COHEN [8] stresses the possibility of devaluing, through surprise inflation, existing government debt under exceptional circumstances as a means of collective insurance.

(4) Several authors have rightly pointed out that a true currency unification is very difficult to achieve by means of a mere commitment to irrevocably fixed exchange rates. See, in particular, SOHMEN [51] and COHEN [8]. But for the present purpose, the problems of currency unification can adequately be analysed as resulting from fixity of bilateral nominal exchange rates.

The present paper addresses these questions within the framework of the "dependent economy" model, in which the equilibrium value of the real exchange rate is defined as allowing the simultaneous achievement, by means of a suitable expenditure policy, of internal and external balance. The type of price rigidity introduced is a generalized downward rigidity of the nominal wage rate. The sectoral structure of the economy is organized around the dichotomy between traded and non-traded goods produced with two factors (labor and capital) and differing factor intensities, whereby a distinction will be made between the case of perfect intersectoral capital mobility and the case of sector-specific capital. The real changes analysed will be endowment and productivity changes, as well as terms-of-trade shocks. Finally, the question will be raised if, and in what sense, factor movements and structural and regional transfers may be seen as substitutes for variability of bilateral nominal exchange rates.

The paper will be restricted to changes in the real fundamentals, or real shocks, and how they can be absorbed with and without changes in bilateral nominal exchange rates. Monetary shocks will not be considered.

2. - Internal and External Balance in the "Dependent Economy"

The purpose of this paragraph is simply to demonstrate how, and under what circumstances, variability of the nominal exchange rate can act as a "surrogate price flexibility" in the presence of certain kinds of wage rigidities, and how the "real" structure of the economy relates to this issue. Use will be made of the so-called "dependent economy" model, which has a long tradition in international economies, but which has not so far been used to address currency unification issues (5). For the time being, we will only analyse a single

---

(5) The paper draws heavily on DORNBUSCH [11], BRUNO [6], HELPMAN [23], [24], JONES - CORDEN [34], CORDEN [10] and BRECHER [5]. More recent applications of the "dependent economy" model are ARNDT - RICHARDSON [1] and EDWARDS [14]. The originator of the internal/external balance analysis is, of course, MEADE [44].

country faced with given terms of trade. The application of the results obtained in this chapter to the currency unification problem and the analysis of terms-of-trade shocks will follow in subsequent chapters.

The country analysed produces traded and non-traded goods, with the prices of traded goods, in terms of a foreign currency (US$, say) (6), being given and independent of the home-country's actions. In addition, producers and consumers of the traded goods are in no way rationed on world markets, i.e., they can export and import arbitrary quantities. Constant relative prices of all traded goods allow their perfect aggregation and this aggregate will simply be referred to as the traded good. For the sake of simplicity, it will be assumed that non-traded goods may also meaningfully be aggregated or that there is only one non-traded good. Choose units of all traded goods such that their foreign currency prices are equal to one. This implies that the home currency price of the traded good P_T is equal to the nominal exchange rate e:

(1) $$P_T = e$$

This is an arbitrage-condition (7). For the following analysis e will be assumed fixed at e^0, unless otherwise stated. Next we introduce the real exchange rate R as the relative price of the traded good:

(2) $$R = \frac{P_T}{P_N} = \frac{e}{P_N}$$

The aggregate price level P is

(3) $$P = e^{\theta T} \cdot P_N^{\theta N}$$

(4) $$= e / R^{\theta N}$$

where θ_j is the share of good j in domestic absorption. If we use a *-superscript to indicate a second country, we can derive a simple

---

(6) In later chapters this will be the third currency, against which the union currency (currencies) can fluctuate (jointly).

(7) We could at this stage introduce trade taxes, but that would not affect the analysis in any substantial way.

relationship between a purchasing-power-parity variable E and the real exchange rates of the two countries.

$$(5) \qquad E = (e / e^*) \cdot (P^* / P), \text{ and}$$

$$(6) \qquad E = R^{\theta N} / R^{*\theta^*}{}_N$$

This last equation is quite important in the present context in view of the fact that Vaubel·[55] has used intra-EC variability of E as a "comprehensive and operational criterion" for the desirability of currency unification (8). The following analysis will argue that R rather than E is the crucial variable for real adjustment. While the above equation does show that diverging movements in R and R^* will also imply changes in E, it also shows that not all movements in E will necessarily involve diverging movements in real exchange rates as defined above. More importantly, however, the key issue of the subsequent analysis is not so much changes in real exchange rates as such, but whether or not these changes will be feasible under certain kinds of wage rigidity, if bilateral nominal exchange rates are fixed as in the case of a currency union.

The following analysis will assume that the two goods are produced with a given endowment of capital and labor, which will conveniently be indicated by the vector V. Following Bruno [6], the core equations of the model can now be written as:

$$(7) \qquad Q_T = Q_T(R, V)$$

$$(8) \qquad Q_N = Q_N(R, V)$$

$$(9) \qquad C_T = C_T(R, C) + D_T$$

$$(10) \qquad C_N = C_N(R, C) + D_N$$

$$(11) \qquad C = Y - S$$

$$(12) \qquad Y \equiv Q_N^e + R \cdot Q_T$$

---

(8) It is perhaps worth remembering the main empirical result obtained by Vaubel on the basis of this criterion: «. . . the conclusion cannot be avoided that the Community has been in greater need of real-exchange-rate adjustment, and is consequently a less desirable currency area, than Germany, Italy and the US».

$Q_j(\cdot)$ $(j = T, N)$ are full employment supply functions, $C_j(\cdot)$ are endogenous private demand functions, and D_j are autonomous demands, which can be thought of as including government demand as well as investment demand (9). C is total endogenous expenditure, which is related to total income Y (both measured in terms of the non-traded good) through S, total "savings" (10). These "savings", however, include taxes T, measured in units of non-traded goods. Hence, we can write $S = S(T, \cdot)$. Other arguments in this savings-function will be introduced below.

It should be noticed that $C_j(\cdot)$ are effective, not notional, demand functions, since the income constraint is formulated using effective supply of non-traded goods, Q_N^e, with

$$(13) \qquad\qquad Q_N^e = \min\{Q_N(\cdot), C_N\}$$

Of course, $C_N < Q_N(\cdot)$ can only occur in the case of some sort of binding price rigidity. More on this in a moment. A final comment regarding the supply functions is in order. We have called $Q_j(\cdot)$ full employment supply functions. Moreover, we have assumed that producers of traded goods are never rationed on the output side, i.e., that they always realize $Q_T(R, V)$. This should not be taken to imply full employment of all resources. What it means is that producers of traded goods will always realize an output level that would also be realized in the case of full employment. But if, at the same time, $C_N < Q_N(\cdot)$, then there will actually be less than full employment.

So far, we have modeled the real side of the economy, and we have only specified flow equations. Adding asset market considerations will now provide the link between the real and the monetary side of the economy. The following remarks will try to do so in the course of considering external balance.

---

(9) These autonomous components of demand are of crucial importance in the papers by HELPMAN [23], [24], who stresses sectoral aspects of fiscal policy. In the present paper, fiscal policy as such will not be considered.

(10) Writing domestic income as the value of domestic production implies that there is no existing foreign debt or credit.

2.1 *External Balance*

In the literature, one can find two approaches to define external balance. One, used by Corden [10] and Edwards [15], is to say that an economy is in external balance, if it does not live beyond its means or, stated somewhat more scientifically, if its expenditure over time satisfies the intertemporal budget constraint. The other, stressed by the monetary approach to the balance of payments and its generalization, the portfolio approach, is to say that any external imbalance represents an adjustment of the actual stocks of financial assets to their desired levels, and that, therefore, external balance is achieved if all stocks of financial assets are at their long-run equilibrium levels. As regards the above model, a version of the monetary approach (without allowing for international mobility of assets, however) has been incorporated by Dornbusch [11] and Brecher [5]. Common to both approaches is the notion that in the short run unbalanced commodity-trade, in itself, is not necessarily "a problem". In the former approach, unbalanced commodity-trade at any one point in time may simply be the result of intertemporal trade, in the latter it is nothing but a stock adjustment, which can either be a pure portfolio shift between financial assets and real capital or an adjustment of total wealth to its desired level.

It seems to me that, in a fundamental sense, the two approaches are actually closer to one another than the above wording might suggest. For one thing, to be operational the portfolio approach needs to determine the equilibrium level of total wealth, and in the case of perfect foresight and a given world interest rate this is nothing but the present value of all future   production (or future incomes). This imposes an intertemporal budget constraint on portfolio considerations (11). Moreover, the (optimal) stock demand for real capital, which is usually modelled in a rather *ad hoc* way in the portfolio approach, should ideally be viewed as a state variable in an intertemporal model (12).

Despite these ties existing on a fundamental level between the two approaches, however, I would argue that the notion of countries

---

(11) On this point, se McKinnon [42], p. 211.
(12) For such an extension of the present model, see the appendix in Bruno [6].

trying to live beyond their intertemporal budget constraints is more
appropriate for practical purposes and short-run policy analysis. This
notion is no doubt of great practical importance, but it is, in a sense,
alien to the portfolio approach, where any trade imbalance is nothing
but a stock adjustment, which will eventually come to an end, thereby
automatically also eliminating the trade imbalance. For the following
analysis, which will be of a short-run nature, it will be assumed that
there is a short-run target value for the trade balance, measured in
units of the traded good and denoted by $\bar{B}$. To keep the analysis
simple, this value will not be derived from an intertemporal model,
but will, instead, be treated as an exogenous variable. The empirical
hypothesis behind this approach is that informed observers do quite
often have a fairly clear notion of whether or not a country with a
given trade balance is living beyond its means (13).

External equilibrium can then be written as excess demand for
the traded good, $U_T(\cdot)$, being equal to $-\bar{B}$:

$$(14) \qquad U_T(\cdot) = C_T(\cdot) + D_T - Q_T(\cdot) = -\bar{B}$$

It could easily be shown that, if the non-traded good market is cleared
(see below), $U_T(\cdot)$ is also equal to the difference between domestic
expenditure and domestic income or to the difference between savings and total autonomous demands, both measured in units of the
traded good.

In order to have expenditure policy in the model, and also in
order to indicate the kind of adjustment emphasized by the portfolio
approach, we next complete the savings function as follows (14):

$$(15) \qquad\qquad S = S(T, Y, i, A/P)$$

---

(13) As we have learned from the debt crisis, the answer to this question crucially
depends on the extent to which domestic absorption is for consumption or investment.
Of equal importance is the interest payment on existing foreign debt. Both of these are
not explicitly modelled here, because the focus is on switching versus expenditure
policy to attain external balance *given* these other influences.

(14) A similar specification of savings can be found in KENEN [36]. There is,
however, no wealth effect in Kenen's savings function. This part of the paper is not
intended as a complete description of the dynamics of stock adjustments. As mentioned
in the text above, the purpose is only to indicate, not analyse, the kinds of adjustments
operating through asset markets. The primary focus of the paper is on flow equilibria,
not stock equilibria.

As regards T, it was already mentioned above that savings in the present definition also include involuntary "savings" via taxes. This is the fiscal part of expenditure policy. Income Y as an argument may be seen as a Keynesian influence of income on savings as well as representing, together with the interest rate, total desired wealth along the lines suggested by McKinnon [42] and Jones [31]. With zero expected inflation, the real interest rate is equal to the nominal interest rate i. It is assumed that foreign and domestic bonds are perfect substitutes. Hence, with capital mobility and no expected change in the exchange rate, i is equal to the given world interest rate. Finally, A/P denotes the real value of actual net financial wealth, which is equal to the given stock of money, M, plus the stock of domestic bonds held by domestic residents outside the central bank, Z_d, minus net foreign indebtedness of domestic individuals, F (in terms of domestic currency):

$$(16) \qquad\qquad A = M + Z_d - F$$

Individuals are assumed to instantaneously adjust their money balances to their desired levels $L\,(\cdot)\cdot P$ by means of swaps between M and foreign securities, such that:

$$(17) \qquad\qquad M = L(Y, i, A/P)$$

whereby $L(\cdot)$ is a standard stock demand for real money balances.

Two aspects of the above savings function are worth mentioning. First, with a given world interest rate, monetary policy can only operate through a wealth effect. Secondly, the trade balance is closely linked to the change in financial wealth:

$$(18) \qquad\qquad e\cdot U_T(\cdot) + i\cdot F = -\,dA$$

This will exert a long-run tendency towards a zero current account (not trade!) balance (15). Indicating steady state variables by a $\tilde{\ }$, we have:

---

(15) The speed of this adjustment processes will also depend on whether or not monetary authorities attempt to follow a sterilization policy. See FRENKEL - MUSSA [19], p. 997-8 and p. 709-14.

(19) $e \cdot U_T(\cdot) = - i \cdot \bar{F}$

The external sector is depicted by the schedules $U_T(\cdot) = - \bar{B} > 0$ and $U_T(\cdot) = - i \cdot \bar{F}$ in Graph 1. The former satisfies the short-run target, the latter is the long-run equilibrium according to the monetary approach. It is assumed that the short-run target implies a negative trade balance. The schedules show the familiar trade-off between expenditure policy, represented in the present specification by $S(\cdot)$, and the real exchange rate (16). An increase in absorption (reduction in S) will increase the demand for traded goods and maintenance of external balance requires an increase in the real exchange rate, which will partly offset this demand effect and also elicit a shift in allocation towards the production of traded goods. Formally, the slope of the $\bar{B}$ schedule can be obtained by differentiating $U_T(\cdot) = - \bar{B}$:

(20) $$\left. \frac{dS}{dR} \right|_{U_T = -\bar{B}} = - \frac{C_{T_C}(1 - S_Y) Q_T + C_{T_R} - Q_{T_R}}{- C_C} < 0$$

whereby it was assumed that the numerator above is negative. This is a stability condition similar to the Marshall-Lerner condition of the partial equilibrium model. The portfolio considerations outlined above imply a long-run tendency towards $U_T(\cdot) = - i \cdot \bar{F}$. But the assumption of the present analysis is that economies do not smoothly adjust to external balance along such a "natural" path. Instead, we postulate the notion of countries trying to resist such an adjustment for extended periods, and this is depicted by points to the right of the $\bar{B}$ schedule in Graph 1.

2.2 Internal Balance

By internal balance we mean nothing but notional equilibrium in the non-traded goods market:

(21) $U_N(\cdot) = C_N(\cdot) + D_N - Q_N(\cdot) = 0$

---

(16) The left hand part of Figure 1 is familiar from DORNBUSCH [11]. More recent expositions of similar models are KENEN [36], p. 650-4 and KRUGMAN [37], p. 30-5.

GRAPH 1

INTERNAL AND EXTERNAL BALANCE,
THE WAGE RESTRICTION AND THE "SWITCHING PROBLEM"

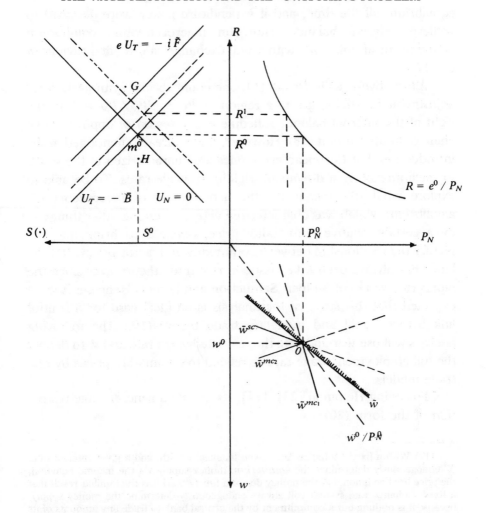

As with external balance, we can depict internal balance by a $U_N(\cdot) = 0$ schedule in the $S - R$ space. Differentiating the above equation gives:

$$(22) \quad \left.\frac{dS}{dR}\right|_{U_N = 0} = -\frac{C_{N_C}(1 - S_Y)\,Q_T + C_{N_R} - Q_{N_R}}{-\,C_{N_C}} > 0$$

At this stage, the price rigidity repeatedly referred to above, has to be introduced in some more detail. If there were no price rigidity whatsoever, then we would expect the economy to be in internal equilibrium all the time, and if expenditure policy were designed to achieve external balance, short-run macroeconomic equilibrium would occur at point m^0, with a real exchange rate R^0 and savings of S^0 (17).

Alternatively, as in Bruno [6], one could specify symmetric price adjustment functions, giving a region of $\hat{P}_N = dP_N / P_N > 0$ to the right of the internal balance schedule and a region of opposite price changes to the left of it (18). However, it was already mentioned in the introduction that European economies are characterized in the short- to medium-run by a downward-rigidity of wage rates. To be able to explore what this means for the achievement of macroeconomic equilibrium, which was characterized above — among other things — by a certain relative commodity price, one has to bring into the picture the relationship between commodity and factor prices. But the latter has always been a key issue in real trade theory ever since the pioneering works of Stolper, Samuelson and Lerner. Hence, it is to be expected that this stage of the analysis is an ideal case for a fruitful link between real and monetary trade theory (19). The following analysis will use $\tilde{w}$ to indicate the restricted wage rate and $\bar{w}$ to denote the full employment wage rate as related to commodity prices by real trade models.

Following Helpman [23], [24], I stipulate a general wage restriction of the form (20).

---

(17) With a fixed exchange rate, given financial wealth, and a given interest rate, R^0 endogenously determines the *equilibrium* money supply via the income equation, the price level equation and the money demand function. This is the familiar result that a fixed exchange rate system will always endogenously determine the money supply, because it is nothing but a commitment by the central bank to trade any amounts of its money against assets denominated in foreign currencies at a fixed rate. $S(\cdot) = S^0$ will then implicitly determine equilibrium taxes T^0.

(18) This notation will be followed throughout the paper: $\hat{x} = dx/x$.

(19) The following analysis is very much in the spirit of DORNBUSCH [11], JONES - CORDEN [34], HELPMAN [23], [24], and BRECHER [5], who have already stressed this link.

(20) Writing the wage restriction in the form of relative changes is meant to reflect the empirical fact that wage bargaining is also always about such changes rather than absolute levels.

$$(23) \qquad \hat{\bar{w}} \geq \omega_T \cdot \hat{P}_T + \omega_N \cdot \hat{P}_N$$

If $\omega_j = 0$ for $j = T, N$, we have a strictly nominal wage rigidity: $\hat{\bar{w}} \geq 0$. If $\omega_j = \theta_j$, we have a real wage rigidity. Of course, cases in between these two extremes are equally possible.

Whether or not this wage restriction is binding, will now depend on the real structure of the economy. From real trade theory, we postulate the existence of a wage function of the following form:

$$(24) \qquad \bar{w} = \bar{w}\,(P_T, P_N, V)$$

The implication is that the given prices of all traded goods alone do not yet determine the factor prices. This is the case if the traded goods produced domestically all have roughly the same factor intensity, which is assumed to differ from that of non-traded goods. Alternatively, one can assume one factor to be sector specific. These are also crucial factors as regards the properties of $\bar{w}\,(\cdot)$ (see below).

An alternative to this approach is to have wage indexing in a wage contract model, as in Marston [40]. In Marston's approach, there is only one good produced at home with a parameterized production function (Cobb-Doublas), assuming that labor is the only mobile factor. With given expectations regarding the output price and the price level (which includes foreign goods) and a given labor supply (or a labor supply function), there is an equilibrium contracted wage, which is the basis for the indexing equation. Feeding the indexed wage into the optimal supply function derived from the production function then gives supply depending on surprise price changes of domestic output as well as surprise inflation. There are two fundamental differences between this approach and the present one. First, the present one does not have uncertainty or expectations, and, therefore, has no surprise effects. Second, instead of wage indexing, which always forces the wage to deviate from its equilibrium value if there are surprises, the present approach has a wage restriction, which need not always be binding. The present approach was chosen primarily on the grounds of trying to highlight the relevance of real production structures for the currency unification issue.

Instead of assuming straight away, as in Helpman [23], [24], that the wage restriction is binding, we start from a situation of macro-economic equilibrium, in which it was not binding, such as the point m^0 in Graph 1. Next we suppose that there is an exogenous change, shifting both the internal and the external balance schedules in such a way that the initial point now exhibits excess supply of non-traded and excess demand for traded goods (21). The new schedules are indicated by dashed lines. The figure is now completed on the right hand side by relating the real exchange rate to P_N through the given nominal exchange rate, and then adding a $P_N - w$ space below. $w^0 = \bar{w} (e^0, e^0 / R^0, V)$ is the initial equilibrium wage rate.

Through point 0 we now draw a line representing the wage restriction $\tilde{w} (\cdot)$ and several other lines representing the wage function $\bar{w} (\cdot)$. Clearly, since $0 \leq \omega_N < 1$, the $\bar{w}$ line will have a slope less than w^0 / P_N^0. Points to the right and above this line are excluded by the wage restriction. The slope of the $\bar{w}$ line will depend on the production structure in the following way. If labor is assumed to be completely mobile as between different sectors, but capital is assumed to be sector-specific, then:

$$(25) \qquad\qquad \frac{\delta \bar{w}}{\delta P_N} = \lambda_N \cdot \frac{w^0}{P_N^0}$$

with λ_N being the elasticity of labor demand with respect to the own real wage rate in the N-sector, standardized to be less than unity and summing to one with λ_T (22). This is depicted by the line labeled $\bar{w}^{sc}$ (*sc* stands for sector-specificity of real capital), where it was assumed in addition that $\omega_N > \lambda_N$ (23). It becomes clear that in this case the wage restriction does not preclude the decrease in P_N necessary for the required real depreciation from R^0 to R^1. If, however, $\omega_N < \lambda_N$, then the wage restriction would translate into an opposite restriction as regards movements of the real exchange rate with the given nominal exchange rate. Only in the knife-edge case of $\lambda_N = \omega_N$ does

---

(21) The next chapter will be concerned with what may lie behind such exogenous changes.

(22) See JONES [32] for a systematic treatment of this case.

(23) These lines should be interpreted as gradients of the above wage-function, which will, of course, in general not be linear in the $w - P_N$ space. The analysis, therefore, is a local one.

the wage restriction not translate into any real exchange rate rigidity. If we assume that capital is also perfectly mobile between the two sectors, then we have, according to the Stolper-Samuelson theorem,

$$
(26) \qquad \frac{\delta \bar{w}}{\delta P_N} = \frac{\theta_{KT}}{\theta_{KT} - \theta_{KN}} \cdot \frac{w^0}{P_N^0}
$$

where θ_{Kj} is the share of capital income in the unit-cost of good-j. The sign of the numerator in the above equation, and hence the implication of the wage restriction for real exchange rate movements, depends on the relative factor intensity of the two sectors (24). If the non-traded good is relatively labor intensive (depicted by the line $\bar{w}^{mc_1}$, *mc* standing for mobile capital), then the required real depreciation is again precluded with the given nominal exchange rate. The opposite applies, if the non-traded good is relatively capital intensive (line $\bar{w}^{mc_2}$). If there is no difference in factor intensities, then factor prices are not uniquely determined in the full employment equilibrium. The wage restriction cannot be binding in such a case.

The above cases are obviously polar in their assumptions as regards intersectoral factor mobility, and these assumptions can, therefore, be criticized. In particular, one might wish to have intermediate, but still given degrees of capital mobility or, preferably still, one might want to endogenize factor mobility along the lines of option pricing theory by focusing on uncertainty about future returns in different sectors (Bertola [3]). But to be able to focus on the general equilibrium relationship between commodity and factor prices, and to highlight the role played by sectoral (or real) aspects for the issue of exchange rate unification, the above assumptions serve reasonably well. It should also be pointed out that the slopes of the internal and external balance loci are affected by differing degrees of factor mobility through the terms Q_{jR}. With given technologies these terms increase with increasing factor mobility. However, this only affects the *amount* of the required real appreciation or depreciation after a real "shock", whereas the present issue is whether a given wage

---

(24) See Jones [30] for this formulation of the Stolper-Samuelson theorem.

restriction translates into an upward or a downward rigidity of the real exchange rate.

If the wage rate restriction should turn out to be a binding one for the real exchange rate movement required for the achievement of a new macroeconomic equilibrium after a real "shock", then the familiar internal vs external balance dilemma arises. An expenditure policy designed to achieve external balance will lead to unemployment or, more precisely, a "temporary equilibrium with rationing" (Neary [48]) in the non-traded goods and the labor market. In the following, countries in such a situation will be referred to as having a "switching problem" (Corden [10]) (25). Now, of course, the question arises, if variability of the nominal exchange rate could conceivably help in solving such a problem. This will be taken up in the next subsection, before finally turning to the currency unification issue.

2.3 *Does Nominal Exchange Rate Variability Help?*

I am deliberately using the term variability, rather than flexibility, in the present context. I simply do not want to address the issue of whether market forces or political processes should be used to bring about desired nominal exchange rate changes. It is well known that the excessive volatility of nominal exchange rates during the past 15 years has led some economists to favor the return to a system of adjustable pegs (26). Krugman [37] is an important example. Others, however, are far less convinced that the high exchange rate volatility of the past decade should be attributed to inefficient capital markets, and place heavy emphasis on the well known problems of fixed but adjustable rates. Accordingly, they favor abstaining from futile exchange rate management and using market forces instead. Two

---

(25) We talk of a "switching problem" only in those cases in which a change in the equilibrium real exchange rate is precluded by the wage restriction.

(26) The above statement implies the existence of a measuring rod against which to judge *excess* volatility. This has frequently been the subject of hot debate in empirically oriented international economics. Against the background of the above model, excess volatility would mean a nominal exchange rate leading to sustained deviations from the flow equilibrium level of the real exchange rate, given the wage restriction.

prominent examples here are Sohmen [50] and Haberler [21]. As regards the exchange rate question for Europe, it seems clear that the alternative to currency unification is not complete flexibility of bilateral nominal rates, but carrying on with the EMS, which is an adjustable-peg-type system. It should be pointed out, however, that this would most probably entail giving up on part of Europe 1992, inasmuch as countries would have to be allowed using foreign exchange controls to fight speculative attacks on their currencies. This has been emphasized by Giavazzi [20].

Suppose that attaining macroeconomic equilibrium as defined above requires, in addition to a suitable expenditure policy, a real depreciation: $\hat{R} = \rho > 0$. Suppose, further, that there is a "switching problem", i.e., we either have $\omega_N < \lambda_N$ in the case of sector specific capital, or $\theta_{KT} - \theta_{KN} > 0$ for mobile capital. The question of whether a nominal exchange rate adjustment can do the job is complicated by the fact that any change in e will also shift all the lines in the fourth quadrant of Graph 1, because the full employment equilibrium wage rate as well as the wage restriction also depend on the price of the traded good. Again, we draw on pure trade theory (Jones [32]) to see that for the case of sector-specific capital and given endowments we get:

$$(27) \qquad \hat{w} = \lambda_T \cdot \hat{e} + \lambda_N \cdot \hat{P}_N$$

We now use this equation plus:

$$(28) \qquad \hat{e} = \rho + \hat{P}_N$$

and the above wage restriction (with an equal sign) to solve for the required change in the nominal exchange rate:

$$(29) \qquad \hat{e}^{sc} = \frac{\lambda_N - \omega_N}{1 - (\omega_N + \omega_T)} \cdot \rho$$

In the case of intersectoral capital mobility, we have (Jones [30]):

$$(30) \qquad \hat{w} = \delta_{KT} \cdot \hat{e} - \delta_{KN} \cdot \hat{P}_N$$

instead of the above equation, where $\delta_{Kj} = \theta_{Kj} / (\theta_{KT} - \theta_{KN})$ $(j = N,$ $T)$. This gives the following required nominal depreciation

$$(31) \qquad \qquad \hat{e}^{mc} = \frac{\delta_{KT} - \omega_N}{1 - (\omega_N + \omega_T)} \cdot \rho$$

It should be emphasized once more that the above equations for $\hat{e}$ are not "exchange rate equations" describing the behavior of flexible rates. They are merely those nominal exchange rate changes that would exactly offset the wage restriction.

The first thing to note is that any wage restriction which is homogeneous of degree one makes exchange rate policy futile as an instrument to solve the "switching problem" characterized above. Such a case can be referred to as the absence of money illusion. This has always been emphasized in the literature (27), and it is not at all surprising in the latter case of mobile capital, because we know from the Stolper-Samuelson effect that a real depreciation would necessarily entail a reduction in any real wage rate, however it may be defined. It is, however, somewhat surprising for the case of sector-specific capital, where the Stolper-Samuelson magnification-effect is absent. Perhaps one would expect that a sufficiently high (low) value for ω_N (ω_T) in the wage restriction might enable exchange rate policy to do the job. The point is, however, that in such a case the wage restriction would not be binding in the first place (28).

The second point is that the required nominal depreciation is less than ρ in the case of sector-specific capital, but greater than ρ in the case of mobile capital. Intuitively, one would perhaps have expected that a greater exchange rate movement is required to compensate for a given wage rigidity if factors are immobile rather than when they are mobile. But here one has to distinguish between the amount of the real exchange rate movement required to establish macroeconomic equilibrium in the face of a wage restriction, and the size of the

---

(27) See, instance, Corden [10], S. 31-3, Tower - Willet [54], S. 37, and Laidler [38], S. 158.

(28) Take, for instance, $w_N = 1$ $(w_T = 0)$, in which case the above condition that $w_N < \lambda_N$ could not arise.

nominal exchange rate change necessary to effect a *given* real depreciation. As already indicated above, the former tends to be greater, for a *given* real "shock", with factor-specificity. But the latter depends on the *relative* mobility of the factor, the price of which is rigid. Labor is equally mobile in an absolute sense in both cases considered above, but it is relatively more mobile in the specific-capital case, where the nominal devaluation is less than the required real devaluation.

Of course, using exchange rate policy as a surrogate for complete flexibility of all commodity and factor prices involves a cost in terms of a rise in the general price level, and this cost will be higher, the lower the degree of money illusion, represented by $\omega_N + \omega_T$ in the above two equations. This was first emphasized by McKinnon [41] in his contribution to the theory of optimum currency areas. He therefore argues that small open economies with a large value for θT in the general price level should not use exchange rate policy in the above sense. The previous analysis suggests that the inflation cost of resorting to exchange rate adjustments will in a crucial way also depend on intersectoral factor mobility. McKinnon also stresses that small open countries will usually find the employment cost of maintaining external balance by means of expenditure policy alone to be less severe, because the traded goods sector has a low leverage on the non-traded goods sector. It should be pointed out here, that we actually have two different criteria that determine the inflation cost of using exchange rate policy and the output cost of abstaining from it. The former is determined by the shares in domestic absorption as indicated above, while the latter is determined by marginal propensities to absorb traded and non-traded goods (29).

Finally, exchange rate policy also affects asset markets. First, one might be tempted to argue that exchange rate policy, in view of its price level effect, has to be supported by accommodating monetary policy. However, with a high degree of capital mobility, exchange rate policy *is* monetary policy. Changing the foreign currency price of one's money will *endogenously* also change the money supply in accordance with the money demand function and the price level effect

---

(29) For a somewhat similar argument within an income-expenditure model, see HELLER [22].

of this exchange rate change. The mechanism bringing this about operates through the "foreign securities window" (30). What is true, however, is that the exchange rate change will have an immediate effect on the real value of net financial wealth with ensuing impacts on savings according to equation *(15)*. Thus, starting from the short-run equilibrium m^0, a nominal depreciation will indeed move the economy towards long-run equilibrium along the internal balance schedule.

3. - Currency Unification

The above analysis has shown that there are limitations to the necessity and the feasibility of using nominal exchange rate changes to overcome a wage rigidity in the desire to attain macroeconomic equilibrium. This already sheds some light on whether, and under what circumstances, currency unification may pose *additional* problems of real adjustment. In this chapter, currency unification will be addressed in a more direct and detailed way.

As far as monetary affairs are concerned, the countries belonging to a European currency union with a single currency must be looked at in precisely the same way as we presently look at regions within a country. The single most important aspect of such a perspective is that these regions will no longer be able to issue and service debt in a money that they can themselves create. This has been stressed by Cohen [8]. In terms of the above terminology, this seems to suggest that civil law alone will fairly quickly force these regions onto their intertemporal budget constraint (31). However, we also have to consider the behaviour of a European Central Bank, which might still allow the union as a whole to live beyond its means. Formally, the type of adjustment emphasized by the monetary approach to the balance of payments will ultimately lead to an equilibrium distribution, among European regions, of any given stock of European money

---

(30) See FRENKEL - MUSSA [19] for more details.

(31) See, however, SCHLESINGER [49], who expresses some reservations based on the idea that "regional" governments may benefit from the notion of bail-out by central authorities of the monetary union, who might face a time consistency problem.

brought into circulation by the European Central Bank. But this stock of money (and its change) might still be such that Europe as a whole would be (remain) in external disequilibrium (32). For the following analysis, I shall assume, however, that Europe as a whole is in external balance. In this case, the above argument would imply that, in the course of adjustment any single European country would indeed move fairly quickly towards the external balance schedule ($\bar{B}$).

For simplicity, the following argument will be cast in terms of only two prospective union countries: Germany, meant to represent the surplus countries and indicated by a G-superscript, and Greece, meant to represent the "southern" deficit countries and indicated by an H-superscript. Although it is by no means essential for the argument, it will also assume that both countries retain their own currencies. According to the triangular arbitrage principle (Marston [40], p. 409-10), currency unification now implies that the two nominal, exchange rates *vis-à-vis* the "third" currency will always have to move together:

$$(32) \qquad\qquad \hat{e}^G = \hat{e}^H$$

It is important to note that, in the event of currency unification, European countries would not forgo using exchange rate policy altogether, because their currencies (or the European currency) could still float against "third" currencies. The point is simply that they could only do so subject to the above restriction. While this observation seems trivial from a practical perspective, it has not always been appreciated in theoretical discussions of currency unification.

3.1 *Real Adjustment with Given Terms-of-Trade*

For the time being, we retain the assumption of given terms-of-trade. This should not be taken as an empirical hypothesis implying that the respective countries are small. The assumption merely serves

---

(32) The US is a good example. Nobody thinks of individual states as living beyond their means, but the US as a whole arguably does. We do, however, observe great differences between states as regards unemployment.

the purpose of separating terms-of-trade "shocks", which will be discussed in the following subsection, from other sources of problems. Under what circumstances, then, will the two countries feel the above restriction as a painful one in the process of real adjustment? We will in this subsection consider adjustments to changes in each country's "real fundamentals", by which we mean factor endowments and productivity. Logically prior to this, however, there is the question of finding the right bilateral rates, with which to start the union (33).

In this connection, the public discussion emphasizes the need for greater convergence of European countries before monetary unification should actually be attempted. In terms of the above model, this can be interpreted as saying that, ideally, the currency union should be formed with all countries initially being in macroeconomic equilibrium, such as point m^0. Suppose that, instead, Germany is at point G, whereas Greece is at point H (34). It might be tempting to argue that the two external imbalances tend to offset each other and that the problem is only one of capital market integration. This is an old argument in the theory of optimum currency areas (Ingram [27]), but it is only concerned with financing, not with adjustment (35). The real adjustment problem in the present case is that after the above mentioned mechanisms will have moved both countries towards their budget constraints there will be excess demand for non-traded goods in Germany and excess supply, i.e., unemployment in Greece. Whether or not the required opposite adjustment in the two real exchange rates will be possible without changing nominal exchange rates (which can only move together!) depends, as we have seen in the previous chapter, on the type of wage rigidity and the real production structures in the two economies. Suppose that capital is specific in the short-run in both countries. We can then conclude from the previous

---

(33) Such bilateral rates are also implied by adopting a common currency.

(34) Any two countries will, of course, not have identical internal and external balance schedules. But assuming that they do makes the argument simpler without affecting its validity.

(35) In another form, this argument also relates to the necessary reserve requirements, which can be lowered by monetary integration of countries with less than perfect correlation of external shocks leading to external imbalances of individual countries. See the two papers by MUNDELL [46], [47] at the Madrid conference. On the difference between the possibility of financing and the ultimate force of the budget constraint, see also COHEN [8].

chapter that real adjustment is possible without nominal exchange rate changes if:

$$(33) \qquad \omega_N^H > \lambda_H^N \text{ and}$$

$$(34) \qquad \omega_N^G < \lambda_N^G$$

These conditions might conceivably be fuilfilled, as illustrated in Graph 2. In the long-run, if capital is mobile, the analogous conditions are:

$$(35) \qquad \theta_{KT}^H < \theta_{KN}^H \text{ and}$$

$$(36) \qquad \theta_{KT}^G > \theta_{KN}^G$$

I.e., the traded good has to be the relatively labor intensive one in Greece, and the other way round in Germany. Note that the traded good is an aggregate, and the two countries will most probably produce different components of this aggregate. Hence, the above conditions are not wholly unrealistic. Alternatively, they may also be caused by factor intensity reversals.

However, if any of the above conditions is not fulfilled, then at least one of the two countries has a "switching problem". Thus, assume that the condition for specific capital is violated in Greece. A nominal devaluation would help Greece, but in a currency union such a devaluation would then also be forced upon Germany, thereby causing a rise in the price level that could otherwise have been avoided.

What we have here is nothing but the familiar tension between inflation and unemployment in two regions of a suboptimal currency area, first pointed out in his pioneering article by Mundell [45]. He argued that a common currency would be more likely to toss the coin in favor of inflation than would a fixed rate system with separate currencies: «In a currency area comprising different countries with national currencies, the pace of employment in deficit countries is set by the willingness of surplus countries to inflate. But in a currency area comprising many regions and a single currency, the pace of

GRAPH 2

WAGE RESTRICTION OF TWO COUNTRIES
WITH NO "SWITCHING PROBLEMS"

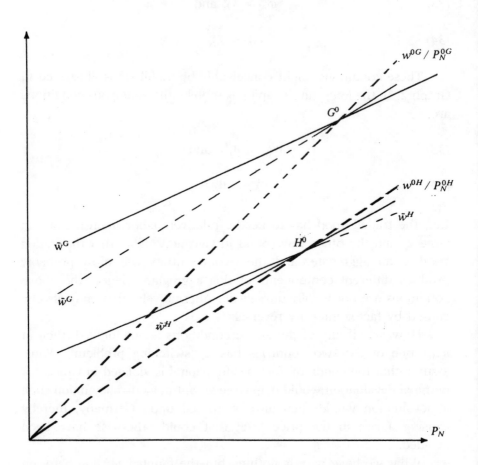

inflation is set by the willingness of central authorities to allow unemployment in deficit regions».

The presently ongoing negotiations on the design of a European central bank system, however, appear to be geared towards being responsible, in an uncompromising way, for price level stability. As formulated by Cohen ([9], p. 197): "monetary policy... should be conducted *independently* of regional disequilibria". At the same time, it is difficult to envisage what other "central authorities" could conceivably develop any pressure in the opposite direction, for the sake of employment in any particular region. Note also that the above mentioned negotiations will most probably shift exchange rate management firmly into the responsibility of the European Central Bank, and it is a devaluation by means of which inflation would be effected in the case just considered (36).

Are present exchange rates the right ones in the above sense? Arguably, at least some of them most probably aren't. Thygesen ([53], p. 361-2) also points out that a problem very similar to the one discussed above might emerge if a further devaluation of the US$ should be necessary for a correction of the US external imbalance. Taking present exchange rates as a starting point, it is highly questionable that all the "southern" countries could "swallow" an appreciation against the US$ as might be necessary for some central countries, like Germany, for instance. Yet, that is precisely what the currency union would force them to do (37).

Strictly speaking, the previous discussion has only been concerned with choosing the right exchange rates at the start of the monetary union, or, phrased somewhat more realistically, with guaranteeing that the currencies converge towards such rates in a transition process, however that may look in detail (Cohen [8], p. 208). On a purely theoretical level, this is only a technical question. More important, and more in the spirit of the theory of optimum currency areas, is the "dynamic" perspective: What is the likelihood that different regions of the union will face conflicting "switching problems" in the course of their development? What are the kinds of changes in "real fundamentals" that would cause problems? The argument will be kept as simple as possible by assuming various scenarios of exogenous changes, and it can also be fairly short because much of what has just been said is also relevant for these scenarios. In particular, it has to be kept in mind that production

---

(36) Again, I want to leave it open to what extent the currency union will use market forces or political processes for changes in the nominal exchange rate of the union currency vis à vis outside currencies.

(37) In a similar vein, it has been estimated that macroeconomic equilibrium in Italy and France would have required their currencies to devalue by a third to a half against the Deutsche mark in the period 1981 to 1985, if the Deutsche mark had remained stable vis à vis the US$ during that period. See THYGESEN [53], p. 362.

structures in the two countries may well be such that diverging trends in equilibrium real exchange rates can be realized without any change in the nominal exchange rate, despite the given wage restriction.

Expansion will have both, a supply and a demand effect, and whether macroeconomic equilibrium requires a real appreciation, a real depreciation, or none of both, in the course of this expansion depends on whether or not supply and demand effects have a different "bias" as regards traded and non-traded goods (38). If the expansion of supply is biased towards non-traded goods, and if the opposite holds true for the expansion, then a real depreciation will be called for, and, depending on the production structure and the nature of the wage restriction (see above), a "switching problem" might arise. But even if it does, the currency union as such will cause *additional* output or inflation cost only to the extent that the required changes in the nominal exchange rates as derived above differ between the two countries. The rest has to be attributed to the wage restriction as such, which has nothing to do with the currency union.

As regards supply effects, a distinction may be drawn between productivity changes and endowment changes, and as regards the latter, between labor growth and capital accumulation. A host of different scenarios could be developed, but this would not really add a great deal of insight, hence only a few remarks will follow before I turn to terms-of-trade "shocks".

Take, for instance, a growth of the labor force. If both factors were mobile, we could think of the adjustment process in two steps. First, the supplies at a notionally unchanged real exchange would show the usual Rybczynski effect: If the non-traded good is relatively labor intensive, there would, *ceteris paribus*, be a more than proportional increase in the production of the non-traded good and an absolute decrease in the production of traded goods. But income, Y, would unambiguously increase, and as a second effect we have increased spending on both types of goods if they are normal hence excess supply of traded and excess demand for nontraded goods. This is one way, in which point m^0 in Graph 1 above might arise as a "switching problem". An opposite situation might emerge if there is a

---

(38) For a formal analysis, see BRUNO [6].

Hicks-neutral productivity increase in the production of traded goods. Considerations analogous to the ones above would lead one to expect that the equilibrium real exchange rate will fall. Again, this may or may not raise a "switching problem" (see above).

In the short-run, if capital is sector-specific, the situation is different insofar as an increase in the labor force will exert a direct downward pressure on the wage rate even at a constant real exchange rate (39). Given the wage restriction, there will be an immediate threat of unemployment. Assume, for the moment, that there is no wage restriction. The supply of both goods will increase at constant commodity prices, with the relative amounts of these increases depending on the elasticities of labor demand in the two sectors and also on factor intensities as measured by distributive shares. Total income and, therefore, expenditure will again increase, and this time it is conceivable that demand and supply effects are equal, in which case no change in the real exchange rate is required. Such an outcome is, however, impossible with a wage restriction, because it would actually involve a nominal reduction in the wage rate. Hence, even if there were no opposite biases in the supply and demand effects of a growing labor force — a case that can practically be ruled out if capital is mobile — the wage restriction would, in itself, constitute a basis for the use of exchange rate policy to trade-off unemployment against a price level increase.

Capital accumulation is different in that it is a direct part of demand, i.e., accumulation is either out of current production or imports. To consider the implication of this simple fact for external balance, we have to recall our assumption regarding international mobility of financial capital. Complete mobility implies that "the allocations among nations of the world's (real) capital stock and its wealth can be independent on each other" (Arndt - Richardson [1], p. 21). Complete immobility, on the other hand, implies that real capital and the respective ownership certificates must always be located in the same country. In this latter case, external balance would, in the long-run at least, require $U_T (\cdot) = 0$. If, however, we have free international exchange of securities, then the situation is drastically

---

(39) See, again, JONES [32] for details.

different in several respects. Arndt - Richardson [1] show that in this case two economies with a given and identical real interest rate can have (offsetting) trade imbalances for indefinite periods of time. Hence, financially integrated *growing* economies cannot be assumed to approach a balanced trade position in the long-run, as the monetary approach of Graph 1 above suggests. What happens in such a situation is that one economy repeatedly trades present against future consumption by means of acquiring ownership titles to part of the other country's *new* capital goods in exchange for its own present consumption, with a mirror image for the other country. External balance (not living beyond one's means) now requires that the amounts traded reflect the given real interest rate, and this again implies an equilibrium real exchange rate. Notice, however, that this equilibrium real exchange rate will be different with financial liberalization and without. Specifically, the country trading future against present consumption (the "deficit" country) will have a lower real exchange rate in the former case than in the latter (Arndt - Richardson [1], p. 21). Moreover, the real endowments V will follow different paths in the two scenarios, since without financial liberalization a country can only trade present against future consumption by accumulating capital stock within its own borders, whereas in the other case it can do so by means of foreign investment. Without going into further details we can now bring these considerations to an end by noting that investment may have a bias towards either of the two sectors (N and T), and this, together with the secondary demand effects, may then obviously lead to a "switching problem", depending on the real production structure as indicated above.

3.2 *Real Adjustment to Terms-of-Trade "Shocks"*

The previous chapter was concerned with "switching requirements" such as may occur due to changes in real fundamentals within different countries of a currency union. The exchange rate restriction of a currency union may, however, also pose a problem in the adjustment of different countries to a common external "shock", such as abrupt and significant changes in the terms-of-trade. In fact, this issue has played a much more prominent role in the theory of optimum currency areas than the previous one, and it will be addressed in the present paragraph.

By terms-of-trade "shocks" we mean changes in the relative prices of the traded goods. A proportional change in the foreign currency prices of all traded goods can, of course, be perfectly offset by a change in the nominal exchange rate, and this will not pose any problem for currency unification, unless different countries want to have different rates of inflation (see above). A change in the relative prices of traded goods, however, first of all destroys the convenient two-goods property of the above model. We now have an n-commodity model, and it is well known that it is difficult to obtain strong results for the effects of a given change in commodity prices on outputs and factor prices in such a model. A few insights can nevertheless be drawn from the model.

There is a well known argument, going back to Kenen [35], to the effect that countries will find it easier to dispense with the nominal exchange rate as a mechanism of adjustment to terms-of-trade "shocks", if they have a well diversified structure of production and exports. The implications of this argument for the currency unification issue are, however, not self-evident and clear-cut. Tower and Willet ([54], p. 50-1) have pointed out that there will, in general, be a negative correlation across countries between the degree of diversification in production and their openness and trade dependence. Small open economies will be less diversified than large and comparatively closed ones. The former will, according to Kenen, want to rely on the nominal exchange rate as an adjustment mechanism, but they will, at the same time, be the ones most severely hit by the price level implications of doing so (see above). I would argue that this dilemma does not necessarily arise.

First, within the present model, the price level effects of nominal depreciations do not depend on the actual amount of trade, but rather on the size of trade*able* goods in domestic absorption. Hence, even large economies with comparatively little actual trade can be very open in this sense.

Secondly, and more importantly, the crucial question is not whether countries of a currency union are at all severely affected by terms-of-trade changes, but rather whether they are affected in such ways that the above exchange rate restriction (31) becomes a problem. Diversification of the union countries, as such, will probably determine the desirability of exchange rate changes *vis-à-vis* third currencies, but it is of little relevance for whether or not different union countries would wish to liberate themselves from the above exchange rate restriction in order to absorb terms-of-trade "shocks" with minimal employment or output cost. What is important in this respect is not so much diversification but a certain degree of similarity in production and demand structures among union countries.

Consider, for instance, the case of sector-specific capital and a strict downward rigidity of the nominal wage rate. Graph 3 illustrates this case for two traded and one non traded good. We have three Marginal-Value-Productivity (MVP) schedules, corresponding to given specific capital stocks, to the initial values for the traded goods prices, P_{T1}^0 and P_{T2}^0, and the nominal exchange rate, e^0. The MVP schedule for the non-traded good and the first traded good are added horizontally, to yield a labor demand curve for these two sectors taken together, $L_N(w) + L_{T1}(w)$. The MVP curve of the second traded good is drawn with the origin on the right hand side. Initial equilibrium is w^0 with full employment of the total labor force $\bar{L}$, indicated by the horizontal difference between the two origins. Now the world prices of the two traded goods change to $P_{T1}^1 < P_{T1}^0$ and $P_{T2}^1 > {}_{T2}^0$. This shifts the MVP schedules, and, by construction, the new production equilibrium would require a lower wage rate $w^1 < w^0$. This is the immediate labor market effect, and it depends on the initial allocation of labor to the different sectors as well as on the elasticies of the MVP schedules (40). Two countries with similar allocations and similar elasticities will observe a similar direct effect on the labor market. Notice, however that with many traded commodities it is conceivable that similarity can obtain despite countries producing different traded goods. A second country could, for instance, have a third traded good playing exactly the role that the first one plays in Graph 3.

Now, w^1 is, of course, not the new general equilibrium wage rate, because the above Graph only shows production effects. In addition,

---

(40) See JONES [33] for a detailed formal analysis of this effect.

GRAPH 3

TERMS-OF-TRADE "SHOCK"
WITH SECTOR-SPECIFIC CAPITAL

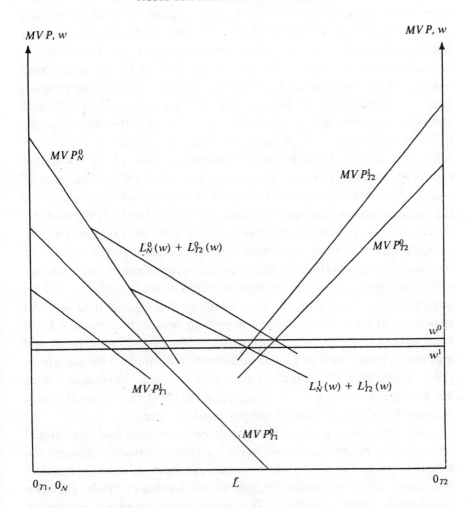

there will be direct and indirect demand effects, including demand for non-traded goods, with respect to which countries can again be more or less similar. Without going into much detail, we can state that the more similar they are, the less likely it is that they would gain by being able to have their exchange rates move independently on each other, in order to compensate for a given wage restriction.

How similar can international production structures be in a world of international division of labor? One would be inclined to think that, if trade is based on orthodox division of labor, countries with a similar structure of production will not heavily engage in trade with each other. Wouldn't monetary integration between such countries tend to minimize the very gains of having a common currency? This paradox is easily resolved, empirically, by observing that in the past three decades or so countries with similar endowments and similar production structures have, in fact, increased significantly their bilateral exchange of goods, and theoretically, by referring to the "new" theory of international trade emphasizing product differentiation, returns to scale and aspects of imperfect competition. One of the principal results of this theory is that, in addition to traditional determinants of comparative advantage, the kind *and amount* of trade depends on *a)* the relative size of different countries and *b)* on the level of, and the differences in, per-capita income (41). To take an extreme case, if product differentiation is modeled in a Chamberlin-type model of monopolistic competition, even countries with identical endowments will to a significant extent engage in bilateral trade and this will be intra-industry trade, with the two countries having identical sectoral structures of production. From the present perspective, then, it is an ideal situation for currency unification. Moreover, there is an old argument, going back to Linder and recently formalized by Markusen [39], saying that differentiated products will gain importance with increasing per-capita income, suggesting that this view is particularly relevant for countries with high per-capita incomes.

The previous argument points to a rather simple and operational criterion that might play a role in the currency unification debate: the extent of intra-industry trade between prospective union countries. The more these countries engage in intra-industry trade between prospective union countries. The more these countries engage in intra-industry trade, the less will they want to resort to nominal exchange rate changes in the process of absorbing terms-of-trade "shocks", while at the same time having a significant amount of

---

(41) See, for instance, HELPMAN [25], HELPMAN - KRUGMAN [26] and MARKUSEN [39] for a detailed demonstration of these results.

bilateral trade through which the welfare gains of having a common currency could be effected (42).

The principal example of a "dissimilarity problem" is, of course, having an oil-exporting country within a union of heavy oil-importers, as is the case for the UK in the EEC. Obviously, the UK and the other European coutries are affected very differently by oil-price shocks, and currency unification may mean imposing inflationary pressure on the UK in the event of further oil-price increases, if unemployment in other countries is to be avoided. Thygesen ([52], p. 168) points out that Norway, in a sense, is a counterexample: Despite a much heavier share of oil production in GDP, the Norwegian krone remained reasonably stable during oil-price increases. But it can hardly be denied that European currency unification will create some potential for adjustment problems of the kind just mentioned.

4. - Alternative Adjustment Mechanisms

It does not make too much sense to talk about European currency unification except as part of a larger integration effort, covering almost all economic aspects and extending well into the political sphere. This larger integration effort also provides for mechanisms intended to alleviate the frictions that might be caused in the course of real adjustment by the exchange rate restriction implicit in a currency union. Two of these will very briefly be discussed in the following: factor movements and the use of structural and regional funds.

4.1 *Factor Movements*

Obviously, an unemployment equilibrium can be turned into a full employment equilibrium if the unemployed leave the region and

---

(42) Existing empirical studies on intra-European trade do support the above view of determinants of intra-industry versus inter-industry trade (BALASSA - BAUWENS [2], and JAQUEMIN - SAPIR [28], but there is, to the author's knowledge, no study systematically investigating the differences between prospective union countries in terms of their trade structure along the lines of the above argument.

migrate to some other region with inflationary pressure. Perhaps a little less obviously, unemployment can also disappear if capital moves into the region. These are somewhat sweeping statements that need a little more detailed analysis below. Both kinds of movements are prime targets of Europe 1992, which is supposed to establish a single market within which persons, goods, services and capital can move freely. It should, however, be pointed out straight away that what we need in the present context is actual factor movements, not just the absence of artificial barriers. Hence, the whole question boils down to whether or not natural barriers to factor movements between different European countries are still significant and, if so, whether or not these natural barriers will eventually disappear as well (43).

The basic argument goes back to the pioneering article by Mundell [45], whose example identifies regions with sectors. This has subsequently led to a discussion on the relationship between inter-regional and intersectoral factor mobility (44). A distinction has to be made here between two questions. First, what is the relevance of intersectoral factor mobility for the use of exchange rate variability as "surrogate price flexibility"? And secondly, does interregional factor mobility imply intersectoral mobility if it is to be a substitute for exchange rate variability in the event of currency unification? The first question has already been addressed above, with the result that equilibrating real exchange rate movements will be greater, the less mobile, intersectorally, factors are, and that the nominal exchange rate change required to compensate a given wage restriction will be less, the more mobile labor is *relative* to capital.

As regards the second question, Kenen [35] has pointed out that interregional mobility implies intersectoral mobility if two regions produce different goods. Hence, if capital is sector-specific, inter-regional mobility of capital will only help to the extent that regions produce the same goods. Besides, what is needed here is physical

---

(43) Of course, the border line between natural and artifical barriers itself is anything but "natural". Indeed, a large scale integration effort as the one presently undertaken in Europe can also be interpreted as an endeavor to shift this border line to the effect that more and more barriers are turned into artifical ones that can then be dismantled.

(44) See, in particular, KENEN [35], and the discussion on Kenen's paper.

capital mobility which, in a static environment, implies shipment of existing capital goods from one region to another. It is immediately obvious that there is little scope for this kind of capital mobility to play the above mentioned role.

Matters improve, however, in the context of growing economies with complete international mobility of financial capital, i.e., international mobility of savings. Such mobility may indeed help accumulating real capital stocks in deficit countries, thus avoiding the persistence there of "switching problems" (45). Again, mobility, defined as the absence of artificial barriers alone, is one thing, but actual movements of savings for long-term investment across borders is another, and what we need is the latter. Here, of course, the Feldstein-Horioka result comes to one's mind, saying that incremental savings do not in any significant amount cross international borders but largely stay within the country of origin (Feldstein - Horioka [16]). The sample of that study, however, does not extend into the more recent past, and it would seem rather important to have an idea as to the extent to which the Feldstein-Horioka result carries over to present day Europe. In addition, note that the monetary adjustment mechanism will lead to increased savings in deficit countries and decreased savings in surplus countries. Hence, for capital mobility to help solving the "switching problem" of deficit countries, the incentives for potential investors of the surplus country to invest in the deficit countries would have to increase sufficiently to compensate for this reduction in surplus countries' total savings. This point was made by Fleming [17]. Overall, it thus seems to be an open question to what extent liberalizing capital movements will contribute to easing the frictions that might be caused by currency unification.

Labor movements appear to be a better candidate in that we do undoubtedly observe much more relocation of existing labor among countries than of existing physical capital stocks. At the same time, it cannot be denied that labor mobility within Europe falls way short of labor mobility within the US, a currency union of roughly comparable economic size. Hence, on this account as well, it is somewhat difficult

---

(45) Obviously, international mobility of existing stocks of financial assets cannot help in accumulating real capital stocks. This distinction is similar to the above mentioned difference between financing and adjustment.

to judge whether factor movements will be sufficient for the EC to be an "optimum" Mundellian currency area.

Recent work on factor reallocation under uncertainty has pointed out that factor mobility may also depend on the exchange rate system, thus introducing a simultaneity into our argument. If a factor movement between two locations is seen as exercising an option in an uncertain environment, then there will be an option price, depending on the amount of uncertainty, and this option price is nothing but the difference between expected earnings in the actual location and the "trigger value" of expected earnings in the other location, i.e., the difference necessary to "trigger" actual movement. The point now is that this option price increases with uncertainty about earnings. With given stochastic disturbances (such as terms-of-strade shocks) in two regions, the variability of expected income, defined as the wage rate times the ratio of employed to total labor force, will be lower in the case of flexible exchange rates than in the case of fixed rates under conditions specified above. Hence the option price will increase with fixed rates, i.e., factor mobility will be increased with flexible rates. This is an argument put forward by Bertola [3].

4.2 *Structural and Regional Funds*

It has always been acknowledged that a system of interregional transfers may help avoid frictions within a currency area or a fixed rate system. Consider the following passage from Johnson ([29] p. 203): «The pressures of competition in the product and factor markets facilitated by the common currency frequently result instead in prolonged regional distress, in spite of the apparent full freedom of labour and capital to migrate to more remunerative locations. On the national scale, the solution usually applied, rightly or wrongly, is to relieve regional distress by transfers from the rest of the country, effected through the central government. On the international scale, the probability of regional (that is, national in this context) distress is substantially greater because of the barriers to mobility of both factors and goods mentioned previously; yet there is no international government, nor any effective substitute through international co-operation, to compensate and assist nations or regions of nations suffering through the effects of economic change occurring in the environment of a single currency».

Without having a central government, the EC has a long tradition of using regional and structural funds to "relieve regional stress". The *Delors Report* explicitly emphasizes that the currency union will need support through an enlarged scope for interregional transfers. And the Council has, indeed, decided in 1988 to double the size of the structural funds by 1992.

From a theoretical perspective, it is very important to distinguish between several different uses that interregional transfers may be put to. First, as pointed out by the *Delors Report*, they can be used to improve infrastructure, communications systems, and education systems, with the aim of establishing similar conditions of production all over the union. Inasmuch as this involves the provision of public goods, little can be said against it. However, a different picture emerges if the transfers are used as subsidies proper. Several different scenarios are possible. Pure income transfers would be equivalent to simply financing the external imbalance that would arise if expenditure were maintained at a level securing full employment. A more differentiated approach would involve lowering subsidies to industrial sectors that produce tradeables in the surplus countries and by increasing subsidies to the traded goods sectors in deficit countries (Thygesen [53], p. 363). However, both of these scenarios are second-best. The reason is that they do not hit the problem at its source, which is a wage stickiness. According to the general principle of first-best policies in the face of distortions, a wage subsidy (to both sectors, if labor is mobile) would be first-best, because it would avoid introducing a "by-product-distortion" (Bhagwati - Srinivasan [4], p. 221-2).

Notice also that there is a fundamental difference between the use of exchange rate policy and the use of regional transfers to deal with "switching problems". The former will lower real wages whereas the latter doesn't. Hence the two policies are not perfect substitutes for each other, as far as distribution is concerned. If lowering real wages in deficit countries is a socially unacceptable means of avoiding unemployment, then variable exchange rates will not make regional funds redundant.

Finally, it might be added that the administration of regional funds will always involve much more bureaucracy and incentives for rent-seeking behavior than does managing exchange rates, and even more so than letting exchange rates float freely. Indeed, if it should turn out that the formation of a European monetary union brings with it a significant increase in interregional transfer activity as a substitute for exchange rate variability, then the above mentioned bureaucracy and rent-seeking costs should also be considered and appropriately weighted in an overall cost-benefit analysis of currency unification.

5. - Closing Remarks

In public as well as academic discussions, the use of the exchange rate as an adjustment instrument is very often associated with a "beggar thy neighbor" policy. It cannot be denied that countries faced with a problem of competitiveness may be tempted to gain a temporary advantage over their foreign competitors by means of a devaluation, if the international monetary system allows them to do so (46). That is, the exchange rate can also be the opposite of an adjustment instrument: it can be used to postpone adjustment, at the cost of inflation and only to make it more painful later. In a similar vein, the possibility of such devaluations may be anticipated by economic agents in their price setting behavior, in particular in a system of more or less centralized wage bargaining and if there is uncertainty about the evolution of prices during the contract period. This was, indeed, one of the prime reasons for Britain to join the exchange rate mechanism of the EMS. It might even be argued that the precise nature of the wage restriction may well depend, among other things, on the exchange rate system.

All this cannot be denied and it may, in the end, be decisive for the choice of an appropriate exchange rate system. However, two points must be stressed. First, the foregoing remarks relate to a system of adjustable pegs, but hardly for truly flexible rates. And

---

(46) The opposite scenario is also possible: Two countries trying, independently, to fight inflation by appreciating their currencies will go through restrictive periods without achieving their inflation target. See COHEN [8].

secondly, on a theoretical level, it would certainly sound very strange to call exchange rate changes designed to bring relative prices closer to their equilibrium values as "beggar thy neighbor policies". The problem, of course, is that, in practical terms, nobody really knows what the equilibrium real exchange rate at any given point in time is. And a given movement of the nominal exchange rate may be regarded by some as an equilibrating movement in the above sense and as "beggaring neighbors" by others. The above model, however valuable it may be as a device of organized thinking, is not operational enough to solve these empirical issues. Being a general equilibrium model it does, however, demonstrate another point that occasionally comes up in academic discussions. Seeing a role for nominal exchange rate variability to play in real adjustment processes does not automatically place one into the realm of the, admittedly, outdated partial-equilibrium elasticity-approach to the balance of payments (47).

It must also be stressed that variability of nominal exchange rates by no means insulates countries against real "shocks". On the contrary, we have seen in all instances above that devaluing one's currency has real effects. Indeed, these real effects are the prime target of such devaluations; The purpose in all the cases considered above is to lower the real wage, which could otherwise not have happened, due to the wage restriction. It would, thus, be a severe misunderstanding, if exchange rate variability were seen as a miracle means of avoiding painful real adjustment (Cohen [8]). Except for hysteresis phenomena, it must even be questioned that the long-run adjustment will be any different with variable exchange rates than without (Laidler [38]). But exchange rate variability may offer an additional degree of freedom in the search for the least costly path of real adjustment.

Finally, much of what has been said above about "switching problems" of countries can, of course, also be applied to regions within existing countries, not just different countries in a European currency area. An oft-quoted example is Italy with its rapidly advancing northern part and the southern part somewhat lagging behind. But breaking up existing currency areas is simply not on the agenda,

---

(47) On this point, see the discussion between McKINNON [43], DORNBUSCH [13], and WILLIAMSON [56], p. 98.

presumably for good political reasons, whereas expanding such areas in Europe is. If a full European Monetary Union is to come despite the above (and other) reservations, it will probably do so because of the same good political reasons. As Mundell ([47], p. 156) noted almost 20 years ago, with respect to the present issue: «... politics in the widest sense of the word has to override economics».

BIBLIOGRAPHY

[1] ARNDT S.W. - RICHARDSON J.D.: «Real-Financial Linkages among Open Economies: An Overview», in ARNDT S.W. - RICHARDSON J.D. (eds.): *Real-Financial Linkages among Open Economies*, Cambridge (Mass.), MIT Press, 1987, pp. 5-32.

[2] BALASSA B. - BAUWENS L.: «The Determinants of Intra-European Trade in Manufactured Goods», *European Economic Review*, n. 32, 1988, pp. 1421-37.

[3] BERTOLA G.: «Factor Mobility, Uncertainty and Exchange Rate Regimes», in DE CECCO M. - GIOVANNINI A. (eds.): *A European Central Bank?*, Cambridge, Cambridge University Press., 1989, pp. 95-118.

[4] BHAGWATI J. - SRINIVASAN T.N.: *Lectures on International Trade*, Cambridge (Mass.), MIT Press, 1983.

[5] BRECHER R.A.: «Money, Employment, and Trade-Balance Adjustment with Rigid Wages», *Oxford Economic Papers*, n. 30, 1978, pp. 1-15.

[6] BRUNO M.: «The Two-Sector Open Economy and the Real Exchange Rate», *American Economic Review*, n. 66, 1976, pp. 566-77.

[7] CANZONERI M.B. - ROGERS C.: «Is the European Community an Optimal Currency Area? Optimal Taxation Versus the Cost of Multiple Currencies» *American Economic Review*, n. 80, 1990, pp. 419-33.

[8] COHEN D.: «The Costs and Benefits of a European Currency», in DE CECCO M. - GIOVANNINI A. (eds.): *A European Central Bank?*, Cambridge, Cambridge University Press, 1989, pp. 195-209.

[9] COHEN D. - WYPLOSZ CH.: «The European Monetary Union: An Agnostic Evaluation», in BRYANT R. *et al* (eds.): *Macroeconomic Policies in an Interdependent World*, Washington (D. C.) Brookings Institution, IMF, CEPR, 1989, pp. 311-37.

[10] CORDEN W.M.: *Inflation, Exchange Rates, and the World Economy*, Chicago, University of Chicago Press, 1977.

[11] DORNBUSCH R.: «Real and Monetary Aspects of the Effects of Exchange Rate Changes», in ALIBER R. (eds.): *National Monetary Policies and the International Financial System*, Chicago, University of Chicago Press, 1974, pp. 64-81.

[12] ——: «The European Monetary System, the Dollar and the Yen», in GIAVAZZI F. - MICOSSI S. - MILLER M. (eds.): *The European Monetary System*, Cambridge, Cambridge University Press, 1988, pp. 23-41.

[13] ——: «Doubts about the McKinnon Standard», *Journal of Economic Perspectives*, n. 2, 1988 , pp. 105-12.

[14] ——: «Real Exchange Rates and Macroeconomics: A Selective Survey», *Scandinavian Journal of Economics*, n. 91, 1989, pp. 401-32.

[15] EDWARDS S.: *Real Exchange Rates, Devaluation, and Adjustments*, Cambridge (Mass.), MIT Press., 1989.

[16] FELDSTEIN M. - HORIOKA CH.: «Domestic Savings and International Capital Flows», *Economic Journal*, n. 90, 1980, pp. 314-29.

[17] FLEMING M.: «On Exchange Rate Unification», *Economic Journal*, n. 81, 1971, pp. 467-88.

[18] FRENKEL J.A.: «Reflections on European Monetary Integration», *Weltwirtschaftliches Archiv*, n. 111, 1975, pp. 216-21.

[19] FRENKEL J.A. - MUSSA M.: «Asset Markets, Exchange Rates and the Balance of Payments», JONES R.W. - KENEN P.B. (eds.): *Handbook of International Economics*, vol. II, Amsterdam, North-Holland, 1985, pp. 679-747.

[20] GIAVAZZI F.: «The Exchange Rate Question in Europe», in BRYANT R. *et* AL. (eds.): *Macroeconomic Policies in an Interdependent World*, Washington (D.C.), Brookings Institution, IMF, CEPR, 1989, pp. 283-304.

[21] HABERLER G.: «The International Monetary System, the European Monetary System (EMS) and a Single European Currency in a "Single European Market"» in BUB N. - DUWENDAG D. - RICHTER R. (eds.): *Geldwertsicherung und Wirtschaftsstabilität*, Frankfurt, Verlag Knapp, 1989, pp. 293-316.

[22] HELLER R.H.: «Exchange Rate Flexibility and Currency Areas», *Zeitschrift für Wirstschafts- und Sozialwissenschaften*, n. 99, 1979, pp. 115-35.

[23] HELPMAN E.: «Macroeconomic Policy in a Model of International Trade with a Wage Restriction», *International Economic Review*, n. 17, 1976, pp. 262-77.

[24] ——: «Nontraded Goods and Macroeconomic Policy under a Fixed Exchange Rate», *Quarterly Journal of Economics*, n. 91, 1977, pp. 469-80.

[25] ——: «Imperfect Competition and International Trade: Evidence from Fourteen Industrial Countries», *Journal of the Japanese and International Economies*, n. 1, 1984, pp. 62-81.

[26] HELPMAN E. - KRUGMAN P.R.: *Market Structure and Foreign Trade*, Brighton, Wheatsheaf Books, 1985.

[27] INGRAM J.C.: *Regional Payments Mechanisms: The Case of Puerto Rico*, Chapel Hill, University of North Carolina Press, 1962.

[28] JAQUEMIN A. - SAPIR A.: «International Trade and Integration of the European Community», *European Economic Review*, n. 32, 1988, pp. 1439-49.

[29] JOHNSON H.G.: «The Case for Flexible Exchange Rates, 1969», in JOHNSON H.G. (ed.): *Further Essays in Monetary Economics*, London, George Allen & Unwin, 1969, pp. 198-222.

[30] JONES R.W.: «The Structure of Simple General Equilibrium Models», *Journal of Political Economy*, n. 73, 1965, pp. 557-72.

[31] ——: «Comment: 'Portfolio Balance and International Payments Adjustment», in MUNDELL R.A. - SWOBODA A.K. (eds.): *Monetary Problems of the International Economy*, Chicago, University of Chicago Press, 1969, pp. 251-6.

[32] ——: «A Three-Factor Model in Theory, Trade, and History», in BHAGWATI J. *et* AL. (eds.): *Trade, Balance of Payments and Growth*, Amsterdam, North-Holland, 1971, pp. 3-21.

[33] ——: «Income Distribution and Effective Protection in a Multicommodity Trade Model», *Journal of Economic Theory*, n. 11, 1975, pp. 1-15.

[34] JONES R.W. - CORDEN W.M.: «Devaluation, Non-flexible Prices, and the Trade Balance for a Small Country», *Canadian Journal of Economics*, n. 9, 1976, pp. 150-61.

[35] KENEN P.B.: «The Theory of Optimum Currency Areas: An Eclectic View», in MUNDELL R.A. - SWOBODA A.K. (eds.): *Monetary Problems of the International Economy*, Chicago, University of Chicago Press, 1969, pp. 41-60.

[36] ——: «Macroeconomic Theory and Policy: How the Closed Economy was Opened», in JONES R.W. - KENEN P.B. (eds.): *Handbook of International Economics*, vol. II, Amsterdam, North-Hoalland, 1985, pp. 625-77.

[37] KRUGMAN P.: *Exchange Rate Instability*, Cambridge (Mass.), MIT Press, 1989.

[38] LAIDLER D.: «Concerning Currency Unions», *Zeitschrift für Wirtschafts- und Sozialwissenschaften*, n. 99, 1979, pp. 147-62.

[39] MARKUSEN J.R.: «Explaining the Volume of Trade», *American Economic Review*, n. 76, 1986, pp. 1002-11.

[40] MARSTON R.C.: «Exchange Rate Unions as an Alternative to Flexible Rates: the Effects of Real and Monetary Disturbances», in BILSON J.F.O. - MARSTON R.C. (eds.): *Exchange Rate Theory and Practice*, Chicago, University of Chicago Press, 1984, pp. 407-37.

[41] MCKINNON R.I.: «Optimum Currency Areas», *American Economic Review*, n. 53, 1963, pp. 717-25.

[42] —— : «Portfolio Balance and International Payments Adjustment», in MUNDELL R.A.- SWOBODA A.K. (eds.): *Monetary Problems of the International Economy*, Chicago, University of Chicago Press, 1969, pp. 199-234.

[43] —— : «Monetary and Exchange Rate Policies for International Financial Stability: A Proposal», *Journal of Economic Perspectives*, n. 2, 1988, pp. 83-104.

[44] MEADE J.E.: *The Balance of Payments*, London, Oxford University Press, 1951.

[45] MUNDELL R.A.: «A Theory of Optimum Currency Areas», *American Economic Review*, n. 51, 1961, pp. 657-65.

[46] —— : «A Plan for a European Currency», in JOHNSON H.G. - SWOBODA A.K. (eds.): *The Economics of Common Currencies*, London, George Allen & Unwin, 1973, pp. 143-72.

[47] —— : «Uncommon Arguments for Common Currencies», in JOHNSON H.G. - SWOBODA A.K. (eds.): *The Economics of Common Currencies*, London, George Allen & Unwin, 1973, pp. 114-32.

[48] NEARY J.P.: «Nontraded Goods and the Balance of Trade in a Neo-Keynesian Temporary Equilibrium», *Quarterly Journal of Economics*, n. 95, 1980, pp. 403-29.

[49] SCHLESINGER H.: «Die Währungspolitischen Weichenstellungen in Deutschland und Europa», (Vortrag bei der Jahrestagung des Vereins für Socialpolitik, Würzburg 1990), *Auszüge aus Presseartikeln*, Frankfurt, Deutsche Bundesbank, 1990, pp. 3-12.

[50] SOHMEN E.: «The Assignment Problem», in MUNDELL R.A. - SWOBODA A.K. (eds.): *Monetary Problems of the International Economy*, Chicago, University of Chicago Press, 1969, pp. 183-98.

[51] —— : «Currency Areas and Monetary Systems», in BHAGWATI J. *et* AL. (eds.): *Trade, Balance of Payments, and Growth*, Amsterdam, North-Holland, 1971, pp. 391-400.

[52] THYGESEN N.: «Is the European Economic Community an Optimal Currency Area?», in LEVICH R. - SOMMARIVA A. (eds.): *Future Developments and Future Prospects of the Eur. Currency Unit*, Massachusetts, Toronto, Lexington Books, 1987, pp. 163-85.

[53] —— : «The Benefits and Costs of Currency Unification», in SIEBERT H. (ed.): *The Completion of the Internal Market*, Tübingen, J.C.B. Mohr (Paul Siebeck), 1990, pp. 347-75.

[54] TOWER E. - WILLET T.D.: *The Theory of Optimum Currency Areas*, Princeton, International Finance Section, Princeton University, *Special Papers in International Economics*, n. 11, 1976.

[55] VAUBEL R.: «Real Exchange-Rate Changes in the European Community: A New Approach to the Determination of Optimum Currency Areas», *Journal of International Economics*, n. 8, 1978, pp. 319-39.

[56] WILLIAMSON J.: «On McKinnon's Monetary Rule», *Journal of Economic Perspectives*, n. 2, 1988, pp. 113-20.

Towards a Common Monetary Policy in the Transition: The Role of the ECU and Required Reserves

Daniel Gros (*)

Centre for European Policy Studies (CEPS), Brussels;
Catholic University of Leuven

1. - Introduction

Two successive European Councils set the date for the beginning of stage two and launched the intergovernmental conference on EMU. Monetary union within this decade (and century) looks therefore increasingly likely. However, it is somewhat surprising that most of the work so far has concentrated on the final stage of EMU and not on the practical questions that arise during the transition.

The *Delors Report* did not give any indication how the transition should be managed except to insist that during stage two the ultimate authority for (national) monetary policy should remain in national hands (1). The preparatory work of the central bank governors has also concentrated on the final stage. Their draft statutes for the European System of Central Banks (ESCB) prepared by the central bank governors are likely to be incorporated in the forthcoming *Treaty* amendment. The most important elements of the final stage of EMU seem therefore to be in place.

It is thus time to begin to think about the practical problems that

---

(*) I wish to thank Lorenzo Bini-Smaghi and Jose Vinals for stimulating discussions. The ideas expressed in this paper have been deeply influenced by the joint work with Niels Thygesen that has stretched over a number of years.

(1) See COMMITTEE FOR THE STUDY OF ECONOMIC AND MONETARY UNION [5].

Advise: the numbers in square brackets refer to the Bibliography in the appendix.

will arise in the transition. Discussion about the transition is particularly important in the area of monetary control since stage two represents an unknown new intermediate stage between the current EMS and the final stage of full monetary union. During stage two a common monetary authority already exists, but the ultimate authority for (national) monetary policy remains at the national level. This is different from the EMS where national authorities also retain ultimate authority, but where in the absence of a common monetary institution the exchange rate mechanism is run on mixture of informal cooperation and leadership by the strongest. It is also different from the final stage when no national authority in monetary matters remains.

This paper therefore analyses how a common monetary policy could be organized during stage two. It focusses on the role of a system of reserve requirements because other mechanisms of monetary control that are used at the national level cannot be used at the European level during stage two when national currencies still exist and financial markets will retain some national characteristics. The European Central Bank will not be able to rely on a stable demand for clearing balances by commercial banks since most clearing will presumably be done at the national level (and in national currencies). Moreover, the European Central Bank will also not be able to control the supply of currency in circulation because the common single currency will be introduced only in the final stage.

The paper assumes the ECU will be the common currency in the final stage of EMU, the ECU is therefore the obvious unit of account for the ESCB and also the obvious unit of account for the reserve requirements to be discussed below. This does not imply any presumption that the ECU will (or should) become a parallel currency. The success of the ECU as a parallel currency has no implications for the system proposed here. The well-known objections against the parallel currency approach (see for example Pöhl [16]) do not apply to the use of the ECU proposed here.

The paper starts in paragraph 2 by briefly summarizing the arguments for using a system of reserve requirements in stage two. It then turns to a discussion of two ways in which the ESCB could operate a system of required reserves. Paragraph 3 describes the two systems: *(i)* a three-tier system under which the European central

Bank (ECB) (shich is at the centre of the entire system called ESCB) would force national central banks to maintain reserve accounts in a special account. These reserves would a proportion of certain national monetary aggregates and would be denominated in «official» ECUs. Under this system the position of the ECB vis-à-vis national central banks would be similar to the position of national central banks towards commercial banks. This scheme is elaborated in Ciampi [4]; *(two)* a two-tier system under which the ECB would impose a uniform Community reserve requirement on commercial banks that would be independent of national reserve requirements. The reserves would also be denominated in ECU. This scheme is elaborated in Gros [8].

Paragraph 4 then discusses a technical problem that would be common to both systems and paragraph 5 discusses the comparative advantages of each system. Paragraph 6 concludes.

2. - Required Reserves During the Transition Towards EMU

Required reserves are not indispensable for an efficient monetary policy as shown by the example of countries that do not have a system of required reserves on commercial banks. For example, in the United Kingdom monetary policy relies on the demand of commercial banks for clearing balances and marginal accommodation of demands for liquidity. These instruments are sufficient to achieve control over domestic interest rates in the short run and the money supply in the long run.

However, this method of monetary control can not be used during the transition to EMU at the European level because as long as national currencies and national financial markets continue to exist most clearing will continue to be done at the national level. This implies that the demand for clearing balances will be in national currencies and go to national central banks.

The same line of reasoning applies to the accommodation of short term liquidity needs. For short liquidity relief commercial banks could in principle go to other national financial markets. However, the foreign exchange transactions that would be needed to do this make this alternative in practice too expensive because of transactions costs.

For example, a bid-ask spread of only 0.1% makes it uninteresting to go to another national financial market unless the weekly interest rate differential exceeds 500 basis points (assuming exchange rates are expected to remain constant). Commercial banks will therefore continue to rely on national central banks for short-term liquidity relief as long as national currencies exist.

The ECB could, of course, just intervene in the ECU market and buy and sell ECU-denominated securities. Given the transactions costs that arise in the bundling and unbundling of ECU the ECB could probably have considerable influence on ECU interest rates in the short run if it did intervene in the ECU market. However, it is difficult to see what purpose (other than short-term interest smoothing) could be achieved by this.

Moreover, the ECB would be able to intervene in the ECU market only if it can either create his own liabilities or has a line of credit with national central banks. In the latter case an intervention by the ECB, say an acquisition of ECU denominated paper, would be equivalent to an expansionary policy in all member countries. In this case the ECB would therefore interfere directly with national monetary policy. In the former case (i.e. when the ECB can issue its own liabilities) the ECB would be able to create money and could possibly undercut the monetary policy of the country that constitutes the anchor for the exchange-rate mechanism. This would not be acceptable for those who wish to maximize the chances that the system aims at price stability.

Another possibility that is often mentioned (see for example De Larosière [6]), is to give the ECB the means to intervene in the foreign exchange markets vis-à-vis third currencies. However, while it is possible for a small open economy to define a monetary policy in terms of the exchange rate this would not be appropriate for the Community as it nears EMU because the Community is a big economy whose trade with the rest of the world accounts to less than 15% of GDP. It would therefore be difficult to provide an anchor for the Community monetary policy by relying only on foreign exchange interventions.

The British proposals for an 'evolutionary approach' (HM Treasury [13]) can also not be considered a viable alternative because it is highly unlikely that the markets would actually use the hard ECU (which is in reality just a fixed basket ECU).

A system of required reserves is therefore the most promising policy tool for the ECB during the transition (2).

3. - The Alternatives: Three-Tier and Two-Tier Systems

As mentioned in the introduction a system of reserve requirements at the European level could take two forms.

Ciampi [4] proposes that the ECB could take a similar position vis-à-vis national central banks as the latter have vis-à-vis commercial banks. This would lead to a three-tier system under which the ECB would force national central banks to maintain reserve accounts in a special account. Graph 1 shows the organizational structure of this scheme.

The reserves to be held by national central banks with the ECB would be equal to a proportion of certain national monetary aggregates and would be denominated in «official» ECUs. The latter requires that the automatic credit facilities of the EMS would have to be discontinued (unless the circuit for the new «reserve ECU» was isolated from the existing official ECU).

Ciampi [4] also mentions that the reserve requirement could be based on the liabilities of national central banks (i.e. the monetary base) or part of their assets, i.e. domestic credit. The former option would allow the ECB to control indirectly the overall monetary base in the Community. The latter option would requires the ECB to coordinate interventions vis-à-vis third currences if it wants to retain control over all sources of monetary base expansion. However, this latter option will not be considered any further in this paper because the part of domestic credit in reserve money varies too much across countries. In the case of the UK applying a reserve requirement on domestic credit (of the Bank of England) would not make sense because this item is negative.

---

(2) BRUNI [3] emphasizes the same point. It should also not be overlooked that the fact that most countries do have some form of reserve requirements suggests that they are a convenient tool for monetary policy at the national level as well.

Daniel Gros

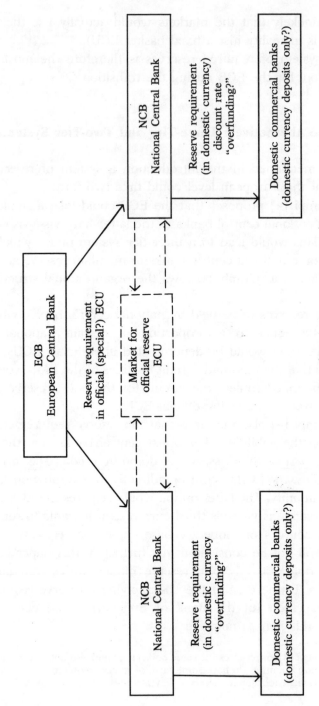

GRAPH 1

THE 3-TIER SYSTEMS

An alternative, analyzed in more detail in Gros [10], would be to allow the ECB to impose a uniform Community reserve requirement on commercial banks. This possibility is already foreseen in article 19 of the draft statutes elaborated by the central bank governors and the draft *Treaty* submitted by the Commission for the IGC on EMU (3).

It is crucial that the European reserve requirement be independent of national reserve requirements, because only in this case would it constitute an independent policy instrument for the ECB.

Commercial banks would be able to satisfy this reserve requirement only by acquiring deposits with the ECB. These deposits might be called «ECU federal funds» in analogy with the federal funds banks in the US need to satisfy the reserve requirement imposed by the Fed. Since the ECB can always control its liabilities it would then be able to control the overall rate of monetary expansion in the Community in the same way a national Central Bank can control monetary expansion in the domestic banking system by limiting the supply of reserve money.

The reserve coefficient could be kept very low to minimize the tax it imposes on deposits within the Community. If the example of the US is a good guide a flat (average equal to marginal) reserve requirement of 1% should not lead to a significant displacement of deposits (it would involve an interest rate loss of only 8 basis points at an interest rate of 8%). But at the same time given that the total commercial bank deposits in the Community amount to over 2 600 billion ECU, a 1% reserve requirement would lead to total reserves of over 26 billion ECU, enough to provide a solid basis for a common monetary policy (4).

---

(3) This does not imply that the governors endorse the idea of using reserves on commercial banks during the transition, the governors might have had principally the final stage in mind for which they wanted to keep the option of using this instrument. Article 19 of the draft statutes mentions that these reserves might have to held with national central banks. However, it is not important where commercial banks would have to hold their reserves. This is just a question of accounting as long as all decisions regarding the reserve requirement are taken by the ECB.

(4) The seigniorage the ECB would gain from a reserve coefficient of this order of magnitude would not be very large. If market interest rates are 8% the ECB would earn about 2 billion ECU per annum on the 26 billion ECU of securities it can buy with the proceeeds from the required reserves. For this reason the fiscal implications of required reserves are not stressed in this paper. For more details on this issue see BRUNI [3] and GROS [8] and [9].

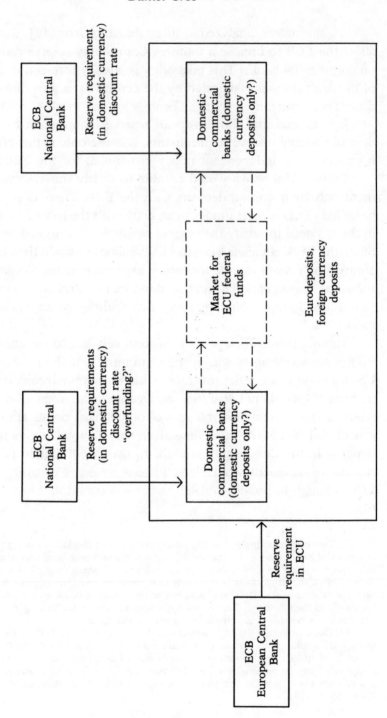

Graph 2

THE 2-TIER SYSTEM

Graph 2 shows the organization structure of such a system under the assumption that the reserves have to be held with the ECB.

An feature that is common to both systems is that they can only provide an *additional* anchor for the common monetary policy. In the present EMS this anchor is provided by a mixture of dominance of the strongest currency and informal coordination. The introduction of a system of required reserves can only put an upper limit on monetary expansion, it cannot therefore be a constrain for any individual country (or even the average of all countries) if it desires to implement a more restrictive policy.

The comparative advantages and disadvantages of the two systems are discussed in paragraph 5 below after a short digression on a technical problem that is common to both systems.

4. - Exchange Rate Changes and the Overall Demand for Reserves

Both systems would have to overcome a technical problem that arises because of the residual exchange-rate changes within the bands that are still possible in stage two. Any intra-EMS exchange rate change would reduce the ECU amount of the reserves to be held against deposits in the currency that is depreciating (this applies to the two-tier system; under the three-tier system the same effect applies to the reserves national central banks have to hold with the ECB). The ECU amount of the reserves held against deposits in the currencies that are appreciating would, of course, increase, but it is not clear which effect will be stronger.

The net effect of exchange rate changes on the overall demand for reserves depends on the relationship between ECU weights and the shares of national monetary aggregates as shown by the following simplified two-currency representation of a reserve system that could be either of the two-tier or three-tier type: The ECU is defined as a basket with fixed amounts of DM (α) and F_2 (β):

(1) $$ECU = \alpha DM + \beta F_2$$

The DM/F_2 exchange rate is denoted by e:

(2) $$DM \equiv eF_2$$

The definitions *(1)* and *(2)* imply that the ECU/DM exchange rate is given by:

(3) $$ECU = (\alpha + \beta/e)\,DM$$

The required reserves, which are expressed in ECU, are equal to a proportion, π, of the Community-wide total of the relevant monetary aggregate, M_{ECU}. This aggregate could be the sum of all commercial bank deposits in the Community (in this case these equations represent the two-tier system) or the sum of national reserve monies (in this case these equations represent the three-tier system):

(4) $$RR = \pi M_{ECU}$$

Denoting the two national reserve money supplies (or deposits with the national banking systems) by M_D and M_F, respectively, and using the DM/ECU exchange rate, equation *(3)*, this can be rewritten as:

(5) $$RR = \pi\,(\alpha + \beta/e)\,[M_D + eM_F]$$

A first question is whether (intra-Community) exchange-rate changes affect the overall amount of reserves. Differentiating equation *(5)* yields:

(6) $$dRR = \pi\,[\alpha M_F - \beta M_D/e^2]\,de$$

The overall amount of reserves changes with the exchange rate if the expression in square brackets is different from zero. After some tedious algebraic manipulations (see Appendix) equation *(6)* can be rewritten in a more revealing form using the weight of the DM in the ECU, denoted by $s_{ECU,D}$, and the weight of deposits with the German banking system in the overall Community money supply, denoted by $s_{M,D}$. In elasticity form this yields:

$$(7) \qquad dRR/RR = (s_{ECU,D} - s_{M,D})\, de/e$$

which establishes that the overall amount of reserves demanded by the Community banking systems is affected by the exchange rate only if the ECU shares differ from the relative weights of the national money supplies. A one percent change in the DM/F_2 exchange rate leads to a change in the demand for reserves equal to the difference between ECU share of the DM and the weight of the German money supply in the overall Community aggregate.

How important is this effect in reality? It depends on the exact definition of «money» used. Table 1 therefore shows the ECU weights (as of the end of 1989) and the share of the major national monetary aggregates in the corresponding Community totals (the monetary aggregates are valued at average 1989 exchange rates) (5). This table shows that the 'monetary' weight of some countries varies considerably according to the aggregate used and that there are considerably discrepancies between the 'monetary' and ECU weights.

These differences are mainly due to the large differences in required reserves since the major differences arise between the ECU weights and the monetary base wieghts. For example, the Italian monetary base accounted for 24% of the overall monetary base of the Community (because of the 25% marginal reserve requirement on commercial banks) whereas the weight of the Italian lire in the ECU was only 10%. Under the three-tier reserve scheme based on reserve money a 1% depreciation of the lire vis-à-vis all other currencies would lead to a reduction in the overall amount of ECU reserves of 0.14% (6).

---

(5) In this table the values for the German monetary aggregates have been increased by 20% to account for the increase that can be expected from unification. At the end of 1990 the part of $M3$ held in eastern Germany was about 14%, with a rapid recovery this proportion should rise to about 20 by 1994. The ECU weights were not affected by this, reflecting the assumption that the ECU weights will not be changed in 1994 and that there will be no major revaluation of the DM.

(6) This is obtained by multiplying $(0.10 - 0.24)$ times 0.01 and converting it back into percentage terms by multiplying by 100.

TABLE 1

ECU WEIGHTS AND SHARES
OF NATIONAL MONETARY AGGREGATES

Share of	Base money	M1	M3	Domestic credit	ECU weights
Belgium	2.4	2.5	2.3	2.8	7.9
Denmark	0.9	3.2	2.1	1.6	2.5
Germany	30.7	22.5	27.1	39.7	30.1
Greece	2.0	0.6	1.3	0.7	0.8
Spain	15.9	7.7	7.7	8.6	5.3
France	12.7	18.5	15.2	12.0	19.1
Ireland	0.7	0.3	0.4	0.4	1.1
Italy..................	24.1	24.5	22.5	13.0	10.2
Netherlands	4.0	4.5	5.8	6.3	9.4
Portugal	1.3	1.0	1.3	0.9	0.8
United Kingdom	5.4	14.7	14.3	14.1	13.0
Sum of absolute difference with ECU share	53.7	38.8	34.0	33.9	0.0
Memorandum item Community total in billion ECU	418.5	1 053.9	2.747.3	3 419.9	

Source: Own calculations based on *International Financial Statistics yearbook,* 1989. Weight of Germany increased by 20% to account for the effects of reunification.

The United Kingdom, which does not have required reserves on commercial banks, is an example of the opposite effects. Its weight in the monetary base of the Community was only 5% whereas the weight of the pound in the ECU was 13%. A one percent depreciation of the pound would therefore increase the overall demand for ECU reserves under the three tier system by 8%.

In general the correlation ECU weights/shares of national monetary aggregates is less weak for the broader based monetary aggregates as can be seen in the last row of this table: the average absolute difference between monetary base and ECU weights was 5.4% whereas the average absolute difference between domestic credit weights (the broadest monetary agregate considered here) and ECU weights was 3.4%.

Graph 3 tries to give an indication of the order of magnitude of the effect of exchange-rate changes. Each line in this graph refers to a different base for the reserves and shows how the total amount of reserves would have varied in 1989 given actual 1989 monthly exchange rates. The line labeled base money therefore indicates the evolution of the total amount of reserves (in official ECU) national central banks would have to hold with the ECB if the reserves were levied on the monetary base. The line labelled domestic credit does the same for the hypothesis that the reserves were levied on domestic credit. The line labelled $M3$ can represent both systems. For a two-tier system is indicates the effect of exchange-rate changes on the overall demand for «ECU federal funds» and for a three-tier system it indicates the effect of exchange rate changes on the demand for

GRAPH 3

TOTAL *EO, DC, M3* AND *BM* IN PERCENTAGE CHANGES USING
MONTHLY CURRENCY/ECU EXCHANGE RATES FROM 1989
(Germany +20%)

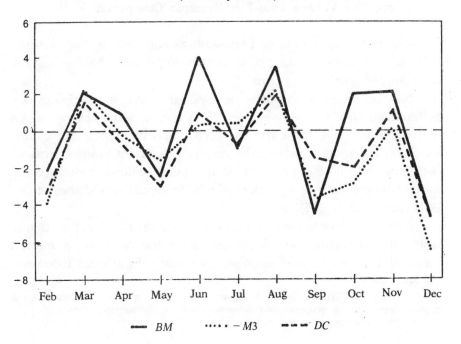

official 'reserve ECU' under the hypothesis that national central banks have to hold reserves with the ECB that are proportional to the national broad money supply (7).

Graph 3 suggests that exchange-rate changes could affect the overall amount of reserves significantly. In some cases the monthly percentage changes exceed 4% at an annual rate. However, movements up and down tend to cancel out over time as long as the central rates are not changed. This effect should therefore be mainly a source of short run 'noise' without implications in the long run. Moreover, since during stage two exchange rates should vary less than in 1989, the effect should be less important than suggested by this data.

This effect should, however, not impair the ability of the ECB to conduct a stable policy based on a system of reserves since the net effect of exchange rate changes can be easily calculated in advance. The ECB could therefore neutralize this source of noise by simply changing the supply of reserves to accommodate automatically the effects of intra-Community exchange-rate changes.

5. - Three-Tier Versus Two-Tier Systems Compared

Although it would not be impossible to combine the two systems it is useful to consider the problems that could arise if either system were implemented on its own (8).

One attraction of the three-tier system is that it anticipates the hierarchical structure between the ECB and national central banks that will arise once full EMU has been reached. If the reserves are levied on the monetary base the reserve coefficient could be raised over time until it reaches 100%. At this point national central banks would become just the equivalent of wholly owned subsidiaries of the ECB (Bini-Smaghi [1]).

A three-tier system would, however, have the disadvantage that it would not eliminate the undercounting of the Community money supply that arises because national definitions of the main monetary

---

(7) THYGESEN [18] also argues in favor of basing the reserve requirement on a broader aggregate, he proposes total domestic credit of the banking system.

(8) This paragraph is based on GROS [10].

aggregates often do not comprise foreign currency deposits and almost never comprise cross-border deposits. For example, despite the Belgium-Luxembourg monetary union a deposit by a Belgian resident with a bank in Luxembourg is not counted in Belgium because it is not with a Belgian bank, nor is such a deposit counted in Luxembourg because it is a deposit of a non-resident. Another example is the United Kingdom which uses explicitly the aggregate «sterling M4» which excludes deposits in foreign currency. It is apparent that imposing the reserve requirement directly on commercial banks would allow eliminate this issue and would allow the ECB to control the total amount of all liquid monetary assets that can be expected to finance expenditure within the Community.

The overall importance of this undercounting is difficult to estimate since there is no systematic data on the currency breakdown of foreign currency deposits and of the country of origin of cross-border deposits. The scarce data that are available suggests that this phenomenon is not yet very important. Bini-Smaghi - Vori [2] show that in the big member countries the ratio of foreign currency deposits to domestic deposits is below 10%. Since the part of these deposits that is in Community currencies is generally below one half this implies that foreign currency deposits are still relatively small in relation to national money supplies.

Cross-border deposits (i.e. a deposit that is denominated in the currency of the bank, but whose owner is a non-resident) seem to be more important. However, most of this international activity is inter-bank business and does not therefore have a direct impact on the size of the liquid assets that are held by the non-banking sector. Cross-border deposits are therefore also still relatively unimportant. For example, at the end of 1989 in Germany sight liabilities of domestic non-banks were equal to 263 billion DM whereas sight liabilities to non-bank non-residents were equal to only 23 billion DM. For time liabilities the share of non-residents was even lower. This implies that for the broader monetary aggregates these deposits of non-residents, which are not considered relevant for domestic monetary policy because their relationship with domestic spending is not clear, are probably also of minor importance.

However, even though the problem of «undercounting» the

European money supply is a present no serious it is clear that it can only increase in importance with the increasing integration in financial markets so that it is likely that it will be an important factor by the time stage two starts.

A three-tier system with reserves proportional to the national monetary base would have to deal with the implications of differences in national reserve requirements and therefore national multipliers. This problem has two dimensions:

(i) if there is a shift in monetary base between countries with different multipliers the overall monetary aggregates would be affected: a shift from a country with a low multiplier (high reserve requirement) to a country with a high multiplier (low or no reserve requirement) would increase the total amount of deposits within the Community unless the ECB reacts to each such disturbance;

(ii) national central banks could conduct an expansionary national monetary policy by reducing the domestic reserve requirements. In order to keep control over the Community total the ECB would again have to react to this development.

This suggests that a reserve requirement on the national monetary base would lead to difficulties unless national reserve requirements have been harmonized. This is different under the two-tier system since the total of deposits in the entire Community cannot increase as long as the ECB does not increase its liabilities vis-à-vis commercial banks (i.e. as long as it does not supply more «federal funds»). The two-tier system could therefore be implemented even before national reserve requirements have been harmonized.

The residual changes in exchange rates that are still possible in stage two are likely to pose another problem to a three-tier system even if they do not affect the overall amount as discussed in the previous paragraph. Under the three-tier system the central bank of a currency that is depreciating would have excess reserves and would therefore be in a stronger position than the central bank of the currency that is appreciating. This would not be a problem if one could rely on the emergence of a smoothly functioning market in these «official reserve ECU». But since central banks are not strictly profit maximizers and since only four central banks would dominate this market it is not likely that a central bank that experiences an appreciation of its own currency would be able to buy the «official reserve ECU» it needs.

In contrast, under the two-tier system there would be a market among commercial banks that would redistribution the «ECU federal funds» smoothly if exchange rates change (or if there is currency substitution).

This market for the «ECU federal funds» provides another argument for the two-tier system. Through its operations on this market the ECB would have, from the start, a direct contact with a Community-wide market. It would therefore immediately start to acquire the expertise that it will anyway need in stage three, when it acquires the exclusive responsibility for monetary policy. The interest rate on the market for «ECU federal funds» would also provide a convenient signal about the stance of the common monetary policy.

Finally, there seems to be no legal basis for the three-tier system. Article 19 of the draft statutes for the ESCB gives the ECB the power to impose reserve requirements on commercial banks, but not on national central banks. The ECB would therefore not be able to use sanctions to make sure that national central banks actually stay within the constraints imposed by the required reserves.

6. - Concluding Remarks

This note has emphasized the usefulness of a system of reserve requirements to provide an anchor for the common monetary policy during the transition to full EMU. Since reserve requirements are a tax on deposits they are not the ideal instrument of monetary control in general, and, as the experience of countries without reserve requirements shows, this instrument is not indispensable for an effective monetary policy. A sound monetary policy can also be based on the demand of the public for cash and the demand of commercial banks for clearing balances with the central bank. However, these two instruments cannot be used as a base for a *common* monetary policy in stage two (probably even during stage IIIA, i.e. before the introduction of a common currency) because cash would still be in national currency and because the clearing in national currencies would still be done at the national level.

Imposing a small, uniform reserve requirement on all deposits held with a commercial bank in the Community would give the European Central Bank a convenient instrument with which it could always put an *upper limit* on total monetary expansion in the Community. The asymmetry in this system would provide a guarantee that it could never be used for a policy that is more expansionary than that of the most stability-orientated member.

Dividing equation *(6)* by equation *(5)* yields:

(A.1)
$$\frac{dRR}{RR} = \frac{\alpha M_F - \beta M_D/e^2}{(\alpha + \beta/e)(M_D + eM_F)} \, de$$

adding and subtracting αM_D to the nominator (and multiplying by e/e) yields:

(A.2)
$$\frac{dRR}{RR} = \frac{\alpha e M_F + \beta M_D - \alpha M_D - \beta M_D/e}{(\alpha + \beta/e)(M_D + eM_F)} \frac{de}{e}$$

after some simplifications this yields:

(A.3)
$$\frac{dRR}{RR} = \left[\frac{\alpha}{\alpha + \beta/e} - \frac{M_D}{M_D + e\beta M_F} \right] \frac{de}{e}$$

The first term in the square brackets is the weight of the DM in the ECU, $s_{ECU,D}$, and the second term represents the weight of the German money supply in the overall money supply of the Community, $s_{M,D}$.

BIBLIOGRAPHY

[1] BINI-SMAGHI LORENZO: «Progressing Towards European Monetary Unification: Selected Issues and Proposals», Roma, Servizio studi Banca d'Italia, *Temi di discussione*, n. 133, April 1990.

[2] BINI-SMAGHI LORENZO - VORI SILVIA: *Competition, Hegemony and Monetary Unification*, mimeo, Roma, Banca d'Italia, July 1990.

[3] BRUNI FRANCO: *Il regime della riserva obbligatoria e l'integrazione europea dei mercati finanziari*, mimeo, Milano, Università commerciale Luigi Bocconi, November 1990.

[4] CIAMPI CARLO A.: «An Operational Framework for an Integrated Monetary Policy in Europe», *Collection of Papers Annexed to Delors Report*, 1989, pp. 225-32.

[5] COMMITTEE FOR THE STUDY OF ECONOMIC AND MONETARY UNION: *Report on Economic and Monetary Union in the European Community (the Delors Report)*, Luxembourg Office of Publications of the European Communities, 1989.

[6] DE LAROSIÈRE JACQUES: «First Stages Towards the Creation of a European Reserve Bank - the Creation of a European Reserve Fund», *Collection of Papers Annexed to Delors Report*, 1989, pp. 177-84.

[7] GROS DANIEL: «The EMS and the Determination of the European Price Level», Brussels, Centre for European Policy Studies, CEPS, *Working Document (Economic)*, n. 34, 1988.

[8] — —: «Seigniorage in the EC: the Effects of the EMS and Financial Market Integration», Washington, International Monetary Fund, IMF, *Working Paper*, n. 7, 1989.

[9] — —: «Paradigms for the Monetary Union of Europe», *Journal of Common Market Studies*, vol. XXVII, n. 3, March 1989, pp. 219-30.

[10] — —: «The Ecu in the Common Monetary Policy», *ECU Newsletter*, n. 32, April 1990, pp. 14-9.

[11] GROS DANIEL - NIELS THYGESEN: «The EMS: Achievements, Current Issues and Directions for the Future», Brussels, Centre for European Policy Studies, CEPS, *Paper*, n. 35, 1988.

[12] — — - — —: «Concrete Steps Towards Monetary Union», Brussels, Centre for European Policy Studies, CEPS, *Paper*, n. 44, 1990.

[13] H.M. TREASURY: *An Evolutionary Approach to Economic and Monetary Union*, Londra, HM Treasury, November 1989.

[14] KNEESHAW JOHN T. - PAUL VAN DEN BERG: «Changes in Central Bank Money Market Operating Procedures in the 1980s», Bank for International Settlements, *Economic Papers*, n. 23, January 1989.

[15] LAMFALUSSY ALEXANDRE: «Macro-Coordination of Fiscal Policies in an Economic and Monetary Union in Europe», *Collection of Papers Annexed to Delors Report*, 1989, pp. 91-125.

[16] PÖHL KARL OTTO: «The Further Development of the European Monetary System», *Collection of Papers Annexed to Delors Report*, September 1989, pp. 131-55.

[17] RUSSO MASSIMO - GIUSEPPE TULLIO: «Monetary Policy Coordination Within the European Monetary System: Is There a Rule?», in GIAVAZZI FRANCESCO - MICOSSI STEFANO - MILLER MARCUS (eds.): *The European Monetary System*, Ch. 11, Banca d'Italia, Centro *inter*-universitario di studi teorici per la politica economica and Centre for Economic Policy Research, Cambridge, Cambridge University Press, 1988, pp. 292-320.

[18] THYGESEN NIELS: «A European Central Banking System - Some Analytical and Operational Considerations», *Collection of Papers Annexed to Delors Report*, 1989, pp. 157-76.

Monetary Union and its Implications for Fiscal Policy

Daniel Cohen
CEPREMAP, Paris; CEPR, London

Introduction

Should monetary union in Europe be accompanied by a tight coordination of the fiscal policies of its member states? Is it the case that, in the long run, monetary integration has to lead to an integration of all European fiscal policies within the framework of, say, a European unified budget? Several authors have answered positively to this question. Sachs and Salai-i-Martin, for instance, have argued that the main difference between monetary integration in Europe and monetary integration in the US had to do with fiscal policy. They show that the federal budget in the US dampens dramatically the fluctuation of income that any one of the US states had to bear. This, in their view, explains why it was apparently so easy to surrender monetary sovereignty: the cost of losing the monetary instrument is overwhelmingly dominated by the benefit of belonging to a supra-regional fiscal area.

Another line of reasoning in favor of fiscal coordination, and perhaps fiscal integration, has to do with the the risk that profligate governments may come to over-borrow if their budget is not kept in check within a European one. Today governments' laxism is kept in check by the exchange-rate constraint. Tomorrow, if this constraint was to be subsumed into a European exchange-rate constraint, which mechanism would keep a government from free-riding on the average quality of its neighbour's fiscal policies?

We intend in this paper to analyze the validity of these arguments and that of others which have been offered in favour of fiscal coordination. We shall first attempt to show that that there is no presumption that monetary integration induces governments to over-borrow. We shall see, however, that the free-rider argument is a valid one that deserves to be answered. We shall then argue that monetary integration in Europe is quite a different story from monetary integration in the US because of a different labor mobility. On this ground, we shall argue that fiscal integration is not a good idea for Europe. In the final paragraph of the paper, we develop an analytical model that tackles some of the questions that we raised before.

1. - Monetary Integration
and the Risk of Fiscal Laxism

Should one fear that monetary integration will induce governments to be more profligate than they would otherwise be? Two types of arguments must be distinguished before one answers this question. There are the arguments that have to do with the seignorage tax, and the arguments that have to do with the exchange rate. They each go in opposite directions.

1.1 *The Seignorage Tax*

By renouncing their discretionary use of money creation, each government surrenders, within a monetary union, to an important tool of economic policy. For that matter, one may conclude that fiscal policy will be more cautious than it would otherwise be. To that extent, monetary integration should make the governments more cautious.

Strictly defined, seignorage tax only amounts to the purchasing power that is gained by the government when it issues money. To that extent however, the empirical relevance of the argument is minor: only 1% of GNP in the case of France.

Defined more broadly, however, the seignorage tax includes the capability for the government to create a surprise inflation that amounts to a capital levy on the holders of government debt (when it is not indexed). For countries like France or Germany, this is again not a major dimension of the government finances. For countries in which the share of public debt in GNP is substantial, the question deserves to be asked: is there a risk that a government such as that of Italy, Greece, or Ireland may become insolvent, i.e., may find themselves incapable of servicing their debt by refinancing it or by raising adequate taxes? As long as a government can issue the money in which the debt is indexed such a risk is literally nil: it can always print what it is asked for (whatever the purchasing power of the money may be). Once it has surrendered its monetary sovereignty, this is not the case any more and the government may technically become insolvent.

What should be the EC's appropriate response to this risk? Some have argued that it should simply do nothing and let each government face its creditors. If necessary, it should let the bankrupt government default just like any other enterprise. So as to keep this bankruptcy from creating too much financial instability within Europe, one may think of imposing regulatory norms on the private investors so as to make sure that they do not invest more than a given fraction of their assets in the debt of any one of the Community's governments (Bishop [1]).

It is hard to believe, however, that one could let Italy's government go bankrupt and it is very likely that, *ex-post*, it will not be viewed in the other government's interest to let it happen. This is indeed the main fear of those who argue that monetary integration has to be accompanied by a strict coordination of fiscal policies, and perhaps by a federal budget. The question that is at stake here, however, is not so much the coordination of fiscal policies as *flows* but rather the determination of a joint policy with respect to the *stock* of debt that is accumulated by a government. If a response were to be given at the level of the Community to this problem, it should amount to some form of surveillance on the level of public debt that is issued by a government. This would endow the EC with some capability of intervention more or less on the model that is offered by the IMF. One could imagine for instance that the Community would accept to guarantee the debt of the member state, conditionally on their acceptance of guidelines on the maximum level of debt to GDP that is acceptable.

1.2 *Fiscal Policy and Exchange Rate*

Let us now assume that the insolvency risk is taken care of, whether by the private investors themselves, or through the EC itself. What to think of the argument according to which the removal of the exchange market may induce governments to free-ride on others and have a more lenient policy than they should?

Once the risk of insolvency is controlled for, it should be clear that a fiscal policy cannot be systematically too loose. It can only be so in response to transitory phenomena. The analysis of the relationship between fiscal policy and the exchange-rate constraint must therefore be reformulated as follows: in response to which (transitory) disturbances can one expect the fiscal policy response to be looser without an exchange-rate constraint than with one? We develop in the last paragraph of this paper a model that responds to this question. Let us here emphasize the main points of the reasoning.

1.3 *Inflationary Shocks*

Let us first assume that Europe is subject to a joint inflationary shock, say an appreciation of the dollar. Let us analyze how the exchange-rate constraint interferes with the design of the best fiscal policy response.

When the country can run its own monetary policy, it will attempt to offset the inflationary shock by appreciating its currency *vis-à-vis* its neighbour's, and, among others, with respect to its European neighbours. If every European country attempts to do the same, one will get an unnecessary contraction in Europe, as each monetary policy will vainly attempt to be tighter than the monetary policy next door.

If each European country surrenders its monetary sovereignty to a European Central Bank, the risk of an undue monetary contraction can be avoided. It still remains however that each country can use its fiscal policy. In response to an inflationary shock, each European country will attempt to use the only instrument that they are left with and will each create a domestic deflationary shock that will not take account of the spill-over effect that it may have on the other country. In such a case, one can see that, in general, the removal of the rate constraint will make fiscal policy tighter than it would be otherwise.

In contrast, faced with a deflationary shock, such as a devaluation of the dollar akin to what is occurring in the early nineties, the reasoning above is inverted, and it then indeed becomes the case that monetary integration may turn fiscal policy into becoming too loose.

2. - Fiscal Integration?

If one can readily accept the idea that the coordination of fiscal policies is in general a good thing, should one go beyond and argue in favor of a supranational budget? We shall first review the argument of those who favor such a line of reasoning by pointing to the US experience. I will then try to show why this argument is not only biased, but could prove very misleading when applied to the European case.

2.1 *Monetary Union and Fiscal Integration*

Many authors have pointed out that the major difference between monetary integration across European states and across US states is the role of fiscal integration. As shown by Sachs and Sala-i-Martin, for instance, every dollar that is lost by a state in the US is compensated at the federal level by a corresponding transfer of about 40 cents. This explains why, according to these authors, surrendering monetary sovereignty is not a bad deal, if it can be compensated by an implicit insurance scheme that is offered by the federal budget.

In order to assess the validity of this argument, it is important to analyze carefully the origin of the loss of income that is compensated by the federal budget.

2.2 *Symmetric Shock*

Let us first assume that a joint disturbance affects Europe. In that case, it must be clear that a federal budget is of little help. Each state is suffering from the same shock and no compensation is delivered by the federal authority. The mechanism that indeed underlies the calculation in Sachs and Sala-i-Martin is the automatic stabilizer that is provided by the increase or reduction of taxes that is mechanically triggered by any fluctuation of income. If all states go through the same reduction of income, no benefit can be expected from a federal budget.

2.3 *Asymmetric Shocks*

Let us now examine what happens when an asymmetric shock hits the nation. It is then certainly the case that the region whose income is reduced benefits from its membership to a federal budget. In order to analyze carefully what this means for monetary integration one must again carefully analyze the nature of the shock that hits the country.

Let us first consider the case when the shock is a transitory one, i.e., let us assume that the shock is not expected to last very long. In that case, a single nation which has access to the world financial markets can very well offset on its own the impact of the shock by borrowing the loss of income until it dies out, or until it is reverted by a shock of an opposite sign.

Let us consider then what happens when the shock is permanent. In that case, and in that case only, a federal budget can indeed deliver an improvement, which is akin to an insurance mechanism, that a multi-country world cannot deliver. The key question however is not so much to investigate whether a federal budget does better (it surely does), but to compare the outcome of a system without a common currency to a system which has one. If an earthquake permanently destroys 10% of a country's wealth, having a currency of its own or not will change little to the welfare of the country. No devaluation can help offsetting a *permanent* loss of income. All that the country can do is reduce its standard of living correspondingly. In order to assess whether a federal budget is needed or not, one must not compare the outcome of a monetary union to the outcome that would be reached if it were not created. There is no point comparing them both to a third outcome.

2.4 *Current Account Disequilibria and Adjustments*

As one sees a federal budget is not a pre-condition to monetary integration. I would now want to argue that it may actually turn out to be counter-productive.

The key question that is raised by a monetary union is simply the following: how to deal with a country's loss of competitiveness without a devaluation? In the theory of an optimal currency area, it was emphasized that the condition of success of a monetary union was the mobility of the factors of production, and particularly of the labor force. Labor mobility, in the work of Mundell in particular, helps avoiding that persistent disequilibria take place on the labor market. Indeed, if a region were to be hit by a labor market disequilibrium — due, say, to a bad productivity shock — migration away from that region would eventually ease unemployment and eventually bring wages back to their equilibrium level.

There is little doubt that Europe is *not* an optimal currency area, if one accepts Mundell's paradigm. While the mobility of capital is about to become very high, there is no prospect of a high mobility of labor, if only because of barriers to speak the same language. This remark, if it is to be accepted, has two related consequences.

The first one is that the taxation of labor can be quite different across European countries. The low mobility of labor makes it indeed possible to have an autonomous fiscal policy.

The second consequence of a low labor mobility is that it makes a differentiated fiscal policy desirable. Indeed, if labor mobility is low and cannot offset easily a labor market disequilibrium, it becomes crucial that fiscal policy keep an autonomous ability to respond to idiosyncratic shocks. If a country were to suffer a loss of competitiveness, and cannot count on a devaluation to coordinate a swift return to an equilibrium point, it is important that it keep a fiscal degree of freedom to achieve that goal (by reducing, say, social security or the like).

3. - A Framework on Analysis

In order to analyze more specifically the questions addressed in paragraph 2, we shall develop here an analytical model based on a joint work with Charles Wyplosz (Cohen-Wyplosz [4]).

We analyze a world composed of three countries which we call France, Germany and the US. France and Germany are referred to as "Europe" and the US as the "rest of the world". We index with a 1 all variables referring to France and with a 2 all variables referring to Germany. France and Germany are two identical countries.

We call e the (log) of the nominal exchange rate of the franc with respect to the mark, e_1 the nominal exchange rate of the franc with respect to the dollar, e_2 the nominal exchange rate of the mark with respect to the dollar. We have:

(1) $$e = e_1 - e_2$$

we assume that each country produces one (representative) good. The (log of the) price of the good produced by country i is $p_1(t)$. The price of the US good is constant and normalized to be 1.

Each consumer in country i consumes a good produced in country i or turned (at a cost) into a product which looks like a country i product.

We can define (in log terms) the corresponding prices as:

(2)
$$\begin{cases} z(t) \equiv p_2(t) + e(t) - p_1(t) \\ z_1(t) = e_1(t) - p_1(t) \\ z_2(t) = e_2(t) - p_2(t) \end{cases}$$

$z(t)$ is the Franco-German real exchange rate; $z_1(t)$ the real exchange rate of country i with respect to the rest of the world.

In response to any deviation of $[z(t), z_1(t)]$ from zero, we assume that some foreign goods are shipped to the least competitive country.

The transportation cost includes the cost of turning a country i good into a country j good. Call $TB_1(t)$ the trade balance which is triggered. We assume a finite response of the following form:

(3)
$$\begin{cases} TB_1(t) = h_1\, z_1(t) + h\, z(t) \\ \\ TB_2(t) = h_2\, z_2(t) + h\, z(t) \end{cases}$$

$TB(t)$ is the trade balance of country i; $h_1\, z_1(t)$ and $h_2\, z_2(t)$ are respectively the trade surplus of country i with the US; $h\, z(t)$ is the trade surplus of France with Germany.

3.1 *Prices*

We assume that prices in each European country are set through a mark-up above labor which depends upon the relative prices $z_1(t)$ and $z(t)$ and upon output.

(4a)
$$\begin{cases} p_1(t) = w_1(t) + a_1\, z_1(t) + a\, z(t) + b\, Q_t(t) + \varepsilon_1(t) \end{cases}$$

(4b)
$$\begin{cases} p_2(t) = w_2(t) + a_1\, z_2(t) - a\, z(t) + b\, Q_2(t) + \varepsilon_1(t) \end{cases}$$

Note that in equation (4b) we have directly set $a_2 = a_1)\, \varepsilon_i(t)$, $i = 1, 2$, are two transitory disturbances. We shall examine the two cases when $\varepsilon_1(t) = \varepsilon_2(t)$ and when $\varepsilon_1(t) = -\varepsilon_2(t)$.

Wages of time t are set at the end of period $t - 1$, before $\varepsilon_i(t)$ are known. We assume that wage earners set a nominal wage equal to:

$$w_1(t) = \varepsilon_{t-1}\, p_i(t)$$

3.2 *Policy Objectives*

We assume that policymakers in country i are elected so as to minimize the following loss function:

$$L_1 = \frac{1}{2} \{\phi_0\, [A_i(t)]^2 + \phi_1\, [Q_i(t)]^2 + \pi_i(t)^2\}$$

in which $\pi_i(t) = p_i(t) - p(t-1)$ is the (current) inflation rate and $A_i(t)$ is domestic absorption. We directly assume that $[\pi_i(t), A_i(t)]$ are the policymaker's instruments. This latter assumption is less stringent than it seems to the extent that we only deal with transitory disturbances.

In order to spell out the equilibrium which will arise from this model we now need to specify the strategic interactions between the decisions of the government of countries 1 and 2.

4. - Non-Cooperative Equilibrium

In this paragraph, we analyse the Nash feed-back equilibrium of the game between the policymakers in countries 1 and 2. Each policymaker responds to the stochastic disturbance $[\varepsilon_1(t), \varepsilon_2(t)]$ through a feed-back $[A_i[\varepsilon_1(t), \varepsilon_2(t)]; \pi_i[\varepsilon_1(t), \varepsilon_2(t)]]$ which is best to apply when to other policymakers response is taken as given and when the expectations of the wage earners are similarly taken as fixed. (This latter assumption amounts to choosing a time-consistent equilibrium of the game between the government and the wage earners, (Cohen and Michel [2]).

Under these assumptions, let us see how the policymaker in country 1 chooses its policy package. Because of the transitory nature of the disturbances $\varepsilon_i(t)$, one can readily conjecture that the private sector's expectations of inflation are constant:

(5) $$w_t = w_t^* = 0$$

Both the government of country 1 and of 2 consequently take the price response of the economy to be given by the following equations:

(6)
$$\begin{cases} \pi_1(t) = a_1 z_1(t) + a z(t) + b Q_1(t) + \varepsilon_1(t) \\ \\ \pi_2(t) = a_1 z_2(t) - a z(t) + b Q_2(t) + \varepsilon_2(t) \end{cases}$$

The government of country 1, on the other hand, takes the response $[\pi_2(t), A_2(t)]$ as given. Since $z_2(t) = z_1(t) = -z(t)$, the government of country 1 is consequently led to take as given the following interaction between $z_1(t)$ and $z(t)$:

(8) $$z(t) = \theta\, z_1(t) + h_2\,[\varepsilon_1(t), \varepsilon_2(t)]$$

in which:

(9) $$\theta = \frac{a_1 + b\, h_1}{(a + a_1) + b\,(h + h_1)}$$

and:

$$h_2\,[\varepsilon_1(t), \varepsilon_2(t)] = \pi_2\,[\varepsilon_1(t), \varepsilon_2(t)] - \varepsilon_2(t) - b\, A_2\,[\varepsilon_1(t), \varepsilon_2(t)]$$

Substituting equation (8) into the equation describing the domestic economy one can consequently write the policymaker's program as one which minimizes L_i subject to the following set of equations:

(9a) $$\pi_1(t) = [a_1 + 2\, a]\, z_1(t) + b\, Q_1(t) + \xi_1\,[\varepsilon_1(t), \varepsilon_2(t)]$$

(9b) $$Q_1(t) - A_1(t) = [h_1 + \theta\, h]\, z_1(t) + \eta_1\,[\varepsilon_1(t), \varepsilon_2(t)]$$

in which ε_1 and η_1 are the stochastic disturbances which are obtained by substituting (8) into the original law of motion of the economy.

Call λ_t and μ_t the shadow prices associated to each of the constraints (9a) and (9b). One can write the first order conditions as follows:

(10a) $$\phi_0\,(A_t - \bar{A}) = \mu_t$$

(10b) $$\phi_1\,(Q_t - \bar{Q}) = -\, b\, \lambda_t - \mu_t$$

(10c) $$\pi_t = \lambda_t$$

(10d) $$(a_1 + \theta\, a)\, \lambda_t - (h_1 + 0\, h)\, \mu_t = 0$$

Out of this system of equations, one can readily find that the policy response will set the economy on the hyperplane:

(11) $$\phi_0\, A_t + \phi_1\, Q_t + b\, \pi_t = 0$$

In order to find the equilibrium feed-back policy which is chosen by the policymaker when the shock $[\varepsilon_1(t), \varepsilon_2(t)]$ hits Europe, we now distinguish the cases when the shocks $\varepsilon_i(t)$ are symmetric or asymmetric. (Cohen and Wyplosz [3] for an empirical analysis).

4.1 Response to Symmetric Shocks

Let us analyze here the case when:

(12) $$\varepsilon_1(t) = \varepsilon_2(t) = \varepsilon(t).$$

At the equilibrium we must necessarily have $z(t) = 0$. In order to find which equilibrium feed-back rules will arise out of the first order condition written in (10), we simply need to substitute these conditions into:

(13)
$$\begin{cases} \pi_1(t) = a_1 z_1(t) + b Q_1(t) + \varepsilon(t) \\ Q_1(t) - A_1(t) = h_1 z_1(t) \end{cases}$$

(and similarly for country 2).

One can write the response of each country i as follows:

(14)
$$\begin{cases} A_i(t) = \alpha \pi_i(t) \quad ; \; \alpha = \dfrac{1}{\phi_0} \dfrac{a_1 + \theta a}{h_1 + \theta h} \\[3mm] Q_i(t) = -\beta \pi_i(t) \; ; \; \beta = \dfrac{1}{\phi_1}\left[b + \dfrac{a_1 + \theta a}{h_1 + \theta h}\right] \end{cases}$$

(15)
$$\begin{cases} \pi_i(t) = \delta_s \varepsilon(t) \\[3mm] \delta_s = \dfrac{1}{1 + \dfrac{a_1}{h_1}(\alpha + \beta) + b\beta} \end{cases}$$

In response, say, to a joint inflationary shock $\varepsilon_t > 0$, each country carries an expansionary monetary policy ($\alpha > 0$) and a tight monetary policy ($\delta < 1$) which brings a recession, creates a trade deficit, appreciates the exchange rate and (partially) eases the inflationary pressure.

One can immediately make the following crucial remark (to which we shall return in the next paragraph). When h is very large with respect to the other parameters, one sees that α, the measure of the fiscal response, tends towards zero. No European country undertakes a fiscal expansion. The intuition is simply the following. Fiscal expansion is undertaken because it eases inflationary pressure through the appreciation of the exchange rate. When h is very large, it means that intra-European trade prevents any substantial deviation from *PPP*. Because its fails to internalize the action of the other European country, no European policymaker will undertake a fiscal expansion. When they are hit by a joint inflationary shock, however, it is the importance of the trade effect with the US, not with Europe which is relevant and makes a joint fiscal expansion (and a larger appreciation of the exchange rate) desirable or not.

4.2 *Response to an Asymmetric Shock*

Let us analyze the response to a shock $\varepsilon(t)$ such that $\varepsilon_1(t) = \varepsilon(t)$, $\varepsilon_2(t) = -\varepsilon(t)$. For instance let us assume that $\varepsilon(t) > 0$. Because of the asymmetry of France and Germany we know Europe's overall trade with the US will be balanced. We consequently know that, at the equilibrium, $TB_1(t) + TB_2(t) = h_1[Z_1(t) + Z_2(t)] = 0$. We can consequently characterize the equilibrium through the following conditions:

(16)
$$
\begin{cases}
z_1(t) = \dfrac{1}{2}\, z(t) \\[4mm]
z_2(t) = -\dfrac{1}{2}\, z(t)
\end{cases}
$$

France will appreciate its exchange rate (to ease down the inflationary pressure), Germany will symmetrically depreciate its exchange rate (to increase output).

At the equilibrium, we must consequently have:

(17)
$$\begin{cases} \pi_1(t) = \left[\dfrac{a_1}{2} + a\right] z(t) + b\,Q_1(t) + \varepsilon(t) \\[3mm] \pi_2(t) = \left[\dfrac{a_1}{2} + a\right] z(t) + b\,Q_2(t) + \varepsilon(t) \end{cases}$$

The response of fiscal policy and output are still characterized as in equation *(14)*. Inflation instead is now a solution to:

(18)
$$\begin{cases} \pi_i(t) = \delta_a\,\varepsilon_1(t) \\[2mm] \text{with:} \\[2mm] \delta_a = \dfrac{1}{\dfrac{a_1 + 2\,a}{h_1 + 2\,h}(\alpha + \beta) + b\,\beta} \end{cases}$$

The same comments are in order. When $h = +\infty$, no European policymaker will undertake an active fiscal policy. In the case of an asymmetric shock, however, this need not be bad if one policymaker expands while the other deflates. The trade disequilibrium is likely to be larger than needed. In order to be more specific, we now turn to the analysis of the fully coordinated response.

5. - Socially Optimum Solution

Let us now investigate how a European central planner would optimally choose the policy mix in Europe in response to the shock $[\varepsilon_1(t), \varepsilon_2(t)]$. More specifically, let us assume that a European policymaker is free to choose, at each period, $[\pi_1(t),\ A_1(t),\ \pi_2(t),$ $A_2(t)]$ in response to a *shock* $[\varepsilon_1(t),\ \varepsilon_2(t)]$ in such a way as to minimize the average loss function of Europe. Let us analyze in turn, the response to a symmetric and to an asymmetric shock.

5.1 *Symmetric Shocks*

Let us assume that $\varepsilon_1(t) = \varepsilon_2(t) = \varepsilon(t)$ and, for easing the discussion, assume that $\varepsilon(t) > 0$.

Contrarily to the uncoordinated response of each European policymaker does internalize the symmetric nature of the shock when he decides of the optimal response to deliver. Here, it is straightforward to see that the European policymaker will simply have to minimize any one of the two European countries' loss function subject to the constraint that $z(t) = 0$.

One can therefore readily see that the optimal response of the European policymaker is simply that which is chosen in the non-cooperative game in the case when $\theta = 0$. One can consequently write the European policymaker's response for each European country $i = 1,2$ as:

(19)
$$\begin{cases} A_i(t) = \alpha_s^* \, \pi_t \qquad \alpha_s^* = \dfrac{1}{\phi_0} \dfrac{a_1}{h_1} \\[4mm] Q_i(t) = -\,\beta_s \, \pi_t \qquad \beta_s^* = \dfrac{1}{\phi_1}\left[b + \dfrac{a_1}{h_1} \right] \end{cases}$$

(20)
$$\begin{cases} \pi_i(t) = \delta_s^* \, \varepsilon(t) \\[2mm] \text{with} \\[4mm] \delta_s^* = \dfrac{1}{1 + \dfrac{a_1}{h_1}(\alpha_s^* + \beta_s^*) + b\,\beta_s^*} \end{cases}$$

As one sees, the comparison between the non-cooperative (*NC*) case and the socially optimum solution (*SOS*) only hinges on the comparison between $a_1 + \theta\, a_1 / h_1 + \theta\, h_1$ and a_1 / h_1. One consequently needs to distinguish two cases.

$$(A) \qquad\qquad \frac{a}{h} < \frac{a_1}{h_1}$$

When inequality A is satisfied, the price effects in Europe are less important than trade effects *relatively* to the corresponding *relative* hierarchy which the rest of the world. The question is *not* to decide whether price or trade effects are important, but rather whether intra-European trade flows are *relatively* more sensitive to exchange rate fluctuations than prices. It is our view that this should be the case. The fluctuations of the dollar have a strong effect on price (through oil or other key commodities) while the fluctuations of the DM have a relatively stronger effect on French trade than on price. We postpone to a forthcoming empirical paper a more qualified answer.

At any rate if inequality *(A)* is satisfied, one sees that $\alpha_s^* > \alpha^*$, $\beta_s^* > \beta$, and $\delta_s^* > \delta$ the *SOS* response to a joint inflationary shock is *less* inflationary than the *NC* response, fiscal expansion is *more* pronounced and the recession is worse. The intuition behind this result was already apparent in the analysis of the *NC* equilibrium. The non-cooperative European policymaker does not internalize the fact that no net intra-European trade will take place at equilibrium and (*sub*-optimally) take intra-European trade into account.

For the European social planner, in contrast, all that matters, in case of a joint shock, is the trade and price effects with respect to the rest of the world.

When inequality *(A)* is satisfied, a European *expansionary* fiscal policy and a *tight* monetary policy (*à la* Reagan-Volcker) can buy a disinflation which is less effective (in trade terms) than the one which is perceived by the individual (non-cooperative) policymaker. If one trusts that such is the case, one also sees that binding fiscal policy (as proposed in the *Delors Report*) would not be a good idea.

Let us now turn to the opposite case, when:

(B)
$$\frac{a_1}{h_1} < \frac{a}{h}$$

In that case, everything said previously is turned around. Non-cooperative yields an over-appreciated exchange rate with respect to the socially optimum outcome. This is simply because of the traditional Hamada-Sachs-Miller-Salmon argument according to which each policymaker vainly attempts to appreciate its currency against the other so as to buy imported disinflation. When inequality *B* holds this creates an undue appreciation with respect to a third country. Cooperation, in that case, implies *more* inflation and a looser monetary policy (a view which was already criticized by Melitz [6] as non-relevant for Europe).

5.2 *Asymmetric Shocks*

Let us now analyze the response of a European policymaker to an asymmetric shock. Let us assume $\varepsilon(t) = \varepsilon_1(t) = -\varepsilon_2(t)$ and, here again, that $\varepsilon(t) > 0$.

In this case, a European social planner internalizes the fact that Europe as a whole will run no trade imbalance with the rest of the world so that one will necessarily have, at equilibrium:

$$\begin{cases} z_1(t) = \dfrac{1}{2} z(t) \\ z_2(t) = -\dfrac{1}{2} z(t) \end{cases}$$

The task of a European social planner is now simply to maximize the welfare of any one of the two countries subject to $z_i(t) = \pm 1/2$ $z(t)$. As one immediately sees, this simply amounts to use the first-order conditions which were calculated in the non-cooperative case and to take $\theta = 2$. The *SOS* can consequently be characterized as follows:

(21)

$$\begin{cases} A_i(t) = \alpha_a^* \, \pi_i(t) & ; \quad \alpha_a^* = \dfrac{1}{\phi_0} \dfrac{a_1 + 2\,a}{h_1 + 2\,h} \\[4mm] Q_i(t) = -\,\beta_a^* \, \pi_i(t) & ; \quad \beta_a^* = \dfrac{1}{\phi_1}\left[b + \dfrac{a_1 + 2\,a}{h_1 + 2\,h} \right] \end{cases}$$

(22)

$$\begin{cases} \pi_i(t) = \delta_a^* \, \varepsilon(t) \\[4mm] \delta_a^* = \dfrac{1}{1 + \dfrac{a_1 + 2\,a}{h_1 + 2\,h}(\alpha_a^* + \beta_a^*) + b\,\beta_a^*} \end{cases}$$

Here again, as one sees, the comparison between the *SOS* and the *NC* equilibrium hinges on the comparison between a_1 / h_1 and a / h. However, as we now show, the conclusions are exactly *opposite* to those which were obtained in the symmetric case.

(A)
$$\frac{a}{h} < \frac{a_1}{h_1}$$

In that case, we see that $\alpha_a^* < \alpha$, $\beta_a^* < \beta$, $\delta_a^* > \delta$. In the country which is hit by an inflationary shock, fiscal policy is *less* active than in the non-cooperative case, the exchange rate appreciates by less, the recession is less pronounced and *inflation is larger*. The reason why the results are opposite to those which were obtained in the case of a symmetric shock is straightforward. A non-cooperative policymaker fails to internalize the fact that the other policymaker will undertake a policy which is opposite to the one which he undertakes. He consequently fears less than he should the trade effect of his European counterpart. When inequality *A* holds (trade effects are relatively more important than price effects), this leads non-cooperative policymaking to be more active than it should. A European social planner will consequently reduce the trade imbalance within Europe, reduce (in absolute value) the intra-European volatility of the exchange rate and engineers more inflation than in the non-cooperative case.

(B)
$$\frac{a_1}{h_1} < \frac{a}{h}$$

This case simply yields the opposite result: here, coordinating economic policy reduces inflation and widens the trade imbalance within Europe. Non-cooperative policymaking fails to internalize the potential disinflationary impact of an appreciation of the exchange rate (or, in the other country, fails to internationalize the potential gain for output of a depreciated currency).

We can summarize the results obtained thus far in the following Table:

	Trade effects dominate within Europe	Price effects dominate within Europe
Symmetric shocks	*SOS* fiscal policy more active than *NC* *SOS* monetary policy tighter than *NC*	*SOS* fiscal policy less active than *NC* *SOS* monetary policy looser
Asymmetric shocks	*SOS* fiscal policy less active than *NC* *SOS* monetary policy looser than *NC*	*SOS* fiscal policy more active than *NC* *SOS* monetary policy tighter than *NC*

Conclusion

We have shown that a fully coordinated economy policy appreciates the exchange rate of one country (in response to an inflationary shock and with respect to a third country) when: *a)* the trade effects dominate the price effects of the exchange rate within Europe (relatively to the rest of the world) *and* when the shocks hit symmetrically *all European countries; b)* when price effects dominate *and* when the shocks hit asymmetrically the European countries. In each instance fiscal policy is more expansionary when economic policy is fully coordinated than when it is set non-cooperatively. Coordinating monetary policy only has been shown to be always more inflationary than when coordinating both instruments.

In the two instances above, however, less inflation than in the non-cooperative case is brought by larger trade disequilibria than in the non-cooperative case.

BIBLIOGRAPHY

[1] BISHOP G.: «La Creation d'une Union à Monnaie Forte dans la Communauté Européenne», *Vers l'Union Économique et Monétaire Européenne*, Paris, La Documentation Française, 1990.

[2] COHEN D. - MICHEL PH.: «How Should Control Theory be Used to Calculate a Time-Consistent Economic Policy», *Review of Economic Studies*, March 1988.

[3] COHEN D. - WHYPLOSZ CH.: «European Monetary Union: An Agnostic Evaluation». in BRYANT *et al.* (eds.): *Macroeconomic Policies in an Interdependent Word*, IMF, The Brookings Institution, CEPR, 1989.

[4] —— - ——: «Price and Trade Effects of Exchange Rates Fluctuations and the Design of Policy Coordination», CEPR, *Working Paper*, 1990.

[5] HAMADA K.: *The Political Economy of International Monetary Independence*, London, MIT Press, 1985.

[6] MÉLITZ J.: «Germany, Discipline and Cooperation in the EMS», in GIAVAZZI *et al.* (eds.): *The European Monetary System*, Cambridge, Cambridge University Press, 1987.

[7] MILLER M. - SALMON M.: «Policy Coordination and Dynamic Games» in BUITER - MARSTON (eds.): *International Policy Coordination*, Cambridge, Cambridge University Press, 1985.

[8] SACHS J.: «International Policy Coordination in a Dynamic Macroeconomic Model», NBER, *Working Paper*, no. 1166, 1983.

A Political Economy of Economic and Monetary Union

Andrew Tyrie
Nuffield College, Oxford

Introduction

Economic and monetary union (EMU) has become a central issue in West European politics today (1). EMU is a linchpin of French foreign and economic policy. Helmut Kohl appears to consider that an EMU treaty, taken together with steps towards European political union, would be his crowing achievement as German Chancellor, sitting alongside the unification of his country. In Britain, the EMU issue has contributed to the downfall of the three most senior and influential figures in British politics in the 1980s: Margaret Thatcher, Nigel Lawson, and Sir Geoffrey Howe.

Why has EMU assumed such a central role in European politics What are the economic benefits of EMU and do they justify the price in terms of loss of control over our own affairs and/or sovereignty?

The first three paragraphs of this paper offer some answers to these questions. The first chapter explains how EMU has come to play such an important role in the politics of Europe. Without first understanding the politics of EMU it is not possible clearly to understand the economics.

The second paragraph examines the view, strongly argued by

---

(1) In this paper I shall use EMU as shorthand for monetary union while recognising, of course, that the economic aspect embodies all those reforms envisaged as a consequence of the *Single European Act*, and probably more besides.

some in Britain, and elsewhere in the Community, that EMU would fundamentally alter member States' sense of national identity, and involve an irrevocable loss of sovereignty.

The third paragraph examines the economic benefits said to result from EMU.

The fourth paragraph examines some other routes to EMU. Not only hve the benefits of EMU been exaggerated, certain types of EMU have been neglected.

1. - The Politics of Monetary Union - Origins of the Present Debate

1.1 *France*

The renewed interest in monetary union can be explained largely in terms of the politics of the Franco-German alliance.

Much of France's interest in EMU derives from many people's belief that it might bolster the Franco-German alliance, the principal means by which France retains a disproportionate influence in Europe. France's position needs bolstering for several reasons.

First, Germany's increasing economic dominance, combined with her growing maturity, has gradually exposed the myth of equal partnership in the Franco-German alliance. Second, the decline of the threat from the Societ Union, combined with the acceleration of detente, provided the opportunity for Germany to look eastwards as well as westwards in her search for security. The long shadow of Rapallo has haunted French foreign policy for decades; it is there once more. Third, partly as a consequence of her greater self-confidence, Germany sought to deepen her alliances with other Western countries. She found, prior to the Gulf war, a more sympathetic ear in Washington. She might also have succeeded with Britain, were it not for periodic rebuff, made more serious by the difficult relations between Helmut Kohl and Margaret Thatcher.

All this was happening even before the unification of Germany. Unification intensified the process. The fear of a larger Germany heightened French awareness of their own declining influence. The collapse of the Soviet empire in Eastern Europe greatly strengthened Germany's hand in her relations with the Soviet Union (2). US foreign policy objectives in Europe increasingly coincided with Germany's attempts to broaden the base of her West European relationships (3).

Faced with these bevelopments the French anxiously sought out other means of retaining their disproportionate power, derived largely from their singular influence over Germany, and (partly through Germany) over the direction of the European Community. EMU is one such way.

Many in the French political and bureaucratic establishment see EMU as one of France's last oppurtunities to tether Germany to a wider and West European framework, one which she has helped so much to shape. The French would rather see the EC develop as a major international player than find themselves excluded entirely from a group of three consisting of the US, Japan and Germany. So a central French objective has been to obtain German signature to a grand European Treaty. They would see it as a kind of insurance certificate. if the Germans were, at some subsequent stage, to resile from part of it the French would then hope to exercies some influence on the direction of policy by pointing to the Germans' «un-European» behaviour.

The Tresor is, perhaps, less persuaded by the political arguments but sees EMU as a means of weakening the power of the Bundesbank. Their dislike of the Deutschmark zone, that omnipresent symbol of German economic ascendancy, is patent.

---

(2) The 2 + 4 negotiations demonstrated vividly for the French the limits of the Franco-German alliance. Helmut Kohl's direct negotiations with Mr Gorbachev were far more important in determining the outcome than any advice or pressure form Paris.

(3) The objectives in Europe of the Bush administration have been twofold. First, it has sought to obtain the withdrawal of all Soviet troops from non-Soviet soil, including East Germany, as soon as possible. In this US interests coincided with those of West Germany and contrasted with the more ambivalent attitude towards a Soviet presence on German soil emanating from France and Britain in the autumn of 1989 and spring of 1990.

Second, the US wished to preserve their role in Europe. The most important vehicle for that was NATO and the best way to secure the retention of a role for NATO and to keep a military presence in continental Europe was by working with the Germans. These objectives took priority over any concerns the US may have had that the unification of Germany might upset the power balance in Europe. The removal of Soviet troops from Europe was of crucial domestic political significance for the US; it was a demonstration of the victory of the West in the cold war.

Some in France also hope that the call of wider European demands might do something to sap the German sense of national identity, enabling it to be subsumed in a wider European framework. However, others in France, at least on the right, have also expressed concern that Europe, and particularly EMU, might weaken their own identity. The desire of the French to obtain German signature to an EMU treaty has been further reinforced by the near collapse of many other aspects of French foreign policy (4).

1.2 *Germany*

French pressure alone would not have sufficed to propel EMU towards the top of the Franco-German and hence the European agenda. Notwithstanding the Germans' attempts to broaden their support by wooing Washington, Germany still needs France. German political self-confidence has not grown to match her economic self-confidence (5). The Gulf crisis is a reminder of the limited capacity of Germany's economic success to substitute for willingness to exercise military power. She remains vulnerable to the charge of recidivism, to the lingering memories of the last war, and to the absence of any clear psychological or territorial limit to the sense of German identity.

That vulnerability might one day be translated into practical terms. The Franco-German relationship was a cornerstone on which

---

(4) Three legs of French foreign policy have recently been gravely weakened, in the Middle East, in Africa and in Europe. First, the invasion of Kuwait exposed its fragility in the Middle East, a policy which extended far beyound decisions on arms sales. The collapse of France's friendship with Iraq shaken the whole structure of her Middle East relationships. Second, France's long-standing relationship with her former colonies in Africa is now being exposed as a costly post-Imperial legacy, one of which the central administration would like to be rid. Third, notwithstanding France's token repudiation of the *de facto* division of Europe decided at Yalta, French security policy had, at least to a large extent, been based on the continued division of the Germanies. With unification that leg of policy has been removed.

(5) Perhaps Helmut Kohl, by explicitly repudiating any further territorial claims on his neighbours (and by his pro-European advocacy) is reflecting the dictum of Bismarck: «Nothing could be more dangerous for Germany than to play the part of a man who has suddenly come into money and now throws his weight around» (quoted in the *Daily Telegraph*, 17.7.90).

the return of the Germans to the international Community and respectability was built. Were a French President ever to accuse a German Chancellor of being un-European or of having repudiated a major European commitment, the effects on German politics could be considerable. Whereas such an attack on a British Prime Minister might easily result in a strengthening of support for his or her Government, in Germany it could just as easily weaken a Chancellor's domestic political base, particularly given the exigencies of German coalition politics. It is often said that the Germans cannot do without the French in their international relations. It is almost as true that they cannot do without the French in their domestic politics.

Unification, at least for the time being, has intensified this need. Much German public opinion (and most of the leadership) is as anxious to find a European solution to the «German problem» as are the French. A pro-European strand is also strong in Christian democratic thinking and owes much to Adenauer.

This goes a long way to explaining how it can be that the Germans appear to neglect their own economic interests. Certainly, from the German point of view the economic arguments in favour of currency union are not strong. The Bundesbank already exercises most of the monetary control which the Germans could wish for under stage one of Delors (6).

The Bundesbank itself naturally sees EMU as a threat to its existence. But its wishes may come to be subordinated to those of the Bundeskanzleramt. Already, the Bundesbank has been overridden once, on the question of German monetary union. Nonetheless, the draft statutes prepared by the central bank governors appear to lean towards the Bundesbank model. This may, of course, merely reflect the influence of Karl Otto Pöhl and the fact that the report was prepared by central bankers.

The acid test of how far the Bundesbank is overridden on EMU will be the extent to which the constitution of any new European

---

(6) Many senior German officials privately expressed reservations about the pace and direction of the drive towards EMU from the start. Some of this surfaced in public and was reflected, for example, in the report of the Board of German Economic Advisers to the Bundesbank.

institution accords «Bundesbank-type» independence to it (7). By contrast, the French have been pressing for greater «accountability» for any new European monetary institution. The more directly that institution is open to influence by politicians, the less satisfied will the Bundesbank be with it. For the French, obtaining «accountability» is crucial to their negotiating position; it is the most effective way to erode what they see as the dominance of the Bundesbank in French monetary and economic affairs.

1.3 *Other Pressures for EMU*

So far, it has been argued that the EMU debate has been driven almost entirely by politics and in particular by the tension of the Franco-German alliance. Of course other developments have played a part.

First, the relative success of the EMS, assisted by a sustained period of steady growth in the mid and late 80s, has strengthened the view that further monetary integration could yield economic gains.

Second, the acceleration of economic integration as a consequence of the *Single European Act* can be said to imply, in economic terms, the need for further progress in the field of monetary integration.

Third, not only France but Italy, Belgium, Holland and others support EMU, partly as a way to curtail the power of the Bundesbank. The Italians also see EMU as a way to obtain a toehold in the Franco-German axis. And several of the poorer, smaller countries look at EMU with an eye to obtaining increased regional assistance.

There is force in these points, but none of them is enough to explain the acceleration of pressure for monetary union. The origins of

---

(7) In a search for that independence last year the Bundesbank quietly negotiated with the French in an effort to obtain agreement to some kind of Schengen group proposal, one in which Germany, and hence the Bundesbank, would remain the dominant partner. A smaller group would also increase the chances of enabling the Bundesbank to secure other objectives, for example binding rules on budget deficits and a lengthy period of adjustment in which non-participating countries' economies were given time to converge.

that pressure lie in politics, not economics (8). Only the exigencies of the Franco-German alliance can fully explain why it is that Germany should want to abandon an arrangement as favourable to them as the ERM (9), why it is that the French seem to be obsessed with the need for «accountability» in EMU, and why it is that German unification, far from leading to calls for slower progress to EMU (as much economic logic would suggest) has if anything led to calls for faster progress. De Gaulle is alleged to have said: «The European Community is a coach and horses; Germany is the coach and horses and France is the coachman». EMU is about a struggle to keep hold of the reins.

The central role of the Franco-German alliance also explains the apparent marginalisation of Britain (and, indeed, other members of the Community). Historically, the British have primarily seen the European Community as a means of securing economic rather than political objectives. Pragmatism had been the hallmark of British policy. The British have sought to examine the economic benefits of EMU and have been less than altogether convinced. Against that, many have argued that there is a high political price: the transfer of control over their own affairs partly at the behest of a European institution which has had, at best, only a mixed record in delivering the policies for which it is responsible. Both these allegations, about the loss of sovereignty as a consequence of EMU and about its economic benefits, will now be examined.

2. - Sovereignty and Monetary Union

It is clear that the creation of a single currency would require the handing over to a central European authority of a large number of functions at present exercised by the Bank of England, often under

---

(8) Karl-Otto Pöhl has made the same point: «Significantly enough, the proposal to create a European currency and a European Central Bank, did not come from the Minister of Economics or Finance, let alone the Bundesbank, but rather from the Minister for Foreign Affairs», Speech in Munich, 3 September 1990, reproduced in Europe's Constitutional Future, IEA, 1990.

(9) Karl-Otto Pöhl put this graphically: «in the Deutshmark we 'the Germans' would be sacrificing a hard currency on the European altar without knowing what we would be getting in return», *op. cit.* (5), p. 36.

the supervision of the Treasury (10). This undoubtedly represents a reduction in British control over its own affairs, but by no means necessarily constitutes a shedding of sovereignty (11).

Those in Britain and elsewhere who have argued on sovereignty grounds against any commitment to a Treaty providing the option of a single currency have greatly overstated their case.

What follows is no more than a somewhat formalised recital of what many instinctively feel, that the first call of people's loyalties in Europe, and particularly in Britain, will remain with nation states for the foreseeable future. Such fundamental loyalties would not be transferred to Brussels by a treaty on monetary union. The ultimate sovereign power of their legislatures, or whatever other constitutional arrangements exist for expressing that power, would not be affected.

2.1 *Sovereignty*

Two essential characteristics of sovereignty would seem to be, first, the right to limit or relinquish control over one's own affairs; second, the right to claw back that control (12). The principle that control over one's own affairs may be eroded by treaty is as old as international relations. Two contemporary examples are signature to the *Charter of the European Court of Human Rights* and signature to the *Treaty of Rome* (13). No new constitutional principle would seem to be established by the further transfer of responsibility for monetary

---

(10) The arguments here are set out with reference to Britain but they are, for the most part, valid for other member States.

(11) definitions of sovereignty abound. Here I shall take Geoffrey Marshall's definition of Parlimentary sovereignty: «Where a parliament is sovereign (as is the parliament of the United Kingdom) it has an unlimited authority, recognised by the courts, to make any law or to amend any law already made. In consequence no other body or court has the right to overrule or set aside its legislation» (Quoted from V. BOGDANOR (ed.) in *The Blackwell Encyclopaedia of Political Institutions*, London Blackwell, 1987).

(12) For an interesting analysis of this question, see, «Sovereignty and the Eurofed», in the *Political Quarterly*, by I. J. HARDEN, university of Sheffield, October 1990.

(13) A striking example of the erosion of control as a result of the *Treaty of Rome* is the recent «Barber decision» of the European Court of Justice which held that occupational pensions are a form of pay for the purposes of Article 119. This requires that men and women should receive equal pay for equal work. The financial implications for the pensions industry could be enormous, running into many billions of pounds.

policy, provided first that it was the free decision of the sovereign power (in Britain's case, Parliament) and second that the sovereign power retained the right to reassert its control should it wish, *in extremis*, to do so. Certainly, such a transfer might entail the loss of accountability of the executive to the Westminster Parliament. It is worth bearing in mind, however, that Parliament has never had a direct responsibility for the creation of money nor for the operation of monetary policy (14). Both the Bretton Woods system and the system of floating rates have been matters for executive or prerogative control. In 1946 nationalisation put the Bank of England firmly in the hands of the executive, not of Parliament. Nor has Parliament ever had a direct role in controlling the level of borrowing.

Parliament's essential «sovereign power» consists of the requirement for annual legislative authorisation for taxation and of the supply estimates, «the power of the purse». This power would probably be unaffected by signature to a monetary union. Indeed, it can be argued that Parliamentary sovereignty has been made vulnerable to a far greater extent by the growth of the Community budget, and by the growth of competence in the field of indirect taxation, than it would be by monetary union (15). But also it could controversially be argued that monetary union would be bound to entail a much greater degree of direct involvement in revenue raising matters by the European Community, in which case there would be further erosion of Parliamentary authority over the «power of the purse».

Nonetheless, by far the clearest test of whether sovereignty has been handed over would be the capacity of Parliament to exercise its sovereignty by repealing any EMU legislation, and if necessary by repealing the *European Communities Act* itself.

The economic price of withdrawal from a possible EMU is of course, hard to estimate but could well be considerable. If it were held that such withdrawal would also require leaving the Community (which is impossible to conclude at this distance), then the price could be enormous. The technical task might also be large and it would be

---

(14) In constitutional theory it could be said that Parliament has always delegated responsibility for monetary policy to an agent.

(15) The Community has, for example, acquired considerable powers in determining the size of the VAT base and the common external tariff.

foolish to belittle it. Difficulties would be likely to grow, the longer the single currency was in place. (Those who believe that withdrawal from an EMU would be impossible on technical grounds are urged to turn to the Appendix, which examines the likely problems).

Nevertheless if the Parliamentary and political will existed to bring back sterling, it could and would be done (16).

Moreover, monetary unions have come and gone over the years. These have included the Latin monetary union of 1865, between France, Italy, Belgium and Switzerland, the Germanic monetary union of 1857, between Austria and members of the Zollverein, and the Scandinavian monetary union of 1873. The most famous union, the gold standard, operated between all the major industrial powers between 1876 and 1913. Since the second world war monetary systems falling short of union came and went, including Bretton Woods and the «snake». The creation of the EMS led to the withdrawal of the Irish punt from union with sterling (17).

If the analysis above is correct it is wrong to suggest, as some have done, that Britain and other countries would somehow cease to be sovereign by entering into a treaty bringing about monetary union (18). There may, indeed, be a high price attached to joining a monetary union, but it is not the price of loss of sovereignty. It is the largely economic price of making a mistake and subsequently having to disentangle oneself from it.

One further implication of the weakness of the sovereignty argument is that those who hope that EMU might somehow subsume «the German problem» in a wider European identity are also probably mistaken. Even after monetary union if, at some subsequent stage, Germany or France decided that its supreme national interests con-

---

(16) It is often held by supporters of EMU that even discussion of any putative dismemberment of an EMU would greatly reduce its chances of success. The irrevocability of a single currency, it is held, is central to its credibility in the markets and elsewhere. There is force in this argument. Nonetheless, whether or not there is widespread discussion of it, Parliament would. possess the sovereign authority to withdraw.

(17) For a succinct description of the recent history of monetary unions and systems see TOMMASO PADOA-SCHIOPPA: *Efficency, Stability and Equity, 1987*, pp. 17-25.

(18) The idea that Britain would no longer be an independent nation after EMU has been trenchantly argued by a wide spectrum of opinion in the House of Commons. Professor Tima Congdon also takes this view in his paper *EMU Now*, 1990, p. 30. Centre for Policy Studies.

flicted with participation it could withdraw, and recreate its own currency. That would be a dramatic step and could entail a high economic and political price. But the option would remain.

2.2 *Loss of Control*

This chapter has, so far, addressed the question of whether EMU would result in a loss of sovereignty. There is, of course, the much wider question of the degree to which membership of an EMU would result in a loss of control of member country's affairs, and whether such loss of control is acceptable.

Clearly, the loss of control involved in an EMU could be considerable. Not only would the direct control of the issue and regulation of money would be lost, it is quite possible that EMU could lead to greater Community involvement in fiscal policy and economic regulation. Furthermore, several countries, particularly Germany and Italy, would like a strong political dimension as a counterpart to EMU, involving the extension of majority voting in the Council, the incorporation of the federal principle of subsidiarity into the *Treaty* (19), and the extension of the Community's role in foreign policy and security matters, amongst much else. Such a package would certainly erode a country's control over its own affairs.

Furthermore the direct loss of control implied by EMU would be accompanied by an end to the traditional methods of accountability. Much of the confused discussion about loss of sovereignty has been fuelled in Britain by some people's instinctive dislike of the idea that a body dominated by «foreigners», on long-term contracts and largely independent of Parliamentary scrutiny, should set British interest rates. Chancellors may make mistakes when they exercise their power to set interest rates; but at least, the argument runs, they are members of elected governments accountable to Parliament.

There may a good deal to these arguments. Nonetheless, their proponents should bear in mind that the «indepenence» which Britain has enjoyed in recent years in setting interest rates might have been to

---

(19) For a cautionary note on subsidiarity see ANDREW ADONIS - ANDREW TYRIE: «*Subsidiarity, as History and Policy*», *IEA*, December 1990.

some extent illusory. The authorities have, of course, been able to set short-term interest rates. However, it is arguable that, beyond the short run, many of the «powers», if Britain ever had them, have been largely surrendered to the markets and to foreign economic policy-makers years ago. Furthermore, whatever genuine independence Britain has enjoyed in recent years has now been further eroded by membership of the exchange-rate mechanism of the EMS (20). Nor is it clear that such independence has delivered better economic decisions. It should be small comfort to argue that at least the mistakes were homegrown.

Those who argue against any change to present arrangements for the scrutiny of Chancellorial decisions on interest rates are also thereby ruling out reforms for giving greater independence to the Bank of England. For any increase in the Bank's independence could not possibly be held to erode control by the British over their own affairs. Yet it is notable that virulent opponents of EMU often also oppose the suggestions recently made for greater Bank independence.

These three questions, the extent to which independence has been enjoyed in the past (and is still enjoyed), the extent to which such independence has been beneficial, and the related question of the independence of the Bank of England, are all very controversial. This chapter does not draw conclusions on them. The limited conclusion is only that EMU would entail some loss of control over a country's own affairs but that this would almost certainly not entail a loss of sovereingnty. The «worst-case» price of joining EMU is the largely economic price that renegotiation or withdrawal might entail. Set against that are the economic benefits which might flow from monetary union, which the next chapter addresses.

3. - The Economic Benefits of Monetary Union

Most economists agree about the economic benefits of monetary union. They are simply stated: the elimination of exchange-rate

---

(20) Nonetheless, even with membership of the exchange-rate mechanism Britain retains the residual power, after consultation, to realign.

uncertainty, the reduction in transactions costs, and all the benefits which flow from these.

However, in deciding whether to go ahead with the prescriptions of the *Delors Report* the benefits of a single currency must be compared with those of the high degree of monetary integration already obtainable with narrow bands in the EMS, the so-called stage one. By far the most comprehensive, not say exhaustive, case for these extra benefits has been made by the Commission itself in a series of papers (21).

Summarising, the benefits are said to include: *a)* greater price stability; *b)* the elimination of exchange-rate uncertainty; *c)* benefits to public policy and the public finances; *d)* benefits to the international economic system.

One cost is held to be that regional imbalances could be exacerbated, largely from the loss of power to devalue.

3.1 *Price Stability*

If one could be sure that monetary union would cure inflation there would be no need to rehearse any other arguments in its favour. That alone would suffice. But there is no necessary connection between the creation of a single currency and the achievement of price stability. On the contrary, it is at least arguable that a Delors-type stage three would be less likely to deliver price stability than a stage one-type system dominated by the Bundesbank. As a paper by HM Treasury made clear, it is very plausible that a stage three-type system could lead to convergence of inflation performance around the average rather than the best (22).

It is natural that countries should like to have more influence over the Bundesbank. And it is reasonable to suppose that those countries whose governments have rarely shown the necessary will to fight inflation domestically might be better served by a Europe-wide institu-

---

(21) for example, EUROPEAN COMMISSION, *Economic and Monetary Union: the Economic rationale and Design of the System*, 1989; and *One Market, One Money: an Evaluation of the Potential Benefits and Costs of Forming an Economic and Monetary Union in the European Community*, 1990.

(22) HM TREASURY: *An Evolutionary Approach to Monetary Union*, November 1989.

tional framework. But, as far as the goal of price stability is concerned, it does seem that they might do better to stick to the Bundesbank's coat-tails than to flirt with an untried European experiment.

There is also another line of argument to suggest that monetary union might lead to greater price stability. Some people, while sceptical about the effectiveness of any European institution, nevertheless see the debate about monetary union as a means by which greater independence may be accorded to their domestic central banks. The greater the independence generated, it is argued, the better will be the delivery of an anti-inflationary performance.

There may be a good deal in this. Several central bank governors in Europe have also pointed to the fact that, even under any form of stage two, greater independence for central banks would be required.

Nonetheless, independent central banks are certainly not the cure for all monetary ills. They are neither a necessary nor a sufficient condition for good anti-inflation performance. Evidence if the former is that Japan, for example, has in the 1980s succeeded in delivering low inflation without an independent central bank. Evidence of the latter is the US, where the substantial independence of the Federal Reserve has delivered a mixed record on inflation.

In sum, European monetary constructs might be able to deliver better anti-inflation performance. On the other hand they might not. Much would depend on the structure of the institution, and the manner in which its directors were made accountable to their respective governments. Anti-inflation performance would also depend, of course, on all those cultural and behavioural factors which have made inflation so difficult to eradicate in inflation-prone economies for decades.

3.2 *Exchange-Rate Uncertainty*

There are two main ways in which variable exchange rates might incur economic costs. First, it is clear that the existence of separate national currencies increases the risk of any transaction by generating uncertainty about its future return. Second, it is clear that while there are separate national currencies, transactions costs will be incurred when exchanging them, whether it is for commercial, investment, or tourist purposes.

3.3 *Uncertainty*

Here the proponents of a single currency probably have a strong case. Exchange rate fluctuations undoubtedly add to uncertainty and so, other things being equal, reduce any given level of trade. Hedging against fluctuations can be expensive; and may not readily be available for periods of more than a year or two ahead, particularly for smaller firms (despite growth in the swaps market). They are, therefore, a deterrent to longer-term investment, particularly investment orientated towards export markets. The creation of a single currency can, in that sense, be considered part of the completion of the 1992 programme, removing a barrier to trade.

Nonetheless, it should not be forgotten that the completion of Delors Stage I, with all currencies in the narrow band exchange rate mechanism, should greatly reduce these uncertainties without recourse to. a single currency. Furthermore, monetary union cannot remove uncertainty for countries, such as Britain, with a high degree of trade with non-EC countries.

A single currency might further increase capital mobility and thus lead to a better allocation of European savings. Certainly, longer term flows of investment and savings may still be inhibited by the uncertainty caused by the scope for realignment in Stage I. There already is a high degree of capital mobility reflected in the persistence of current account imbalances within Europe, but there may be scope for more.

Labour is likely to be more mobile when people are sure of being paid in the currency which they normally use, or which they may wish to repatriate, even when working abroad. As in the case of trade, a decision to take a job abroad involves an element of investment; a reduction in the uncertainty of the return to this type of investment would presumably lead to more of it. Interestingly, the Commission does not mention this gain from a single currency, perhaps because, from the point of view of the poorer countries, risk of losing skilled labour is hardly an attraction. The Commission want to keep the poorer countries on board the Delors train. Equally, the wealthy countries might not be very enthusiastic about limitless migration from their poorer neighbours (23).

In any case customs, nationality, fiscal regimes and languages are more likely to impede labour mobility than the existence of separate currencies.

3.4 *Transactions Costs*

The Commission paper argues that only full monetary union can eliminate transaction costs. It estimates their cost to be between ECU 13 billion and 19 billion, or 0.3 to 0. 4% of the Community's GDP (24). In addition to the cost of conversion services performed by banks, companies bear internal costs through doing business in many currencies. Companies would also bear indirect costs from the lack of complete transparency of price comparisons which only full monetary union can bring. Transactions costs would undoubtedly fall with monetary union but it is important not to exaggerate this (25).

First, many of the gains will come with stage one of Delors. Increased competition generated by the completion of a single market in banking services is likely to reduce the average cost of currency transactions, and by a substantial amount. The Commission comes close to accepting this by saying: «the relatively high expenses and

---

(23) It might be argued that such migration, the right to which is embodied in the original *Treaty of Rome*, might ultimately pose a far greater threat to national identity than new constitutional arrangements for monetary policy.

(24) *One Market, One Money*, p. 251.

(25) In passing, it can be argued that the *City of London* case for EMU has been exaggerated. At first sight one might imagine that parts of the City would find the prospect of the removal of opportunities for intra-EC exchange dealing as deeply concerning. Perhaps surprisingly, the «City view» has been that they would greatly benefit from EMU and London's reputation as a financial centre would be tarnished if britain stood aside. This argument is not entirely convincing.

The City has benefited enormously on occasion by being outside a major centre of regulation. For example, Wall Street regulation brought much of the Eurodollar market to London. Nor is it necessarily true that a particular economic zone necessarily maintains its financial centre within that zone. For example, Switzerland is one of the financial centres of the German speaking world; Luxembourg also benefits from being outside the German regulatory sphere. A quarter of the international German bond market is traded in London; about a third of French equity business is traded there. These examples also show that it is not necessary to operate in the same currency in order to obtain the business.

long delays cross-border payments in the Community suffer from are in the first place due to the existence of several technical barriers that need to be removed in the internal market framework» (26).

Second, the Commission's estimate may well inadvertently include some costs which are merely the cost of transferring funds (in whatever currency they may be denominated) rather than exchanging currencies. If money is transferred from one bank to another, by banker's order, there is likely to be a charge for it, whatever the currency. Transactions costs in the United States, for example, can be substantial across single state frontiers, even though of course conducted in a single currency. On transactions costs Karl Otto Pöhl has summed things up forcefully: «The repeated references to alleged huge savings in transaction costs for the countries of a single currency area are not in the least convincing» (27).

3.5 *Public Policy and Finance*

The Commission and others have argued that by preventing governments from obtaining access to central bank finance (in the current jargon this is known as monetary financing of deficits) they would have to evaluate borrowing at its true cost and therefore there would be strong pressure to reduce and then eliminate public sector borrowing requirements. There is something in this but, again, much of the benefit could probably be obtained through the existing exchange-rate mechanism, with ever narrower bands. The exchange-rate mechanism may already be imposing some discipline on the fiscal policies of the participating states.

Controversially, another benefit which may come as a by-product of EMU is the need to impose binding budgetary rules. Proponents argue that without rules the Community would be underwriting the creditworthiness of each Member State's fiscal stance, a massive temptation to borrow irresponsibly. This is the Bundesbank's view. Opponents, including Britain, argue that by denying the existence of guarantees, by means of the so-called «no bail-out» rule, the market would discipline potential miscreants.

---

(26) See *One Market, One Money, op. cit.* p. 262.
(27) See *IEA Readings, op. cit.* p. 36.

It is implausible to suppose that an ESCB could permit a member State to go bankrupt, in which case a «no bail-out» rule is not enough. This points to the need for some binding rules for limiting budget deficits, which was proposed by the original *Delors Report*, later dropped, to the chagrin of the Germans (28). A possible alternative to binding rules might be to issue firm guidelines backed by tough sanctions such as withholding Community regional or agricultural spending.

The Commission also argues that the debt interest element of government budgets would be reduced as interest rates came down in previously inflation-prone economies. However, reductions in nominal interest rates that simply correspond to reductions in inflation do not make government finance any easier because the reduction in debt interest payments is fully offset by a reduction in the so-called «inflation tax»; or, put another way, by a reduction in the size of budget deficits that is consistent with a sustainable fiscal position. Moreover, it should be remembered that long-term debt with a 10 or 12% coupon becomes extremely difficult to service at zero inflation.

Another minor public finance gain would be savings in the use of foreign currency reserves. Foreing·exchange would no longer be needed to finance trade within the EC. The gain is unlikely to be great: how much, if any, would depend on the difference between the return earned by marginal reserves at present (eg. the US Treasury bill rate) and their return in alternative uses.

3.6 *The International Economic and Financial System*

There is perhaps something in the argument that monetary union would give European countries leverage *vis-à-vis* the dollar and the yen and that, inasmuch as benefits are to be had from international economic and monetary co-operation, monetary union would enable such benefits to be delivered more easily than under the existing multi-currency system. There may also be some seigniorage gains generated by increased holding of the EMU currency by third parties.

---

(28) No doubt the Commission's initial enthusiasm for budgetary rules was also fuelled by the hope that some central authority might acquire broader powers of fiscal co-ordination, parhaps for the purpose of demand management.

Nonetheless, none of those gains could on their own be considered worth the risk and upheaval of creating a single currency.

3.7 Regional Imbalances

The Commission implies that the regions, by which they mean poorer areas, could get hit by monetary union. It admits that a potential cost of monetary union would be the exacerbation of already existing regional imbalances and suggests increased regional funding as compensation.

Naturally, the loss of exchange-rate flexibility removes the opportunity for countries to use monetary policy as a means by which to absorb shocks. (Of course, shocks are only of concern if they affect some countries more than others. A discreet rise in the price of a commodity which all countries, per capita, used roughly equally, would not have much relevance for the debate on monetary union).

Remember that shocks such as an oil price hike can, in principale, affect the richer countries of the Community as much or even more than the poorer countries. European monetary policy is still available to deal with such Europe-wide shocks.

It is a myth, however, to suppose that nominal exchange-rate depreciation (or appreciation for that matter) can ensure a permanent adjustment/improvement to competitiveness. Any initial gain in competitiveness from depreciation may well be eroded in time by subsequent inflation. Higher import costs will see to that. Likewise the old argument, that monetary union would inhibit countries from keeping to an optimal inflation/unemployment trade-off, has been discredited. This dismisses a whole body of economic literature associated with belief in a long-run Phillips curve, but at least it follows the orthodoxy of the majority of economists in the 80s (29).

A far more effective way of restoring competitiveness is to create the conditions in which factor costs, particularly wage costs, can adjust to any shocks. However it would be difficult to sustain the view that exchange rates can never play a role in helping to adjust to

---

(29) An early exponent of the view that the cost of joining a monetary union would be small if monetary policy could not sustain a higher of unemployment was Professor PARKIN. See his *An Overwhelming Case for European Monetary Union*, banker, 1972.

shocks: the exchange rate can probably assist adjustment to very big shocks, so big that even fairly flexible economies would find them difficult to absorb quickly. Nor can it be concluded that exchange rate depreciation will always be inflationary. The fall in sterling in 1981 and the dollar in 1985 can both be said to have assisted adjustment in ways consistent with reducing inflation.

There will inevitably be more shocks in the future. We are experiencing one from the Middle East now. Perhaps one day Europe (and the US and Japan) might finally grasp the nettle of eliminating agricultural support. That would be a shock in more ways than one. More shocks may yet emanate from German unification. And without doubt there will be further ones, as yet unforeseeable.

It is, of course, true that the more inflation-prone countries in the European Community might find themselves faced with particularly difficult economic problems in the short term. But the case for additional regional funding (or indeed any regional funding at all) to alleviate this is quite unproven.

There is a strong case for saying that, in general, the more regional aid is given the less likely it is that the structural adjustment takes place, if only because aid distorts the market signals which can spur adjustment. In theory at least, one should ask all countries, and partucularly the more inflation-prone ones, to undertake radical reforms guaranteeing more flexible cost structures, particularly wage rates, as a condition of entry into full EMU. There should be no restriction of ways in which regional labour markets can compete and adjust. In other words, a very sceptical eye should be cast at the *Social Charter*.

That is what the theory says. It is also what history says. Japan was a poor, trade-dependent country. She caught up without depreciating the exchange rate: quite the contrary — the yen has appreciated over the years.

On economic grounds the problems of regional imbalances should not stand in the way of EMU. All the same, the fact that several countries might persuade their partners to indulge in massive fiscal transfers (despite the economic arguments against), is a good reason for those countries which may face paying the regional bills to hesitate. Furthermore, EMU has already led to calls for measures to co-ordinate EC-wide wage setting which would reduce wage flexibility and wage differentials between the regions. Were those calls to be heeded then EMU, far from being associated with more flexible cost and wage structures which would tend to erode regional differences, could have the opposite effect, bringing with it an extension of *Social Charter* legislation and the social action programme. These twin dangers, of higher and probably pernicious regional spending and of greater regulation of labour markets, are not negligible.

3.8 *Summary*

The benefits of monetary union have been exaggerated, but then so have the costs. Of the economic benefits listed by the Commission and others, the capacity of EMU to deliver sound money is by far the most important.

Monetary union is not a cure-all for inflation. It might lead to greater price stability, it might lead to less. And the yardstick by which we must judge it is not some Latin American style inflation-prone region, but a highly successful anti-inflationary strategy dominated by the Bundesbank. That is what we have at present. Whether monetary union would deliver price stability would largely depend on the structure of the European Central Bank and, in particular, on how far the French ensured the direct political «accountability» of that institution to European politicians. If they did get their way my guess is that it would be inflationary, at least compared with the ERM. On the other hand, if Bundesbank dominance and independence were to be replicated at a European institutional level there might be real hope, in the medium term, for price stability, comparable to that of the ERM in Europe.

Even the strongest advocates of EMU would be hard put to argue that it would do better than the ERM. It must also be remembered that Bundesbank type credibility cannot be created by fiat. The success of the Bundesbank owes much to their record for taking tough decisions (30) and relative independence. The jury of the

---

(30) As William McChesney Martin, US Federal Reserve Chairman from 1951-1970, said: «The Fed's job is to take away the punch-bowl just when the party is getting going», *IEA Readings, op. cit.*, p. 39.

markets would be out. Only after a number of years would they deliver their judgment.

As for the other alleged economic benefits of EMU, monetary union would reduce but certainly not remove transactions costs. But some of these costs would be removed as a result of the 1992 programme, anyway. The public finance gains of monetary union have also almost certainly been exaggerated; and, again, many of the pressures making for prudence in fiscal policy already obtain under stage one. The benefits of a European role in the international financial and economic system are easily exaggerated; the Commission's rehearsal of these arguments may reflect their desire, common to all institutions, to create a role for themselves, rather than their belief in the arguments. Only the removal of exchange rate uncertainty would seem to have survived detailed scrutiny as an important economic benefit of monetary union. That benefit is not susceptible to measurement, though it may be substantial.

Finally, the problem of regional imbalance as a cost of monetary union is largely false. It is true that monetary union would require the more inflation-prone countries to make substantial adjustments. But that is an argument against a headlong rush into EMU.

More generally, there is a case for saying that the single market process cannot be completed, particularly on the capital side, without monetary union. But moving to monetary union prematurely would also cause problems: the need for adjustment generated by the 1992 process may threaten any new monetary structure.

In sum, the economic case for monetary union is there, but it is by no means overwhelming. And this is particularly true when considered against the background of the reforms already undertaken as a consequence both of the *Single European Act* and of the development of the exchange rate mechanism of the EMS.

4. - Other Routes to Monetary Union

The idea that monetary union should be defined only in terms of a single currency administered by an independent European Central Bank is a recent one. In the 1970s proponents of monetary union put forward a raft of other proposals. In the 1970s Roland Vaubel, amongst others, proposed a move to monetary union through currency substitution and a parallel currency (31). F.A. Hayek proposed the «privatisation» of money to enable currencies to compete (32).

Another contribution came in the so-called «*All Saints' Day Manifesto*», first published in *The Economist*, a form of non-inflationary parallel currency not dissimilar to Britain's proposals for the hard ECU (33). Indeed, many of those who proposed these ideas did so because EMS-type schemes such as «the snake» and the Werner Plan, to which many had been attracted, seemed to have failed (34).

The completion of what is now known as stage one of the *Delors Plan* would probably have been looked upon as monetary union in the 1970s. This is hardly surprising since, as is shown in *Chapter Two*, most of the benefits commonly ascribed to the creation of a single currency are obtainable under those arrangements.

The defects of the *Delors Report* have been very widely discussed and examined. The call for restrictions on the size of budget deficits, for increased regional spending, the lack of accountability for monetary policy to any democratic authority and the weakness of its analysis of the transition from stage one to stage three have all provoked controversy and criticism (35).

A rival to the Delors scheme is not prescribed here. However, some other schemes which have not received due consideration are briefly examined.

---

(31) See ROLAND VAUBEL: «Choice in European Monetary Union», IEA *Occasional Paper*, n. 55, 1979.

(32) See F. A. HAYEK: «The Denationalisation of Money - the Argument Refined», *IEA Hobart Paper*, February 1978.

(33) Set out in *The Economist*, November 1, 1975.

(34) The snake was an exchange-rate system with adjustable parities, which operated between some West European currencies between 1972 and 1978. The *Werner Plan* was a report by the then Prime Minister of Luxembourg, Pierre Werner, for the achievement of economic and monetary union. This *Plan* proposed an increase in Community spending, extension of regional policy and a common monetary policy with the intention of creating the conditions in which the margins of fluctuation between member currencies could be gradually reduced. The monetary aspect of the *Werner Plan* bore considerable similarities to the exchange-rate mechanism of the EMS.

(35) For a good brief analysis of these and other points see *An Evolutionary Approach to Economic and Monetary Union, op. cit.*

4.1 *Strengthening the EMS*

If economic arguments were the prime movers in the pressure for greater monetary integration, one would expect a good deal of support for building on the currency system we have at present. However, as has been explained, the pressure for further monetary integration is largely political, not economic. Sir Leon Brittan seemed to acknowledge this when he dismissed building on the ERM by saying: «this is politically difficult for both countries that have to follow the lead and also for the leading country itself which finds itself saddled with a reserve currency role which it may not be willing or able to undertake effectively» (36).

There has not, so far, been a great deal of evidence to suggest that the Bundesbank has been carrying out their role in the ERM ineffectively, nor does it seem unwilling to continue to do so.

There is certainly scope for building on the ERM.

With the abolition of capital controls, the completion of the single market in banking, the move to 2.5% exchange rate bands for all currencies and, as has been the case in recent years, eschewal of realignments to accommodate inflation, there will be strong pressure on the domestic monetary authorities to bring about convergence of monetary policies.

In addition, a move to narrower bands of, say, 1, or even 0.5%, would impose a tough monetary discipline and might also encourage governments to consult on anti-inflation objectives and interest rate policy (37). Narrow bands are likely to generate convergence of policy, with or without consultation, as has happened between France and Germany, making realignments rarer.

Market expectations would play a crucial role in the success of such further monetary integration. Markets would need to be convinced that inflation rates were converging and, along with building upon stage one in this way could be complemented by consultation to

---

(36) Sir LEON BRITTAN: *Monetary Union*, CPS, 1990.

(37) An informal 1% band has operated between Germany and Benelux for several months. The French have also tried to limit fluctuations with the narrow band but without much success latterly.

develop a common policy for currencies in the ERM *vis-à-vis* the dollar and the yen, building on the informal understandings which have already grown up. It is conceivable, although perhaps not necessary, that such close consultation could be formalised. Formalisation of the process might serve to protect member States against the possibility that external exchange-rate policy was being decided largely by the Bundesbank.

The consultations described above could be formalised through an enhanced Monetary Committee, Committee of Central Bank Governors or some other body, perhaps with some of the powers envisaged for the European Monetary Fund under the British hard-ECU proposals (38). It could additionally, but perhaps unnecessarily, be given powers to manage foreign exchange reserves and to intervene in foreign-exchange markets in order to deliver agreed exchange-rate policies.

4.2 *British Proposals*

Two approaches have already been put forward, both by the British Government. The first, the proposal for allowing currencies to compete to provide a non-inflationary anchor in the EMS, has been widely criticised on at least two grounds.

First, if it were successful, it would probably lead to the ascendancy of the Deutschmark. (It is not clear that this would necessarily be so unacceptable to most Governments of Europe. Many would be only too happy to be able to share in the success of West Germany's post-war monetary stability). Second, it has been pertinently pointed out that good currencies tend to drive out bad only where the bad currency suffers hyperinflation. Both these criticisms have some force, the first political, the second economic.

---

(38) Although it might transpire that there was no need for a new institution, its absence would leave the proponents of highly institutionalised Delors stage three-type monetary union very dissatisfied. Whatever the economic merits, «ERM building» of the type described above would probably carry little political support except inasmuch as it was seen as a development of stage two.

4.3 *The Hard ECU*

The British Government's second proposal builds on a long pedigree of non-inflationary parallel currency ideas (39).

The British have proposed the creation of a European Monetary Fund (EMF) which would have responsibility for issuing hard ECUs. The most attractive aspect of this proposal is that it should be non-inflationary. The hard ECU would be as strong as the strongest Community currency. It would never devalue against another Community currency. The EMF would have to set interest rates at the level required to meet that obligation, however high that might be. A discipline on inflation-prone countries would be that member States would be required to repurchase their own currencies from the EMF with the hardest currency then prevailing in the Community, or as specified by the EMF. This would prevent the creation of hard ECUs from adding to the money supply. It is these key features which distinguish the British parallel currency proposal from most other parallel currency proposals (40). Most parallel currency schemes have foundered on the problem that adding an extra currency would be inflationary, as both the *Delors Report* and the Bundesbank were swift to point out.

The EMF could also manage the exchange-rate mechanism of the EMS, and co-ordinate exchange-rate intervention aginst the dollar and the yen, amongst other tasks.

Besides being non-inflationary, the proposals have the merit of being gradual and evolutionary. This would give more time to the more inflation-prone countries to make the necessary structural adjustments.

To some extent, the same criticism that is made of the competing currencies proposal can be made of the hard-ECU proposal, that the gap in inflation rates would not be enough to drive out other

---

(39) See, for example, the earlier references to *The All Saints' Day Manifesto*, and to Vaubel. It was recently resuscitated by Sir Michael Butler of Hambros Bank. According to John Williamson, of the Institute for International Economics, the idea bears a close similarity to a Japanese proposal for the valuation of the SDR, put forward in 1973. See *Britain's Role In EMU, Open Forum of the Liberal Democrat Party*, 1991.

(40) As with *Chapter 2* the arguments here are set out with reference to the British case, though for the most part they apply to any country wishing to leave an EMU.

currencies (41). Of course, it is arguable that massive currency substitution is not a necessary condition for delivery of greater discipline in countries with lax policy. Merely the potential for a large switch into a hard currency may be enough to exert discipline.

It is likely, too, that the hard ECU would have little advantage over the Deutschmark so long as the latter retained its anchor role in the ERM. Indeed, until the hard ECU became widely traded the Deutschmark would be a preferable asset since its wider circulation would almost undoubtedly deliver lower transactions costs.

4.4 *Gold or Commodity-Based Standards*

One of the forms of monetary union with the longest pedigree is, of course, the gold standard. Volumes have been written for and against gold over the years. Whatever the theoretical merits and notwithstanding the relatively good track record of gold, it is extremely unlikely that most member States would wish to tie their currencies to a commodity with such a vulnerable price history and which is so susceptible to shocks. Few countries would be prepared to see their competitiveness eroded by civil war in South Africa or unrest in the Soviet Union, for example.

A more stable variant of the gold standard would be a commodity-based standard in which the value of a currency would be defined according to a basket of commodities. These would be selected and weighted with the express objective of finding that mix which best stabilised price. The best commodities for this purpose would probably be those which are the key determinants of inflation/deflation.

World demand would be a major determinant of the value of the commodity basket. High demand would lead to the appreciation of European currencies against the dollar and yen and vice versa. This would, of course, stabilise activity and prices in the European economies, but not in the US and Japan. It could lead to pressure from

---

(41) *The All Saints' Day Manifesto* proposal would be akin to «a super-hard ECU», because in their proposals the parallel currency would be required to increase in value by the inflation rate of the basket of currencies.

those countries to join the commodity basket or, alternatively, to international economic friction. The problems of storing commodities would probably greatly reduce the opportunity for destabilising speculation in the markets, a problem inherent with gold.

Sir Alan Walters, a former economic adviser to Margaret Thatcher, has recently proposed a form of commodity-based standard (42). He argues that it is sufficient to make currencies redeemable against a financial asset which carried the power to purchase a given basket of commodities, or services. With the use of this «indexed reserve asset» it would not be necessary physically to store commodities.

Much detailed work is needed before any commodity-based standard could become a serious option. Nevertheless it is extraordinary that the Community should have done so much work on monetary union without having given consideration to this option, which has some theoretical advantages and which, because of its proximity to the gold standard, can be said to have a historical pedigree.

Conclusion

This paper has sought to make four points: first, the debate about EMU and the European Community is not primarily about economics, but about politics, largely the politics of the Franco-German alliance; secondly, those who argue that forms of monetary union, and even the highly prescriptive form proposed by Delors, would lead to an *irrevocable* loss of sovereignty, are probably mistaken. Neither the hopes of the French, that monetary union might erode Germany's sovereignty and sense of national identity, nor the fears of the British, that EMU would mean the end of «nation-states as we know them», are likely to be fulfilled; thirdly, the economic benefits of further monetary integration are probably nothing like as great as the Commission and others have alleged, and certainly not great in comparison with the benefits already enjoyed as a result of monetary integration in the exchange-rate mechanism of the EMS.

---

(42) See Sir ALAN WALTERS: *Sterling in Danger*, 1990, pp. 114 ff.

Finally, it has been shown, if only in outline, that the *Delors Plan* is but one of many routes to greater monetary integration and the economic benefits that could flow from it. It is perhaps a reflection of the extent to which the real motive for EMU is political that these other possibilities have not been given the consideration they deserve. For the alternatives to Delors all have one feature in common, they involve a far smaller degree of surrender of control over one's own monetary affairs than stage three of Delors. That surrender, more than the economic benefits, would seem to be the principal objective of the Commission and some others in these negotiations.

Technical Problems of Withdrawing from EMU

Clearly it would be possible to extricate oneself from monetary union if the disentangling process took place while separate currencies, albeit fixed, continued to exist. Even the strongest proponents of EMU expect this to be the case for several years to come. The unbundling of a single currency would be harder. For example, what would be Britain's (41) monetary base? What would be her reserves?

On the question of the monetary base, if the ESCB (the European System of Central Banks) was «federal» in character, with identifiably separate balance sheets for national central banks, and most of the system's assets held in them rather than in the Central Bank, that would greatly assist the disentangling process.

If, furthermore, British clearers held their operational reserves at the British branch of the Central Bank it would be possible to identifly the monetary base for the national currency and to establish those deposits of the commercial banking system which should be denominated in the new currency.

On the other hand, if the British portion of deposits in the banking system could not be readily identified, and there were no such reserves, individual holders would perhaps have to be given a choice between keeping their deposits in ECUs or transferring to the new currency. If so, the size of the new currency would be decided in part by market choice.

There would be the further complication of the ownership of deposits with British banks put there by Community residents. These depositors might well object to the redefinition of their deposits as pounds, rather than ECUs. It would, of course, be open to them to withdraw their deposits.

The above outlines some of the considerable problems of disentangling broader measures of money. As for narrow money, notes and coins issued in Britain would presumably be distinguishable in some way, following the practice of US Federal Reserve district banks, perhaps marked by some British symbol such as the Queen's head. This would greatly simplify the task of establishing whose money was whose.

Considerable instability could attend the creation of a new currency. Presumably it would be necessary, on divesting day, to attempt to start with a one-to-one exchange rate. Depending on the circumstances of the withdrawal from monetary union, there could be a massive and disruptive exodus from the new currency, for example if it were thought that the new pound would be more inflationary than the ECU which it was leaving. Conversely, if the pound was leaving an ECU perceived to be inflationary, there could be a massive influx of funds.

Interest rates would bear the main burden in any attempt to bring a measure of stability. They would need to vary to compensate for any of this immediate pressure. Sharp rises in interest rates might result and these could have severe destabilising and disruptive influences, not only for individuals but for businesses as well.

As for the depooling of foreign-exchange reserves, some guidance might be given by the central bank statutes. In the recent draft of the central bank governors, it is proposed that there should be a «key» for the establishment of reserves by each national central bank. That key could determine who owned what (42).

This might still leave the awkward question of who owned the accumulated undistributed profits on the reserves. However, the statutes of the central bank are also likely to provide guidance on this, perhaps on the basis of contributions to the system's capital base.

The ESCB may develop supervisory responsibility for some truly cross-frontier financial institutions with business in a number of Community countries, and this it would presumably retain. It should be possible also to maintain the existing clearing and settlement system to cope with the revival of sterling. There would, of course, be considerable problems for firms, and to some extent individuals, who would have to re-establish facilities for handling foreign currency where previously they had required none.

Another approach to the unscrambling of sterling from a

European single currency might be to take advantage of the British proposals on the hard ECU, but in reverse. The British Government could decide to issue a hard pound as a competing currency which it declared would never devalue against the single currency from which it was leaving. This could prove a useful approach if it had been decided to take sterling out of the single currency because of fears of European inflation. Furthermore, it is likely that there could be considerable demand for the new hard sterling if it was backed by the firm commitment of the British Government to press ahead with the recreation of a British currency. Certainly, the substitution would probably be far swifter than from individual currencies to the new hard ECU.

From the EMS to the EMU:
The Role of Policy Coordination

Francesco Farina
Università di Siena

1. - Introduction

The problems of the transition of the European Community to the Monetary Union (EMU) are both more numerous and more complex than the ones that have accompained the functioning of the exchange rate mechanism (ERM) of the European Monetary System (EMS). However, the EMS experience is an important guide to understand the difficulties that the ERM will encounter on the way to a common central bank and to a single currency, particularly with regard to policy coordination.

This paper, in paragraphs 2 and 3, assesses the main features of the fixed but adjustable exchange rate regime and criticizes — on the basis of the available empirical evidence — the hypotheses of a "symmetric EMS" and of the "monetary discipline" which maintain, respectively, a very high and a very low degree of monetary policy autonomy in initially high-inflation and weak-currency countries like France and Italy. In paragraph 4, the interpretation is put forward according to which capital controls and interest rate differentials with Germany have been utilised as complements and not as substitutes of the anti-inflationary monetary stance aimed at pursuing convergence to Germany.

Paragraph 5 is then concerned with the problem that this strategy is no more available in the transition to EMU. The persistent weaknesses of the EMS, reflected by the huge trade imbalances of France and Italy vis-à-vis Germany, and the exposure of the system to asymmetric shocks, might collide with the increase in policy coordination required by complete capital mobility and by the process towards irrevocably fixed exchange rates. Under the circumstances, the solutions proposed by the two competing approaches to EMU — the "gradualist" and the "radical" ones — have both serious contra-indications.

The first approach proposes a two-step strategy, where full convergence of inflation rates is the precondition to further moves towards monetary unification; this strategy, however, does not take into account the fact that the convergence process is still menaced by the possibility of defection and will not be completed but through an increase in monetary and fiscal policy coordination. The second approach points instead to the necessity to accelerate the process towards full convergence. This view, however, lays stress on the lack of credibility of national monetary authorities and governments and advocates a fast drift to a single currency. Yet, the drastic abolition of divergences in the fundamentals brought about by a currency reform might augment the risk of defections from the unification process and widen discrepancies in productive structures among the Community members.

The paper comes instead to the conclusion that — differently from the *Delors Report* — more precise guidelines should be imposed on monetary and fiscal policies by the coming European System of Central Banks (ESCB). Policy coordination furthered by a Board of Governors credited with authority could succeed in the elimination of the currency "risk premium" which slows down the convergence to interest rates' parity. In divergent countries, the output-inflation trade-offs should then improve and the move to the currency reform will be favoured.

2. - The Exchange Rate Mechanism of the EMS

The functioning of the EMS can be better understood by looking at its evolution throughout the eighties than by the rules which were set up at the moment of its creation. In fact, two major questions related to the exchange rate mechanism were not clearly stated.

The first one is the well-known problem according to which in a system of N interdependent countries only $N - 1$ members of the agreement must peg their exchange rates, so that there is an extra instrument with respect to the number of policy targets. The solution to this "redundancy" problem (hereafter, the "$N - 1$ problem") will be "symmetrical" if central banks peg a basket of goods — for instance, to the price of gold — and will instead be "asymmetrical" if one country plays the role of *leader* and pegs the price of the basket in units of its own currency, whereas the other countries peg the exchange rate with respect to the *leader*'s currency (1).

The second question deals with differences in the productive structures among countries participating in a monetary agreement: in the EMS case, the most important difference was the inflation differentials due to unit costs divergences between Germany on the one side and France and Italy — the two countries which were members of the ERM since its inception, whose economies are comparable in size with the German one — on the other side. The problem (hereafter dubbed the "divergence problem") concerns the necessity to set up a strategy to cope with exchange rate tensions generated by the inflation differentials with Germany. The "cooperative" solution points to evenly shared interventions aimed at sustaining the weak currencies; the "hegemonic" solution is instead represented by the privilege of the *leader* country to dictate monetary policy without any obligation to intervene marginally or intramarginally. Besides, whenever a realignment can no longer be postponed, the "cooperative" solution will bring to a multilateral exchange rate change and the "hegemonic" solution will consist in the sole realignment of the divergent currencies.

These two questions are closely related. With regard to the first question, whenever one country stands out as the best performer in the fulfillment of the low inflation target, and its central bank is in the position to dictate the monetary stance, the "asymmetric" solution turns out to be the most favourable as for the exchange rate stability. Should this country become the *leader* of the system, the central bank will fix monetary policy independently from the partners and, because

(1) See GIAVAZZI-GIOVANNINI [8], pp. 193-5.
Advise: the numbers in square brackets refer to the Bibliography in the appendik.

of high anti-inflationary reputation, its currency will perform the role of "nominal anchor" for the whole area. By pegging their exchange rates to this currency, the other countries participating into the agreement will be forced to curb the inflation rate so that the system should become stronger (2). This seems to be even more true in the EMS case. As we will now see, the existence of the "divergence problem" has in fact rendered the "asymmetric" solution not only the most efficient but also without alternative.

Let us start by recalling that, from the inception phase of the EMS, France and Italy have renounced to accelerate money growth and use "surprise" inflation for internal objectives (for instance, to reduce the real wage rate), and have then put their efforts in the opposite strategy to pursue a real appreciation of the currency *vis-à-vis* the mark. As well-known, workers forming rational expectations (in order not to be "fooled", as it had happened in the late seventies, by non-announced inflationary monetary expansions) and the growing impact of import prices on manifacturing goods prices (following the second oil shock) convinced monetary authorities — since 1980 in Italy, three years later in France — to undertake a shift to anti-inflationary policies.

Once low inflation is a target shared also by the divergent countries and becomes the "general interest", a currency agreement which is formally among "equals" can function under the *leadership* of the low-inflation country if this "asymmetry" is strengthened by the adoption of the "hegemonic" solution to the "divergence problem". The rationale is the following. For the task to provide the "nominal anchor" of the system and further the public good represented by low inflation to be accepted by the *leader*, this country has to make sure that the divergent countries will not try to behave as free-riders and shift the "divergency problem" on it. It has been demonstrated that a currency area in which all central banks contemporaneously adopt a non-cooperative deflationary strategy will suffer from a deflationary bias, evenly distributed among its members (3). Yet, consider a system

---

(2) See GIAVAZZI-GIOVANNINI [8], pp. 195-6.
(3) The deflationary bias brought about by central banks contemporaneously attempting to reduce inflation through a "surprise" money contraction have been shown by CANZONIERI-GRAY [1].

in which divergent countries retain the power to manage their exchange rates vis-à-vis the center currency, whereas the *leader* country sticks at the "asymmetric" solution to the "$N - 1$ problem" and keeps fixing monetary policy: in this case, a "beggar-thy-neighbor" deflationary strategy from divergent countries, aimed at provoking an exchange rate change, will bias deflation at a disavantage of the *leader* country (4). Therefore, in the EMS strategic game, the *leader* country had to obtain guarantees that France and Italy will abide by the "hegemonic" solution. A refusal of these countries to bear the major burden of intervention — not only in defence of their own currencies, but also in the case of weakness of the DM inside the ERM parity grid due to a dollar's appreciation trend — would have in fact exposed Germany to unilateral strategic behavior, such as France or Italy overcontracting money supply in order to reduce their inflation rate at a low cost in terms of output.

This need for the "hegemonic" solution can also be demonstrated *a contrario*. Had the EMS worked according to the "symmetric" solution to the "$N - 1$ problem" and, correspondingly, to the "cooperative" solution to the "divergence problem", a very unstable ERM would have resulted. Owing to divergences in unit costs among members, a currency agreement in which no country sets monetary policy and all countries intervene in defense of the weak-currency's parities brings about a paradoxical outcome: the countries whose currencies are prone to depreciation suffer from the depletion of reserves and, correspondingly, the strong-currency countries experience an automatic increase in their money supply and lose control over their money growth. This happens because, in the "cooperative" solution, the even distribution of the intervention burden has to be accompained by the prohibition to sterilize possible increases in the money supply, so that the monetary stance of the strong-currency countries is jeopardized by capital inflows (5).

Therefore, a currency agreement among countries whose unit costs widely diverge has to be dependent upon the following features:

---

(4) See GIAVAZZI [6], p. 6.

(5) As ROUBINI [17], (pp. 18-20) demonstrates, central banks refraining from sterilization is a necessary condition for an exchange rate mechanism of this kind to be "symmetric".

1) a necessary *but not sufficient* condition for the exchange rate regime to be stable is the adoption of the "asymmetric" solution to the "$N - 1$ problem" (the system shall not survive once the "symmetric" solution, with which the "cooperative" solution to the "divergence problem" necessarily combines, were implemented); by consequence: 2) the required mix of solutions to the two problems above discussed is the couple "asymmetry plus hegemony". The conceptual framework so far described then accounts for the two main features evolved in the ERM during the working of the EMS: that is, the German "asymmetric" position into the system due to the "nominal anchor" role of the DM, and the German "hegemony", due to the Bundesbank's virtual abstension from marginal interventions and systematic sterilization of any increase in the monetary base caused by the high-inflation countries' interventions (6). It can then be said that the so called "German leadership" is a *structural* condition of the EMS functioning, as the stability of the system hinges upon it.

Let us now analyse the impact of these two key-features of the EMS on national monetary policies. As for the initially high-inflation countries, it is widely recognized that the couple of solutions "asymmetry plus hegemony" have sheltered the system from the risk that exchange rate tensions were used by these countries to pursue selfish objectives. Indeed, both features of the EMS helped in preventing the ERM of the EMS to be transformed from a regime of adjustable parities to a "managed" exchange rate regime. By pegging the exchange rate to the currency the central bank of which has the highest anti-inflationary reputation, France and Italy put themselves in the position to exploit the advantage stemming from monetary authorities' augmented independence vis-à-vis both the public and the private sectors. At the same time, the inflationary cost attached to currency devaluation — because of the virtual obligation, implied by the "hegemonic" solution, to bear the whole burden of the bilateral parities' adjustments — has rendered even less desirable to defect from the anti-inflationary strategy. For these reasons, an agreement like the EMS framed by the "asymmetry plus hegemony" couple of

---

(6) See GIAVAZZI-GIOVANNINI [8], Ch. 4, and MASTROPASQUA-MICOSSI-RINALDI [13], pp. 269-74.

solutions gave to France's and Italy's central banks the incentive to gear the monetary manoeuvre to the slackening of the nominal depreciation of their currencies and to pursue the real appreciation of their currencies, thus inducing their governments to enforce deflationary policies aimed at accelerating the adjustment of the productive structure and the convergence of the inflation rate to the German one (7).

On the other hand, German national interest in the EMS comes from the need to protect its low inflation rate from erratic shifts in monetary policy pursued by the divergent European countries. The EMS functioning described above has allowed Germany to be shielded from selfish behaviors which could have endangered from outside the Bundesbank's monetary stance. Moreover, the negative impact of the dollar/DM fluctuations on the German competitiveness has been substantially dampened. Therefore, the Bundesbank's privilege to dictate the monetary stance and to counteract external disturbances to domestic money supply has permitted Germany to benefit from a non-inflationary growth triggered by the DM real undervaluation.

3. - Alternative Views
on the Functioning of the EMS

This theoretic framework can be compared with two different approaches to the EMS functioning. One of the more vexing questions concerns the degree of monetary policy autonomy in initially high-inflation countries like France and Italy. With regard to the extent in which the *U*-turn to the anti-inflationary strategy has forced monetary policy coordination with the centre country of the system, opinions differ sharply. These opinions range from the extreme view according to which the EMS has worked «symmetrically» (that is, Germany did not independently set monetary policy and no constraint was then imposed on the autonomy of France's and Italy's monetary policies) (8), to the opposite extreme view according to which by pegging the

---

(7) See GIAVAZZI [7], p. 95.
(8) See COHEN-WYPLOSZ [2], DE GRAUWE [4] and VON HAGEN-FRATIANNI [18].

exchange rate to the DM, because of the Bundesbank's tight monetary stance, the autonomy of these countries' monetary policy has
tended to zero (9).

Let us start from a discussion of the first view. By virtue of
econometric estimates of the money growth and interest rates in the
EMS countries mainly based on Granger-causality tests, some authors
have derived the conclusion that there is no evidence of a German
monetary policy «dominance» (10). Yet, the absence of any prevailing
influence of German monetary policy cannot be proved by this type of
test: the more "contemporaneous" and the more stringent is this
influence, the less the phenomenon will be detected (11). Therefore,
we will stick at the "asymmetric" interpretation of the EMS functioning described in paragraph 2, and will be concerned only with the
piece of evidence provided by one of these authors relative to the
comparison between the short run behavior of the *offshore* and the
onshore interest rates on the occasion of speculative crises (12). In
fact, as we will see, even though this evidence shows the relevant role
performed by capital controls in countries like France and Italy, the
soundness of the "asymmetric" interpretation is by no means put in
doubt.

The following equation is the "closed interest parity condition":

$$(1) \qquad\qquad\qquad r = r^* + f$$

where r and r^* are, respectively, the domestic and the German
interest rate and f is the *forward premium* of the mark with respect to
the domestic currency. Capital controls seem to have shielded the
domestic money markets of the weak-currency countries from the
consequences of the speculative crises that have characterized the
EMS, especially in the first phase of its functioning. Formally, capital

---

(9) See GIOVANNINI [10].

(10) See COHEN-WYPLOSZ [2], pp. 324-31, DE GRAUWE [4], pp. 16-22, and VON
HAGEN-FRATIANNI [18], pp. 362-70.

(11) In particular, the empirical method used by COHEN-WYPLOSZ [2] has been
questioned by GIOVANNINI [11], pp. 340-2.

(12) See DE GRAUWE [4].

controls have the effect to create a "wedge" in the "interest parity condition":

$$(2) \qquad\qquad r = (r^* + \mu) + \pi$$

where π represents the "wedge", and the *forward premium* which appeared in the "closed" condition has been replaced by μ, the expected rate of change of the exchange rate (under the assumptions of efficient markets and *risk premium* equal to zero). Any expected devaluation of the franc or of the lira *vis-à-vis* the mark will be expressed by a positive μ in equation *(2)*, which will be offset by a proportional change in π, so that no variation of the *onshore* interest rate will be required. According to this critique of the "German dominance" hypothesis, whenever exchange rates tensions arise, data would suggest that *forward premia* of the DM (with respect to the franc and the lira) and French and Italian *offshore* rates of the Euromarket soar, while domestic interest rates — not only, as expected, in Germany, but also in France and Italy — barely react (13). Therefore, taking into account that Germany, by making recourse to sterilization policies, has managed to set independently its money supply, while France and Italy have used capital controls to insulate their domestic markets from speculative disturbances, the conclusion that the EMS has worked in a relatively «symmetric» way follows.

This «symmetric EMS» view can be criticized on the basis of the long run observation of the «covered» interest rate parity condition relative to France and Italy:

$$(3) \qquad\qquad c = f + (r - r^*)$$

The computation of the annual means of the equation (3) variables shows that c rarely exceeds one point in the period 1984-1990 in both countries (14). Interest rate differentials almost as high as the *forward premium* of the mark demonstrate that capital controls did not

---

(13) See DE GRAUWE [4], pp. 2-6.
(14) See FARINA [5], pp. 120.

free central banks from the necessity to take issue with depreciation expectations held in the financial markets and to augment domestic interest rates. Therefore, this long run evidence successfully questions the claim that the EMS does not appear to deviate from a "symmetric" functioning. On the other hand, evidence showing a low degree of correlation between movements in the *forward premium* and movements in the domestic interest rates in the short run, that is at the moment of speculative attacks, is perfectly compatible with the "asymmetric" interpretation of the EMS functioning described in paragraph 2: the more the autonomy in determining the domestic interest rate levels is reduced by the participation in the ERM, the more monetary authorities will attach importance to instruments capable to lower the volatility of *onshore* short-run interest rates.

The opposite viewpoint on the degree of autonomy retained by monetary policy in France and Italy is the so called "monetary discipline" view. This view stresses the importance of the shift in expectations induced in the initially high-inflation countries by the decision to peg their currencies to the DM. The hypothesis is the following. Once the commitment to a lower inflation rate is perceived by financial markets as a decision to renounce to monetary policy independence and subdue to the Bundesbank's monetary stance, the disinflation cost is reduced, because the "importation" of the Bundesbank's reputation changes inflationary expectations and eases the success of a deflationary monetary policy.

The evidence of a prompt revision of inflationary expectations at the inception of the EMS is weak (as is well-known, France's and Italy's inflation rates started shrinking only after a lag which has lasted four or five years). However, the growing stability recently gained by the two currencies inside the ERM, despite the completion of the capital movement liberalization process, has strenghtened this view. It might be argued that the change in market expectations has been determined precisely by the drift to a new phase of the EMS. The rationale for this change is that, in recent years, financial markets started expecting a stronger commitment to exchange rate fixity. Once capital controls are abolished, monetary authorities have to be aware that a defection from convergence to the Bundesbank's rigorous monetary stance would no more cost just a realignment but the abandonment of the system, as after an unilateral exchange rate adjustment their credibility would be irremediably compromised (15).

Therefore, on the basis of the "monetary discipline" view, the hypothesis can be put forward according to which, the more the capital movements' liberalization process has gone on, the more monetary policy coordination has been boosted in France and Italy. By assuming that the forward exchange rate is an unbiased predictor of the future spot rate, it is possible to verify if speculators have become more and more confident in the monetary authorities' commitment to disinflate in order to cope with complete capital mobility. To test the hypothesis, an estimate of the coherence of the DM/franc and DM/lira *forward premia* with the expected exchange rate change in the subsequent period can be carried out:

$$(4) \qquad\qquad (Es_t - s_{t-1}) - f = 0$$

where Es_t is the expected exchange rate and s_{t-1} is the current one.

Under the assumptions of rational expectations (i.e. the hypothesis that foreign exchange markets are efficient) and of absence of *risk premium* (i.e. assuming perfect substitutability), no deviation from the equality between the *forward premium* of the DM and the subsequent period depreciation of the franc and of the lira should result. Annual means of the *forward premia* of the mark and of the exchange rate variations in the subsequent period, however, show that even in the last years of increasing exchange rate stability the *forward premium* have exceeded — by far in Italy, to a lesser extent in France — the expected exchange rate change for the next period (measured, according to the rational expectations hypothesis, by the *ex post* spot rate) (16).

The origin of a *forward premim* of the mark higher than the *ex post* depreciation of these currencies is not easy to detect. If the rational expectations hypothesis is maintained (otherwise, we should think of a long run sequence of systematic errors, in the absence of

---

(15) See GIAVAZZI-SPAVENTA [9], pp. 73-4.
(16) See FARINA [5], p. 122.

any *learning* process), this excess in the expected depreciation might be traced to a *risk premium* required by speculators. In other terms, the lack of credibility of the monetary authorities' commitment to defend exchange rate stability leads to a less than perfect degree of substitutability of the two currencies with respect to the DM. Be that as it may, since the high levels of the *forward premium* of the mark demonstrate the sluggishness of foreign exchange markets' expectations, the "monetary discipline" view is not confirmed either as regards the functioning of the EMS in the recent years.

4. - The Degree of Autonomy of National Monetary Policy

The above discussion of the two extreme views on the EMS functioning suggests the following remarks. The participation in the ERM has not compelled France and Italy to full monetary policy coordination; at the same time, it has by no means allowed an equal status with Germany as far as the monetary stance and interest rates are concerned. Therefore, starting from the key-features of the EMS sketched in paragraph 2, an interpretation alternative to both these extreme views can be suggested.

The "asymmetric" solution to the "$N - 1$ problem" obviously causes monetary policy autonomy to tend to zero in the weak-currency countries; but the "hegemonic" solution to the "divergence problem", just because puts the whole burden of adjustment on the weak currency countries, actually allows "room for manoeuvre" through the use of policy instruments aimed at avoiding recourse to realignments. The possible outcome is the partial relaxation of convergence to the Bundesbank's monetary stance. In principle, less-than-full coordination of monetary policy is then compatible with the couple of "asymmetric" and "hegemonic" solutions. For the speculative attacks to be restrained and the deflationary objectives to be fulfilled, the required condition is that capital controls and interest rate differentials are used as *complements* and not as *substitutes* of the anti-inflationary monetary stance.

The experience of France and Italy inside the EMS supports this interpretation.

The evidence to which we made reference above in criticizing the "symmetric EMS" view also shows that annual means of the interest rates are much higher in Italy than in France. In fact, despite the *forward premium* of the DM is higher *vis-à-vis* the lira than against the franc, the franc/DM interest rate differentials are generally less close to the *forward premium* values than the lira/DM ones.

This diversity does not mean that monetary policy has been tighter in Italy than in France, but has probably to be traced back to the high public debt problem which characterizes the former country. In fact, after the shift to the anti-inflationary monetary stance, Bank of Italy has pursued the objective of a higher bond-financing of the PSBR. The drift to largely positive real interest rates, for the widening stock of debt to be accepted in the savers' portfolios, has opened a large nominal interest rate differential both with Germany and USA. Since 1985, while "temporary" capital movement restrictions kept shielding domestic markets in the occasion of speculative crises (17), "permanent" capital controls have mainly worked inward. Capital inflows, which have overfinanced the current account deficits, forced monetary authorities to continue in the policy of high interest rates, in order to curb the domestic credit expansion triggered by the low-cost foreign funds, which were responsabile for the monetary aggregates' growth rates continuously exceeding the announced targets.

France, on the other hand, have been relying more than Italy on capital controls; besides, because of the lower domestic interest rate level, the Bank of France has been in the position to benefit from a higher interest rate flexibility, as the franc's larger degree of volatility with respect not only to Germany but also to Italy demonstrates (18). However, the domestic market's insulation provided by restrictions to capital movements has been far from complete: because of the adoption of the ERM normal band and of lower capital inflows (the interest rate differential with Germany has been less large than in Italy), current account deficits have impinged on the exchange rate

---

(17) See MICOSSI-ROSSI [16], p. 209.
(18) See GIAVAZZI-SPAVENTA [9], pp. 75-6.

stability more heavily than in Italy, so that monetary authorities have been compelled to make frequent recourse to marginal and intramarginal interventions (19).

In short, in dealing with the contradiction between inflation differentials with Germany and the obligation to defend the bilateral parities of their currencies, France has mainly used capital controls, whereas Italy has mainly made recourse to the interest rate differential with Germany. However, the deflationary monetary policy has been more effective in the former country, with a virtually full convergence to the German inflation rate, which has been accompained by the continuous shrinking of the *forward premium* DM/franc and of the interest rate differential with Germany, and by the franc's move towards nominal appreciation against the mark. In Italy, on the other hand, the credit expansion continuously exceeding the announced targets, and the persistence of a rate of growth of the unit labour costs higher than in Germany, stopped the elimination of the inflationary differential with Germany as well as the reduction of the *forward premium* DM/lira and of the interest differential.

These outcomes seem to show that financial markets trust in the · monetary authorities' commitment to pursue low inflation, as long as the "degree of freedom" retained by monetary policy through capital controls and interest rate differentials is not used as an opportunity to escape from the anti-inflationary strategy but as a provisional support on the way of full convergence. If France, differently from Italy, has been able to convince financial markets to reduce the *forward premium* DM/franc, is just because of the convergence to the German inflation rate, the fulfillment of monetary and credit targets, and its very low public debt.

While this interpretation points to a positive evaluation of the EMS experience, two weaknesses of the system are nevertheless to be stressed. The first one stems from the contradiction embedded in the working of the EMS according to the "asymmetric" and the "hegemonic" solutions: the impact of the virtual obligation to avoid realignments on the trade balance between the *leader* and the divergent countries. Even though the degree of autonomy retained by

---

(19) See MASTROPASQUA-MICOSSI-RINALDI [12], p. 273.

means of capital controls and interest rate differentials is not turned to domestic objectives but is geared to further the convergence, so that the inflation rate is progressively reduced, the divergence of a particular country's unit costs from the best performer's ones will anyway impinge on its current account balance. The real appreciation of the franc and of the lira has brought about the accumulation of trade deficits in France and Italy and trade surpluses in Germany. Compensative capital movements have till now offset these imbalances, but their size makes the correction in the "fundamentals" no more postponable.

The second weakness is the exposure of the EMS to external shocks which hit asymmetrically the system. The most important source of a *nominal* shock, the dollar/DM fluctuations, is doomed to lose relevance as a cause of destabilization of the ERM of the EMS. After the 1992 abolition of residual barriers in goods markets, the financial markets' integration will even more speed up and the utilization of the ECU should expand. Therefore, more credible exchange rates and the increased degree of substitution among the EMS currencies should guarantee that the impact of the dollar/DM fluctuations will not cause tensions in the ERM bilateral parities. The enduring danger then comes from *real* shocks. Presently, the German economic and monetary unification process is demonstrating how difficult is to cope with unilateral real shocks of high intensity. Indeed, due to sharper competition, the 1992 goods markets integration will probably affect unevenly the output and inflation levels among the Community members, thus becoming a source of unilateral shocks on single countries, so that monetary authorities might claim that an exchange rate adjustment is justified. The consequences of the divergent monetary and fiscal policies implemented by countries hit by an unilateral shock, especially in a system that works according to the "asymmetric" rules above discussed, can then be very dangerous for exchange rate stability.

Moreover, these weaknesses are doomed to worsen. Whereas the functioning of the EMS has been mainly shaped by the relationship between Germany (and the countries traditionally belonging to the "DM area") on the one side, and France and Italy on the other side, the inception of the monetary unification process will reckon with the special approach followed by Britain, Britain's and Spain's adoption of the "wider" band, and the lack of participation in the ERM of the late comers high-inflation countries (Greece and Portugal).

5. - Policy Coordination
   in the Transition to EMU

In the current debate on the transition to EMU, the centre of attention are the problems contained in the blueprint presented by the Committee for the study of economic and monetary union (the so called *Delors Report*) (20). The establishment of the ESCB should be the main achievement of Stage II of the transition to EMU. The role envisaged fro this organism is to strenghten the national monetary authorities' commitment to boost convergence in inflation rates, public deficits and exchange rates, in order to smooth the path to irrevocably fixed exchange rates at the end of Stage II.

Yet, the coexistence of the ESCB with national monetary authorities, and with governments autonomously setting fiscal policy, can put the transition process in disarray. In fact, one of the main shortcomings of the *Delors Report* is that the planning of the ESCB has not been backed by the provision of precise guidelines for monetary and fiscal policies. On the one hand, the instruments through which France and Italy retained a certain degree of monetary and fiscal autonomy in dealing with the ERM constraints will no more be available, so that the risk of non-cooperative behaviors is far from disappearing. On the other hand, monetary control is doomed to be weakened along the transition process to EMU.

As for monetary policy, due to the increasing substitutability among the EMS currencies triggered by capital movements liberalization, demand for money in each individual country might be destabilized and a money supply increase in a single country will tend to be equal to a monetary expansion of the whole EMS. Owing to the exchange rate stability achieved along with the financial markets integration, the incentive might arise to exploit the reduced risk of

(20) See COMMITTEE FOR THE STUDY OF ECONOMIC AND MONETARY UNION IN EUROPE [3].

currency depreciation. In principle, a single country could accelerate money growth — provided that the reserve depletion following the internal inflation could be afforded — in order to augment the claim on real resources at the other countries' expense.

As for fiscal policy, the elimination of governments' access to direct financing by central banks proposed by the *Delors Report* is not a sufficient measure either to force governments to reduce the public debt growth rate below the real income growth rate or to cancel out the temptation to pursue a bond-financing fiscal expansion. Even though the *Delors Report* also forbids the accumulation of a particular country's public debt by the ESCB, the increase in the cost of borrowing will spill over from a single country to the whole EMS. Should the interest rates have not fully converged yet, the deflationary bias that will follow will be unevenly distributed among countries with negative consequences on the move to irrevocably fixed exchange rates.

The problem is that capital controls have been abolished and interest rate differentials — due to growing currency substitution — cannot be relied upon as before. On the other hand, the establishment of the ESCB does not consist in a transfer of authority from national central banks to an institution which inherits the Bundesbank's credibility. During Stage II, more "symmetry" will then be introduced in the ERM functioning during Stage II, without at the same time enforcing policy coordination. In the present integrated financial market, speculators are not disposed to interpret the artificial maintainance of interest rates higher than the *leader* country's ones as a provisional support to the anti-inflationary strategy. Instead, they tend to consider this instrument as an expedient which enveils the monetary authorities' impotence in forcing convergence in unit wage costs and public debt/GNP ratios. Financial markets could then fear that national monetary authorities might not be able to cope with the rise in convergence required by the transition process to EMU. Therefore, central banks and governments will have to come to terms with the financial markets' expectation of an *increase* in policy coordination, but for this objective to be met the *Delors Report's* Stage II does not devise suitable instruments.

The supporters of the "gradualist" approach to the EMU — in particular the authors belonging to the "symmetric EMS" view, who now oppose a fast transition to the monetary unification — underestimate these shortcomings of the *Delors Report* strategy. According to them, the rules imposed by the EMS have not been effective in boosting convergence to the best performer; likewise, a rapid shift to more stringent constraints would not bring welfare gains to the EMS members. Since monetary integration will not *per se* further the removal of trade imbalances and enforce a cooperative response to asymmetric shocks, policy flexibility should be longer allowed through the maintainance of adjustable exchange rates (21).

The sequence suggested by the "gradualist" strategy points to the completion of the convergence process, with the elimination of the persistent inflationary differentials, as the necessary precondition to further moves towards monetary unification. Even though it turns to real problems, the "gradualist" approach is not convincing. As we have seen above, just because of the lasting unit costs differentials impinging on trade imbalances, and of the instability stemming from possible asymmetric shocks, divergent countries might be taken by the temptation to make recourse to strategic non-cooperative behaviors. Therefore, it is by the possible implementation of discretionary policies in a changed scenario in which instruments oriented to smoothen convergence are no more available — and not by the imposition of more stringent rules on central banks and governments — that the unification process can be endangered.

Let us turn to the opposite view, that is the "radical" approach to monetary unification. This view regards monetary policy credibility — similarly to the central role attributed to the central banks' reputation by the "monetary discipline" view — as the cornerstone of the transition to EMU. The lasting evidence of positive *ex post* rate-of-return differentials of the franc and of the lira vis-à-vis the mark (the sum of expected rate-of-return differential and unexpected changes of exchange rates) is attributed to interest rate distorsions due to the lack of full credibility of the governments' commitment to maintain bilateral parities (22). Not only in the present regime of fixed but

---

(21) See COHEN-WYPLOSZ [2], pp. 331-2.

(22) See GIOVANNINI [8], pp. 22-5. The author calculates the net profits yielded by means of the following strategy: the representative operator, after shorting the mark in favour of the franc and the lira, invests in assets denominated in these currencies, and finally changes in marks the francs and the liras obtained spot at maturity.

adjustable exchange rates, but also in the irrevocably fixed exchange rates envisaged in the *Delors Reports* Stage II, realignments aimed at evening out a particular country's imbalance are always possible. According to this view, until a single currency will be introduced the system will be exposed to a shift in speculators' expectations due to fear of "surprise" devaluations. The announcement of a fast move to a currency reform, by replacing national currencies with a single currency, is then advocated as the sole strategy capable to eliminate both the persistence of inflation differentials and the interest rate distorsions imposed by the rigidity of speculators' expectations.

However valuable is the analysis of the credibility problem on which this approach is founded, dangers originating from the single currency's "superimposition" to the persistent inflation differentials cannot be overlooked. The introduction of a currency reform is equivalent to put full policy coordination before the convergence in the fundamentals. By consequence, a real appreciation of the "new" currency should be forced in the divergent countries, and soon after the change of the currency standard full wage and price flexibility would be required. Moreover, differently from the present experience of the Eastern part of Germany, no recourse to redistributive policies aimed at mitigating imbalances could be made, as most transfers are prohibited by the *Delors Report*. Therefore, a rapid introduction of a currency reform, by implying the sudden move to full convergence, might cause de-industrialization processes and thus heavily worsen the economic conditions of the backward regions of the European Community.

Therefore, the argument from which the "radical" approach starts — the causal relationship that has to be established between the need to increase policy coordination and the need to accelerate convergence — is surely to be shared. As for the following proposal of a fast leap to the single currency, a monetary reform would obviously do away with the credibility problem which threatens national monetary policies in markets characterized by full capital mobility. Yet, the risk cannot be underestimated that a too early transition to EMU might bring about excess welfare losses in some countries. The question which has then to be addressed is to define a viable strategy aimed both at the increased policy coordination required by full capital mobility and the amelioration of the output-inflation trade-off in divergent countries.

The theory of "optimal currency areas" (23) provides assignment rules for national policies. In accordance with this approach to policy coordination, a common money supply target could be fixed at the ESCB level by agreeing on a common inflation target, so that monetary authorities would be forced to conform their national monetary growth rates to the common money supply target; besides, fiscal policy should be used to tackle unilateral shocks and to implement compensatory adjustments. However, conditions for following this strategy are not mature: the enduring presence of inflation differentials and the instability of the EMS-wide demand for money might undermine the common money supply target, while "activist" policies are at odds with the need to level out national fiscal stances.

A more realistic starting point to further policy coordination is provided by the Lamfalussy's [12] proposals aimed at opening the way to a transfer of authority from national central banks to the ESCB: mainly, the pooling of instruments like interventions in third currencies (notably, the US dollar), changes in reserve requirements on national money creation, and the adjustment of relative short-term interest rates. However, if profound institutional changes like these are to be implemented, it is crystal clear that the transfer of authority to the ESCB cannot be set as an objective. For the needed acceleration of the policy coordination process to be obtained, the transfer of authority to the ESCB has then to be considered as a pre-requisite.

Therefore, in order the two objectives on which we have focused attention — the financial markets' confidence in central banks' stronger commitment to full convergence and the minimization of welfare costs of the transition to EMU — to be fulfilled, rigid guidelines are to be imposed on national policies. Even the sanction of exclusion from further steps towards monetary unification might be reckoned among possible instruments to enforce full policy coordination. Indeed, if the Board of Governors of the ESCB is entrusted with authority, thus inheriting the Bundesbank's credibility as for monetary stability and

---

(23) The reference is to Mc KINNON [14], Mc KINNON [15] and WILLIAMSON-MILLER [19].

independence from fiscal authorities, divergent countries will restrain from postponing policy coordination to a slow completion of the convergence process. The credibility problem should thus be solved, and financial markets will probably start accepting the abolition of the "risk premium" that has made the DM/franc and DM/lira *forward premia* higher than the *ex post* depreciation of the two currencies. In turn, this move towards the annulment of the interest rate differentials might allow divergent countries to improve their output-inflation trade-offs and reduce risks of heavy welfare losses resulting from monetary unification.

This strategy to EMU, which is an alternative to a drastic currency reform, then depends on the enforcement of policy coordination as a precondition to the restoration of the "interest parity condition". This convergence of the EMS divergent countries to lower interest rates, by meeting both the needs of a safe passage to irrevocably fixed exchange rates and of the reduction in welfare costs, can be considered the intermediate step required to pave the path to EMU.

BIBLIOGRAPHY

[1] CANZONIERI M.B. - GRAY J.: «Monetary Policy Games and the Consequences of Non-Cooperative Behavior», *International Economic Review*, n. 26, April 1985, pp. 547-64.

[2] COHEN D. - WYPLOSZ C.: «The European Monetary Union: An Agnostic Evaluation», in BRYANT R.C. - CURRIE D.A. - FRENKEL J.A. - MASSON P.R. - PORTES R. (eds.): *Macroeconomic Policies in an Interdependent World*, Washington (DC) The Brookings Institution, 1990.

[3] COMMITTEE FOR THE STUDY OF ECONOMIC AND MONETARY UNION: *Report on Economic and Monetary Union in the European Community*, Luxembourg, European Communities, 1989.

[4] DE GRAUWE P.: «Is the European Monetary System a DM-ZONE?», CEPR, *Discussion Paper*, n. 297, 1989.

[5] FARINA F.: «I tassi di cambio dello Sme e l'autonomia della politica monetaria», in «Inflazione, disavanzo pubblico e politica monetaria», Supplement to *Rivista di Politica Economica*, 1991.

[6] GIAVAZZI F.: «The Exchange-Rate Question in Europe», CEPR, *Discussion Paper*, n. 298, 1989.

[7] GIAVAZZI F.: «The EMS: Lessons from Europe and Perspectives in Europe», in FERRI P. (ed.), *Prospects for the European Monetary System*, London, Macmillan, 1990.

[8] GIAVAZZI F. - GIOVANNINI A.: *Limiting Exchange Rate Flexibility: the European Monetary System*, Cambridge, Cambridge University Press, 1989.

[9] GIAVAZZI F. - SPAVENTA L.: «The New EMS», in DE GRAUWE P. - PAPADEMOS L. (eds.): *The European Monetary System in the 1990s*, London, Macmillan, 1990.

[10] GIOVANNINI A.: *European Monetary Reform: Progress and Prospects*, Washington (DC), The Brookings Institution, 1990.

[11] — —: «Comment to "The European Monetary Union: an Agnostic Evaluation" by D. Cohen e C. Wyplosz», in BRYANT R.C. - CURRIE D.A. - FRENKEL J.A. - MASSON P.R. - PORTES R. (eds.): *Macroeconomic Policies in an Interdependent World*, Washington (DC), The Brookings Institution, 1990.

[12] LAMFALUSSY A.: «A Proposal for Stage Two Under Which Monetary Policy Operations Would be Centralized in a Jointly-Owned Subsidiary», in Collection of Papers of *Delors Report*, 1989.

[13] MASTROPASQUA C. - MICOSSI S. - RINALDI R.: «Interventions, Sterilization and Monetary Policy in European Monetary System Countries, 1979-87», in GIAVAZZI F. - MICOSSI S. - MILLER M. (eds.): *The European Monetary System*, Cambridge, Cambridge University Press, 1988.

[14] MC KINNON R.I.: *An International Standard for Economic Stabilization*, Cambridge (Mass.), MIT Press, 1984.

[15] — —: «Monetary and Exchange Rate Policies for International Financial Stability: A Proposal», *Journal of Economic Perspectives*, n. 2, 1988, pp. 83-104.

[16] MICOSSI S. - ROSSI S.: «Restrictions on International Capital Flows: The Case of Italy», in GORDON I. - THIRWALL A.P. (eds.): *European Factor Mobility. Trends and Consequences*, London, Macmillan, 1989.

[17] ROUBINI N.: «Leadership and Cooperation in the European Monetary System: A Simulation Approach», NBER, *Paper Series*, n. 3044, 1989.

[18] VON HAGEN J. - FRATIANNI M: «German Dominance in the European Monetary System: Evidence from Interest Rates», *Journal of International Money and Finance*, n. 4, December 1990, pp. 358-75.

[19] WILLIAMSON J. - MILLER M. «Target and Indicators: a Blueprint for the International Coordination of Economic Policy», Washinghton (DC), Institute for International Economics, *Policy Analyses in International Economics*, n. 22, 1987.

The Role of the European System of Central Banks in the European Integration Process

Lucio Valerio Spagnolo
Università di Salerno

Introduction

At the European summit of December 14th-15th, 1990, proposals were presented for the revision of the *Rome Treaty*, regarding the European Political Union (EPU) and the Economic Monetary Union (EMU). Their ratification by National Parliaments should happen before the end of 1992, according to the meeting of Dublin of April 18th, 1990. There seems to exist a general agreement on the principles underlying a European political and economic union, although the achievement of a political union will take longer than an economic one. Some reserves still persist on the proposals of the Commission for a monetary union.

The reserves do not relate to specific aspects of the proposals of revision, but represent rather a result of alternative approaches on the answers to give to three questions: what end should be reached, when will it be reached and by what means?

If the answer to those three questions is identical, it is possible to believe that national Parliaments will have no difficulties in ratifying the proposals of the Commission accepted by the European Council. If it is not, then national Parliaments of those countries that follow a different line of thought will not be able to ratify the proposals about which they disagree and, in this case, the definition of the new image of Europe will not yet appear clearly homogeneous. It is worth while therefore to discuss briefly these three questions regarding the realization of the Economic and Monetary Union.

1. - What End?

The end consists in realizing «. . . an economic and monetary union founded on one money, the ECU, and a social development and a common policy on external relations and defence. It is founded on the respect of democracy and fundamental rights, and on the principle of subsidiarity. . . .» (*Draft Treaty Containing Revision of the Treaty Founding the European Economic Community for the Achievement of an Economic and Monetary Union*, Part One: *Principles*, Art. 2).

The action of the Community implies «. . . *g)* the establishment of a common economic policy founded on a definition of common ends, on a strong coordination of the economic policies of the member States and on an application of other common policies; *g bis)* the definition and the putting into effect of one monetary policy whose primordial end is a price stability and, in respecting such an end, maintaining of a common economic policy. . .» (Part One, *Principles*, Art. 3).

2. - When?

«. . . The economic and monetary union is founded on a strong economic integration and one monetary policy. It will be developed progressively during a period of time divided into two stages preceding a final stage, maintaining a parallelism between economic policy and monetary policy. Continuing the developments verified after the beginning of the first stage on July 1st, 1990, the second stage, that is a transitory period of time, will commence on January 1st, 1994. During this period of time the regulations contained into the articles from 109 *B* to 109 *E* are to be applied. The existence of the conditions for passing to the final stage is verified by the European Council in accordance with the article 109 *F*». (Part Three, *The Policy of the Community*, Art. 102 *A*).

3. - How? (1)

«. . . Monetary policy is to be designed and realized by the European System of Central Banks, that in what follows will be denominated Eurofed, acting in the respect of the Treaty and the Statute. . . (Part One, *Principles*, Art. 4).

«. . . Member States cannot restrict capital flows of residents in the member States or discriminate the conditions on the basis of nationality, residence or place of investment.

«. . . Payments regarding capital flows among member States are free» (Part Two, Head 4 *Capitals*, Art. 67).

«. . . The cases recognized incompatible with the economic and monetary union and thereby forbidden are: *a)* public deficits financed directly by Eurofed or by privileged access to capital markets to public authorities; *b)* unconditioned warranty given by the Community or by a member State in favour of the public debt of a member State.

«. . . Excessive public deficits are to be avoided» (Part Three, Head 1 *Community Policy*, Art. 104 *A*).

«. . . The monetary union implies one money, the ECU, the achievement of one monetary policy and the institution of Eurofed» (Part Three, Head 2 *Monetary Policy*, Art. 105).

«. . . The community and the member States refrain from exerting influence on the European Central Bank, on the Central Banks of the member States and on their personnel when executing their task respecting their independence. To this end member States have to adjust their laws concerning the relationship between Central Banks and national Governments.

«. . . The European Central Bank can allow in no case to the Community or to one of the member States or to any public institution a loan or any other facility to fill a deficit» (Part Three, Head 2, *Monetary Policy*, Art. 106 *A*).

---

(1) The «how» is here summarised, of course, only in brief.

Advise: the numbers in square brackets refer to the Bibliography in the appendix.

The revision proposals of the *Treaty* are the result of intensive preparatory works carried out, in particular, by the Central Banks of the member States, by the commission for the Ministers of Finance (*Christophersen Report*), by the Commission and by the Monetary Committee (*Sarcinelli Report*). These works, substantially, accept the *Delors Plan*. However the British point of view expressed in a document of November 1989 (2) and not modified significantly in its philosophy is clearly an alternative to the *Delors Plan* (3)».

4. - The «Delors Plan»

The *Delors Plan* aims to realize an economic and monetary union through a gradual approach and in respect of a number of principles, such as: *a)* the division of the integration process into a limited number of separate but evolutionary stages; *b)* the parallelism between the monetary integration process and economic convergence of member States; *c)* the timing to be respected, [although not specified exept in the indication of the first stage (July 1, 1990)], to coincide with the coming into force of the law governing the total liberalization of capital movements; *d)* the participation of all member States.

The first stage aims to realize a greater convergence of economic results through a stronger coordination of economic and monetary policies inside the existing institutions. At the moment of the passage to the second stage it should have been prepared and ratified by the revision of the *Treaty*.

In the economic field actions are directed to the completion of the internal market and to the attenuation of the differences still existing through more effective regional and structural policies and programmes directed to reducing public deficits where existing.

In the monetary field actions are to be directed to the elimination of all the obstacles to financial integration and to the intensification of cooperation and coordination of monetary policy. The end to be

---

(2) See H.M. TREASURY [12].
(3) See DELORS J.: *Rapport sur l'Union Économique et Monétaire dans la Communauté Européenne,* Submitted to the Committee for the Study of Economic and Monetary Union, 1989.

reached is one financial area in which all monetary and financial assets are free to be moved and in which banking services and all those connected to movable and insurance values are offered on the same conditions all over the Community area. The autonomy of central banks is to be strengthened. All the Community monies are to be included in the European Monetary System (EMS) and the obstacles to the use of the private ECU are to be eliminated. The Committee of Central Banks Governors has been given new tasks of expressing its opinions on monetary and exchange policies to single governments and to EEC Council of Ministers and producing an annual report on its own activities and on the Community monetary integration to the European Parliament and to the European Council.

The second stage will start only after the ratification of the new *Treaty*. The existing institutions would have to be reformed and the new ones installed. It should be considered a transitory stage towards a final stage and a stage of arriving at a common decisional process.

In the economic field the European Parliament, Council of Ministers, Monetary Committee and Commission itself must strengthen their action on the subjects of one market, competition policy, regional and structural policies and macro-economic policies towards the convergence.

In the monetary field the most important initiative is the establishment of the European System of Central Banks, absorbing the European Monetary Cooperation Fund, the Committee of Central Banks Governors, the subcommittees for the analysis of monetary and exchange rate policies and for the control of banking activity. The fundamental task of ESCB is to organize the start of the transistion, coordinate the international economic policies, elaborate and establish one common monetary policy. The difficulty of the transition lies in the realization of a progressive transfer of national monetary authority decisional powers to ESCB. The intervals of fluctuation inside the exchange rate mechanism will have to be reduced with a view to eliminating them at all in the final stage.

The third stage starts with the passage to an irrevocably fixed exchange rate system and attribution of full monetary and economic powers to the Community institutions.

In the economic field it is possible to forecast three developments:

a) a further strengthening of community regional and structural policies; *b)* a strengthening of powers to the Council of Ministers, that in cooperation with the European Parliament, has authority of imposing constraints to national deficits to assure monetary stability, of modifying discretionary use of resources, of imposing constraints and conditions to regional and structural policies to improve the adjustment and convergence process; *c)* a taking upon the Community of the capacity of representing itself in the international cooperation policy.

In the monetary field the ESCB is to take upon itself the full powers given to it by the *Treaty* and to manage the passage to one European money.

5. - The British Proposal
(The Money Competition Approach MCA)

The *Delors Plan* is based upon the idea that a monetary union needs one monetary policy, that such a policy can be effective if it acts in parallel with one economic policy. Both of them can be realized correctly by filling up the present democratic deficit existing in the Community institutions. One monetary policy needs a centralized non-hegemonic institution and such an institution can manage the process of creation of one European money.

The MCA is based upon the idea that community policies should be in competition. Experience will determine whether such competition will imply a hegemony of one monetary policy or a continuation of a number of different policies, and in the second case it will not be possible to fix irrevocably the exchange rates. According to MCA, the realization of a European monetary union, needs a full interaction between real economy and monetary economy, whose premise is perfect capital and financial services mobility and, in particular, a full elimination of any residual restriction in the insurance field and regarding to diversification and international management of insurance and pension funds. The realization of one market, according to MCA, needs a much longer time than 1992 and in any case not before exchange risks will have been eliminated by the existence of one money. At the same time, as interaction between real economy and monetary economy is still to come, the use of one money will take a long time. As for the idea of creating a ESCB that by statute should pursue the end of price stability, and that should be independent from political power, according to MCA, it is simplistic and illusory. No central bank, as a matter of fact, however formally independent it may be, can escape from public opinion pressures. The Bundesbank, it is said, has obtained credibility after a long time of wise monetary management during which the aversion of German people to inflation (coming from historical experience) was made stronger by the certainty that a price stability is the best warranty for a steady and lasting economic growth. The existence among member States of divergences in inflation rates and public deficits implies different levels of competitivity that sooner or later will involve increasing rates of unemployment first of all in less competitive countries. The existing differences in income levels, volume of unemployment, regional differences, inefficiency in the redistribution mechanism inside the Community, differences in public deficits, all that will imply strong inflationary pressures on the Central Bank and it will not be able to ignore such pressures if it does not want to lose its political legitimacy.

MCA, it is said, aims to help the Community in realizing a monetary union putting it on guard against *a)* a fixing of exchange rates that could appear premature in absence of an adequate convergence of economic results and *b)* an eventual confusion of responsibilities between national monetary authorities and Community. Hence the alternative of MCA to *Delors Plan a)* of creating a monetary unity, the hard ECU, whose central rate could not fall compared with other EEC monies and that should be an option over the existing monies, *b)* of establishing a new institution, the European Monetary Fund (EMF) having the power of creating the hard ECU and *c)* of assigning to EMF the task of maintaining price stability through the value of the hard ECU, and of using intervention techniques to assure the substitution of national monies with the hard ECU without adding it to them.

The advantages of MCA would consist *a)* in hooking up EEC monies to a monetary community unity and not to a national money, *b)* in giving the possibility to EMF to acquire an experience and a

credibility in sight of one monetary policy, *c)* in avoiding the risk that
a monetary policy carried on by the central bank of the national
money-anchor be not coincident with the monetary policy needed by
the whole Community, *d)* in the possibility given to EMF of managing
a reserve policy in order to facilitate the convergence.

MCA implies a preoccupation with the risk of realizing a process
«accelerated» towards the economic and monetary integration rather
than a «lasting» one. The success of the integration process cannot be
assured, finally, by fixing dates or compulsory behaviour.

6. - Consideration on MCA

In the idea of MCA member States exercise their own monetary
sovereignty in the presence of a perfect capital and financial services
mobility. Only future experience will be able to verify the possibility of
fixing irrevocably the exchange rates and it is not certain that this will
happen. A full integration of markets will be realized only after having
eliminated exchange risks through the use of one money. One money
is therefore a means by which exchange risks will be avoided. It is the
result of a full substitutability among monies, which will be able to
happen only with a full integration of financial services and one
market. One money needs one market and at the same time one
market needs one money. The hard ECU is, as gold was at the date of
the Gold standard, the reference of ultimate request of the monetary
assumed system. The hard ECU has nothing to do with the ECU of the
Delors Plan. The ECU is the natural consequence of the irrevocable
fixing of exchange rates. Fixed exchange rates in MCA could not take·
place. Fixed exchange rates in the *Delors Plan* are the result of a
process of convergence. The hard ECU is a means through which it is
possible to realize a process of convergence. The European Monetary
Fund is a negation of the idea of ESCB. ESCB aims to realize a
coordination of Community policies to reach a fixing of exchange
rates and one money. EMF is a means by which it is possible to realize
a necessary experience to formulate in the future a common monetary policy. MCA assumes a perfect substitutability among techniques.
The *Delors Plan* assumes implicitly a discontinuity of techniques. In

MCA there exists only one stage: the first one. In *Delors Plan* the first stage is an acknowledgement of a will of continuing the path designed by the EMS pushed to an extreme consequence of avoiding realignments and of including all monies of member States. In MCA the first stage appears to be a world to be built *ex-novo* rather than the result of a path gone over by EMS. EMS has been a first stage towards a realization of a coordination of national monetary policies. In MCA monetary sovereignty is not modified. In ESCB the objective of price stability is involved, first of all, by the independence of monetary decisions from political power, and above all forbidding financements of public deficits. In MCA EMF has the institutional task of maintaining a price stability independently of eventual expansions of public deficits and on monetary consequences involved by them. In the idea of MCA the independence of Bundesbank by political power, assumed it exists, is the result of a long and wise monetary management directed to control the rate of inflation having always in mind historical experience. In the idea of *Delors Plan* the independence of ESCB is an indispensable condition, although not sufficient, to realize a price stability. The independence of Bundesbank from political pressures is the reason, *ab initio*, not the effect, of the possibility of following a wise monetary policy.

A competition among national monies, for MCA, reduces in fact the necessity of institutional overnational coordination of monetary policies. It should aim to control the growth of nominal magnitudes in the community countries and consequently assure exchange rate stability and reduce interest rate differentials. If this would have been the case, neither it would have been necessary create the EMS nor it would make sense to say that the fundamental task of ESCB is a realization of such an end.

As matter of fact EMS starts (march 1979) for restoring a certain exchange rate stability among European monies inside a growing international monetary instability, and for supporting an integration of European national markets and a renewal of growth. International monetary instability, although already existing, appeared evident after setting up international flexible exchange rate system. In EMS the aim of an exchange rate stability is a result of a convergence of national economies obtained through the coordination of national economic policies. The convergence is expressed by a reduction of divergence among inflation rates and by containing price increases. During the seventies, in a flexible exchange rate system, those divergences and increases had involved a fall in investment, employment and production. If national policies are not coordinated, and if there is not an institution coordinating them, in the presence of perfect capital mobility the end of an exchange rate stability is almost impossible to be reached. To say that money competition will imply exchange rate stability is in antithesis with the reasons that have determined the creation of EMS. In summary, the MCA implies a rejection of coordination and the institution that aims to realize it. It implies a rejection of the ends, the when and the how.

7. - ESCB and Paper Exchange Standard

But there is a further issue. Money competition, if accepted, would develop itself inside the existing paper exchange standard. The EMS represents a reaction of Europe to international monetary instability brought about by an excess of international liquidity denominated in dollars and made worse by persisting USA deficits. As central banks of the rest of the world have been and are disposable to finance such deficits, there is no reason to believe that they could be reduced until the behaviour of central banks (of the rest of the world) is modified. The growth of those deficits, in the meantime, continues to let reserves of central banks (of the rest of the world) and international liquidity grow.

The maintaining of a paper exchange standard contrasts with the elementary rule that advises against the financing of deficits through an increase of the money supply (to avoid inflation pushes) and with the evident ethical fact that the rest of the world, that needs financial capitals for its own development, is forced to contribute to the standard of living of the citizens of the richest country of the world (4).

---

(4) See TRIFFIN R., [28].

The privileged position of the dollar, the only international money, will continue to be such provided that three considerations are accepted. The first is implied by the USA contribution to a common defence in a greater measure than any other country; the second is involved by the threat of recession in the world economy consequent on an eventual elimination of USA deficits not balanced by a corresponding expansion of investments abroad by Germany and Japan or by a reduction of their surpluses; the third is the acknowledgement of the international rôle of the dollar in the existing international monetary system.

The irreplaceable rôle of the dollar depends on four main factors: the first is that it is the most important money as a reserve and as a supply of international liquidity; the second is that it is the main money used in international trade; the third is implied by interest rates in dollars being a key variable in the international financial market; the fourth is the predominant rôle of financial flows both on USA balance of payments and on dollar exchange rates (5).

The additional consideration that the financements of USA deficits (by the rest of the world) should be interpreted as a loan appears to be ambiguous and diverting. In fact they are loans to the USA by the rest of the world without any possibility of remboursement and not, as sometimes said, loans by the USA, considered as a bank to the rest of the world to be transformed into goods and services or in increasing liquidity.

If the considerations explaining the maintaining of the paper exchange standard continue to be accepted and if the reasons for the international rôle of the dollar continue to be valid, the prospect of the international monetary system does not seem to be indeed a path towards either stability or an income redistribution closer to the international real economic development capacity.

Some optimism might nevertheless be felt in the international context of a possibility of modifications able to reduce the validity of the first and third considerations and consequently a reduction in the importance of the second one. The progressive reduction of defence expenses (that we hope will not increase again in the near future) by

---

(5) See EMMINGER O., [11].

leading countries consequent to the end of the cold war, the opening
to the west for eastern countries, the reunification of Germany, the
EEC efforts towards an economic, monetary and political integration,
the perspective of widening the Community to other countries, are all
elements that can or, if successfully managed, will be able to avoid an
international crisis of the international monetary system and of the
world economy. The decrease of defence expenses reduces in fact the
importance of the first consideration in favour of the maintaining of
the privilege of the dollar and the paper exchange standard, as does
the condition that other countries take their own responsibilities
together with USA in maintaining defence. The other modifications
are all moving towards the realization of a united Europe.

A united Europe will be realized if the coordination of economic
policies of member countries produces the expected result of establishing inside the growing community area a convergence of all of its
economies; an irrevocably fixed exchange rate system; one money.

This result is unthinkable in the absence of an institution,
accepted by all, as ESCB is, that coordinates those policies and
manages the passage to one money.

8. - ESCB and One Money

One money for Europe, controlled in its quantity, and therefore
not liable to the volatility of the dollar, will inevitably be considered, in
the world economy, better than the dollar. The USA will be compelled
to finance in a greater measure than now, their own deficits through
national saving, as it happens in any other economy that aims for
stable growth and cannot export its deficits.

If the USA propensity to save is low and is becoming lower
(probably due to their high expenses for education and professional
qualifications and for life insurance) evidently that passage will not be
painless. Historically it will certainly not be the first time that a strong
money, at a certain point, starts its decline and another one substitutes for it. It was the case of the Orient Empire Bisante, the
Florence fiorino, the Venetian ducato, the Dutch florin, and the
British pound.

The establishment in Europe of an irrevocably fixed exchange rate system and of one money is desired apparently only by firms, whose costs would come down, and not by banks, whose profits would come down. In fact, if one money is an advantage for firms, that can expand their activities in the absence of exchange risk and in the presence of price stability, the whole economy grows and the volume of banking operations and bank profits grow without reducing the oxygen to the expansion of the real economy.

Independently of the impossibility of imagining a united Europe without one money, the use of one money is an expression of the political will of creating a united Europe. The way of imagining today one money for Europe is the most important and wise contribution Europe can give to itself and a correction to the rôle of the dollar as it has been developed in the international monetary system.

The credibility of one European money starts from its origins. It represents a major modification in the history of monies and of States. The idea of a State is in fact indissolubly connected to the idea of monetary sovereignty. There has never existed a State without a power of determining the supply of money. State money is accepted by all and is considered legal. Inevitably monetary sovereignty, an expression of State sovereignty, has coincided with State power of financing its deficits by increasing the money supply. If a State's power goes beyond its boundaries its money is accepted by all those who recognize its power. As the money supply grows, so grows the power of the State that creates it. Its power continues to grow with the money supply accepted by all. Such an expansion of money supply, nevertheless, menaces the stability of an international monetary system. Either the country creating it maintains fixed (if possible, and it will not be possible forever) exchange rates by using monetary policy interventions and financing chronic deficits of other countries by its own surpluses, or the exchange rates are left to fluctuate freely. Both cases are not compatible with a lasting peace. They involve an increasing uneasiness in other countries and at the same time in that of the leader a behaviour of unrest and disengagement (in the absence of particular strong reasons) on the international scene. Sooner or later that uneasiness will explode and in the leader country will lack the capacity of opposing pacifically that explosion or of maintaining its leadership in the case of an eventual modification of the international equilibrium.

The right solution is institutional cooperation inside a fixed exchange rate system. Whatever leadership it cannot substitute a policy necessary for its own ends with a different policy.

The institutional function of ESCB is essential even in the presence of fixed exchange rates. An irrevocably fixed exchange rate system is not equivalent to a system with one money. The absence of one money, though in the presence of fixed exchange rates, cannot produce a perfect substitutability among monies as it does not eliminate the costs of monies substitution. In this case it is not possible that the demand of the national money will come down and the one of any other money will increase. The creation of one money is an indispensable step to realize a monetary integration and ESCB is an indispensable means to realize one money.

One European money is the result of the action of ESCB in an irrevocably fixed exchange rate system. This type of fixed exchange rates has nothing to do with the exchange rate systems outlined above. An irrevocably fixed exchange rate system involving one European money is the result of a will to belong to one political reality and to cooperate with the rest of the world for an international monetary system stability; to coordinate the economic policies of single member countries; to give up their own monetary sovereignty to the new emergent reality of a united Europe. From a defence position against international monetary instability expressed by the European monetary snake before and by the European Monetary System later, Europe, with its proposal of ESCB and one money, aims to have an active rôle in reducing that instability.

9. - The Independence of ESCB

The credibility and validity of that rôle are implied by the credibility and validity of one money. ESCB gives credibility to one money. The credibility of ESCB is bound up with the separation of powers of ESCB from those of governments. The affirmation that ESCB cannot finance public deficits implies an acknowledgement of a limitation of single State monetary sovereignties in name of a common interest. If such a limitation of monetary sovereignty is directed to eliminate the danger involved by the idea that a State has power of financing its deficits by increasing the money supply, as history teaches, that limitation of sovereignty should be welcome.

In support of the independence of ESCB from political power, the *conditio-sine qua non* for the existence of ESCB itself, is often quoted the German historical experience. It is not clear why the experience of dollar should not be mentioned only because it has had the priviledge of being accepted by all.

The priority to price stability given to the tasks of ESCB has not only a monetary nature. It is known in fact that price instability creates conditions for increasing unemployment. ESCB independence creates conditions for growth and employment increases. Expansion of public deficits, explained by increase of public sector employments implies inflation, unemployment and, in any case, a growth lower than an economy is able to realize and, at the same time, an unfair income distribution.

ESCB independence necessarily involves a control of public deficits and their financing through national savings existing in the economy. In this case, if it is true that an high saving propensity reduces the risks involved by increasing deficits, it is also true that persisting anomalous deficits neither reduce those risks nor allow a stable and possible growth.

The diffusion of one money could be realized, in priciple, without a ESCB. Central banks have been created only in XIX century whereas monies have practically always existed. What gives credibility to a European money is rather the condition of independence of ESCB from political power.

10. - ESCB and Substitutability Among Monies

The credibility and the consequent progressive achievement of one European money, in the presence of increasing USA deficits, will involve sooner or later a return of direct investments and net capital flows of the rest of the world in the USA, and a preference for the transformation of international liquidity and dollars reserves into assets denominated in European money (or in an alternative one).

A fixed exchange rate system does not reduce the incentive to money substitution. If using alternative monies the exchange risk comes down, the opportunity of substituting one money for another one increases. The choice of the right money depends on the efficiency of structures and financial markets. A perfect capital mobility, condition for European integration, will imply a greater efficiency in payment systems and higher demand for European money.

A modification of the international portfolio in the light of the disadvantages of dollar assets and the advantage of alternative money (yen or European money) assets does not imply however an economic expansion, unless USA disinvestments are not substituted by new investments elsewhere. If it is difficult to say at present that those new investments can be directed towards eastern Europe, it is equally difficult to exclude it. It is true, neverthless, that in maintaining the paper exchange standard there is a risk that the third consideration referred to above about the international rôle of the dollar, might reduce in perspective its validity and that, in the presence of USA disinvestments and in the absence of new investments substituting for those, it is possible that a recession in the world economy could appear on the horizon. ESCB, through a creation of one European money and a greater efficiency in the European financial markets may really play a rôle against that possible recession.

Concluding Remarks

There has been much discussion on the process of European political, economic and monetary integration; on the ESCB and on a single money. Specific aspects and general ones have been analysed and discussions are certainly not finished as the new Europe is still to be built.

My brief observations, that cannot be exhaustive of the subject, aim only to offer a contribution to the idea of a united Europe in which single countries, on one hand do not limit themselves to delegate European institutions to look for solutions to their internal problems, and on the other hand bind themselves to accept the principles according which those institutions have to design a common policy.

I am convinced that the rôle of the ESCB will be seen as irreplaceable. It is such for the realization of the coordination of monetary policies, of the fixed exchange rate system and of one money. The highest cost for the realization of monetary integration is of course the loss of the use of exchange rate policy for the adjustments, whereas the greatest benefit is the credibility of one common economic and monetary policy.

The MCA coexistence of all national monies, the hard ECU, exchange rate stability and perfect capital mobility is deeply different from that of the *Delors Plan*. According to MCA competition among national monies involves a reduction of the importance of policies and an acknowledgement of that of financial markets. The experience involved by it could show further developments. The Delors approach implicitly admits an incompatibility of coexistence of a fixed exchange rate system and perfect capital mobility in the absence of policy coordination and control of one money by ESCB.

The establishment of ESCB is however a necessary but not sufficient condition to give credibility to one European money. The credibility of one European money and of the same ESCB is bound up with the achievement of European political union objectives regarding the realization of one common external defence policy, the strengthening of powers of European Parliament, an extension of the Community competences, a European citizenship and a redistribution of responsabilities between the Commission and the European Council.

It should appear evident that the credibility of one money and of ESCB is undoubtly conditioned by the progressive reduction and elimination of the democratic deficit at present existing in the Community. The elimination of the democratic deficit and the acceptance of one money are, in fact, two aspects of the same reality: the consciuosness and the will of the peoples of member countries to belong to a United Europe. No decision independent of it will be able to produce the expected effects, as any decision directed to realize it constitutes the right path to be followed to one money. ESCB contributes to realize that reality. From this point of view the current history of Europe is somewhat different from similar cases happened in the past. Now both the unions, monetary and political, are preceding altogether, as it should be, whereas in the past, usually, monetary unions have preceded political ones. The maintaining of this tendency might lead to a convergence of two lines of thought: one for which a State has to manage political processes, which are still very sceptical about the creation of one European money, the other for which a State has to manage also economic processes, that consider the creation of one European money and ESCB to be inevitable.

The possibility of convergence of those two lines of thought is demonstrated by a full collaboration of the United Kingdom in the drafting of the ESCB statute, although preferring the alternative of MCA. If the two lines of thought do converge, the path towards a united Europe will be more rapid than it might appear. And as the credibility of an economic and monetary union lies in the realization of a political union, the contextuality of the processes of realization of both of them could eliminate the remaining obstacles existing for a convergence of the two lines of thought.

But Europe has little time to decide that convergence. The modification of the paper exchange standard, the cooperation asked by eastern Europe and developing countries, the necessity of establishing an orderly international monetary system, the existence of persisting and increasing uneasiness in many areas all over the world, cannot wait further. Tomorrow's historians, telling today history, when asking themselves why Europe waited so long to become a United Europe, might find a number of reasons but not a satisfactory justification.

BIBLIOGRAPHY

[1] AGLIETTA J.: «L'Ecu et la Vieille Dame. Un Levier Pour l'Europe», Paris, Cepii, *Economica*, 1986.

[2] — —: «Des Principes Keynesiens Pour un Pole Monétaire Européen» in ZERBATO M. (ed.): *Keynesisme et Sortie de Crise*, Parigi, Dunod, 1987.

[3] ALLEN P.R.: *The ECU and Monetary Management in Europe*, Conference ECU, University of Leuven, 12-13 June 1987.

[4] AUME: *A Strategy for the ECU. A Report prepared by Ernst & Young and the National Institute of Economic and Social Research on behalf of the Association for the Monetary Union of Europe*, London, Kogan Page Ltd, 1990.

[5] BASEVI G. - FRATIANNI M. - GIERSCH H. - KORTWEG P. - O'MAHONY O. - PARKIN M. - PEETERS T. - SALIN P. - THYGESEN N.: «The All Saint's Day Manifesto for the European Monetary Union», *The Economist*, November 1975, reprinted in FRATIANNI M. - PEETERS T. (ed.): *One money for Europe*, London, MacMillan, 1978.

[6] BINI SMAGHI L. - VONA S: «The Effects of Economic Convergence and Competitiveness on Trade among Ems Countries», in HODGMAN WOOD G. (ed.): *Macroeconomic Policy and Economic Interdependence*, London, MacMillan, 1989.

[7] COMMISSION OF THE EUROPEAN COMMUNITIES (COMMITTEE FOR THE STUDY OF ECONOMIC AND MONETARY UNION): «1. Report on Economic and Monetary Union in the European Community, 2. Collection of Papers Submitted to the Committee for the Study of Economic and Monetary Union», *Delors Report*. Luxembourg, Office for Official Publications of the European Communities, 1989.

[8] COMMISSION OF THE EUROPEAN COMMUNITIES: «One Market, one Money», *European Economy*, 44, October 1990.

[9] DE CECCO M. - GIOVANNI A. (eds.): *A European Central Bank? Perspectives on Monetary Unification After Ten Years of the Ems*, Cambridge, Cambridge University Press, 1988.

[10] ELTIS W.: «The Obstacles to European Monetary Union», *De Pecunia*, vol. I, October 1989.

[11] EMMINGER O.: «The International Role of the Dollar», *Economic Impact*, n. 4, 1986.

[12] GROS D. - THYGESEN N.: «Towards Monetary Union in the European Community: Why and How», in atti del Convegno su *Mercato interno e Unione monetaria in Europa*, Trento, September 1990.

[13] TREASURY H.M.: *An Evolutionary Approach to Economic and Monetary Union*, H.M. Treasury, London, November 1989.

[14] KINDLEBERGER C.P.: *Il dollaro: ieri, oggi e domani*,revised version of the *George W. Stocking Memorial Lecture* tenuta alla Vanderbilt University, Nashville, Tennessee il 17 October 1985.

[15] LOEHNIS A.D.: «European Money and European Central Bank: a British View», in OTMAR FRANZ (ed.): *European Currency in the Making*, Sindelfingen, Libertas Verlag, 1989, pp. 76-88.

[16] MENTRÈ P.: «Vers une Banque Centrale Européenne», Relazione presentata al Congrès: *Trente ans d'Europe Economique: Bilan et perspectives*, Lille, March 1986.

[17] MUNDELL R.P.: «A Theory of Optimum Currency Areas», *American Economic Review*, vol. 51, 1961, pp. 657-65.

[18] PADOA SCHIOPPA T.: «The European Monetary System: A Long Term View»; in GIAVAZZI F. - MICOSSI S. - MILKER M. (eds.): *The European Monetary System*, Cambridge, 1988.

[19] — —: «Politica economica nazionale e concorrenza tra sistemi», Roma, Banca d'Italia, *Bollettino economico*, vol. 15, October 1990.

[20] PADOA SCHIOPPA T. - PAPADIA S.: «Competing Currencies and Monetary Stability», in MASERA R.S. - TRIFFIN R. (eds.): *Europe's Money*, Oxford, 1984.

[21] POHEL K.O.: «Europe Needs a New Currency», *European Affairs*, n. 1, 1987.

[22] — —: «Banque Centrale Européenne: Les Réticences du President de la Bundesbank», *Problems Economiques*, June 1988.

[23] SARCINELLI M.: «Verso l'unione monetaria europea», *Analisi per i mercati finanziari*, Milano 1990.

[24] SPAGNOLO L.V.: «Considerazioni sul Sistema monetario europeo nel regime internazionale dei tassi di cambio flessibili», in *Il mezzogiorno d'Europa*, Napoli, Isveimer, 1988.

[25] THYGESEN N.: «The Emerging European Monetary System: Precursors, First Steps and Policy Options», in TRIFFIN R. (ed.): «The Emerging European Monetary System», *Bullettin de la Banque Nationale de Belgique*, April 1979.

[26] — —: «Decentralization and Accountability within the Central Bank: Any Lessons from the US Experience for the Potential Organization of a European Central Banking Institution?», in DE GRAUWE P. - PEETERS T. (eds.): *The Ecu and European Monetary Integration*, London, 1989.

[27] TOBIN J.: «La teoria keynesiana è uno strumento ancora utile nella realtà economica odierna», in BALDASSARRI M. (ed.): *Keynes e le politiche economiche degli anni '80*, Roma, Sipi, 1989.

[28] TRIFFIN R.: «Il sistema monetario europeo nell'economia mondiale», in BALDASSARRI M. (ed.): *Verso il grande crack? Lo squilibrio globale nell'economia mondiale*, Roma, SIPI, 1989.

[29] ZOLOTAS X.: *The European Monetary System, the Dollar and the Need for Reform*, Atene, Bank of Greece, 1987.

The Political Economy
of the Hard ECU Proposal (*)

Peter Bofinger
Landeszentralbank in Baden-Württemberg and University of Kaiserslautern

1. - Introduction

The paper discusses the British hard-Ecu proposal (1), which was developed as an alternative to the Delors Committee's blueprint for European monetary integration.

The analysis is based on the theory of political economy which is the main theoretical basis of parallel currency approaches in general. After a short description of the principle of institutional competition and its main preconditions, paragraph 3 presents a microeconomic analysis of the process of currency competition in the traditional functions of money. The microeconomic evaluation is supplemented by a discussion of the macroeconomic implications of the *Hard ECU Plan* (paragraph 4). Such considerations play an important role in the argumentation of British officials, who expect a significant contribution of the hard-ECU scheme to a stable price level in Europe.

(*) Research conducted under the auspices of the CEPR's research project on *Financial and Monetary Integration in Europe*. I thank Norbert Kloten and Manfred Neldner for valuable suggestions. All views are those of the author.

(1) The following analysis is based on two British papers: A technical paper of the Bank of England with the title *The Hard ECU in Stage 2: Operational Requirements* (BANK OF ENGLAND [1] and a Bank of England Statement published in the *Financial Times*, June 21, 1990 (BANK OF ENGLAND [2]).

Advise: the numbers in square brackets refer to the Bibliography in the appendix.

Paragraph 5 gives a short summary and discusses the future of parallel currency approches.

2. - Istitutional Competition as an Exploratory Device

Institutional competition is one of the main theoretical principles of the Commission's *Internal Market Programme*. It replaced the *ex-ante* harmonization approach, which was unsuccessfully practised in the first three decades of the Community, by the so-called «country of origin» principle: on the basis of some minimum standards all national regulations are acknowledged in the whole area of the Community. It is expected that the coexistence of diverging regulations will lead to a selection process at the end of which those regulations will survive which are in the best interest of consumers. In the fields which are covered by the *Internal Market Programme* the merits of using competition as an «exploratory device «in the sense of Hayek were widely acknowledged among economists and politicians (2).

The *Hard ECU Plan* as well as its predecessor, the so-called «evolutionary approach», translates the principle of institutional competition from goods and services markets to the field of money. Not the politicians and the bureaucrats in Brussels, the markets should find out the optimum monetary order for Europe, which includes the timing of a currency union, the definition of the single currency at the end of the process and the number of member countries. Of course, the British ideas are not new. They were developed in the late 1960s and early 1970s under the heading of the parallel currency approach (3). Even the specific proposal of a «hard» parallel currency which cannot devalue against any of the Community currencies dates back to the year 1969 when it was proposed by Wolfgang Stutzel (1969) in a mimeographed paper (4).

---

(2) See in more detail SIEBERT [12].

(3) For a survey, see VAUBEL [15].

(4) In the last few years this specific variant of a parallel currency was put forward by RUSSO [10].

The theoretical basis of the parallel currency approach and also of its British version is the theory of political economy. The general hypothesis of this theory is that even in a democracy politicians have only very little knowledge of the «true» preferences of the pubblic (5). In the context of European monetary integration the crucial hypothesis is that economists and politicians do not have enough theoretical knowledge of the advantages and disadvantages of a common currency. As Roland Vaubel [16] puts it: «Since there is no scientific procedure of determining whether, and which countries ought to combine in a currency union, a discovery procedure is needed». This ignorance assumption, which criticizes adherents of other integration approaches of a «pretence of knowledge» is of central importance for the evaluation of British proposal. it is the most important argument for objecting a procedure determined by administrative fiat, which characterizes the Delors Committee's plan and which has now been widely adopted by the eleven other EC countries at the EC Conference in Rome on October 27-28, 1990.

Thus, for an assessment of the hard ECU proposal two questions have to be answered: 1) How much do we know about the advantages and disadvantages of the final stage of monetary integration with a common and single European currency compared with an arrangement with independent national currencies?; 2) Is a process of currency competition between national currencies and the hard-ECU a procedure which will lead to the survival of the most efficient monetary arrangement in Europe? In other words: Can the process of institutional competition be transferred from the field of regulations for goods and services markets to the area of a European monetary order?

An answer to first question goes far beyond the scope of this paper. A very recent study of the EC Commission [5] discusses these issues in detail and comes to the result that the introduction of a single currency could have growth effects in an order of magnitude of

---

(5) A second basic assumption of this theory is that politicians are not motivated by the social welfare but by their personal well-being (prestige, influence, etc.). Applying this assumption to the «hard ECU proposal» one would have to answer the difficult question why politicians should be interested to install a scheme which might deprive them of their national currency and the associated seignorage.

about 5 of the Community GNP, which are similar to those of the *Internal Market Programme*. While the microeconomic advantages of a single European currency are evident, its macroeconomic aspects can be discussed quite controversially. The outcome depends on the assumptions about the nature of future shocks (symmetric or asymmetric) and about the future constitution of a European Central Bank System, which will determine the overall inflation rate in Europe.

The focus of this paper is on the *process* of currency competition. The most important question is whether competition can be used as exploratory device in the field of money. As the discussion of the *Internal Market Programme* shows, the main requirement for this process is the absence of externalities (Siebert [12]). If externalities can be identified in the process of currency competition, it would not be an efficient mechanism for creating a common European currency. A political decision would be indispensable on the basis of the existing theoretical wisdom.

3. - Microeconomic Aspects of Currency Competition

To evaluate the functioning of market processes in the field of the monetary order we have to distinguish between the three traditional functions of money: *a)* means of exchange; *b)* store of value, and *c)* standard of value.

3.1 *The Hard ECU as a Means of Exchange*

In the means of exchange function the competition process concerns non-interest-bearing monies, above all sight deposits, banknotes and coins. For an analysis of the determinants of this process it is useful to start with banknotes, which means that the issuing institution of the hard ECU, the hard ECU bank, will operate as a currency board. The implications of interest-bearing sight-deposits held with private banks or the hard ECU bank will be discussed in the following sub-paragraph. Two dimensions are relevant in this process: transaction costs and the wealth effects of switching from one currency to another. While the exchange of one currency against another has normally no wealth effects, the exchange of national banknotes in hard ECU banknotes immediately increases the financial wealth of the hard ECU holder. This effect in due to the specific definition of the hard ECU, which links this currency by definition and guaranteed by the hard ECU bank to the respective strongest erm-currency. Thus, the hard ECU shall never depreciate against any national European currency. The logic of this definition can be explained in terms of option theory, which shows that risk positions, which are created specific instruments, can always be replicated by synthetical positions.

In the case of the hard ECU it is quite obvious that a hard ECU banknote can be replicated by combining a national currency note (with a corrensponding ECU value) with a currency call option. This option provides the right to exchange the national currency at the present exchange rate in the strongest currency of the ERM at any future point in time. According to the British plan this option, which is an American option without a final exercise date, is sold for free to every private agent who is willing to switch from his national currency to the hard ECU. The coasts have to be borne by the writer of the option, which is the hard-Ecu-bank. In order to safeguard the issuing bank's solvency, the British proposal prescribes that each European national central bank would have to accept an obligation to maintain the ECU value of the hard ECU-bank's holdings of its respective currency (6).

For the competition process the value of the option is of central importance. The value of an option is the sum of its intrinsic and its time value. At the moment of the exchange from the national currency to the hard ECU, exercising the option immediately would be of no value; the so-called intrinsic value of the option is zero. The time value of the option depends on the expected volatility of the exchange rate between the national currency and the respective strongest currency of the ERM. As long as there exists no hard ECU market, it is difficult to assess this time value. In order to see the orders of magnitude, it is assumed that the future maximum yearly

---

(6) This can be regarded as a redistribution of seignorage gains, which accrued to national central banks by an inflationary policy, to the public.

exchange-rate adjustments in the ERM are identical with the present inflation differentials. Thus, from a British point of view the maximum appreciation of the pound *vis-à-vis* the DM would be about 7% p.a. For a British citizen, the value of the implicit option of a 1 ECU banknote is 0,07 ECU p.a. If one also assumes that a household has an average stock of national banknotes of an equivalent of, say, 200 ECU, the maximum gain, that a British household can achieve by switching all its currency in the hard ECU is 14 p.a. The value of the option is considerably lower in EC countries with low inflation rates, such as the Netherlands, Germany, France and Belgium. The likelihood of a depreciation of each of these currencies against the prospective strongest currency is very low. In the case of the DM the value of the option would be close to zero. Because of the strong regional differential of the option value between the group of low inflation countries and the group of the remaining EC countries, the incentives for choosing the hard ECU are markedly different in Europe and could lead to a two-tier Europe in terms of circulating currencies — a development which the British officials explicitly tried to counter with their proposal (7).

The additional information and transaction costs, which are associated with using the hard ECU instead of national currencies, are the second main determinant of the competition process. This issue can be addressed in categories of game theory: Two players (buyer and seller) can use either the hard ECU or a national currency for their mutual payments transaction. It is assumed that a player does not know *ex ante* which currency is used by the other player. The possible outcomes in terms of the cooperation rent of both parties are shown in the payoff matrix:

SELLER CHOOSES

Buyer chooses	Hard ECU	National currency
Hard ECU	1	−1
National currency	−1	0

---

(7) See Leigh-Pemberton [9].

It is assumed that a mismatch of currencies leads to a negative outcome, which reduces the cooperation rent of their mutual transaction. If the seller does not accept the buyer's currency the latter has to find another supplier or has to go to a bank. Both alternatives lead to additional transactions costs and possibly to a complete loss of cooperation rent for both sides. If the supplier is ready to accept a currency which is not his preferred one, he has to hold higher stocks of cash or he also has to go to the bank more often. In the matrix it is also assumed that the use of the hard ECU by both parties is superior to the use of the national currency, which is due to the implicit currency option. As the matrix shows the Pareto-efficient arrangement would be characterized by both parties using the hard ECU. However, as long as both currencies exist side by side, the players do not know which currency the other side wants to use. How will they react in this prisoners' dilemma situation? In the starting period of the hard ECU obviously the only successful strategy is to use the national currency. This outcome can be explained by the concept of «prominence», which has been developed by Schelling [11]. Sudgen ([14], p. 90) puts this general principle as follows: «If people coordinate behavior without communicating with one another, the must be drawing — consciously or unconsciously — on some fund of ideas they have in common. The most important source of such ideas, I suggest, is common experience».

A coordination mechanism on which people normally rely in such situations are conventions. Because the national currency order is such a convention, a buyer can expect that the seller will accept the national currency. The specific disadvantage of the hard ECU is that it does not start in situation without a convention. Instead, it has to compete with an existing convention, the national currency order, which is self-perpetuating after it has been established. An important result of game-theoretic approaches is that such conventions can be evolutionary stable if they are not Pareto-efficient (Sudgen [14], p. 93). Of course, this would not be the case if a convention (or a European currency order) would be deliberately chosen by politicians, an approach which is explicitly rejected by the British government. Thus, if a monetary order, which is a very important convention, can be successful without being Pareto-efficient, currency competition cannot be regarded as a superior organizing principle for the European monetary order. In terms of the *Internal Market Programme*, the individual advantages of using a «second-best» convention instead of the Pareto-efficient arrangement constitute an important externality which impairs the functioning of institutional competition in the field of the monetary order.

It is important to note that the uncertainty, which necessitates a convention, cannot be reduced by legal tender laws, which would legally oblige sellers to accept the hard ECU as a means of exchange at a fixed rate *vis-à-vis* the national currency (8). For suppliers this would not improve the situation in the case of a currency mismatch. For buyers the risk remains that a supplier, which does not understand the whole concept of legal tender, does not accept the hard ECU, even if it has been declared legal tender. Although the buyer could force the seller to provide the good against hard ECUs, this would require time-consuming legal procedures.

In sum, the competition process between the hard ECU and national currencies is determined by the positive effect of the implicit currency option and by the negative transaction cost effects, which reflect the natural monopoly of national currencies within their traditional currency areas. The question remains, whether the wealth effect would be high enough to compensate hard ECU holders for situations, where a currency mismatch arises. Because the option has almost no value in low inflation countries, the «prominence» of their national currencies will suffice to avoid a significant market share of the hard ECU. In EC-countries with higher inflation rates it is more difficult to forecast the outcome of currency competition. However experience with hyperinflations shows that it requires extremely high inflation rates to drive out the national currency as a means of exchange. Benjamin Klein ([8], p. 72) puts this as follows: «The switching by the public to a new medium of exchange appears to be highly inelastic to the currency's inflation rate. Even in the extreme cases of post-world war I hyperinflations or the moderately rapid but

---

(8) The definition of a «legal ratio» (JEVONS [6], s. 97) for the discharge of debts in hard ECUs is necessary in order to avoid an indirect refusal of the hard ECU by exchanging it at an exchange rate, which is extremely disadvantageous rate to the buyer.

decades-long Latin American inflations, individuals did not switch to competing currencies. Although in these cases individuals often drastically reduced their real holdings of the inflating currency, competing currencies were not held as alternative media of exchange».

Thus, in the field of banknotes institutional competition seems not an adequate mechanism for creating an efficient monetary order in Europe. The only large EC country where the hard ECU could have some positive market prospects would be the United Kingdom, which would certainly not be in the interest of its inventors.

Under aspects of political economy the subsidy, which is provided to holders of the hard ECU by offering them a free currency call option reveals a remarkable inconsistency of the British proposal. If politicians pretend not to know whether a common currency is good or bad for Europe, it is difficult to understand why they want to subsidize a specific common currency by offering a free currency option to its holders. The distortion of the competive process, which it creates, would considerably reduce the informational content of observed market outcomes. A subsidy for a specific currency could only be justified by the (allegedly unknown) merits of a single currency. In this respect the proposal of H.M. Treasury which was put forward in November last year (the so-called «evolutionary approach») was much more consequent as it suggested a currency competition, which is limited to existing national currencies without any specific subsidies. However, all other flaws of the hard ECU approach would also apply to this alternative. Here, the competition process would focus on the DM, which would have similar difficulties as the hard ECU to drive out the other national currencies in their established currency domains.

3.2 *The Hard ECU as a Standard of Value*

The second function of money is the standard of value function, above all as a standard of deferred payments in contracts specifying financial obligations. The determinants of an optimum standard of value are not easy to assess, because its quality depends on its specific context. It is evident that the US dollar is on average a better standard of value for Americans than the DM, while for Germans the opposite is true. This is due to the fact that the riskness of financial assets or obligations is normally seen in relation to expected future income or expenditure flows. If his income is denominated in dollars, a risk averse debtor will prefer the dollar as standard of value for its debts. And if future expenditure streams are also denominated in dollars, risk averse savers will have a preference for the dollar as their investment currency. Because the currency denomination of incomes and of many expenditure streams (rents, mortgage payments, etc.) is determined by contracts concluded in the past, this creates a stickiness in the choice of optimum standards of value which works against a newcomer such as the hard ECU. For instance, for a British wage earner it might be cheaper to denominate his mortgage payments in hard ECU instead of pound sterling. However, ad long as his wage is not denominated in hard ECU he has to bear the full risk of a pound depreciation, which is due to his position ad the writer of the implicit option during the whole investment period.

The stability of the hard ECU in terms of the ERM currency with the lowest inflation rate does not improve its quality ad a standard of value for domestically oriented households and firms. Because a specific subsidy for users of the hard ECU is not possible in this money function, it is not expected that it will overcome the inertia which is created by the network of contractually determined financial flows.

3.3 *The Hard ECU as a Store Value*

How are the market prospects of the hard ECU in the store of value function of money! With interest-bearing hard ECU assets issued by private debtors and banks the value of the implicit option would have to be reflected in a negative interest rate differential of hard ECU assets in relation to the strongest ERM currency. The subsidy element would necessarily disappear in private contracts.

Thus, hard ECU sight deposits held with private banks wold have to carry a lower interest rate than deposits in one of the national currencies. Therefore a conversion from the national currency deposits to the hard ECU deposits would not offer an increase in wealth. In the starting period the transaction cost disadvantages of using a currency as a transactions medium which differs from the national currency would be pervasive.

In the store of value function the hard ECU would be one among several foreign currencies which are used by internationally oriented investors. An important difference between the means of exchange function and the store of value function is that in the latter standardization is of much less imnportance. With longer investment periods and increasing technical sophistication in international banking transactions costs of exchanging a foreign asset into the national currency lose their significance for investment decisions. Thus, in this field the tendency towards a single currency unit is generally much less pronounced than in the means of exchange function.

A significant contribution to a unified European currency cannot be expected from the workings of competition in this segment of currency competition. In purely private contracts, i.e. without a subsidy, the hard ECU would have a similarly low potential for driving out a national currency as all other foreign currencies, which is mainly due to the fact mentioned above that foreign currencies are more risky standard of value than the domestic currency. Moreover, for many investors the hard ECU would be a very close substitute for the DM. Such a relationship favours corner solutions. Because of the very liquid and highly developed financial markets of DM it is to be expected that this currency would be superior to the hard ECU. Markets would favour the DM instead of its shadow, the hard ECU. Compared to the traditional basket ECU, the hard ECU would lack one specific advantage of this composite unit: it could not provide the European portfolio diversification, which the basket ECU offers today at relatively low transactions costs. Seem from this perspective the transition from the basket ECU to the hard ECU could easily lead to an end of a separate ECU circuit. Present ECU markets could break down after the basket ECU loses the strong official support it could enjoy in the past, while the hard ECU is not traded at all, because it is regarded as a «DM in disguise».

The negative prospects of the hard ECU on private financial markets could only be improved by an interest rate subsidy on ECU deposits held with the hard ECU bank. According to the British papers the hard ECU bank would not only be a «currency-switching» but also a «deposit-taking» institution. If the hard ECU bank is willing to pay, for instance, an interest rate on its hard ECU liabilities wich equals or even exceeds the interest rate for comparable DM deposits, it is very likely that a strong conversion of national currencies in hard ECUs will occur. However, in this case an increansing marked share of the hard ECU would not reflect private preferences for a single currency but subsidized deposit rate of the hard ECU bank. It is obvious that such a policy would again be absolutely incompatible with political economy approach wich underlies the whole strategy.

3.4 *The Hard ECU in International Transactions*

The evaluation of the demand for the hard ECU in the three traditional functions of money was so far based on private agents which do not operate internationally. One can expect that the advantages of using a common European currency are higher if it is used by travellers and firms which are importing and exporting at the European level. But also in this context, the transactions costs of the hard ECU in the starting period should not be neglected. In the present setting, normally either the importer's or exporter's currency is used for invoicing and payments so that at least one party can use its domestic currency. With the hard ECU, both sides would have to deal with a foreign currency for which they need forward cover and which requires additional bank charges for payments transactions. This may be an explanation why the basket ECU, which already today provides the option of using a common currency in European trade, plays almost no role as a means of exchange in this context (Table 1).

For travellers the EC Commission ([5], p. 66) has calculated that the currency transactions losses in a hypothetical roud-trip through 10 countries total 47%. However, with credit cards and Eurocheques the amount of cash can be reduced to a minimum. In addition, if a journey covers only one or two countries the transaction cost disadvantages of not using a national currency will outweigh the cost of bank charges for conversion.

TABLE 1

CURRENCY DISTRIBUTION (%) OF PAYMENTS (1) BY (OR TO) DOMESTIC RESIDENTS TO (OR FROM) EC MEMBER STATES (CURRENT ACCOUNT TRANSACTIONS AND FOREIGN)

	Economic union Belgium-Luxembourg		Italy (2)		France (3) (4)		Germany (5)		Denmark (6)	
	receipts	payments	receipts	payments	receipts	payments	receipts	payments	receipts	payments
BFR.........	30.8	25.5	2.1	2.4	9.2	2.9	1.7	1.4	other	other
FF	12.5	11.8	17.6	15.6	59.1	51.9	6.3	7.5	other	other
UKL	5.9	5.0	7.1	4.3	5.5	4.6	4.7	5.1	7.0	4.0
HFL	8.0	8.6	2.6	4.9	1.7	1.8	1.6	2.9	2.0	3.0
DM	19.3	23.2	26.4	31.0	9.8	11.2	77.6	59.7	14.0	17.0
LIT	3.1	2.8	37.1	28.8	3.0	3.2	3.6	3.4	other	other
DKR	0.6	0.5	0.5	1.3	0.0	0.1	0.5	0.6	37.0	33.0
ESC.......	0.02	0.03	0.1	0.0	0.0	0.0	0.0	0.0	other	other
PTA.......	0.6	0.9	2.6	2.1	0.1	0.3	0.1	0.3	other	other
DR	0.01	0.1	0.0	0.1	0.0	0.0	0.0	0.0	other	other
IRL.......	0.1	0.2	0.1	0.2	0.0	0.1	0.1	0.2	other	other
USD	16.0	19.0	3.2	8.4	15.2	16.4	2.6	10.7	21.0	23.0
ECU	1.6	1.0	0.4	0.5	1.3	1.4	0.0	0.2	other	other
YEN	0.6	0.5	0.1	0.3	other (7)	other	0.1	0.2	other	other
Other	0.9	0.9	0.1	0.2	2.1	6.5	1.2	7.8	19.0	20.0

Legend:
(1) Payments executed through the banking sector. Banknote payments are as a general rule not included.
(2) Payments arising from intra-EC trade account transactions and technology transfers.
(3) Payments arising from current account transactions only.
(4) Own computations on the basis of trade statistics according to the country of destination or origin and of the currency distribution of global current account transactions. Figures should therefore be seen as indicative in particular as it proved hard to distinghish between the EC and the rest of OECD-Europe.
(5) Trade account transactions only.
(6) Global current account transaction.
(7) Subsumed under Other.
Source: EC COMMISSION ([5], p. 258).

4. - Macroeconomic Aspects

A macroeconomic assessment of the proposal is necessary, because the British Treasury regards the hard ECU plan not only as an exploratory device for identifying the «true» currency preferences of the public but also as «a powerful lever for the extension of a collectively agreed, non-inflationary monetary policy among member States» (Bank of England [2]).

The mechanism for achieving this aim is an asset settlement obbligation of national central banks in relation to the hard ECU bank. The underlying assumption is that inflationary policies at the national level will lead to an increased conversion of such national currencies in hard ECUs. According to the British scheme each national central bank is obliged to redeem balances in its own currency, which are acquired by the hard ECU-bank in the conversion process, against hard currency. The transfer of dollar reserves, or a «hard» European currency which can be designated by the hard ECU bank, reduces a central bank's currency reserves. Because of limitations on central banks' reserves and their ability to borrow on international markets, a loss of reserves is unsustainable. Therefore, the central bank which loses reserves has to change its policy in order to stop the conversion and to protect the level of its reserves. This mechanism is identical with the «reserve constraint», which operates in the ERM (Bofinger [4]) and which has proved a very efficient disincentive for central banks with inflationary policies.

4.1 *The Rationale of an Additional Nominal Anchor for Europe*

For an assessment of this additional policy constraint at the European level one has to identify the main macroeconomic difference between the indirect ERM-coordination mechanism under the status quo and the British blueprint (with an ERM which is supplemented by the hard ECU and the hard ECU bank). In the ERM setting of the 1980s the average inflation rate of the system has — to a large extent — been determined by the central bank with the strongest currency. Such a system has a nominal anchor, as long as the country with the lowest inflation rate has a strong currency and as long as its inflation rate is compatible with price stability. Both conditions were fulfilled during the last decade. The need for an additional anchor is therefore not obvious. One could argue that inflation differentials have become less important for exchange-rate expectations in the last few years, which impairs the working of this indirect coordination mechanism. However, the increasing fixity of ERM parities, which considerably reduced exchange rate expectations of market participants, would be also be a problem for the hard ECU. The demand for this currency, which would by definition have the lowest interest rate of all European currencies, would be extremely low if intra-ERM exchange-rate expectations were absent.

The only rationale for an additional anchor is that the present anchor could fail. Theoretically one could think of a scenario where all national central banks (including the Bundesbank) decide collectively to pursue an inflationary policy. In this situation the nominal anchor of the ERM arrangements would become a drag anchor, the system would lack an efficient mechanism for inflation control. Only under such extreme circumstances the hard ECU bank could play a useful macroeconomic role acting, as it were, as a nominal anchor for the last resort: its managers could raise the interest rates on ECU deposits to a level which induces a strong conversion from all national currencies in the hard ECU. This would set in motion the above mentioned asset settlement process. The loss of foreign exchange reserves would exert a disciplining effect on all national central bank with the strongest currency of the ERM.

4.2 Why Should the HEB Behave Differently!

However, from the perspective of the theory of political economy one has to ask why the managers of the hard ECU bank should behave so entirely differently from their colleagues in all other central banks. Such an outcome would only be plausible if the statues of the hard ECU bank provide very stringent incentives and disincentives for the bank managers, which enhance their resolve to pursue a stability-oriented monetary policy. In particular, the statutes should be at least as stringent as the statutes of the present dominant central bank, the Deutsche Bundesbank. This would include, above all, a complete independence of the hard ECU bank from political directives to guarantee the stability orientation of the HEB. To guarantee the anti-inflationary resolve of the HEB in a situation where even the Bundesbank begins to inflate, some additional regulations would be required. Above all, one would have to design specific microeconomic incentives (e.g. salaries which are not inflation-adjusted) which would contribute to a strong stability orientation of the HEB's management. Having in mind the overall political economy approach of the British proposal it is surprising that its authors did not discuss this important point at all. Again, one gets the impression that although the strategy is based on the theoretical assumptions of political economy, it does not apply its principle and methods in a consequent way.

4.3 *Microeconomic Implications*
of a Macroeconomic Role of the HEB

Theoretical inconsistencies becomes also evident if one analyses the microeconomic implications of an anti-inflationary monetary policy of the hard ECU bank. As already mentioned, the principle of institutional competition requires that the interest rates the hard ECU bank offers for its depositors do not deviate from the rates which are determined by private markets. However, this neutrality requirement is incompatible with a macroeconomic role of the HEB. The microeconomic analysis has shown that market processes will by themselves not lead to a significant conversion in hard ECUs, at least as long as national inflation rates remain out of the range of hyperinflations. A strong conversion, which is required to discipline national central banks, will only occur, therefore, if the HEB pursues an active interest rate policy, which is equivalent with a subsidy for hard ECU depositors. Therefore, a macroeconomic role of the HEB has the negative side-effect that it strongly biases the process of currency competition in favour of the hard ECU. The macroeconomic functions, which the British government attributes to the hard ECU bank, are obviously not compatible with its main intention to use currency competion as an exploratory device.

4.4 *Relationship Between the HEB and the Bundesbank*

A consequent application of the theory of political economy reveals a further macroeconomic drawback of the proposal, which is due to the extremely competitive relationship between the DM and the hard ECU. On the basis of the theory of political economy one would be tempted forecast that this rivalry could lead to too high an interest rate level in Europe.

One has to expect that the managers of a newly established institution like the hard ECU bank will be interested to gain prestige and public influence. This will depend above all on the increase of the amount of ECU notes and ECU deposits held with bank. If one agrees with the microeconomic analysis of this paper and if one assumes that the Bundesbank will continue its stability-oriented monetary policy and that no interest rate subsidies will be paid on the hard ECU interest rate, the conversion process will remain very limited, especially between strong EC currencies and the ECU. Thus, there exists a permanent temptation for the managers of the hard ECU bank to gain a stronger public profile by raising their deposit rates in order increase the hard ECU's market share. Of course, the Central Bank Council of the Bundesbank would not be willing to allow a considerable conversion of DM in ECU ad this would undermine not only the DM's international reputation but also the prestige of the members of the Central Bank Council. In the end an interest-rate war between the Bundesbank and the hard ECU bank would not be totally implausible with the effect of too high an interest rate level in Europe. Such negative implications of the hard ECU scheme could only be prevented if the statutes of the HEB prescribe a limit for the bank's losses. However this could prevent the HEB from exerting an effective disciplining influence on national central banks if they pursue a common inflationary monetary policy.

4.5 *Implications for Monetary Policy in the Transition Phase*

A succesful penetration of national currency areas by the hard ECU would also have negative implications for the national monetary management in the transition phase. The coexistence of the national currency and a common European currency would make it very difficult for national central banks to determine a non-inflationary money supply for their currencies. in the case of Germany, for instance, the Bundesbank would not know the amount of hard ECUs circulating in their currency area. Of course, there would be information available on the amount of DM which were exchanged in hard ECUs at the hard ECU bank. However, the public in Germany could also obtain hard ECUs against DM from private agents in other countries. According to the expectations of the adherents of the proposal, these hard ECUs could be used in the same way as the DM for domestic payments. Thus, with an increasing market velocity of money, which is a main determinant of the Bundesbank's monetary targets, would lose its significance. During the transition to a single currency these conceptual difficulties would create a serious void in the management of monetary policy in Europe. Although the British proposal intends to maintain the formal independence and responsibility of national central banks for their own national monetary policies, it would become more and more difficult to achieve this task in an efficient way. What would be required in this situation is coordinated management of Europe's money by the hard ECU bank and national central banks. Because of the indivisibility of monetary responsibilities this could be only realized under the aegis of an integrated European Central Bank System, where all responsibilities lie with a common decision-making body. Thus, even in the unlikely case of a success of the hard ECU, the coexistence of national currencies with the hard ECU would require at an early stage of the transition process an institutional set-up which has now be laid down in the draft statute of the Committee of Governors and which until know has been firmly rejected by the British government.

5. - Summary

The main institutional innovation of hard ECU proposal is its combination of a traditional banknote with a free option for its holders.

However, this subsidy is absolutely incompatible with the philosophy of institutional competition, which is propagated by the British government. But even with this specific definition, the hard ECU would not be able to out-compete established national currencies, especially those with low inflation rates. The only larger country where the national currency might be driven out of circulation is the United Kingdom. In the two other monetary functions, the hard ECU is one among other foreign currencies for national investors. In this field only a deliberate interest subvention by the hard ECU bank could provide the ECU a larger market share.

The macroeconomic role of the hard ECU bank is theoretically not very well founded. The only situation, where an additional nominal anchor for Europe's money might be useful, is a collective inflationary policy of all major central banks in Europe. However, this would require an explanation why the management of the hard ECU bank would behave entirely different from its colleagues in other central banks. In addition, a deliberate macroeconomic management of the hard ECU bank would lead to a serious distortion of the process of currency competition, which is incompatible with the political economy approach of the British government. Finally, even if the hard ECU were successful, the coexistence of national currencies with the hard ECU would require common management of the European money supply under the aegis of a European Central Bank system, which now has been firmly rejected by the British government.

The main arguments of this paper are not limited to the concrete British variant of a parallel currency approach. The central result that currency competition does not necessarily lead to a Pareto-efficient monetary order and that the coexistence of a national and a common currency will seriously complicate the task of national monetary policy is also of relevance for present proposals, which were developed by Soviet economists as a solution to the monetary problems of their economy (Kazmin and Tsimailo [7]).

BIBLIOGRAPHY

[1] BANK OF ENGLAND: *The hard ECU in Stage 2: Operational Requirements*, mimeo, 1990.

[2] — · — : «Statement Stable Princes Sees as Major Goal for EC Monetary Integration», *Financial Times*, June 21, 1990.

[3] BOFINGER PETER: *Wahrungswettbewerb*, Koln et Al, 1985.

[4] — · — : «The EMS and Monetary Policy Coordination in Europe», Tilburg SUERF, *Papers on Monetary Policy and Financial Systems*, n. 7, 1989.

[5] COMMISSION OF THE EUROPEAN COMMUNITIES: *One Market, One Money, European Economy*, n. 44, October 1990.

[6] JEVONS W.S.: *Money and the Mechanism of Exchange*, New York, 1898.

[7] KAZMIN ANDREI - TSIMAILO ANDREI: *Towards Ruble Convertibility: The Case for a Parallel Currency*, Washington, Paper presented at a Conference of the Istitute for International Economics, October 24, 1990.

[8] KLEIN BENJAMIN: «Competing Monies, European Monetary Union and the Dollar», in FRATIANI M. PEETERS T. (eds.): *One Money for Europe*, London and Basingstoke, 1978, p. 69-94.

[9] PEMBERTON-LEIGH: «The United Kingdom and Europe, Speech on the Occasion of The English-Speaking Union's Churchill Lecture», November 22, 1990, reprinted in KEUTSCHE BUNDESBANK: *Auszuge aus Presseartikeln*, n. 92, November 27, 1990.

[10] RUSSO MASSIMO: «Coordination and Coordination in the EMS: The System at a Crossroad», in DRAGER C. — SPATH LOTHAR (eds.): *Internationales Wahrungssystem und Weltwirtschaftliche Entwicklung*, Baden-Baden, 1988 p. 281-312.

[11] SHELLING THOMAS: *The Strategy of Conflict*, Cambridge, (Mass), 1960.

[12] SIEBERT HORST: *The Completion of the Internal Market*, Tubingen, 1989.

[13] STUTZEL WOLFGANG: *Eurofrank-Bank Als Europaische Rediskontbank*, mimeo, 1969.

[14] SUDGEN ROBERT: «Spontaneous Order», *Journal of Economic Perspectives*, vol. 3, n. 4, 1989, p. 85-97.

[15] VAUBEL ROLAND: *Strategies for Currency Competition*, Tubingen, 1978.

[16] — · — : «Currency Competition and European Monetary Integration», *The Economic Journal*, vol. 100, 1990, pp. 936-46.

Aspects of the British Debate on EMU (*)

John Williamson

Institute for International Economics, Washington

European monetary union is a much more controversial issue in Britain than elsewhere in the European Community. Two issues are of major concern: the greater difficulty of securing adjustment in response to real shocks in the absence of the ability to vary the exchange rate, and the loss of monetary sovereignty. Those who hold the latter concern (like Mrs Thatcher) tend to have an opposition that is visceral and impervious to economic reasoning. In contrast, to those of us who worry about loss of the exchange-rate instrument, the question is very much one of economics.

I have contributed to this debate in a pamphlet shortly to be published by Britain's Liberal Democrat Party (Williamson [10]). In the first section of this paper I outline the scope and content of that longer study, before taking up two issues that are of particular concern to those of us who believe that exchange-rate flexibility remains a useful instrument.

1. - An Overview

I start my paper for the Liberal Democrats by surveying the benefits and costs of EMU, very much on the lines of *One Market, One Money*

(*) Copyright 1990. Institute for International Economics, Washington, (DC) Reprinted by permission.

Advise: the numbers in square brackets refer to the Bibliography in appendix.

(European Commission [7]). I conclude that monetary union would offer some quite significant benefits but that, as already indicated (and as recognized in *One Market, One Money*), it carries with it one potentially important cost, loss of the ability to devalue in order to facilitate adjustment to a real shock. (I explicitly reject the view that this is of no consequence because it requires the presence, in some sense, of money illusion, since the form of money illusion required is merely that it be more difficult to achieve a cut in the real wage needed to reestablish macroeconomic equilibrium by reducing money wages than by devaluing.) How important that cost is depends on two things: on the ability to develop alternative mechanisms that can facilitate adjustment, and on the frequency with which nationally differentiated real shocks are likely to arise. As one might expect in a study being published by what is by far the most European-minded of Britain's political parties, I conclude that the goal of monetary union is worth pursuing; but also argue that caution is called for.

The next paragraph of the paper discusses the choice between irrevocably fixed exchange rates and a single money. I argue in favour of a single currency, on the ground that irrevocably fixed exchange rates carry all the costs of a single money but forego many of the benefits, both those concerned with eliminating transactions costs and those stemming from complete credibility. However, this makes a case for going the whole way once the conditions are right, not for jumping into monetary union without making sure it is safe.

My paper also touches on the benefits that the countries of Eastern Europe could gain from an early association with the EMS, essentially on the lines suggested by Peter Bofinger [1]. These benefits would come from the reinforcement of their liquidity resulting from EMS membership, and in the increased credibility of their macroeconomic policy commitments as a result of requiring EMS agreement for realignments. Mrs Thatcher may have tried to use the cause of the East Europeans as a way of banking the momentum toward monetary integration, but that is not a good reason for rebuffing the Eastern countries.

I go on to discuss the British proposals for a hard ECU as an alternative to the *Delors* proposals for a European System of Central Banks. I express scepticism about this proposal, even though the

British government went to considerable lengths to lay to rest the fears about the potential inflationary impact of a parallel currency that were aroused by its earlier version. I question whether a hard ECU has any particular virtues as a unit of account and, like Peter Bofinger in his paper for this volume, draw attention to the subsidy likely to be involved. Even with a subsidy, it is doubtful whether the hard ECU will in fact out-compete the existing currencies and thus lead to a single currency — which is, of course, the proposal's principal attraction to its sponsor, a Conservative government that does not want to end up with a single currency (but hesitates to say so directly for concern about Britain's relations with its partners).

One other topic discussed in my study but not spelled out at length here is the need for an ERM realignment. I argue, as did the paper of Jürgen Kröger for this volume, that German reunification and the resulting desire of Germany to run down its current account surplus in order to supply the real resources for the reconstruction of Eastern Germany has created an acute need for an appreciation of the DM. Note that this is precisely the sort of nationally differentiated real shock — and a massive one, equal to some 7% of GNP according to Kröger's estimate — that *One Market, One Money* argues to be best accommodated by an exchange-rate change, something that is explicitly still permitted during Stage one of the program for achieving EMU. I also argue that Britain made a mistake in entering the ERM at an exchange rate that significantly overvalued sterling, creating a need to realing the pound downwards. It would of course be crucial to accompany such a devaluation of the pound by a credible package of anti-inflation measures. An implication of the need to realign both the DM and the pound in real terms is that the French franc would need to be treated as the nominal anchor for the time being.

2. - The Vexed Question of Fiscal Coordination

The most controversial recommendation in the *Delors Report* was its call for each country's fiscal deficit to be subject to «binding limits». This proposal has been almost universally criticised in Britain, even by Liberal Democrats. Is the idea really without merit!

One possible danger of a monetary union is the scope that it will give to national governments to over-borrow. The Delors Committeee proposed that the ESCB should be prohibited from monetising government debt, and so far as I am aware no one has challenged this very prudent recommendation (1) But even if this is done investors might believe that the Community was underwriting the creditworthiness of each of the individual national governments, thus giving them an ability to over-borrow. It is often argued that one way of meeting that danger would be to make it transparently clear that there are no such guarantees, and allow national governments to be disciplined by the market. The Delors Committee (par. 30) anticipated this argument:

Rather than leading to a gradual adaptation of borrowing costs, market views about the creditworthiness of official borrowers tend to change abruptly and result in the closure of access to market financing. The constraints imposed by market forces might either be too slow and weak or too sudden and disruptive.

It is wildly unrealistic to suppose that countries that did run up a debt that they subsequently found it difficult to service could be allowed to go «bankrupt». The debt crisis has shown just how impossible it is to decide whether goverînents that are having difficulty servicing their debts are doing as much as they should be expected to do, thus entitling them to debt relief, or whether they are looking for default as an easy option. The alternative approach to resolving the problem advocated by the Delors Commitee, that of imposing limits on each government's borrowing rights, seems altogether more realistic.

Nor is this the only reason advanced by the *Delors Report* for arguing that fiscal coordination may be desirable within a monetary union. Views still differ sharply on the legitimacy of using fiscal policy to manage demand, from the Nigel Lawsons and Helmut Kohls and Ronald Reagans who make it a point of anti-Keynesian virility to deny any role to contra-cyclical considerations in determining budgetary policy, to old-fashioned Keynesians who still wish to use tax policy to

---

(1) The Delors formulation does not preclude the ESCB *holding* government debt, provided that it does not *increase* its holding of a particular government's debt in response to an increase in supply.

pursue an unemployment target. In between is a growing school who accept that fiscal policy cannot achieve «fine tuning» as was sought in the 1960s and also recognise that it is important to have any target formulated in nominal terms so as to place proper weight on the control of inflation, but who nonetheless regard it as desiderable to look to some help from fiscal policy in keeping the level of money demand increasing at a rate aimed at sustaining growth while gradually reducing inflation to near-zero. The Delors Committee seem to fall in this third camp, which is a very sensible place to be.

What they argue is that, without any conscious coordination at the Community level, there is no reason why the fiscal policies individually chosen by national governments need sum to a fiscal outcome that would make sense on this criterion at the Community level where the other half of demand-management policy — monetary policy — is going to be determined. The temptation would typically be for individual governments to plump for over-expansionary policies, and leave the ESCB to rein in demand by high interest rates, thus generating the same sort of lop-sided policy mix from which the United States has suffered for the last decade. But circumstances may also arise where it is desirable to have more expansionary overall policies in order to keep money demand growing fast enough to avoid a recession. To have any confidence of being able to put such polices into effect, we will again need some mechanism for influencing the fiscal policies of individual national governments. (Note that this problem is very different in existing federal governments, where the bulk of public spending is done by the central government, than it will be in Europe, where the intention is, following the principle of subsidiarity, to keep the vast bulk of spending out of the hands of Brussels.)

A third reason for fiscal coordination stems from the concern expressed earlier about inability to use exchange-rate changes to facilitate adjustment to real shocks. When Texas was hit by the 1986 oil price decline, the impact on Texan income was moderated by the reduction in tax payments and increases in federal expenditure directed to Texas. Indeed, it has been estimated that between 30 and 40% of the loss in income was offset in this way, which presumably helps explain why there was not even a murmur in Texas suggesting

that it would be desirable to establish a separate Texan currency so as
to be able to devalue. In contrast, a European country suffering a
comparable shock would today receive no more than about 1% of its
lost income through automatic fiscal transfers from Brussels, which is
not much of a compensation for loss of the exchange-rate instrument.
Jacques Delors [5], in a paper submitted to the committee he chaired,
noted that «... in all federations that might have written monetary
unions the different combinations of federal budgetary mechanism
have powerful 'shock-absorber' effects, dampening the amplitude
either of economic difficulties or of surges of prosperity in individual
states». Should we really tempt history by defying all precedents and
failing to incorporate any automatic redistributive mechanism into the
Community's institutions?

Hence there are three reasons which point strongly toward the
need for a measure of fiscal coordination or centralisation. This does
not necessarily require a wholesale transfer of responsibility for
taxation or expenditure from national capitals to Brussels, but some
trasfer is inescapable in order to create a redistributive mechanism.

One expenditure function that should certainly be transferred to
Brussels is payment of a minimum level of unemployment benefit, an
idea mentioned by David Begg and Charles Wyplosz as reported in
CEPR ([3], p. 23). If the payment were pitched at a level that would
provide reasonable support in the Community's poorest countries,
comparable to that already provided from national sources, it would
avoid adding to the disincentive to seek new jobs. The richer countries
would be free to supplement the minimum unemployment benefit by
additional national payments, but the Community would not reim-
burse those extra payments. Since the immediate manifestation of an
adverse shock that creates a need for adjustment is almost inevitably a
rise in unemployment, this mechanism would ensure an automatic
trasfer that would help to compensate countries or regions within
countries that suffer ill fortune (2).

How significant such a transfer would be! In 1987 Portuguese
wages were about 23% of British wages, so if the replacement ratio

---

(2) How the programme would be financed is not a key issue. The simplest
procedure would be to transfer an extra tranche of VAT revenue to Brussels.

was 50 per cent in Portugal it would be only some 12% in Britain. Perhaps 60% of a loss in income takes the form of lost wages in Britain, giving a total automatic transfer of some 7%. That is a big improvement over 1%, but still meagre compared to the level of transfers that glues the US monetary union together. Hence it might be wiser to tranfer the whole system of unemployment compensation to Brussels. The very least that should be contemplated is a uniform system of minimum unemployment benefits.

The first rationale for coordination demands not more expenditure from Brussels but rather the imposition of some limit on how much a national government can borrow. That limit should, however, relate to the stock of debt rather than to the annual deficit (as contemplated by the Delors Committee), a conclusion that Daniel Cohen also argues in his paper for this volume. The limit should be pitched at a level where it would ordinarily not be binding, perhaps somewhere around a 60% ratio of national debt to GDP. A country like Italy that currently has a higher debt/GNP ratio should obviously be allowed a path that would permit it to adjust gradually and non-disruptively. But the Community will do Italy a great service if it pressures the country to eliminate its budget deficit promptly, before the crisis hits, rather than allow it to continue following the path of least political resistance until it is too late. Indeed, many Italians are strongly in favour of EMU and an associated Community role in determining fiscal policy percisely with the hope of creating a mechanism that will induce their political system to act responsibly before a major crisis erupts.

The appropriate response to the second reason for coordination is different again. In this case in is not the stock of debt that needs to be controlled by limits that ought to be binding (on the rare occasions that a country needs to be bound), but rather the *sum* of the deficits of all members of the Community that ought to be influenced in a way that will serve the collective interest. This requires an ability to persuade member countries to take into account the Community's overall position when formulating their target budget deficit or surplus. The country's individual position is also highly relevant in this context, since one of the responses that one would expect and hope to see when an adverse shock hits is a larger budget deficit; the need for a flexible fiscal response to shocks is actually enhanced by monetary union, since the option of a stabilising monetary (and hence exchange-rate) response is lost (Goodhart [9]). Binding limits on budget deficits, which almost inevitably have to be uniform across countries and which by definition cannot be used to ecourage more expansionary policies when the need arises, are not the answer to this problem (as the European Commission [7] has recently recognised in *One Market, One Money)*.

For all their weaknesses, mutual discussion and moral suasion are altogether more suitable. If they are judged insufficiently forceful, one might explore the possibility of constructing a formula for the «appropriate» budget deficit, and then penalise countries that overshoot their target, perhaps by payment of an additional percentage of their value-added tax revenue to Brussels. (In the abnormal case where the Community was aiming to encourage more expansionary fiscal policies, one would penalise countries that undershoot the norm).

Hence I conclude, contrary to the thrust of Daniel Cohen's paper for this volume, that EMU will create a very real need for Community coordination of fiscal policy, in several dimensions. Without a fiscal dimension, particularly to create automatic fiscal transfers to help offset real shocks, a monetary union would be a distinct gamble. However, none of the initiatives that seem called for — a system of unemployment benefits financed from the EC budget, binding limits on national debt relative to GNP, and mutual agreement on targets for budget deficits — take the particular form called for in the *Delors Report*, which was a binding upper limit on each country's budget deficit (par. 33).

3. - The Question of Phasing

Ever since EMU was first mooted in the late 1960s, it has been envisaged that progress toward monetary union would be in phases. The *Werner Report* of 1970, the plans for the EMS drawn up in 1978, and the *Delors Report* in 1989, all proposed three stages. So far Europe has never got beyond Stage one, but this time intentions seem altogether more serious.

Stage one of the *Delors Report* encompassed an abolition of all capital controls, entry of all EC members into the ERM, and strengthened coordination. This stage started on 1 July 1990, and the more concrete conditions have already been met except for Spain, Greece and Portugal. The principal characteristic of Stage two was envisaged as the founding and working in of the ESCB. It is now proposed that this will start at the beginning of 1994. Stage three would be inaugurated by the irrevocable locking of exchange rates, and it is generally assumed that this will be followed in due course by the replacement of the national moneys by a single European currency. No dates have yet been set for Stage three.

Some British critics of the Delors Committee who endorse its objective of monetary union (e.g. Goodhart [8]) have argued that it would be better to jump from Stage one to Stage three, omitting Stage two. The logic is a variant of that used above to argue for a single currency rather than an «irrevocable» locking of exchange rates: namely, as long as the possibility of exchange-rate changes exists, the promise of fixed rates will lack full credibility and hence the system will not get a fair trial.

That is true, but there is nonetheless an important counterargument. While it is probable that Europe will succeed in making inflation rates converge, and ultimately in reconciling convergent inflation rates with equilibrium levels of competitiveness, it is much less certain that it will be able to cope without using exchange-rate changes to adjust to real shocks. The usual adjustment mechanism (labour mobility) is extremely weak. The usual transfer mechanism (through the fiscal system) is virtually absent, and even if it is strengthened as urged in paragraph 2 — and *a fortiori* if it is not — prudence demands a lengthy trial period before exchange rates are locked. Nothing could be worse for the future of EMU than a premature locking of exchange rates which confronted the Community with a choice between unscrambling what were supposed to be irrevocably locked exchange rates and imposing indefinite depression on an important region. One must be sure this is not going to happen before proclaiming exchange rates to be irrevocably locked.

A second factor that argues for caution in moving to full monetary union is the continuing fiscal disarry in some members of the

Community, as documented in *One Market, One Money* (European Commission [7], p. 109). Italy is the most important case in point, but the situation is even worse in Portugal and especially in Greece. These countries have high ratios of debt to Gnp and large fiscal deficits thatare causing the debt/GNP ratios to increase further. This is a situation that has traditionally ended with the Central Bank being called on to monetise the debt and inflate away the debt burden. If that escape route is blocked by monetary union, then either the ESCB will have to bail out the over-indebted governments or the latter will be driven into a financial crisis. The former has rightly been ruled out, but it seems most imprudent to risk forcing Community governments into bankruptcy-type crises early in EMU's history. To avoid this danger, one needs to delay monetary union until all member countries have brought their fiscal deficits under control and are at least within sight of the specified maximum debt/GNP ratio that was suggested earlier.

The Commission itself has been having second thooughts about the *Delors Report's* timetable. In *One market, One Money*, it reports (European Commission [7], p. 40): «The *Delors Report* placed emphasis on the gradual transfer in Stage two of responsibility for monetary policy. After discussion, the emphasis has since been placed more on the technical preparation of the Eurofed institution [the ESCB] in Stage two, on the grounds that policy responsibility must be clear-cut. For this reason it is now widely considered that Stage two should be quite short».

That seems persuasive. However, on present plans a short Stage two that starts in January 1994 cannot be reconciled with a prudent caution in delaying the commitment to irrevocably fixed exchange rates until it can safely be made. The «convergence tests» that prudence suggests need to be satisfied are budget deficits firmly under control, low inflation rates, and exchange rates that are close to equilibrium in real terms. Europe is not there yet, and clearly not all countries will be there by the mid-1990s. Something must give.

It already seems to be generally accepted that Stage three will be broken down into two stages, with the second sub-stage being marked by introduction of the single currency. One way of squaring the circle would be to replace the «irrevocable fixing» of exchange rates by the «fixing» of exchange rates. Stage one (and the short Stage two) would provide the breathing space that is needed to achieve fiscal discipline, convergence of inflation rates and properly aligned currencies, after which an experiment in the feasibility of managing without parity changes would start. The fact that parity changes were not absolutely forbidden would mean that the credibility benefits of union would not accrue, which would actually make such a dry run an over-strong test of the feasibility of dispensing with the exchange-rate weapon — but given what is at stake that has some merit. Assuming that the experiment was succesful and the system got through 5 or 10 years without a parity change or any sentiment that countries were paying an excecsive price for avoiding such a change, the national currencies would be called in and replaced by the ECU.

Should all the currencies of EC members participate from the start in the locking of exchange rates and replacement of their national currencies by the ECU, or should one contemplate the possibility of a multi-speed EMU? The answer is surely that a single-speed EMU is much to be preferred but may not prove feasible. It is inconceivable that the whole of Europe will allow further progress toward monetary union to be held hostage until Greece manages to sort out its public finances. And it would be irresponsible to exclude the Eastern European countries from the Community, or the EMS, because they found it impossible to achieve inflation convergence with Western Europe in a fraction of the time that Western Europe has taken. Hence one must recognise the probability that not all EC members will be in a position to make the commitment to exchange-rate fixity at the same time.

Calls are already being made for a hard core of countries that have succeeded in achieving convergence to go ahead without waiting for the rest (Brittan [2], Dornbusch [6]). Most British opinion is very reluctant to see Britain assigned to a slow track, in part because of fears as to what this might do for the City's position as the major financial market in Europe. Such an outcome will presumably be inevitable if the Conservative government continues to drag its feet despite the replacement of Margaret Thatcher: in that event the rest of the Community will have little option but to go ahead without Britain, which will doubtless repeat its customary performance of coming along with its tail between its legs a few years later. But if Britain should adopt a more positive attitude, one hopes that other coutries will be willing to show some flexibility on the question of timing. Indeed, it would be very silly for even the hard core of the ERM to rush into an irrevocable locking of exchange rates at this moment, just when there is an acute need for a realignment of the DM to cope with the biggest nationally differentiated real shock experienced in many years. (If I thought that shocks of that magnitude were likely to come along more than one every half-century or so, I would find it difficult to support EMU).

Monetary union is a goal worth pursuing. But it should not be attempted until convergence has been achieved in fiscal performance, inflation and competitiveness, and untile a redistributive fiscal mechanism that can proved an alternative to devaluation has been put in place, or, failing that, until experience has demonstrated the ability to cope without the exchange-rate weapon. When the time comes, the move should be complete and irrevocable, into a single money rather than irrevocably fixed exchange rates. But the desirability of making a big leap when it is safe to do so does not excuse one from the duty to look first to see if it is safe to leap.

BIBLIOGRAPHY

[1] BOFINGER PETER: «The Role of Monetary Policy in the Process of Economic Reform in Eastern Europe», CEPR, *Discussion Paper*, n. 457, 1990.

[2] BRITTAN SAMUEL: *Europe Without Currency Barriers - An Update*, Social Market Foundation, 1990.

[3] CEPR: *The EMSA in Transition*, London, Centre for Economic Policy Research, 1989.

[4] COMMITTEE FOR THE STUDY OF ECONOMIC AND MONETARY UNION: *Report on Economic and Monetary Union in the European Community (Delors Report)*, Luxembourg, European Communities, 1989.

[5] DELORS JACQUES: «Regional Implications of Economic and Monetary Integration», appendix to the *Delors Report*, 1989.

[6] DORNBUSCH RUDIGER: «Two-Track EMU, Now» in *Britain and EMU*, LSE, 1990.

[7] EUROPEAN COMMISSION: «One Market, One Money» *European Economy*, n. 44, October 1990.

[8] GOODHART CHARLES: «The Delors Report: Was Lawson's Reaction Justifiable!», LSE, Financial Markets Group, *Special Paper*, n. 15, 1989.

[9] — - — : «Fiscal Policy and EMU», *Britain and EMU*, LSE, 1990.

[10] WILLIAMSON JOHN: Britain's Role in EMU, Open Forum Series, West Yorkshire, Hebden Royd Publications, 1991.

The Fluctuations of the Mark/Dollar Exchange Rate and their Impact on European Rates: The Case of the Lira and the French Franc (*)

Massimo Tivegna
Università «Tor Vergata», Roma

1. - Introduction

The international role of the US dollar, the huge amount of financial assets denominated in this currency, its important role in the invoicing practice of international trade have all been considered to be a limiting factor for the establishment of a homogenous area of exchange rate stability in Europe.

To the "convulsions" of the free-floating US currency have been attributed a potentially distruptive role for the stabilization of the bilateral European exchange rates and for their joint float versus the dollar. The basic reasons are represented by the different "structural" inflation rates of the original — and today's — members of the EMS and by the different reactions of growth and inflation to an external shock (like the two oil shocks of 1974-1975 and of 1980-1981).

Following the old adage "when the US sneezes the rest of the world catches pneumonia", most market comments seem to consider — even today — the European exchange rate events and realignments as local consequences of dollar episodes, which keep a central role. The results of this paper and of other analyses on the same topic (e.g.

(*) The research was partially financed by a grant from the Ministry for the University and Scientific Research administered by the University of Perugia.
Advise: the numbers in square brackets refer to the Bibliography in the appendix.

Giavazzi - Giovannini [20], especially chapters 3 and 6) show, quite the contrary, that the EMS has important insulation properties for the intra-European rates — which have gained further strength in recent times — and that it is infact the effective dollar rate to fluctuate sharply around EMS realignments.

All this is particularly relevant for short-term fluctuations. It is to be noted also that a monetary and exchange rate discipline could take shape in Europe in the eighties, in a period when the dollar rose by 96.2% from its lower quotation before the maximum in February 1985 and then fell again from there by 52.5% to its lower value towards the end of the decade.

In this paper we will make some estimates of the conditional variance of the DM/$ exchange rate as a measure of volatility of this rate and we will compare it with measures of volatility of two key European rates, between the Italian lira (Lit) and the DM and between the French franc and the DM. These two rates are quite central in the history of the EMS as belonging to original member countries of the EEC and as being two rates generally more deviant with respect to the DM (see also Giovannini [21].

The conditional variance of the DM/$ exchange rate will be derived in paragraph 2 from the error structure of a monthly, monetary specification exchange rate equation with an ARCH error structure estimated on monthly data in maximum likelihood between 1974 and 1988 (Daddi-Tivegna [8]). To the variables appearing on the right-hand side of this equation will be attributed the role of "fundamentals", whereas volatility will be estimated by the time-varying standard error of residuals generated by the ARCH (AutoRegressive Conditional Heteroskedastic) error structure. The behaviour of this volatility will be examined (paragraph 3) in close reference to the market events summarized chronologically in the Appendix drawn from various market commentaries (1). Paragraph 4 will contain a

---

(1) The economic and econometric literature in the background of this paper is well represented, among acedemic economists, by BAILLIE-McMAHON [1], MACDONALD [27], MACDONALD-TAYLOR [28], and among the professional economist working in financial institutions by DUNIS-FEENY [12]. As we shall see later, this paper makes also an extensive reference to the best commentaries on the foreign exchange markets produced by research institutions (e.g. Wharton E.F.A., London Business School, Prometeia), by financial entities (e.g. Goldman-Sachs, Morgan-Stanley, Merril-Lynch) and by economic and financial dailies and periodicals.

brief summary of some results on the relationship between the dollar and the European currencies and some other empirical evidences. Some conclusions will be proposed in Paragraph 5.

2. - Fundamentals and Volatility in an Exchange Rate Equation

The literature, on the determination of exchange rates which mostly dates from the beginning of the seventies, when the fixed exchange rate system displayed the first signs of crisis, can be classified in three basic schools (Kenen [26], Frenkel and Mussa [18], Macdonald [27]: *a)* approaches based on balance of payments flows, derived from the Mundell-Fleming model; *b)* monetary approaches with fixed prices or flexible prices; *c)* portfolio approaches.

In approach *a)* the exchange rate is determined by the equilibrium of the flows which constitute the overall balance of payments result and is therefore linked to the economic variables which influence imports, exports and capital movements, i.e. the relative levels of economic activity, relative inflation rates and interest rate differentials (on this point see Kenen [26]; Macdonald [27], Chap. 3). The monetary approach to exchange rate determination is based on monetarist theories of inflation whereby, for a constant velocity of money, price changes are determined in the short term (in the flexible price model, Frenkel [17], Bilson [3]) or in the long term (in the rigid price model, Dornbusch [11], Frankel [15], [16]) by changes in the monetary aggregates. By equalizing the processes which generate inflation in the two countries linked by the exchange rate, assuming PPP (Purchasing Power Parity), we obtain this latter variable as a function of the relative values of money, economic activity, expected inflation and — depending on the price formation hypothesis — of the interest rate differential (2). In the portfolio approach — which we

---

(2) Flexible price monetary models have been estimated principally by BILSON [3], and rigid price models mainly by FRANKEL [15], [16]. Comparative results of estimates of these specifications and of others nested into them are to be found in BAILLIE-MCMAHON [1], Chapter 8, BOUGHTON [4], MACDONALD [27], Chap. 9, MEESE-ROGOFF [29], SOMANATH [33].

mention only briefly here — the exchange rate is determined by the supply of and demand for domestic and international saving instruments combined according to interest rate differentials in the portfolio of investors in the two countries linked by exchange rates (Branson [7], Frankel [16]).

We thus see that the "fundamentals" in the determination of exchange rates vary, to some extent, in the three different approaches outlined above. Volatility can be considered to be captured by the error term of an econometric equation. In the estimation techniques used in this paper we will allow for the time variability of volatility — as commonly observed in foreign exchange markets — assuming heteroskedasticity in the error term, which will be modelled through ARCH techniques (to be briefly examined later). We will make reference to the monetary approach with sticky prices as outlined in the work of Frankel [15], [16] according to the following specification (3):

$$(1) \quad s(t) = b_0 + b_1 \cdot dum \cdot m(t) + b_2 \cdot (1 - dum) \cdot dom(t) +$$

$$+ b_3 \cdot dum \cdot dom(t) + b_4 \cdot (1 - dum) \cdot p(t) +$$

$$+ b_5 \cdot dum \cdot p(t) + b_6 \cdot (1 - dum) \cdot es(t) +$$

$$+ b_7 \cdot dum \cdot es(t) + e(t)$$

The variables appearing in this equation (reported in Table 1 under OLS and Maximum Likelihood Estimation with ARCH error structure) are:

s = logarithm of the average nominal mark-dollar exchange rate;

m = logarithm of the ratio between the German and American seasonally adjusted stock of money;

dom = logarithm of the ratio between the German and American deseasonalized indexes of industrial production;

---

(3) For an analytical derivation of this specification see also DADDI-TIVEGNA [8], par. 2.2.

p = logarithm of the ratio between the German and American rate of inflation;

es = logarithm of the expected exchange rate according to the uncovered interest rate parity formula;

dum = dichotomic variable which is equal to zero from January 1974 to September 1979 and to one from October 1979 to August 1988.

These are the reasons for dichotomization: the estimation of this equation gives two fairly separate systems of exchange rate determination which are partly ascribable to the difference in financial market integration in the seventies and eighties and partly to the introduction of the European Monetary System and to the new monetary policy launched by the US Federal Reserve in October 1979 (see Appendix).

The first and most important variable requiring dichotomization is that relating to the demand differential, which is approximated here by the industrial production differential between Germany and the United States: this variable changes sign in the two estimation periods (Table 1). This would suggest that in the first sub-period the monetary specification is not satisfactory, probably because trade flows continue to have a greater effect on the exchange rate owing to the smaller degree of financial market integration. It should be noted that in all the equations estimated in dichotomic form the absolute value of this variable's coefficient is consistently higher in the period when it captures the effect of trade flows than when it represents economic activity in the demand for money (hence the negative coefficient, Table 1).

The inflation differential enters in the equation very significantly and is also dichotomized (Table 1) thus showing a coefficient that is more than twice as high in the seventies as in the eighties. This aspect is consistent with the earlier hypothesis that in the first sub-period the exchange rate is affected more by the economic activity and relative price variables, representing the price of two goods, while in the second sub-period it is more responsive to financial variables owing to the changed economic and institutional context, thus becoming the price of two monies.

We turn at last to the expected exchange rate, which has by far the most predominant coefficient and significance. Most of this variable consists of the previous period's exchange rate (the rest being the interest rate differential). When it is dichotomized, this variable has a much higher coefficient in the eighties than in the seventies, a fact which is due, as we mentioned earlier, to the greater importance of financial variables during the period.

Let's now turn to the error term in equation *(1)*. In recent years the closer international integration of financial markets and the speed with which information on their performance is divulged have had major repercussions on the daily, weekly and monthly behaviour of exchange rates. This fact has caused the statistical properties of exchange rate series to converge to those of the prices of financial assets in general. One of these seems especially important: the

TABLE 1

OLS ESTIMATES AND STATISTICAL TESTS ON THE RESIDUALS OF EQUATION *(1)* (*)

$$s_t = b_0 + b_1 dum \cdot m_t + b_2 (1 - dum) \cdot dom_t + b_3 dum \cdot dom_t + b_4 (1 - dum) \cdot p_t + b_5 dum \cdot p_t + b_6 (1 - dum) \cdot es_t + b_7 dum \cdot es_t + e_t.$$

b_0	0.212	(5.05)	b_4	3.04	(2.94)	
b_1	0.283	(5.08)	b_5	1.47	(2.01)	
b_2	0.336	(2.64)	$b6$	0.762	(16.0)	
b_3	-0.276	(-3.23)	b_7	0.958	(46.7)	
R^2	0.965		Arch$_1$:	χ_1^2	6.71	(0.010)
σ	0.0323			$F_{1;166}$	6.62	(0.011)
$F_{12;156}$	1.14	(0.325)	Arch$_2$:	χ_2^2	7.25	(0.027)
Q_{12}	14.0	(0.301)		$F_{2;164}$	3.56	(0.030)
Q_{12}^2	15.2	(0.231)	Arch$_3$:	χ_3^2	9.09	(0.028)
b'_1	-0.011	(0.525)		$F_{3;162}$	3.00	(0.032)
b'_2	3.52	(0.079)	Arch$_4$:	χ_4^2	9.25	(0.055)
$T_{\lambda=0.6}$	0.028	(0.041)		$F_{4;160}$	2.27	(0.063)
D	6.65	(7.23)	Arch$_8$:	χ_8^2	11.4	(0.178)
$Ks1$	0.003	(0.954)		$F_{8;152}$	1.39	(0.206)
$Ks2$	1.72	(0.189)	Arch$_{12}$:	χ_{12}^2	12.8	(0.385)
Ks	1.73	(0.421)		$F_{12;144}$	1.01	(0.439)

(*) The t test is in brackets next to the estimates of the regression parameters. For Seigel's T test and Kolmogorov-Smirnov D test the figures in brackets indicate the critical term of the respective distribution under the null hypothesis at the 5% probability level. The other bracketed statistics refer to the likelihood of error of the corresponding statistics. The b'_1 asymmetry test and subsequent tests are calculated on standardized residuals.

TABLE 1 *continued*

MLE/ARCH ESTIMATES AND STATISTICAL TESTS
ON THE RESIDUALS OF EQUATION *(1)* (*)

$$s_t = b_0 + b_1 dum \cdot m_t + b_2 (1 - dum) \cdot dom_t + b_3 dum \cdot dom_t + b_4 (1 - dum)$$
$$\cdot\, p_t + b_5 dum \cdot p_t + b_6 (1 - dum) \cdot es_t + b_7 dum \cdot es_t + e_t.$$
$$h_t = \alpha_0 + \alpha_1 \varepsilon_{t-1}^2$$

b_0	0.195	(4.52)
b_1	0.264	(4.74)
b_2	0.251	(1.45)
b_3	−0.272	(−3.14)
b_4	2.86	(2.37)
b_5	1.30	(1.76)
b_6	0.782	(15.4)
b_7	0.963	(52.7)
α_0	0.00078	(6.71)
α_1	0.178	(1.29)
$1/\upsilon$	0.056	(33.6)
$Log1$	353.1	
Q_{12}	11.5	(0.487)
Q_{12}^2	7.17	(0.846)
ϑ_1	−0.07	(0.661)
ϑ_2	3.82	(0.013)
$T_{\lambda=6}$	0.018	(0.041)
D	6.12	(7.23)
$Ks1$	0.247	(0.619)
$Ks2$	6.49	(0.011)
Ks	6.73	(0.034)

(*) The *t* test is in brackets next to the estimates of the regression parameters. For Seigel's *T* test and Kolmogorov-Smirnov, *D* test the figures in brackets indicate the critical term of the respective distribution under the null hypothesis at the 5% probability level. The other bracketed statistics refer to the likelihood of error of the corresponding statistics. The tests on residuals are calculated on conditional variance standardized residuals, *h* (*t*).

extreme volatility and its variability in time, which can be defined more formally as heteroskedasticity of the variance of exchange rate series. These phenomena appear to become more marked in certain periods, in conjunction with sudden or unexpected changes in the variables which economic theory says should influnece exchange rates, or with persistent violations of the relations supposedly linking the two (Tivegna [34]).

In this paper we have therefore used maximum likelihood estimation methods of structural-type linear models, borrowed from

economic theory (the monetary approach with sticky prices to exchange rate determination), with heteroskedastic error variance
(Autoregressive Conditional Heteroskedastic, ARCH). These methods
can effectively combine in a single context the study of structural
relations between economic variables and the study of variability (or
volatility).

The ARCH processes were originally proposed by Engle [13] and
have been used extensively in the economic and finance literature (see
Bollerslev and others [6] for a comprehensive survey). The ARCH
scheme can be attributed to the error structure of equation *(1)* and
represented in the following way:

(2) $$\varepsilon_t | \varepsilon_{t-1}, \varepsilon_{t-2}, \ldots, \varepsilon_{t-p} \sim N(O, \sigma_t^2)$$

(3) $$\sigma_t^2 = \alpha_o + \sum_{i=1}^{p} \alpha_i \varepsilon_{t-i}^2$$

with $\alpha_o > 0$, $\alpha_i \geqslant 0$ and $i = 1,2,3, \ldots, p$ and estimated by
maximizing the following likelihood function

(4) $$\ln L(b_i, \alpha_i, S, m, dom, dum, p, es) =$$

$$= CONST - \sum_{t=1}^{T} \ln \sigma_t - \frac{1}{2} \sum_{t=1}^{T} \frac{\varepsilon_t^2}{\sigma_t^2}$$

where the b_i represent the parameters of model *(1)* containing the
structural variables affecting the exchange rate (*m, dom, dum, p, es*,
defined above) entering in the model through the squared error terms,
$e^2(t)$, the α_i are the parameters of the ARCH process *(3)* — used to
model volatility — and T is sample size.

Model *(1)* was estimated by OLS (without any correction for the
ARCH structure of the errors) and in maximum likelihood through
(4). The results are reported in Table 1 together with some dynamic
specification tests. For a thorough discussion of both estimates and
tests with references see Daddi-Tivegna [8].

3. - Fluctiations of the Mark/dollar French Franc/Mark and Lira/Mark Exchange Rates: 1978-1989

In this paragraph a brief history of the fluctuations of the DM/$, Lit/DM and FrF/DM exchange rates will be carried out to investigate heuristically — but with respect to the volatility estimates stemming from the ARCH mechanism *(3)* of equation *(1)* in the previous section (4) — the relations between volatility, market events and market sentiment or expectations. A specific aim of this paragraph is to examine the possibile causes of fluctuations in the international value of the DM, here represented by the DM/$ rate, and of two of its key European parities, those vis à vis the Italian lira and the French franc. As we pointed out in the introduction, these two rates are quite central in the ERM (European exchange Rate Mechanism) as "founding members" and as frequently deviant with respect to the DM.

We will comment in the following pages on seventeen episodes of abnormal fluctuations in the currencies here considered; these episodes generally refer to the DM/$ but also to the Lit/DM and FrF/DM after the start of the EMS in March 79. As we shall see the European fluctuations of the DM play an important role both within and outside Europe. These episodes refer to the following periods:

October 1978	— January	1979
September	— December	1979
March	— June	1980
February	— November	1981
April	— July	1982
November 1982	— April	1983
January	— March	1984
July	— October	1984
February	— April	1985
July	— October	1985
March	— August	1986

---

(4) In this paper we will model the conditional variance only of the DM/$ rate. The volatility of the Lit/DM and FrF/DM rates will be estimated by means of a moving variance of monthly observation over a three-month period. This indicator catches the major volatility peaks fairly well. See DADDI-TIVEGNA [8], Graph 4.

January	— February	1987
October 1987	— February	1988
June	— August	1988
November	— December	1988
July	— August	1989
October	— December	1989

In the following description we will make reference to Graphs 1-3 and to the Appendix which contains a more detailed account of events occurred in the years 1978-1989 in the world foreign exchange markets.

October 1978 - January 1979

This is the period where the highest volatility peaks of exchange rates are recorded both for the DM/$ rate and for the Lit/DM and FrF/DM (Graphs 1-3). These peaks occur at the end of a long period of devaluation of the dollar (initiated in November 1975 with temporary breaks) as the monetary authorities seek to halt the slide through an increase of the interest rate differentials in favour of the US unit. In November the discount rate is increased in the US by one percentage point to its historical maximum; a squeeze on bank liquidity is also imposed by the Fed (see Appendix). The dollar reacts with a surge in November after the strong depreciation in October. These gyrations of the US currency, at a time when interest rate differentials move sharply in its favour, cause strong volatility increases in November and December, till January, to the three currencies here examined (Graphs 1-3, upper panels).

September - December 1979

Important policy measures are announced in October by the Fed in the US on the techniques of money management with a targetting of bank free reserves instead of the Federal Funds rate (Appendix).

GRAPH 1

MARK/DOLLAR VOLATILITY

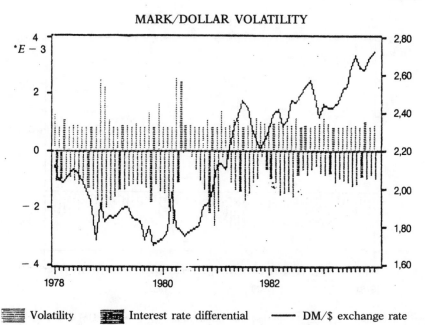

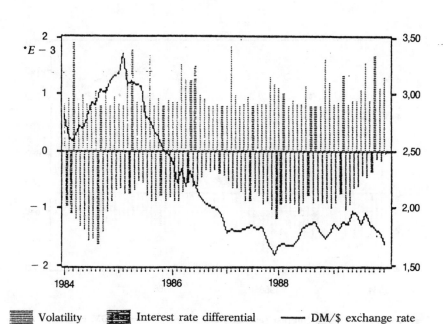

GRAPH 2

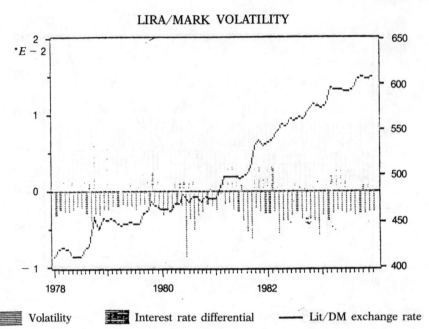

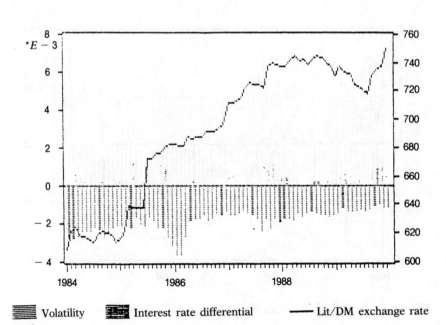

GRAPH 3

FRENCH FRANC/MARK VOLATILITY

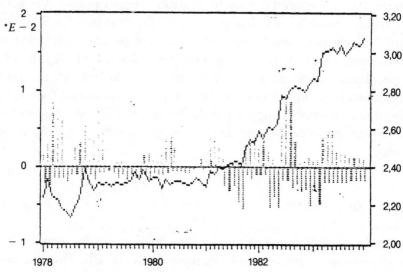

▤ Volatility   ▨ Interest rate differential   —— FrF/DM exchange rate

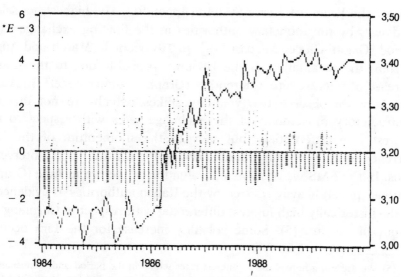

▤ Volatility   ▨ Interest rate differential   —— FrF/DM exchange rate

The dollar, after a weakening in August-September goes up in October then falls again in November even though interest rate differentials with the DM had moved favourably (Graph 1, upper panel). A possible explanation could lie in the occurrence of the first two EMS realignments in September and November, which are generally preceded by a weakening of the dollar (see also Giavazzi-Giovannini [20], p. 137) as speculative funds move out of dollars and into DM. These events cause an increase in volatility of the dollar in October and then again in December (Graph 1, upper panel). Some volatility increase occurs also in Europe over the two realignments (Graphs 2 and 3, upper panels).

March - June 1980

The new techniques of money management by the Fed imply a strong increase of interest rate fluctuations in the US. This phenomenon appears evident right from the beginning of 1980, continuing for the rest of the year and into 1981. In March 1980 an important anti-inflation package is announced in the US and an increase in compulsory reserves in imposed upon the US banks, both inside and outside the Federal Reserve System (Appendix). The highest net sales of dollars by the monetary authorities in the floating exchange rate period (Gaiotti-Giucca-Micossi [19], p. 19) occur in March and April to stem the revaluation of the US unit, probably due to the sharp increase of interest rate differentials (Graph 1, upper panel). In April and May we observe two volatility spikes, which are not due to contradictory movements of the exchange rates with respect to its interest rate differentials, but only to the momentum of the US currency in the preceding months and to the central banks' interventions. In the EMS we observe a devaluation of the lira in June (Graph 2, upper panel) heavily resisted by the Italian authorities as evidenced by the historically high interest differential with respect to Germany in favour of the lira (5). Some volatility increase for the Lira occurs

---

(5) We are using here Eurolira interest rates which in the period under consideration might have reflected the expectations of the markets on the lira more than the attitudes of the Italian monetary authorities.

around this episode (Graph 2, upper panel) and also the French franc shows some increase in volatility amid a context of substantial interest rate and exchange rate stability (Graph 3, upper panel).

February - November 1981

There are two realignments in 1981, in March and October; the volatility of domestic US interest rates, following the new techniques of money management of the Fed from October 1979, keeps on being rather high. In January and February 1981 the dollar gets stronger even though the interest rate differentials with Germany diminishes for the US. In March President Reagan survives a murder attempt and there is the first realignment of 1981: both events seem to contribute to weaken the dollar, notwithstanding the more favourable US interest rate differentials and the interventions in the foreign exchange markets by the Fed to support the US currency (Appendix). There are volatility peaks for all the three currencies examined between February and May; another set of volatility peaks occur also in the fall, following the second EMS realignment of the year on October 5th (Graphs 1-3, upper panels).

April - July 1982

Another two EMS realignments occur in 1982, in February and June. The one in February does not produce any visible consequence in the volatility of the exchange rates here examined. In May the dollar gets stronger even though the interest rate differentials with the DM move unfavourably; in July there is an important bank crisis in the US (collapse of Penn Square, see Appendix) which causes an injection of liquidity in the US banking system, as a precautionary measure by the Fed. There are two important peaks of volatility in the DM/$ rate in June and July, around the EMS realignment (Graph 1, upper panel); the Lit/DM volatility is normal (Graph 2, upper panel) whereas the FrF/DM volatility abnormally high and interest rate differentials between the DM and the French franc increase sharply before the realignment Graph 3, upper panel).

November 1982 - April 1983

In the central part of 1982, till October, the dollar revalues continuously even though interest rate differentials in its favour become smaller and smaller (Graph 1, upper panel). The markets explain this episode as due to "flight to quality" for the uncertain climate of international investment (Appendix). At the end of the year the interest rate twist against the dollar obtains the expected result and the US currency weakens also because of shifting expectations (Appendix) which are not confirmed by interest rate differentials, so there is a substantial volatility peak in January for the DM/$ (Graph 1, upper panel). In March 1983 another EMS realignment occurs which does not seem to produce any reaction on the DM/$ (Graph 1), whereas both the European currencies show a peak of volatility and a rather sizable devaluation (Graphs 2 and 3, upper pannels).

January - March 1984

No realignments in 1984 as the two European currencies obtained substantial nominal adjustments from the five parity changes of 1981, 1982 and 1983 (+ 26.4% for the Lit/DM and + 26.3% for the FrF/DM). This is the year of the strong revaluation of the US currency which can't be explained by standard international economics theory (the "speculative bubble" theory is thus proposed). There is a peak in the DM/$ volatility after a series of contradictory movements of the exchange rate and the interest rate fundamentals between December 1983 and March 1984 (Graph 1, lower panel). The spike of the DM/$ rate in January 1984 has probably a psychological motivation after the political and military events of November-December 1983 (Appendix). The fall in February is also abnormal given the increase of US interest rates. All these events produce the volatility peak in March 1984

(Graph 1, lower panel) as the European currencies remain quiet (Graph 2 and 3, lower panel).

July - October 1984

The dollar seems to fly on a "speculative bubble" in this period. The crisis of continental Illinois is considered to be handled quite succesfully (this is the perception of market participants) between June and July (Appendix); the resulting increase of bank liquidity in the US causes a slight temporary reduction to US interest rates but not an arrest of the dollar in the period (Graph 1, lower panel). In July it is annuounced that US real fixed investment has increased by 20% in the previous quarter on a yearly basis (see Appendix also for other events bullish for the dollar). The temporary stop of the US unit in August is attributed by the markets to fears of another bank crisis in the US (Appendix). In September-October there are large and well publicized net sales of dollars by the Bundesbank with large daily swings of the dollar (Appendix); which remains on an irresistible upward trend (Graph 1, lower panel).

February - April 1985

We observe high values of DM/$ volatility in March and April, after the historical maximum of this exchange rate in February (Graph 1, lower panel). Substantial interventions by the monetary authorities (Gaiotti-Giucca-Micossi [19], p. 19) weaken the dollar in March as interest rate differentials remain substantially stable and this gives rise to the volatility peak in April (Graph 1, lower panel).

July - October 1985

There is an EMS realignment in July which produces some modest volatility peaks of the two European currencies and an

increase of the interest rate differentials in favour of the two depreciating currencies vis à vis the DM (Graphs 2 and 3, lower panels).
In the same month the US monetary authorities announce a rebasing
of $M1$ targets over a more expansionary period (Appendix): which is
interpreted by the markets as an indication of aquiescence to the new
downward trend of the dollar: as a result of the realignment and of
this perceived attitude of the US policy makers the value of one dollar
loses three pfennigs in the month, even though interest rate differentials become more favourable to the US currency. A strong volatility
peak of the DM/$ thus results in August (Graph 1, lower panel) and
other smaller values follow around the famous G-5 meeting at the
Plaza in New York on September 21-22; this tendency is not observed
in Europe (Graphs 2-3, lower panel).

March - August 1986

It is a period of large swings of the dollar on a downward path.
The February drop is not generated by interest rate fundamentals but
rather by the perception that the US trade deficit has indeed become
unmanageable and by the new "talking the dollar down" practice of
the US Treasury Secretary (Appendix). In April we have the EMS
realignment and the drop of the dollar generally (Giavazzi-Giovannini
[20], p. 137) associated to it (Graph 1, lower panel). In Europe we
have no volatility spikes for the lira (which remains stable versus the
DM, see Graph 2, upper panel) and some volatility spikes for the
French franc, which undergoes a substantial parity adjustment (Graph
3, lower panel).

January - February 1987

We have an EMS realignment in January and the dollar drops
immediately before (as it does in general, an increase of interest rate
differentials notwithstanding) also over the markets' psychological
reactions to the publication of the *Tower Report on Irangate*, very

critical of President Reagan (Appendix). From this realignment till the end of 1989 both the lira and the French franc remain stable within their EMS bands (larger for the lira which experiences some low frequency swings up and down) and we do not have any appreciable spike of volatility (Graphs 2 and 3, lower panels).

October 1987 - February 1988

Generalized crash of the major world stock exchanges in mid-October. The dollar drops sharply and there is a suspension of the informal target zones agreed upon at the Louvre summit. The pick-up of the dollar in January 1988 is determined by supportive interventions of the monetary authorities which offset the lower US interest rates, determined by the Fed to protect the US financial markets. There are volatility peaks of the DM/$ between November 1987 and February 1988 (Graph 1, lower panel) and some turbulence of the French franc in the same period (Graph 3, lower panel) as the lira remains quiet (Graph 2, lower panel).

June - August 1988

We observe DM/$ volatility peaks in July as central banks intervene in favour of the dollar (Appendix) which records a three month surge not supported by favourable interest rate differentials (Graph 1, lower panel). In Europe moderate volatility peaks of the French franc in the period (Graph 3, lower panel).

November - December 1988

The November presidential election and the victory of a Republican candidate does not seem to offer any relief to the dollar (Appendix) which depreciates on stable interest rate differentials. This produces the volatility spikes in the period.

July - August 1989

The strong upward movement of the dollar against interest rate differentials causes the two volatility peaks of July and August.

October - December 1989

The dollar settles on a downward trend once again against interest rate differentials following the events of the October (Appendix) and the new "Eurocentric" sentiment following the quick pace of economic reforms in Eastern Europe. In the two years 1988 and 1989 volatility of the Lit/DM and FrF/DM exchange rates is very low.

Some conclusions of this section could be the following:

a) the DM/$ volatility peaks in general when there is a contradictory movement of the exchange rate and the interest rate differentials;

b) the peaks of DM/$ volatility generated by non-economic factors are rather the exception than the rule for this exchange rate: they occur probably in January 1983 (Appendix) and in the period of the speculative dollar bubble in the second part of 1984;

c) a standard determinant of DM/$ volatility spikes is represented by the proximity of an EMS realignment (Giavazzi-Giovannini [20], Chapter 6) as the dollar drops in the imminence of the event and rebounds thereafter;

d) point *c)* implies that the chain of causation and the transmission of disturbances go rather from EMS episodes to the DM/$ volatility and not vice versa (Giavazzi-Giovannini [20]), Chapter 6 pp. 143-4);

e) the EMS realignments cause some volatility of the Lit/DM and of the FrF/DM — but not an excessive one and sometimes an absence of it — depending on the peculiarities of each of them;

f) from the last important realignment in 1987 onward, volatility and interest rate differentials among the European currencies here examined stabilize, together with the exchange rates, whereas volatility remains quite high for the dollar: this fact points to a tangible success of the EMS as a rate stabilization mechanism (other shortcomings being outside the scope of this paper) and to the emergence of an European monetary area which has been able in the recent past to insulate nominal-bilateral and real-effective exchange rates of ERM participants (Giavazzi- Giovannini [20], Chapter 6).

4. - The Dollar and the EMS

A certain number of empirical results on the relationship between the fluctuations of the — effective or bilateral, nominal or real — dollar and of some bilateral European exchange rates have been proposed by the economic and econometric literature in recent times. A non-exhaustive list of them is the following:

a) the EMS has decreased the bilateral DM exchange rate volatility of both the French franc and the Italian lira (Giavazzi-Giovannini [20], par. 3.2; Diebold-Pauly [10]; Bollerslev [5];

b) for France and Italy there has been an increase in the volatility of real effective exchange rates after 1979, contrary to Germany, where the fluctuations of real effective exchange rates are lower after 1979 than in the previous twenty years (Giavazzi-Giovannini [20], par. 3.4);

c) the EMS "might have limited the effects of the fluctuations of the DM/$ rate on Germany's competitiveness" (Giavazzi-Giovannini [20], par. 3.4);

d) the exchange rates of the French franc and the Italian lira with the DM tend to appreciate or depreciate as the effective dollar rate appreciates or depreciates (i.e. when the dollar is strong the DM is weak in the EMS) and this tendency is more visible in the years preceding the EMS (Giavazzi-Giovannini [20], Chapter 6);

e) «almost all EMS realignments (which resulted in an appreciation of the DM *vis à vis* the European partners) are preceded by a large fall in the effective dollar index and are followed by a recovery of the dollar» Giavazzi-Giovannini [20], Chapter 6);

f) the variability of the intra-European exchange rates is explained the by variability of the foundamentals a lot more than the freely floating rates (e.g. the DM/$, the yen/$, etc., Gros [23]);

In the preceding chapter we have shown another — and quite central — result on this argument:

g) the fluctuations of the dollar seem to have a limited impact on the bilateral fluctuations of the FrF/DM and Lit/DM whreas the EMS realignments seem to have a more sizable impact on the fluctuation of the dollar.

We will examine in this paragraph some empirical evidence which should confirm these results and highlight some new elements.

Graph 4 compares overtime the bilateral volatility (expressed by moving variances centered on the current observation) of the DM/$ with that of the Lit/DM; Graph 5 does the same for the FrF/DM. The Lit/DM graph indicates that the highest DM/$ volatility peaks are not matched by those of the Lit/DM; the latter shows some specific peaks around the realignments of October 1981 and of April 1986; after 1986 both first and second moments of the lira exchange rate with the DM are quite stable in the EMS. Table 2, which reports average values per year of these moving variances, shows values of the Lit/DM

TABLE 2

MEASURES OF VOLATILITY
AND COVARIATION OF EXCHANGE RATES

Year	Volatility (1)					Covariation (2)	
	DM/$	Lit/DM	FrF/DM	Lit/DM	FrF/DM	L/DM-L/$	F/DM-F/$
1974 ..	0.7650	0.7804	..	0.5115	..	− 2.3034	..
1975 ..	0.9048	0.2981	..	0.2329	..	− 4.8129	..
1976 ..	0.1503	1.3506	..	2.1497	..	− 3.8069	..
1977 ..	0.2929	0.0091	..	0.1623	..	− 3.5324	..
1978 ..	1.4503	0.4345	0.6819	0.4321	0.5753	− 10.7477	− 10.2811
1979 ..	0.9612	0.4270	0.6992	0.1681	0.2411	− 2.7829	− 1.3600
1980 ..	1.7060	1.0560	1.1879	0.0743	0.1249	− 4.2236	− 3.6422
1981 ..	0.8634	0.4932	0.9260	0.2021	0.2120	− 3.8109	− 1.7244
1982 ..	0.5295	0.5764	1.1380	0.1044	0.3043	0.5393	2.0928
1983 ..	0.5274	0.4530	0.6003	0.0977	0.1893	− 0.9079	− 0.4570
1984 ..	1.0331	0.6531	1.0296	0.0505	0.1066	− 2.4103	− 0.4064
1985 ..	1.2020	0.4809	0.9614	0.2198	0.1768	− 5.2493	− 1.4795
1986 ..	1.1265	1.1856	1.0732	0.0101	0.1719	0.2906	− 1.1971
1987 ..	0.7613	0.3356	0.3547	0.0614	0.1702	− 2.6418	− 2.9183
1988 ..	0.8512	0.9756	1.0283	0.0193	0.0685	0.4311	− 0.0899
1989 ..	1.2527	0.9252	1.1539	0.0427	0.0423	− 2.7887	− 0.6815

(1) Yearly average of moving variances over three months.
(2) Yearly covariances on monthly data.

exchange rate much lower than that of the DM/$; also the moving variances of the Lit/$ are in general lower than those of the DM/$.

Comparable results are also obtained for the FrF/DM volatility vis à vis that of the DM/$, even though the French currency has a couple of extra volatility peaks with respect to the lira (Graph 4). Also the levels of volatility are in general higher for the FrF/DM than for the Lit/DM (Table 2).

Let's look now at the issue of the positive comovements of the effective dollar rate and of our bilateral FrF/DM and Lit/DM (point *d*, this paragraph), examined through the covariances among these exchange rates. The evidence in the last two columns of Table 2 and 3 confirms the tendency of closer comovements of the two European exchange rates with the DM/$ before the start of the EMS (as indicated under point *c)* above) and the tendency of negative comovements is confirmed in general for the whole period under consideration, even though to a slightly lesser degree in recent years (Table 3).

TABLE 3

MEASURES OF VOLATILITY AND COVARIATION OF EXCHANGE RATES OVER VARIOUS PERIODS OF DOLLAR FLUCTUATIONS

	Before EMS (a)	EMS period (b)	Dollar depreciat. (c)	Dollar appreciat. (d)	Dollar depreciat. (e)
Volatility (1)					
DM/$	0.9158	0.9527	0.3847	1.0678	1.0642
Lit/$	0.5864	0.6796	0.4968	0.6388	0.8006
FrF/$ (3)	0.6526	0.9041	0.2429	0.9581	0.9291
LIT/DM	0.8738	0.0893	0.8107	0.1503	0.0720
FrF/DM (3)	0.4952	0.1516	0.3092	0.2293	0.1248
Covariation (2)					
Lit/DM	− 6.0624	− 2.2251	− 4.7061	− 2.7745	− 2.2643
FrF/DM	− 4.4237	− 1.0348	− 5.1208	− 1.2069	− 1.3146

(1) Averages of moving variances over three months.
(2) Covariances on monthly data.
(3) From July 1977.
(a) July 1973 - February 1979.
(b) March 1979 - December 1989.
(c) September 1975 - October 1978.
(d) November 1978 - February 1985.
(e) March 1985 - December 1989.

Table 3 indicates how volatility changed before and after the beginning of the EMS (point *a*) of this paragraph) and in correspondence of episodes of appreciation or depreciation of the dollar. We see that the volatility of the DM/$ did not change substantially, on average, before and after 1979 whereas the FrF/$ and the Lit/$ exchange rates became more volatile after the beginning of the EMS: this result is consistent with point *b* above for France and Italy (even though we are here examining bilateral rates and not effective real rates). The dollar volatility of the DM seems to be unaffected by the EMS which, on the contrary, sharply reduces the bilateral volatility of the DM vis à vis the French franc and the lira: this result confirms point *a*) and is consistent with a reduction of the real effective rate of Germany (under point *b*) above) and with point *c*) on the EMS-induced insulation of the effective real DM from DM/$ fluctuations.

The empirical elements assembled in this paragraph and in the previous one thus confirm all the results outlined above, except that under *f*), which is not explicitly examined in this paper.

5. - Conclusions

The main findings of the analysis carried out in this paper confirm most previous research results on this topic (paragraph 4).

The principal purpose for the establishment of the EMS, i.e. the objective of insulating the intra-European bilateral exchange rates from the fluctuations of the free-floating dollar has been fulfilled in the course of last decade. In the last three years considered in our analysis the fluctuations of the Lit/DM and FrF/DM rates have been virtually non-existent whereas the dollar has shown rather sharp peaks of volatility. This insulation property of the EMS implies that it is infact the dollar to be influence by European monetary and exchange rate events rather than the opposite.

The attainment of the result of limiting the exchange rate flexibility in Europe is only a first and partial success on the road towards full economic integration. The strucutural differences of the European economies — well represented by those existing among Italy, France and Germany — in inflation, private and public productivity, labour market and wage dynamics, to mention a few, the substantial risk premium embodied in the high real interest rates of countries like Italy and France (Giovannini [21]), the resulting misalignment of the exchange rates of these countries with Germany, all represent major challenges in the years ahead before a lasting and meaningful economic integration can be reached in Europe.

Foreign Exchange Market Events: 1973-1989

1978

Continuation of unfavourable differentials of growth and inflation for the US dollar. Increasing attempts to counteract the devaluation of the dollar by rising US interest rates. Massive interventions in the foreign exchange markets by the Bundesbank and the Fed from the last quarter of 1977 through the first quarter of 1979 to counteract the depreciation of the dollar.

Events and market sentiment: June: introduction in the US of 6-month *CD* with floating rates indexed to the *T*-bills; August: elimination of the 4% US bank reserves on foreign liabilities to make it cheaper borrowing in the Eurodollar markets; September: US Fed supervision over the US branches of foreign banks; November: in the US, increase of the discount rate by one percentage point to the historical maximum, increase of reserves by commercial banks on deposits above $100 000, establishment of $30 billion swap facility with other Central Banks for foreign exchange markets interventions; December: introduction of "NOW" accounts (checking facilities on saving deposits).

1979

The dollar stabilizes after a three-years fall. The movements in the course of the year are largely determined by interest rate differentials and by a swing from net purchases to net sales of dollars by the Monetary Autorities. Oil price increase lend support to the dollar in the first part of the year.

Events and market sentiment: March: formal implementation of the EMS; July: increase of the discount rate by the US and Germany; September: first EMS realignment on the 24; October: important policy measures by the Fed: *a)* new operating policy with a shift in emphasis from the federal funds rates to the growth of bank reserves as the operating target of monetary policy; *b)* increase in the discount rate by 1 percentage point and imposition of a marginal reserve requirement of 8% on managed liabilities of US banks (including borrowing from the Eurocurrency markets); November: second EMS realignment on the 30th.

1980

Sharp "spike" of the dollar in the first quarter determined by higher interest rates in the US. Latter movements determined by interest rates differentials.

Events and market sentiment: March: announcement of an anti-inflation program by the US; April: Strong net sales of dollars against DM by the monetary authorities in the last two months.

1981

Up and down of the dollar over the year. Net sales of dollars against DM by the moneatry authorities over the year.

Events and market sentiment: March: assasination attempt of President Reagan and subsequent intervention by the Fed on the foreign exchange market. Third EMS realignment on the 22nd; October: fourth EMS realignment on the 5th.

1982

The dollar begins its unprecedented climb sustained in the first part of the year by record interest rate differentials in its favour. Temporaneous drop in the last two months of the year.

Events and market sentiment: February: fifth EMS realignmment on the 22nd; April: uncertainties about the management of $M1$ by the Fed and the degree of interest rates variation connected to it dominates the foreign exchange markets leading to a depreciation of the dollar when interest rate differentials move in favour of the dollar; May: the dollar strenghth occurs despite declines in the US domestic interest rates. The factors that seem to have been important in this occurrence are the continued concern over the medium-term outlook for US interest rates — due to the confusion surrounding the proposed federal government budget for 1983 — and indications that some economic authorities abroad (in particular president Mitterrand and the Governor of the Central Bank of Canada) may be no longer committed to strongly support their currencies against the dollar; June: the sixth EMS realignment of June 12 contributes to the further strenghtening of the dollar in the month. Interest rate differentials widen in favour of the US while expectations of high US rates get confirmed by the announcements of $M1$ and the perceived difficulties of the Treasury refunding; July: failure of Penn Square in the US and injection of liquidity into the banking sector by the Fed, drop in the Federal Funds rate and a reduction in the discount rate. Long positions mantained in the exchange market given the continued uncertainty over interest rates in the US and abroad; August: in spite of the continued downtrend in US short term interest rates, the dollar remains on an upward trajectory for "flight to quality" reasons determined by the Mexican liquidity crisis and widespread uncertainties concerning AEG, Poland and the Middle East; October: the dollar tends to revalue because of the $M1$ figures much above Fed targets and of the continuous substantial inflows of funds into US capital markets determined by the perceived risk of holding non US-dollar denominated financial instruments; December: dollar declines in November and December determined also (besides lower interest differential on US assets with respect to the beginning of the year) by the conviction gradually materializing in the markets that the Fed is indeed not prepared to raise short term interest rates in response to the high growth of $M1$. Orderly rescheduling negotiations of the debt of major international borrower also eases concerns over world liquidity crises.

1983

Dollar broadly stable in the first three month of the year when interest rates begin to raise in the US setting the stage for the increase of the dollar from April through August, when it peaks for the year. A drop in September, stability in October then revaluation that will go on through January 1984.

Events and market sentiment: January: expectations of higher US interest rates, following higher than planned $M1$ growth in the second half of 1982 and higher than expected US Treasury funding requirements for the first half of 1982, set the stage for a later revaluation of the dollar; March: seventh EMS realignment on the 21st; April: sustained rise in the US stock market, declining US interest rates and first concerns over the US trade deficit, as offsetting elements for a stable dollar in the month; June: $M1$ growth higher than expected in May and June. A deteriorating trade deficit does not influence the dollar; July: higher than expected growth rate of GNP in the second quarter in the US; August: three consecutive $M1$ declines change expectations from higher to flat or lower US interest rates; September: dollar drops following lower and expected lower interest rate differentials; November: higher dollar and fluctations following political events (200 marines killed in Lebanon, invasion of Grenada, anti-missile demonstrations in Western Europe, increased tension in the Persian Gulf). Higher interest rates expected in the US because of the strength of the economy.

1984

This is "the" bull year for the dollar. Following a strong drop in February and March in a period of rising interest rates differentials in favour of the US and further consolidation in the growth of the economy, the dollar goes up like a rocket through February 1985 ending 22% higher than December 1983. From September 1984 interest rates differentials are actually falling for the dollar: this is the period of the "speculative bubble".

Events and market sentiment: May and June: a confidence crisis hits Continental Illinois and the high US interest rates provoke repeated protests from debtor countries in Latin America which threat to default even on debt servicing. Fears of bank crises trouble Manufacturers' Hanover and other US institutions. Cash injections by the Fed make the Federal funds rate fluctuate sharply. Stronger than expected growth of the US economy; July and August: a 20.7% rise of US real business fixed investment, rising real interest rates differentials, removal of the US 30% withholding tax and strong capital inflows into the US, especially from Japan, satisfaction on how the Continental Illinois crisis was resolved; August: another case of financial uncertainty and perhaps collapse at Financial Corporation of America and quiet trading causes a temporary arrest to the rise of the dollar; September and October: foreign exchange market intervention by the Bundesbank (estimated at $2.0 billion in the month) causes sharp fluctuations of the dollar over a rising trend.

1985

The dollar begins in February its downtrend for the rest of the year after lowering interest rates differentials have begun in September 1984 and will last till mid year. In December the dollar is 25% lower than in February.

Events and market sentiment: May and June: earlier in the year (till February) the dollar rose sharply on perceptions of continued high growth and rising interest rates. Since that time the US rates have dropped by more than the European ones shifting expectations towards a lower US growth and lower interest rates; July: Paul Volcker announces in a Congressional testimony that the Fed has decided to accommodate the high growth if $M1$ in the first part of the year by re-basing its new targets in the second quarter. Industrial production is rebounding up sharply in West Germany. Eighth EMS realignment on the 21st; September: Over the September 21-22 weekend the monetary authorities of the five major industrial countries announce an agreement to coordinate their economic policies with the aim to lower the dollar. The dollar loses immediatly 4% of its effective value; November: the markets disregard a positive revision of US growth rate of GNP for the third quarter to 4.3% and later in the year there seems to be further evidence of swinging and deterioration on the relative cyclical positions of the US and some European countries.

1986

It was another bear year for the dollar consistent with declining interest rates differentials. In the first part there was a roller-coaster ride of the US currency, following the strong declines of oil prices and the associated fears for stability of some US banking institutions heavily exposed in the oil sector. At the end of December the dollar was 21% lower than a year before.

Events and market sentiment: January and February: the market begins to experience a series of "stunning" negative news about the US trade deficit and the "new" fashion of exchange market interventions by the US minister Baker (not shared by the Fed Governor), "talking the dollar or down", in order to counteract and pacify the protectionist lobby in Washington, due to the virtual "rubbing-out" of large industrial segments in the US; April: Ninth EMS realignment on the 7; July and August: the dollar's continued declines seem to be caused by a disappointing set of economic factors both within the US and in Europe and by another decline in oil expected to set a new record in both value and volume terms; November: Irangate. With the disclosure that the White House had been covertly shipping arms to Iran the markets believe that the President has violated his own "firmness" principles and caused a breach of faith with the electorate. Further evidence of lower growth prospects in the US and higher in Europe.

1987

The DM/$ rate stabilized somehow in the first seven months of the year, while the yen/$ was still deteriorating for the US. The generally increasing interest rate differentials over the year helped to achieve this result on the stock market crash of October and the following "free fall" of the dollar.

Events and market sentiment: January: Tenth EMS realignment on the 19; February: the continuing bearish sentiment for the dollar is still being fuelled by: *a)* the release of the *Tower Report over Irangate* sharply critical of president Reagan; *b)* Brazil's debt moratorium and consequences for the US banks; *c)* a disappointing 7.5% fall of durable goods orders; *d)* the widening US trade deficit; March: growing protectionist sentiment in the US Congress is weighing on the dollar. The frequently heard argument is: as long as Japan and Germany do not take substantial measures to stimulate their economies and thus help narrow the huge US trade deficit, the US administration will let the dollar fall (especially against the yen) as a weapon against protectionist legislation in Congress; June and July: support for the dollar in the recent past and in the month is provided by the trend back to US investment by international investors, attracted by the

favourable interest differentials, by the strong stock market performance and by the perception that the dollar has entered a stable period.
The escalating instability in the Persian Gulf following the reflagging of
Kuwait Tankers also helps the dollar; October: stock market crash
and subsequent fall of the dollar which loses all remaining support
when the Fed injects liquidity and pushes interest rates lower to
support the stock market; November and December: free fall of the
dollar continuing because of the Fed policy on interest rates and the
announcement of a $ 17.6 bill trade deficit for October.

1988

The dollar rallied in the first eight months of the year then
subsided a little thereafter ending the year on an upward trend.
Interest rate differentials in favour of the dollar were not a factor as
they moved up and down around a stable level. The year began with
supporting interventions from the Central Banks which then turned
the other side during the summer sending the dollar on a downard
trend.

Events and market expectations: January: concerted interventions throughout the month succeed in bolstering the value of the
dollar and changing the markets' sentiment from bearish to bullish for
the support to the dollar thus shown by the monetary authorities of
various countries; March: strong statements in favour of the dollar by
US Treasury Secretary Baker, who in the past had frequently "talked
the dollar down"; August: higher US interest rates and an increase in
the discount rate support the dollar. Indications that a strong US
growth and incipient inflation might force the interest rates still higher
send the dollar up in the summer months; September: G-7 Finance
officials reveal that they had spent over $10 billion in July and August
to stem the dollar climb and warn that they would oppose another
rally; November: the dollar continues to plunge after the US presidential elections. Though the currency markets expect a Bush administration to be staunchly free trade and receptive to business interests,
they view it as unlikely to quickly restore confidence in the long-term
prospects of the US economy. The markets remain unimpressed by
the President's assurances that the administration will negotiate with
Congress to reduce the budget deficit.

1989

The dollar has a bell-shaped behaviour over the year: in the beginning a series of favourable releases on the health of the US economy and an apparent nonchalance of G-7 countries to be consistent with their warnings about the excessive strength of the US currency send the dollar higher; at the end of the year the new developments in Eastern Europe convince the markets that Germany is going to benefit the most from the new situation and prices the DM up accordingly.

Events and market sentiment: January: the dollar surged in January as US short-term interest climbed and the inauguration of president Bush generated optimism that the budget deficit might somehow be reduced. The considerable interest rate differential enjoyed by dollar-denominated assets creates a very strong demand for the US currency; May: very strong demand for dollars which blasts past DM 2.00. Speculative factors feeds the seemingly insatiable demand for dollars. Some international investors reportedly purchase dollars to realize capital gains on expected future interest rate reductions on Government debt as the economy seems to slow down; June: speculative dollar bubble; September: the dollar crashes in the last week of the month from the level that G-7 finance ministers complain to be too strong. The markets had dismissed earlier interventions and warnings by the central banks that their meeting would produce a new impetus to curb the dollar strength; October: quite a lot of action buffeted the foreign exchange markets in the month. G-7 central banks continued to sell dollars heavily. Germany led a substantial lifting of European interest rates. Japan raised its discount rate. The US and European stock markets slid sharply, which forced the Fed funds rate slightly lower. The US trade position deteriorated. The DM benefited most from these events and from repeated Bundesbank calls for a stronger currency; November: the DM continue to surge in the month. The widespread perception that a peaceful political and economic transformation of Eastern Europe would greatly benefit the German economy boosted speculative capital flows already drawn by high nominal interest rates.

BIBLIOGRAPHY

[1] BAILLIE R.I. - McMAHON P.C.: *The Foreign Exchange-Market Theory and Econometric Evidence*, Cambridge, Cambridge University Press, 1989.

[2] BANCA D'ITALIA: *Relazione annuale*, Roma, Banca d'Italia, various issues.

[3] BILSON J.F.O.: «The Monetary Approach to the Exchange Rate: Some Empirical Evidence», International Monetary Fund *Staff Papers*, n. 25, 1979, pp. 48-75.

[4] BOUGHTON J.M.: «Tests of Performance of Reduced-Form Exchange Rate Models», *Journal of International Economics*, n. 23, 1987, pp. 41-56.

[5] BOLLERSLEV T.: «Modelling the Coherence in Short-Run Nominal Exchange Rates: A Multivariate Generalized Arch Approach», *Review of Economics and Statistics*, 1990.

[6] BOLLERSLEV T. - CHOU R.Y. - JAYARAMAN N. - KRONER K.F.: *Arch Modelling in Finance: A Selective Review of the Theory and Empirical Evidence with Suggestions for Future Research*, Mimeo, 1990.

[7] BRANSON W.H.: «Exchange Rate Policy After a Decade of Floating», in BILSON J.F.O. - MARSTON R.C.: *Exchange Rate Theory and Practice*, Chicago, The University of Chicago Press, 1984.

[8] DADDI P. - TIVEGNA M.: «Stima di equazioni di tassi di cambio: specificazioni GARCH mensili del cambio marco-dollaro», *Note economiche*, n. 3, 1990, translated as: *Estimation of Exchange Rate Equations: Monthly GARCH Specification of the dollar-DM Exchange Rate*, Roma, Centre for Research in Finance - IMI Group, n. 3, September 1990.

[9] DE GRAUWE P. - VANSANTEN K.: «Deterministic Chaos in the Foreign Exchange Market», CEPR, *Discussion Paper*, n. 370, 1990.

[10] DIEBOLD E.X. - PAULY P.: «Has the Ems Reduced Member-Country Exchange Rate Volatility», *Empirical Econometrics*, 1988, pp. 81-102.

[11] DORNBUSCH R.: «Expectations and Exchange Rate Dynamics», *Journal of Political Economy*, n. 84, 1976, pp. 1161-74.

[12] DUNIS C. - FEENY M. (ed.): *Exchange Rate Forecasting*, Londra Woodhead-Faulkner, 1989.

[13] ENGLE R.F.: «Autoregressive Conditional Heteroskedasticity with Estimates of the Variance of UK Inflation», *Econometrica*, n. 50, 1982, pp. 987-1008.

[14] FAMA E.: «Forward and Spot Exchange Rates», *Journal of Monetary Economics*, 1984, pp. 319-38.

[15] FRANKEL J.A.: «On the Mark: A Theory of Floating Exchange Rates Based on Real Interest Differentials», *American Economic Review*, n. 69, 1979, pp. 610-22.

[16] ——: «Tests of Monetary and Portfolio Balance Models of Exchange Rate Determination», in BILSON J.E.O. - MARSTON R.C.: *Exchange Rate Theory and Practice*, Chicago, The University of Chicago Press, 1984.

[17] FRENKEL J.A.: «A Monetary Approach to the Exchange Rate: Doctrinal Aspects and Empirical Evidence»», *Scandinavian Journal of Economics*, n. 78, 1976, pp. 255-76.

[18] FRENKEL J.A. - MUSSA M.L.: «Asset Markets, Exchange Rates and the Balance of Payments», in JONES R.W. - KENEN P.B.: *Handbook of International Economics*, Vol. II, Amsterdam, North-Holland, 1985.

[19] GAIOTTI E. - GIUCCA P. - MICOSSI S.: «Cooperation in Managing the Dollar (1985-87): Interventions in Foreign Exchange Markets and Interest Rates», Roma, Banca d'Italia *Temi di Discussione*, n. 119, 1989.

[20] GIAVAZZI F. - GIOVANNINI A.: *Limiting Exchange Rate Flexibility; the European Monetary System*, Cambridge (Mass.), MIT Press, 1989.

[21] GIOVANNINI A.: «European Monetary Reform: Progress and Prospects», preparato per il Brookings Panel on Economic Activity, Washington (DC), 13-14 September 1990.

[22] GOLDMAN-SACHS: *The International Economics Analyst*, monthly, various issues, London.

[23] GROSS D.: «On the Volatility of Exchange Rates: Tests of Monetary and Portfolio Balance Models of Exchange Rate Determination», Weltwirtshaftliches Archiv, 1989, pp. 273-95.

[24] HODRICK R.J. - SRIVASTAVA S.: «The Covariation of Risk Premiums and Expected Future Spot Exchange Rates», *Journal of International Money and Finance*, 1986, pp. 55-522.

[25] INTERNATIONAL MONETARY FUND: *Annual Report*, various issues, Washington.

[26] KENEN P.B.: «Macroeconomic Theory and Policy: How the Closed Economy Was Opened», in JONES R.W. - KENEN P.B.: *Handbook of International Economics*, vol. II, Amsterdam, North-Holland, 1985.

[27] MACDONALD R.: *Floating Exchange Rates: Theories and Evidence*, London, Unwin-Hyman.

[28] MACDONALD R. - TAYLOR M.P. (eds.): *Exchange Rates and Open Economy Macroeconomics*, Oxford, Basil Blackwell, 1989.

[29] MEESE R.A. - ROGOFF K.: «Empirical Exchange Rates Models of the Seventies: Do they Fit out of Sample?», *Journal of International Economics*, n. 14, 1983, pp. 3-24.

[30] MERRIL-LYNCH: *International Economic and Currency Review*, monthly, various issues, London.

[31] MORGAN-STANLEY: *Global Perspectives*, monthly, various issues, London.

[32] PROMETEIA: *Rapporto di previsione*, various issues, Bologna.

[33] SOMANATH V.S.: «Efficient Exchange Rate Forecast: Lagged Models Better Than the Random Walk?», *Journal of International Money and Finance*, n. 5, 1986, pp. 195-220.

[34] TIVEGNA M.: «Elementi per una valutazione della volatilità dei tassi di cambio: un'applicazione ai cambi del dollaro», *Note economiche*, n. 3, 1989, pp. 463-89.

[35] TULLIO G.: «Validità e limiti dei modelli applicati del tasso di cambio», in PADOA-SCHIOPPA T. (a cura di): *Il sistema dei cambi oggi*, Bologna, Il Mulino, 1986, pp. 41-54.

[36] WHARTON ECONOMETRIC FORECASTING ASSOCIATES (WEFA GROUP): *Foreign Exchange Rate Outlook*, monthly, various issues, Philadelphia.

Sequencing and Timing of Stabilization Policies: the Case of German Monetary Union

Emil-Maria Claassen
Université Dauphine, Paris

Introduction

The year 1989 is probably as decisive for world history as the year 1789 200 years ago. The political democratization and the economic liberalization of the East constitute a challenge to any third-way solution between capitalism and socialism. Forty-five years after the Second World War, fifty-five years after the former nazi and later communist regime in Central Europe, and even seventy years after marxism-leninism in the Soviet Union had to pass in order to recognize that democracy and the market economy are the least evils for the political and economic organization of society.

We are concerned with the sequencing and timing of stabilization policies during the transition period. Stabilization policies are broadly defined as monetary, fiscal and exchange rate policies. The sequencing of stabilization policies is associated to the specific order of succession of monetary, fiscal and exchange rate policies. Their timing refers to the speed with which the necessary adjustment policies are brought about.

The policy priorities of the former German Democratic Republic (GDR) constitutes a benchmark for sequencing and timing. On the one hand, stabilization policies were installed first and microeconomic or structural policies were envisaged afterwards in terms of the legal and fiscal framework, of privatization and property rights, of commercial banking and financial markets, of the relative price structure of factors of production and of tradable/nontradable goods. On the other hand, the proper sequencing of stabilization policies should have been first the re-establishment of internal convertibility via an adequate monetary and fiscal policy mix. Afterwards, external convertibility would have been introduced step by step with the liberalization of commercial transactions followed later by the liberalization of capital transactions. As we know, the proper timing of these stabilization measures took place for the GDR on July 2, 1990. Other countries like Poland and Yugoslavia have chosen a more moderate, but still radical timing for their stabilization program.

In paragraph 1 we shall begin with the description of the internal and external currency status within a planned economy. Paragraph 2 is concerned with the proper monetary and fiscal policy mix for establishing the internal convertibility either by a currency reform or by open inflation. The introduction of the external convertibility dealt with in paragraph 3 raises the question of whether the foreign exchange rate should be chosen as the nominal anchor of the monetary system. Another issue to be analyzed in paragraph 4 concerns the real exchange rate which should be appreciated rather than depreciated. Finally, in paragraph 5, we present our interpretation for the timing of the German experiment which has its roots in the disequilibrium of the German labor market.

1. - Internal and External Inconvertibility

In the presence of rationing and price controls (repressed inflation), the domestic currency in any former socialist economy is deprived of its functions as a means of payment and a store of value. Consequently goods take over the functions of money. On the one hand, a great part of domestic transactions takes the form of barter trade. On the other hand, goods are hoarded by households and firms as a store of value. Thus, we have the paradoxical situation that goods are in abundance as far as their hoarding is concerned and that they are simultaneously in shortage since they are purchasable in a limited amount of (soft) goods against the domestic currency. Ronald McKinnon [7] (*) has estimated the inventories of firms for the Soviet Union for 1985. They amounted to 82% of national income while US firms accumulated inventories equal to 31% for the same year.

The share of Eastern Europe and of the USSR in total world trade was under 8% in the late 1980s (Lavigne [6]). Roughly half of it was traded among the members of the Council for Mutual Economic Assistance (CMEA). Despite the formal existence of a "common socialist currency" called the transfer ruble, trade among CMEA members was basically bilateral (which is nothing else than barter trade) while multilateral trade accounted only for 1% of total CMEA trade. The basic idea of the transfer ruble was that a country could be a net exporter to one type of country and use its transfer ruble surpluses as a net importer of another CMEA country. However, that type of multilateral trade arrangement (except for the above one percentage point) was never achieved, simply because a country, having acquired balances in transfer rubles, could not use yhem for buying goods in another member country, the latter not disposing of any available goods. In reality, the transfer ruble was not convertible in goods and thus was not transferable. In a similar way, the domestic currencies on the internal market were neither convertible into domestic goods as a result of the shortage of goods.

In early 1990, the members of the CMEA agreed (or expressed the pious hope) to shift toward foreign trade based on world prices and settled in convertible currencies from 1991 onwards. The dominant view in the West is that Eastern Europe should be integrated increasingly into the world economy while the Soviet Union may be disjointed from Eastern Europe because of uncertainty about its future economic reform. Consequently, a revival of the CMEA as a regional union would not be desirable. External currency convertibility would be an important part of the transition process toward a market economy and toward integration into the Western world economy such that any extra efforts for intra-regional convertibility within Eastern Europe would be redundant.

However, this view is not shared by all economists. Some (Lavigne [6]) are concerned by the time profile of the transition process

---

(*) *Advise:* the numbers in square brackets refer to the Bibliography in the appendix.

which they conceive rather as a gradual process, in particular as far as the intra-regional trade relationships are concerned. According to them, a reduction by 50% of trade within the CMEA would be devastating since foreign would not be diverted to the West due to the lack of competitiveness. One possible scheme for providing additionally multilateral trade would be monetary arrangements in terms of settlements in domestic currencies provided that they become progressively convertible within each economy, within the CMEA area and outside the area.

2. - Internal Convertibility:
Currency Reform versus Open Inflation

In the case of repressed inflation, the price level is fixed (in the sense of price controls) with a simultaneous excess supply of money which is the monetary overhang and with a corresponding excess demand for goods. This phenomenon expresses the shortage of goods within the economy or the imperfect convertibility of the domestic currency into domestic goods. This overall disequilibrium of socialist economies is represented in Graph 1 by the shaded area for which there is simultaneously an excess demand for tradables and nontradables and an excess supply of money.

Graph 1 illustrates the Australian model elaborated by the Australian economists Salter [11], Swan [12], and Pearce [10]. There are three markets: the market for tradable goods (*T*), the market for nontradable goods (*N*) and the money market (*M*). The real sector (*NN* or *NN-TT*) determines the relative price between tradables and nontradables ($q = P_T/P_N$). This relative price is defined as the real exchange rate. The money market determines the general price level.

Tradables and nontradables are considered as gross substitutes in production and consumption. Their supply and demand depend only on the relative price q (and the demand functions on other real macroeconomic variables like real income, the real interest rate and real cash balances which are not taken into account explicitly in Graph 1). Any point which is located leftward from the equilibrium schedule *NN* describes a situation of excess demand in the market for

GRAPH 1

TOTAL MACROECONOMIC DISEQUILIBRIUM

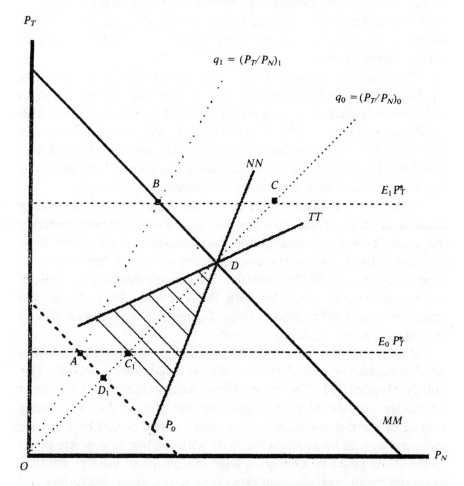

nontradables. Similarly, points rightward from *TT* indicate an excess demand in the market for domestic tradable goods. At the same time, the *TT*-schedule is assumed to reflect an equilibrium in the trade balance such that an excess demand for *T* corresponds to a trade balance deficit. The equilibrium value of the real exchange rate is q_o represented by the Oq_o-ray. The precise point of the Oq_o-ray at which the *TT*-schedule intersects the *NN*-schedule depends on the monetary sector.

The MM-schedule is drawn for a given quantity of money. There is only one general price level which brings about equilibrium in the money market. This precise equilibrium level of P is represented by MM. Its equilibrium value can be accompanied by various combinations of P_T and P_N. Any situation leftward from MM reflects an excess supply of money.

The intersection point D illustrates one possible macroeconomic equilibrium of internal convertibility as a consequence of a series of stabilization policies. Assume that the initial situation of total disequilibrium is at point A. The price level is at P_o with the specific mix of a high price level for tradables and an extremely low price level of non-tradables. The intensity of repressed inflation at point A is measured by the distance AB which represents the monetary overhang.

Open inflation would imply the maintenance of the outstanding quantity of money (MM). On the contrary, if one wants to maintain the price level P_o (including the corresponding wage level) by a currency reform, the otustanding quantity of money has to be reduced by the rate of BA/BO such that the new equilibrium schedule of the money market coincides with the P_o-curve. The TT-and NN-schedules would shift through point D_1 because their slopes depend only on the relative price $q = P_T/P_N$.

If one opts for a currency reform, there are many technical ways for eliminating the monetary overhang as it has been emphasized by Robert Mundell [9]. The most simple, but probably also the most unpopular way would be to confiscate one part of the outstanding volume of bank deposits. A less harmful method would be to freeze them and to wait to decide what to do with the frozen deposits in the future. They could be converted later into property titles of physical assets during the privatization process of state-owned enterprises and land. They could also be converted into new government bonds implying a fiscal deterioration as far as future debt service is concerned. Until now (early 1991), no Eastern European country has chosen to confiscate or freeze deposits except Eastern Germany. The conversion rate of East mark prices and wages (flows) into West mark prices and wages was 1 : 1 while the conversion rate of East mark currency (stocks) into West mark currency was 1.8 : 1; (the conversion rate of East mark debt to West mark debt was 2 : 1).

Two important observations have to be made with respect to a price level peg P_o. On the one hand, after the elimination of the monetary overhang, prices of tradables can and should be decontrolled in order to introduce the necessary change in relative prices. At that stage the price level peg can be replaced by an exchange rate peg such that the domestic relative prices of tradable goods would reflect those of the international economy. However, the prices of nontradables (housing, public transport, energy) could still remain unchanged in order to prevent a radical fall in real wages. Prices of nontradables are still at A, but they should move later to C_1 or D_1. On the other hand, as Robert Mundell [9] has emphasized, a monetary overhang cannot be eliminated by cancelling one or two zeros of the outstanding quantity of money (examples are the new French franc or the new pesos) and by degrading prices also by the same proportion since the excess supply of money would be maintained, but only expressed by another numéraire.

Open inflation constitutes an alternative to equilibrating the money market via decontrolling prices. It is not the money supply which is reduced, but the money demand which is increased as a result of rising prices. The subsequent (hopefully short-lived) hyperinflation (as in the Polish or Yugoslavian case) could also be regarded as a (silent) confiscation of the monetary overhang since its real value is reduced to zero via the price level increase. The inflation method $[- \Delta M = - \Delta M/P]$ is usually preferred to the direct confiscation method $[- \Delta M = - \Delta M/P]$ since it operates by deceit on an unsuspecting public. However, according to Brenner [1], the confiscation issue via open inflation is not all that dramatic since people were used already by high prices in black markets such that the official price level was largely underestimated and real wages overestimated. The high prices in black markets were nominal bribes which avoided long lines or years of waiting.

Having maintained point A by a currency reform or having reached point B by open inflation, there are still other potential sources of inflation during the transition phase. This aspect has been demonstrated by Ronald McKinnon [7] for the case of the Soviet Union, buts it is equally applicable to other Eastern countries. In the absence of any elaborated fiscal system, the main government revenue of socialist countries was provided in former times by the surpluses of enterprises. The central planning authorities fixed prices according to cost (labor, intermediaries) plus the so-called surplus being transferred to government. When the first price deregulations emerged and certain enterprises were allowed to set prices freely, the surpluses disappeared. The Soviet budget deficit rose from 1.8% of GNP in 1985 progressively to 10% in 1989. To indicate another figure, according to Frydman-Wellisz-Kolodko [4], the Polish budget deficit was 7% of GNP in 1989 and it is estimated to be reduced to 1.5% in 1990 due to various fiscal reforms and to the cut of subsidies.

There is still a third inflationary source in many Eastern countries provided that the banking system has not been reformed as McKinnon [7] and Brenner [1], have indicated. In the planned economies firms had full access to bank credits at zero or low interest rates in order to finance the purchase of inputs they needed to fulfil the plans. In the terminology of the Hungarian economist Kornai, enterprises had «soft» budget constraints. To the extent that bank reforms are retarded, this specific lack of financial constraint constitutes another source of inflation.

3. - External Convertibility: the Issue of the Nominal Anchor

Having opted either for a currency reform as in the German case or for an open inflation like Poland and Yugoslavia, the next decision concerns the issue of external convertibility. All three countries have realized it by having eliminated foreign exchange controls and by having chosen a fixed exchange rate regime. The German case of monetary unification can be conceived in terms of three separate analytical stages which in reality took place at the same time, but which the other countries followed step by step. The first stage consisted of the elimination of the monetary overhang and it re-established internal convertibility. The second analytical stage for East Germany would have been to maintain the east German currency and to fix the exchange rate of the East mark to the West mark at the ratio 1 : 1. In terms of Graph 1 the appropriate exchange would have been E_o. In the mind of many German economists this procedure was considered as the most favourite one since it allowed to dispose still of a policy instrument for the hypothetical case of a necessary change in the foreign exchange rate. The third stage would have been the change of the underlying currency standard either by choosing a new one or by selecting an existing one.

With the option for an open inflation, the fixing of the exchange rate can only be introduced after the adjustment of the money demand toward the money supply has been taken place via the rise in the price level (E_1 in Graph 1). As Frydman-Wellisz-Kolodko [4] have described the Polish situation, on January 1, 1990 the exchange rate was set above the free market rate at 9500 zloties for one dollar. Zloties were freely convertible into dollars. In the first months of 1990 there was a considerable shift from dollars into zloties since the latter were made attractive by high interest rates on zloty deposits. Poland's open inflation took place mainly from August 1989 to February 1990 with a retail price index of 1640 (December 1988 = 100) while afterwards monthly inflation rates were less than double digit.

Yugoslavia's open inflation represented several thousand percentage points in 1989 and early 1990. It then introduced a new convertible dinar for 10,000 old dinars and pegged the new dinar to the deutschemark at 7 : 1. As in the Polish case there was a considerable exchange from deutschemark holdings into holdings of the new dinar since the latter shared equally high returns on deposits. The Yugoslavian currency reform resembles very much the German currency reform of November 1923 (Claassen [3]) when one trillion paper marks were exchanged for one gold mark (or Rentenmark) and where the exchange rate of the gold mark to the dollar was set at 4.2 : 1.

Among the lessons one could draw from open macroeconomics over the last three decades is the recognition that policy makers can fix only one nominal variable, while the others become endogenous provided that markets clear. According to Robert Mundell [9], among the nominal variables one can choose as the single exogenous one — being nothing else than the nominal anchor of the system — the quantity of money, the nominal exchange rate, the price level and the nominal wage rate. For our Western industrialized countries, we are normally used to choose between the first two variables, i.e. to target either the outstanding quantity of money or the exchange rate. The first monetary system is that of a fixed quantity of money and of a flexible exchange rate. The second system is just the contrary, a fixed exchange rate and a flexible quantity of money.

The idea of targeting the money supply can be ascribed to the monetarist school. By fixing the rate of growth of the money supply, all other nominal variables have to adjust as endogenous magnitudes: the price level, the nominal exchange rate, and the nominal wage rate. Furthermore, these three endogenous nominal variables have to move such that the resulting real exchange rate and real wage assure an equilibrium in the real sector of the economy (goods market and labor market, respectively). The money supply target can be motivated by the ultimate goal of price level stability or of low inflation rate. The three present monetary areas in the world economy (dollar, deutschemark and yen area) could be interpreted such that each of the centre countries fixes the growth rate of its money supply according to its desired price level evolution and all other nominal variables float correspondingly.

The second monetary system is that of a fixed nominal exchange rate by letting all other nominal variables float. Its ultimate goal could also be price level stability or the realization of a low inflazion rate. Since a country can only fix one exchange rate among the $(n - 1)$ independent exchange rates (n representing the number of currencies in the world), it should choose the exchange rate of that country with whom it has important trade relationships and which succeeds relatively well in pursuing price level stability. The evolution of the European Monetary System (EMS) toward a German monetary area is one striking example in this respect. The choice between a fixed and a floating exchange rate is not a matter of indifference if the monetary authorities of the concerned country have a lack of credibility as a consequence of their past inflation prone behavior. Pegging to the deutschemark involves following the monetary policy of the Bundesbank, which has gained a high level of credibility with respect to the maintenance of price level stability over the last four decades.

The possibility of pegging the price level is probably the most inconvenient method since it would not only imply the price control of thousands if not millions of goods, but it would primarily result in the distortion of relative prices. The control of a single price would be the other extreme consisting of pegging the exchange rate as the simplest device to the extent that the concerned currency is convertible on the domestic and international level. The choice of nominal wages is the ultimo ratio in the Keynesian case of wage rigidities.

If the nominal exchange rate is to be used as the nominal anchor for avoiding inflationary pressure, confidence in the newly convertible currency can only be built up provided that a future devaluation is absolutely excluded. There will be no difficulty in maintaining the exchange rate with conservative monetary and fiscal policies. As far as Poland and Yugoslavia are concerned, their currencies are «newly created» ones since their former status was deprived of any «moneyness». Their respective monetary authorities cannot rely on any past monetary performance because there was none. Their credibility can only be based on future monetary policy. With a fixed and immovable exchange rate they could gain the credibility of the currency to which they have pegged. This insight is valid at least for the small open economies of Central Europe in contrast to the big and relatively closed economy of the Soviet Union.

4. - Real Exchange Rate

Another reason for choosing a fixed exchange rate as the anchor of the monetary system is the fact that a devaluation will not have a lasting impact on the competitiveness of the domestic tradable goods sector with respect to foreign tradable goods. What a devaluation is able to bring about concerns a change in the real exchange rate in terms of q. However, for all the former socialist countries, it is not a real depreciation but a real appreciation which is of primary concern.

In early 1991 citizens of East Berlin who use the local transport system of West and East Berlin still pay one-tenth of the price paid by citizens of West Berlin. Similar ratios exist for postal services and energy. As far as housing is concerned, rents are diverging between one-tenth and one-twentieth. The price liberalization of nontradable goods would decrease considerably the real purchasing power of salaries within the production sector of tradables with the subsequent danger of higher wage claims in this sector and higher unemployment.

When we analyzed the realization of internal and external convertibility, the macroeconomic equilibrium was reached at point A for Eastern Germany and at point B for Poland and Yugoslavia (Graph 1). The real exchange rate (q_1) is still a disequilibrium one. There is the need for a real appreciation (q_o) which would change the production structure in favor of nontradable goods. In the case of East Germany, the price level of nontradables has to rise by AC_1. Consequently, the quantity of money for East Germany has to increase such that the new P_o-schedule passes through point C_1.

With respect to other countries which have maintained their proper currencies (point B), there are two ways to realize real appreciation, namely point D or point C. Solution D implies a fall in P_T via a nominal revaluation and an increase in P_N such that the general price level would remain unchanged. Solution C is analogous to the German case. The quantity of money has to increase (taking place even automatically according to the monetary approach of the balance of payments) and the new MM-schedule has to pass through point C.

5. - Labor Market and the Timing of Stabilization Policies: the Case of Germany

«*Kommt die DM, bleiben wir. Kommt sie nicht, gehen wir zu ihr.*». (Slogan in Leipzig and East Berlin in early 1990). The literature on currency areas is rich and bewildering because of so many various criteria according to which countries should establish a currency area. We shall refer to one of the first theoretical contributions in this field written in 1961 by Robert Mundell [8]. We choose that particular model because it seems to perfectly fit the actual situation of both Germanies. According to this model, countries should join a currency area if there is perfect factor mobility between them. Before July 2, 1990 we had already perfect labor mobility within both Germanies. Capital mobility followed afterward. Factor mobility would avoid unemployment in the member countries of the currency area. If there is unemployment in one country, labor would move out to the other country. If labor is not mobile, a separate currency standard is required. By devaluating its currency, unemployment would be absorbed provided that wages are not pushed upwards. Furthermore, capital would flow in to sustain the extension of production.

The Mundell model is only valid when the labor movement does not create unemployment in the other country. However, increased unemployment is the situation with which the Federal Republic and the former GDR will be confronted in the very near future. The final reasons for the rising unemployment rate are twofold: the considerable potential wage differential between both economies and the firm opposition of West German trade unions to any decline in their real wages. Thus, at first sight, Mundell's model does not seem to apply at all to either Germanies, since in each currency regime unemployment will persist. There seemed to be only one option: the currency union. Under *whatever* currency regime, the labor outflow and inflow continues. Consequently, one has to reduce the labor productivity differential as quickly as possible by the most radical reform program.

In Graph 2 we illustrate the unified labor market with three possible outcomes for labor migration from East to West. Before migration starts, we assume that there is no unemployment in neither of the two countries. The active population in the West (P_w) is measured from left to right and the active population in the East (P_e) from right to left. The marginal productivity of labor of each region is represented by the downward sloping schedules, MPL_w and MPL_e. Before the fall of the wall, the distribution of the active population was at P at which labor productivity in the East (point B) is estimated to be one-third of the Western labor productivity (point A).

By opening the West German labor market to the Eastern part, the optimal migration level would be determined by the intersection point C at which both marginal labor productivities are equalized. The Eastern labor of PP_0 would migrate to the West and the whole area would have a net benefit in terms of an additional GDP equal to the triangle ABC. At the same time, a considerable number of Eastern firms would close which produced in former times one part (i.e. BPP_0C) of the total Eastern GDP, which shrinks now to the level of $CP_0O'D$.

GRAPH 2

MIGRATION MODEL

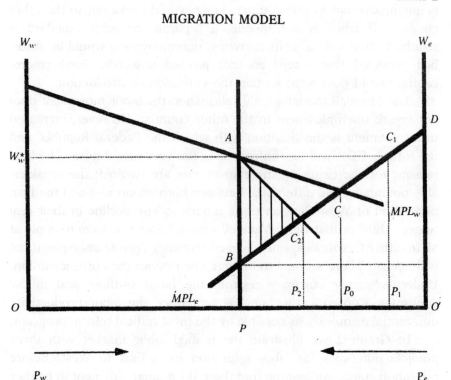

However, the optimal solution of *C* is unlikely to happen. What is optimal for both regions taken together is not optimal from the point of view of West German trade unions. The West German level of real wages would fall from *A* to *C* (but, correspondingly, the real wage level of all East Germans would rise from *B* to *C*). Take the assumption that West German trade unions succeed in maintaining their original real wage level at W_w^*. This outcome is even more likely to happen if one takes into consideration that future West German real wages after taxes will probably decrease to the extent that the tax burden has to rise in order to finance part of the public expenditures in the East. With an unchanged real wage rate of W_w^* situation C_1 may take place: a massive unemployment in both regions (with or without migration) of the size PP_1 and a total net loss of GDP for both regions equal to the surface of BPP_1C_1.

Fortunately, situation C_1 can be disregarded as being likely since in the case of migration, Eastern emigrants must take into account the considerable risk of unemployment when they search the Western labor market. At this stage we can resort to a model elaborated by Harris-Todaro [5] for developing countries which regards labor migration from a low productive rural sector to a high productive urban sector. The main considerations for labor migration are wage differentials, but in the Harris-Todaro framework the wage differentials must be the expected and not effective ones. By applying their model to the German economy, the effective real wage differential is $W_w\text{-}W_e$ while the probable or expected wage differential is $pW_w\text{-}W_e$ where p represents the probability degree of finding employment within the west German economy. The coefficient p can be proxied by the ratio of employment (E_w) over the total active propulation (P_w). In Graph 2, the schedule AC_2 illustrates the evolution of $pW^*{}_w\text{-}W_e$ where p is assumed to fall increasingly with rising migration. The shaded area ABC_2 represents the shrinking expected wage differential. The migration stops at point C_2. Total migration amounts to PP_2 creating unemployment of the same size in Western Germany. The net loss of GDP for the whole territory is the area BPP_2C_2. It has been assumed that Western wages remain at the rigid level W_w^* and that Eastern wages have risen from B to C_2.

The above geometrical model represents an oversimplification of the united German labor market. It abstracts from many other determinants of the expected wage differential, the latter having constituted until now the single and decisive force for labor migration. There are factors which could enlarge the expected wage differential and others which attenuate it. Unemployment benefits granted by the West to the emigrants for the duration of one year dampen the fall in p but recently they have been abolished and Eastern unemployed emigrants receive their proper unemployment benefits from the former GDR. Existent unemployment in the East of the static and disguised type will also enforce labor movement. Other elements shorten the expected wage differential. Depending on how one measures real wages in the East, they may be higher than generally estimated if one takes into account more distinctively certain nontradable goods which are cheaper for the moment in the East than in the

West. A possible fall in the real wage rate of Western Germany should also not be excluded. A rapidly raising unemployment rate could exercise a downward pressure on real wages.

The Federal government could also envisage a premium for staying in a similar way as the (former) «Zitterprämie» granted to the population of West Berlin. Furthermore, the migration may stop already at a certain threshold value of a positive expected wage differential to the extent that potential emigrants take into account positive nonpecuniary elements such as those of remaining in their home. Finally, life (i.e. permanent) income will be the decisive element of migration and any radical program which shortens the transition period will also decrease the permanent wage differential between West and East.

The most decisive argument for the German monetary union and thus against all other solutions consists precisely in its radical form in opposition to measures of gradualism. One could argue that the choice of a radical versus gradual reform program would be a matter of indifference to the extent that the results are identical except for timing. However, during the adjustment process, radical programs may cause more credibility than gradual ones, since the latter, in particular in democracies, can always be altered, attenuated, put into doubt such that their final outcome is less satisfactory. The ultimate economic reason for Germany's radical timing of the stabilization policies lies in the unified labor market creating the enormous threat of increasing unemployment provided that one does not succeed in shifting the MPL_e-schedule upward via investment as quickly as possible.

Concluding Remarks

The sequencing of stabilization policies could be imagined in four successive steps: internal convertibility (elimination of the monetary overhang), external convertibility (choice of the monetary anchor), designation of the currency standard, and real appreciation of the currency. For countries like Poland and Yugoslavia, the monetary overhang was eliminated by open inflation. Any further inflationary source in form of the monetary finance of budget deficits was avoided by fiscal reforms (at least in the case of Poland). After the «hyperinflationary» jump in the general price level, external convertibility was introduced. A fixed exchange rate was chosen as the nominal anchor. At the same time, both countries had to select the currency standard. Poland maintained its old currency while Yugoslavia decided to cancel four zeros of its dinar. The last step of a real appreciation of their currencies (in terms of the relative price of nontradables) is still an operation to be realized gradually over the future.

In the case of the German monetary union, instead of open inflation the quantity of money was reduced from 1.8 to 1. In principle, the sequencing of the first three steps was the same but their timing coincided on July 2, 1990: reduction of the quantity of money; a fixed nominal exchange rate of one East mark to one West mark; the replacement of the East mark by the deutschemark. The real appreciation of the deutschemark in the Eastern part of Germany has still to be accomplished in the future.

BIBLIOGRAPHY

[1] BRENNER R.: *The Eastern Bloc: Legal Reforms First, Monetary and Macro-economic Policies Second*, in CLAASSEN E.M. [2].

[2] CLASSEN E.M.: *Exchange Rate Policies in Developing and Socialist Countries*, San Francisco, ICS Press, 1991.

[3] — —: *Gradual versus Radical Transformation: the Case of the German Monetary Union*, in CLAASSEN E.M. [2].

[4] FRYDMAN R. - WELLISZ S. - KOLODKO G.: *Stabilization in Poland: a Progress Report*, in CLAASSEN E.M. [2].

[5] HARRIS J.R. - TODARO M.P.: «Migration, Unemployment and Development: A Two-Sector Analysis», *American Economic Review*, 1970.

[6] LAVIGNE M.: *Intraregional Convertibility in Eastern Europe: is it still an Issue?*, in CLAASSEN E.M. [2].

[7] McKINNON R.I.: *The Problem of Internal Convertibility*, in CAASSEN E.M. [2].

[8] MUNDELL R.: «A Theory of Optimal Currency Areas», *American Economic Review*, 1961.

[9] MUNDELL R.A.: *Stabilization Policies in Less Developed and Socialist Countries*, in CLAASSEN E.M. [2].

[10] PEARCE I.F.: «The Problem of the Balance of Payments», *International Economic Review*, Jan. 1961.

[11] SALTER W.E.: «Internal and External Balance: The Role of Price and Expenditure Effects», *Economic Record*, Aug. 1959.

[12] SWAN T.: «Economic Control in a Dependent Economy», *Economic Record*, Mar. 1960.

German Monetary Union: Experiences and Problems

Norbert Walter
Deutsche Bank, Frankfurt

1. - No Political Alternative to GEMU

The German Monetary and Economic Union ("GEMU") came into effect on July 1, 1990. Its establishment was intended as a milestone on the road towards the political unification of Germany which was completed on October 3, 1990 with the accession of the five new Federal States — the former GDR — to the Federal Republic of Germany. Key elements of the monetary union were the introduction of the DM as sole legal tender in East Germany (replacing the «mark of the GDR», the transfer of full responsibility for monetary policy from the "Staatsbank" to the Bundesbank as well as the fixing of the conversion rate between the DM and the Eastmark. The other side of the GEMU coin was, of course, the creation of an economic union, i.e. East Germany also adopted the fully-fledged (legal) framework of the smoothly functioning social market economy ("soziale marktwirtschaft") of West Germany. Despite the creation of GEMU, there remain two different economic areas in Germany for the time being, with different economic starting points and degrees of dynamism and a substantially higher standard of living in the West.

The GEMU approach contrasts with traditional economic wisdom which, given uncertainty and a wide discrepancy of economic status, suggests to employ a piecemeal approach. From a purely academic point of view, a gradual move towards convertibility of the

East German mark through phased plans with German monetary union as the "crowning achievement" of the process would have seemed advisable because the exchange rate would have been available for some time as a means of mitigating adjustment pressure. Such a process, however, is based on the assumption of two separate "entities". This gradual approach could not be applied since the situation changed dramatically in the former GDR in the aftermath of the fall of the Berlin wall on November 9, 1989. It soon proved doubtful whether such a time-consuming transitional process would have been politically acceptable for East Germans. It became more and more obvious that it would not have worked without the creation of new protective economic walls between East and West Germany including strict "border" controls. Despite the problem of the lack of international competitiveness on the part of East German companies, there was no political alternative to the rapid introduction of an economic and monetary union. Residents of the GDR expressed their deep-rooted distrust of the viability of the so-called socialist system by voting "with their feet": in the four months to January 1990 alone, more than 300,000 East Germans left their country. Another clear signal was the famous slogan shouted at the Leipzig demonstrations at that time: «Kommt die D-mark, bleiben wir, kommt sie nicht, gehen wir zu ihr!» (Roughly translated: «If the DM does not come to us, we will go to the DM»).

The continued lack of an improved outlook in East Germany could easily have led to unabated migration to the West and increasing economic and social tensions in both parts of Germany. Therefore, it was a politically reasonable decision by the Federal government to offer GEMU at an early stage of the process (on February 6, 1990) and to reach an agreement on GEMU with the newly elected East German government within a short time span (completed by the "Staatsvertrag" on May 18). There were also sound economic arguments in favour of GEMU. The introduction of the DM gave East German companies and households immediate access to a fully convertible currency, thus creating confidence in a better future and providing new economic and individual freedoms like full availability of western goods and services and, most important, legal certainty. Furthermore, monetary union is deemed an important prerequiste for speeding up the flow of private capital into East Germany which is badly needed to restructure the stagnating economy.

2. - Monetary Implications of GEMU

2.1 *Monetary Union Without Inflation*

One important issue in creating GEMU was the fixing of the conversion rate between the DM and the East German mark. In this context, neither the inadeguate statistical data of the former GDR nor the various official exchange rates and the strongly fluctuating free market rates of the East German mark (M) provided economically reliable clues. In the end, multiple conversion rates were agreed more or less by a political decision (e.g. recurring payments like wages, rents etc. at a rate of 1:1, also savings accounts, depending on the account holder's age, to maximum amounts of M2,000, M4,000, and M6,000; all other assets and liabilities at a rate of M 2:DM 1; the average conversion rate was M 1.8:DM 1). By such arrangements, the monetary supply created remained small enough to avoid significant inflationary risks. The 2:1 conversion of financial obligations of the business sector was designed to restrict the burden for enterprises resulting from the transition into the market system. The wages agreed upon seemed low enough so as not to render East German firms uncompetitive, especially considering the potential productivity jump after the economic reform.

There were strong sentiments, above all abroad, that GEMU would have inflationary effects because of an expected spending spree from East Germany and very high budget deficits caused by the tremendous public transfers from the West to the East. However, such fears proved unfounded. A sizeable spending boom on the part of East German consumers did not occur, partly because of the increasing risk of unemployment. The additional demand concentrated on a few goods (like cars, consumer durables etc.) which could easily be satisfied by increasing imports. Furthermore, Deutsche Bundesbank continued with its restrictive monetary policy. The rise in the West German inflation rate from 2.3% in June to 2.7% in December 1990 (peaking at 3.2% in October) was mainly due to the oil price hike and remained well below projections by highly esteemed experts in the financial world.

In the process of GEMU East German prices were rapidly adjusted to market conditions (with a few exceptions, e.g. rents and some energy prices). While prices of 'basic goods' like food rose sharply, those of consumer durables and semi-luxuries (e.g. coffee) decreased substantially. On balance, the East German price level remained some percentage points below the pre-year average (until November) and the level of May 1990 (when the new price statistics started). East Germans also benefitted from a substantial, increase in the quality and availability of goods and services which cannot be covered by a year-on-year comparison of price statistics. This means that GEMU was associated with a gain in purchasing power in East Germany and an improvement in the standard of living, a fact wich is particularly visible when examining the car fleet of today compared to a year ago.

2.2 *Monetary Policy in the Enlarged DM Area*

All in all, the Bundesbank very successfully managed the conduct of monetary policy in the enlarged currency area. It was particularly skillful in dealing with the complex transition problems. Before the introduction of GEMU on July 1, 1990, the Bundesbank set up a «provisional administrative office» in Berlin and 15 branches in the former GDR to take care of the technical aspects of monetary union. The conversion of East German marks into DM was carried out only via bank accounts. Around 24 million bank accounts were converted at the beginning of July. In order to supply the 16 million East German residents with an initial stock of currency the Bundesbank provided DM 28 billion in coin and notes.

The DM money supply ($M3$), which comprises currency in circulation, domestic banks' sight deposits, time deposits with less than 4 year maturity and savings deposits at statutory notice increased in the wake of the currency conversion by 15%; this certainly marks the high end of the spectrum of estimates for the East German productive potential as percentage of that of West Germany. This caused, however, no inflationary problems because a portfolio adjustment has been under way in East Germany and monetary wealth formation has increased disproportionately, i.e. banks' clients' assets (included in $M3$) have been replaced by the purchase of securities or other forms of long-term saving which are not included in $M3$. In other words, the increase of the effective money supply did not surpass the German economic potential, especially considering the — internationally desired — substantial reduction of net exports.

The West German monetary target for 1990 of 4% to 6% for $M3$ will have been met, though monetary expansion accelerated somewhat after the introduction of GEMU (to 5.5% in November compared to the fourth quarter of 1989). The analysis of money supply can no longer be restricted to West German figures as was the case during the first few months after the introduction of GEMU because of a lack of data in the former GDR. One reason is the growing interdependence: many West German companies are increasingly keeping deposits with East German banks whereas many East German inhabitants have deposited their money with banks in West German. Consequently, in December 1990 the Bundesbank announced for the first time a money supply target for the enlarged currency area (of again 4-6% for 1991 against Q4 1990). In this context, the Bundesbank indicated that the rate of monetary expansion will preferably be kept at the lower end of the band. There is no doubt that such a target implies a clearly anti-inflationary policy.

The conduct of monetary policy in East Germany is in principle based on the same instruments and techniques as in the West. However, during the initial phase of GEMU the rudimentary character of the East German banking system had to be taken into account. For instance, trade bills eligible for rediscount or marketable securities that might serve as a basis for repurchase agreements or Lombard loans were not available at East German banks. Therefore, Deutsche Bundesbank has granted them so-called refinancing quotas which — in contrast to traditional rediscount credit — can be utilized not only on the basis of trade bills but also on the basis of bank promissory notes. These refinancing loans are settled at the discount rate (currently 6%). East German banks may also submit bank promissory notes as collateral for Lombard credit (currently 8.5%). These special refinancing facilities are to be abolished gradually by the end of 1991.

The improvement in the conduct of monetary policy in the East goes hand in hand with the development of a more efficient banking system which is well under way. To begin with, a two-tiered banking system distinguishing between a central, bank and commercial banks was already implemented on April 1, 1990 in the former GDR. The State Bank's ("Staatsbank") commercial banking activities were transferred to the newly-founded Deutsche Kreditbank AG while it retained its central bank function until the beginning of GEMU. Cooperative banks, savings banks and some special banks were also allowed to operate as independent institutions. These institutions were actively supported by the corresponding West German banking groups e.g. as far as the transfer of modern banking know-how is concerned. Foreign banks were allowed to start local business in East Germany with the beginning of GEMU. Especially West German private banks entered the market by founding joint ventures (e.g. Deutsche Bank and Dresdner Bank with Deutsche Kreditbank AG) and/or establishing new branches. At the turn of year 1990-1991 about 35 private West German banks are operating in the East with more than 430 branches. The East German banking system tends to assume a similar structure as in the West; each bank is basically allowed to offer the full range of bank services. The quality of bank services has been substantially improved since the beginning of GEMU and is expected to catch up with western standards in 2 to 3 years.

2.3 *Monetary Policy, Budget Deficits and Interest Rates*

The Bundesbank is obviously more and more concerned about the possible inflationary risks due to the substantial increase in public-sector deficits. In fact, the combined budget deficit of central, regional and local authorities (including the German unity fund) amounted to DM 110 billion or 4.0% of GNP in 1990 and is expected to increase to some DM 140 billion (approx. 5% of GNP) in 1991, provided that there are spending cuts in the order of DM 35 billion.

The main cause for increased budget deficits is massive public transfers to the East partly necessary because of the collapse of the tax
revenues in East Germany. Temporary public transfers are a "natural"
corollary of GEMU, needed to alleviate the adjustment pressure by
boistering the social security systems and establishing an efficient
infrastructure in the administration, in telecommunications, transport
etc. The transfer amounts to approx. DM 65 billion in 1990 and is
expected to rise to DM 90 billion to DM 100 billion in 1991. As the
Federal government does not want to raise the level of taxation for
good reasons, there is enormous pressure on politicians to cut government expenditure and subsidies.

At present, DM interest rates include a major risk premium for a
continuously lax fiscal policy. If the Federal government proved able
to constrain public deficit by cuts, concerns of the Bundesbank and
the financial markets would subside and a major reason for raising
German central bank rate in the months to come would disappear and
long-term interest rates could begin to decline. Normally, real interest
rates moved between 2 and 4 percentage points.

There is no reason to dramatize an increase in the budget deficit if
if is only a temporary one. Given the chance for a further substantial
cut in net exports — the current account still has a surplus of 3% of
GNP — and the favourable outlook for West German growth and
hopefully from 1992 onwards also in the eastern part, which means
rising tax revenues, a reduction of public deficits should be possible
after 1992 at the latest. German capital markets are expected to be
efficient enough to smoothly secure the financing of public-sector
borrowing requirements. In 1990, current savings by West German
households increased substantially to more than DM 200 billion and
East German households probably added another DM 25 billion.
Thus, current savings were more than double the amount of the
budget deficit in 1990. In the past few years West Germany has
incurred a high surplus on current account (in the order of DM 100
billion p.a.), i.e. it exported its surplus in current savings to finance
economic development and growth abroad. In the years to come,
German savings will have to be reallocated partly in order to meet
increasing domestic public-borrowing requirements and partly to
finance additional private investment. In the process, the high Ger-

man current account surplus will shrink further (from around DM 75 billion in 1990 to DM 35 billion in 1991).

3. - Impact on the Real Economy

Germany is currently a "split economy". While business activity in West Germany is booming, the East German economy is in a process of fundamental restructuring with shrinking production and increasing unemployment. West German GNP increased by around 4.5% in 1990 and is expected to grow by approx. 3% in 1991. Domestic demand will continue to be the source of dynamism. Steeply rising new order intake in the capital goods sector and the double-digit increase in retail sales after the introduction of GEMU clearly indicate that the West German economy is strongly benefitting from East Germans' pent-up demand and their focus on Western products. All in all, the West German economy seems to be well prepared to integrate the five new Federal States.

GEMU immediately highlighted East German companies' lack of international competitiveness. On the one hand East German firms suffered from a steep decline in domestic demand because Western products were clearly preferred by the East German population. There was no lack of demand but a shift in demand in East Germany. On the other hand, East German exports to the traditional Comecon markets have come under increasing pressure due to the problems connected with economic reform in these countries and the decision to settle intra-Comecon trade in convertible currencies as of January 1, 1991.

As a consequence, East German companies have had to adjust to market conditions via shock therapy. They have been compelled to reduce their production to actual demand, to improve quality and styling of products and to attach particular attention to cost-oriented pricing. In the process, industrial output declined by 45% from the second to the third quarter 1990, thus falling short of the pre-year level by 9.5% and 48% respectively. Unemployment increased substantially (to 6.7% or 590,000 in November 1990); in addition to that around 1.8 million people are working short time.

No doubt, this painful process of "creative destruction" is necessary to clear the way for market-related structures and to establish a sound basis for future growth and higher employment. In order to alleviate the adjustment pressure, East German state-owned enterprises were initially granted so-called liquidity loans by banks which were guaranteed by the Treuhandanstalt, the public-sector agency set up to handle the reprivatization of the 8,000 state-owned enterprises in the former GDR. These credits will expire at the end of March 1991. Then Treuhandanstalt will have to decide on the basis of the opening balance sheets which companies have a chance of surviving and which do not, i.e. another decrease in production and employment is in the pipeline from this side.

Many international economists said that it would have been wiser to secure the competitiveness of East German firms by a conversion rate much lower than M 1.8:DM 1. Such an analysis is not particularly well-founded given the almost complete mobility of labour within Germany — which would have led to massive continued migration within the country — and the almost complete information about goods and services. The perception of quality differentials was so great that price differentials to compensate for the preferences would have left East German incomes at the level of marginalisation. This held true for Trabis as well as for soap or toothpaste.

An economic turnaround in East Germany is to be expected around the middle of 1991, as activities in the construction and the services sector will continue to pick up and the shrinkage of the industrial sector will slow down. As far as the medium term economic prospects of East Germany are concerned there is reason for optimism. Following a contraction of GNP of more than 10% in 1990 and a further reduction in 1991, there will be a prolonged period of growth in the order of 10% p.a. (similar to the Federal Republic in the '50s). There is already "good news" for East German private initiative, i.e. the economic incentives given by GEMU are beginning to work. In the first ten months of 1990 approximately 227,000 new businesses were registered and about 3,000 small and medium-sized firms nationalized in the last big campaign of 1972 have been reprivatized. In addition to that, Western companies, especially West German firms are increasingly interested not only in selling in East Germany but also in setting up plants. For 1991 direct investment of more than DM 20 billion have already been announced. And contrary to the perception abroad, non-German firms are also welcome. Impediments to invest have to be reduced further. For instance, public administration has to be improved with regard to clarification of private property and provision of land for new plants. Treuhandanstalt can do even more to promote the process of recovery by emphasising rapid privatization rather than the reconstruction of firms.

While most prices for goods and services are converging in the enlarged German single market, the integration of the two labour markets is proving much more difficult. The final outcome, of course, will be a rough approximation of wage levels which today are on average half of those in the West. Only a small step towards integration is the increasing number of commuters (est. at several 100,000). However, despit redundant East German labour no significant pressure on West German real wages is visible which should have occurred according to textbooks on a single market. On the contrary, real wages continue to increase rapidly by a good 3% in the West and there are a number of double-digit wage claims in the negotiations ahead. The reason for such a development is above all a lack of modern professional skills as well as a lack of vocational mobility in East Germany. Therefore, besides retraining, a productivity-oriented wage policy is a key element in improving the competitive position and employment prospects in the East. In general, wage settlements since spring 1990 have been too generous compared to the situation in productivity. More important, however, is the fact that they have not been sufficiently differentiated. Wage increases should be increasingly differentiated according to productivity and scarcity of the labour force.

4. - International Implications of GEMU

No doubt, the GEMU-induced stimulus is not only propping up German GNP but also supporting growth in our partner countries via increased German imports. In the current phase Germany is playing the role of a "growth locomotive" in a slackening world economy. On the other hand the tremendous fiscal expansion in Germany should lead to relatively higher interest rates abroad with detrimental effects on already weaker business activity, It is, however, not particulaly convincing that the bail-out of 16 million people, i.e. the bail-out of a city like New York, should shake-up world financial markets and keep international interest rates high in view of a world recession. A slackening of business activity in most industrial countries gives some scope for easing interest rates as the example of the US has demonstrated. On balance, the stimulating effect of GEMU is expected to prevail internationally, as the Reagan policy mix stimulated the world economy in the first half of the '80s.

An interest rate dilemma was felt by come EMS partner countries that are interested in stable EMS parities and therefore not able to lower their interest rates because of high DM rates. Usually the leading role of the anchor currency is a key rule of the game in every workable fixed exchange rate regime. In this context Germany has been recommended to change the policy mix and to increase taxes to finance the public transfer to the East. However, is there really an alternative to a restrictive monetary policy and an expansive fiscal policy in Germany at the moment? I do not think so. More public spending cuts are desirable, not so higher taxes which would either increase inflation rates and thus interest rates and/or dampen business activity. Critisism of the German policy mix, i.e. its unwillingness to increase taxes, is ill-founded.

In some quarters, Germany is reproached of pursuing Reaganomics as far as the policy mix and its effects are concerned. There are some similarities with the US in the early '80s like strong growth and a strong currency which supports the stabilization of the domestic price level. However, the differences are also obvious: currently Germany's huge current account is being reduced substantially but is expected to remain positive, while the US experienced mounting external deficits in the early 1980s; Germany's inflation is low whereas the US combatted double-digit inflation rates at that time.

As far as the exchange rate of the DM is concerned fears of a GEMU-induced weakening have not materialized. On the contrary, the DM tends to be strong against the US dollar and the yen. Within the EMS the DM has also strengthened since the introduction of

GEMU owing to the perception of DM interest rates remaining high and increasing growth differential in favour of Germany. Against this background the DM is expected to remain the stability anchor of the EMS to the benefit of the process of monetary integration in Europe.

With regard to the impact of the enlarged DM area on the European integration process there are, however, two conflicting schools of thought. One argues that the integration of East Germany will bind up West Germany's energy with detrimental effects especially on the creation of EMU. According to the second school of thought, GEMU and unification will speed up European integration because the EC partner countries aim at firmly linking the enlarged Germany into the EC. Obviously, the Federal government continues to have a strong interest in strengthening European integration, as has been proved at the various EC summits in 1990. Therefore, GEMU is expected to accelerate rather than retard the process of monetary integration towards EMU.

Opinions are also divided whether and to what extent GEMU and unification will enhance Germany's role in the process of European integration. To my mind, the united Germany will remain firmly committed to the creation of European economic, monetary and political union because it is finally in its own political interest. Given the pivotal role of the DM in this process, the success of GEMU creates an important precondition for an effective implementation of EMU in the years to come.

EMU and Greece: Issues and Prospects for Membership

Miranda Xafa (*)

Princeton University - The International Monetary Fund

1. - Introduction

The EC's recent initiative to integrate its market for goods, services, labor and capital, has been accompanied by progress toward establishing a monetary union within the EC. As part of this process, the European Council appointed a Committee to study and propose concrete stages leading to monetary union. The *Delors Committee Report* [7] proposed a three-stage approach to full monetary union. The first two stages involve the gradual elimination of all barriers to free capital mobility within the EC and greater coordination of monetary policies among EC members under the present system of separately managed currencies. Stage one would involve the participation of all EC members in the exchange-rate mechanism of the EMS, including those who do not presently participate (Greece, Portugal and the United Kingdom). Stage two would require coordination of monetary policies and an understanding that exchange-rate realignments would be made only in exceptional circumstances. Full

(*) This paper was not presented at the International Economic Conference Building the New Europe. I have benefited from discussions with Bill Branson, Alex Cuckierman and Rex Ghosh. I would also like to thank Peter Kenen for detailed comments on an earlier draft of this paper, and participants at the Sloan-IFS workshop in international economics at Princeton University for helpful suggestions. The views expressed are my own and do not necessarily represent those of the IMF.

Advise: the numbers in square brackets refer to the Bibliography in the appendix.

unification would be achieved in stage three, which involves the transfer of monetary management to a European System of Central Banks (ESCB) and a single EC currency.

The issue of European monetary integration has received considerable attention from policymakers and academics much before the *Delors Commission Report* was issued, insofar as the desirability establishing a nominal anchor by joining the EMU can be assessed on the same basis as the desirability of joining the existing European Monetary System (EMS). The issues addressed include the desirability of fixed nominal exchange rates in the presence of independent demand or supply shocks that affect member countries asymmetrically; and concerns about an overly restrictive fiscal policy under an exchange-rate system anchored on the Deutschmark (see Van der Ploeg [14], for a summary of the advantages and disadvantages of European monetary union).

This paper focuses on the narrower issue of the feasibility of fixing the nominal exchange rate in an EC country with a large fiscal deficit which is the source of money creation and above-average inflation (1). This issue, arises, to various extents, in all the South European countries, but is particularly relevant to Greece, which has the highest inflation rate and fiscal deficit among the EC countries. Dornbusch [8] advocates a «crawling peg» under which the currencies of the Southern European countries would gradually depreciates *vis-à-vis* the nothern countries in order to maintain competitiveness. Underlying his proposal is the concern that the loss of . revenue from monetization under the EMU would require a fiscal adjustment in the Southern European countries to ensure the sustainability of their public debt. If the loss of revenue from monetization cannot be easily made up through other revenue sources (because a larger black economy reduces the tax base), it may be preferable to accommodate the existing inflation differential through currency depreciation. This argument is strengthened if some of the South European countries start from an unsustainable fiscal position:

---

(1) Even if the European Central Bank is less conservative than the Bundesbank, so that the EC average inflation rate rises, the EMU would imply lower inflation for EC countries with above-average inflation rates.

for these countries, the loss of revenue from monetatization under the EMU adds to the deficit reduction required to attain a sustainable fiscal position.

Gros [11] has argued that the crawling peg proposal overlooks the benefits of low inflation and monetary discipline that the EMU anchor would entail. France has reaped these benefits by pegging to the Deutschmark since 1986 and «importing» the German inflation rate. A tight fiscal stance and a clear signal that the French monetary authorities will not accommodate any wage settlements that emerge from the negotiating table contributed to the success of this policy. Among the South European countries, Spain has opted to reap the credibility gains associated with the Bundesbank's past performance by joining the EMS in 1989. Italy, whose currency has tended to depreciate in past EMS realignments, has recently narrowed its fluctuation band in the EMS and eliminated all remaining exchange controls. Portugal remains outside of the EMS, but acts as if it is in, by targeting a reduction in the inflation rate toward the EC average. By contrast, monetary policy in Greece remains severely constrained by the size of the fiscal deficit. Paragraphs 2-4 of this paper provide an overview of policies and economic performance in Greece in the 1980s compared with the rest of the EC, and use a simple framework to assess the fiscal adjustment required to reach a sustainable fiscal position under different inflation targets.

While the credibility gains of pegging to a low-inflation currency area are no doubt substantial, a credible commitment to join the EMS or the EMU requires a sustainable fiscal position. If the size of the required adjustment to sustainability is very large, this commitment will not be credible. Moreover, a trade-off will arise between the gains from disinflation and the resulting loss of revenue from inflation. Although the government budget constraint exists independently of the exchange rate regime chosen, this constraint becomes more severe if government revenues from inflation are foregone, as noted above. Additional costs would be incurred if the — yet unspecified — timetable for implementation of the EMU is short. Branson [3] points out that if the output cost of rapid disinflation is high, it may be preferable to join the exchange rate arrangements after the rate of inflation has been reduced to the range of existing members.

Another issue that arises in the context of the EMU is the required degree of fiscal policy coordination through the various stages of EMU and the need for systemic limitation of the fiscal autonomy of member States. The *Delors Committee Report* ([7], Article 59), proposed limits on budget deficits of member countries «to the extent that this was necessary to prevent imbalances that might threaten monetary stability». The underlying presumption is that the preservation of price and financial stability in the EMU requires a regulatory framework to prevent overlending and overborrowing: private creditors may not base their lending decisions on country risk analysis alone if they perceive the ESCB as a lender of last resort. Although an analysis of the moral hazard issue in the EMU is beyond the scope of this paper, paragraph 2 of the paper notes that Greece has had access to spontaneous external financing from international capital markets on a larger scale than countries in a similar situation which are not members of the EC (Mexico and Turkey are chosen as examples). It could thus be argued that the moral hazard issue may arise independently of the existence of the EMU; all that is required is that private creditors perceive that the EC will «stand behind» any of its members through the provision of financing and guarantees.

The Delors Committee ([7], Article 59) proposal to impose limits on budget deficits was accompanied by a recommendation to apply to Community loans (as a substitute for the present medium-term financial support facility «terms and conditions that would prompt member countries to intensify their adjustment efforts». Because the substitution of EC resources for market-based lending would shift the risk of default from individual member countries to the EC as a whole, the EC would undertake to monitor and contain fiscal imbalances through some form of conditionality. The financial stability of the EMu could still be threatened under this risk-transfer scheme depending on how strictly this conditionality is imposed. The experience with the existing EC medium-term financial support facility shows that the degree of adjustment undertaken ultimately depends on the member country. France, which used this facility in 1983, overperformed with respect to the macroeconomic targets specified and repaid the EC loan early; Greece, which used the facility in 1985, is now facing larger macroeconomic imbalances than in 1985.

2. - Economic Policies and Performance in Greece in the 1980s

The period since 1981, when Greece joined the EC, is characterized by a market divergence in both policies and performance relative to the rest of the Community. Since 1981, Greek economic policy has pursued the sometimes contradictory objectives of growth, price stability, and social equity. The autorities' growth strategy relied on expansionary fiscal and incomes policies, while policies in the rest of the Community generally aimed at disinflation and fiscal consolidation. The need to finance budget deficits averaging 14.5% of GDP in the 1980s gave rise to a sharp increase in external and internal public debt and to a sustained increase in money growth well in excess of the EC average. The inflation differential with the EC thus widened in the 1980s, leading to continued depreciation of the nominal effective exchange rate. Throughout the 1980s the announced inflation targets were consistently exceeded, as were the announced budget targets. Expansionary financial policies in Greece did not elicit a sustained output response; on the contrary, they crowded out private investment, with the result that GDP growth in the 1980s slowed considerably more than in the EC as a whole.

Chart 1 compares Greece's growth and inflation record to the EC average in the 1970s and the 1980s. GDP growth in Greece fell from an above-average annual rate of 4.75% in the 1970s to a below-average 1.5% in the 1980s. Similarly, the divergence of inflation rates between Greece and the EC became much more marked; inflation in Greece was only marginally above the EC average in the 1970s, but rose to three times the EC average in the 1980s.

Macroeconomic policies in Greece in the 1980s can be assessed with reference to three periods: an initial phase of expansionary fiscal and incomes policies in 1981-1985, the 1986-1987 stabilization phase, and the period since 1988 which has been characterized by adjustment fatigue and pre-election spending, followed by a sequence of coalition governments since mid-1989. The initial rise in budgetary outlays reflected discretionary increases in social benefits and public sector wages, and was accompanied by a sharp increase in minimum wages which affected wage settlements in the private sector. These

GRAPH 1

GREECE AND EC:
GDP GROWTH

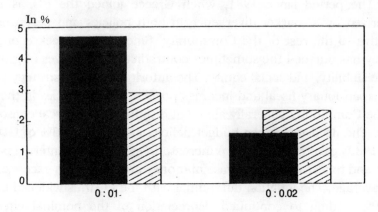

Source: EC COMMISSION: *European Economy.*

GRAPH 1*a*

INFLATION RATES

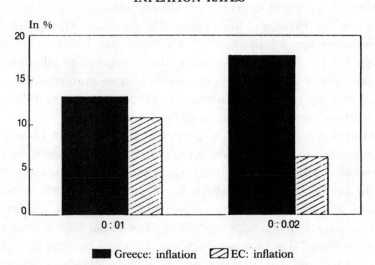

Source: EC COMMISSION: *European Economy.*

policies contributed to large increases in the fiscal and external deficits (Graphs 2 and 3) as most of the stimulus benefited Greece's trading partners. Real wages rose considerably faster than productivity, reducing profit margins and the incentive to invest and produce (Graph 4). This trend continued until 1985, when the current account deficit peaked at 10% of GDP and a stabilization program was undertaken, supported by a $2 billion loan from the EC.

The 1986-1987 stabilization program was successful in reducing somewhat the fiscal and external deficits — though by less than the amount targeted — but not on a lasting basis. First, it relied entirely on a sharp reduction in wages through a modification of the wage indexation scheme, and on the implicit «taxation» of oil products by not passing on to consumers the benefit of the oil price decline in 1986. But the reduction in real wages was achieved by compressing the wage scale to protect lower incomes. Continued compression in the wage scale could not be sustained without reducing the incentive to work and acquire new skills; its microeconomic effects were thus negative and made the policy counterproductive over the medium term. Similarly, there was no lasting reduction in public expenditures or increase in revenues: the fiscal revenue from the taxation of oil products has dissipated as oil prices rose in the world market since 1987 with no corresponding increase in the domestic price of oil products. Second, the stabilization program attempted to correct the macro imbalances without paying attention to the efficiency of resource use. Addressing long-standing structural weaknesses caused by over-regulation of private sector activities would have helped increase private investment and the output response to demand stimulus. These structural issues are discussed below.

The adjustment effort was abandoned in 1988 in favor of a more «growth-oriented» policy. There was a renewed fiscal expansion accompanied by wage increases well in excess of productivity. As was the case in the 1981-1985 period, the relaxation of financial policies had an only transitory impact on GDP growth, while compounding the underlying disequilibria through further increases in the public debt relative to GDP. A stabilization in the debt/GDP ratio would have required a primary fiscal surplus. Instead, the primary deficit remained in deficit throughout the 1980s; its servicing has therefore

GRAPH 2

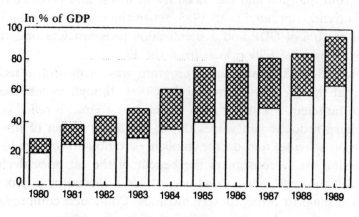

TOTAL NET PUBLIC DEBT
(in % of GDP)

Source: BANK OF GREECE and WORLD BANK.

GRAPH 2*a*

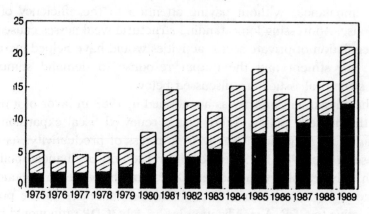

PSBR AND INTEREST PAYMENTS
(in % of GDP)

Source: BANK OF GREECE.

GRAPH 3

TRADE DEFICIT
(in % of GDP)

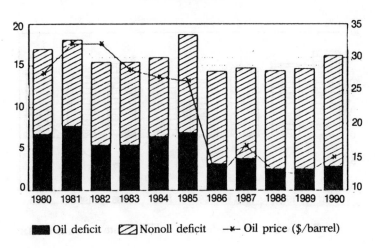

■ Oil deficit ▨ Nonoll deficit —✳— Oil price ($/barrel)

Source: BANK OF GREECE and IFS.

GRAPH 3*a*

CURRENT ACCOUNT DEFICIT
(in % of GDP)

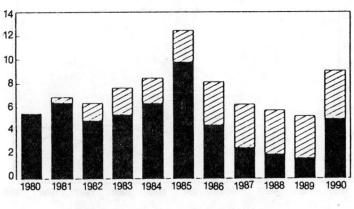

■ Incl. EC transfers ▨ EC transfers

Source: BANK OF GREECE.

GRAPH 4

WAGES AND PRODUCTIVITY
(in %)

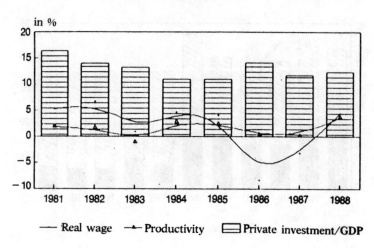

Source: OECD.

GRAPH 4*a*

NOMINAL AND REAL EXCHANGE RATE
(index, 1985 = 100)

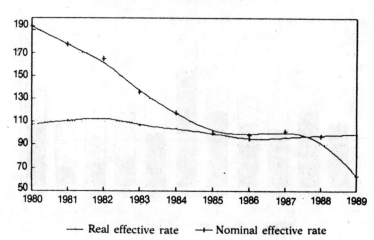

Source: IMF.

been achieved through further borrowing, causing the deficit to feed on itself. The primary deficit resumed its upward trend in 1988 and rose to 8% in 1989 the same level that was reached in 1985, just before the stabilization program was undertaken (Graph 2). But because the stock of public debt was considerably higher in 1989 than in 1985, the total deficit (including interest payments) rose well above the previous peak reached in 1985. The deficit amounted to just over 21% of GDP in 1989 and the total net public debt rose to almost 100% of GDP, about a third of which is foreign debt.

Throughout the 1980s, external conditions were favorable to Greece. Oil prices declined sharply and EC net transfer payments started flowing in (mainly agricultural subsidies under the CAP) in growing amounts. Exchange rate policy essentially accommodated the inflation differential between Greece and its trading partners. Two successive devaluations, in 1983 and 1985, did not have a lasting imact on the real exchange rate in the absence of a sustained reduction in the fiscal deficit. The trade deficit peaked in 1985 at 18% of GDP, and its subsequent reduction under the 1986-1987 stabilization program was due entirely to the decline in oil prices on the world market (Graph 3). The current account deficit similarly peaked at about 10% of GDP in 1985; its subsequent reduction was due mainly to rising EC transfer payments and an increase in private transfers attracted by high nominal interest rates and the perception that the authorities would not devalue again following two devaluations in 1983 and 1985. This perception waned in 1989, when there was a further sharp increase in the current account deficit fueled by a reduction in private transfers, stagnating exports, and booming imports, which may partly reflect capital flight through under-invoicing of exports and over-invoicing of imports.

Gross external public debt rose to an estimated $19 billion at end-1989, equivalent to 35% of GDP (Graph 5). The debt service ratio has tripled since the beging of the decade to 30% of foreign exchange receipts in 1989. These figures exclude military debt and short-term debt, and they also exclude some $11 billion of foreign currency liabilities of the Greek banking system (only a portion of which is subject to reserve requirements). These liabilities are owed to domestic residents and can therefore be considered a domestic rather than a foreign liability.

Foreign borrowing in Greece has financed public and private consumption rather than investment (Graph 6). The shares of both public and private investment in GDP fell sharply in the 1980s, with a brief interruption under the 1986-1987 stabilization program. Rising interest payments on external debt have become larger than the inflows of workers' remittances since 1985, causing GNP to exceed GDP for the first time irr the post-war period.

The bulk of Greece's external debt is due to commercial banks. Since 1989, foreign financing has shifted away from bank borrowing toward ECU-linked bond issues, which carry an interest rate of about 100 basis points above the risk-free rate. As these issues have been oversubscribed, Greece's access to financial markets seems to have remained intact — albeit at a higher price — despite an external imbalance which would appear excessive on the basis of any intertemporal optimization model. On a cross-country basis, Greece's external position in 1989 was similar to that of non-EC members which have experienced debt servicing difficultues in the past.

Subject to the caveats that apply to cross-country comparisons of external positions (2), Graph 7 and 8 compare Greece's external position with that of Mexico in 1982 and Turkey in 1979. Both countries experienced liquidity crises in those years, followed by debt rescheduling and concerted lending packages or syndicated balance of payments support loans. The Graphs show that the ratio of external debt to GDP and the debt service ratio in Greece is comparable, if not higher, than in these countries at the peak of their liquidity crises. The maintainance of access to external financing in Grece, in contrast to Mexico and Turkey, may also partly explain why the inflation rate in Greece has remained well below its level in the other countries during their liquidity crises.

---

(2) Cross-country differences in the openess of the economy and in the growth of foreign-exchange receipts can have an impact on the ability to service debt, although this would be reflected in different debt ratios to some extent. Differences in saving rates could similarly affect debt servicing ability. The maturity structure of external debt could also play a role by precipitating a liquidity crisis.

GRAPH 5

EXTERNAL PUBLIC DEBT
(medium/long term)

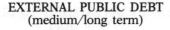

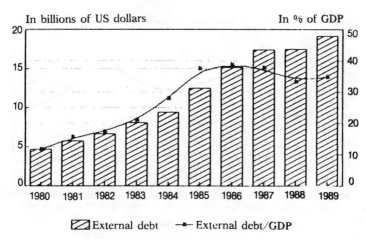

Source: BANK OF GREECE and WORLD BANK.

GRAPH 5*a*

EXTERNAL DEBT SERVICE
(in % of exports)

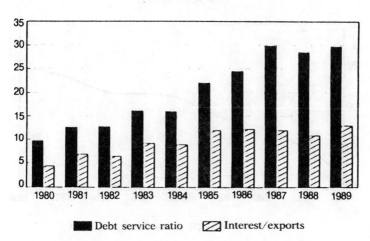

Source: WORLD BANK and BANK OF GREECE.

GRAPH 6

RATIO OF INVESTMENT TO GDP
(in % of GDP)

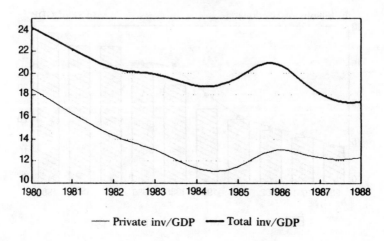

——— Private inv/GDP   ——— Total inv/GDP

Source: OECD.

GRAPH 6*a*

RATIO OF CONSUMPTION TO GDP
(in % of GDP)

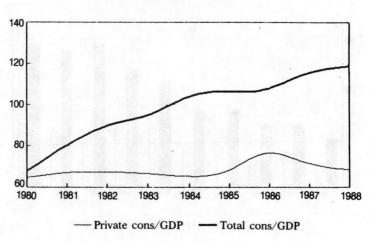

——— Private cons/GDP   ——— Total cons/GDP

Source: OECD.

GRAPH 6*b*

RATIO OF IMPORTS AND EXPORTS TO GDP
(in % of GDP)

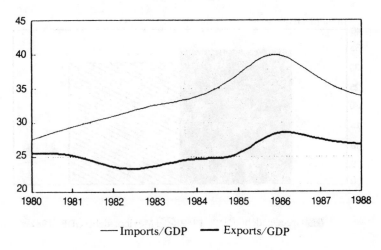

— Imports/GDP   — Exports/GDP

Source: OECD.

GRAPH 6*c*

RATIO OF NET FACTOR INCOME TO GDP
(in % of GDP)

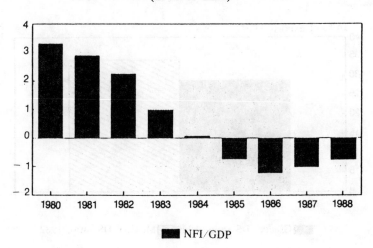

■ NFI/GDP

Source: OECD and IMF.

GRAPH 7

GREECE AND MEXICO:
EXTERNAL DEBT, 1989 AND 1982

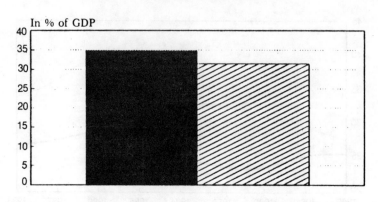

Source: WORLD BANK and BANK OF GREECE.

GRAPH 7*a*

GREECE AND MEXICO:
DEBT SERVICE RATIO, 1989 AND 1982

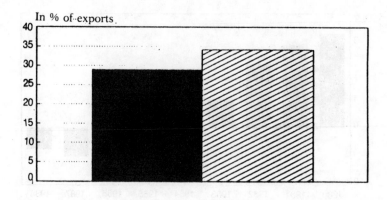

Source: WORLD BANK and BANK OF GREECE.

GRAPH 8

GREECE AND TURKEY:
EXTERNAL DEBT, 1989 AND 1978

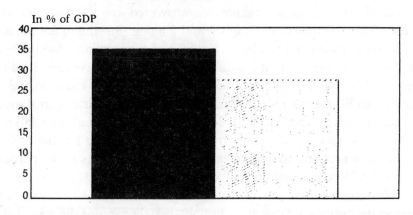

In % of GDP

■ Greece: debt/GDP, 1989 |⋯| Turkey: debt/GDP, 1978

Source: WORLD BANK and BANK OF GREECE.

GRAPH 8*a*

GREECE AND TURKEY:
DEBT SERVICE RATIO, 1989 AND 1978

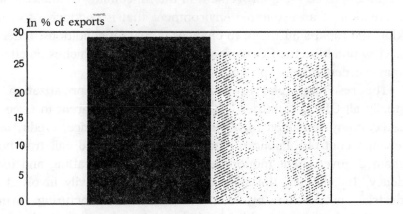

In % of exports

■ Greece: DS Ratio, 1989 |⋯| Turkey: DS Ratio, 1978

Source: WORLD BANK and BANK OF GREECE.

This raises the moral hazard issue: To what extent has Greece's membership in the EC (which coincided with the adoption of unsustainable fiscal policies in 1981) helped preserve access to financial markets? This question cannot be answered on the basis of the information contained on Graph 7 and 8 alone. But the maintainance of access to external financing in the face of ever-growing disequilibria in the 1980s suggests that capital markets may not base their lending decisions on country risk analysis alone; they may be more willing to lend to an EC member than to non-members in similar circumstances if they perceive the EC as a lender of last resort through its medium-term support facility or other means. If so, the case for the Delors Committee proposal to impose limits on budget deficits in the context of the EMU be strengthened.

Turning to structural issues, it should first be noted that budgetary outlays in Greece do not adequately capture the size of the government in terms of its impact on the economy. Numerous regulatory impediments to market entry, exit and competition raise the cost of producing goods and services, thus shifting the burden of government intervention from taxpayers to consumers and producers. By contrast, over the past decade most OECD countries have reassessed the cost of direct and indirect government involvement in the management of productive activities; they now perceive the role of government to be the improvement in the functioning of markets and the creation of an economic environment that is conducive to risk-taking and rapid adjustment to changes in market conditions. Indeed, this view underlies the EC internal market program which is, in effect, a massive deregulation program.

The resulting trend toward deregulation and privatization in virtually all OECD countries in the 1980s is not apparent in Greece. The economy remained highly regulated through price, credit, and exchange controls. Public utilities as well as air and rail transport remained government monopolies, promoting overstaffing and inefficiency. In addition, the state continued to be heavily involved in industrial production by controlling 56 manufacturing firms, accounting for about a third of industrial output, in which state-owned banks have a controlling interest. Cumulative losses of these firms since 1983 are estimated at $1.2 billion (3% of GDP), not counting numerous loan capitalizations which have reduced the profitability of state-owned banks. These losses should in principle be added to the fiscal deficit to get a more complete picture of the size of the required fiscal adjustment. Although direct interveniton by the government in the pricing and employment policies of these firms has not been conducive to a turnaround in their profit position, about half of them have been declared non-viable even in the absence of restrictive government regulations which limit their profitability.

Another area in which the efficiency of resource use could be improved is the tax system, which is far from neutral in its resource allocation effects. The OECD notes the large divergence between tax rates, which remain at or above the OECD average, and tax receipts relative to the taxable base, which are below the OECD average because of numerous exemptions and tax benefits granted to both households and corporations (OECD [12]). The tax base is further reduced by statutory exemptions for some groups (e.g. farmers, who are not subject to income tax) and inadequate enforcement of tax laws for others (e.g. professionals who routinely understate their incomes). In addition to its resource allocation effects, a broadening of the tax base and a removal of tax exemptions would make any stabilization program more even-handed and therefore more easily sustainable.

3. - Fiscal Deficits and Macroeconomic Targets

This paragraph presents an analytical framework that can be used to calculate the sustainable deficit given certain macroeconomic targets. The framework draws on the theoretical literature relating public deficits to inflation (Phelps [13]; Fischer [10]; Buiter [4]; Drazen and Helpman [9]), and on the framework used by Anand and Wijnberger [1] and [2] to assess the sustainability of fiscal policy in Turkey.

We start with the budget constraint of the public sector relating public spending to available sources of financing:

$$(1) \qquad D + iB + i^* B^* E = \Delta B + \Delta B^* E + \Delta DCg$$

On the LHS of *(1)* is the public sector deficit (PSBR): the primary deficit D, plus interest payments on domestic *(B)* and foreign *(B*)* debt.

E is the nominal effective exchange rate and i and i^* are the domestic and foreign nominal interest rates. On the RHS of *(1)* are the financing items, which consist of changes in domestic and foreign debt plus domestic credit to the public sector by the Central Bank, ΔDCg.

To consolidate the public sector with the Central Bank, to which a portion of government expenditures may be shifted through accounting practices, we can introduce a simple Central Bank balance sheet identity:

$$(2a) \qquad\qquad M = C + RR$$

$$(2b) \qquad\qquad M = DCg + NFA^* E - NW$$

Base money M equals currency in circulation C plus required reserves RR on the liability side of the Central Bank balance sheet (equation *(2a)*), and it is also equal to domestic credit to the government plus net foreign assets minus the Central Bank's net worth NW on the asset side (equation *(2b)*). Assuming that the Central Bank earns no interest on its loans to the government, Central Bank profits will be equal to interest earned of foreign exchange reserves, $i^* NFA^* E$ (3). Subtracting these profits from the PSBR, and its counterpart, ΔNW, from from the increase in government liabilities in equation *(1)* yields:

$$(3) \qquad\qquad \begin{aligned} D + iB + i^* B^* E - i^* NFA^* E = \\ = \Delta B + \Delta B^* E + \Delta DCg - \Delta NW \end{aligned}$$

Noting from *(2b)* that $\Delta DCg = \Delta M - ANFA^* E + \Delta NW$ at any given exchange rate E, and substituting in (3) yields:

$$(4) \qquad\qquad \begin{aligned} D + iB + i^* (B^* - NFA^*) E = \\ = \Delta B + (\Delta B^* - \Delta NFA^*) E + \Delta M \end{aligned}$$

Equation *(4)* establishes a dirct link between the fiscal deficit on the *LHS* and base money, on which the inflation tax is levied, on the

---

(3) Gains or losses on foreign exchange reserves due to exchange rate movements, which also affect Central Bank profits, are introduced at a later stage in the analysis. At this stage it is assumed that the exchange rate remains fixed.

RHS. The equation thus considers the inflation tax on the monetary base as fiscal revenue accruing to the government.

Next, we express equation *(4)* in real terms, noting that $E = ep/p^*$ (where e is the real effective exchange rate). It is also useful to decompose the nominal interest rate, i, into a real component, r, and an inflation component, $\dot{p}$. Using lower-case letters to denote real variables:

$$(5) \qquad d + (r + \dot{p})\, b + (r^* + \dot{p}^*)\,(b^* - nfa^*)\, e = \\ \Delta b + (\Delta b^* - \Delta nfa^*)\, e + \Delta M/p$$

where: $\qquad i = r + \dot{p}$ and $i^* = r^* + \dot{p}^*$.

A final adjustment that needs to be made is to include in equation *(5)* capital gains or losses on the net foreign debt due to changes in the real exchange rate. These losses can be expressed as $\Delta e\,(b^* - nfa^*)$, or equivalently as $\dot{e}\,(b^* - nfa)\, e$. Adding this expression to both sides of equation *(5)*, and using the identity:

$$(6) \qquad \Delta[(b^* - nfa^*)\, e] = \\ = (\Delta b^* - \Delta nfa^*)\, e + \dot{e}\,(b^* - nfa^*)\, e$$

to simplify the *RHS*, we get:

$$(7) \qquad d + (r + \dot{p})\, b + (r^* + \dot{p}^* + \dot{e})\,(b^* - nfa^*)\, e = \\ = \Delta b + \Delta[(b^* - nfa^*)\, e] + \Delta M/p$$

Equation *(7)* states that the fiscal deficit in real terms equals changes in the real value of domestic and foreign debt plus revenue from monetization (the «tax» levied on the monetary base). A depreciation in the real exchange rate ($\dot{e} > 0$) as part of a stabilization program raises the cost of servicing the foreign debt in domestic currency terms and correspondingly reduces the primary deficit, d, compatible with the available financing under different macro targets.

The last term in equation *(7)*, which represents the portion of the deficit financed through inflation, can be decomposed in two parts: seigniorage, $\Delta n = \Delta (M/p)$, and the inflation tax, $\dot{p}m$. Although these terms are often used interchangeably to refer to total revenue accruing to the government through inflation, it is useful to distinguish between the two insofar as revenue from seigniorage depends primarily on the growth rate and accrues to the government even in the absence of inflation, while revenue from the inflation tax depends primarily on the inflation rate.

Some authors have suggested that a further adjustment needed to establish a link between the fiscal deficit and the authorities' inflation target is the adoption of an «operational» deficit concept (Anand and van Wijnbergen [1]). It is now widely accepted that in an inflationary environment, interest payments partly reflect compensation for the erosion of the real value of the outstanding debt; they thus constitute an implicit repayment of principal which represents a financing item and should be excluded from the fiscal deficit (4). Netting out of the fiscal deficit the inflation component of interest payments yields the socalled operational deficit, which equals the conventional deficit as defined on the *LHS* of equation *(5)* minus pb and $\dot{p}^*$ $(b^* - nfa^*)$; correspondingly, Δb and $(\Delta b^* - \Delta nfa^*)$ would be defined as *net* of the inflation component of net government borrowing on the *RHS*. However, it has been argued that this may give a misleading picture of the sustainability of fiscal deficits under any of the following behavioral assumptions: *a)* money illusion causes holders of domestic debt to spend rather than save the inflation component of interest payments, thus fueling inflation under a policy of monetary accommodation; *b)* inflation is perceived to increase the risk of default, thus causing bond holders to demand a higher real premium; if so, the inflation component of interest payments cannot be refinanced on existing terms; and *c)* a highly liquid domestic debt is used as a substitute for money (Tanzi *et* Al [15]). While the third argument can be expected to be relevant only in situations of hyperinflation in which debt is replaced for money for transactions purposes, the first two could plausibly apply to relatively low-inflation countries. It can thus

---

(4) The rationale for the exclusion of the inflation component of interest payments from the fiscal deficit is that its impact on aggregate demand is different from the impact of other components of fiscal spending: insofar as it merely safeguards the real value of existing wealth without increasing it, it is more likely to be saved than spent. This argument implicitly assumes that the inflation component of interest payments can be refinanced on existing terms; if not, then it will have an impact on real interest payments and thus on the operational deficit.

be argued that although in an inflationary situation the conventional fiscal deficit may overstate the size of the required adjustment, the operational deficit will almost certainly understate the size of that adjustment. The calculations shown in the next paragraph are therefore carried out on the basis of the conventional deficit.

The next step needed to compute the sustainable deficit given certain macro targets is to incorporate these targets in equation *(7)*. Sustainability is usually defined with reference to the scale of borrowing to which it gives rise and the terms of such borrowing: a sustainable deficit is one that can be financed through borrowing at market rates indefinitely. An additional constraint on the financeable (as opposed to sustainable) deficit is introduced if the authorities target a reduction in the inflation rate, which limits financing through money creation.

An increase in total debt relative to GDP cannot be sustained indefinitely without a rise in borrowing costs, crowding out of the domestic private sector, and eventual loss of access to financing if there is a perceived risk of default. Accordingly, two constraints must be introduced in equation *(7)*, namely, stabilization of the internal and external debt relative to GDP. These constraints can be expressed as:

(8a)
$$\Delta b = \dot{y} b$$

(8b)
$$\Delta\,[(b^* - nfa^*)\,e] = (\dot{y} - \dot{e})\,(b^* - nfa^*)$$

where $\dot{y}$ is the growth rate of real GDP. Incorporating *(8a)* and *(8b)* in *(7)* and noting that revenue from seigniorage, Δm, will equal $\dot{y} m$ in the steady state, yields:

(9)
$$d + (r + \dot{p})\,b + (r^* + \dot{p}^* + \dot{e})\,(b^* - nfa^*)\,e =$$
$$= \dot{y} b + (\dot{y} - \dot{e})\,(b^* - nfa^*) + (\dot{y} + \dot{p})\,m$$

Equation *(9)* states that the primary deficit plus interest payments on domestic and foreign debt must equal new borrowing compatible with the maintainance of the existing internal and external debt/GDP rations, plus revenues from monetatization (with all variables expressed in real terms). A debt strategy involving a reduction in debt relative to GDP would obviously reduce the financeable deficit further.

It is clear from equation *(9)* that if r, $r^* > \dot{y}$, the deficit will rise faster than available sources of financing, ceteris paribus. It is also clear that a real depreciation ($\dot{e} > 0$) will unambiguously reduce the financeable deficit by raising the local currency value of interest payments on external debt on the *LHS*, and also by reducing the new external debt that can be contracted at a constrant debt/GDP ratio on the *RHS*. The opposite policy (real appreciation, i.e. $\dot{e} < 0$) would alleviate the financing constraint in the short term for any given primary deficit, but would undermine confidence in the sustainablility of exchange-rate policy over the medium term.

The last term on the *RHS* of *(9)* must be evaluated at its equilibrium value, i.e. at the point where the supply of real balances, m, equals the demand for real balances at the inflation rate targeted by the authorities. To ascertain what this level is, we need an estimate of the demand for money function. We turn to this now.

4. - Money Demand, Inflation Revenues, and Fiscal Sustainability

This paragraph derives estimates of the financeable deficits in Greece under alternative target inflation rates and assuming that internal and external debt remain constant relative to GDP at their 1989 levels. Variants of this scenario are presented based on different GDP growth rates and different assumptions about movements in the real exchange rate.

The following Cagan-type specification of the demand for base money is used:

$$(10) \qquad\qquad m = a_0 \, y^{a1} \, e^{a2c}$$

where $m = M/p$ are real money balances, y, is real income, and c is the expected return (or negative opportunity cost) of holding money, which is a function of the expected rate of inflation, $\dot{p}^e$, or the nominal interest rate on interest-bearing assets, i, whichever is higher. Deposit rates in Greece have remained negative in real terms throughout the 1980s, and should thus not affect the demand for base money.

Alternative financial assets offering market-related returns did not exist until 1985, when T-bills and bonds of short maturity carrying positive real returns started being sold to the nonbank public, while deposit rates continued to be set administratively. The following equation was therefore estimated over the period 1977:2 to 1988:1:

$$(11) \qquad \ln m_t = -5.66 + 0.54 \ln y_t - 0.52 \dot{p}_t +$$
$$\quad (-6.04) \quad (6.77) \qquad (-1.41)$$

$$+ -0.71 \, DUM + 0.72 \ln m_{t-1}$$
$$(-3.06) \qquad (9.15)$$

$$\bar{R}^2 \quad = 0.753$$
$$DW \quad = 2.07$$
$$SEE \quad = 0.053$$

When the rate of inflation increases, the demand for money normally diminishes (or velocity rises), eroding the base on which the inflation tax is levied. The coefficient on the expected inflation rate (assumed equal to the actual rate) thus has the expected sign. A *dummy* variable was introduced to capture the effect of the introduction of T-bill sales to the nonbank public since 1985:3. The dummy is significant and has the expected negative sign, indicating that the introduction of a financial asset with a positive real return has reduced the desired money holdings at any given inflation rate and real income level; a higher inflation rate would thus be required to derive any given amount of revenue from the inflation tax. Finally, the estimated money demand equation assumes a partial adjustment of actual money balances to their desired level, captured by the lagged real money balances term, m_{t-1}. When the (administratively set) deposit interest rate is inserted in equation *(11)*, it is not significant either individually or jointly with $\dot{p}$.

Using the target values for internal and external debt growth incorporated in equation *(9)*, the elasticity estimates obtained from equation *(11)*, and estimates of inflation revenues derived from the banking system, we can now estimate the sustainable deficit corresponding to different target inflation rates.

TABLE 1

GREECE: ACTUAL AND SUSTAINABLE DEFICIT IN 1989
(in percent of GDP)

	Deficit	
	actual	sustainable (1)
Revenues from monetization	5.6	5.6
Seigniorage	0.3	0.3
Inflation tax	5.3	5.3
Domestic borrowing	13.3	1.1
Foreign borrowing	2.4	0.6
At fixed *e*	(3.2)	(0.6)
Capital gain (−)/loss (+)	(− 0.8)	(−)
Total financing	21.3	7.3

(1) Assumes GDP growth and inflation at their actual levels of 18 and (2) percent, respectively, and stabilization of both domestic and external debt relative to GDP at their end-1988 levels.

Table 1 compares the actual and sustainable deficit in Greece in 1989 at the present inflation rate of 18% (5). The actual public sector deficit reached 21.3% of GDP, about one fourth of which was financed through revenues from monetization. At the same inflation rate, stabilization of the internal and extenal debt relative to GDP would have required a deficit of only 7.3% at the actual growth rate of 2%. Underlying this estimate is the assumption that the real appreciation which occurred in 1989 cannot be sustained without undermining confidence in the consistency between fiscal and monetary policy.

Turning to projected outcomes, Table 2 shows the estimated financeable deficit at different inflation rates, assuming the domestic and external debt stabilize at their end-1989 level. At a 2% growth rate, stabilization of the external debt at its end-1989 level of 33% permits external financing of 0.7% of GDP per year. Similarly, stabilization of the domestic debt at its end-1989 level of 65% permits domestic borrowing of 1.3% of GDP per year.

_____

(5) The figures presented in Tables 1-3 are expressed as a percent of GDP. This involves a straightforward normalization of equation *(9)* using real GDP.

TABLE 2

GREECE: FINANCEABLE DEFICIT
UNDER DIFFERENT INFLATION TARGETS (1)
(in percent of GDP)

	$\dot{p} = 18$	$\dot{p} = 12$	$\dot{p} = 6$
Revenues from monetization	5.6	4.0	2.4
Seigniorage	0.3	0.4	0.5
Inflation tax	5.3	3.6	1.9
Domestic borrowing	1.3	1.3	1.3
Foreign borrowing	0.7	0.7	0.7
Total financing	7.6	6.0	4.4

(1) Assuming GDP growth at 2 percent, no change in the real exchange rate, and stabilization of both domestic and external debt relative to GDP at their end-1989 levels.

The third possible source of financing, monetization, provides the revenues shown on Table 2 at different target inflation rates. This is broken down in two parts: *ceteris paribus*, GDP growth permits an increase in real money balances with no impact on inflation. This is revenue from seigniorage. In Greece this can be estimated at 0.3% at a growth rate of 2% and inflation at 18%. A lower inflation rate would increase the demand for real balances at any given real income level, thus raising the revenue from seigniorage. The second source of revenue from inflation is the inflation tax levied on money balances. Inflation reduces the demand for real money balances at any given real income level. However, moneyholders must build up their nominal money balances to offset to some degree the erosion of their real balances through inflation. This buildup in money balances represents revenue from the inflation tax. As long as we are operating on the left side of the inflation tax Laffer curve, revenue from the inflation tax will rise with the inflation rate, and correspondingly decline in a period of disinflation. Revenue from this source in Greece is estimated to decline from 5.3% of GDP at the current inflation rate of 18% to 1.9% of GDP at an inflation rate of 6%.

On this basis, the financeable deficit is estimated at 4.4% of GDP at the EC average inflation rate of 6%. A higher growth rate would ease the debt burden by permitting higher borrowing at constant debt ratios and by providing greater revenues from seigniorage. By contrast, a real depreciation would reduce the deficit that can be financed at any given inflation and growth rates by raising the cost of debt service in local currency. The financeable deficit based on different assumptions about growth, inflation and real depreciation are shown on Table 3. At the present inflation rate of 18%, the required deficit reduction amounts to 14% of GDP. A doubling of the growth rate would reduce the required reduction to just under 10% of GDP. By contrast, a 4% real depreciation would raise this reduction to nearly 16% of GDP at the present growth rate.

The estimates presented above do not depend on how long it takes to reach a sustainable fiscal position. The cost of waiting is reflected only in the rise of interest obligations relative to GDP that will occur if the constraints on debt accumulation are not observed. A rise in interest obligations would make it more difficult to reduce the fiscal deficit because it implies a correspongly larger reduction in the primary deficit relative to GDP.

Broadly similar conclusions about orders of magnitude for the required adjustment are reached by Catsambas [5]. Using a financial programming framework base on alternative «inflation target-

TABLE 3

GREECE: REQUIRED DEFICIT REDUCTION
UNDER ALTERNATIVE MACRO TARGETS
(in percent of GDP)

		$\dot{y} = 2, \dot{e} = 0$	
Inflation target	18	12	6
Required deficit reduction	14	15.5	17
		$\dot{p} = 18, \dot{e} = 0$	
Growth target	2	3	4
Required deficit reduction	14	12	10
		$\dot{y} = 2, \dot{p} = 18$	
Real depreciation target	0	2	4
Required deficit reduction	14	15	16

required deficit» simulations, his analysis confirms the tradeoffs presented in Tables 2 and 3. Clearly, changes in growth and inflation rates will affect not only the sustainable deficit but also the actual deficit, through changes in the taxable base and in cyclical components of spending. A higher growth rate will reduce the actual deficit relative to GDP, while a lower inflation rate will have an ambiguous effect depending on the degree of indexation of the tax and financial systems and the strength of the «Tanzi effect».

5. - Conclusions

This paper has used a simple framework to evaluate the size of the fiscal adjustment required to reach a sustainanble fiscal position in Greece. The discrepancy between the actual and sustainable deficit is estimated at 14% of GDP at the present inflation rate of 18% and growth rate of 2%. A credible commitment to join the EMS — as required under the first stage of EMU — would require a further reduction in the fiscal deficit to a level compatible with a reduction in inflation to the EC average level. Opting for a «hard currency» policy would entail a loss of revenue from monetization estimated at 3% of GDP. This revenue loss would raise the size of the required fiscal adjustment by an equivalent amount. These figures provide a basis for evaluating the feasibility and desirability of joining the EMU or for estimating the compensation required (say, through the EC regional and social funds) to make up for the foregone inflation revenues.

The analysis presented here could be extended by addressing the moral hazard issue in greater depth. It has been suggested in this paper that Greece has had greater access to external financing compared to other debtors with a similar external position outside the EC. This would indicate that the moral hazard issue may arise even in the absence of EMU, just by virtue of membership in the EC. If so, the case for systemic limitation of fiscal autonomy under the EMU would be strengthened.

BIBLIOGRAPHY

[1] ANAND R. - VAN WIJNBERGEN S.: «Inflation, External Debt and Financial Sector Reform: a Quantitative Approach to Consistent Fiscal Policy with an Application to Turkey», NBER *Working Paper*, n. 2731, 1988.

[2] —— : «Inflation and the Financing of Government Expenditure: An Introductory Analysis with an Application to Turkey», *The World Bank Economic Review*, vol. 3, 1989, pp. 17-38.

[3] BRANSON W.H.: «Financial Market Integration Macroeconomic Policy and the EMS», London CEPR, *Discussion Paper*, n. 385, 1990.

[4] BUITER W.H.: «Measurement of the Public Sector Deficit and its Implications for Policy Evaluation and Design», IMF *Staff Papers*, vol. 30, 1983, pp. 306-49.

[5] CATSAMBAS T.: *The Greek Economy: An Alternative Approach*, Athens, Credit Bank, 1990.

[6] CUCKIERMAN A.: *Descretion, Precommitments and the Prospects for a European central Bank*, manuscript 1989.

[7] DELORS COMMITTEE: *Report on Economic and Monetary Union in the European Community*, Committee for the Study of Economic and Monetary Union, 1989.

[8] DORNBUSCH R.: «The European Monetary System, the Dollar and the Yen», in GIAVAZZI FRANCESCO - MICOSSI STEFANO - MILLER MARCUS (eds.): *The European Monetary System*, Cambridge, Cambridge University Press, 1988.

[9] DRAZEN A. - HELPMAN E.: «Stabilization with Exchange Rate Management», *Quarterly Journal of Economics*, vol. 102, 1987, pp. 835-56.

[10] FISCHER S.: «Seigniorage and the Case for National Money», *Journal of Political Economy*», vol. 90, 1982, pp. 285-313.

[11] GROS D.: «Seigniorage versus EMS Discipline: Some Welfare Considerations», Brussels, CEPS, *Working Document*, n. 38, 1988.

[12] ORGANISATION FOR ECONOMIC COOPERATION AND DEVELOPMENT: *OECD Economic Surveys*, Greece, 1989, 1990, Paris, 1990.

[13] PHELPS E.: «Inflation in the Theory of Public Finance», *Swedish Journal of Economics*, vol. 2, n. 1, 1973.

[14] PLOEG F. VAN DER: «Towards Monetary Integration in Europe», in *De Europese Monetarie Integratie: Vier Visies*, The Hague (The Netherlands), The Netherlands Scientific Council for Government Policy, 1989.

[15] TANZI V. - BLEJER M. - TEIJEIRO M.: «Inflation and the Measurement of Fiscal Deficits», IMF, *Staff Papers*, vol. 34, 1987, pp. 711-38.

IV - NEW EUROPE
AND WORLD ECONOMY

Europe in the World Economy

Charles P. Kindleberger
Massachusetts Institute of Technology, Cambridge (Mass.)

I have taken on an impossible assignment. How can one feel in any way confident in describing the role of Europe in the world economy in the months and years to come, if one is unclear about the economic prospects facing Europe, Japan, the Middle East, the so-called Third World and the United States, in the light, especially as I write, of: the deadline facing Iraq in Kuwait in less than a week; the threatened collapse of the Soviet economy, especially in the production and distribution of consumer goods and food; frustration in Eastern Europe; a new government in Britain; deepening recession in the United States, apparently spreading to Japan and parts of Europe; continuing problems in Third World debt, raw-material prices, and so on. If various elements of the picture are obscure, it takes a prophet or the son of a prophet to see the whole picture as they come together. The task is made particularly difficult as I write on the last day of the Uruguay-round negotiations without knowing whether Europe, the United States, Japan and the grain-exporting countries will reach agreement or let the negotiations fail.

My diffidence in forecasting is not universally shared. Two highly-respected political scientists in the United States, Henry Nau and Joseph Nye, brush away signs of American weakness that others think may lead to a reduction of the US role in the world economy. The first calls American decline a myth with the subtitle *Leading the World Economy into the 1990s*. Nye's book is called *Bound to Lead*, though it is concerned as much with political as with economic leadership. A third entry in the debate, by Myron Ross, relies on Kondratieff long-wave theory to predict a *Coming Economic Boom, 1992-2020*. For the moment I reserve my positions on these views, to turn first to the general problems facing the major national and regional economies in the provision of public goods, and then discussing how the world economy has been and may in future be organized and world public goods produced.

Adam Smith thought in terms of only three public goods (which he called the duties of the sovereign): national defense, the administration of justice, and the few works so large that they could not be undertaken by the private market. Modern economists have added to this list. Public goods, I may remind you, form that class that cannot be exhausted short of some very high degree of congestion, and from which no one can be excluded so that they are available to all, whether they pay for them or not. They are produced by government with the power to tax, since if they were produced by the market, inability to exclude consumers would lead individuals to ride free without payment for the cost of production. For international public goods, where there is no government with power to tax, there is a grave risk that the goods may not be produced at all. The difference between private and public goods is akin to that between a market and a budget. Values are exchange in a market. In a budget funds are expended on some basis, perhaps need, perhaps to favor political interests, and raised by taxation on some basis, perhaps by borrowing, or by the inflation tax.

Within an economy with a government, the public goods beyond defense, justice and infrastructure may include competitive markets, stable money, standards, and perhaps some means of softening the harsher results of competitive markets by providing certain services at a resonable standard, as in health, education, perhaps housing, and social security. At times of crisis the list may be extended, My list of international public goods includes, on trend, open markets, stable exchange rates, access to supplies in acute shortage and to markets in glut, and a lender of last resort in financial crisis. In the absence of international government, other means have to be provided if these public goods, including the most important of all, peace, are to be produced at all.

Before I come back to public goods, I offer a brief *tour d'horizon* of the economic problems facing Europe, Japan and the United States, and then move to the role of Europe in the world economy. Everything I say is provisional, subject to change without notice. If no economist to my knowledge predicted the implosions of the stock market in Octobers 1987 and 1989, or the collapse of the socialist economies in Eastern Europe in 1989, you will understand my insistence on not rushing in where angels fear to tread.

First Europe. The Continent is embarked on two great journeys, one to assimilate Eastern Europe into the European economy as a whole, the other to complete the forging of a single economic community, begun in this city in 1957. I am concerned that the two journeys are substitutes rather than complements. The current and capital costs of absorbing Eastern Europe into the market system of the West will be substantial. The crisis problem of feeding the Soviet Union has been assisted by the adventitious existence of stocks of food assembled years ago in Berlin in defense against another Soviet blockade. Provision of stocks against possible disaster is one sort of public good, exemplified by the grain offices of Italian city-states and the US petroleum reserves. Sometimes, as in US stockpiles of grain and cotton built up in the 1930s to support farmers, but invaluable during the war, serendipity comes to the rescue. But subsidies for eastern Germany, for moving out Soviet troops, for equalizing the social security systems, and the like will be expensive currently. And the capital demands for deferred maintenance and obsolence in the East, for correcting cumulative pollution, for accomodating the migrants to the West, will be on top of the current expenditure.

Capital requirements in Europe are virtually certain to raise world interest rates, cut off the flow from Europe and perhaps Japan to the United States. Optimists are not troubled that this will intensity recession or depression in the United States because the cut-off of capital can be offset in the foreign-exchange market by further depreciation of the dollar. Much further depreciation of the dollar, however, poses an inflationary danger as the rise of foreign-trade prices spreads through the cost of living and wages. The choice between further depreciation and inflation, or higher interest rates and deflation, is not an agreeable one.

The other mobile factor of production, labor, poses a question, and perhaps a problem. The *Treaty of Rome* provided for free movement of labor across national boundaries, although apart from South Italians among the original six, little movement took place. Migration to the West from Eastern Europe, however, is now substantial; indeed, that from the People's Republic to the Federal Republic through Hungary and Austria in 1989 precipitated the Socialist collapse. With the razing of the wall, it was anticipated that this would dry up. It appears not to be doing so. East Germans, moreover, are being joined by citizens of other Eastern countries, both those of ancient German origin and those with no ethnic claim on the West. Austria faces a harrowing problem of whether to send refugees back to such a country as Romania or to let them stay.

There is a danger that this migration may go so far as to deprive Eastern Europe of the minimum of professional, semi-professional and skilled cadres needed for a modern economy. A riot in Leipzig in November 1990 could not be contained because of the absence of adequate numbers of police. Rapid economic recovery in Eastern Europe that gives the populace sufficient hope in the intermediate run of matching Western productivity and standards of living may be difficult or impossible to achieve. Bear in mind that this movement of population is different in its effects than that that produced the wall in 1961. In the 1950s, the refugees and expellees moving to the Federal Republic, and the guest workers, proved stimulating to economic growth, holding wages down and profits up, with the profits reinvested in further productive capital, along the lines of the Lewis model of growth with unlimited supplies of labor. These migrants were originally single men for whom infrastructure in the form of housing, shools and hospitals need not be provided beyond simple barracks. The migration of whole families produces a different result. The earlier movement from the South stimulated the sending economies, as well as the receiving, as disguised unemployment was cleared away, and rising wages encouraged both savings and labor-saving investment. Today the risk is that the wholesale movement of workers East to West may hurt growth in both areas.

If we turn from these immediate issues, building the complete common market by 1992 on which the experts here have been discoursing promises to be difficult enough. Harmonization of tax systems, social security, regulations in pure food and drugs, safety standards and the like is a tedious, specialized and time-consuming task. Building the European Monetary System with a common currency, European central bank, and consistent fiscal policies seems moving along nicely after twenty years of set-backs and new starts, but questions remain that will take economic expertise and especially political will to solve. How rapidly will Europe move how far: to a confederation? Federation? United States? Union?, how much sovereignty, that is, are the constitutent countries ready to surrender to the Continent as a whole? Different visions of the future are held by the leading protagonists, Germany, France, Italy, Britain, with some uncertainty remaining in the last instance after the change in conservative leadership. Mrs Thatcher's resistance to grants of sovereignty seemed to me to have provided a cover behind which President Mitterrand and Chancellor Kohl could assert more devotion to the European ideal than perhaps they felt at heart. The new twist in Ostpolitik, and the problem of Eastern European recovery, reconstruction and integration into the East seem likely in my uninformed judgment to extend the achievement of current goals of Western integration beyond 1992.

There are problems enough in the economic field, to be sure, but an American may be pardoned if he mentions the differing responses of the Community's members to the military crisis in the Middle East. Creating a European political Community may be even more difficult than building the economic one.

On Japan, I am, again, far from expert. Like Germany, Japan has had a superb record of economic growth since the end of the second world war. More than Germany, it has made economic hay under the American defense umbrella, Americans are impressed by Japanese innovative prowess, saving habits, export drive, and faithful support of American economic leadership in the past, at the same time that many insist that Japanese support for free markets is limited in particular respects, such as competition for rice farmers, ease of entry of foreign direct investment, readiness to streamline wholesale and retail distribution. In a number of financial circles, moreover, there is worry that security and real estate prices remain still dangerously high, despite the substantial 1990 declines from 1989 levels.

In the last few years, Japan has become mone economically assertive, making the point, for example, that with its new high status in international finance, it should have enhanced voting power in the International Monetary Fund and World Bank. (Parenthetically, the same could also be said about the United Nations Security Council where both Germany and Japan will one day obtain permanent membership in recognition of the realities). The rise of the yen has continued for five years with substantial paper losses for the Bank of Japan and Japanese insurance companies that have been financing a large proportion of the United States cumulative budget deficit. Japanese investment in the US has increasingly moved from debt into real assets like direct investment and real estate, in the latter case not always with exquisite timing. I have nonetheless been surprised that Japanese lenders to US bodies have not insisted on denominating the loans in yen, rather than dollars, to shift the exchange risk to the borrowers.

A word or two about my own country before getting to the world economy. Wide differences of opinion exist not only over whether the United States is in secular decline, but also over the short-term prospects of recession or depression. Long-term decline, of course, may be merely relative to faster growing countries or areas elsewhere. Despite Nau, Nye, Ross and others, I view the United States as an aging economy, its interests shifting from trade and industry to finance, from capital accumulation to consumption, from individual enterprise to what Mancur Olson calls «distributional coalitions» or vested interests, that seek to protect what the French used to call in the pre-war days of Malthusianism, *positions acquises*. I detect a decline of team-play, not only in sport but in business and professions, as takeovers break up existing management structures, firms in law, accounting, advertizing reshuffle partners and even liquidate. Even academic departments appear to be succumbing to the star system that so dominates sport and entertainment.

Moreover, the short-run outlook looks dangerous with its fragile financial structure of high levels of debt owed by government, industry, real estate, Third World countries and consumers. Insurance companies and banks are awash with defaulted real-estate loans and depreciated junk bonds. While low by 1930 standards, bankruptcies are rising. The possibility that government has to take over a huge load of debt as lender of last resort poses a threat of inflation. If on the other hand banks and insurance companies work their way out of the problem by a return to conservative lending and investing, the prospects for rapid and extensive recovery become less than bright. I hasten to warn you, however that I have been bearish on the immediate economic outlook in the United States for some years, and am only recently begun to find a swing of opinion in my direction. Roger Babson predicted a crash of the stock market in 1928. He found it did not pay to be right prematurely.

There are then short-run problems of absorbing the shock of the collapse of Eastern Europe, financial tensions in Japan and the United States. Assuming these difficulties can be overcome, we have a longer-run question of how the world economy is to be organized, and the place in it of the New Europe, how, that is, international public goods will be produced in the absence of world government.

The primary international public good, as noted, is peace. Its provision poses problems well beyond my capacity to expound. I restrict myself to economic public goods, starting with five I have discussed many times before: open markets, stable exchange rates, co-ordinated or at least not inconsistent macro-economic policies, international capital, and a lender of last resort. To these can perhaps be added some of the intractable issues already mentioned: economic breakdown as in Eastern Europe, hunger because of breakdown, drought, pestilence, disease, earthquake; the settlement of massive numbers of refugees or would-be refuges; and economic development in general. In all these first responsibility rests with the countries concerned. Once their capacities are overwhelmed, however, the threat of human, economic or political disaster becomes a challenge to the world.

Assume that national governments are moderately successful in providing domestic public goods. International public goods may not be furnished at all if countries free ride, each looking after its national interest whatever the cost to other countries. This is international anarchy under which the strong and aggressive exploit the weak and the passive, a condition of the world not without historical precedent. If, on the other hand, international public goods are to be provided, a number of ways lie open. One country may be a hegemon, as political scientists like to term it, what I prefer to call a leader to dilute the implication of force; second, instead of one leader, duoply of power, or an oligopoly or cartel, what is thought of today as trilateralism, with Europe, Japan and the United States sharing the world's burdens; third, regional blocs; fourth, «regimes», another concept of political science, described by Stephen Krasner as «principles, norms, rules and decision-making procedures around which actor expectations converge in a given issue area»; fifth, a system of functional international organizations. Apart from anarchy, these are of course not mutually exclusive. I may also add that any system decays over time. Entropy is endemic, if you can abide a short sentence of Greek roots.

Anarchy, the absence of international economic order, is abhorred in the same way that nature abhors a vacuum. I have lately been studying monetary anarchy in the seventeenth century in the Holy Roman Empire, and been struck by how the many territorial units detested the inflation that followed the gradual breakdown of rules for minting coin under the imperial ordinance of 1559. The breakdown was initially gradual, picked up speed and culiminated in hyperinflation in 1618 to 1622. Even as the Thirty Years' War broke out, various circles covering usually one or more principality, duchy, bishopric, city, etc. reached out to agree with its neighbors to restore monetary order. There are economists who think an absence of authority is desirable because of normal government malversation or blundering. By historical revealed preference, some provision of the public good of stability is sought in anarchy. It may evolve in Darwinian fashion; it is probably desirable to plan it.

In due course, as the world continues to get smaller, world government will evolve. After World War II there were idealists or utopians who wanted to write constitutions to install one immediately. For as far ahead as one can now see, the notion is premature. The road probably lies through international organizations such as — to name a few in alphabetical order in English — BIS, ECOSOC, FAO, GATT, IBRD, ICAO, IFA, IMF, IPU, UNESCO, WHO and dozens more. Experience going back to the League of Nations, if not earlier, reveals that few of such organizations adequately fulfill their purposes unless they are pushed by powerful nations. Most too are paralleled by similar regional organizations, or by additional organizations in the less-developed world, or both. GATT, for example, has a counterpart in UNCTAD in the EEC, and in the North American Free Trade Area, now in embryo. In finance, in addition to the World Bank there are regional funds for Latin America, Asia and Africa, plus the European Social Fund, European Investment Bank and the European Overseas Bank for investment in former colonies. Nor do most of them have the powers that inhere in national ones. The IMF is far from a world central bank in its inability to create money. No opinion that has come to my attention has suggested that the hunger problems of the Soviet Union should be turned over to the rather moribund Food and Agriculture Organization.

Regimes are one step down in tems of organization than these formal bodies, just as they are a long step down from world government. In a well-known book, *After Hegemony*, Robert Keohane notes that regimes are sometimes habits formed in a period of hegemony. On the whole, the world economy has performed fairly well on trend and in crisis since the perceived (by some) decline in the hegemonic power of the United States. Rampant protectionism has been held in check even if there has been some backsliding. Oil crises in 1973 and 1979 have been overcome — the returns are not in for 1990-1991 — with the help of the international oil companies in the first instance. Third World debt presents an on-going crisis in some views, or is being muddled through on another. The Uruguay round underlines the limits of dependence on old habits, however, whether it squeaks through or fails. Without injections of national energy in the international interest rather than the national or parochial, regimes run down.

Regionalism has been put forward as a solution for the organization of the world economy for many decades, and expecially since World War II. It calls for fairly tight regional arrangements, such as are under construction in Europe, and less rigorously in North America, for the most part only talked about in the rest of the world — with little structure among the separate blocs. There is a good deal to be said in favor of regional coopeation, close cooperation in relevant instances, but I think it a mistake to raise an expedient into a principle. Many individual countries trade more outside the geogaphic confines of a region than within them — Australia, for example, though both Australia and New Zealand may be cited for the affirmative in the debate as they have increased their trade and cultural ties with Asia since they were orphaned by Britain's joining the Common Market. While Brazil has close trade ties with the United States because of coffee, Argentine connections run to Europe. The prospect for close regional cooperation in the Middle East looks dim. A recipe for close African integration is one for turmoil. It is unclear whether Mexican adherence to a North American trade arrangement would help or hurt Mexican growth. Evolutionary regionalism is desirable; forced regionalism is not.

We come to trilateralism, the notion that Europe, Japan and the United States should lay out the lines along which the world economy organizes caucus in international bodies to decide what needs doing, and rig the voting arrangements, mostly weighted, to ensure that the agenda is followed. One variation of this might be the G-5, G-7 or the G-8 with the inclusion of the Soviet Union, raising the question of vetoes as in the Security Council. Another question is whether the European vote would be cast by the Community as a whole (the EEC) or by Germany. After the success of Ostpolitik, the German role in the Common Market seems dominant in much the same way that Prussia dominated the path leading to the unification of the Reich, and Piedmont that of Italy. If regional units have to arrive at decisions before tackling world problems, the process becomes time-consuming and extremely awkward in crises when decisions may be required in weeks, days or even hours. The Federal Republic has acted like a leader of Europe in relation to the problems of the Eastern bloc, taking on major costs in the integration of the two Germanies and the payment to hasten the removal of Soviet troops.

The trilateral solution can work for the lender-of-last-resort function since the swap arrangements are conducted by central banks, some of which are independent of governments (in the short run). For the other international public goods, trade, exchange rates, capital flows and macro-economic coordination, the troika solution assumes either that the three participants are prepared to serve the international rather than the national interest, in cases where they conflict, or that the national interests of the three coincide. Both assumptions seem unlikely to be fulfilled.

This takes me back to the hegemonic or leadership solution. As I noted at the outset, scholars such as Nau and Nye think that the United States is «bound to lead» in future, «leading the world economy into the 1990s» as it did from 1945 to some uncertain date in the 1970s. US leadership in the military field was demonstrated when after the rape of Kuwait, President Bush moved to shield Saudi Arabia from Iraqi aggression. US policies, moreover, obtained international support from the United Nations. In the economic arena, however, the record is one of weakness and following along. American contributions in aid of Eastern European relief and reconstructions have been derisory, and organized by other countries. The country has passed the hat to get substantial contributions to pay for the costs of its deployment. Assistance to the USSR has taken the form of grain exports which serves a parochial interest. United States preoccupation with Third World growth of the 1950s and '60s has given way to attempts to collect debts and hold down restrictions on some leading US exports, such as computers in Brazil. From its position as economic leader of the world in the third quarter of this century, the United States has slipped back into the pack, while Germany (Europe?) and Japan have moved up.

Some. of you may know that I ascribed the length, depth and width of the world depression of the 1930s to the fact that Britain was no longer capable of acting as world economic leader and the United States then was unwilling to assume the role. There is a danger — how serious I am at a loss to measure — that with its problems of debt, productivity, savings and the rest, the United States is becomings like Britain in the interwar period, with no replacement in sight. Germany and Japan have been faithful followers of the United States lead after World War II, and while they are becoming more assertive, neither seems poised to claim a dominant and expansive world role. That the position bears a resemblance to the 1930s is seconded by a passage from José Ortega y Gasset's *The Revolt of the Masses* which I recently reread. To bring it up-to-date, I substitute the United States where he writes Europe, and Germany and Japan for his New York and Moscow. The book appeared in 1930, more than 60 years ago:

«United States commandments have lost their force, though there is
no sign of any other on the horizon. The United States — we are told
— is ceasing to rule, and no one sees who is going to take her place...
It would not matter if the United States ceased to command, provided
there was someone to take her place. But there is not the faintest sign
of one. Germany and Japan represent nothing new... one does not
know what they really are... United States loss of command would not
worry me if there were in existence another group of countries
capable of taking its place in power and in the direction of the planet».
Ortega thought that provincial England, Germany and France were in
decay, but that a United States of Europe could overcome the
suffocation caused by the narrow boundaries of the separate countries. This notion, wildly premature in 1930, has a new lease on life
two generations later.

I have no great optimism that Europe will recapture its
«command» of the world as Ortega put it, or take its rightful share of
the responsibility for the international public goods of peace and
economic stability and growth in the immediate future. It is fully
occupied at the moment with more parochial concerns, completing
the common market and integrating Eastern Europe into the West.
For the years immediately ahead, it would appear we have to rely on
all the methods of producing public goods, trilateralism, regional-bloc
building, international organizations, and perhaps especially regimes.
It embarrasses me to confess that I do not fully share the American
predilection for drawing up and attempting to implement written
constitutions. The most interesting economic institutions of the
postwar period, in my judgment — the Euro-currency market and the
swap network — were not the result of complex negotiations as at
Bretton Woods, but evolved. I am a wobbly — not firm — believer in
proceeding as the way lies open, muddling through, unwritten constitutions. But it is important to have a fairly clear idea of the direction
one wants to go In the longer run, the world economy wants an
institutional equivalent of world government to produce international
public goods. I fervently hope that the experience of the next years in
building the new Europe — to which this conference is contributing,
will provide a pattern that can be followed with necessary variations
in moving to the needed larger scale.

The New Europe
and the Japanese Strategy

Ippei Yamazawa
Hitotsubashi University, Tokyo

There is a big economic entity emerging in Europe resulting from EC'92, EFTA's approach to it, and the recent liberalization of Eastern Europe. It is a big concern of outsiders what external policy will be implemented. Since the EC will continue to be the core of the New Europe, the EC's policy will be focused upon. While the EC Commission states that the single European market will create greater import from outsiders, many outsiders are concerned about the possible diversion of their export from the EC due to the strengthened protectionism within it. The government of Japan as well as those of other Pacific countries have been expressing the latter concern of the outsiders on various occasions and warning against any move toward a fortress Europe. However, on a careful overview of the recent Japan-EC economic relations, one can easily see that Japanese MNCs have already participated in the moves toward EC'92 and it would not be to the EC's benefit to sever this co-existence. Japanese MNCs look less pessimistic than their government's statement.

Nevertheless, private firms of Asian NIEs and ASEAN countries are not well-prepared and seriously concerned about the possible exclusion from one of their major markets. There has been recently proposed an Asian trade bloc in case a fortress Europe does emerge. However, it will contradict with the Japanese strategy and retard further development of the Asia Pacific. The Japanese strategy should be extended to incorporate other Pacific firms into their European business and to connect the two fast-growing regions.

Throughout the 1980s, the Japan-EC economic relationship was activated toward a new direction with a shift from export to direct investment in local production. This trend has not been initiated by the EC'92 program. Indeed, the EC'92 program has stimulated Japanese MNCs, but their active participation in Europe has continued since the 1970s, being attracted by the gradual completion of the EC. Japanese MNCs have been concerned about both the protection and growth potential aspects of the EC market, and EC'92 has strengthened these two aspects and accelerated the new Japanese approach to the EC. This trend also reflects changes on the Japanese side, especially the rapid globalization of the large Japanese firms. They have been investing in North America and South-East Asia as well as Europe and their participation in Europe is a part of their global strategy. The new Japanese approach should be correctly understood in this global context.

This paper aims to elaborate the new Japanese approach to EC. Starting with an overview of the Japan-EC relations, paragraph 1 will present the new Japanese approach. Paragraphs 2 to 5 will elaborate its various aspects: changes in the Japanese economy underlying rapid globalization of Japanese firms (paragraph 2), Japanese firms' response to the EC policies (paragraph 3), MITI's international cooperation program (paragraph 4), and Japanese banks' participation in Europe (paragraph 5). Paragraph 6 will summarize the Japanese strategy and conclude the paper with a suggestion for mutually beneficial ties between Europe and the Pacific (1).

1. - Japan-EC Relationship: an Overview

Commodity trades between Japan and EC used to be less intensive mainly because of similar factor endowments and similar stages of industrial development. The trade intensity between Japan and the EC (EC's share in Japan's total export relative to EC's share in the world total import and vice versa) was around 0.4 in both ways in

---

(1) I benefited from comments made by Richard Blackhurst. An earlier version was also presented at the WWZ Conference on «The EC After 92: Perspective for the Outsiders», in Basle, Switzerland, on August 22-24, 1991.

comparison with 2.0-2.4 with the United States and 2.7 to 4.5 with raw materials exporters in the Pacific. Both trade and investment were activated during the 1980s. Between 1980 and 1989, Japan's trade with the EC expanded much faster than its total trade and the EC's share increased from 12.8% to 17.4% of total Japan's export and from 5.6% to 13.3% of Japan's total imports. Trade intensity between Japan and EC has been on increase in both ways accordingly.

The trade expansion was contributed by sophisticated machineries and chemicals reflecting the emerged complementarity at higher income level between Japan and the EC. Table 1 lists Japan's major export items, which cover 85-90% of total exports to the EC. Machineries accounted for 81% of Japanese exports. Automobiles, office machinery, optical machinery, and semi-conductors increased or kept big shares, while tape recorders, radio, metals, and textiles decreased their shares. Column *B* gives the EC's shares in individual export items. The all commodity average increased from 12 to 17%,

TABLE 1

COMMODITY COMPOSITIONS
OF JAPAN'S EXPORT TO EC (*)

	1980		1985		1989	
	A	*B*	*A*	*B*	*A*	*B*
Machineries	72.3	14.8	79.3	12.6	81.4	19.0
Automobiles	16.0	11.0	15.2	8.8	17.6	17.4
Auto parts	n.a.	n.a.	2.6	9.8	1.9	9.3
Generators	1.0	6.4	1.4	7.2	2.0	12.6
Office machinery	3.5	25.8	8.8	22.5	11.0	27.4
Optical mach	9.3	34.3	9.1	26.8	7.6	32.6
Semiconductors	2.6	18.8	4.1	17.2	4.4	14.9
Tape-recorders	7.2	52.0	7.0	16.7	3.3	20.5
Radio	3.5	19.3	1.2	21.3	1.3	27.6
TV	1.3	13.3	0.7	5.4	0.6	16.6
Chemicals	4.2	10.4	4.7	12.2	5.0	16.2
Metals	6.8	5.3	2.7	2.9	2.3	5.1
Textiles	2.5	0.3	2.3	7.3	1.7	12.0
All commodities	100.0	12.8	100.0	11.4	100.0	17.4

(*) *A:* Commodity composition (%) of Japan's exports to EC;
B: EC's shares (%) in industrial commodity exports.

Source: Compiled by the author from Mɪᴛɪ: *White Paper on International Trade*, 1980, 1985, and 1989.

but many items listed here exceed the average. More than half of
Japanese tape-recorders were shipped to the EC in 1980 and more
than a quarter of optical machinery, office machinery, and radio went
to the EC in 1989. The EC provides a major market for the Japanese
high-tech products. Table 2 shows major import items to Japan from
the EC, among which machineries occupied only 30% of the total. But
its column *B* indicates a greater contribution of the EC than in the
case of Japanese exports. The EC provided 87%, 77%, and 49% of
Japan's imports of automobile, spirits, and pharmaceutical products
respectively. Both the increase and pattern of the Japan-EC trades
show an emerging complementarity between the two at higher income level.

The trade expansion, however, was lopsided and accompanied by
widened trade imbalance, i.e. persistent surplus on Japan's side.
Japan's trade surplus increased from 8.8 billion US dollars to 20.0
billion US dollars during the 1980s, causing serious trade frictions on
the bilateral over-all relation, and an increase of imports to Japan has

TABLE 2

COMMODITY COMPOSITION
OF JAPAN'S IMPORTS FROM EC (*)

	1980		1985		1989	
	A	B	A	B	A	B
Machineries	33.0	26.3	26.3	18.9	30.7	26.7
Industrial mach	14.0	28.9	10.5	19.8	9.4	23.1
Electronic mach	5.9	16.7	5.6	12.8	5.2	12.8
Transport mach	9.3	32.6	7.8	26.9	14.6	59.2
Automobile	4.3	74.3	5.6	92.0	12.3	86.6
Precision instrument	3.7	28.8	2.4	18.2	1.4	16.3
Chemicals	21.0	26.5	24.0	26.4	17.7	31.2
Pharmacultical	5.6	41.2	4.9	33.5	4.8	49.0
Textile	9.0	22.1	7.6	17.3	8.6	18.2
Clothing	3.9	20.1	3.1	14.0	4.8	15.2
Spirituous	3.7	86.7	2.5	77.7	3.6	77.5
All commodities	100.0	5.6	100.0	6.9	100.0	13.3

(*) *A:* Commodity composition (%) of Japan's imports from EC;
    B: EC's shares (%) in industrial commodity imports.
Source: The same as Table 1.

been requested by the EC side on various occasions of Japan-EC dialogue. It also tended to aggravate frictions between EC producers and Japanese exporters and Japanese exporters in individual sectors. Individual trade frictions started with France's import restrictions on colour TVs in 1968 and on autmobiles, VTRs, and working machinery in 1981-1982, followed by anti-dumping procedures against miniature ball-bearings, copying machines, printers and VTRs, and further followed by anti-dumping procedures against parts of those machineries because of alleged "screw-driver production".

The new Japanese approach was accelerated in the course of aggravated trade frictions. It entailed a shift from commodity export to foreign direct investment (FDI). Japan's FDI in Europe ranked only after the United States in its cumulative total amounts for the years 1950-1989, but two-thirds of it was undertaken over the last three years. Table 3 gives the Japanese FDI in Europe classified by country and industry. It concentrated in machineries among manufacturing, whose commodity exports were most rapid and affected by serious frictions with EC producers. It should also to noted that Japanese FDI was also active in the non-manufacturing sector. Four times as much as manufacturing was invested in commerce and services, especially in finance, which will be analysed in some detail in paragraph 5.

There are two aspects of this shift from exports to direct investment in local production. One is to decelerate export growth and shift to assembly production at first and further to parts production later so as to circumvent such restrictive measures as anti-dunping procedures and screw-driver allegations. Another is to pursue the advantages of local production, such as production close to customers and savings in long-distance transportation costs.

The EC'92 programme tends to affect both aspects and accelerate the Japanese FDI in the EC. On the one hand, in case EC'92 should lead to fortress Europe, they have to complete their shift before the restrictions are strengthend. On the other, the enlarged single market resulting from EC'92 will enhance the advantage of local production within the EC.

To sum up, Japanese firms see aspects of both increasing protection and an enlarged integrated market in the EC'92 pogram and the two aspects jointly accelerate the new Japanese approach toward EC.

Country / Industry	EC	%	UK	%	Luxembourg	%	Netherland	%	West Germ
Foodstuffs	295	94.9	101	32.5		0.0	39	12.5	9
Textiles	462	94.5	36	7.4		0.0	125	25.6	
Wood and pulp	9	52.9		0.0		0.0	1	5.9	8
Chemicals	1,084	97.7	108	9.7		0.0	271	24.4	376
Metal	305	77.2	69	17.5		0.0	72	18.2	0
Industrial mach.	1,313	98.1	507	37.9	18	1.3	252	18.8	138
Electric machn.	1,945	96.5	778	38.6	4	0.2	485	24.1	343
Transport mach.	1,348	99.7	454	33.6		0.0	151	11.2	24
Miscellaneous	828	90.3	228	24.9		0.0	112	12.2	101
Manufactures tot.	7,588	95.5	2,281	28.7	21	0.3	1,510	19.0	998
Agricult and forest	8	100.0	0	0.0	3	3.75	0	0.0	1
Fishery	2	11.1	0	0.0		0.0		0.0	
Mining	924	65.3	850	60.0		0.0		0.0	
Primary tot.	934	64.8	850	58.9	3	0.2	0	0.0	1
Construction	84	100.0	32	38.1		0.0	17	20.2	21
Commerce	5,053	93.5	1,230	22.8	2	0.0	1,209	22.4	1,365
Finance insur.	19,772	93.0	8,267	38.9	5,186	24.4	5,072	23.9	456
Services	2,362	95.0	426	17.1	17	0.7	994	40.0	79
Transportation	126	80.3	55	35.0	31	19.7	15	9.6	7
Real estate	3,524	96.0	1,695	46.2	22	0.6	1,200	32.7	21
Others	950	90.0	708	67.0	101	9.6	49	4.6	58
Commerce/services	31,871	94.4	12,413	36.4	5,359	15.7	8,556	25.1	2,007
Branches	1,422	99.4	234	16.4		0.0	4	0.3	437
Real estate	35	92.1	13	34.2		0.0	0	0.0	5
Total	41,857	93.1	15,793	35.1	5,383	12.0	10,072	22.4	3,448

Source: Compiled from MINISTRY OF FINANCE'S STATISTICS. Reproduced from KUME G.: *Japanese Manufact*

TABLE 3

-1989 CUMULATIVE TOTAL
ollars)

France		Spain		Belgium		Ireland		Italy		Portugal		Europe
	%		%		%		%		%		%	
132	42.4	3	1.0	2	0.6	0	0.0	8	2.6	1	0.3	311
107	21.9	49	10.0	0	0.0	104	21.3	19	3.9	22	4.5	489
0	0.0	0	0.0		0.0		0.0		0.0	0	0.0	17
37	3.3	121	10.9	147	13.2	0	0.0	23	2.1	1	0.1	1,110
67	17.0	62	15.7	25	6.3	6	1.5	3	0.8	1	0.3	395
232	17.3	35	2.6	65	4.9	21	1.6	44	3.3	1	0.1	1,339
119	5.9	100	5.0	24	1.2	37	1.8	52	2.6	3	0.1	2,016
52	3.8	564	41.7	32	2.4		0.0	62	4.6	9	0.7	1,352
103	11.2	14	1.5	178	19.4	25	2.7	31	3.4	36	3.9	917
848	10.7	949	11.9	472	5.9	193	2.4	242	3.0	74	0.9	7,947
4	50.0	0	0.0		0.0	0	0.0		0.0		0.0	8
	0.0	1	5.6		0.0	1	5.6	0	0.0		0.0	18
57	4.0		0.0		0.0	17	1.2		0.0		0.0	1,416
61	4.2	1	0.1	0	0.0	18	1.2	0	0.0	0	0.0	1,442
8	9.5	5	6.0	1	1.2		0.0		0.0	0	0.0	84
613	11.3	116	2.1	276	5.1	7	0.1	207	3.8	28	0.5	5,404
291	1.4	16	0.1	405	1.9	13	0.1	58	0.3	8	0.0	21,258
296	11.9	185	7.4	22	0.9	325	13.1	18	0.7		0.0	2,487
5	3.2	0	0.0	13	8.3		0.0	0	0.0		0.0	157
487	13.3	58	1.6	5	0.1	4	0.1	30	0.8	2	0.1	3,669
17	1.6		0.0	11	1.0	1	0.1	5	0.5	0	0.0	1,056
,717	5.0	380	1.1	733	2.1	350	1.0	318	0.9	38	0.1	34,115
259	18.1	216	15.1	148	10.3	2	0.1	122	8.5	0	0.0	1,430
15	39.5	1	2.6	0	0.0	0	0.0	1	2.6	0	0.0	38
,899	6.4	1,546	3.4	1,353	3.0	565	1.3	684	1.5	114	0.3	44,972

stment in EC: Present State and Future Prospect, (in Japanese), *Kaigai Touschi Kenkyuujoho*, July 1990.

2. - Mechanism of Active Japanese FDIs

Active Japanese FDIs have been destined not only to EC but also to North America and Asia Pacific and should be regarded as a part of their global strategy. It is also related to their restructuring efforts at home, which originated as their response to the global adjustment common to all industrialized economies during the last two decades. Restructuring efforts by Japanese firms was their response to changed patterns of Japan's comparative advantage resulting from such factors as price hike of energy and raw materials, increased labour costs, catching-up by late-starting Asian neighbours, rapid appreciation of yen, and so on, all of which occurred over the past two decades.

The restructuring effort took three forms: rationalization, diversification, and globalization of their business activities. The rationalization was implemented typically by metal and chemical firms badly affected by higher energy and material prices and low utilization of their large scale factories under slowed growth after the oil shock. Many firms scrapped obsolete factories and equipment and reduced employment so that they could run competitive capacities at reduced scales. Saving of energy and material use was another aspect of rationalization effort, for which Japanese integrated steel firms were highly credited (2).

The diversification consists of up-grading and sophistication of their production toward higher value-added and of switching-over to related industries with higher technological possibilities. The success of this effort hinges upon new product innovation which was promoted actively in Japan through the 1980s and also helped by the new consumer taste which emerged at the higher income level. The globalization is characterized by a shift from domestic production-cum-export to overseas production-cum-exports to third countries and import to Japan. The globalization is only feasible for firms with superior technology and efficient resources. Let me call these firms Japanese MNCs (Japan-based multi-national corporations).

---

(2) Refer for details IPPEI YAMAZAWA: *Economic Development and International Trade: the Japan model*, University of Hawaii Press, 1991.

FDI is a core element of the globalization effort. Japanese FDI has been oriented mainly towards three regions; North America, Western Europe and Asia Pacific. But the motivation and pattern of investment in America/Europe and Asia are quite different. The Japanese investment in Asia is mainly motivated by saving labour costs, while those in Europe and North America are motivated by market potential and trade conflicts. The two are complementary and have increased in parallel. They promote the global operation of Japanese MNCs.

Japanese investment in the EC is motivated by both trade frictions and the economic advantage of local production but a shift from the former to the latter has been observed. Japan's export of sophisticated machinery went to the EC as one of the promising high-income markets. Japanese MNCs preferred at first to produce at home and export in the form of completed products because the cost and quality advantage of their domestic production with its total productivity control and just-in time procurement system more than offset the high transportation costs of exporting from a distance. However, strengthened restrictions and pressures by individual EC member governments urged them to change to local production and local sale in spite of their economic disadvantage.

Although originally motivated by circumventing restrictions, Japanese MNCs have recently become more oriented to the advantage of the EC market than for its protection. Table 4 summarizes a recent survey of 270 Japanese firms operating in Europe and their motives of investment. Sample firms are classified into assembly, parts and material production, but their numbers are not reported. Listed motives interact with each other and multiple answers were allowed. At least half of all sample firms cited "trade friction", while two-thirds gave "global operation". Such related motives as "switch from export to local production" and "customer's demand" were given by many firms. As regards future prospects for EC'92, "protection" exceeded "large scale benefit", but the positive expectation for EC'92 seems to be included in "global operation" and related motives. Many motives are common to assembler, parts and material producers but relatively more assemblers cited "trade friction" while relatively more parts and material producers cited "advantage of European production" and "global operation".

TABLE 4

JAPANESE MANUFACTURING FIRMS IN EUROPE BY COUNTRY AND INDUSTRY
(January 1990)

	Total	UK	France	West Germany	Spain	Nether-land	Italy	Bel-gium	Ire-land	Portu-gal	Gre-ece	Den-mark	Lu-xem-bourg	Aus-tria	Swit-zer-land	Swe-den	Fin-land	Ice-land	Nor-way
Total	529	132	95	89	55	34	28	25	22	13	3	3	2	12	5	6	4	1	0
Foodstuff	21	3	15	1	1	1													
Textiles	8	3		2	1	1			1										
Clothing	7		3	1			2			1									
Furniture	4	1	1	1	1														
Pulp and paper	4		1							1							1		
Chemicals	83	11	11	9	11	10	8	6	4	3	1	1		2	3	3			
Pharmaceutical	14		3	4	3		1	1	2								1		
Rubber prod.	18	1	4	4	3	2		1		1	1							1	
Ceramics	13	2	2	2	1	1		4	1										
Iron and steel	5					1		1	1	1	1								
Nonferrous metal	14	5	5	2	2														
Metal products	20	7	2		3		1						1	4					
Industrial machnry	66	16	14	16	8	6	3	1	6							1			
Electric machnry	86	25	18	19	7	3	6	2	5	1		1							
Electric parts	53	20	4	14	2	2	1	3					1						
Transport equipmt	14	4	2		5	2	1	1											
Transport parts	24	14	1	1	2	2	2		1	1				1		1			
Precision instrument	22	4	3	7				1	1	1		1		1	1	1	1		
Others	53	16	6	6	5	3	3	4	1		1			4	1		1		
Design centre/R&D	73(23)	29(9)	11(4)	14(6)	11(0)	3(0)	3(2)	4(1)	1(0)	0	0	0	0	0	1(1)	1(1)	0	0	0

Source: JETRO: *Survey of Japanese Manufacturing Subsidiaries in Europe: 1990*, reproduced from KUME G., *op cit.*

3. - Strategy of the Japanese Manufacturing MNCs

We have seen in the previous paragraph that the Japanese MNC's participation in Europe is a part of their global strategy and that it has been promoted by such macro economic conditions as the appreciation of the yen, persistent trade surplus Japan's, the policies of the EC governments, and the growth potential of the EC market. Nevertheless their active globalization in response to the macro economic conditions was possible only because Japanese industries and firms had reached the stage of enabling the shift from export to FDI (3).

3.1 *Development Stage and Globalization Strategy*

This does not mean, of course, that all Japanese industries reached that stage as once. In such industries as textile and shipbuilding have already lost their competitive edge, entered a reverse import stage, and are no longer able to promote further FDI. On the other hand, the electronic and automobile industries achieved import substitution in the 1960s, expanded export in the 1970s and have entered the investment stage in the 1980s. This is a typical pattern of industry development followed by Japanese and Asian NIEs' firms and is named the "flying wild-geese" or "catching-up product cycle" development *vis-à-vis* the "product cycle" development by R. Vernon, where foreign MNCs, instaead of local enterpreneurs, take the initiative (4). Both the textile and steel industries typically followed this pattern and have reached the last stage of reverse import. Many Japanese firms have resorted to rationalization and diversification rather than to globalization against the rapid catching-up by Asian NIEs firms.

The Japanese automobile industry achieved import substitution in the late 1950s and 1960s, during which import was restricted at a low level, European production technology was actively introduced, and the efficient just-in-time subcontracting system of parts procurement was established. The industry achieved the output/consumption ratio

---

(3) The analysis in this paragraph is based on the author's interview study with major Japanese MNCs in 1989-1990.

(4) See YAMAZAWA, *op. cit.*, for details of the catching-up product cycle model.

of 3.5 in 1988 and has entered the mature (FDI) stage. On the contrary, the Japanese household electronic industry did not experience a clear stage of import substitution buth developed their star products for domestic consumers. It started to export after its domestic market was satiated, which was consistent with Vernon's "product cycle" model. Nevertheless, both the automobile and electronic industries have been engaged actively in globalization strategy throughout the 1980s and led the Japanese participation in the EC market.

Successful FDI requires competent managerial resources (management personnel and technology) and Japanese automobile and electronic firms accumulated those resources at the import substitution and export stages. They are characterized by severe oligopolistic competition on the domestic market and they have extended similar competition to FDI abroad. They have typically pursued the swich from export to FDI, but one can observe a greater variety in their spatial dispersal of FDI, coordination among dispersed subsidiaries, and degree of localization.

The performance of Japanese MNCs in the EC is affected by the interaction between the following factors, as was pointed out in the previous paragraphs: 1) policies of EC member governments and EC Commission; 2) market size and growth potential of host countries; 3) industry characteristics as well as competition with local rival firms.

3.2 *EC's Policy to Japanese MNCs*

The EC's policy to Japanese firms was at first implemented by individual member governments and has been coordinated by the EC Commission recently. One can observe a new element affecting foreign exporters differently from traditional trade policy. It has emerged from the interaction between the EC governments/Commission and Japanese MNCs and its effect should be understood in a dynamic context of the changing strategies of Japanese firms in response to the escalated EC policies.

First came import restriction with tariffs, but low-bounded tariffs were not effective and quickly replaced by such restrictive arrangement as Voluntary Export Restraints (VER) and Orderly Marketing Arrangements (OMA) as was imposed on passenger car imports by several member governments. In response to effective import restrictions, Japanese MNCs switched from export of domestically produced products either to local production or to export from third countries. FDI in local production suits the need of some member governments which are eager not so much to restrict import as to keep domestic production and employment by foreign MNCs.

The rule of origin has been strengthened in response to Japanese firms moves to relocate assembly production abroad and to export to the EC from there. The rule requires that "last substantial process" needs to be carried out within EC but it has become more strictly applied (local value-added more than 45% of the ex-factory price) and the possibility of further strengthening in future has discouraged moves by Japanese firms to export from their SouthEast Asian bases. The treatment of exports from other member country bases has been argued between exporting and importing member countries as was evidenced by exports of Japanese cars made in the UK to France and Italy and has not yet been settled.

Another group of member countries has been making frequent use of anti-dumping/counter-veiling duties (AD/CVD) rather than VER and OMA. The former is a legal safeguard measure against unfair practice under the GATT article VI. But its application criterion is not transparent and so arbitrary that it has been selectively imposed on individual firms and had more direct impact on them. AD/CVD has been extended to imports of parts for assembly production in order to urge existing foreign firms to increase the local value-added of their production.

How far will this interaction continue between EC governments and Japanese MNCs? There seems to be a tendency to converge to a form beneficial to both parties. On the EC side, the EC Commission tends to restrain further escalation of regulatory policies. Discretionary application of AD/CVD has recently been refuted by the GATT panel and the stricter local content requirement has been discussed in the TRIM negotiation of the current Uruguay Round, and the EC Commission seems to be oriented for their liberalization. On the other hand, Japanese MNCs tend to promote localization in the single

European market and try to be insiders and good citizens so that they can apply for national treatment in their business operation there.

Greater fluctuation of exchange rates gives another incentive for Japanese MNCs to increase local production in Europe. Under the present flexible exchange rate system, the yen-European currency rates fluctuate more widely than anticipated, while European currencies move together within a narrow band under the ERM. To give an example, the yen-pound rate fluctuated between 215 and 265 yen per pound and the yen-mark rate fluctuated between 85 and 100 yen per mark during the two years 1989-1990. The appreciation of the yen makes imported parts dearer for Japanese assemblers in Europe. The less imported parts are used, the less will be the exchange rate risk. This encourages many Japanese MNCs to increase the use of local components in their European production. In Table 4, 10% of Japanese MNCs in Europe gave this motive.

3.3 *Industry Characteristics and Spatial Dispersal*

The performance of Japanese firms in the EC is also affected by industry characteristics. Both automobile and electronic industries consist of assembly production but they differ significantly in some aspects of local operation.

The automobile industry has a limited number of product variety. Automobiles are classified into passenger cars and commercial vehicles, each of which are usually produced by different firms. Individual passenger car manufacturers produce several different sizes and designs but they tend to specialize in a few major types in their overseas production. Its minimum optimum scale of production is usually big and it requires a big investment fund. This is especially the case if major parts are to be supplied locally.

On the other hand, the electronic industry has a great diversity of products. They are broadly classified into household electronics, industry electronics, and components, all of which are often covered by major electronic firms. Each group is further divided into major product groups and handled by separate product division systems. Each product variety has a far smaller minimum optimum size than in the case of car production and requires a much smaller investment fund, which enables electronic firms to adopt a more flexible investment strategy than car producers.

Table 5 gives the spatial dispersal of Japanese FDIs in various manufacturing activities in Europe in terms of number of cases. By comparing this table with the corresponding figures in terms of amount in Table 3, one can see that investment in automobiles requires a greater amount of fund per case and is concentrated in two countries, UK and Spain. Investment in electronics requires a smaller amount and is dispersed to such major markets as the UK, France,

TABLE 5

MOTIVE TO INVEST IN EUROPE
(270 Japanese firms in Europe, 1990)

	Total	Assembly	Parts	Material	Others
Total	773	317	141	220	95
1. Trade frictions	144	98	25	12	9
Quota restriction to Japanese	48	36	7	3	2
Anti-dumping	31	25	4	2	—
Anti-dumping (parts)	20	9	6	2	3
Protection after EC'92	45	28	8	5	4
2. Advantage of local production	245	89	38	84	34
Cheap material supply	7	1		4	2
Reduction in production cost	34	7	6	15	6
Investment incentives (tax, etc.)	44	14	9	16	5
European designs	10	5	2	2	1
Switch from exports to local prod	97	34	11	35	17
Large scale benefits after EC'92	37	19	5	10	2
R&D in Europe	16	9	4	2	1
3. Global operation	355	125	68	113	49
Global strategy	179	62	31	65	21
Exchange rate risk	29	12	2	13	2
Customer's demand	91	40	15	21	15
Accompanying parents	11	3	3	1	4
Supply to Japanese in Europe	45	8	17	13	7
4. Others	29	5	10	11	3

Source: The same as Table 4.

Germany, and the Netherlands in response to the policy and market potential of individual countries. In general, further dispersal of Japanese MNC's subsidiaries over more member countries is desirable. The present concentration in a few countries reflects mainly the in response to the compartmentalized EC market by member governments' policies as well as the small size of individual member country markets, language barriers, and the lack of their acquaintance with some member countries. The EC'92 program will resolve those barriers and encourage ·Japanese MNCs to further disperse thier subsidiaries.

As they disperse their subsidiaries over individual countries, Japanese MNCs have started to recognise the need for reshuffling their overseas operations. In 1989-1990 major electronic firms announced one after another plans for changing their traditional system of independent product divisions controlling global operations from the Tokyo headquarters to a new system of three to four regional headquarters coordinating all product divisions within each region. Regional headquarters are located in Tokyo, New York, London or other European cities, and Singapore. This tendency will promote the localization of European subsidiaries in both greater local value-added, more local R&D activities, and more local management personnel. Some firms have moved ahead in this direction but most of them have only started, so that their European HQs serve only liaison functions at present.

3.4 *Local Procurement of Parts*

Successful procurement of parts and components is the biggest problem machinery assemblers face in their localization efforts. This is especially the case for Japanese MNCs in automobile and electronics, the series which acquired their competitive edge on the basis of a efficient procurement system, that is, high standard of quality control and subcontracting with just-in-time delivery covering a great variety of parts and components. A majority of part suppliers are small - and medium-scaled and are not connected with their parent assemblers by equity shareholding. They have their own business decisions but are less prepared for overseas operations. This was a major reason why Japanese MNCs relocated assembly processes overseas at first and relied on parts imported from Japan.

However, as the need for greater localization increases, Japanese MNCs have to solve the problem of efficient local procurement of parts and components, which is far more difficult than the relocation of the assembly process. There are a few alternatives, all of which are being attempted in parallel. The first is to bring Japanese subcontracting firms to Europe through which they continue to rely on the same subcontracting system. However, only a few medium part suppliers can respond to this request and another few suppliers are integrated into part production within assembly subsidiaries. FDI by parts suppliers have become active in Asia and the US and the percentage share of medium-sized firms is higher than in Europe.

The second is to organise local part supplying firms which need to be assisted in upgrading of their technology and skills and in adjusting to the Japanese style operation. Host governments certainly welcome this move since they expect Japanese FDIs will help the industrial revival of their depressed areas. The UK's invitation of a Japanese car producer to a traditional industrial area in Midland provides a good example of this. However, it is time-consuming to organize a network of part suppliers and upgrade their technology.

Then there is the third, new alternative, i.e. strategic alliance with local rival competitors with a competent local part supplying network. A Japanese assembling subsidiary switches from part supply from Japan to procurement from a rival's part supplier and gives technical assistance to the latter to meet its standards. Similar strategic alliances have been reported recently between such long-time rival competitors as Sony and Philips, Fujitsu and Siemens, Matsushita and Grundig (Philips).

4. - MITI's International Cooperation Program

Major Japanese electronic and automobile firms have announced a common principle in their long term plans called "International Cooperation Program (ICP)", which is attributed to the MITI's (Ministry of Industry and International Trade) administrative guidance. It seems to be based on the MITI's scenario of how to resolve trade frictions with North America and EC. Figures differ between individual firms but it has three common pillars: 1) to reduce the company's export by 30 percent by 1993 an d to a half by 2000; 2) to increase the company's overseas production so as to replace export, thereby raising its proportion to total sales abroad accordingly; 3) to double the company's import by 1993 and double it again by 2000, thereby increasing the proportion of import supply of parts to domestic assembly up to 10% and more.

With its ICP, MITI aims to decrease Japan's trade imbalance with the US and EC and persuade major firms to make their overseas operations consistent with it for the sake of "national interest". MITI's administrative guidance covers the major automobile and electronic firms, which account for three quarters of Japan's export earnings, and MITI expects that if its guidance is followed faithfully, Japan's trade surplus will be reduced substantially. This is a managed trade and is criticised at home for its inconsistency with market mechanism. Besides, there will be feedbacks in opposite direction and one cannot be sure about its net final effect. But MITI appears to be determined to rely on it in order to supplement insufficient macro-economic adjustment.

It is, however, incorrect if one considers it as evidence of "the Japan Incorporated" still working in its international activities, with the government serving as a brain and the private sector following its instruction. It reflects the reality that Japan's trade frictions with the US and EC have been aggravated to such an extent that their pressure for adjustment is felt not only at the government and industry levels but also at the individual firm level and individual firms find it consistent with their interests to follow MITI's instructions both for easing pressure and for pursuing their new global strategy.

This ICP was originally aimed at trade frictions with the US but is equally applicable to Japanese MNCs in North America and Europe. They have been confronted with the similar policies in the US and concern about protectionistic moves by the US Congress as well as fortress Europe. There are major aspects common to Japanese FDIs in the US and EC. Both were undertaken in order to take advantage of big market and to circumvent protection. Japanese MNCs have been in the US much longer and their cumulative impact is much greater than in Europe as is evidenced by the following figures; total cumulative investment for the years 1950-1989 was 104.4 billion dollars in the US vs 41.9 billion dollars in EC; total employment by Japanese affiliated firms was 215 thousand in the US vs 94 thousand in EC; the number of automobile factories is 8 factories with one million cars per year in the US vs 2 factories with 100 thousand cars in EC. Both big and medium Japanese firms have invested in the US, while only big firms have invested in Europe.

5. - Strategy of Japanese Banks

Not only manufacturing firms but also Japanese financial firms have been active in FDI in Europe as was shown in Table 3. The pre-requisite for globalization discussed in paragraph 2 and 3 are well met by Japanese banks and securities firms as well as manufacturing firms. In addition, accumulated current account surplus in the 1980s has enabled Japanese financial firms to emerge as a big creditor group in the world financial market. Let me overview the participation by Japanese banks and securities firms in Europe. Table 6 shows it in chronological order.

Europe used to be less attractive market for Japanese banks than the US and South-East Asia. Following the tradition of heavy reliance on trade credit business, Japanese banks went to South-East Asia in the 1960s in accordance with the trade expansion there and to the US in the 1970s, while the limited expansion of Japan-EC trade delayed the Japanese banks' participation in Europe. The US market had a big attraction. Its big integrated market with a single currency assured Japanese banks stable business. Increasing securities prices in a bullish small market could attract foreign banks for a while but once the boom has finished prices tend to fall quickly and provide only low profits. Although the Euro-dollar market attracted Japanese banks as the fund source of loans and issuance of bonds, the EC did not attract Japanese investment when compartmentalized by country and currency. Nevertheless, 70% of the existing branches, subsidiaries, and liason offices were established during the years 1970-1985. The same figure in London alone was as high as 80%. (Table 6).

The EC will provide a single big market comparable to the US if EC'92 creates an integrated market with a stable monetary union. The EC'92 program encouraged Japanese financial firms to participate in the European market for the management of accumulated funds in Japan. Securities firms have been more active than banks since 1986 as is shown in Table 6. Major banks had already established branches and subsidiaries in London by 1985 and only extended their network to other financial centres like Frankfurt and Paris thereafter, while securities firms delayed and established their subsidiaries in London only after 1985.

However, the financial market situation is much less profitable for Japanese banks in Europe than elsewhere, reflecting severe competition there. First, local merchant banks still monoplise business with European firms. Second, participation by Japanese manufacturing firms tends to break this monopoly, but the issuance of bonds at the start of these Japanese firms are not to be handled by subsidiaries of Japanese banks according to the administrative guidance of the Ministry of Finance. Third, competition in the Euro-dollar market is so severe as to yield only a low profit margin. Thus many banks have recorded no profitable business, including some short of break-even point. On the other hand a European network requires competent personnel, and high personnel expense. A major bank is less enthusiastic and has not invested much in its European business yet. Besides, due to the new BIS's regulation and their depreciated asset values resulting from the rapid decline of stock prices, Japanese banks have become less active in their foreign investment everywhere in the past year.

What is the impact of the EC's policy on Japanese banks? The EC Commission announced in 1988 the second banking directive, under which existing banks in a member country can operate freely in other member countries and are subject to regulation only by their home country government. So long as it is applied to foreign banks' subsidiaries already admitted, Japanese banks with a well-established branch and subsidiary network have no worries about their operations throuhgout the EC. Their only concern is about the stricter applica-

TABLE 6

NEW ESTABLISHMENTS BY JAPANESE BANKS AND SECURITY CORPORATIONS IN EUROPE
(number of establishments) (*)

Japanese banks	1950-1959	1960-1969	1970-1979	1980-1984	1985	1986	1987	1988	1989
Branches	8 (6)	8 (4)	25 (12)	7 (1)	2 (0)	4 (0)	5 (0)	7 (0)	2 (0)
Subsidiaries	0 0	4 (2)	39 (18)	22 (6)	8 (2)	9 (4)	9 (5)	11 (0)	3 (0)
Liason offices	0 (0)	2 (0)	13 (0)	22 (7)	13 (6)	4 (1)	4 (1)	9 (3)	5 (1)

Japanese security corpor.		1970-1974	1975-1979	1980-1984	1985	1986	1987	1988	1989
Subsidiaries		14 (6)	10 (4)	11 (3)	5 (1)	12 (8)	8 (4)	6 (3)	5 (0)
Liason offices		2 (0)	1 (0)	2 (0)	2 (0)	3 (1)	7 (2)	7 (2)	5 (0)

(*) Figures in parentheses show establishments in London alone.

Source: Classified by years of establishment by SAKUMA H. from data compiled by MINISTRY OF FINANCE, INTERNATIONAL FINANCE BUREAU, published in *Kinyu Zaisei Jijou*.

tion of a "reciprocity rule" to the lack of a universal banking system in Japan which may give the EC member governments an excuse of not admitting national treatment to existing Japanese subsidiaries. However, considering that the global acute shortage of loanable funds will continue throughout the 1990s, it will not be beneficial for the EC member governments to exclude Japanese banks from their markets.

6. - Concluding Remarks

The Japanese strategy toward EC'92 is summarized as follows. In spite of its official warning against moves toward a fortress Europe, Japanese firms will continue their FDIs in Europe and localize their operations so as to be insiders and good citizens in the new Europe. With their well-established subsidiary network, they can operate efficiently through Europe and connect their business with outside world even if a fortress Europe emerges. They are confident that they will not be excluded from Europe so long as they contribute to the development of the single European market. MITI's international cooperation program aims to mitigate trade frictions and is consistent with the strategy of the Japanese MNCs.

However, not all firms and governments outside EC are well-prepared for EC'92. In particular, private firms in Asian NIEs have been expanding their business beyond their home region but have not reached the global investment stage yet. They are seriously concerned about the possibility of being excluded from the new Europe. Some suggest that Asia Pacific economies should form a trade bloc in order to counterbalance the European trade bloc (5). The suggestion, however, contradicts Japanese global interest and strategy. Japanese firms have been investing in the US, EC and in Asia Pacific, with different motives between the former two and the last. Both are complementary and one cannot be substituted by the other. The

---

(5) Some Pacific scholars have been suggesting that in case the GATT Uruguay Round fails and the EC pursues restrictive policies to outsiders, Pacific countries promote liberalization on a conditional MFN basis. A Malaysian minister recently proposed an Asian Trade Bloc on a similar logic. See NIPPON KEIZAI: *Shinbun*, December 7, 1990.

Pacific trade bloc would also contradict with the benefit for Asia Pacific economies by detering the long-term development of their trade-oriented growth.

What is the welfare implication of the Japanese strategy for both the Asia-Pacific region and the world as a whole? There will be both negative and positive aspects and it is the future course of EC'92 that will determine which of these aspects will prevail over the other. If the EC promotes free-trade with outsiders, Japanese MNCs and their global intra-firm network will serve as an efficient conduit through which two dynamic growths in Europe and Asia Pacific will be interconnected with each other. If on the other hand, fortress Europe does emerge, major Japanese firms will survive in a compartmentalized world market, while minor suppliers in both Japan and other Asia Pacific economies will be let out and the Pacific dynamism will be substantially constrained. It is imperative that the Japanese strategy be extended to keep Euro-Pacific relations as open as possible and to encourage these minor but dynamic Asian Pacific firms to participate in Europe.

The new Europe cannot be built in a fortress. It needs the contribution of all outsiders with capital, technology, and vitality. The new Europe should be built global blessing for its open policy both within and with outside Europe.

Can New Europe Compete with Japan and the United States?

Gianni Fodella (*)
Università di Milano

1. - Major Changes in the World Economy

If we consider the dynamics that characterized foreign trade in the post-war period we can easily see that during the sixties, seventies and eighties while the percentage of US exports on world exports declined, that of Europe remaind stable while that of Japan together with other East Asian countries (1) almost doubled in the span of time of the three decades considered.

More precisely while East Asia has seen its share of world exports grow from 9% in 1950 to 22% in 1988, the share of the less developed countries halved from over 30% to less than 15% over the same period, while that of the developed Western economies remained almost stable showing a slight increase in Europe and a slight decrease in North America.

At the same time the gap between the already developed and the highly promising economies on one side, and the less developed countries on the other, in terms of overall economic performance, has considerably widened.

(*) Gianni Fodella is working on a book *Europe, Japan, United States Economies on Trial* to be published in 1991.

Advise: the numbers in square brackets refer to the Bibliography in the appendix.

(1) East Asia is the area dominated or strongly influenced by Chinese civilisation, or by important minorities of Chinese origin. The centre of East Asia includes China (with Taiwan, Hong Kong, Macao), Japan, Korea (South an North), Vietnam, Thailand, Malaysia with Singapore and Brunei, Indonesia.

Several factors have contributed to such a situation: *a)* the ever-diminishing contents of raw materials and energy in products and services. Such a de-materialization, coupled with the increased accessibility to raw materials has damaged the relative position of all primary goods producers; *b)* the introduction of microelectronics in production processes has discouraged direct foreign investments in the less developed countries. This has enabled companies belonging to industries once labelled as «mature» to remain in the developed countries, and has deprived the developing countries of a flow of capital from the direct foreign investment in manufacturing induced by the low cost of labour; *c)* the availability of technology through the purchase of patents or licensing. This has reduced the importance of technological monopolies giving the most dynamic technology makers that were not as able to fully exploit their own technological innovations.

It is a framework that has favoured the more agile trasforming economies of Japan, Germany, France and Italy, all technology takers that in addition are heavily dependent on imports of raw materials, but that were able to respond with vitality to a challenging situation and even to severe constraints like the one caused by the energy crises of the Seventies.

2. - Europe's Economy Matches America
but Growth Rates are Higher in East Asia

In a classical work (Denison [1]) the 1960 situation of some of the most developed among the European economies (Italy was not included) was compared to that of the United States of 1925. The per capita income levels of 1925 USA were roughly similar to those of 1960 Europe, but the growth rates were higher in Europe than in the United States. As a result of such of different dynamics in 30 years a 35-year gap has been filled, since today the income levels in the United States and in New Europe are almost equal, if not in dollar terms at least in terms of purchasing power parities.

The growth rates have continued to be higher in Europe than in the United States. For example in the 24 years from 1965 to 1988 the average annual growth rate of real GNP per capita grew 3.5% in Norway, 3.4% in Yugoslavia, 3.2% in Finland, 3.1% in Portugal, 3% in Italy, 2.9% in Austria and Greece, 2.5% in Belgium, France and West Germany, and by 1.6% in the United States and 4.3% in Japan.

In 1965 the GDP of the United States was 701 billion dollars, that of the European Community (12 members) was 457 billion dollars and that of Japan 91 billion dollars. In 1988 the figures had respectively become 4847, 4614 and 2844 (World Bank [8]). In 1990 the European Community, including the 12 member countries plus the 13th «hidden member» (Fodella [4], p.8), has overcome the United States while Japan has considerably reduced its gap with them.

The most surprising economy has undoubtedly been that of Japan, although the brilliant performance of China and of the four Asian NIES (to be read in my opinion: *Now Industrialized Economic Systems)* South Korea, Taiwan, Hong Kong, Singapore, should not be overlooked.

American GDP grew, in dollar terms using current exchange rates, between 1965 and 1988 about seven times and that of 12-country Europe ten times; but Japan's GDP grew over 31 times and that of South Korea over 57 times: Japan has not been alone as a brilliant performer of East Asia, since also China, Taiwan, Hong Kong, Singapore, Korea, Indonesia, Thailand and Malaysia experienced in 1965-1988 real GNP per capita rates of growth equalling or exceeding an annual average of 4%. Only Hungary (5.1%) performed equally well, while the United States scored a meagre 1.6% and even the most dynamic ones among the European countries did not approach the performance of East Asia as a whole.

Europe has been able to grow at a pace quicker than that of the United States — that seems therefore a competitor new Europe may be able to cope with in future as well ad it did in the past — but slower than that of Japan and the «magnificent seven» of East Asia. Although the future is not to be assumed as a simple extrapolation of the past, it might be relevant to investigate the reasons behind the trend that developed in order to see what new Europe may have to do in order to deal with Japan's economic challenge effectively. The reasons behind Japan's ability to thoroughly diffuse within the companies of its economic system the technology produced elsewhere, in making

Accessible to its companies the world natural resource it needs, to
manage its monetary and exchange-rate policy and its long-term industrial and trade strategy imply not only the adoption at different levels
(country, industry, company) of highly efficient policies, but also the
operating of *orgware* (structural organization that stems out of the institutions, rules and behaviours that characterize an economic system)
of far superior quality than that of Europe or the United States.

3. - Have the Traditional Rules of the Game Become Obsolete?

When the United States became (after Britain) the most powerful
economic system of the world it had by definition no external threats
to fear and its only problem was to protect its own system through the
rules of the game that it had inherited from Britain.

These rules were essentially concerned with the mechanisms of
competition within a free-trade framework and were aimed at protecting both citizens (as consumers) and entrepreneurs (as producers)
from the power of domestic monopolies, the only visible menace to
welfare and to healthy competition.

The institutions, rules and behaviours being almost identical in
the British and America economic systems, there were no reasons to
consider orgware as an element deserving of special interest or
attention when dealing with competitivity or other aspects peculiar to
the economic system.

In other words all companies were considered to be competing
on an equal footing, since each economic system was considered to be
based more or less on the same type of structural organization.
Companies belonging to less developed economic systems had the
«advantage» of reduced labour costs to balance other shortcomings
that might characterize their own economic system, and in any case
such companies were not in the world top list. The most competitive
companies belonged to the Western world. In the last few year, with
Japan and also with Korea, we have experienced a different situation.
Not all companies competing in the world market come from
economic systems that have the same type of institutions, rules and
behaviours of the Western world and we have begun to suspect that

structural organization may positively affect their competitivity, and not only their style of behaviour.

Maybe *orgware* has always beeen important, and for example the causes of underdevelopment might have their roots there, but so far economic theory has failed to recognize even its existence. This problem requires investigations that go beyond the scope of this paper but I would like to use this conceptual framework as a provisional tool in investigating the competing ability of the United States, Japan and New Europe in a comparative perspective.

4. - The Emergence of a New Competing Power Having Odd Behaviour

In the 1950s Japan was largely ignored by the major industrial countries of Western Europe and North America. It was thought to be an unimportant country, forced by military defeat to play but a marginal role in world affairs. As a producer of manufactures, Japan was widely considered to be destined to reproduce foreign goods and to export cheap, low quality, industrial products.

In the 1960s Japan's near miraculous economic growth was generally attributed to the low wages paid to Japanese industrial workers. As a product of cheap labour, Japanese industrial growth was generally believed to be based on social dumping and probably short-lived.

In the 1970s, when Japanese growth rates, though smaller in the previous decades, remained much higher than in the other major industrial nations, the prevailing expectation was that soon the Japanese people would start enjoying life like everybody else and stop being so productive and thrifty. Wages were increasing in Japan and living conditions were improving rapidly. Yet Japan was still competitive with the rest of the world in manufactures and services, notwithstanding the continuous revaluations of the yen, due in large part to a sustained current account surplus. The popular explanation of Japan's continuing success then became «Japan Inc.», a kind of unholy alliance between the private sector and government aimed at fostering production and exports, made possible by the acquiescence of labour.

In the 1980s, also the appeal of «Japan Inc. waned, and no other explanation of the success of Japan found acceptance. The general conclusion in the West seems then to be that Japan has become invincible, and companies, both from America and from Europe, have become even more eager to establish ties with Japan.

The most innovative Western firms, for example, leave to Japanese firms the production and especially the commercialization of new products that they do not feel confident enough to market by themselves. Many Western government authorities (including many state governments in the United States) seek direct investments from Japan, offering all kinds of incentives for the location of productive enterprises within their jurisdictions. Western firms in increasing numbers seek joint ventures with Japanese firms to produce in and for the Western markets.

European and American companies alike export to Japan by making use of Japanese general trading companies, who have in their hands almost two thirds of Japanese imports and that develop the local market according to their strategies, not always coinciding with the interests of the foreign company for which they market the products in Japan.

The main trading companies are part of informal groups of companies (*keiretsu*) that have continued to exist after the formal dissolution of pre-war *zaibatsu*. This fact helps the well-known and practiced capacity of Japan to substitute efficient domestic production for imports. Every time a foreign product attracts a growing number of Japanese consumers, local companies are ready and able to produce it for the domestic market (in general under license), usually adapting it specifically to Japanese consumers. Advertising and packaging of the products are part of this process of adaptation to the domestic market. This type of import substitution does not stem from government policies, but from a spontaneous reactions of the market. This helps to explain why, while foreign trademarks are increasing in number in the Japanese market, there is no corresponding increase in imports.

Foreign products have traditionally been considered expensive in Japan, something made for special occasions and not for daily use. Although this attitude is changing, it is still deeply rooted. The consumption of wine and of whiskey, for example, is expanding in Japan, but this new demand has been met by increased supply of domestic products, rather than by imports. Japanese consumers also feel more confident with products fabricated in Japan. This is not a problem of quality, but of acceptance. In some cases, the traditional quality problem has been reversed; for example, Japanese producers of Italian-type pasta claim their product is better than that produced in Italy and, while this is unlikely, it has increased acceptance of the product.

No doubt Japanese consumers may believe that locally produced goods are better than equivalent foreign products, for they are proud and sure of the manufacturing ability of their country, which is proving superior to that of all other countries in many areas.

The low volume of import of manufactured goods in Japan can also be due in part to the internal distribution system which does not favour foreign products. Foreign firms do not offer wholesalers and retailers the same benefits (for example, credit) and guarantees (for example, stability of supply and service) offered by local producers. Yet, it would be misleading to see in this a major reason for the poor performance of foreign exports in Japan. Some responsibility lies in the foreign companies themselves, which often rely on Japanese general trading to enter the local market, without realizing that this approach may be appropriate only when the targeted market is seen as a marginal one. The Japanese general trading companies especially when they belong to a group that represents Japanese manufacturers of products similar to the foreign ones, may lack the incentive to push aggressively the sales of foreign-made products that could displace directly or indirectly products manufactured within the group to which they belong.

Japan in the 1930s was still a relatively small exporter of manufactures, never accounting for more than 4% of total world trade. Its sudden emergence on the world scene was not due to low wages (wages had always been low), but to gains in productivity. The new circumstances which strengthened Japan's competitive abilities «were the marked gains in technical efficiency and business organization achieved through the decade 1926-1936 and the violent dislocation of costs, prices and exchange rates precipitated by the Great Depression» (Lockwood [6]; p. 68).

In the 1990s Japan is no longer a new entrant, willing to transfer to foreign consumers the benefits of currency depreciations, tied to the export of cheap manufactures and shying away from direct investments outside Asia. Japan has become an established industrial power, willing to assert some of its weight in the world. With a great market power — 11% of world exports — maintained compatible with a strong national currency, Japan's weight in world trade and invest-ments, and gains from this participation in the world economy, are far greater than the simple market shares indicate. The situation today is sharply different from that of the 1930s, when an investment-shy and weak-currency Japan provided cheap exports to the rest of the world largely benefiting foreign consumers.

Yet, the growth of Japanese exports frightens the United States and the EC in ways that are strongly reminiscent of the 1930s.

5. - The Secrets of Japan's Economic Success

The near hysteria aroused by Japanese trade surpluses in the United States (as if they did not have any apparent relation to the net outflows of capital from Japan) and the more muted, but nonetheless critically important, European preoccupation with further possible Japanese penetration of EC markets after 1992 — from automobiles to financial services — appears to be unjustified on the basis of the traditional factors. The yen is hardly undervalued. Japanese wages are not those of a labour-rich developing country. Japanese tariff, and probably also non-tariff, barriers do not seem to be significantly higher than those of the other main industrial countries.

Then what is the secret of Japan's continuing trade expansion and the reason for the strongly protectionist response of the main trade partners to Japan's success in trade? The «secrets» of Japan's industrial success are many. Rationalization of industrial output, within the framework of a superior structural organization, which allows a thorough diffusion of technology in the economic system, is a primary one, while fast growth of labour productivity is another.

Japan uses trade and industrial policies in a way different from its main industrial competitors. Trade policies in the United States and trade and industrial policies in Europe are mostly directed at protecting declining industries. They are, in other words, defensive and *status quo* oriented. Japan, on the other hand, encourages by all means the groth of the most promising industries, while reducing at the same time the weight of declining ones.

Japan, moreover, is rather protective of the technologies developed by its companies and is probably the country that offers the least access to the results of its own technological research. On the contrary, many Japanese companies obtain licenses for the use of advanced technology produced by foreign companies, often at bargain prices. Research institutions as well as private researchers do not generally consider the potential damage to the competitiveness of their countries done by the sale of licenses to overseas producers. In the West the interest of the individual company, researcher, consultant, etc. comes first, not that of the economic system. One of Japan's assets lies in the ability of diffusing the technology that Japan has gained (Fodella [3]). Very often Japan has been able to fill a technology gap in a particular field: 1) by sending to the most advanced countries promising young people ready to learn and bring home the results of their learning; 2) by offering attractive contracts to young foreign experts who, though not yet well known in their own countries, have valuable knowledge in their fields; 3) by hiring as consultants promising researchers in fields of special interest, or buying, in full or in part, innovative foreign companies endowed with efficient research structures.

Joint ventures are a particularly useful vehicle for acquiring technology. In general, after a few years, the joint ventures with Japanese partners dissolve, since the Japanese partner either has grown too strong or has learned enough not to need its foreign counterpart any longer.

In entire sectors where Western technological leadership (for example, home electronics, personal computers, optical equipment, automobiles) was the rule, Japan has in recent years eroded the position of both the North American and European industries.

This is explained in part by remarkable increase in R&D outlays occured in Japan. Today R&D expenditures are five times greater in Japan than in the United Kingdom, three times greater than in France and Germany, and one-third greater than in the Soviet Union. This indicator, though generally unsatisfactory in explaining technological diffusion — the only aspect of technology that matters in economic terms — is quite appropriate in this case since Japan devotes resources specifically to the «development», and therefore the diffusion of technology. The fact that Japan is the main world buyer of foreign consultancies also contributes to the same final result.

Paramount in permitting the diffusion of technology in the most important sectors of the economy have been the institutions, rules and behaviours that form the *orgware* of Japan. The very key to economic success is to be found in having equipped with the most efficient technologies the greatest part of productive units belonging to the most important industries of the economic system.

In certain cases the diffusion has required *hardware*, material and financial resources, or more skilled labour that had to be formed (again using resources and precious time). In other cases the icrease in efficiency has come solely or almost exclusively from a better way of making things happen following a pattern devised to increase efficiency, a blend of *orgware* and of *software* (technology and management).

If in an economic system like that of Japan communication networks (from rail to mail, from telex to fax) work well, it is easier for companies to be punctual in their deliveries. If all companies are punctual it is not necessary to stock spare parts in large numbers or may not be necessary at all, as it happens with the JIT (Just-in-Time) system of production. Thus costs are reduced and, being all other conditions equal, competitivity is enhanced.

If we consider another element of competitivity, the cost of capital, *orgware* plays an important role here too, since borrowing and lending rates may have huge differential (like in the case of Italy) or be less apart (like in the case of Japan).

The strategy of Japan seems to be moving from direct exports of goods totally produced domestically (still prevailing in most instances, but heavily exposed to the danger of protectionism), to the overseas assembling of parts produced in Japan (the so-called screwdriver factories, well represented by typewriter and motorbike factories), to total overseas production of industrial goods on a project basis, often considered by Japanese as necessary to serve markets that are differentiated in needs and tastes.

This strategy is being pursued for at least two good reasons:

1) economies of scale are possible even with less than gigantic units of production. This makes decentralization possible and even desirable purely from the point of view of private costs. This trend is also desirable in order to reduce the social costs caused by the increased congestion of most urbanized areas and to contain social overhead expenditure for transportation and other networks;

2) large scales remain important in the marketing phase, since the success of a brand is often strongly correlated to market power, exemplified by the image attainable only through massive advertisements or to the type of market presence possible only for firms operating on a worldwide scale.

Mergers and acquisition of foreign firms have also become widespread in recent years favoured by the appreciation of the yen, which renders foreign assets relatively more attractive to Japanese firms. Japanese firms have in this way acquired existing firms in Europe and the United States. While the big acquisitions actually completed — Firestone Tire and Rubber acquired by Bridgestone — or attempted — Fairchild Industries sought by Fujitsu — attract the most attention, this new important facet of Japanese foreign investment is best exemplified by the acquisition of small and medium-size companies operating in sectors or industries such as electronics, specialty manufactures and computer software, that do not result in big news but that enhance the competing ability of Japan in many new fields paving the way to incremental or even breakthrough innovation.

6. - Can Differentiated Protectionism on the Basis of Orgware be the Appropriate Answer?

A large, efficient and relatively isolated economic system — like that of the United States at the beginning of this century — needed protection from within. From the overwhelming power of monopolies in industry, trade, services that would penalize new initiative and the ordinary citizens seen as consumers. The antitrust legislation that was passed is still in force after a century, but the situation at world level has dramatically changed and now the USA needs protection from without, since it has ceased to be the most important industrial country of the world as it was.

Japan, where after the defeat in the Pacific war a Fair Trade Commission was established in order to prevent the resurgence of monopolies, did not consider the protection of consumers as a priority and acted accordingly giving more attention and protection to the national producers, with the result that they were able to establish perhaps the most efficient economic system on earth, one that does not need any longer protection from without and can now embrace free trade in earnest: a change that Japan is now ready to adopt in order to avoid blame and protectionist actions from the part of its partners. On the contrary the USA should adopt a more matter-of-fact attitude towards monopolies and free trade in order to cope with the challenge coming from Japan.

Whenever institutions, rules and behaviours reciprocally contradict themselves or do not match the actual needs of the economic system in any given moment, the efficiency of the economic system decreases in terms of less-than-potential rates of growth, or in terms of bottlenecks or imbalances that the ill-performing *orgware* causes the economic system to occur.

Economists used to point to terms of trade as a source of inequality among economic systems exporting mainly primary products or manufactures. Today many developed economies export products of the primary sector and almost all developing countries also export manufactures (even if they may often do so as subcontractors for companies of the developed countries). The attention must be shifted to exchange rates, keeping in mind that it is always possible to manage one's exchange rate when the country has a surplus, enjoys credit and can afford to borrow. Not when it has a deficit, unless it is for a short period. It is not the level of debt that matters, but how the financial resources are being used.

Once more the problem of development shows the importance of the qualitative aspects. Since it is difficult, not to say impossible, to measure them, economists tend to ignore them, concentrating on the quantitative aspects only. It is time to reconsider this approach that has led to the misuse and waste of resources because the qualitative aspects, those pertaining to *orgware*, had been overlooked.

The fact that in the Euro-American world a contractual type of relationship prevails among companies, while in Japan relations between companies are often based on mutual trust, on confidence rather than on contract, has led us to suspect that this may change the time horizon of the company and its perspective to such an extent as to become a serious factor of differentiation also in terms of competing ability.

The Japanese economic system did not, in the past, observe the rules of the game set at world level by the West, but so far all efforts to ptove that this is continuing have failed. It is also possible — and indeed likely — that, although Japan be trying to follow these rules, under labels familiar to the West operates a quite distinct reality giving origin to an *orgware* that supplies the economic system with a more efficient basis for the operation of its companies.

Ron Dore points out that mutual trust, sincerity and goodwill are the basis of the *relational contracting* that prevails in Japan, rather than of the spot-contracting that prevails in the West «There are some good reasons — writes Dore — for thinking that it might be *because of*, and not *in spite* of relational contracting that Japan has a better growth performance than the rest of us» (Dore [2] pp. 174-92).

After the difficult post-war years (1946-1964) Japan's GDP ranked fifth after USA, USSR, West Germany and France. During the easy years of economic prosperity (1968-1986) it ranked second and the world was shocked when the average income of the Japanese became higher than that of the Americans: 17,000 dollars a year compared with 16,000 (*The Economist* [7] pp. 15-6). During the decade after the years of triumph (1989-1998), thanks to the yen/dollar exchange rate and to the differentials in growth rates, Japan's GDP might even become equal, in dollar terms, to that of the United States. That result will have to be attributed to the ability of diffusing technology and marketing technological products as factors responsible of a high speed economic growth and although in both these abilities, largely due to the quality of its *orgware*, Japan's excellence is well known, there is more to it.

It is important to analyze and to understand fully the reasons for Japanese competitiveness, not only as an intellectual exercise, but also as a necessary condition for appropriate policy responses by new Europe (and the United States) to a vital challenge coming from Japan and the other NIES of Asia. The challenge is no more and no less than the transfer of the centre of gravity of the world industrial power from the West to East Asia.

It is therefore extremely important that a problem of such relevance be discussed, debated and properly understood both in America and in New Europe. In America, the official tendency to single out Japan as the most deviant trading partner, and to force it to make bilateral concessions usually with final disastrous effects for the United States, not only threatens the foundation of the world multi-lateral trading system, but also limits the range of policy responses to the trade and other macroeconomic imbalances that exist between the two countries. In the EC, the general policy response to the Japanese challenge in manufactures, banking and insurance services will likely shape the overall trade and industrial policy posture of post-1992 Europe.

What is needed is a better understanding of both the strengths and weaknesses of Japan's economy, of the available policy response options, both competitive and collaborative, and of the time horizons within which results can reasonably be expected. There are certainly areas where competition with Japan is inevitable. Bur there are for sure areas where cooperation is mutually profitable, either now in the future. Japan bashing, as well as «if you can't beat 'em, join 'em'" types of responses — the first strong at the government level, the second at the firm level — are equally inappropriate in isolation. The illusion of beating back Japan by resorting to confrontation on a large scale is probably as dangerous as that of Japan's invincibility, with the invevitable corollary of unequal cooperation. Both approaches in-evitably foster delusions, based on results that fall short of expecta-tions, and lead to collissions whose effects may not be controllable, with devastating consequences on world welfare.

Rationalization of production, adoption and thorough diffusion of the latest technologies, together with outstanding marketing abilities, made Japan one of the most efficient exporters of manufactured products in the world. As time goes by Japan is increasingly sharing this performance with other East Asian economies, and New Europe will have to take this into consideration when envisaging measures capable of dealing with the mounting competing pressure from East Asia now mainly if not solely represented by Japan.

To recognize the existence of *orgware* would allow New Europe and the United States to adopt a *differentiated protectionism* as a substitute for free trade, an ideology based on Darwin's principle of the «survival of the fittest», that has proven to be instrumental in preserving an economic order favourable only to the dominating powers, and that has been unable to solve or even direct toward solution the probem of inequality among economic systems, as the growing distance in the economic conditions of countries shows.

Free trade has accentuated existing trends making the rich richer and the poor poorer. Only those countries that have not applied free trade to their own case (like Japan, Korea, Taiwan), but that have taken advantage of the free trade practiced by others, have been able — when assisted by an *orgware* of high quality — to break that vicious circle and have succeeded in developing their economies. Only the very strong can afford free trade, and Japan in now ready to apply it, while the rest of the world (with few exceptions like Germany) is no longer able to afford it.

Japanese companies succeeded in competing because their economic system helped them in that direction. American companies did not need any help to succeed, but times were different and the situation has changed.

The United States might be forced by Japan to become a more redoubtable competitor in the market arena. But such a path so far has beaten wrong tracks.

The joint ventures with Japanese companies have caused a substantial technology transfer. Many American firms in difficulty have been «saved» by Japanese companies that bought them in full or in part.

The Japanese are creating manufacturing facilities in the United States making use of methods that have successfully been experimented at home. Those companies may be a revitalizing addition to the American industrial scene, but may also threaten it.

Japanese foreign direct investments are welcome, but should they not be reciprocated the market power of Japanese companies (and of Japan) will grow to control larger and larger shares of world production. A perspective worse than that of having Japan controlling large portions of exports, since exports can be checked and are more vulnerable than production made with foreign capital.

Many American companies have already recognized the strength of the Japanese economy by becoming their devout customers, while the suppliers of Japan still in American hands decrease every day in number and importance while increase those owned by Japan.

American companies are sometime lured by Japan into joint ventures that often lead to nothing, except for the experience gained that allows the partner from Japan to save time and money before replacing the less efficient partner.

But there is an unbeaten track more likely to be taken perhaps by New Europe than by America: that of co-operation in third countries. But since parity is a concept difficult to be understood in East Asia — perhaps because it does not exist in reality — true cooperation is rare.

At this stage however it seems difficult to find solutions that may reverse the trend. Whatever action is taken it results in a strengthening of the Japanese side.

The quality of *orgware*, the dimensions of the market, the educational level of the labour force and the experience in using the resource with the appropriate methods and technologies make the Japanese system unbeatable.

This is the reality we have to recognize and face.

As a consequence we have either to create a barrier to control that system in order not to be dominated by it, or accept the rule of «the survival of the fittest» even when the «fittest» is not in the West, and Darwin's approach is out of date.

If we have to seek protection from a system that combines an advanced stage of economic growth with a high of *orgware*, we have to accept at the same time the protection that other less fortunate economic systems in Africa, Asia and Latin America are seeking against us.

The world is not made of equals and we have to devise some discriminating tools to be used as handicaps that guarantee equality of development opportunities, to the strong (discriminated against) and to the weak (that can discriminate against others) alike.

The cumulative experience of New Europe — where market forces have operated under social control, or where the market had but a marginal role — might be more favourably biased toward a *differentiated protectionism* where the weak are protected and the strong are kept under control rather than toward Darwin's approach which seems to be typical of the United States.

A *differentiated protectionism* might be worth a try since it would operate in favour of those economic systems where both the low level of economic conditions and the poor quality of orgware indicate the relative disadvantage of the economic systems having these characteristics, and might do what so far the invisible hand has been unable to.

7. - Conclusions

Data and projections seem to indicate that New Europe will be able to successfully compete with the United States, but will not match the competing power of Japan. The reasons seem to lie not so much in unfair practices, but rather in the different behaviour of the various components of the economic system. While in Japan the reasons of the economic system followed by those of the producers seem to prevail, in the United States the reasons of companies and of consumers seem paramount. Europe is probably in between.

It is a conflicting *weltanschauung* that is compelling economists to think and eventually recognize that the rules of the game on which we have geared the operating of the economic systems might not be universal and to admit that they have not been very efficient in making world welfare grow evenly.

The invisible hand has operated — to say the least — below capacity, and companies competing in the market arena have discovered that their international efficiency was influenced by something more than management and externalities.

Japan could base its economic growth on policies that systematically disregarded the rules of the game set by the West, and by doing so it succeeded in becoming the most competitive economic system of the world.

Now Japan is ready to practice free trade more fully than Europe or the United States, but it might be time to recognize that better tools are needed and may be devised, after having experienced the traditional ones, if we really want to avoid that the strong become stronger and the weak weaker: a law of nature that human beings are trying to mend in order to build a less wild world.

Index